If These Pots Could Talk

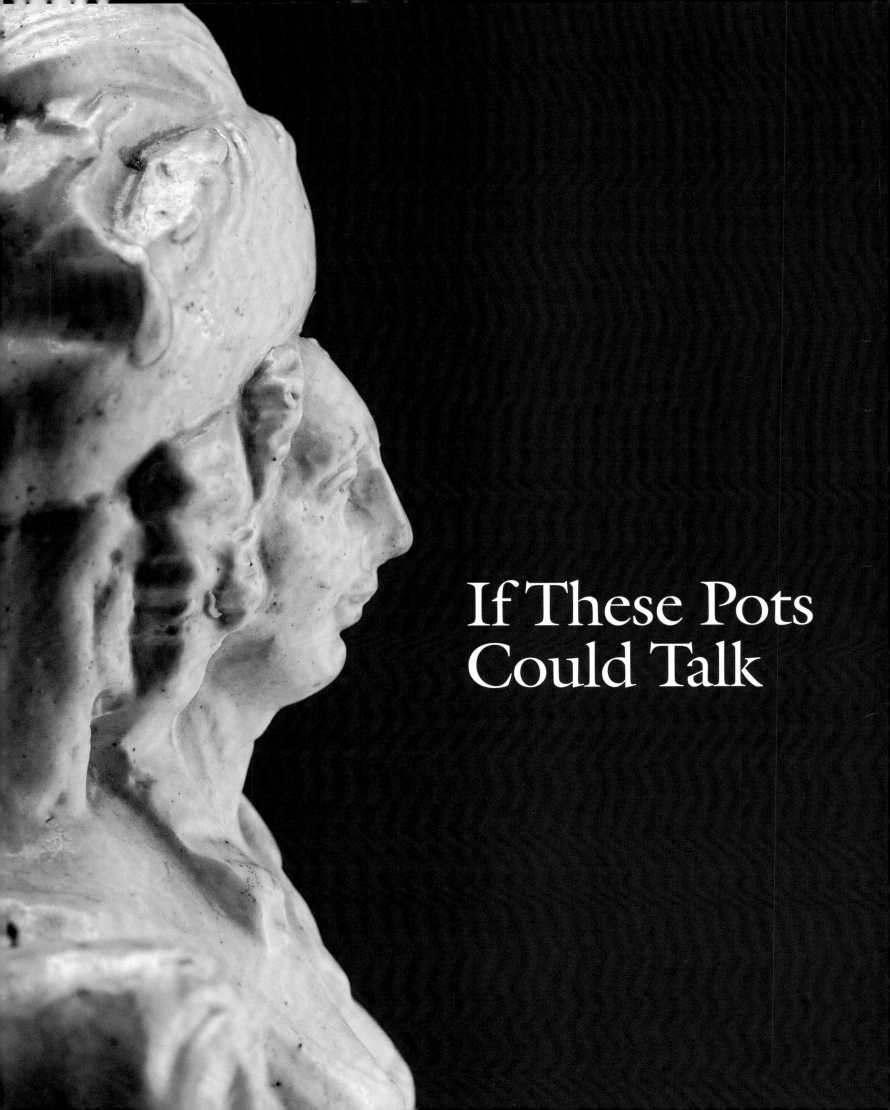

If These Pots
Could Talk

Ivor Noël Hume
O.B.E., F.S.A.

*Collecting 2,000 Years
of British Household Pottery*

Published by the Chipstone Foundation

Distributed by University Press of New England

Hanover and London

Published by the Chipstone Foundation
7820 North Club Circle, Milwaukee, WI 53217

Distributed by University Press of New England
Hanover, NH 03755

Library of Congress Cataloging-in-Publication Data
Noël Hume, Ivor.
  If these pots could talk—collecting 2,000 years of British household
pottery / Ivor Noël Hume.
    p. cm.
Includes bibliographical references (p.   ).
ISBN 1–58465–161–x (alk. paper)
1. Great Britain—Antiquities. 2. Pottery, British—Collectors and
collecting. I. Title.
DA90 .N57 2001
738'.0941'075—dc21
                                        2001001795

A Meditation on a Quart Mug

How often have I seen him compell'd to hold up his Handle at the Bar, for no other Crime than that of being empty; then snatch'd away by a surly Officer, and plung'd suddenly unto a Tub of cold Water. How often is he hurry'd down into a dismal Vault, sent up fully laden in a cold Sweat, and by a rude Hand thrust into the Fire! How often have I seen it obliged to undergo the Indignities of a dirty Wench; to have melting Candles dropt onto its naked Sides, and sometimes in its Mouth; to risque being broken into a thousand Pieces, for Actions which itself was not guilty of! How often is he forced into the Company of boisterous Sots, who lay all their Nonsense, Noise, profane Swearing, Cursing, and Quarreling, on the harmless Mug, which speaks not a Word! They overset him, maim him, and sometimes turn him to Arms offensive or defensive, as they please; when of himself he would not be of either Party, but would as willing stand, still.

. . . And yet, O Mug! If these dangers thou escapist, with little injury, thou must at last untimely fall, to be broken to Pieces, and cast away, never more to be recollected, and form'd into a Quart Mug. Whether by the Fire, or in a Battle, or choak'd with a Dishclout, or by a stroke against a Stone, thy Dissolution happens; 'tis all alike to the avaritious Owner; he grieves not for thee, but for the Shilling with which he purchas'd thee! If thy Bottom Part should chance to survive, it may be preserv'd to hold bits of Candles, or Blacking for Shoes, or Salve for kibed Heels; but all thy other Members will be for ever buried in some miry Hole; or less carefully disposed of, so that little Children, who have not yet arrived to Acts of Cruelty, may gather them up to furnish out their Baby Houses; Or, being cast upon the Dunghill, they will therewith be carted into Meadow Grounds; where, being spread abroad and discovered, they must be thrown to the Heap of Stone, Bones and Rubbish; or being left until the Mower finds them with his Scythe, they will with bitter Curses be tossed over the Hedge; and so serve for unlucky Boys to throw at Birds and Dogs; until by length of Time and numerous Casualties, they shall be press'd into their Mother Earth, and be converted to their original principles.

Benjamin Franklin F.R.S., *Pennsylvania Gazette* (Philadelphia),
July 13, 1733

For Audrey and Carol
Two Wives, Two Loves
One Lucky Man

Contents

Foreword

I FIRST ENCOUNTERED Noël Hume in a barrel or, to be more precise, in about ten barrels. While doing graduate work at the College of William and Mary in Virginia, my wife, Katie, and I liked to visit nearby Carter's Grove, an eighteenth-century home along the James River that now is part of the Colonial Williamsburg Foundation. Among the attractions still there is a wonderful re-creation of a seventeenth-century settlement called Wolstenhome Towne. Comprised only of suggestive wooden outlines of buildings and surrounding fences, the site features an audio tour whose electronic components are hidden in wooden barrels. The press of a button activates an authoritative yet poetic British narrative voice that seemingly transcends time and place. Before long, I had the pleasure of getting to know the man behind the voice, the legendary archaeologist Ivor Noël Hume, and it is a great pleasure to be involved with his latest and most ambitious book project.

If These Pots Could Talk: Collecting 2,000 Years of British Household Pottery is a historical memoir that tracks the professional adventures and collecting exploits of Noël and his late wife, Audrey, who passed away in 1993. Engaging and highly informative, this work sheds important new light on our understanding of early British pottery. The involvement of the Chipstone Foundation as publisher reflects not only a deep admiration for the Noël Humes, but also a shared interest in this important story of British ceramic usage in early America.

Chipstone is the creation of Stanley and Polly Stone of Fox Point, Wisconsin, who in 1946 began collecting decorative arts—a passion that would be a main focus of theirs for the next half century. In addition to buying early American furniture and historical prints, the Stones also sought premier examples of seventeenth- and eighteenth-century British pottery. By the 1960s, their collection was impressive enough to capture the attention of Charles Montgomery, then Senior Research Fellow and former Director of the Henry Francis DuPont Winterthur Museum. At Montgomery's urging, the Stones established the Chipstone Foundation with the dual purpose of preserving their collection and, on a wider level, supporting American decorative arts scholarship. Following Stanley Stone's death in 1987, the foundation was activated by an initial endowment provided by Mrs. Stone, and since has steadily broadened its activities.

Chipstone formally got together with Noël and Carol, his present wife, in 1999, with the initiation of this book project and its corresponding exhibit at the Milwaukee Art Museum (October 5, 2001–January 20, 2002), as well as the planned bequest of the Noël Hume Collection to the foundation. For Chipstone the appeal of this association is multilayered. Of central interest, of course, is the distinctive nature of the Collection itself. Whether in the field or in antique shops, Noël and Audrey invariably looked at artifacts through the lens of archaeology. While their connoisseurial skills were first-rate, they always were primarily interested in real British pottery—pretty or not. This archaeological perspective, with its scientific approach to the gathering of evidence, is the reason for the remarkable scope of the Noël Humes' collection. From wheel-thrown Roman pots to crudely formed medieval earthenwares to ornamented chamber pots to porcelain World War I tanks, the story of British pottery is richly told.

Much of the allure of this new relationship also centers around Noël himself. In addition to being an internationally known scholar and teacher with impeccable credentials and numerous awards, including his designation in 1992 by Queen Elizabeth as an Officer of the British Empire, Noël brings to all that he does unbridled enthusiasm and drive. As the author of more than a dozen books and many more articles, Noël has done more than any other scholar to bridge the long-standing divide between the realms of archaeology and the decorative arts world. *If These Pots Could Talk* gracefully accomplishes this task, and offers much to ceramic scholars and enthusiasts alike.

The interpretive potential for the Noël Hume Collection at Chipstone is considerable. The foundation recently joined forces with the Milwaukee Art Museum, an institution nationally known for its extensive art collections and also its exciting new architectural addition designed by Santiago Calatrava. The joint venture between the museum and the foundation initially was motivated by the fact that the Stones' colonial revival home lies in a residential area that precludes its use as a public museum. In other words, the foundation needed a place to show its collections, and the museum, in return, saw merit in the foundation's scholarly and financial support. May 2001 saw the opening of the reinstalled decorative arts galleries, which bring together in novel thematic displays the Milwaukee Art Museum's collections with the Chipstone Collection and the Layton Art Collection, whose significant holdings have long been shown at the museum.

Another new facet of the foundation's educational mission is *Ceramics in America*. This journal, whose first issue is due out in the fall of 2001, joins Chipstone's journal *American Furniture,* edited by Luke Beckerdite. Internationally acclaimed by scholars and enthusiasts alike since its inaugural issue in 1993, *American Furniture* has substantially raised the bar in the area of American decorative arts scholarship. *Ceramics in America* promises to offer similarly thoughtful analysis for ceramic enthusiasts through essays by American and British scholars, including Noël Hume. The journal is guided by Robert R. Hunter, Jr., who has considerable experience as both a curator and an archaeologist at Colonial Williamsburg and the College of William and Mary. And like so many other ceramics scholars, he also happens to be a former student of the Noël Humes'.

A final Chipstone activity linked to the Noël Hume project is the recent association with the University of Wisconsin at Madison. In 1998 Dr. Ann Smart Martin was hired to be the Stanley and Polly Stone Professor of American Decorative Arts, a position funded by the foundation. Like Rob Hunter, she too is a former student of Noël and Audrey's. Along with her creative colleagues at the university, Ann is developing a cross-disciplinary program centered around the study of American material culture and artifacts used in the American context. The program also is augmented by a newly created two-year visiting professorship and a material culture graduate fellowship named in honor of Dr. James Watrous, the long-time professor of Art History at the University of Wisconsin.

These new initiatives underlie the reasons why America's best-known historical archaeologist has teamed up with a private foundation in the Midwest. Noël Hume is universally hailed for his contributions to the fields of archaeology and decorative arts and his efforts to raise public awareness through his entertaining writings and lectures. *If These Pots Could Talk: Collecting 2,000 Years of British Household Pottery* not only synthesizes Noël and Audrey's half-century devotion to research and collecting, but also provides insights that will benefit scholars for decades to come.

Jonathan Prown

Preface

IT WAS ON A FRIDAY that the collector died. His family mourned; his friends remembered him, and would—for a while. We recalled his erudition. Wasn't it he who told us that in the 1660s manganese was first used to color pottery? Or was it he who proved it wasn't so? We remember his friendship and the jokes he told, none of whose punch lines we can recall. But we do remember how he made us laugh. We miss him, of course we do. But life goes on and so must we.

Few if any of us were aware that on that Friday, on that hour, and in that instant his collection died with him. The pots, the bowls, the cups, the mugs, were still on their shelves just as he had left them, but the reason for their being there had gone. The memories that had made each piece important, the jubilation of their discovery, the reason why this bowl revealed something about that one: all this had been lost. Each piece faced an uncertain future. Evicted from the safety of their shelves, they would be together as a family one last time, numbered tags around their necks, to be stared at and their monetary worth assessed by steely-eyed and cold-hearted dealers as they awaited the auctioneer's hammer. Each piece was about to begin a new life that started with its description in the sale catalog. Many would pass through several hands so that within a few months even the circumstances of the sale would be unknown to the last buyer.

My wife Audrey and I had built our ceramic collection across some forty years of hunting and finding, and when she died in 1993, I was made suddenly and painfully aware that I was now the sole custodian not only of the collection itself but of all the knowledge that bonded it together. Ours was a *teaching* collection in the truest sense. We had learned much from it and had been able to share what we knew with others. I am ashamed to admit, however, that at Audrey's untimely death most of the collection

Audrey Noël Hume, 1927–1993

was still uncataloged, both of us having naively believed that in our retirement there would be plenty of time to work on it. But to what purpose? The existence of a catalog would certainly help the auction house describe what it would be selling, but once dispersed nobody would have a need for our catalog and no one would think it worth publishing—unless the collection could escape the hammer and remain together. But what institution or museum would be willing to take it?

Although we always described the collection as being of English or British pottery, we interpreted the nationality in its broadest sense, thereby embracing such wares as were normally to be found in Britannic and colonial homes from almost then to nearly now, but not necessarily made in the British Isles. Stonewares from Germany, delft from Holland, faience from France, and porcelain from the Orient, all had, and have, a place in the collection, the principal criterion being that we had come in contact with such diverse wares either in the course of our archaeological work or as the result of initially unrelated historical research.

Had the collection been all of one period or even of the two centuries of American colonial history, an organization specializing in the seventeenth or eighteenth century might have been interested in it. But this assemblage embraced two thousand years of British ceramic history. Because we had been senior and professional members of Colonial Williamsburg's staff throughout much of Audrey's and my careers, seeking a permanent home for the collection in Williamsburg seemed the logical starting point. However, at that time the foundation's educational and curatorial interests focused primarily on the American decorative arts of the eighteenth and early nineteenth centuries. Chief curator Graham Hood agreed that he could foresee no future broad-based ceramics-related programs that would make use of so diverse and seemingly eccentric a collection.

Over the course of her working life Audrey had amassed large quantities of documentary material, much of which she had assembled into files devoted to specific classes of objects that ranged from apple scoops to zithers. Although much remained unassimilated at her death (another task planned for our retirement years), her on-paper collection needed a safe haven where it could be used by research students looking for information about objects that began with A or Z. At this point my old friend Dwight Lanmon, then director of the Winterthur Museum in Delaware, agreed to accept the numerous albums and file folders into his research library, where—I am relieved to know—they have been preserved and put to use. He also stressed the need for a catalog of our ceramics collection. I knew that he was right. I also knew that it would be a long task, one made more difficult by the loss of Audrey's shared memories of when and where some of the pieces had been obtained.

Catalogs come in varying levels of detail; some, like those of auction houses, limit themselves to two or three lines of description sufficient only to enable a buyer to recognize what is being offered. At the next tier comes the museum registrar's catalog card, which lets a photograph do most of the talking; and last is the ultimate catalog that not only describes the object in exhaustive detail but includes everything known about its history and conservation. Our catalog belonged in this last category, running as it did to two large and tightly spaced volumes and several hundred photographs. Although I have long contended that a good actor can even make readings from the telephone directory exciting, this catalog would defeat the best of them.

In the midst of my uncertainty about the future of the wide-ranging collection and its cumbersome catalog, Jonathan Prown, the newly appointed director of the Chipstone Foundation, along with his predecessor Luke Beckerdite, came to me with an unexpected proposal. Their foundation would offer to house and use the collection in the way Audrey and I had intended, and drawing on the already completed catalog manuscript I should write a book about the collection telling the story of its acquisitions and their meaning.

My initial reaction to this proposal was less than enthusiastic; but the more I thought about it, the more appealing the challenge became. All those experiences and adventures that were part of the collection's history, which otherwise would die with me, could be woven into the tapestry. But like most tapestries, the uniformity of its weft and weave soon becomes obscured by a plethora of colors and design elements that go off in all directions before coming together in the final picture. Mine is a panoramic view of pottery in Britain and her colonies from the landing of the Romans to the bad intentions of the Germans in 1939. The picture is by no means complete, with its selectivity governed in large measure by Audrey's and my archaeological interests. While most books on ceramics (*Keramics* if one wants to be internationally pedantic) discuss each ware in its totality before going on to the next, this book does not. Instead, it looks at relationships that may at times be technological and at others sociological. Pots played their part in the lives of their users, and nowhere beyond the shops of chinamen did they exist in a vacuum. Find them in an eighteenth-century trash pit and they emerge in the company of glass bottles, rusted cutlery, clay pipes, broken tumblers, lost buttons, and much else, while themselves running a gamut from bed pans to wine cups. If, therefore, you want to find a single word to describe these chapters, the kindest may be *discursive*.

Now, with the book written, I remain too close to the collection and the memories it invokes to judge whether or not I have succeeded. Let's face it, to most people, being a pot detective isn't half as exciting as catching killers; but I am assuming that you are not "most people" or you wouldn't be reading this sentence. But even if you gain nothing more from these pages than vicariously sharing in the joy of the hunt and the stimulus of looking past the pots to the people who made and lived with them, I shall be content—*more* than content. I shall be as happy as the proverbial clam!

Just as computer wizards, anthropologists, physicians, indeed, every profession has its own nomenclature and jargon, so pot people—particularly archaeological pot people—have their own terminology. They don't always agree on whether to call a shallow one-handled bowl a porringer or a bleeding bowl, and talk about *marlies* when most people are happy to call a rim a rim; nor may they agree on how big a platter must be to be called a charger, or the difference between a pitcher and a jug. So rather than slow your reading down to a tiresome crawl by qualifying and reexplaining every term, I have taken refuge in a glossary at the back. It is to the back, too, that you'll need to turn if you care how big a pot is or want to know precisely what wording appears on a porcelain model of the ill-fated *Lusitania*. The same goes for bibliographic details. You'll find them at the back. So, too, is all the really stuffy stuff that would otherwise be dangling as page-end footnotes.

Writing to be readable has its drawbacks, not the least of them being the need to avoid jarring word repetition. That is more easily achieved in fiction than in fact. In technical writing precision is paramount, and yet to refer to a jar as an *olla* three times in one sentence is akin to walking through brambles that snag at every step. Consequently, I am guilty of a crime that pedants will call terminological inexactitude when I alternate in calling a mug a tankard or a plate a dish. A slightly different problem had to be faced when distinguishing between the awkwardly named Ivor and Audrey Noël Hume Collection and those of other collectors. My solution has been to omit the proper names and to capitalize the "C" in Collection when referring to ours.

Connoisseurs who strive to obtain the best of whatever it is they collect and who limit their interests to a finely focused period or a single ceramic ware may be appalled to discover that Audrey and I rejoiced as much in finding a not-so-great example as we did in discovering others of better quality and greater intrinsic worth. Placing us even further beyond the pale is the fact that the sphere of our collecting begins long before most collectors think it should and continues well past the moment in time when antiques give way to "collectibles."

But how old must old be before it's old enough?

We contended that within the historical parameters that guided our interests and our acquisitions, there is no evidentiary difference between a 1782 pearlware figure of Lord Rodney and a porcelain model of Edith Cavell executed in 1915. Similarly, a 1780 creamware jug reminding us of the histrionic excellence of David Garrick sends the same message, no more no less, as does a stoneware flask recalling the 1836 performance of American entertainer Thomas Dartmouth Rice. Were Audrey still alive, she would make no apology for our collecting philosophy. On the contrary, she would argue that our example may prompt others to find unexpected pleasures in looking over and venturing down the overlooked byways of ceramic history.

And then there are the fragments. What excuse do we have for illustrating these? Simply this: To an archaeological historian, an antiquary, and even a serious collector, a potsherd can have more to tell us than may an intact pitcher that echoes no more than the thud of the last auctioneer's hammer. More often than not, the shard breathes life into the whole. It does not follow, however, that when the shards go together to rebuild a pot, honesty requires that we must be visually reminded of them. For me the pot is king, but we do not need to see him warts and all. Consequently, when repairs detract from the whole I have urged that cracks and unintended blemishes be photographically minimized.

Photographs from museums and private collections are credited in the captions; so, too, are those images of objects not necessarily owned by the supplier. Details from originally published engravings or woodcuts are assumed to be in the public domain and therefore are uncredited. Objects in the Collection acquired either directly or indirectly from other collections are so indicated, not for copyright reasons but to preserve their ancestry.

Captions aim at brevity and a degree of formality, recognizing that many details are to be seen in the photographs and that the items are discussed more fully in the text. Also in the interest of brevity is the omission of measurements at the close of each caption. Instead, these are listed at the back of the book along with details of such inscriptions as have not previously been quoted either in the captions or in the text. Unless otherwise indicated, *a, b,* and so on read from left to right, then from top to bottom.

The Chipstone Foundation is the legacy of Stanley and Polly Stone of Milwaukee, both keen collectors whom Audrey and I knew slightly through their many visits to Williamsburg's Antiques Forum. At the time of Stanley's death they had been developing an interest in English ceramics of the seventeenth and eighteenth centuries and had acquired no small number of fine pieces. That facet of the Chipstone Collection continues to grow, and since the foundation's acceptance of Audrey's and my much more diverse collection, director Jon Prown and his advisor Robert Hunter have focused on acquiring pieces that augment and impart additional depth to it. For that reason, this book, though built around our own collecting and researches, also discusses and illustrates several of these related pieces.

With all that said, unless you are among the many people who have helped Audrey and me in our half-century of ceramic research, this is the moment to skip to chapter 1.

Audrey would unhesitatingly agree that our premier debt is to Adrian Oswald, who not only shaped my career, but taught me how to look at potsherds and read their testimony. He also taught me the rudiments of archaeology as we toiled together in the first big hole to be dug in London in the immediate post–World War II years. At the Victoria and Albert Museum, Robert Charleston, keeper of ceramics and glass, was unstintingly gracious and patient with two young disciples who had so much to learn. My career-long love affair with German stoneware stemmed from my friendship with collector Frank Thomas and his daughter Margaret. My introduction to medieval earthenwares was aided and fostered by Britain's Inspector of Ancient Monuments, John Hurst, and my knowledge of Romano-British ceramics was expanded through working alongside the

Guildhall Museum's assistant curator, the late Ralph Merrifield. In America C. Malcolm Watkins, the Smithsonian Institution's curator of cultural history, introduced me to New England earthenwares as well as to old England's West Country pottery. Along with Adrian Oswald, the U.S. National Park Service's regional director J. C. "Pinky" Harrington opened our eyes to the nuances of clay tobacco-pipe dating. John C. Austin, retired curator of ceramics for Colonial Williamsburg, was for many years my ever helpful colleague across the parking lot, he with his whole pieces and me with my previously despised fragments. At Jamestown, Association for the Preservation of Virginia Antiquities curator Bly Straube has been no less generous with her rapidly expanding knowledge as the Jamestown Rediscovery project goes excitingly forward.

Although we had been permitted to view many private collections over the years and had learned from all of them, I am particularly mindful and appreciative of those collectors who have helped me with information or with pictures during the preparation of this book. Among them are stoneware collector Nicholas Johnson of New Haven, Connecticut, and in Milwaukee, Dudley Godfrey, Jr., and his wife Constance, as well as Anne and Fred Vogel III.

Our career-long friend J. Douglas Walton shared our adventures on the Upchurch Marshes as well as our annual treks around England and through the London street markets in search of pertinent pots; and in Bermuda, across more years than I care to count, E. B. "Teddy" Tucker, Allan J. "Smokey" Wingood, Dr. Edward Schultz, and restorer par excellence Bill Gillies all generously made their shipwreck discoveries available to us, took us diving from their boats, and hosted us on land. We have been grateful, too, to London ceramics dealers Jonathan Horne, Garry Atkins, Alastair Sampson, and John May for spending much time with us in their shops even when they knew that our pockets were not deep enough to make us desirable customers.

I know that had she lived, Audrey would have joined me in placing American ceramics expert Robert Hunter high on our altar of ikons, for it has been through his encouragement and wise counsel that the Collection goes to the Chipstone Foundation and this book becomes a reality.

We were no less indebted to Sir David and Lady Burnett, whose potsherd collection they generously gave to us to help in our studies of London delftware. Most of their fragments from the Pickleherring delftware kilns are now in Colonial Williamsburg's ceramics collection, while a wide-ranging trove of assorted earthenwares has been willed through us to the Chipstone Foundation. From Audrey's and my first days as grubby archaeologists, David Burnett, then chairman of perhaps the largest slices of real estate on the south bank of the Thames, became one of our dearest and closest friends, with whom we have scoured the river foreshores in search of potsherds and roamed the markets in pursuit of bigger pieces.

Just as archaeological directors get credit for the hard work done by their excavators and assistants, so authors win all the laurels (if laurels there be) for writing their books. No garlands drape the shoulders of the editors who have turned their literary meanderings into readable prose, nor is there champagne for the copy editors who made the authors appear to know how to parse or punctuate. Consequently, I would be derelict and downright churlish if I did not record my gratitude to my University Press of New England production editor Janis Bolster and my incredibly focused copy editor Elizabeth Dugger. Among my less admirable talents has been the ability to open the first copy of a new book, find a typo, slam it shut, and never look at it again. Here opportunities for self-loathing have been minimized thanks to the eagle eye of my proofreader Nicholas Mirra. This, however, is a book wherein I am but a partner with my photographer, Gavin Ashworth, who, for the first time to my knowledge, has given the commonplace of ceramic history the artistic treatment usually reserved for the grand and costly. Although he would be the last to claim it so, this is as much his book as it is mine. But words and pictures gel only when they are set out in felicitous juxtaposition. For that achievement, both Gavin and I pay homage to designer Wynne Patterson, who put our Humpty Dumpty so seamlessly together.

And then there's Carol—Carol who picked up the shards of my life when Audrey died and who managed to put them back together in something approaching the right order. Neither *Webster's* nor the *Oxford English Dictionary* has words to adequately express my gratitude.

July 26, 2000   I.N.H.

If These Pots Could Talk

I   Khnum and Ptah, and the Clay of Life

Time's wheel runs back or stops: potter and clay endure.

Robert Browning, "Rabbi Ben Ezra," 1864

THE SPLENDOR of London's St. Paul's Cathedral, the grandeur of the Coliseum in Rome, and the intricacies of the temples at Angkor in Cambodia are among many architectural wonders that evoke jaw-sagging awe on the part of peripatetic tourists. Countless times I have asked, "But have you seen the Hypostyle Hall at Karnak?" When they answer "What's that?" I tell them that until they have traveled the Nile from the Pyramids to Abu Simbel they have no yardstick against which to gauge the greatness of Man's architectural accomplishments. The same may be said of the potter's art, and to make the point I show students a small conical beaker that dates from the fourth millennium B.C.—six thousand years ago if we elect to abandon the Christian calendar as politically offensive.

The hieroglyphically recorded history of Ancient Egypt is younger by perhaps a thousand years than is our pot. But from the earliest recorded time, the ram-headed god Khnum was worshiped in his temple on Elephantine Island at modern Aswân. It was he who sat down at his potter's table, slapped a lump of clay onto it to fashion the father and mother of us all. Just as Khnum (or Khnemu) fashioned people, another Egyptian god, Ptah, took to the potter's wheel to create the world, not flat as would be so long supposed, but as an egg-shaped oval.[1] Later potters, particularly those in England in the seventeenth century, were thinking of a quite different couple. But if, as some Creationists may yet believe, the seventeenth-century Irish theologian James Ussher was right in determining that the Garden of Eden materialized on October 23, 4004 B.C., then a beaker like mine might well have been held in Adam's other hand. The beaker belonged to Upper Egypt's Chalcolithic culture of El-Badari that lasted for about six hundred years, between approximately 4000 and 3400 B.C. (Fig. I.I).

FIGURE I.I. Predynastic Egyptian beaker characteristic of the Badarian Culture of the Middle Nile valley, demonstrating the effect on clay fired in both reducing and oxidizing atmospheres. Hand shaped and burnished, fourth millennium B.C.

In 1937 or thereabouts, ten-year-old Audrey Baines visited the Early Egyptian Rooms at the British Museum and was captivated by the rather ghoulish exhibit featuring a very parched Egyptian buried in a crouching position surrounded by a bevy of Badarian beakers. Shortly before or afterward I too visited the British Museum, and the memory of this mummified, but never wrapped, man with gingerish hair was still in my mind when I told my guardian that I thought I'd like to be an archaeologist. I had just bought and was still clutching a copy of Gaston Maspero's *Ancient Egypt*. My uncle angrily dismissed this notion by informing me that archaeology was an avocation and not a profession—and in those prewar days it often was.

Two years later, in the summer of 1939, Audrey Baines was taken to view the ongoing excavations of the Saxon burial ship at Sutton Hoo in East Anglia, arguably the most important discovery in Britain in the first half of the twentieth century. She was unimpressed. It so happened that I was already there as a Boy Scout camping nearby. I too went to see the vast oval hole in the ground and although asked to empty a bucket, I thought the experience singularly uninteresting—until I saw pictures of the dig on the back page of *The Times* and realized that I had been a witness to, even a participant in, something really big.

Early in January 1950, Audrey Baines and I would meet in a much larger hole in the ground amid the ruins of bombed London. We would be married in September, and the rest, as cliché writers are wont to say, is history—albeit archaeological history. But back to the Badarian pots.

Decades later, while sitting outside a tomb at Sakharra not far from the Pyramids, we asked our eminent Egyptologist companion[2] what she knew about the bared burial in the B.M. We learned that the fake-grave's occupant was known to the staff as "Ginger," and that he had been acquired earlier in the century when the museum curators contacted a well-known Cairo antiquities dealer and asked him to find them a pre-predynastic burial for exhibition in the Mummy Room. With unexpected rapidity the crouching and highly desiccated corpse arrived in London. Once in his case and in his mock grave, and packed around with an assortment of Badarian pots brought from the department's store rooms, "Ginger" became one of the museum's most photographed attractions (Fig. 1.2). However, suspicion grew into a legend that this Ancient Egyptian was not nearly as old as he was labeled, and that instead, in the Cairo dealer's eagerness to please, he had dug up and shipped his own uncle.

More certain is it that not all Badarian-style pots are six thousand years old, for once established the style may have continued to be made for a thousand and more years. For my purposes, however, the beaker that I bought while sipping incredibly strong coffee amid the mummies and pots of a Luxor dealer exhibits attributes that make it ideal as a teaching aid. Predating the use of kilns, after being shaped and sun dried, the "green" pot was baked upended in an open fire,[3] rendering it black inside and one third black on the outside, while the rest of its exterior fired red.

FIGURE 1.2. The British Museum's reconstructed Badarian burial with its reassembled funerary vessels.

IF THESE POTS COULD TALK

The absence of oxygen within the pot as well as around that part of the rim and wall buried in the hot ashes turned it black, while the exterior above the slow-burning fire was oxidized and thus fired red.

Although Khnum appears much later spinning his creations on a hand-turned wheel, the Badarian wares were made without it and instead were either built up from rolls of clay or draped and shaped downward over a mandril, before being smoothed and externally burnished to a pleasingly high gloss.[4] Essentially the same atmospheric variants would be employed thousands of years later by Josiah Wedgwood when manufacturing wares he named *Black Basaltes* and its cousin the red *Rosso Antico*. My point is simply that just as students of architecture need to be careful with their superlatives, so in learning about pottery as Audrey and I did, we needed a measure, a point of departure, to help us better understand and evaluate the wares that were to interest us most, namely those of the sixteenth, seventeenth, and eighteenth centuries. But they were not the eras wherein our passion for pots was born. It began in the mud of that hole on a London bomb site and amid the destruction debris of the city's first great disaster.

Audrey was a classics and archaeology graduate of Bristol University and already had experience of digging on Romano-British sites. I, on the other hand, was as green as copper glaze. Through the summer of 1949 I had worked as a volunteer to the then keeper of London's Guildhall

FIGURE 1.3. The Guildhall Museum's Adrian Oswald and his youthful assistant uncovering the remains of a fourth-century Romano-British mosaic in London's Ironmonger Lane, 1949.

Museum, Adrian Oswald, and became his paid assistant only ten days before he was taken ill and left the museum (Fig. 1.3). To my dismay I found myself with the lone responsibility for salvaging what I could from the jaws of the mechanical excavators whose digging was the historically destructive prelude to rebuilding the city.

Fortunately, Audrey's professor at the Institute of Archaeology, Sir Mortimer Wheeler, had gone to India to help set up a state-sponsored archaeological program and had left her with instructions to keep busy in his absence.[5] She, therefore, became my first volunteer helper, and shortly thereafter my assistant on the Guildhall staff and coordinator of a team of other volunteers who ranged from a somewhat flaky Peer of the Realm and a disbanded Home Guard major, to a library assistant and a meat packer with the unlikely name of Charlie Lefevre. Together we gave new meaning to the term "a motley crew." By the summer of 1950 the museum had appointed a new keeper and a senior assistant, but Audrey and I continued to be its archaeological arm, aided by our often rain-soaked and mud-caked, yet intensely loyal, volunteers.

Lacking traditional museum training (I had wanted to become a playwright), I came to what turned out to be my career-long profession unencumbered by the stuffiness and arrogance then characteristic of antiquarian scholars. Consequently, it seemed strange to me that the museum-going public should be allowed to be intimidated and befuddled by case labels that only an insider could understand:

Terra sigillata bowl, OF CRESTIO, *Drag. 29, La Graufesenque, Flavian.*

The aforesaid insiders would instantly know that Terra Sigillata[6] was the name given to the red-gloss pottery generally (but erroneously) known as Samian Ware. Crestus was the potter; La Graufesenque the name of the place in southern France where he made it; and Drag. an abbreviation for Hans Dragendorff, the German scholar who, in 1895, had established a numbered typology for the vessels' shapes—hence Form 29. Finally, Flavian referred to the series of Roman emperors who reigned between A.D. 69 and 96 (Fig. 1.4).

While visiting a provincial museum at Rochester in Kent I saw a case filled with identical Samian Ware bowls and dishes, one of whose labels told me something to the effect that this was the kind of bowl out of which a Roman centurion would have slurped his gruel. With that thought in mind, it was no stretch for me to imagine a legionary officer sitting on a roadside rock, his bronze helmet with its scarlet plume set aside, and his boots unlaced, as his column paused for lunch on its way north to help chase the Druids out of Wales or the barbarian Scots back where they belonged. In short, this was the kind of image I would later term "people stuff," one that would remain at the core of my educational efforts throughout my career.

When I returned from Rochester I was naive or brash enough to ask the Guildhall Museum's new keeper, Norman Cook, why we wrote labels

FIGURE 1.4. Examples of Gaulish, red gloss Terra Sigillata (Samian Ware) of the first century A.D. (*a*) Bowl Form 29, and (*b*) cup Form 27. (*a*) Guildhall/Museum of London.

FIGURE I.5. Copper-alloy (orichalcum) dupondius of the Roman Emperor Vespasian (A.D. 69–79) dredged from the River Thames below London Bridge, 1955.

about La Graufesenque and Drag when we could be telling viewers something they could understand. "Young man," Cook answered, "our labeling is designed to keep small boys from coming in and breathing on the cases."

Like the Rochester label writer, I was beginning to look past the pot to the people who had made, owned, used, and broken it, and in so doing created an imaginary but very personal bond with the long-dead somebody who had been the last to hold it. Alas, many a modern computer-literate scholar will scoff at such romantic nonsense and snort, "What do you expect from a guy who came to the profession out of the theater?" And they are right; but at the same time wrong, dead wrong, for I would have had it no other way!

Fifty years later I still vividly recall the moment when, standing on a Thames dredger as it dumped river silt in front of me, I saw a coin shining yellow in the mud. On picking it up, I stared into its portrayal of the face of Flavius Sabinus Vespasianus, commander of the Second Legion in the Claudian invasion of Britain in A.D. 43 and twenty-six years later ruler of the mighty Roman Empire (Fig. I.5).[7] I knew that no one had seen what I was seeing since a citizen of Roman Britain had tossed his coin into the water as a good luck offering to the river god. It was possible even that it had been thrown from the very bridge that Vespasian himself had crossed as the army with its elephants and cavalry entered an undefended London. For me, that and countless other encounters with the people of the past were what archaeology has always been about.

Only very rarely can an archaeologist be sure of what happened, why, and precisely when. But on March 2, 1950, I had just such an opportunity, and although it preceded the "Why Drag?" exchange, I am certain that it cemented my desire to abandon my theatrical ambition and remain an antiquary the rest of my life.

The first major building project in postwar London was begun in the center of the city only a few yards from the mayoral Mansion House. Where several offices and the hall of the Worshipful Company of Salters had stood before the bombing there was now a huge hole that occupied most of a city block, one that grew bigger with every swing of the contractor's mechanical drag lines (Fig. I.6). The excavation reached to a depth of about twenty feet, cutting through two thousand years of London's history and then dug even deeper into the natural gravels of the Thames Valley. Exposed in profile were the remains of buildings destroyed in 1940, and under them, others consumed in the Great Fire that burned the heart of London in 1666. Below that red welt of burned brick were chalk-built foundations of medieval buildings, and below them yet

FIGURE 1.6. Baptism of fire. The author (bending right) salvaging Roman remains exposed during construction of London's St. Swithin's House, 1950.

another red scar left by the fire that ravaged Londinium around A.D. 120 in the reign of the emperor Hadrian. And under that there was one more.

Through the twenty years since the Roman army had invaded Britain, its procurators and generals had fought, threatened, and bribed the British tribes into at first grudging submission. As for most invaders, paydays were less appealing than were opportunities for rape and pillage, and in A.D. 61 Queen Boudicca (or Boadicea), the female ruler of the East Anglian Iceni, and her two daughters became the subjects of such brutish legionary attention. The humiliated and enraged Boudicca called on her tribe to repel the invaders and regain her independent sovereignty.

Taken completely by surprise, the Romans evacuated their base at Camulodunum (modern Colchester), leaving it to be sacked and burned. Then, emboldened by her initial success and her ranks swollen by contingents from neighboring tribes, Boudicca and her warrior army pressed on to the brand new but lightly defended city of London, whose inhabitants took to their heels as soon as the smoke from burning suburban homes drifted their way.

Virtually unopposed, the Iceni and their allies torched the city, turning its mostly clay-walled dwellings into a blanket of scorched dust—but not before they had enjoyed the satisfaction of wantonly smashing everything that wouldn't burn. At one modest house they ransacked the kitchen and carried its pots and jars outside to an open trash pit and hurled eighteen of them down into it so that each shattered as it landed atop the growing pile of shards. With that done, one (or probably two) of the destroyers seized a heavy amphora and threw that down, crushing the remaining partially broken pots (Fig. 1.7). One more item, a gracefully twin-handled wine jar, remained to be thrown. It landed on the amphora, cracking one of its handles, and in doing so the jar's neck and handles broke off to fall on one side of the amphora and its body on the other. Later, when the shaken Londoners came back to assess the damage, the burned debris was shoveled flat as a prerequisite for rebuilding, thereby sealing the pit and its vandalized contents with the fire's bright red clay. And that was how we found it on a cold March afternoon, some of us drawing, digging, and brushing, while others did their losing best to keep the press at bay, word having spread to nearby Fleet Street that something exciting was afoot in the City (Fig. 1.8).

Although still an archaeological novice, I was even less prepared to handle the press. The following morning, pictures and stories were in every London newspaper. The *Daily Telegraph*'s headline announced "Two Roman Wine Vessels Dug Up In City," and went on to claim that "There are believed to be only four similar amphorae in existence." The *Daily Herald* went one better.[8] Under an even larger headline reading "Two-Pot Luck Found on Bombed Site" it printed that preposterous statement as a direct quote. What I actually said was that to my knowledge there were only four others in the museum collection. To an old-guard museum and archaeological fraternity already infuriated by the amount of press interest my city salvage work was receiving, this was proof that I was a young loose cannon who should have been spiked at birth.[9]

Our cold-water lab was at the often-frozen top story of the historic Guildhall, and through a door that opened into thin air (the abutting art gallery having been destroyed in 1940) we could look down onto the civic pomp that erupted once in a while to greet visiting dignitaries. The afternoon we excavated the "amphora pit" was such an occasion. Unaware of it, and pushing three builders' cement-caked wheelbarrows laden with the amphora and all the broken pots, we trundled up King Street in the

FIGURE 1.7. Roman amphora and wine jar when first seen after having been smashed during the sacking of Londinium in A.D. 61.

FIGURE 1.8. The "Day of the Amphora." Cartoon from the London *Evening News*, and B.B.C. Arabic publication of the discovery.

FIGURE 1.9 The unwitting reception committee that met the arrival of the amphora at London's Guildhall, March 1950.

gathering dusk, leaving a trail of mud behind us. Ahead lay Guildhall Yard and rolled out across it a rich red carpet. Beyond, under a red and white striped awning, stood the Lord Mayor of London, his fur-hatted mace bearer, aldermen, common councillors, sergeants-at-arms, and a phalanx of yellow-and-gold liveried trumpeters, all awaiting the arrival of an honored guest (Fig. 1.9). No less astonished than the august reception committee, we halted at the edge of the carpet, not sure what to do. Several policemen closed in on us demanding that we should leave instantly if not sooner. I replied that I was the city's archaeologist and pointed up to the lab door upon which an anonymous wit had tacked a large sign that read "Heavenly messengers Only." That, I told the officers, was where I worked and now needed to be. The policemen were evidently surprised by this revelation and before they could decide what to do with us, we trundled on up the length of the carpet and under the awning where aghast City Fathers parted like the Red Sea to let our people pass. I think it fair to say that no museum ever received a new ceramic acquisition with more unintentioned pomp and ceremony.

The resulting exhibit that Audrey and I mounted in the Guildhall created considerable interest in the exploits of the Amazon-like Icenian queen as well as in our archaeological salvage work, which at that time operated with no budget, no vehicles, only borrowed tools, and a camera held together with duct tape.

In 1967 the Guildhall Museum and the London Museum were incorporated into the present Museum of London, where the two collections reside together. As so often was the case, there existed a deep and significant gulf between archaeologists and curators, the former insisting that properly excavated ceramics and other artifacts are contributions to history and should be kept together as such, while curators prefer to see each pot in catalogable isolation. Thus, medieval earthenware pitchers are on separate shelves from sixteenth-century dishes, while the latter are separated yet again from stoneware mugs of the same period. Similarly, excavated eighteenth-century jugs are in one cupboard and delftware plates in another. This widely adopted housekeeping policy does not, however, explain why on a visit to the Museum of London's storage rooms I found the Boudiccan ewer sitting on a shelf with an eighteenth-century French stoneware storage vessel and several other distinctly un-Roman pots. The amphora, however, was on exhibition in the Roman gallery with a label saying from whence it came but without any reference to its dramatic role in London's early history.

The problem of lost association is by no means confined to archaeological material. Nine tenths of all objects that aspire to being ancient or antique have been divorced from their pedigrees by the time they pass through the hands of collectors and auction houses. Curiously, however, Victorian antiquaries and collectors were much better at attaching handwritten labels to identify where objects were found than are their modern successors. This is explainable, perhaps, by the fact that eclectic collectors of the second half of the nineteenth century were more likely to enjoy the fact that they were holding a piece of history than are, say, modern ceramic collectors whose aim is to secure every conceivable variation in pearlware cow creamers or the broadest range of stoneware gin flasks.

For obvious reasons, already wealthy collectors are the most likely to covet the rarest and most expensive items in their chosen field, and the same is true of art museums the world over. It was ever thus. In 1913 the keeper of ceramics at London's famed Victoria and Albert Museum warned his superiors of the need to acquire only masterpieces because they alone "are the source of inspiration—and by the number of its masterpieces a collection is finally judged."[10] In implementing this elitist policy the chipped, cracked, and mundane are eliminated, and in so doing we are left with a totally false impression of who had what, and when. The same is true of historical restoration projects whose curators felt safest when acquiring only the most costly furnishing examples in the belief that if they were expensive they must be genuine. However, hindsight (often aided by ultraviolet light) frequently demonstrates that so-called ceramic masterpieces are less pristine than the dealers had led their ingenuous customers to believe. But more on that anon.

When I first found myself as the Guildhall Museum's lone and incredibly ill-prepared "excavations assistant," my knowledge of Roman artifacts was minimal. My months as Adrian Oswald's volunteer had largely been spent with him on the south side of the Thames in the ancient borough of Southwark where the Bankside Power Station was under construction, a site limited to medieval and later artifact sources—the handling of which would eventually prove invaluable as my archaeological career progressed. At the time, however, that educating experience was of little or no use to me when faced with the buried ruins of Roman London.

Archaeology, no matter into what age one is delving, is governed by two simple rules: We peel the ground away in the reverse order in which it had been built up. Thus, the last in has to be the first out. The second cardinal rule is that we date each layer, pit, or whatever it may be by the most recent artifact we find in it. If we think we are excavating a refuse dump from the 1650s and come upon a copper halfpenny of 1750, it's time to think again.

FIGURE I.10. A lithographed ceramic pot lid from the Upchurch Marshes and its incorporated 1857 registry mark.

FIGURE I.11. Mason's Ironstone China marks both discreetly printed and impressed on the underside of a transfer-printed plate. Ca. 1820.

Theoretically, every artifact offers us a date of manufacture—providing we have the knowledge to recognize it. Pottery, be it earthenware, stoneware, or porcelain, is second only to coins in providing its date of manufacture. Just as in the nineteenth century between 1842 and 1867 English registry data can tell us that a ceramic pot lid so marked was made soon after January 5, 1857 (Fig. I.10), so back through time many pieces exhibit clues that can range from actual dates painted into the design to known time brackets wherein identifiable factories were in operation. Although some Staffordshire slipwares manufactured in the latter half of the seventeenth century bear the names of the potters,[11] it fell to Josiah Wedgwood to be among the first to recognize that in the mass marketing of the Industrial Age his name sold dishes. Like virtually all marks on crockery to this day, Wedgwood and many of his competitors stamped or printed their names discreetly on the underside of their wares (Fig. I.11). Not so the Roman-era Gaulish potters who displayed the same marketing acumen and, as brazenly as modern T-shirt advertising, stamped theirs on the upper surfaces of their Samian Ware dishes and bowls where no one could miss them (Fig. I.12)!

FIGURE I.12. Romano-Gaulish Samian Ware potters boldly applied their marks where they could best be seen. BITVRIX.F[ACIT]. Early second century.

IF THESE POTS COULD TALK

Archaeologists working on Roman sites of the first and second centuries, be they in Britain or in continental Europe, have long relied on the classifications of Dragendorff and others as well as on the seminal studies of potter's stamps and relief design elements by Felix Oswald, father of my early mentor Adrian. Thus, if one found (as we did) a dish bearing the name STATVTVS F[acit], a quick check in "Oswald" would reveal that Statutus's factory was located at Rheinzabern in the second half of the second century and that he made both plain and relief-decorated wares.[12]

I, and to a lesser degree Audrey, knew that we had much to learn about Roman pottery if we were to become knowledgeable excavators in Roman London. But the question was, how were we to do that? The shelves and exhibit cases of the Guildhall Museum were loaded with Romano-British pots, but all of them shorn of their contexts and thereby robbed of their ability to tell us how long they had been in use. That is not to say that there were no reports and books illustrating pottery previously found in controlled excavations at such places as St. Albans, Colchester, and Silchester,[13] but outline drawing and old black-and-white photographs were no substitute for holding a pot in one's hand. Not even the best of illustrations can show you how the walls may vary from one side to another or reveal a hitherto unrecognized scoring line suggesting that several pots were made by the same man with the same tool.

We needed to learn not only where and when the countless Roman pots found in London had been manufactured, but also *how* they were made. We needed to see the spoiled pots (wasters) whose testimony to what went wrong in the kiln would be more technically revealing than what went right. But nobody had ever reported finding a kiln site in the square mile of our archaeological jurisdiction. For that we would have look further away to the flat, salt-washed marshes of the kind that Dickens so graphically described in the first chapter of *Great Expectations.* Pip's encounter with the runaway convict Abel Magwitch was on the Essex marshes, but ours was in the southeastern county of Kent near the mouth of the River Medway where sedge-grassed islands stretched for miles. Taking their name from the nearest village, they are known as the Upchurch Marshes. Some of the islands were large and others small, all separated by narrow rills that quickly flooded, making passage from one to another impossible until the tide again receded. So fast would it rise that seawater out of sight one minute could be racing toward us the next, instantly concealing pockets in the mud that once stepped in held you in their suctioning grip (Fig. 1.13). The Upchurch Marshes had been used for gunnery practice during the Second World War, as well as becoming repositories for occasional bombs dropped by Luftwaffe pilots who turned back before reaching their assigned targets. Filled with loose mud, these holes lay in wait, hidden beneath the smooth surface to trap anyone unlucky enough to step their way. One's immediate reaction was to stand up straight and struggle to drag one's boots free. We soon learned, however, that the more we struggled, the further we sank. For the enlightenment

of any reader who may inadvertently step into quicksand, the correct procedure is to fall forward and claw one's way toward what one hopes is the hole's edge.

In the latter part of the nineteenth century, sailing barges laden with London's garbage offloaded their noxious cargoes into the gaps between the marsh islands, creating strayways that allowed hunters of duck and wild geese to pass from one patch of solid ground to another. But by the time Audrey and I, and the two youngest of our London volunteers,[14] first ventured out onto the marshes, wind and tide had destroyed most of these causeways, allowing pottery, glass, and other imperishable trash to spew out across the surrounding mud flats.

It was hard to believe that such inhospitable marshes had once been to southeast Britain what Staffordshire would be to eighteenth-century England. But such was the case. A potting industry that began on the low, coastal ground early in the first century A.D. and continued until early in the third had been a major source of household wares for London and

FIGURE 1.14. Local antiquaries sent servants into the mud in search of Up-church pots while they picnicked on the high ground. Engraving, ca. 1870.

other Roman cities and villas of the region. By the mid-nineteenth century Kentish antiquaries were aware of the kiln sites' existence, and many a happy afternoon was spent picnicking on the adjacent high ground while servants waded and probed about in the mud in search of Roman pots (Fig. 1.14).

So vast had been the potting industry that its debris was to be found across several miles of marshland. However, the areas mined by Victorian antiquaries had been exhausted by the time we first ventured out in the spring of 1950. A survey of the once-revealing Otterham Creek proved disappointing, yielding nothing but a fifteenth-century bronze purse frame. However, the adjacent Slayhills Marsh was strewn with pottery—but not all of it Roman. Excitedly, Audrey (a fervent animal lover) picked up a small cylindrical bottle, and on rubbing the mud from the name impressed into its side, she knew at once who had owned it, where, and why. The inscription read A. HENDERSON, VETERINARY SURGEON, NO. 8. PARK LANE —one of the most exclusive addresses of Victorian London (Fig. 1.15).

FIGURE 1.15. Audrey's first stoneware-focusing find from the Upchurch Marshes: a medication bottle impressed A. HENDERSON, VETERINARY SURGEON, NO. 8. PARK LANE. Ca. 1870–1880.

Audrey's first foray into London's Victorian garbage became a catalyst extending our still-embryonic ceramic interests forward another eighteen hundred years and to a lasting interest in the evolution of English brown stonewares. Stretched out before us was a sea of shattered and intact crockery of varieties that today comprise the stock of countless shops advertising "Antiques and Collectibles." Within minutes, Audrey's large backpack was filled with stoneware ink bottles, printed pot lids, blacking jars, seltzer and ginger beer bottles of all manner of sizes, and yet we had only advanced a few hundred yards out on the Slayhills strayway. I, however, was less easily beguiled. We had come in search of Roman kilns and it made no sense to burden ourselves with Victorian trash. But not until Audrey had sunk knee deep into the mud under the weight of her treasures were we able to persuade her to temporarily abandon her trove and proceed with our intended mission.

About half a mile from shore and after the Victorian garbage had petered out, we sighted what in the distance appeared to be a beach of still-wet

pebbles glistening in the sunlight. As we drew nearer we realized that the glistening pebbles were Roman-era potsherds—thousands of them! We felt like mice, albeit cold and wet ones, who had fallen into a cookie jar (Fig. I.16). Our first inclination was to start picking every fragment that looked interesting, but we soon realized that to do so we would need a fleet of trucks to haul it away. And then what would we do with it all?

As I recall, we came away from that first visit with very few Roman fragments but most of Audrey's retrieved brown stonewares. The down side of our discovery (and we certainly were not the first to make it) was that while all this pottery could tell us a good deal about methods of manufacture, the fragments were no more datable or interrelated than were the mute pots on London museums' shelves. To accomplish anything meaningful we had to find a kiln or a pit containing wares that had all been in use together—in archaeological terms, a discrete and stratified group.

Contacting the marshland's owner, Francis Webb of nearby Hartlip, and gaining permission to excavate was the mandatory next step. Fortunately, he proved instantly amenable and even helpful in that he told me where, when he was a boy, he had found deposits of broken pots. So many shards littered the marshes that it seemed ridiculous to hope that sufficient

FIGURE I.17. Out of hundreds of shards recovered, only two dishes could be pieced together. Both early second century.

pieces of any one vessel could be found and put together. Nevertheless, Audrey and I agreed that we would see what would happen if we retrieved every fragment we could find of one kind of shallow, highly burnished dish. Over a period of six years we brought back hundreds of pieces, and out of them came two specimens, one of them of an apparently characteristic Upchurch Ware type and the other of a variety less well represented among the fragments (Fig. I.17).[15] That, of course, made the latter's shards easier to recognize and isolate.

As late as the 1950s, few, if any, archaeologists recognized the value of what has since come to be known as *cross-mending*. Because major Romano-British sites yielded so much broken pottery, project directors would retain only rims and bases, thereby rendering cross-mending impossible.[16] The procedure means taking the sum of each ceramic type from a site, laying out all the rims, bases, handles, and body fragments, and by a process of elimination gathering together all the shards from any one vessel. Although the end product may be a pieced-together pot that can be exhibited, what we are really looking for is an association of the previously applied numbers that record precisely where on the site each piece was found. Thus, joining shards whose numbers show that one piece was under a wall and another in a refuse pit tell us that the pot was broken and thrown away before the wall was built, and therefore that the contents of the pit predate the building. It is as simple as that. What is not so simple is the long and space-hungry process of sorting that brings those telltale shards together. Alas, cross-mending the Upchurch wares gave us dishes but no dating information or site relationships, for none survived.

FIGURE 1.18. (*a, b*) Large and small carinated beakers, gray bodied and with highly burnished surfaces, together representative of the best of Romano-British potting in the first century A.D. (*c*) As first revealed after being foot-found in the Upchurch mud.

From time to time we found intact or mendable pots, discoveries usually made by the highly unscientific method of unwittingly stepping on them in the mud. That was how I found one of the finest examples of early British potting that I have ever seen (Fig. 1.18 *b*). Known as a carinated beaker, it is almost eggshell thin and decorated above its shoulder with the kind of impressed rouletting that would be "engine-turned"[17] into the surfaces of teaware in the late eighteenth century. A second smaller carinated beaker with a large chip out of the rim lay alongside the first and left no doubt that both had been thrown away together—though why an undamaged beaker of such superlative quality would have been discarded remains anyone's guess.

Almost as common on the marsh sites as the black carinated beakers were others whose shape led them to being called *poppyheads*. Although most were thin-walled and black, some exhibit an attractive silvery sheen. But common to all of them are the rows of dots applied in vertical panels around their walls, with the uniformity of placement probably created by a template made from a strip of pierced leather (Fig. 1.19). This applied dot technique is familiar to ceramic scholars as being *en barbotine,* a French term meaning, according to the *Oxford English Dictionary,* "a paste of kaolin clay used to ornament pottery." If nothing else, this proves that even the august *O.E.D.* is fallible.[18] No kaolin (white Cornish "china clay") was available to the Upchurch potters, who achieved their designs by using the same clay for their dots as they did for their pots. On the contrary, the first news of kaolin's availability would not reach England until about 1740, after potter Andrew Duché had discovered it in the Cherokee territory of Georgia!

It soon became apparent that on the Upchurch Marshes we were finding pots thrown into pits dug before the land surface eroded, leaving only the last foot or so undisturbed beneath the sea of mud. But as the entire region was submerged twice a day, causing the natural clay to be converted to mire, we were unable to detect the outlines of any pit. Nineteenth-

FIGURE I.19. Poppyhead beaker in a high-gloss gray ware typical of the better quality Upchurch wares. Ca. A.D. 60–100. Restored.

century reports had told of actual sealed layers of broken pottery being exposed in the banks, but we were not that lucky. Nevertheless, we did find seven gray-bodied jars of the late second to third centuries standing erect in the sides of banks and distributed in an arc spanning about eighty feet (Fig. I.20). Each pot contained charcoal and the bones of puppies later tentatively identified as akin to the Russian Laika, a form of husky work dog known to have been domesticated in Northern Europe "from remote times."[19] Clearly these were relics of Romano-British ritual, and several explanations were put forward by different experts, the most convincing being the likelihood that the burials were associated with rites to placate Robigus, the god of mildew in wheat. As recently as the nineteenth century, superstitious Devonshire farmers believed that they could rid their fields of weeds by burying three puppies "brandiswise."[20]

In the summer of 1956 Audrey and I had visited Virginia's Colonial Williamsburg as consultants and returned to England in October of that year. In the succeeding winter months before moving permanently to the United States, we returned to the Slayhills marshes for a final farewell. We took no digging equipment with us, as we expected only to recall past adventures and revel in the aroma of the salt sea air.[21] But on reaching the area of the puppy burials I was astonished to find the side of another jar protruding, this one capped by Statutus's inverted Samian dish (Fig. I.21).

FIGURE I.20. Six of the coarse, gray, Upchurch ollae used as burial urns for puppies. The smallest would appear to be the latest in date, but all were undoubtedly buried at approximately the same time. Donated to the British Museum in 1957. Second to third century A.D.

FIGURE I.21. An Upchurch Ware burial urn with its Samian Ware lid stamped STATVTVS.F[ACIT]. Partially decanted and as found. Ca. A.D. 150–180. Found in December 1956.

The bones in the pot had clearly been cremated and came from an animal much larger than the puppies. However, in the midst of packing to move to America there was no time to do anything but add this new discovery to the list of "things to go" and to study it later.

When eventually we took the cremated bones to a local veterinarian to see if he could suggest the size of the dog, he replied that it had been a big one. "It had relatively little hair, walked on two legs, and probably woofed in Latin." The bones had turned out to be those of a person. But why he or she came to be buried amid the puppy pots has never been determined.

When Audrey and I knew that we would soon be leaving England we set about finding homes for the most archaeologically significant material, some of it in the British Museum and some in the Kent county museum at Maidstone. But one group of repairable pots we had found together in the late fall of 1956 had yet to be studied. As it had been clustered together in the mud and isolated from any other broken pottery, we were sure that this had at last been the associated context that had so long eluded us. The numbers of vessels and the variety of shapes seemed sufficient to provide a significant and related assemblage meriting publication. So these, too, came with us with a view to our drawing them and sending the resulting report to the editor of *Archaeologia Cantiana* to be printed along with other papers I had previously contributed.[22]

In contrast to the splendor of the carinated beakers, the marshes yielded several pots that almost certainly were the work of apprentices whose master hurled them away in disgust—the pots, not the apprentices (Fig. I.22).

IF THESE POTS COULD TALK

FIGURE I.22. Apprentice pots from the Upchurch Marshes. Both probably second century A.D.

FIGURE I.23. A toy barrel with filling and spigot holes. The color of the clay and the presence of sedge grasses in it suggest a date in the first century A.D.

Two examples remain in the collection, one a squat and grossly thick copy of a Samian Ware cup, and the other a small bowl better in its exterior appearance but hiding the thickness of a base out of all proportion to the rest. Appealing though these early failures are as an evocation of one's own kindergarten ceramics class, more intriguing is a toy barrel complete with bung hole (Fig. I.23). One wonders whether Romano-British children had dollhouses.[23]

The vast majority of the Upchurch pottery was a smoky-gray earthenware and unquestionably of local manufacture; but in addition there were wares that, like the Statutus dish, were almost certainly imported from France or Germany. The same is probably true of a frilled-rimmed tazza or incense burner in a gritty, gray to buff ware. A jug in the same or a very similar ware is of a type common throughout Roman Britain, and although there is a single shard from a much larger vessel of the same ware from the above-mentioned pit, I'd still bet on its being imported (Fig. I.24). Not so a second, smaller jug dredged up by a local fisherman (Fig. I.25). This has a pink body originally coated with a slip that gave it a smooth, pale yellow surface. That the jug is of local manufacture is attested to by our finding

FIGURE 1.24. (*a*) White jug and (*b*) brazier from the Upchurch mud, but likely to have been imported from France or Germany. Late first to early second century A.D.

FIGURE 1.25. Pink-bodied jug originally yellowish-slip coated. Dredged up by a local fisherman off the tidal Upchurch Marshes. First half of second century A.D.

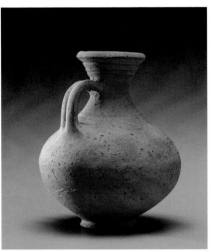

FIGURE 1.26. Fragments from a jar *(a)* and bowl *(b)*, both pink-bodied and yellow-slipped before being painted in red ochre. An extremely rare Upchurch type. First half of second century A.D.

FIGURE 1.27. Wall fragment from a highly burnished Upchurch bowl with incised decoration. Though sometimes called *Weymouth Ware,* it undoubtedly was made in one of the Upchurch potteries. Early second century A.D.

part of an underfired bowl coated with the same slip but overpainted with a remarkable range of red chevrons and dots. Another example, this time the rim of a similarly slip-coated bowl, has its red paint applied in a series of swags (Fig. 1.26). A recent report on Upchurch pottery by archaeologist Jason Monaghan states that "Upchurch Painted Ware is rare and appears to be experimental in nature; possibly being for the potter's personal use only."[24] However, the two very different decorative devices coupled with the vessels' relatively sophisticated shapes do not, in my view, support either supposition. Rare, yes; but experimental—no.

We picked up and retained another fragment because of its remarkable quality. Although previous marsh searchers had found more complete examples, this one serves as a demonstration of the quality that was achieved by polishing the surface to create a high-gloss black and incising decoration through it with a pair of dividers (Fig. 1.27). The bowl's shape emulates that of the best molded Samian Ware, and Audrey and I would have given several right arms to have found the rest of it (Fig. 1.28). Just as discoverers of American Indian sites have named pottery types previ-

FIGURE 1.28. A Victorian rendering of a typical group of Upchurch vessels, among them poppyhead, carinated, and "Weymouth" forms. Engraving ca. 1877.

ously unknown to them by the place where they were found, so this glistening black earthenware has had several names, beginning with those who thought it was imported from Belgic Gaul. They called it *Belgic Terra Nigra*. Others who thought it English and found it near a resort on the south coast called it Weymouth Ware, while yet others who have found a kiln in London give it that name.

The contents of the pit that came with us to America, and that I hoped one day to publish, remained unattended for the best part of forty years. When, at last, I found time to set to work on it, I wrote to the editor of *Archaeologia Cantiana* telling him that at last I was beginning the task that had been a needle in my conscience for far too long, and that once published I would donate the collection to whichever Kent museum would look after it. To my surprise and dismay, back came a letter informing me that Roman pottery strewn across the marshes had nothing new to say,

FIGURE I.29. The Upchurch wares came in a great variety of shapes and sizes, many of them extremely well potted, but most in distressingly small pieces. First to second century A.D.

and furthermore, the county museum needed no more Roman pots. The editor presumably failed to understand that this was not a strewing of shards but rather a discrete assemblage dating from the latter half of the second century. However, it seemed pointless to protest. So the Romano-British collection remains where it can do the most good—as a prelude to the glory days of British ceramics and a constant reminder that more than sixteen hundred years before the rise of the Staffordshire industry, highly skilled Upchurch potters were mixing clays, throwing, decorating, and firing wares that ranged from coarse cooking pots for the country kitchen to tablewares fit for the toga-wearing elite of London (Fig. I.29).

Were Audrey still alive, she would be the first to admit that hunting for pottery on the Upchurch Marshes was the greatest fun she ever had, and I would agree with her. We were both young, strong, and thrilled by the adventure of it all. Nevertheless we recognized from the start that although there was enormous excitement to be drawn from the *Eureka!* of finding, in the long run *finding out* was the real joy of both archaeology and collecting. This was the ultimate thrill that was to stay with us throughout our lives, one I shall try to recapture on these pages as we follow our careers and ceramic collecting (the two umbilically entwined) through the centuries of British and colonial American history.

IF THESE POTS COULD TALK

II In and Out of the Dark Ages

Hath not the potter power over the clay, of the same lump to make one vessel unto honor, and another unto dishonor?

Romans 9:21

YOU MAY HAVE already realized that an archaeologist's lexicon is liberally and irritatingly supplied with weasel words that we can use to escape being downright wrong. *Probably* is one of them. It means could be, might be, ought to be, should be, or conceivably isn't. *Circa* is another. It looks better than *about,* and abbreviates easily to "ca." or just plain "c." Either way, it carries an air of authority and suggests that we are really sure but are being meritoriously cautious. In truth, however, it may mean that we don't know whether our dating is off by one year or fifty. Then there is the equally evasive word *flourished,* usually abbreviated to "fl." and applied to the working life of a potter or any other artist or artisan. In its strict sense it means the point whereat the person reaches the height of fame or excellence, but more often than not it translates as "we never heard of the guy before the given date."

Simple logic should teach us that, just as in human evolution, technological progress means what it says. However, this was not so of the evolution of British ceramics, which took several steps backward when the last Roman headed home. To understand how that happened we need to go even further back—back twenty years before the first cohorts of Julius Caesar's legions fought their way ashore. At some time around 75 B.C., Belgic tribes whose origins were in the Iron Age La Tène culture of the Marne and Aine valleys escaped Roman harassment by crossing the English Channel into southeast Britain, settling primarily in the modern county of Kent, which takes its name from the tribe known to Caesar as the Cantii. They were an industrious and by "barbarian" standards a civilized people, who established farms and villages, linked them with roads, and introduced the heavy plow, as well as coinage and the potter's wheel. With one turn of that wheel the Belgae transformed the crude coil-built

FIGURE II.I. Belgic Upchurch, pedestal beaker with bitumen-burnished collar. Late Iron Age, ca. A.D. 1–50.

wares of the Bronze and early Iron Ages into the often eye-pleasing products that we have seen in the previous chapter.

After two probing campaigns into Britain in 55 and 54 B.C., the second of which got Caesar little further than a hotly contested crossing of the Thames, nearly a hundred years would slip away before the Romans would be back. In the long lull before that storm, British tribes fought among themselves and shaped new alliances, but economically changed very little. To call the Upchurch potters an industry in this early period is to suggest a trading cohesion that probably did not exist. Some of their wares, though wheel thrown, were poor heralds for those to come, and in all our years of combing the marshes we were able to reconstruct but one pre-Roman example and that dated somewhere in the half century between A.D. 1 and A.D. 50 (Fig. II.I).

If you have ever slapped a ball of clay onto a potter's wheel and tried to draw it up into a cylinder, you will have discovered that centering the clay is the first essential, and the second is to catch your cylinder as it flies off onto the floor. An old potter once told me that an apprentice potter takes as much as a year to learn to successfully turn a pot more than six inches in height. By that standard, the best of the Upchurch potters were highly

IF THESE POTS COULD TALK

skilled—with their success reliant on first taming and then mastering the wheel. When the Romans left Britain around A.D. 422, the technology of the wheel is said to have gone with them. But like so many long-held historical truths, there were sufficient exceptions to play havoc with the rule.

In a book devoted to ceramics, the details of how all this came about may seem irrelevant. Because, however, pottery is itself a memorial, we need to understand what kind of Britain the Romans had intended to shape and what really happened in the four hundred years that they were there.

From contemporary historians like Tacitus and Dio, and in our own time from fiction-writing authors like Edward Bulwer-Lytton and Robert Graves, we see a level of civilization and culture that would not be paralleled until the mid-nineteenth century. The key to that Roman high society was commerce, the selling and buying of goods, and by conquering Britain, the emperors hoped to expand their trading empire. What they failed to realize was that Britain had very little to export other than small quantities of corn, Cornish tin, and much larger supplies of slaves. The Britons were a turf-protecting agrarian people ruled by kings, priests, and senior warriors, but lacked a mercantile middle class; nor were there planned towns in the Roman sense. Tribal communities lived within isolated hill forts or on scattered farmlands and had very little truck with their neighbors. Wisely, the conquering Romans preferred not to destroy the fortified settlements, for to have done so would have resulted in huge numbers of displaced, vengeance-seeking nomads scattered throughout the island—a situation not unlike that of the Kosovo refugees in 1998–1999.

Without a prospering middle class to be taxed, the cost to the Romans of policing the island colony would eventually prove too high to be sustained. Consequently, the heyday of Romanized Britain reached during the reigns of the emperors Hadrian and Antoninus Pius (A.D. 117–161) faded all too soon. Towns fell into ruin; private homes built in the Roman manner with central heating, glazed windows, and bathhouses were abandoned to squatters, leaving the military garrisons to waste their lives policing urban slums.[1] Generalizations are always dangerous, and any attempt to put the whole of Britannia into the same cultural box can be grossly misleading. In the southeast, which remained the European gateway to the island, Romanization was more successful and longer sustained. It was in the more distant, western, heavily forested and hilly regions that old Iron Age levels of skills continued uninterrupted. One might argue, therefore, that claiming the loss of the potter's wheel in the fifth century is at best a half truth, for in the wilder parts of the country the peasants may never have used it nor even seen its products.

Wheel-turned or not, there is no denying that pottery making in Britain took a prolonged technological and artistic "time out" in the Anglo-Saxon period, and would take centuries thereafter to come even close to the Romano-Belgic wares of the first and second centuries. Decoration of low-temperature fired urns and cooking pots was limited to ornamental stamps, incised and slashed chevrons, and sometimes with impressed lines

scored by means of a cord spirally wrapped around a stick in the manner of American Indians in the late Woodland Period.[2] The Anglo-Saxon potters of eastern Britain often added bosses or lugs to the exteriors of their wares, a decoration achieved by pressing the clay wall outward from the inside (Fig. 11.2). The result was not very far removed from the projections that had ornamented Bronze Age urns more than two thousand years earlier (Fig. 11.3). The principal difference, however, had been that the Bronze Age vessels had their lugs applied from the outside in essentially the same way that sprig-molded ornament would be applied several millennia later. In short, the Anglo-Saxon potter's craft had advanced very little. In marked and dramatic contrast, however, metalworking and glass making rose to levels that were a match for anything produced in the provincial empire of Rome. The standard explanation for the potters' shortcomings is that the majority of people entering the shadows of the Dark Ages were content to drink out of horn or leather and eat off wood. Consequently, the potters' primary market was in storage vessels and cooking pots that needed no aesthetic appeal. Most of the surviving Anglo-Saxon pots have come from graves, though it is unclear whether they started life as food storage vessels and ended it as cinerary urns or whether they were purchased specifically for the latter purpose.

In ceramic terms, the Anglo-Saxon tradition overlapped into Britain's post-1066 medieval era, but aspired to little beyond convex-bottomed cooking pots. When something better was needed, it had to be imported

FIGURE 11.3. Typical coil-built, early Bronze Age urn with applied lugs and incised decoration. 1800–1200 B.C. Photo: Jonathan Horne.

from modern Belgium, the Rhineland, or Norman France. Only very rarely does any of this pottery, be it imported or homemade, find its way into private collections for virtually all of it has come from archaeological excavations, and in modern times such digging is highly controlled and its "finds" are destined for public museums. That was not the case in the eighteenth and nineteenth centuries (and even in the early part of the twentieth), when amateur archaeo-treasure hunters dug their way through ancient burial mounds in search of funerary pots that then went into the finders' own cabinets of curiosities (Fig. 11.4). More often than not, this unattractive loot would be inherited by kinfolk who, failing to appreciate its importance, threw it out, gave it away, or (if posterity was lucky) donated it to the local museum (Fig. 11.5). Needless to say, there are no such wares in Audrey's and my Collection. A few such pots do occasionally come onto the market, and the example in the Chipstone Collection is one of the best (Fig. 11.2). In truth, however, such wares are of much greater interest to ceramic historians than to the public. Nevertheless, in the timeline of British ceramic usage, the legacy of these early craftsmen has an

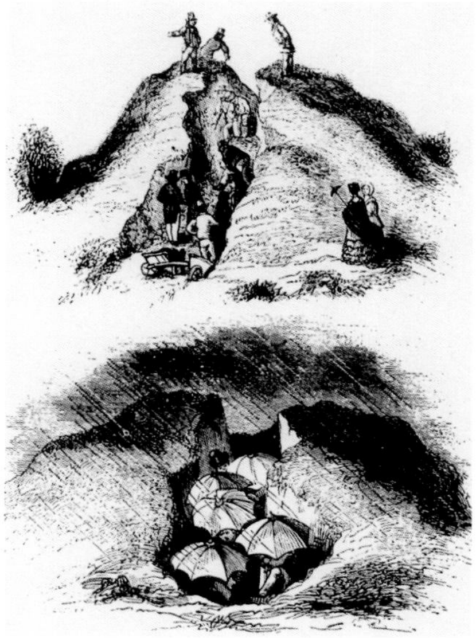

FIGURE 11.4. In the 1870s burial mound robbing was an all-weather sport.

FIGURE 11.5. A grouping of typical Anglo-Saxon cinerary urns unearthed in East Anglia. Second from left similar to Fig. 11.2. Sixth century. Engraved 1877.

FIGURE 11.6. An example of lead glazing in the first century A.D. Jug from St. Rémy-en-Rollat in France. Stolen from the Rochester Museum in Kent and never recovered. Photo: Rochester Museum, U.K.

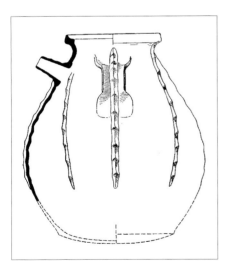

FIGURE 11.7. Drawing of a yellow, lead-glazed pitcher with applied handles and strapped decoration found by the author on the site of the Lloyd's of London building. French, twelfth century. Guildhall/Museum of London.

important role to play, for like any other study of the useful and decorative arts, we cannot appreciate the best as such unless we can measure it against the yardstick of the not-so-good and even the downright bad. In 1877 ceramic historian Llewellynn Jewitt put it this way: "Pottery, as in nothing else, [provides] an unbroken chain, connecting us in our present high state of civilization with our remote barbarian forefathers."[3] Jewitt's idea of his Victorian high state of civilization differed more than a little from our own as we enter the twenty-first century, but so too should our interpretation of barbarism, for like the word *civilization,* it is an essentially comparative term reliant on there having been contemporary alternatives. The same is true of British pottery, whose long history is one of uneven progress that accelerated in the seventeenth and eighteenth centuries with such rapidity that many an old-school potter was left behind in the rush, each innovation distancing the new from the still persisting old.

Few will deny that the most important step forward in the history of English ceramics was the art of lead glazing, although, like the Belgic wares of the Medway, it had its immediate origins in France rather than in Britain.[4] In the first century A.D., kilns near the small modern town of St. Rémy-en-Rollat were producing buff-colored bowls and jugs coated with a pale yellowish-green or amber-colored lead glaze. Scattered fragments of this exotic ware have been found across most of Britain. However, the finest example, an intact St. Rémy jug, was excavated at Bapchild in Kent and became one of the treasures of the county's Rochester Museum (Fig. 11.6). Not nearly as eye-catching as many another pot in that collection, it nonetheless appealed to a thief. At some date around 1950 the exhibit case was forced open and the jug stolen. It has never been retrieved.

As I have noted earlier, my archaeological work in London focused (at least at first) on the plentiful supplies of Roman artifacts that turned up on virtually every construction site. Relics of Saxon London were few and far between, but in 1955 while salvaging all I could from the dauntingly vast site of a new building to house Lloyd's insurance business, I found a large bag-shaped vessel in a buff earthenware coated with a yellowish-orange lead glaze. It possessed both strap handles and a tubular spout, and was vertically decorated beneath the glaze with applied strips of thumb-impressed clay (Fig. 11.7). Made, I supposed, as a wine or beer pitcher, it was a classic example of the superior pottery reaching England, probably from Belgium, in the twelfth century.[5] The shape with its characteristic sagging base and separately applied tubular spout was to be copied by English potters and must have been one of the standard decanting vessels of the early medieval period. At that time, although generally wheel turned, most English utilitarian wares were unglazed. But so, too, were some of the imports, notably the hard sandy wares, iron-slip splashed, from Pingsdorf in the Rhineland, that were reaching eastern England in the ninth and tenth centuries. One fragment from the Thames has its place in the Collection and exhibits potting rings both inside and out that identify it as a product of the foot-driven wheel (Fig. 11.8).[6]

By the end of the twelfth century the wheel had regained its place as the potter's friend. Although early medieval English potters were not renowned for either their decorating skills or design originality, their slow wheel would retain a place in the much later history of English ceramics both as a decorating tool and as an auxiliary to bat molding.[7]

In its earliest form, lead glazing was achieved by dusting the still moist-surfaced pot with lead sulfide (galena), which in bonding with silica from the clay produced the glassy surface. However, the twelfth-century technical writer Eraclius stated that the green ware was first coated with a thin film of flour and water paste to help lead filings adhere to the body.[8] Either way, this dry application resulted in a patchy and uneven coating of the exteriors of medieval pitchers and was characterized by a stippling effect, with each speck of lustrous glaze having a tiny hole in its center (Fig. 11.9). Although, in principle, glazing serves to render earthenware vessels impervious to otherwise leaching liquids, the glazing of most medieval pitchers was insufficiently uniform to provide such a seal. Furthermore, the wares were glazed neither internally nor on their bases. All in all, therefore, most medieval glazing was more for eye appeal than for impermeability. Nevertheless, it is true that the harder an unglazed pot is fired, the more water-resistant it becomes.

Medieval lead glazing came, as I have previously noted, as dry-dusted galena adhering to a moist surface, later mixed with a slurry of clay and painted onto the pot when leather hard; and later still by dipping the green pot into a galena-enriched slip to create an easily washable bib of

FIGURE 11.8. Shard of Pingsdorf ware from the Thames foreshore. The hard-fired, wheel-turned body is painted in random strokes with an iron oxide–based slip. Twelfth century.

FIGURE 11.9. Jug demonstrating the pitted effect of dry galena glazing over a white slip on a red earthenware body. Thirteenth century.

FIGURE 11.10. Typical lead glazing without an underlying slip on a late medieval Surrey jug. Ca. 1375–1475.

glaze below the pitcher's spout. This last was most common in the latter years of the Middle Ages. However there is still some dispute as to the date at which this dipping practice began. The Staffordshire ceramic historian Simeon Shaw gave the credit to experimental potter Enoch Booth (ca. 1750), who, he said, "first introduced that most important improvement on the manufacture of pottery—the fluid Glaze."[9] This, however, was something quite different, being a mixture of lead and flint that was essentially colorless, and unthickened by the clay slurry. Shaw explained that the wares so dipped had first been subjected to a preliminary firing that brought them to the *biscuit* stage, meaning that a second firing was necessary to melt and bond the subsequently applied glaze.[10] Most medieval vessels were fired only once (Fig. 11.10).

Although in some instances medieval glazes were deliberately colored, such as with iron oxide or manganese to render red earthenware dark brown or a purplish black, the color of the end product depended on the character of the clay, and on atmospheric and temperature vagaries in the kiln. Experiments conducted at the Williamsburg Pottery in Virginia have shown that atmospheric variations coupled with impurities in the clay could render a lead-glazed pot red-brown on one side and greenish yellow on the other. Similar inconsistencies could also result from the use of different kinds of fuel wood, as well as through firing variations from oxidation to reduction, and often back again. Most kilns were circular and, like a late-seventeenth-century example found in Westmoreland County, Virginia, had flues and ash pits dug into the ground and so survived for archaeologists to uncover (Fig. 11.11).

Just as London and the Upchurch Marshes had been our learning centers through the first six years of our professional careers, circumstances that could not be foreseen or even imagined were to bring Audrey and me to Virginia to continue our antiquarian schooling through the rest of our

FIGURE 11.11. Virginia potter Morgan Jones's kiln substructure excavated in Westmoreland County. In use 1677. Photo: William Kelso.

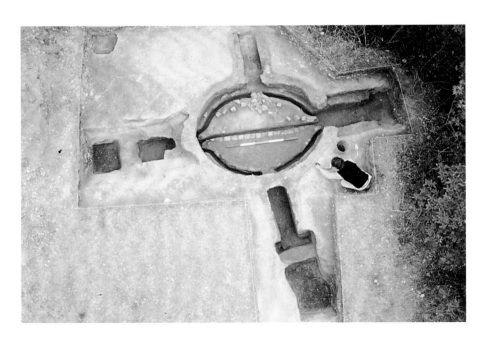

IF THESE POTS COULD TALK

working lives.[11] While our primary responsibility was to study the earth and artifacts of eighteenth-century Williamsburg, the foundation's acquisition of the Carter's Grove plantation some seven miles east of the city on the James River shifted our focus to the plantation's early-seventeenth-century beginnings when the tract was know as Martin's Hundred. Its administrative center, named Wolstenholme Towne, was destined to be destroyed by Indians in 1622, whereafter the studied settlements limped along with a greatly reduced population until about 1645. Our excavations, sponsored by Colonial Williamsburg and the National Geographic Society, began in 1976 and continued through the springs, summers, and falls of the next seven years.[12] Throughout that time, Audrey and I were to focus almost exclusively on Martin's Hundred, she as curator and project historian and I as archaeological director. In the process we learned more about the possessions of Brits at home and abroad in the seventeenth century than would ever have been possible had we stayed in London.

On two of the Martin's Hundred sites we found a potter's waste products: broken pots (both overfired and underfired) and even baked clay from the kiln itself, but no sign of the kiln's foundation. This was by no means the first time that clear evidence of a potting operation has been found but without a trace of the kiln itself being discovered.[13] The usual explanations are (a) that the kiln is nearby but beyond the limits of the excavation, or (b) the waste has been brought from somewhere else and used as landfill. Either can be true; but there is a third possibility, one that was provided at a place where we least expected it.

Having been up and down the Nile several times, both Audrey and I had become enthralled by the splendors of Ancient Egypt, so it seemed an obvious extension of that interest to visit the pyramids of Mexico's Yucatán Peninsula. While staying in a hotel at Uxmal we examined reproduction antiquities being sold in its gift shop and asked whence they came. "Out back," came the answer (or words to that effect), and sure enough, in a grove beyond the gardens we found the potters and their kiln (Fig. 11.12).

FIGURE 11.12. A primitive but effective pottery kiln at Uxmal on Mexico's Yucatán Peninsula, making tourist souvenirs in 1978. The kiln had no below-ground flues or foundation and once dismantled would leave no structural traces. 1978.

FIGURE II.13. An earthenware potter in his workshop. Outside, his kiln resembles the one photographed at Uxmal. Originally a German woodcut, reused in England. Seventeenth century.

FIGURE II.14. Conjectural section through a hog-back kiln, interpreted with the help of Virginia master potter James E. Maloney and ceramic evidence from the kiln site of Edward Challis. Ca. 1690–1730.

The clay-walled structure was circular, domed, and looked for all the world like one we had seen in a seventeenth-century woodcut (Fig. II.13). It had a hole in the roof covered by a removable trash-can lid, and an entrance at one side large enough for a man to crawl through to load and remove the products. But this kiln had no flues, nor any below-ground foundation. It simply stood on the land surface. The pots and figurines were set on shelves at either side, and the fueling billets of wood lay between them. Once the fire was burning, the entrance was sealed by an iron door, and the air circulation was controlled by the trash-can lid. Nothing could be simpler, yet the potters told us that this kiln had been in use for six years without having to be rebuilt. Once dismantled, however, it would leave nothing in the ground for archaeologists to excavate—other than the craft's clay pits and waster dumps.

Not all kilns were circular or even square; some were long and narrow with a firebox at one end and a chimney at the other. These "hog-back" kilns were often cut into the side of a hill and situated to take advantage of the prevailing wind. In such kilns (Fig. II.14), pots closest to the fire

FLASH WALL BUILT AGAINST NATURAL CLAY

SANDSTONE SLABS

NATURAL CLAY

HUMUS

HUMUS

SCALE 1 3 5 7 FEET

SECTION THROUGH POTTER'S KILN OF TYPE BELIEVED USED ON THE CHALLIS SITE, CIRCA 1690 - 1730

source were likely to be harder and darker than those at the chimney end. More often than most early potters would have liked to admit, some pots became so heated that they warped and cracked to a degree that no one would buy them even as *seconds*, while others received too little heat and emerged soft with their glaze unbonded. Similar variations were common to the brick-making trade: bricks burned too hard were called *clinkers*, while those furthest from the heat emerged underfired and were known as *samels*.[14]

For all these reasons it is extremely hard to distinguish local characteristics on the basis of color alone. More reliable are the results of neutron-activation or spectrographic analysis to determine a pot's chemical composition. To prove that the Martin's Hundred shards really were made from the local clay, Dr. Stephen Clement, professor of geology at the College of William and Mary, conducted extensive tests not only on Martin's Hundred pottery but on other samples from England and Europe to plot their alkali-to-titanium ratios. When compared with a series of such charts derived from tested wares whose places of origin are certain, it is possible to narrow the field of possibilities. But narrowing is not pinpointing. Although in the 1970s this kind of analysis was still in its infancy, the testing showed that while an English pot made in Staffordshire might read differently from another made in Essex, it may have a match in Virginia or even in Italy. And there's another snag.

While attempting to associate a Martin's Hundred slipware dish with fragments of others from a nearby kiln site, we were dismayed to find that there was no spectrographic match. The reading had been taken from the surface of the dish. When we tried again using a sample from beneath the surface, the ratios matched both shards from the kiln site and samples of the natural clay. The explanation was this: When finishing the shaping process and smoothing the outer surface, the potter dipped his hands once again into his water bucket—water already clouded with clay slurry. The lighter clay particles remained elevated in the water, while the titanium and other heavy elements separated out and sank, and as a result a thin skin of the purer clay coated the surface of the dish, concealing its true chemical identity.[15]

Without resorting to chemical analysis, there is still much to be gleaned from the careful visual examination of chipped medieval pitchers—or even from the chips themselves. No matter what their age, more can be learned from broken specimens than from those that have survived unblemished. Consider, for example, the use of clay slip. Once lead glazing became the norm, it was not unusual to find that between a glassy green surface and the pinkish red of the body there was a coating of clear white slip. That there is such separation can be much more easily recognized by examining the edge of a shard than by looking only at the finished surface. The purpose of this intermediate step was to separate the glaze from impurities such as iron oxide that could leach out in firing and discolor the surface, and at the same time to make a green glaze appear more brilliant (Fig. 11.15). Though used in England, this technique was common in

FIGURE 11.15. Detail showing the appearance of copper-enriched lead glazing above and below a white slip on a sixteenth-century English chafing dish.

FIGURE 11.16. Medieval pitcher fragments, illustrating the use of slip (*a*) as a base for glazing and (*b*) as matt, unglazed, painted stripe ornament. Thirteenth to fourteenth century. Ex Burnett Collection.

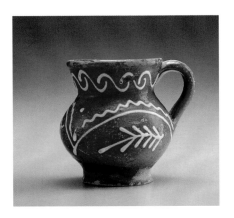
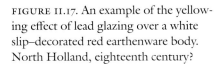

FIGURE 11.17. An example of the yellowing effect of lead glazing over a white slip–decorated red earthenware body. North Holland, eighteenth century?

northern France in the thirteenth to fifteenth centuries where redware exporting potters strove to emulate the most colorful wares of competitors using white-firing clays (Fig. 11.16 *a*). By the end of the fifteenth century the higher priced ceramic products of both countries were often slip-coated in their entirety, thus giving them a totally yellow appearance.

Before going any further, a word of caution: When we talk (and write) about *yellow* slip decoration—which will come up more frequently in the seventeenth century—we are really meaning a whitish (or at least lighter) clay being applied over a darker. It was the yellowness of the "clear" lead glaze that colored the light slip yellow, and at the same time turned a red earthenware body a rich brown (Fig. 11.17).

If the mistress of an affluent medieval household in England wanted pottery jugs somewhat more ornamental than the home-thrown variety, it was to French imports that she would turn. Using whiter clay than was then available to most English potters, the French produced a wide range of color combinations. A fourteenth-century example from my London salvage excavations was made from an almost white French clay coated with a lead glaze that turned the exterior a rich yellow (Fig. 11.18). Relief ornamentation had been added in the form of orange-firing vertical ribbons of clay, with the space between them punctuated with similarly created dots. An additional example of "styling" was provided by the crest of the handle, whose anchoring clay was smeared and drawn upward into a pair of separated tabs. This handle detail on an English jug is represented in the Collection by a fragment that exhibits another decorating technique, namely, the painting of white slip designs on an otherwise unglazed body (Fig. 11.16 *b*).

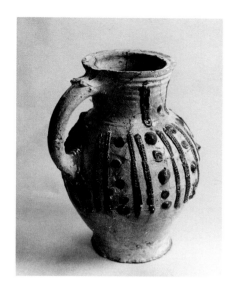

FIGURE II.18. White to buff ware pitcher decorated with applied red clay strips and bosses under a yellowing lead glaze. Found by the author at the site of Watling House in London. Probably from Saintonge, France. Fourteenth century. Guildhall/Courtesy of the Museum of London.

FIGURE II.19. Whiteware pitcher with thin strap handle and parrot-beak spout. Decoration in green, yellow, and black. From site of Watling House, London. Saintonge, late thirteenth century. Guildhall/Courtesy of the Museum of London.

From another London site I retrieved an even more flamboyant French pitcher, its pale gray ware harder fired than was usual and painted with a noticeably complacent bird and pseudo-heraldic arms in green and brown. No less striking were its relatively thin strap handle and its separately applied "parrot bill" spout (Fig. II.19). This jug was made at Saintonge in southwest France in the fourteenth century, a major potting center where at least fifty kiln sites have been located. Archaeologist and ceramics expert John Hurst has written that "From the 13th century the Saintonge was one of the primary production centres for supplying pottery to Britain and northern Europe," and he links it to England's annexation of Gascony and the developing cross-channel wine trade.[16] One can well imagine a French entrepreneur concluding that "if the English want our wine then they are an easy mark for our pots to put it in." Although that may have been true at the outset of the trade, by the time we get to the late fifteenth and sixteenth centuries, the French export products had shifted to more sophisticated forms with levels of embellishment never previously seen. Decorated with characteristic splashes of bright green and orange, they came in an infinite variety of shapes that ranged from relief-decorated dishes and double-handled barrels to incense burners and bird whistles. Particularly popular were bowls and jugs decorated with pre-molded human faces and even with entire heads and upper bodies attached to the rims of pitchers. The French also produced a unique form of chafing dish with four upward-looping handles, a form that, alas, is represented in the Collection by no more than its base (Fig. II.20).

From France, too, came another technical and artistic innovation involving a buff-colored body coated first with a red (iron oxide) slip and then with a white. The latter was carefully cut through to expose the red using a fine-toothed comb for broad cuts and a square-ended burin to incise concentric circles as the dish rotated on the slow wheel. The usually foliate decoration was splashed with a deep blue smalt and with copper green before lead glazing. Like the illustrated fragment that Audrey found

FIGURE II.20. (*a*) Base from a French strap-handled chafing dish from the Burnett Collection. (*b*) An intact parallel found at Delft in Holland. Probably Saintonge, sixteenth century. (*a*) Ex Burnett Collection; (*b*) Museum Boijmans Van Beuningen, Rotterdam.

FIGURE II.21. Examples of double and single sgraffito–decorated dishes. (*a*) Pale yellow body with red slip under white and splashed with copper, with the white slip carved through to expose the red. Beauvais, France. Found in the Thames, sixteenth century. (*b*) North Devon single sgraffito, white slip over red body, found in Bristol, ca. 1620–1660.

FIGURE II.22. Anthropomorphic molded spout from a pink-bodied pitcher. Found by the author at site of St. Swithin's House, London. Probably imported, ca. A.D. 120. Guildhall/Courtesy of the Museum of London.

on the Thames foreshore (Fig. II.21 *a*), the rims were usually ornamented with comb-incised mottos. This complicated technique was characteristic of kilns at Beauvais in northern France in the first half of the sixteenth century but continued into the first half of the eighteenth century. Because the coloring process involved two layers of slip it is known as *double sgraffito,* in contrast to using a single coating of white-to-buff slip and cutting through that alone to expose the red ware beneath. The latter much simpler process is illustrated by a typical mid-seventeenth-century fragment from North Devon, a type frequently found in America on sites of the second quarter of the seventeenth century (Fig. II.21 *b*).

Although the slipwares of Beauvais were made from a light-firing clay, as were other forms, and regardless of the fact that its potters made yellow-glazed bird whistles and other toys, none were as elaborate as those from Saintonge, where relief ornamentation reached levels unmatched since the heyday of Imperial Rome.

The popularity of "face pots"—those possessing what might pompously be described as *anthropomorphic ornament*—can be traced back in Britain into the second century, as an example I found in London attests (Fig. II.22). Although the concept came from Europe, English potters were inspired to turn some of their pitchers into people, and did so as early as the thirteenth century. However, most examples date from the next century, and along with human figures as spouts one finds applied clay horses and other animals charging around the sides, an application sometimes reminiscent of Roman Castor Ware (Fig. II.23). However, the latter was not applied in strips but was squirted onto the pot like writing "Happy Birthday" on cake icing, in short, *barbotine* decorating. That attractive Romano-British pottery is attributed to second-century kilns in Northamptonshire, and as the best of the medieval humanoid jugs are thought to have been made in neighboring Nottinghamshire, one might be tempted to reach for a continuing decorative tradition. But as the Dark Ages intervened to stand astride a time lapse of more than a thousand years, any similarity has to be coincidental.[17]

FIGURE II.23. An example of barbotine decoration, applied like cake-icing ornament and characteristic of fine-quality wares produced at Roman Castor in Northamptonshire. Second century. Guildhall/Museum of London.

FIGURE II. 24. Anthropomorphic jug, green-glazed redware. English or French, thirteenth century. Private Milwaukee collection.

What is not coincidental, however, is the prevalence of anthropomorphic pitchers on exhibition in English museums and illustrated in their catalogs (Fig. II.24). Commonplace, too, are photographs of such vessels to serve as illustrations in archaeological reports. Taken at face value, therefore (and no pun is intended), one might be persuaded that humanoid jugs were as widely used as any other. That, however, is yet another example of artistic selectivity on the part of curators, publishing archaeologists, and ceramic collectors. The common wares are locked away or thrown out, and in archaeological studies are represented only by outline drawings. The bitter truth, therefore, is that plain isn't pretty.

That certainly is true of what may or may not be the earliest medieval object in the Collection and whose purpose is no more certain than its age. Purchased in a London street market, this globular and spouted bowl is made from a hard gritty gray ware of the kind commonly associated with crucibles (Fig. II.25). That may, indeed, be what it is. An alternative theory is that the bowl was an oil lamp whose spout served as a cradle for the wick. One might well wonder, however, why a lamp would have a rounded bottom and be unable to stand unless seated, say, in sand. In my years of London archaeology, I found three others, one of about the same size in a fourteenth-century context and two more much smaller examples in an earlier well on the same London building site that yielded the relics of Boudicca's vengeance. In neither instance was there evidence of assaying, distilling, or metalworking, and none of the specimens retain any of the dross that one associates with used crucibles. The two small examples were no more than two and a half inches in diameter, and were found with a strange oval glass "gem" pale blue-green in color and internally dappled

FIGURE II.25. Crucible or lamp in a hard, sandy, unglazed gray ware characteristic of crucibles as late as the eighteenth century. A street market purchase. Medieval?

FIGURE 11.26. *(b)* Large green-glazed and slip-banded pitcher with *(a, c)* associated small crucibles found together in a well at the site of St. Swithin's House, London. Thirteenth century. Guildhall/ Courtesy of the Museum of London.

with a darker blue pigment. Present also was a heavy, green-glazed pitcher of a type characteristic of the thirteenth century (Fig. 11.26) and that thereby provided an approximate date for the well's abandonment.

My emphasis on pitchers is not the product of hierarchical selection but stems simply from the fact that throughout the Middle Ages English glazed wares were limited almost exclusively to pouring vessels, to the exclusion of dishes, bowls, or drinking mugs. Those needs, as I have noted, were available to the peasantry from the hands of workers skilled in other media, such as the turners of wooden (treen) trenchers and bowls, and to the makers of horn and leather bottles and mugs. For the rich and powerful there was silver-gilt, and for those lower on the social ladder, pewter. But in the kitchens and butteries of the great as well as on the tables of their liegemen, as well as in monastic refectories, there was always a need for beer and wine pitchers. To serve this market, English potters did their often clumsy best to make their wares attractive and even amusing. I found good and not so good examples of these decorated jugs in a London trash pit, their bulbous walls enhanced with chevron-patterned yellow slip around manganese-colored triangles dotted with more yellow slip (Fig. 11.27). Although the decoration of the two medieval jugs is much the same, light

  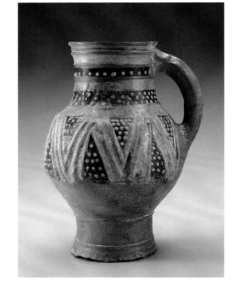

FIGURE 11.27. English redware versions of Rouen slipware pitchers decorated with applied chevron strips, the triangles infilled with manganese slip under applied pellets. *(a, b)* Found by the author together at the site of Watling House, London. The spout of *(b)* was almost certainly incorrectly reconstructed. *(c)* Parallel to *(a)* purchased in the antiques trade. Fourteenth century. *(a, b)* Guildhall/Courtesy of the Museum of London; *(c)* Chipstone Collection.

chevrons bordering purplish triangles, the difference in quality is plain to see. But there is another significant difference. The larger of them has a projecting spout while its companion does not. I believe I am right in recalling that this spout was one of Audrey's restorations—or more accurately, her *creations*. I remember my own embarrassment on taking a visitor through the Guildhall Museum's pottery store and producing an English fourteenth-century jug with the type of "parrot bill" peculiar to the previously mentioned French jug (Fig. 11.19).

"Isn't this a remarkable hybrid?" I declared—and only then remembered that in my archaeological infancy I had reconstructed the jug and given it a plaster-built spout of that shape for no better reason than I thought it looked interesting. That recollection has remained with me throughout my career and taught me that honesty in reconstruction allows us only to put back what we can prove to have been there. If neither the vessel itself nor other surviving examples give us any such assurance, then the rule is to rebuild only what we can see—even if we know that some significant feature is thereby omitted.

The ethics of ceramic restoration have grown increasingly murky as techniques improve in an attempt to keep one jump ahead of the latest scientific devices to unmask them. Some years ago while roaming the Portobello Road antiques market I was asked by a dealer (who apparently knew me by sight), "What do you think of this?" She pointed to an eighteenth-century creamware cruet set whose yellow body was enriched by green flowers in overglaze enamel. "Well," I replied, "the cruet is as right as rain, but the heaviness and tone of the green bothers me."

"I know," the dealer replied. "We're working on it." She had bought a genuine but undecorated cruet set and was adding enameling which, had it been genuine, would have tripled the value of her investment. Museum-quality ceramic restoring is not intended to deceive—at least not for monetary gain. In the 1950s the British Museum's policy regarding the restoration of medieval pitchers was to paint the plastered replacement parts a silvery gray. However, the result took the viewer's eye to the bright bits in preference to the real ware, which, of course, was not the intent. My own approach—once it got over its bogus spout fetish—was to do my best to paint the outside of a hollow vessel or the upper surface of a dish as close to the original as I was able, while leaving the inside of the jug or back of the plate unpainted. By my so doing, anyone with a need to see how much was original and how much plaster had only to look inside or turn it over. I argued that the public was far more interested (if interested at all) in the kinds of vessel its ancestors had put on their tables or under their beds, than in admiring our skill at putting Humpty Dumpty together again (Fig. 11.28).

FIGURE 11.28. Audrey in 1960 in-painting plaster-repaired Pennsylvania slip-decorated bowls, found in Williamsburg, Virginia, excavations. Late eighteenth century. Colonial Williamsburg Foundation.

To the antiques trade, "museum-quality" restorations are rarely, if ever, good enough. The aim is to hide cracks and put back missing parts so skillfully that the buyer will not be aware of them if the dealer chooses not to point them out. This raises another highly debatable question: Setting aside the purely arbitrary value placed on the presence or absence of cracks, does it really matter that a jug or a dish has been invisibly repaired? If the end product is a specimen visually as good as new, and if a buyer has not been tricked into paying too much for it, one might argue—as I do— that an accurate restoration does nothing to diminish a vessel's aesthetic or historical value. If naught else, our espousal of that credo has enabled us to add pieces to the Collection that Audrey and I as impoverished archaeologists could not otherwise have afforded.

We have never shied from buying broken pieces and over time have been given pots with feet missing or rims incomplete, and from these I have derived particular pleasure. Repairing and reconstructing a broken pot, no matter what its ware or age, is a slow job that provides an opportunity to study it and the way it was made with greater and more prolonged attention than would most curators or collectors (Fig. 11.29).

FIGURE 11.29. Burnett Collection earthenwares in the process of reconstruction in the author's ceramic workshop, 1999.

There's time to wonder about the person who made it and what he (or she) may have been thinking while pulling the clay as the wheel turned. My powdered plaster of Paris reveals strange striations in the pot's surface that otherwise would have gone unnoticed. But what caused them? A single swirling pattern holds the answer. It is the potter's fingerprint, and it was this that created tiny tram lines as the pot spun between his smoothing hands. Suddenly we have an affinity, his fingers making the pot and mine remaking it. A young man in love, an old one with little left of his life but to watch the wheel turn and the clay rise? Would this pot be his only legacy? Idle thoughts on my part, you may say. But putting new life into that pot has a satisfaction all its own. For me, using two hands to restore a forgotten potter's creation is far more gratifying than raising one hand to bid on an intact item or another the catalog describes as having "some restoration."

IF THESE POTS COULD TALK

When one is assembling a collection, be it of furniture, glass, ceramics, or whatever, no dealer, no matter how impressive his address, should be considered above suspicion. On the contrary, one is less likely to be misled when buying from a market stall whose owner relies on a quick turnover, than from a high-end dealer who can afford to pay for costly and sales-delaying restoration. A single cautionary tale will serve to make the point:

On a visit to a well-known London dealer, Audrey spotted a Tudor earthenware candlestick, a form not yet represented in our collection. The shape was well known and comprised a tall socket above a flat, median drip tray beneath which the lower stem and foot flared outward to approximately the same diameter as the tray (Fig. 11.30). Such sticks are usually either clear-glazed overall or colored an apple-hued Tudor green—but never, in my experience, both. But this stick was green above the drip tray and yellow beneath it. Closer inspection revealed another unusual feature: the drip tray, instead of being a single, flat disk, had a W-profiled outer edge. The reason was all too apparent, as Audrey explained to the dealer's assistant. "This is a married piece," she said.

"What's a married piece?" the assistant countered.

Audrey went on to explain that the base and drip tray from a yellow-glazed stick had been skillfully bonded to the green socket and tray of another. The price was high even for an intact original, so we did not buy it. Later, however, it occurred to me that having such a hybrid in the Collection could be useful as a teaching aid, so I wrote to the dealer reminding him of its message and asking him to sell it at a reasonable price. He at first denied that there was anything wrong with the stick, but later wrote in some chagrin saying that he had put it through his dishwasher whereupon it fell apart at the bonded drip tray. He was prepared to offer it to us at a somewhat reduced price. We still considered the price too steep, but we both felt sorry for the dealer and concluded that he had bought the stick in good faith and had not known of the deceit until Audrey pointed it out. However, when we were next in London we found the yellow and green candlestick remarried and back on its shelf along with its original exorbitant price tag.

With the growing popularity of selling antiques through the Internet, the buyer's need for caution cannot be overstated. The same applies to buying unseen through auction catalogs as well as doing so only on the basis of a dealer's photographs and descriptions. A Tudor green money box came into the collection by the latter route. The dealer admitted that the globular box had been broken, a revelation that should surprise no one, for the slots to receive the money were too narrow for the coins to be extracted without breaking the box open. The dealer added that the fractured piece had been found with it and had been replaced. That, too, made sense. After the coins had been retrieved, the broken fragment was tidily put inside the box just as one might dispose of the shards of a broken wine glass by putting them within the remains of its bowl. What the money-box seller did not tell us was that although one fragment had been

FIGURE 11.30. A typical "Tudor green" Border Ware candlestick. Late sixteenth century. Photo: Courtesy of the Museum of London.

FIGURE 11.31. Buff-bodied and lead-glazed candle holder with drip tray partially restored. Early seventeenth century.

put inside, another larger fragment was missing and had been replaced with painted plaster.

The case of the patched money-box is an example of a reconstruction that, even for a museum, could not be left unpainted without adversely impacting the visual recognition of what it is—an Elizabethan money box.[18] The same is true of the only early candlestick in the Collection, part of whose deep, basal drip tray was missing (Fig. 11.31). There are instances, therefore, wherein leaving one plaster-built side unpainted would create the visual distraction that one hopes to avoid. The Collection's sixteenth-century brazier or chafing dish (Fig. 11.32) is just such an instance. When I bought it, the upper tier of the perforated wall was missing, and jagged projections that remained had been filed down to make it appear that the dish was open and had a crenelated rim. Fortunately, the British Museum possessed a close parallel that made restoration both legitimate and necessary.[19] To have left the interior unpainted would have meant that the white plaster would have been visible through the several apertures—in my view, a result less acceptable than a modicum of subterfuge.

In London, at the beginning of our museum careers, Audrey's and my jobs depended on speedy restorations at a rate of a dozen or more each month. To this end we set up a slow wheel in tandem with a pot- or dish-profiling template that enabled us to rebuild them even if we had found as little as a third of the original. Thus our laboratory in the attic of Guildhall became a restoration factory that was often working far into the night. Why, you may ask.

FIGURE 11.32. London green-glazed redware chafing dish, the upper terrace largely restored on the evidence of another in the British Museum. Second half of sixteenth century.

IF THESE POTS COULD TALK

At the outbreak of World War II the contents of the Guildhall Museum had been packed up and shifted out of London for storage in the safety of a country mansion.[20] The prewar museum had been part of the City's world-renowned library whose books, in 1945, took precedence over pots and bones. In consequence, at the war's end the library absorbed what was left of the museum's space and was reluctant to release it. However, the head librarian, Raymond Smith, did not go along with members of his library committee who proposed doing away with the museum and giving its treasures to the London Museum, which had reopened in its temporary home in Kensington Palace.[21] Smith therefore told me that I had to demonstrate to his committee that our museum was worth saving by displaying at its monthly meetings the best of the artifacts found in the previous weeks. This meant, of course, that it was no use trying to impress City businessmen with a display of bits and pieces. If we were to survive we had to show them whole pots—hence the attic restoration factory (Fig. 11.33). Covered in building-site mud in daylight and caked with plaster at night, our efforts paid off. The library committee withdrew its proposal to shut the museum, and although its exhibits would later be shifted from one City-owned building to another, it remained open for several years after Audrey and I emigrated to Virginia.[22]

FIGURE 11.33. Audrey at work in the Guildhall Museum's attic restoration factory, ca. 1952.

III   Adam, Eve, and a Bishop's Geese

And they cried out and said,

O thou man of God

there is death in the pot.

II Kings 4:40

THERE ARE TIME periods whereof any historian or collector may say "I really would like to have lived back then" and proceeds to explain why Classical Greece or maybe Victorian Baden Baden would have been the ideal time and place. I have never felt that way about the English Middle Ages. Clanking about in armor or sitting in a great hall trying to keep warm, while wreathed in smoke that declined to exit through the hole in the roof, seemed a grim existence, one best left to Ivanhoe and to Robin Hood and his insufferably merry men. In ceramic terms, England before the Tudors had no place in the evolving story of world technology, having aspired to nothing that had not been accomplished better or earlier on the Continent.

The Chinese had been producing white, translucent porcelain while the British were still floundering around in the Dark Ages. Although it was not until the beginning of the Ming dynasty in the fourteenth century (1368–1644) that the Chinese developed the quality wares for which they became so justly famous, they were not alone in producing ceramics that consciously combined beauty with utility. From the twelfth century onward, potters in Persia and Afghanistan inspired by Chinese exports were producing slip-coated and painted wares covered with clear lead glazes, which at a distance had the decorative appearance of porcelain. Not only had Near Eastern potters mastered the ornamental use of metallic oxides, by the ninth century they had developed the technique of luster-painting that would eventually work its way westward along with the whitening of lead glaze with tin oxide to create the Renaissance products of Arab Spain. Hispano-Moresque and polychrome-painted maiolica dishes and albarelli became high art in Italy in the late fifteenth century. From Florence potters emigrated northward, taking maiolica production techniques into

Flanders, and began shipping their Italianate wares into England early in the sixteenth century. I excavated a pit of that period in London that held three examples, a large maiolica pitcher that may have been Florentine and two flower vases that I was convinced were Netherlandish. One was decorated with the YHS monogram of Catholicism painted in cobalt and characteristic of the first quarter of the sixteenth century (Fig. III.I). These, and others like them, marked the beginning of tin-enameled earthenware usage in England, and where there were markets there soon would be makers.

The first major study of the sixteenth-century wares came from the pen of Bernard Rackham, the distinguished keeper of ceramics at the Victoria and Albert Museum whose 1926 book *Early Netherlands Maiolica* became the sextant for Audrey and me when we first ventured into the poorly charted waters of sixteenth-century domestic pottery.[1] Fifty years later I learned that we had been steering in the wrong direction. The British Museum's Department of Scientific Research was to pioneer a new technique called neutron activation analysis (NAA), which would become as crucial to ceramic detective work as DNA has to prisoners on Death Row.[2]

Although we were able to benefit from Stephen Clement's spectrographic analysis of alkali to titanium ratios separating the local clay from others used in pottery from known production sources in England and Europe, the new NAA technique is more refined and has left no doubt that many of the early vases cited by Rackham (as well as those we found) were not Netherlandish in an Italian style but were actually from northern Italy. Although neutron activation is not confined to the British Museum's laboratory, discriminant analysis requires that there be a broad enough base of comparative material relative to the specific question being asked. Nor is it cheap. Consequently, cautious and penurious archaeologists now hedge

IF THESE POTS COULD TALK

their bets and refer to tin-glazed wares that look as though they ought to be from the Low Countries as Italo-Netherlandish maiolica.

Just as Belgic potters had retreated into southeast Britain as the Romans tightened their grip on Gaul in the first century B.C., so in the sixteenth century A.D. another wave of emigrants crossed the North Sea into England, most of them Protestants escaping the clutches of Catholic Spain. Some followed the Belgae into Kent, but others landed further north in East Anglia. In 1567 two maiolica potters from Antwerp, Jasper Andries and Jacob Janson, resumed their craft in Norwich but soon realized that their marketplace was not in a small provincial town but in the country's greatest population center. Consequently, they moved as close to London as the city fathers would allow, and in 1570 set up in business outside the north wall at Aldgate. In so doing they launched the London delftware industry that was to endure for two hundred years, and one with which I would become umbilically associated.

In the summer of 1949, while I was still a volunteer helper to the Guild-hall Museum's Adrian Oswald, I worked with him on the site of the first major, postwar building project, the construction of the previously mentioned Bankside Power Station. Located on the south side of the Thames just below Blackfriars Bridge, this had to have been one of the ugliest buildings ever erected in sight of the city. Though it was scheduled to be demolished in 1999, the Millennium's arbiters of taste decreed that the complex described as "Sir Giles Gilbert Scott's gloomy power station" should be saved to become the shared home to Britain's principal center of contemporary art, the world-renowned Tate Gallery.[3] The site bordered on a narrow street called Gravel Lane where, from the late seventeenth to the mid-eighteenth century, along with glass making, two entirely different styles of pottery were in production. They were the tin-enameled wares now familiarly called delftware and brown stonewares, which together met the household needs of British and colonial families through much of the latter century. It was there, beside Gravel Lane, that I learned about the potter's aids known as *kiln furniture* and discovered that *saggers* were something other than things that drooped, that not all *biscuit* was to be eaten, that *stilts* were not restricted to making short people tall, and that *wasters* did not necessarily refer to those who were profligate, or *seconds* to pugilistic assistants.[4]

The lessons learned on the power-station site were to stand me in good stead when my beat as the City's salvage archaeologist took me further downriver into the boroughs of Southwark and Bermondsey, which border the south bank of the Thames. The waterfront buildings both above and to a lesser extent below London Bridge were known as the Bankside, and from medieval times through to the nineteenth century were made both famous and infamous as the home of theatrical and one-on-one nocturnal entertainments.

The river, which until the Second World War had been the hub of British maritime commerce, had fallen on hard times. Many of the warehouses

FIGURE III.2. Lady Elizabeth and Sir David Burnett, ca. 1997. Photo: John Burnett.

on both sides of the Thames had been gutted by German incendiary bombs and none had been rebuilt. No less damaging to Thames-side wharfingers was the growing reliance on containerization, which reduced export and import costs by loading factory-filled containers, thereby cutting out the need for riverside warehousing. One of the largest of the old companies was Hays Wharf, whose management owned several acres of idle wharfside real estate and which needed to diversify to survive. This necessitated the clearance of bombed properties as prelude to erecting office blocks and other remunerative commercial buildings. The company had been owned and managed through three generations by members of the Burnett family, with the second chairman having also served as Lord Mayor of London. In 1953, the CEO was Sir David Burnett, whom I first met on one of Hays Wharf's bombed properties. David was to become one of Audrey's and my closest friends, for it turned out that we shared the same interest in London history and more specifically in the archaeology of ceramics.

David Burnett is the quintessential nineteenth-century English gentleman (Fig. III.2). Trained as an architect, and an accomplished watercolorist, he had traveled through the Middle East in the 1930s, drawing and painting ancient monuments in Palestine and Syria. An acknowledged expert on fungi and a keen botanist whose library shelves are rich in volumes of his botanical sketches as well as his not always too kind cartoons of City dignitaries, David was unquestionably the most attuned landowner I ever tried to interest in whatever might lie buried on his property. And that was just as well, for Hays Wharf owned land once occupied by an emigrant Rhenish entrepreneur named Christian Wilhelm, who settled there in 1604, renting part of a house at Pickleherring Quay.[5]

Although Wilhelm was involved in a variety of commercial enterprises that ranged from making blue starch to vinegar and the distillation of potable spirits, by 1612 he was cited as a "galley pott maker"—which brings me rather belatedly back on ceramic track. In 1628 Wilhelm secured a patent that, among much else, stated that he had been making galley ware in England for the past twenty years. Along with galley pots (small pharmaceutical ointment jars) of kinds represented by two examples in the Collection (Fig. III.3), Wilhelm was authorized to manufacture the aforesaid "earthen gallie potte and dishes called by the name of Galliware . . . And all kinde or sorte of bottell[s] of all Colos[,] basons & ewers[,] salte dishes of all sorte[,] drinkinge pott[,] pavinge tyles[,] Apothecaries & Comfittmakers potte of all sorte & all kinde of earthen worke as he the said Christian Wilhelme hath heretofore invented and made."[6]

Besides its need for punctuation, that wording requires clarification. The term *galley ware* was used throughout the seventeenth century to describe tin-enameled earthenware that later would be called delftware—with a small "d," big "D" being reserved specifically for the products of Delft in Holland. More confusing than helpful, the same glaze and body combination was called Faenza in Italy, maiolica (or majolica) in both

IF THESE POTS COULD TALK

FIGURE III.3. English delftware "galley ware" pharmaceutical pots. Southwark, ca. 1610–1630.

Spain and the Netherlands into the early seventeenth century, and faience in France from then until now. The derivation of "galley ware" remains debatable, although most scholars are prepared to accept the explanation that in the early sixteenth century the wares were first shipped into England from the Mediterranean aboard rowed galleys.[7] However, if ships were the derivation, they were not bound for England. As early as 1513, Italian potters working in Antwerp were identified as *galeyerspotbackers*, making it clear that the name came to England with the first Netherlandish tin-glazed wares. Although galley ware remained the generic name for all manner of shapes through most of the seventeenth century, the term "galley pot" was reserved from the vessels defined as *Apothecaries and Comfittmakers*. These pots were cylindrical jars from which to dispense pharmaceutical potions or in which to preserve fruits and pickles, the former often small and similar to the two examples in the Collection.[8] In the last decades of the sixteenth and the first of the seventeenth centuries these galley pots were invariably decorated in blue, orange, and/or manganese, but by the second quarter of the latter century the small pots were being made in such quantities that the factories ceased adding decoration, having discovered that their customers were more interested in the contents than the pots. However, the larger pots and jars, intended for shelf display in the pharmacy or kitchen, would continue to be decorated, albeit in ever-decreasing elaboration, through into the mid-eighteenth century.

The Wilhelm patent's reference to *pavinge tyles* highlighted a major production line, although as the wording stated, these were tiles primarily intended for floors rather than for chimney cheeks and surrounds, as they would be in the later seventeenth and eighteenth centuries. Like the

III ADAM, EVE, AND A BISHOP'S GEESE   49

FIGURE III.4. Southwark-style delftware paving tiles paralleled by fragments from the Pickleherring kilns site. Ca. 1610–1630.

pharmaceutical pots, the tiles' supposed source earned them the name *galley-tile*.[9] As a rule these early domestic tiles were thick, heavily glazed, and painted in geometric designs repeated in units of four like the illustrated examples from the Collection (Fig. III.4). Whether these particular tiles are English or Dutch has not been determined, for virtually every motif produced at the Pickleherring factory was copied from Netherlandish maiolica—which is hardly surprising when the transplanted workers had learned their craft both as potters and painters on the other side of the North Sea.

Because the borough of Southwark had always been considered part of the original City of London, the monitoring of its postwar construction sites was considered my responsibility. It was, of course, absurd to expect one struggling-to-learn archaeologist to stay on top of every building project, the cranes of which, by 1952, were popping up like mushrooms from one end of the city to the other. Consequently, my efforts focused primarily on the largest sites within easy walking distance of my Guildhall

IF THESE POTS COULD TALK

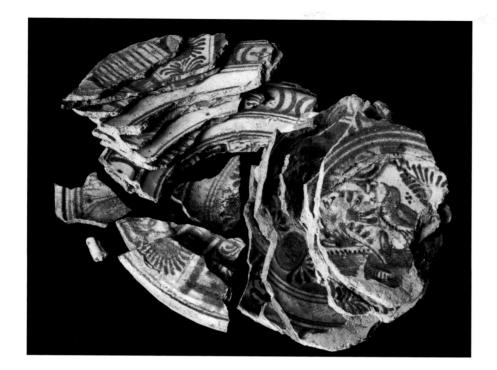

FIGURE III.5. Waster delftware dishes in the Wan Li "bird on rocks" style in monochrome, but one amid the batch in polychrome and in pomegranate design. Ca. 1620–1635. Ex Burnett Collection/ Colonial Williamsburg Foundation.

base, and while there I devoted my time to the being-bulldozed Roman remains that the City fathers and the ever-hovering press considered of the greatest interest. Consequently, the long walk to Hays Wharf was justified only at such moments that the inner city was quiet—which wasn't often. Thus it fell to David Burnett and his people to salvage what they could from his properties. In short, there was no formal archaeological recording and analysis there at a time when it was most needed. We therefore have only David's undocumented recollections of seeing the last traces of Christian Wilhelm's delftware factory being swept away, and cannot be sure of the contexts and exact locations from which its waste products were retrieved (Fig. III.5).

When Audrey and I accepted permanent posts at Colonial Williamsburg, it meant that after January 1957 we would have nothing further to do with London archaeology—beyond annual visits with David and Betty Burnett to view and to discuss the significance of their boxes of broken pots and dishes. Regardless of its lack of archaeological context, there was no denying the Burnett Collection's historical value as a key to the most important ceramic industry in England through most of the seventeenth century. The problem was what to do with it. Having it sit in boxes, first at Hays Wharf and later at David's home, accomplished nothing. The question was being asked at a time when the Guildhall Museum was on hold in the knowledge that its merger with the London Museum was not far off. Consequently, I urged David to offer the collection to the Victoria and Albert Museum, where my friend and mentor Robert Charleston was curator of ceramics and glass. It turned out, however, that Robert was unwilling to accept the whole collection but would accession a selection of key pieces. I, however, argued that the large and readily appreciated

FIGURE III.6. Wan Li style delftware charger, tin-glazed on the obverse, clear lead-glazed reverse and suspension hole through the foot ring. Ca. 1620–1640.

specimens should not be divorced from the rest of the collection, and David agreed. Twelve years later his solution was to give the entire collection to me. I, in turn, arranged to ship it to Colonial Williamsburg, where ceramics curator John Austin was working specifically on delftware. The agreement, therefore, was that I would donate the collection to Colonial Williamsburg on David's behalf, and that in return the Foundation would publish a book that I would write and that would illustrate all the significant material, regardless of whether it came in whole pots or tiny shards.[10]

In the course of studying the collection and then writing about it, I learned much more about London delftware than I could have in any

IF THESE POTS COULD TALK

other way, and in the process of doing so Audrey and I added several key pieces to our own Collection, among them a charger with a geometric design in the Chinese Wan Li style characteristic of the Pickleherring products (Fig. III.6). How, one might ask, can we be certain that such pieces are not Dutch or Flemish? The simple answer is, "Not easily." One thing is certain, however. When two dishes are found that have the same decoration, one being discovered in England and the other in a Dutch collection, the inspirational flow was from Holland to England and not the other way round. The Collection's Wan Li style charger presents one such design, but differs from published Dutch examples by its central "daisy" petals having deteriorated to a series of straight, radiating lines, suggesting that the painter was unaware of the motif's floral ancestry.

A long-held belief had it that in the seventeenth century, English charger glazers conserved tin oxide by saving it for the painted upper sides while settling for a clear lead glaze on the undecorated backs. There is no denying that this is indeed an English characteristic, but unfortunately, as some fragments unearthed in Dutch Limburg demonstrate, tin saving was not a parsimony peculiar to the English.

Another detail to be found on the backs of English chargers is one and sometimes two holes poked through the foot ring when the clay was still pliable, to enable the chargers to be hung as decoration on walls or dressers. But when one examines the finished products, the majority of the holes are not located in positions that enable the designs to be seen the right way up—a necessity when, for example, displaying a charger decorated with a royal portrait or the popular scene of "The Fall." Over the years we have heard two explanations, the less credible being that after firing to biscuit stage the painter was required to align the holes to the top before applying the decoration, but often failed to do so. Much more plausible is the assumption that the holes were only intended to help secure the suspension cord or wire to the foot ring, leaving the hanging loop to be positioned by the purchaser.

The Collection's two dishes depicting "The Fall"—better known as "Adam and Eve" chargers—have a story of their own to tell that has nothing to do with apples or with snakes.[11] Instead, they are an example of the kind of luck that some people have and others do not. I realize that such a statement may sound unattractively conceited, but nevertheless, as many colleagues know, I have had more than my share of million-to-one chances. As proof, I submit the Adam and Eve chargers as exhibits A and B.

Each year from 1957 onward, Audrey and I returned to England to see our families and to travel around the country visiting historic houses and their art collections. It was only natural, therefore, that we should visit any antique shop with an "open" sign on its door. On many of these safaris we were accompanied by our old London and Upchurch cohort, timber broker Douglas Walton, who was with us in 1959 when we visited the shop of Michael Legg in Dorchester. Legg was an antique furniture dealer from whom I had previously purchased a seventeenth-century Bible box

FIGURE III.7. The early "type fossil" Adam and Eve delftware charger illustrated in Rackham and Read's *English Pottery* (1925). Lead-glazed reverse and pierced foot ring. Southwark, ca. 1635–1645. Ex Beaumont Collection.

and three unusually large eighteenth-century glass bottles. Scattered around the shop more as decoration than anything else, he had several brass candlesticks and assorted bric-a-brac which, to our astonishment, included a splendidly early London Adam and Eve charger, which Legg had priced at a distinctly affordable £20 (Fig. III.7). Glued to the lead-glazed back was a faded label bearing a long description attributing the charger to London and more specifically to Lambeth, saying that it had been in the Beaumont Collection and referencing it to page 48 of Bernard Rackham and Herbert Read's seminal 1924 book *English Pottery*. Two days later we were prowling London's Portobello Road antiques market and found another Adam and Eve charger, a much later example, but this, too, bore a label citing the same book (Fig. III.8). The price for the second charger

was the same as the first, but by that time I was short of money and so decided that I could not afford it. Douglas, on the other hand, had no such cash-flow problem and so promptly bought the charger to add to his own ceramics collection.

When we obtained a copy of Rackham and Read's book we found that both chargers were illustrated in Plate 56, with the Legg example representing the "best period" of Adam and Eve painting and the Portobello charger the later. The authors noted that among renderings of "The Fall," "the younger members . . . show a marked tendency to degenerate." They attributed the second dish to Bristol, but warned that "it would be unwise in the present state of our knowledge to try to make too precise a separation between the Lambeth and Bristol dishes of this type."[12]

FIGURE III.8. The late "type fossil" Adam and Eve charger illustrated in Rackham and Read's *English Pottery* (1925). Pale bluish tin-glazed reverse and no suspension hole. Bristol, ca. 1700–1720. Ex J. Douglas Walton and Beaumont Collections.

FIGURE III.9. "The Temptation" engraved by Crispin van de Passe (1564–1637), the primary source for English delftware's Adam and Eve designs. The British Museum.

Not until the 1940s would ceramic historians and collectors recognize that not all London delftware was made across the river from Westminster in the borough of Lambeth, where, in reality, delftware production did not begin until the late 1670s. However, Rackham and Read were right in attributing the second charger to Bristol, where "The Fall" remained a production subject as late as 1750. Current thinking attributes the Portobello charger to a date between ca. 1685 and 1700. But how could one tell the difference between the London and Bristol examples?

Both chargers are of approximately the same diameter,[13] but one is heavy and the other light, or to be more precise 3 lb 10 oz versus 2 lb 4 oz. The early has a pierced and undercut foot ring while the late has no suspension hole and a shallow foot ring. In addition, the Bristol charger has a pronounced ridge below the underside of the rim, and this, too, is a Bristol characteristic. Rarely, if ever, does a museum exhibit both sides of a ceramic plate, believing instead (and in most instances, rightly) that the public wants to see the pretty side and cares nothing for the story hidden behind. But even if these two chargers were to be exhibited with education as well as admiration in mind, the key clue—that of the disparity in weights—could only be appreciated by handling the objects themselves.

There are other significant differences that separate these two chargers in both time and place. The figures on the London example were treated in a consciously naturalistic manner and belonged to a genre that had its genesis in a Crispin van de Passe engraving of "The Fall"—though wisely omitting van de Passe's flea-scratching dog (Fig. III.9).The earliest dated Adam and Eve charger is one from 1635 in the Victoria and Albert Museum's collection. It is also one of the largest, 19 inches in diameter, and being initialed and dated it was intended for show rather than utility. We may reasonably see our smaller charger as its standard-sized offspring,

FIGURE III.10. Pickleherring kiln site trivets and a conical stilt used to separate delftwares during firing. Mid- to late seventeenth century. Ex Burnett Collection.

FIGURE III.11. Detail of Fig. III.6 showing central trivet scars.

and, though simplified in its painting, probably not much later in date. By 1650, delftware renderings of the First Couple had degenerated into almost cartoon-like people. Indeed, the painter of one inscribed T.M. 1650 had given Adam a Van Dyck beard and mustache that resemble modern posters defaced with "Magic markers."[14]

In the mid-seventeenth century, run-of-the-mill plates, dishes, and chargers were usually stacked one on top of another in the kiln and separated by triangular stilts or trivets flat on one side and with the other having three extremities drawn down into points (Fig. III.10). The latter stood on the upper, painted surface, while the flat side supported the foot ring of the charger above. After firing, the three points resting on the thick glaze had to be carefully broken away, thereby leaving small scars that extended through the glaze to the body beneath (Fig. III.11). It is my belief that these blemishes differentiate what we might call "trade wares" from the personalized and dated pieces which were either fired unstacked in the kiln or placed at the top of the stilt-separated pile and so escaped the triple scarring. However, both of the Collection's Adam and Eve chargers exhibit the triple stilt marks.

The extraordinary coincidence that led us to finding both of Rackham and Read's illustrated examples in shops close to a hundred miles apart did not end there. The authors' captions stated that both examples had been in the same collection, that of Dr. W. M. Beaumont of Bath, and presumably were in his collection in 1924 when *English Pottery* was published. However, they cannot have been there very long—five years at the most. How do we know that?

The first and only book devoted specifically to these large dishes was written by the Reverend Edward A. Downman (familiarly known as Father Downman) and published in 1919 under the title *Blue Dash Chargers,* with the adjectives referring to the slashes of blue that ornamented the rims from the beginning almost to the end of the series. Downman listed all the chargers then known to him in public and private collections and cited Dr. W. H. Beaumont as having only one, and that a William and Mary portrait example.[15] The obvious next step in the history of the Dorchester and Portobello chargers was to determine when the Beaumont collection was broken up, and for that I turned to Sotheby's fount of all auction knowledge, the late A. J. Kiddell, who sent me relevant pages from a Sotheby's sale catalog for Thursday, July 2, 1931, which opened with "The Well-known Collection of Lambeth and Bristol Delft Chargers and Dishes, the Property of E. J. Beaumont (Decd.), 1 Staverton Road, Oxford." E. J. was not W. M. Beaumont, nor did he live in Bath. A mandatory hunt through the pages of the *Dictionary of National Biography* led to only one W. Beaumont, but as he was listed as a warrior and feudal statesman who died in the year 1166, I had to conclude that our Beaumont had done nothing to merit a place in the who-was-who of British history. I fared no better with E. J., who I assume to have been the son or brother of Dr. William.

If you have been following this rather tortuous tale with an inquiring and still alert mind, you will have detected a typographical error—which it may be, but not in *this* book. Rackham and Read gave the ownership as Mr. W. M. Beaumont, but as noted here, Father Downman called him Dr. W. H. Beaumont. Regardless of who was right and who wrong, when the collection went to the auction block it belonged to E. J. And what a collection it was! On that summer day in 1931, 104 chargers were for sale in Bond Street, fourteen of them Adam and Eves, an assemblage that today would have every ceramics dealer frothing at the mouth and bidding through the ceiling. But not so in the aftermath of the Wall Street Crash that had beggared England's banking wealthy along with their American cousins. My father, as European representative for New York's Central Hanover Bank and Trust Company, was one of them. Unless one *had* to, this was no time to be selling anything. Of the 104, forty-three found no buyers, among them our London and Bristol chargers. Lot 30 included not only the latter but an immensely rare portrait charger of Civil War hero Sir Thomas Killigrew, but both were withdrawn at £17.10s. Lot 40 paired our London charger with another painted with an equestrian portrayal of the Duke of Marlborough, yet failed to attract a bidder above the buy-in figure of £4.10s. For a pathetic investment of £260 one could have bought all 104—an expenditure that would have worked out at £2.10 per charger![16]

Several questions remain unanswered: How did the Beaumont Collection grow from one charger in 1919 to 104 by eleven years later? Who was E. J. Beaumont? What became of our chargers after they were withdrawn in 1931, and what happened to separate them in 1959, sending one to Dorchester and the other into the Portobello market? We shall probably never know. But the last chapter is no secret. When Audrey and I bought one and Douglas Walton the other, we agreed to a modified tontine whereby the last survivor inherits the other's charger. But when I began to take steps to ensure the intact survival of the Collection, Douglas agreed to sell his charger to me at a very nominal price to see to it that the two would be reunited and would remain so.

I have already noted that the Bristol charger is markedly lighter than the London example, that the foot ring is shallower, and that there is a distinctive ridge around the underside close to the rim. However, there is a more obvious difference: the green and blue foliage had been applied with a sponge rather than drawn leaf by leaf as were the earlier London examples. This specimen also has a feature that sets it apart from all the others, be they from London or Bristol, and it relates to what we may euphemistically term Adam's "begatter." From the van de Passe engraving onward into the eighteenth century, anatomical propriety was maintained by a conveniently located tree branch, by Eve's flowing locks, or by each figure holding a fan made from a sufficiently large leaf. The Portobello charger's painter, however, was not one to beat about the bush and instead chose to provide Adam with an enormous tuft of purple pubic hair.

In movie editing, that somewhat indelicate observation is known as a segue, and it prompts me to recall one of the most remarkable ceramic discoveries of my career. It occurred in the late fall of 1956, shortly before I was due to surrender my Guildhall Museum post and move to Virginia. On a Thames Street bombed site occupied before the Great Fire of 1666 by the church of St. Martin Vintry, I found a fairly well-preserved wooden coffin and in it the skeleton of a man.[17] His hands were not crossed over his chest as was usual, but were extended to cover a delfware plate inverted over his lower abdomen (Fig. III.12). Although I had been involved with maybe a hundred or more seventeenth- and eighteenth-century interments during my London years, I had never before seen a coffin with a plate inside it. Furthermore, I had never previously seen a delft plate emerge from the ground completely undamaged. Even more surprising and, indeed, unique was the fact that on the plate being removed and turned over, most of the deceased's perfectly preserved pubic hair adhered to it.

FIGURE III.12. London delftware plate tin-glazed both back and front, painted in monochrome with "Chinaman and rocks" design. Found by the author in a coffin in the graveyard of the Thames-side church of St. Martin Vintry. Ca. 1680–1690. Guildhall/Courtesy of the Museum of London.

Various scenarios have been put forward to explain the plate's presence in the coffin, the most persuasive relating to the folklore practice of placing a dish of salt on a corpse. A description of burial practices on the Isle of Man (1845) included setting a trencher of salt on the chest. An earlier account (1777), from southern Ireland, described how a plate of salt was placed over the heart as the symbol of incorruptibility. Yet another, this time from Scotland, recalled how friends of the deceased placed on the breast "a wooden platter containing a small quantity of salt and earth, separate and unmixed: the earth an emblem of the corruptible body, the salt the emblem of the immortal spirit." There is no denying that salt is a preservative, and in this curious incident it might have had that effect. However, in 1785, a contributor to the *Gentleman's Magazine* observed that in many parts of England the salt had a more practical purpose. Placed on a pewter plate, it was laid on the corpse "to hinder air from getting into the bowels, and swelling up the belly, so as to occasion either a burst, or, at least, a difficulty in closing the coffin." That explanation serves to shift the salt dish down from the breast to the pelvis, but it doesn't explain inverting it beneath the shroud and then expecting the dead man to hold it in place for all eternity.[18]

As a warning against the dangers of oversimplification, I should add that the conjectured salt on the St. Martin Vintry plate has been accepted by at least one modern writer who stated (without attribution) that "It was a custom to place a receptacle of salt on a corpse in the belief that it prevented swelling or purging," adding that "this is the only known instance of delftware so used." Thus can an unproven hypothesis be corrupted into dogma. Undeniable, however, is the fact that the plate is an excellent example of the growing taste for things Chinese in the later decades of the seventeenth century and of a type produced in several Thames-side factories by the mid-1670s.[19]

The St. Martin Vintry plate is characteristic of the second generation of chinoiserie on English delftware, with the first being represented by wasters from Christian Wilhelm's Pickleherring factory. There, the decoration

FIGURE III.13. Small delftware dish, tin-glazed on both obverse and reverse and with foot-ring suspension hole; monochrome "Chinaman and rocks" design. Said to have been found in Westminster. Southwark or Vauxhall, ca. 1680–1690.

was copied from designs on Chinese dishes commonly called *kraak* ware and featured "bird on rocks" designs.[20] The later motifs reflect the tremendous increase in the last quarter of the seventeenth century in imported Chinese porcelain whose elements commonly included people—hence the generic name *Chinaman and rocks*. This is represented in the Collection by a single small dish reportedly found on a building site in Westminster (Fig. III.13). What makes this example unusual (indeed, seemingly without recorded parallel) is its small diameter (6¼ inches) and the fact that its foot ring is pierced for suspension, suggesting that regardless of its size, its purchaser might think it worthy of display.

Although ceramic collectors have trawled long and deep in search of every conceivable variety of seventeenth-century English delftware, there are still some that have yet to be identified. That thought brings me to another of those coincidences that seem almost occult in their improbability. On one of my many searchings of the Thames north foreshore between Queenhithe Dock and Southwark Bridge, I found the base of a small vessel that I took to be part of a salt. What made it "keepworthy" was its interior cartoon-like portrait of what looked like a Carolian-era cavalier wearing a twirled mustache worthy of a lecherous Victorian villain (Fig. III.14 *a*). Who was this man, and what was he doing inside a salt dish where he would rarely be seen?

For years I dismissed this fragment as the "one off" creation of a delft painter with a sly sense of humor—until we found another basal fragment

IF THESE POTS COULD TALK

 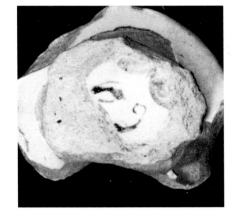 

FIGURE III.14 (*a*) Pedestal base and interior surface of an open delftware salt (?) found by the author in the Thames at Queenhithe and decorated with what was long assumed to be the head of a cavalier. (*b*) A closely matching base with similar decoration, found by Audrey in an excavation at Tutter's Neck Plantation in Virginia. (*c*) A third example found by a latter-day "mudlark" searching the Thames foreshore, with the shard retaining sufficient decoration to prove that the profile is not that of a cavalier, but of a Turk's head, resembling (*d*) an illustration from a children's book of the 1780s. Fragments *a, b, c,* ca. 1675–1700. (*b*) Smithsonian Institution; (*c*) Private collection.

exactly like it, twirled moustache and all (Fig. III.14 *b*). But this one wasn't from the Thames; it came from an archaeological site half the world away at Tutter's Neck in Virginia.[21] Although the context dated as late as ca. 1730, the history of the site showed it to have degenerated into a slave quarter where many of the hand-me-down artifacts dated from the latter years of the seventeenth century. It seemed hardly possible that I could have found the only two examples of these little dishes ever made, but with my kind of luck, I was prepared to conclude that anything was possible. But in this instance it wasn't.

Twenty years later another Thames searcher named Graham Slater found a third fragment. Although broken in precisely the same way as the other two, the new discovery's painted head was more complete. The mustache was longer but still curled, and the hair was partially covered by a turban. Around the neck was a robe instead of a cavalier's linen collar. There was little doubt, therefore, that this was the head of a Mohammedan or rather a "Turk's head," which in late seventeenth- and eighteenth-century London was the sign most often used to identify a coffee house (Fig. III.14 *c* and *d*).[22] It seemed reasonable to deduce, therefore, that all three little delftware objects had something to do with the dispensing of coffee. But what was it?

London's first coffee house was opened by the son-in-law of an importer named Edwards who was described as a "Turkey merchant" and whose business took him to the Middle East, where he acquired a taste for the drink. He also acquired a Turkish servant named Pasqua Rosee, whose job was to make his morning coffee. When Edwards's relative opened his coffee house in St. Michael's Alley, Cornhill, "the sign was Pasqua Rosee's own head"—hence the first Turk's head connection.[23] The new drink quickly caught on and coffee houses began to compete with taverns as gathering places for men of literary and political bent. By the beginning of the eighteenth century there were said to be 3,000 coffee houses in London alone, out of which emerged the social clubs that would reach their greatest popularity later in the late eighteenth and nineteenth centuries. From that information we garner two facts: first, that the Turk's head fragments cannot date any earlier than the mid-seventeenth century, and second, that with so many coffee houses in business by the end of it, the market was sufficient for delftware potters to be making and decorating ceramics specifically for their use. The next step was to find documentation to prove it.

In 1699 the death of John Robins, owner-manager of Christian Wilhelm's old Pickleherring factory, called for the inventorying of its stock and left no doubt that wares specifically designed for the drinking of coffee and chocolate competed with chamber pots for predominance. Although the listing included several hundred vessels in various stages of manufacture, three consecutive entries under the waiting-to-be-fired heading "Clay Ware" make the point:

> 2000 Coffees at..............3.0.0
> 300 eard Coffees at......... 9.0
> 1450 Chocoletts at.........2.17.0[24]

You may well expect that having followed the clues this far, a dramatic revelation is imminent. But it isn't. Although the Robins inventory lists thousands of items, there is no way of knowing which of them had a short pedestal foot, a thick dish or bowl base, and a Turk leering up from it. Thus the three examples' shape and purpose remain (at least for me) a mystery—as does the reason for them all being broken in the same way.

Thanks to the researches of ceramic historian Frank Britton, John Robins's 1699 inventory is made available to every delftware collector and curator and allows us to read into it (or rather out of it) whatever we like. Four men, two of them master potters, were assigned to the tedious task of inventorying the Pickleherring stock, which they performed with great care, separating the finished and unfinished wares under several headings. The delftware was listed under such headings as White and Painted Perfect Ware, Clay Ware, Biskett Ware, Ware Given White, and Ware Given and Painted. The first identified under 230 separate headings those that were ready for sale. *Clay ware* referred to items thrown, sun-dried (green wares), and waiting for their first firing to biscuit hardness. Then came more that had received their coating of tin-enriched opaque white, and lastly those that had been painted rather than being left undecorated. Together, both the white and decorated wares were ready for their second firing.

We tend to think of preindustrial potteries as being run by a single turner with a couple of apprentice decorators, and an output of a few hundred pots a year. It is easy, too, to equate the sum of examples in museum and private collections as being a fair sampling of what was actually made. Archaeologists who see a broader cross-section of the wares being used and broken know better, but even we find it hard to realize that in John Robins's factory at one moment in time 22,984 pieces of plain and decorated delftware were ready to sell, another 22,723 awaited their first firing, 11,630 pieces waiting to be glazed, and another 2,915 were ready for their second firing, in all 60,252 ceramic objects to be launched into the marketplace. And that was not all. Robins was also in the brown stoneware business. Add his "Perfect stone ware" and his "Stone Clay Ware" and you have a stock of close to 121,000 vessels. Multiply that by the number of the several other delft and stoneware potters in the London area at the close of the seventeenth century and the numbers become even more mind-boggling.[25]

Not only did the Robins inventory provide us with accurate numbers, it also gave us names of shapes that have never made it into collections or that, once there, have not been identified by their contemporary names. What did the appraisers mean by *sawcer scollop bowls* and how did they differ from *sawcer basons*? And what were *slite sawcers* and, for that matter, what was meant by *Dutch slites*?

FIGURE III.15. Small London delftware caudle or posset pot, apparently without surviving parallel. Ca. 1630–1660.

FIGURE III.16. London delftware jar painted in Wan Li "bird on rocks" design and dated 1632. The ring handles parallel those on Fig. III.15. The Nelson-Atkins Museum of Art, Kansas City, Missouri (Gift of Mr. Frank P. Burnap) 57-11.

Luck once again played its part in bringing another delftware item into the Collection, though in this instance its catalyst was the experience needed to recognize what we were seeing. During Audrey's and my annual trips to England we visited the same London antique shops again and again. On an earlier visit to the Beauchamp Place gallery where we had found the "married" Tudor candlestick, we discovered a small, ring-handled and spouted caudle pot of the kind suitable for feeding invalids (Fig. III.15).[26] It was a dark, brownish black and was labeled "stoneware." Two things were immediately apparent: It wasn't stoneware, and recognizing it for what it was, we knew it had to be as rare as ice cubes in Hades. The black surface had resulted from the pot's burial in organic soil, probably in a cesspit or an abandoned well. Having worked with a great deal of material from those sources, we knew that the pot was really delftware and that we had a technique for returning it to its original white.[27]

Finding an object for which there are no known parallels is wonderfully stimulating and exciting, arousing, as it must, the Sherlock Holmesian instincts that lurk within even the soberest of collectors. In the case of the delft caudle pot, the ware's identity was easily proven, but determining *when* it was made was something else entirely. The clue resided in the unusual ring-shaped handles, a detail to be found first on early Italo-Netherlandish maiolica altar vases, several of which have been found in London and attributable to dates between ca. 1490 and 1525.[28] Another ring-handled vase found at Delft would be attributed to the second half of the sixteenth century.[29] Our caudle pot, however, has no decoration, and to my knowledge tin-enameled wares were not produced in plain white until 1610 or thereabout.

It seemed likely, or so I thought, that the ring handles were metallic in origin, for in the seventeenth and eighteenth centuries it was not unusual for potters to copy designs from other media. A mazer bowl with such handles in silver and marked with a London date letter for 1585/86 was illustrated in a 1933 exhibition catalog,[30] and that date paralleled the Delft attribution. However, the same catalog also illustrated a ring-handled silver cup stamped with the London hallmark for 1657/58.[31] The mazer bowl's

IF THESE POTS COULD TALK

date seemed much too early and the silver cup too late. More convincing evidence came not from London but from Kansas City, whose museum houses a bird-on-rocks decorated jar or vase with similar ring handles and dated 1632 (Fig. III.16).[32] That date coincided with my estimated dating for a biscuit fragment from a shallow, ring-handled bowl from David Burnett's Pickleherring trove.[33] Putting all that together, a date of circa 1645 for the white posset pot seems about right.

The trouble with any kind of research is that if we arrive at wrong conclusions and then are fool enough to publish them, the negative spin-off can be far-reaching and persists like a computer virus until someone has the temerity to deduce that the supposed pot pontiff didn't know what he was talking about. The old cliché that a little knowledge can be a dangerous thing is nowhere more worthy of recognition than in the field of archaeology, and more specifically in the study of its ceramics.

To the novice student of ceramic history, documentation put on record by the potters themselves, by their heirs, or by their customers may be thought to be truths written in stone. But they are not. A case in point: In 1673/74 a committee hearing in the House of Lords regarding the draft of an Act for encouraging the manufactures of England elicited testimony from both potters and pot sellers, and much had to do with tin-glazed earthenware. On what grounds, the Lords wanted to know, should Dutch imports be restricted and what damage would a continuance of such imports do to the English manufacturers? The potters' answer was little short of a bald-faced lie. They contended that "The Dutch knew not how to make these kind of fine things, till some English artists went to Holland, for want of employment and taught them." Furthermore, "The Dutch could not make this ware without English earth." When the retailers had their say, their enthusiasm for the English wares was scarcely wholehearted. On February 20, a spokesman for the Wardens of the Company of Earthenwares declared that "it was indifferent to the Company whether they had it by English or foreign manufacturers." He added that "The Potters made dishes and painted ware, but not the sixth part of what the shopkeepers would vend," and that their "blue ware" was double the price of the Dutch. Mr. Sadler, a retailer of tiles, complained that "He could have no tiles from them, though he had waited long for them. They could not supply them." Another merchant, Mr. Green,[34] testified that "he had ordered tiles of the Potters, but never could have any of them." He added that "they made some other kind of painted ware, but not so good as what came from Holland."

The potters' unidentified spokesman responded to the "no tiles" charges by explaining that "The tiles they ordered were to be supplied in the declining time of the year, and they required much drying. They could in a short time make tiles enough."[35]

From all this arguing there emerge several interesting questions and a few facts. That the merchants did not care whether their pottery was English or Dutch, and insisted that the Dutch wares were cheaper and more readily available, flies in the face of the visual evidence presented by museums and in private collections where the vast majority of surviving examples from the mid-seventeenth century are deemed to be English. So what happened to all those Dutch imports, and were they sufficiently different from the English wares to be recognized? Or, to put it another way: Are there Dutch specimens made for the English market that have failed to be recognized as such?

Archaeological testimony from the kiln sites does suggest that tile making was not nearly as prevalent in the second half of the seventeenth century as in the first. By 1673, when the Lords were debating the importation issues, the early thick and highly decorated paving and wall-surround tiles that are well represented among Southwark wasters had disappeared. Taking their place was a new generation of tile makers catering to the growing popularity of thinner tiles for use in fireplace surrounds (Fig. III.17).[36] This brings us back to John Robins and his 1699 inventory, which was taken in October in "the declining time of the year."

FIGURE III.17. London delftware tile fragments from the Burnett Collection demonstrating thickness differences between those of the early to mid-seventeenth century, and (*right center, on edge*) a manganese-decorated "landskip" shard of ca. 1700–1760.

Delftware tile making differed from the rest of the trade in that it called for no skilled potters, but did require large, flat drying areas and shelving for tiles at the clay, biscuit, and whiting stages. Robins used at least one loft for this purpose. Nevertheless, his stock was relatively small, and none of it in a finished, salable state. Altogether, in unfired clay and in first-fired biscuit, he had 2,122 tiles in production with a total value of only £2.19s.0d.

The potters' spokesman summarized their position in calling for an embargo on the importation of delftware and made these points:

> They did not pretend to make Cologne ware, tiles, and Chinaware. What they claimed to make was white and painted ware, i.e. Gallaway ware. They sent great quantities of ware to Scotland, Ireland, Barbadoes, and the King's plantations.[37]

After hearing all the testimony the Committee ordered that "all white and painted ware, or Gallaway ware" should be prohibited by the Act. Thus the

IF THESE POTS COULD TALK

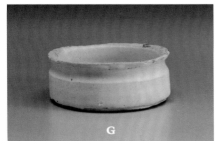

FIGURE III.18. Examples of white delft-ware pharmaceutical pots ranging from (*a–g*) ca. 1620–1680, (*h*) ca. 1680–1710, and (*i*) ca. 1710–1775. Most are from the Thames.

English delftware potters (many of them Dutch emigrants) were granted protection destined to remain in effect for a hundred years.

In the space of seventy-five years, the term *galley ware* had been corrupted into *galleware* and thence into *Gallaway* (which sounds like Irish Galway) and resulted in the word "ware" being twice used, thus Gallaway ware.[38] This not particularly useful piece of information serves, nevertheless, as a convenient segue to bring us back to pharmaceutical gallipots.

As I have previously noted, the early, small ointment pots were decorated with swags, chevrons, and V-shaped stacks of lateral strokes in blue, orange or purple. Later, however, similarly shaped pots were all in white. Those are among the most common of delftwares from archaeological sites dating from the later seventeenth and eighteenth centuries, and are to some degree datable (Fig. III.18). The early shape is essentially cylindrical, regardless of whether the pot is broad and shallow or tall and thin, with the tube constricted above the base and again below the rim, the latter to enable a cover to be tied over and around it.[39] This shape continued throughout the seventeenth century, but early in the eighteenth a new profile evolved, with the base becoming smaller and the rim everted, as demonstrated by the examples illustrated. I firmly believed that the smaller the base became, the later the pot had to be, and for years I used that belief as a dating guide. I had forgotten that in London I had found one such "late" pot in a context of the 1730s, the same shape I was attributing to the closing years of the eighteenth century!

FIGURE III.19. Thick-walled, redware pharmaceutical pots reputed to have been intended as containers for mercury: (*a*) exhibiting the remains of a poorly secured, heavily pitted and colorless glazer; (*b*) a similar but smaller pot with a better bonded lead glaze, dark green in color. Each is glazed internally as well as on the underside of its pedestal foot, both of which features are unusual. Found in Southwark. Probably Spanish, sixteenth century. Ex Burnett Collection.

The dating of ointment pots has suffered from a fishy infusion of red herrings injected by decorators who have taken genuine, undecorated delftware galley pots and supplied them with dates and other value-elevating ornamentation. Because several of these pots have been in collections assembled before World War II, it is probable that the improvements were made by a single individual early in the last century. Nevertheless, it is safe to say that if dates and shapes don't match, it is more likely that one is being offered a fake rather than a ground-breaking revisionist discovery.

Although for 200 years delftware was the principal ceramic container for pharmaceutical nostrums, other small pots were used in the sixteenth century for what purported to be curative substances. Two of these have a treasured place in the Collection, not because they are beautiful (which they are not) nor for the efficacy of their content, but solely as a commentary on sixteenth-century mores (Fig. III.19). Both were found by David Burnett on Hays Wharf property, land on or adjacent to London's red rush-light district, and the ribbon of theaters, taverns, and brothels that had existed along the Bankside (to the pious horror of City fathers) since the Middle Ages (Fig. III.20). Nobody made any real effort to rid London of this blight for two very compelling reasons: first because watermen derived much of their income from ferrying City gentry across the river to escape the rigors of respectability, and second because most of the brothels (called stews) were on land in the fiefdom of the Bishop of Winchester where the loose ladies were known as the Bishop of Winchester's geese. The price of casual copulation has always been high—as the geese well knew, as also did their apothecaries who prescribed ointments that contained mercury, dispensed from small, thick-walled bottles like these. I long thought them to be French, a fitting source, one might think, for

IF THESE POTS COULD TALK

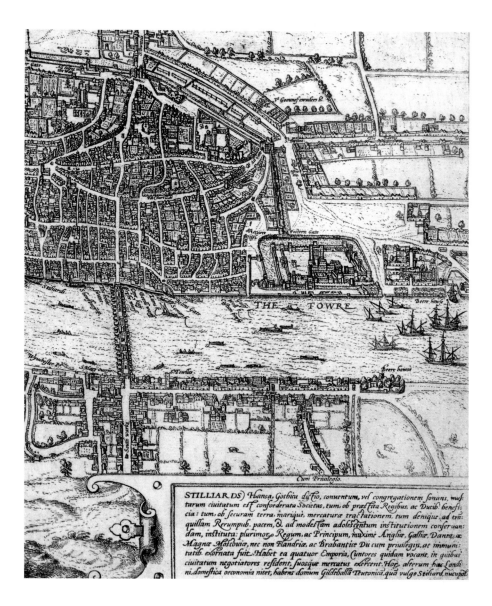

FIGURE III.20. Southwark above and below London Bridge, ca. 1560, as shown on a German map first published in 1572. The "Beere House" is to the right, and beyond it stretch the open fields of Horsely Downe.

STILLIARDS) Hansa, Gothica dictio, conuentum, vel congregationem sonans, mus-
turam ciuitatum est confoederata Societas, tum, ob praestita Regibus, ac Ducib. benefi-
cia: tum, ob securam terra, marique, mercaturae tractationem. tum denique, ad tran-
quillam Rerumpub. pacem, & ad modestam adolescentum institutionem conseruan-
dam, instituta: plurimor, Regum, ac Principum, maxime Angliae, Galliae, Danniae, ac
Magnae Malcouiae, nec non Flandriae, ac Brabantiae Du cum priuilegiis, at immuni-
tatib. exornata fuit. Habet ea quatuor Emporia, Cuntores quidam vocant, in quibus
ciuitatum negotiatores resident, suosque mercatus exercent. Hor. alterum haec Londi-
ni, domestica oeconomia nitet, habens domum Gildehalla Teutonica, qua vulgo Stilhard, nucupat.

FIGURE III.21. Pewter syringes for mercury injection; both found on the Southwark shore of the Thames. Seventeenth or eighteenth century.

containers holding a cure for the Bishop's benefice that the English called the French pox. They are, however, far more likely to be Spanish, for in the seventeenth century the mines of Almaden in Spain were a principal source of mercury for Western Europe.[40]

In the introduction to his 1585 treatise "touching the disease called *Morbus Gallicus*," royal surgeon William Clewes blamed the disease on "the filthy life of many lewd and idle persons, both men and women, about the City of London, and the great number of lewd Alehouses, which are the very nests and harbours of such filthy creatures."[41]

Two pewter urethral syringes in the Collection that I found in the Thames adjacent to the notorious Bankside speak loudly to the price of pleasure (Fig. III.21). Used to inject a honeyed solution of mercury "if the grief be in the passage of the yard as in the case of Gonoree," the cure was both painful and dangerous. John Woodfall in *The Surgeon's Mate* (1617) added that he preferred a mercuric lotion applied "never within the passage but betwixt glans and praeputium."[42] But inserted or applied, the mercury treatment was the standard cure across more than 200 years, thereby siring the adage "Thirty minutes with Venus and thirty days with Mercury."

Private collections of English pottery invariably begin with delftware for the very good reason that prior to its production in the last third of the sixteenth century, nothing else was readily identifiable or decorated to look pretty and thereby collectable. Because ceramic collectors have been far more interested in the wares than in the people who had owned and used them, nobody really cared about the English kitchen and dining table before there were Netherlandish maiolica and its English copies to provide mealtime eye appeal. Visual reconstructions in paintings or movie sets put silver gilt and pewter on the tables of the wealthy and wooden trenchers, horn cups, and nondescript earthen jugs on those of their retainers. With rare exceptions, not until the late 1940s did English archaeologists begin to take an interest in the ceramics of the early Tudor sixteenth century. Museums like the Guildhall, where Audrey and I worked, could boast shelf upon shelf of medieval jugs and the occasional coarse earthenware cooking pot, but they had all been salvaged from construction sites by builders' laborers and so had no archaeological association one to another. By and large, museum curators do not like broken stuff. Potsherds take up a great deal of space. They have to be cataloged. They are meaningless to the general gallery-going public, and when exhibited foster the popular belief that museums are temples of pointless pedantry.

At Hays Wharf, CEO David Burnett was not intimidated by potsherds. Although his interest was in delftware manufacturing, he realized that he couldn't expect his contractor's workmen to separate delft from other wares and so instructed them to salvage anything they unearthed. In his spare moments David separated out and washed the dirt from the delftware, but the rest of the potsherds went into boxes unwashed and remained there for more than forty years. Late in 1999 when he was talking about sending the boxes to the dump I asked David to let me have representative fragments of the coarse earthenwares for use as "pass around" teaching aids to students of ceramic technology. Not until some time after the boxes arrived in Williamsburg did I discover that they offered a wealth of information about the range of Elizabethan earthenwares and provided a new perspective on the stylistic sources for pottery being made and used in Virginia in the early seventeenth century. For the first time I was seeing the range of lead-glazed earthenware shapes in production in the London area in the mid-sixteenth century, most of them types that could easily be mistaken for Dutch imports (Fig. III.22).[43] There were bowls, double-handled cauldrons, three-legged pipkins, oven pans, chafing dishes, porringers, a printed paving tile, and even an armorially decorated and tracery-edged niche tile from a box-shaped, freestanding stove, a type hitherto considered to be of continental European origin (Fig. III.23).[44] All these fragmentary objects had one striking characteristic in common. Seen in section they emulated the Predynastic Egyptian beaker illustrated in chapter 1 (Fig. I.1), being a combination of kiln-controlling oxidation

FIGURE III.22. A miscellany of English kitchen wares from Southwark. Ca. 1500–1560. Ex Burnett Collection.

FIGURE III.23. Corner fragment from an elaborately three-dimensional niche tile made in London redware akin to those of Fig. III.22 in the style of Flemish imports. First half of sixteenth century. Ex Burnett Collection, since donated to the British Museum.

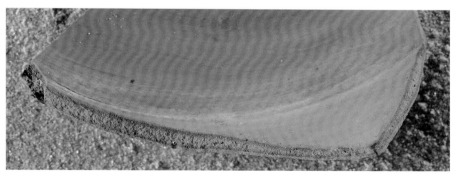

FIGURE III.24. Sectional view of a sixteenth-century London redware shard showing the sandwich effect of external oxidation after early firing in a reducing atmosphere. Ex Burnett Collection.

(red) and reduction (black) that gave them a sandwich-like appearance (Fig. III.24). Furthermore, the presence of a few shards that had cracked in firing hinted that there might have been an unrecorded earthenware kiln nearby.

With so many questions raised and so many tantalizing possibilities perhaps still hidden in the rest of David Burnett's crumbling boxes, studying their contents in their entirety became a responsibility, even a duty. When they arrived, the first to be opened turned out to have been a long-time residence for mice who had torn the wrapping newspaper to shreds. From the outset the primary need was to try to determine when and on which of the several Hays Wharf Company building sites those newspaper-wrapped bundles of potsherds had been found. The largest scrap of newspaper provided a list of the movies running in London on that still unknown date, and so finding out when James Dean's *Rebel without a Cause* was released in England seemed to be my best bet. Fortunately, however, several much smaller shreds when pasted together told me that the paper was *The Times* for February 8, 1956. The second box contained an envelope postmarked to the twenty-fourth of the same month, strongly hinting that much of the pottery came from one site at much the same time. I was lucky, too, that in that year David Burnett had begun keeping a detailed journal, which showed that work was in progress beside Vine Lane in the heart of the Pickleherring industry. With so many of the fragments dating from the early to mid-sixteenth century, my next step would be to find and study such maps of Southwark as existed for that time period in the hope that they would delineate existing pottery-related buildings.

Although modern city maps show only streets and the shape of blocks between them, those of the sixteenth, seventeenth, and eighteenth centuries often included elevations of actual houses. Consequently, it should be possible to guess which of them could have been large enough or open-spaced enough to support a ceramics factory—or so I thought. At this point my skein of evidence and supposition began to unravel. The earliest map published in 1572 showed not a single building in the pertinent area.[45] The ribbon development alongside the river had ended in a fenced and moated "Beere House" some distance to the west. Even though the map had almost certainly been drawn in the mid-sixteenth century (before the spire of St. Paul's was struck by lightning in 1561 and not rebuilt), it was still too late to explain how the mass of early to mid-Tudor pottery came to be where it was found.

The 1572 map showed the Beere House directly across the river from the Tower of London's Lanthorn Tower and with an open sewer immediately to the west of it. With all that in mind, when we look at a detail from Flemish visitor Joris Hoefnagel's ca. 1582 painting of the same juxtaposition of tower and sewer we may be seeing the trash-clogged watercourse whose upkeep would be cause for recrimination and litigation in the following century (Fig. III.25).[46] Twenty years had seen much building in the area, but the Beere House was still there and so was the corner of the adjacent Horsleydown fields, then grass covered and showing no indication of being or becoming the Southwark city dump. On the contrary, they were the setting for archery practice as well as of some surprisingly public private activity. Further muddying already dirty water is the fact that Southwark was assigned its own dunghill ground in 1550 or thereabouts.[47]

Potting entrepreneur Christian Wilhelm's Pickleherring factory lay to the east of the Beere House. In 1638, eight years after Wilhelm died, his son-in-law Thomas Townsend was taken to task by the parish and ordered to clean out the sewer and drain "on the west and south sides of his Potthouse and grounde neare Pickleherringe"—the key words here being *and grounde*.[48] Thomas Townsend had been in trouble on and off through the

FIGURE III.25. Detail from Joris Hoefnagel's painting *The Wedding Feast*, ca. 1580, showing what may be the "Beere House" complex to the right of the lane. Original painting in the Hatfield House Collection. Courtesy of The Marquess of Salisbury.

previous seven years for dumping soil in a channel as well as for keeping hogs, and for "laiding of sand and gravell in the highewaies nere his house."[49] This last seems to have been his way of disposing of sand and gravel extracted during the preparation of his clay. In 1640, Townsend was again fined for failing to "repaire wharfe and fill up four rods of the banke of the sewer in the west side of [the] Potthouse neare Pickleherringe."[50] On the one hand, therefore, Townsend was being harassed for dumping his trash into the open sewer, and on the other for not depositing it as fill behind the sewer's revetment. Although this explains the large quantities of delftware debris recovered by David Burnett, it does nothing to account for the presence of the much earlier lead-glazed earthenwares.

From these scraps of documentary evidence we know that there was open ground to the south of Townsend's pot-house where, presumably, he kept his hogs. That equates well with the 1571 map, which showed cattle grazing there. And there's another clue. A later map, this one of 1682, showed a large open area to the east marked "Potts Fields."[51] It is true that land so named defined a burial place for the neighborhood indigent, but it is highly probable that this particular field had earlier been dug for its

FIGURE III.26. Salt-glazed stoneware mugs and jugs from the Rhineland were plentiful in Southwark taverns and brothels in the first half of the sixteenth century. Ex Burnett Collection.

potting clay. That such use may have been of long duration is suggested by a late-thirteenth-century jug neck in the Burnett collection that had a label tied around its handle inscribed "Found in clay."[52]

Because the contents of the Burnett boxes seemed to fall into two groups, namely, ca. 1500–1550 and ca. 1590–1670, it seems reasonable to suggest that the dung and garbage from Southwark west of London Bridge ceased to be dumped in the Potters' Fields area once the ca. 1550 dunghill ground had been allocated and that the later material represents waste from Southwark's growth east of the bridge in the seventeenth century. All this is speculation, but it is a good example of the kind of thinking that can be generated when potsherds become a signpost to history and not just a bunch of bits in a box.

Assuming that the few pot-house wasters came from much further afield and that the bulk of the shards were domestic trash, that scenario can explain the presence of large quantities of broken, late-fifteenth- and early-sixteenth-century Rhenish stonewares (Fig. III.26) as well as the fact that many of the redwares exhibit evidence of kitchen-related usage—which is a delicate way of saying that they are burned on their bottoms.[53]

In the 1990s, increasing attention was being paid to this hitherto neglected facet of English household ceramic history, in part because American archaeologists and museums were shifting their focus from the Revolutionary years to the founding decades whose story began on Roanoke Island in 1585 and finally took root at Jamestown in 1607. New scientific

IF THESE POTS COULD TALK

techniques that include neutron activation are making it possible to identify both similarities and differences among the Tudor earthenwares found in London and are thereby attributing their manufacturing to specific locations. For the time being, however, the lead-glazed red earthenwares are lumped together as *London redware,* a term that really tells us only that the tested samples were made in the vicinity of the metropolis.[54] With sixteenth-century kiln sites having been found downriver at Deptford and Woolwich and upriver at Lambeth, it should surprise no one that pottery manufacturing might have been going on simultaneously or perhaps earlier in the vicinity of the Pickleherring delftware and stoneware kilns.[55]

Although the full significance of the Burnett material will take time to analyze, to have all this evidence unfold so many years after it was unearthed was akin to opening a cultural treasure chest and, for me at least, provided a glimpse of the ceramic needs and taste of middle-income Londoners in the reigns of Henry VIII and of Mary whose henchmen stoked fires for quite another purpose.[56]

Just as armor became lighter and more elegant as the sixteenth century progressed, so it seems did the everyday pottery in English homes. Vessel shapes, some copying metalwork, came in a breathtaking variety of types, sizes, and degrees of elaboration. An increasing interest in gardens and gardening prompted the manufacture of flowerpots for both outdoor and indoor use. Drinking vessels, as we have seen, copied the imported Rhenish

FIGURE III.27. In London the reign of Elizabeth I saw green and bright yellow replacing the drab redwares of the medieval and earlier Tudor centuries. (*b, d*) Ex Burnett Collection.

stonewares. Bowls, cups, candleholders, even chamber pots came in red, yellow, and green, and sometimes in a mixture of all three. As in the seventeenth century, delftwares transformed the home and colonial table and kitchen dresser into a smorgasbord of blue and white, so in the second half of the previous century apple green and lemon yellow brightened tables long used to the drabness of wood, leather, and horn (Fig. III.27). No less significant was the shift from thick and heavy to thin and light, an aspect best appreciated by archaeologists who have the opportunity to recognize the thinness of Tudor shards—while secretly (and unprofessionally) longing to find their pots unbroken.[57] However, the job of an archaeologist is not just to examine shards, but to try to reconstruct the kind of life of which they were part. The small, handled double dish (Fig. III.27 *b*) is telling us that condiments or relishes were to be handed from one diner to another. You can almost hear an Elizabethan housewife saying, "Prithee Master Thomas, wilt thou pass the pickles?" Here, then, in a single ceramic object we can detect the dawn of civility in British table manners.[58] Gone is the grabbing of food from a communal wooden bowl—and going, if not gone, the debris scattered around the rimless trencher. In such a changing climate, the two-tined fork and the delftware plate could not be far behind.

IV   Mentioning the Unmentionable

He beareth sable, a chamber pot a bed Pot argent...
This is borne by the name of Chamberley.

Randle Holme, *Academie of Armory*, 1682[1]

WRITERS ARE ALWAYS urged to begin the next chapter where the last left off, and not wishing to ignore such wise counsel it seems appropriate to begin with those coarse wares that, not too long ago, were considered unmentionable. Although chamber pots are among the most common ceramic relics of the postmedieval centuries and were present in every household, under most beds, and even in dining rooms where cupboards were provided specially for them (Fig. IV.1), museums and collectors have been as reluctant to speak the noun as actors are to name "the Scottish play." Although there were numerous examples in London's Guildhall Museum, its 1909 catalog listed not one specimen. A 1954 archaeological report on a kiln site at Buckley in Flintshire avoided the unmentionable by drawing it and referring to it only as a "Toilet article in high gloss glaze."[2] Such reticence was not an exclusively English hangup, however. Jan Steen's ca. 1660 painting of a woman preparing for bed had been "restored" in Holland in the nineteenth century, with touchup work that painted over a metal chamber pot and substituted a not very well delineated flagon.[3] To modern historical archaeologists unencumbered by the burdens of Victorian prudery, the evolution of the chamber pot is as sequentially diagnostic as glass wine bottles or clay tobacco pipes. Nevertheless, only one treatise has been devoted to it. Published in 1968 as *Some Domestic Vessels of Southern Britain*, its author, Dr. Francis Celoria, preferred to hide his not inconsiderable accomplishment behind a pseudonymous P. Amis.[4]

It is important to remember that archaeological techniques that treat the recent centuries with the same level of care as was once reserved for the Romans and Saxons did not develop in England and Europe until the 1940s, and that in America (in spite of Thomas Jefferson's admirable example)

FIGURE IV.1. English oak chair-table with chamber-pot cupboard beneath the seat. Seventeenth century. Feathers Hotel, Ludlow.

FIGURE IV.2. Miniature whiteware chamber pot. Probably a fairground "toy." Second half of nineteenth century.

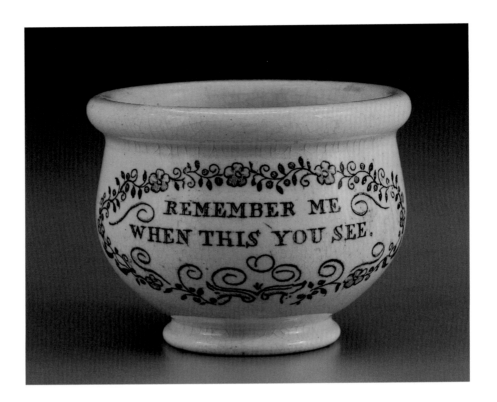

digging stuff up as a by-product to uncovering foundations for reconstructable buildings remained the norm until the late 1950s. Consequently, the notion that chamber pots might have more to say than "here I am" did not readily take root. Along with P. Amis, therefore, Audrey and I had the dubious distinction of being among the first to see these ubiquitous objects not only as worthy of study but as standing front and center in our growing ceramic collection. The inscription on the smallest of them admirably defines our collecting philosophy when it begs

Remember me
When this you see

The pot is only 2⅝ inches in height, and the style of the lettering and the whiteness of the ware suggest a date in the mid- to late nineteenth century (Fig. IV.2). It was almost certainly made as a joke item to be sold at country fairs, leaving us wondering who bought it and for whom. And how did the recipient react to such a gift, and what might it tell us about

FIGURE IV.3. Typical, red-bodied Metropolitan slipware chamber pots found in London. Third quarter of seventeenth century. Guildhall/Courtesy of the Museum of London.

IF THESE POTS COULD TALK

the sense of humor of both giver and receiver? That the pot dates from the stuffy moralistic Victorian Age may be taking us behind the lace curtains and the front parlor aspidistra into a sphere that someone (probably Shakespeare) referred to as *country matters*. However, they could also be urban concerns, as several surviving chamber pots of the mid-seventeenth century attest. Made in a red earthenware produced north of London in the vicinity of modern Harlow and known as Metropolitan ware,[5] they are decorated with inscriptions in white slip that range from the pious "Praise God and Honor the King," to the philosophical and prurient "Be Merry and Wis[e] and Peff!"[6] (Fig. IV.3). Another offers the kind of warning disclaimer that today comes with every appliance: "Break Me Not I Pray in Youer Hast[e] for It [to] non[e] will Give Destast," which can be interpreted as: Drop it and nobody will thank you. Another with an inscription by the same erratic speller is in the Museum of London. When first recorded, the authors of an 1891 book on dated English slipwares could not bring themselves to say the distasteful word, so listed it as "A Pot with Handle."[7]

Unfortunately, Metropolitan slipwares rarely come on the market, and although we were never lucky enough to find a chamber pot, another of our strokes of luck led us to a dish for which we have found no parallel (Fig. IV.4). It came out of a bag of miscellaneous fragments I bought from

FIGURE IV.4. Red-bodied Metropolitan slipware dish, said to have been found in the vicinity of Holborn, London. Ca. 1670–1690.

FIGURE IV.5. (*a*) Buff earthenware chamber pot, green lead glaze, strap handle and flat rim with beaded lip. (*b*) Small plate of same ware, glazing and lip bead, and unquestionably of the same date, though not nearly as early as some have suggested. Ca. 1700–1730. Ex Burnett Collection.

a London laborer for an incredibly nominal sum. When later we sorted through the pieces we discovered that we had virtually all of the dish.[8]

But back to chamber pots.

As I have intimated, up to the mid-twentieth century, knowledge of postmedieval ceramics tended to stem from guesswork, some of it more educated than others.[9] Thus, for example, any earthenware having a bright green glaze was long thought to date from the second half of the sixteenth century and thus came to be known as *Tudor green*. Consequently, when chamber pots were dug up that were also green glazed, it was assumed that they, too, dated from the reign of Elizabeth I (Fig. IV.5 *a*). The Collection's green-glazed pot is one such example, and a small plate in the same clay and same color would be accepted as Tudor were it not for its beaded rim, which betrays it as being kin to the similarly rimmed chamber pot (Fig. IV.5 *b*). However, had anyone taken the trouble to record the contexts wherein such wares were being found, it would have been instantly obvious that they were being dated more than a century too early. That misconception aside, it is reasonable to ask: At what date did chamber pots take the place of peeing into the fire or retreating to a drafty garderobe?[10]

It goes without saying that ever since the first potter turned a vessel capable of holding water he recognized its nocturnal potential, and several late medieval woodcuts show handleless pans under the beds of the sick. Although none resemble the chamber pot as we know it, by 1519 vessels made specifically for that purpose were being traded in Portuguese West Africa, 149 of which were listed as "defective small chamber pots."[11]

The year 1545 would seem to have provided us with England's earliest closely datable metal chamber pot. It came from the wreck of the *Mary Rose* and is shaped almost exactly like another in the Museum of London there attributed to "probably 17th–18th century"—which is probably a century and more wide of the mark.[12]

IF THESE POTS COULD TALK

The dearth of other early pewter or silver survivals can be explained by those of silver being converted into coinage in the 1640s and sacrificed on behalf of the Royalist war effort, while others of pewter got so battered that they, too, would have been melted and recast into something more appealing. In the absence of evidence to the contrary, it seems fair to see metal chamber pots as first appearing in silver as a service to the rich and famous, and fairly soon descending the social ladder to pewter parallels for the middle classes. Elizabeth I's household books (1576–1580) listed "a round basin and Ewer wth a pisspot of Silvr weighg 57. Oz." As for early pewter pots, in 1598 the poet John Marston may have been the first to focus on the hierarchical significance of silver over pewter, asking:

> A silver pispot fits his Lady dame?
> Or i'st too good? a pewter best became.[13]

Although it is hard to tell from an engraving whether a pot is silver or pewter, the pig-, goat-, hog-, and goose-headed topers behaving badly in the title-page woodcut for the 1635 *Philocothonista, or, The Drunkard Opened, Dissected, and Anatomized* (Fig. IV.6), are all drinking out of pewter goblets and covered tankards, so it's reasonable to deduce that the pot in the foreground is also of pewter.[14]

None of the surviving metal chamber pots resembles those made in earthenware in the first half of the seventeenth century, the earliest of which may be the one that I found in a well on the site of the Virginia's Martin's Hundred, whose Wolstenholme Towne was destroyed in an Indian massacre in March 1622 (Fig. IV.7). Among the many artifacts recovered from the Hundred's renewed occupancy in the second quarter of the century were several locally made chamber pots (Fig. IV.8). They were telling us

FIGURE IV.6. Woodcut from a satire on drunkenness with a handy chamber pot in the foreground. Published in London, 1635.

FIGURE IV.7. Virginia-made, lead-glazed earthenware chamber pot discarded into a well at Wolstenholme Towne ca. 1622. Colonial Williamsburg Foundation.

FIGURE IV.8. Virginia, lead-glazed earthenware chamber pots by Thomas Ward of Martin's Hundred. Ca.1625–1635. Colonial Williamsburg Foundation.

that Virginia colonists placed hygiene and convenience fairly high on their domestic agenda, and were not, as one might suppose, satisfied to take short trips into the nearby woods. Perhaps they remembered what happened to one of their number on June 4, 1607:

> 3 of them [Indians] had most adventurously stollen under our Bullwark and hidden themselves in the long grasse; spyed a man of ours going out to do naturall necessity, shott him in the head, and through the Clothes in two places.[15]

It seems safe to conclude that the first Virginia settlers were not well supplied with chamber pots, and that when at sea and "naturall necessity" called, each man made his way out onto the beak-head at the prow of the ship to a seat designed for that purpose.[16]

Excavations begun at Jamestown in the 1990s will eventually tell us how early chamber pots were arriving at or being made in Virginia. In the meantime, the excavation of later seventeenth-century Virginia sites makes it clear that alongside local products, English chamber pots were being imported. Of these the Collection's example with its buff-colored and ribbed exterior and yellow interior glazing is typical of the style (Fig. IV.9). Cooking pots (pipkins) and porringers were simultaneously produced in the same clay and glaze in several kilns in England's western Surrey and the abutting eastern parishes of Hampshire. These yellow or apple-green wares used to be called *Surrey Tudor,* while their predecessors at the beginning of the century were known as *Cheam Ware,* a generally gray-surfaced earthenware with ribbed necks commonly augmented with a frontal bib of white slip or painted as feathery decoration in randomly applied brush strokes. But like so much else in this revisionist age, the generic name has been changed to *Border Ware*, a term I find less helpful. It was true that the bibbed jugs were likely to have been made in more than one pottery, just as the Tudor Green wares were still in use and probably in production for some time after Elizabeth I, the last of the Tudors, died in 1602.[17] In both cases, however, anyone hearing or reading the names had an immediate mental image of the types. But Border Ware

FIGURE IV.9. Typical Border Ware chamber pot, white to buff body coated internally with a clear (yellowing) lead glaze, everted and thickened rim, and single reeded handle. Mid-seventeenth century.

IF THESE POTS COULD TALK

came both in white and red bodies, with the latter continuing in production into the nineteenth century. Thus are we left with a vague idea of where, but not of when or what.

The "married" candlestick discussed earlier was typical of this Border Ware, and while it gave itself away by its glaze being both green and yellow, those color variants imply neither differing period nor places of manufacture. A typical Tudor dish in the Collection (Fig. III.27 *c*) was intended to be covered with a clear lead glaze over its buff-to-white body, but while being coated it had come in contact with another vessel that was green, and so has a wide stripe of "Tudor green" running down its back.

Households in the West of England (the counties of Somerset, Devon, and Cornwall) were in no less need of chamber pots than were their more easterly neighbors. Kilns on the North Devon coast at Barnstaple and Bideford produced them in two varieties that might be dubbed plain and fancy. The latter was well represented among the mid-seventeenth-century sgraffito-decorated slipwares found at Jamestown in the 1950s. This technique, you may recall, involved ornamentation incised through an outer coating (slip) of white clay to the red body beneath. When lead glazed, the result was a yellow pot with red-brown decoration (Fig. II.21 *b*). The plain, on the other hand, used another technique that focused less on aesthetic appeal than on sturdy utility. By mixing fine gravel into the thrown clay, the fired body achieved a domestic-crisis-averting durability.[18] Known as gravel-tempered, the North Devon ware was first discussed in a paper by the Smithsonian Institution's Malcolm Watkins in 1963, at which time the earliest documentation for North Devon ceramic exports to America was 1635.[19] We now know from archaeological evidence that both the plain and fancy wares were reaching Virginia as early as 1622.

Devon's neighboring county of Somerset was also a pottery-producing source. Kilns in and around the village of Donyatt had been in production from late medieval times into the twentieth century, and most of them had been producing chamber pots for local farmers and families. The Chipstone Collection includes an example dating from the first half of the eighteenth century. Coated with white slip and "feather" decorated, this unique pot seems to have been copied from Staffordshire slipwares of the same period. Adding to its interest is an exploded side that appears to render it a casualty of the kiln rather than of usage (Fig. IV.10).

Although no Donyatt or North Devon chamber pots have yet been found in contexts of the early seventeenth century, an infinitely rare gravel-tempered example in the Chipstone Collection can be attributed to its middle years (Fig. IV.11). Further evidence of North Devon wares reaching America even earlier than the 1622 context comes from a third body variety known to archaeologists as *North Devon Plain,* which at first crossed the Atlantic as containers for crew's and settlers' supplies rather than as a purely ceramic export. This fabric is essentially the same as that used to make the sgraffito wares and came in the form of tall, baluster-shaped jars, which have been found aboard the 1609 wreck of the *Sea*

FIGURE IV.10. Lead-glazed earthenware chamber pot with white external slip decorated with unusual zigzag combed decoration reminiscent of early Staffordshire slipwares, but found at Donyatt in Somerset and showing evidence of being a kiln waster. Probably late seventeenth century. Chipstone Collection.

FIGURE IV.II. Gravel-tempered earthenware chamber pot with internal lead glazing; typical of North Devon factories at Barnstaple and Fremington. Probably second half of seventeenth century. Chipstone Collection.

Venture at Bermuda (Fig. IV.12)[20] as well as in our excavation at the site of the abortive 1585–1586 English settlement on Roanoke Island in what is now North Carolina.[21] Until examples began to be found in irrefutable New World contexts, British archaeologists were content to date them to the "17th century or later."[22]

Because the West Country potters served both their own region and England's American colonies, neither the sgraffito-decorated or gravel-tempered wares had a market in London. The latter's citizens were by no means bereft of chamber pots, however. Although much remains to be learned about the simpler Tudor and early Stuart earthenwares, my belated opportunity to study all the shards contained in David Burnett's many boxes from his Hays Wharf properties leaves no doubt that undecorated—one might say—"everyday" chamber pots came in many colors from plain brown to green, red, orange, tortoiseshell, gray, and black. Some of the colors were the inadvertent product of kiln placement and erratic firing, but others were deliberately two-toned, having been washed internally with a white slip. Before the introduction of white and painted delftwares, Londoners who could not afford silver or pewter had to be content with either the heavy red earthenwares made in the immediate vicinity of the City or the thinner and usually better potted buff-bodied and green or yellow glazed wares from kilns along both sides of the dividing line between the counties of Surrey and Hampshire.

The number of domestic ceramic objects that have survived from the seventeenth century is incredibly small. When we see them in museums they are in isolation. Rarely, if ever, do we consider how numerous they had been in their day. The population of London in 1650 is said to have been about 350,000 (up from 200,000 in 1600) and to have increased to 600,000 by 1700. Let's suppose that the average London household was made up of a master, his wife, two children, and four servants, eight in all and requiring a minimum of four ceramic chamber pots between them. That would have meant 175,000 pots in service in 1650 and 300,000 in 1700. With nocturnal accidents more frequent than crockery dropped in daylight, the chamber pot attrition rate may well have been the highest of any.

When John Robins, manager of the Pickleherring Pottery, died in 1699, the inventory of his stock then in hand included more than 3,000 delftware chamber pots in various stages of production. The number is large but not out of line with the size of the user population. It is, however, a figure very different from the at-death inventory of another potter four decades later and an ocean away. He was William Rogers of Yorktown, Virginia, whose stock was not in the thousands nor even hundreds. His executors listed only six. Much has been made of the fact that Governor Gooch in his reports to the Lords of the Board of Trade in England invariably referred to Rogers as the "poor potter" whose work was so inconsequential as to have no adverse impact on the sale of ceramic imports from England. The perceived implication has been that the Governor was downplaying Rogers's manufacturing so as to avoid having to take action

IF THESE POTS COULD TALK

against a prominent Yorktown businessman. To be sure, the inventory shows Rogers to have been sufficiently affluent to own a new sloop worth ninety pounds sterling, have twenty pictures hanging in his hall, and own twenty-seven head of cattle. But his total stock of salable ceramics was worth only £17.2s.0d out of a total inventory amounting to £1,224.5s.6d. As for his six chamber pots, those were valued at a mere fourpence each.[23] By Board of Trade standards, therefore, Governor Gooch was being completely honest in considering Rogers's potting of no account. If nothing else, this demonstrates the kinds of collateral research that can grow out of studying ceramics—and even chamber pots—as societal sign posts.

But back yet again to the pots whose name some dare not speak. In museums and among collections they are almost certainly the rarest of all, thereby giving us an entirely false impression of the scope of household ceramics in the seventeenth or, indeed, the eighteenth and most of the nineteenth centuries.

Although it is relatively easy enough to tell the difference between a lead-glazed earthenware chamber pot of the mid-seventeenth century from another of the early eighteenth century, establishing viable dating for delftware examples of the second half of the seventeenth century versus those of the first decade or so of the next is much more tricky. Surviving pewter pots should point the way, but they do not, and for two reasons: first, that museum exhibits of pewter shy away from displaying them, and second, that those illustrated by Dr. Celoria are so bashed about that rim and base details are hard to interpret.

I had long supposed that delftware chamber pots began to be made around the year 1700, and that the first period examples were characterized by an everted and slightly thickened rim. I made much of my argument that with delft being more fragile than lead-glazed earthenware, the latter's sharply angled rims were impractical in delft—hence its more durable, outward-curving lip shape (Fig. IV.13). However, in 1999, when David Burnett gave me additional fragments from the Pickleherring site, I found among them part of a biscuit-fired chamber pot of remarkable thinness and a sharply flattened rim that made nonsense of my previous thesis (Fig. IV.14). It also paralleled a hitherto undated example in the

FIGURE IV.12. Audrey and *Sea Venture* project director Allan J. Wingood, examining West of England plain earthenware "butter" jars from that 1609 Bermuda shipwreck.

FIGURE IV.13. London delftware chamber pot with gently everted rim, vestigial shoulder cordon, and concave strap handle. Early eighteenth century.

FIGURE IV.14. Biscuit delftware (*a*) can, (b) chamber pot, and (*c*) cylindrical salt, from the Pickleherring kiln area. Second half of seventeenth century. Ex Burnett Collection.

Museum of London that may well have owed its squat and angular design to a pewter version of the second half of the seventeenth century. The white tin glaze of early-eighteenth-century pots frequently appears pinkish as it nears the base, but whether that coloration has anything to do with the fact that biscuit delft from the Pickleherring kilns is found both in yellow and a deep pink can only be determined by chemical analysis.[24] It appears, however, that this coloring of the essentially white glaze is not peculiar to English delftware—if Michael Archer, ceramics curator at the Victoria and Albert Museum and England's leading delft specialist, is right in claiming a Dutch source for a small, pedestaled vase in the Collection that was bought as English on the evidence of its pink-tinted glaze (Fig. IV.15).[25]

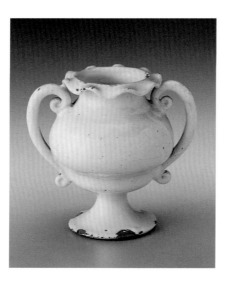

FIGURE IV.15. Globular and pedestal-based posy holder with frilled rim and round-sectioned handles. Dutch or English, ca. 1680.

FIGURE IV.16. White salt-glaze chamber pot with everted and rolled rim, strap handle with beaded edges. Staffordshire, mid-eighteenth century.

By the mid-eighteenth century, delftware chamber pots had become taller and their rims less everted, but their most obvious characteristic was a loss of the rich white glaze in favor of a dirty, eggshell blue singularly lacking in charm. It was small wonder that by the 1740s, the declining quality of utilitarian delftware encouraged erstwhile customers to turn to the new white salt-glazed stoneware pots, which at first were very similar in profile to the earlier white delftware. But perhaps because the rims were fragile, the shape soon evolved into one akin to the later delft, first being folded outward and later rolled under to create a gently rounded edge, as one can see in the Collection's example (Fig. IV.16).

Because the vast majority of English ceramic chamber pots of the eighteenth century were undecorated, few displayed what I call a "Keep Me" factor, meaning that none had any heirloom quality that would foster their preservation sufficiently long to become antiques.

Although I do not recall finding fragmentary chamber pots in Chinese porcelain, we know that pots resembling them were reaching Europe (or rather, *trying* to reach Europe) in the 1750s, because several hundred of them were recovered from the wreck of the *Geldermalsen*, a Dutch East

Indiaman lost in the South China Sea in 1752 (Fig. IV.17) and auctioned in Amsterdam in 1986. I wrote "resembling them" because the ship's inventory did not endorse that identification.

For whatever reason, in 1749 the Dutch East India Company (VOC) listed no chamber pots when it placed its order for arrivals in 1751, but did list 1,300 vomit pots (*spuijgpotjes*), which were described "as shaped like a small chamber pot, the contents those of an ordinary slop bowl."[26] The *Geldermalsen*'s shipping inventory showed 606 such pots, of which 495 were salvaged and auctioned under the heading of "Children's chamber pots in blue and white."[27] The sale also included 245 cuspidors (*quispedoren*), the ancestors of the ubiquitous American Rockingham-glazed spittoons of the nineteenth century. The VOC's order for 1,300 *spuijgpotjes* may be construed as saying something uncomplimentary about Dutch cooking or about an unattractive aspect of Netherlandish table manners. Either way, Christie's was wise to skirt the issue.[28]

There seems to be no information regarding the availability or popularity of Chinese porcelain chamber pots in mid-eighteenth-century England, but nor, for that matter, is there much written about the homemade variety in delftware, white salt-glaze, or whatever. Consequently, virtually all survivors have been retrieved from trash deposits of one sort or another. Just as delftware was succeeded by white salt-glazed stoneware, so the latter could not long compete with the yellow Staffordshire cream-colored wares whose invention is usually attributed to Josiah Wedgwood.[29] Creamware became the chamber-pot fabric of choice from about 1765 to 1800, and several of those that have survived have done so because the faces of political villains were transfer printed onto the insides.[30] Alas, no such treasure is to be found in our collection. In its turn (i.e., around 1780) a new Wedgwood-conceived fabric emulating the appearance of Oriental porcelain began to replace creamware, a whitened ware that he called *pearl*. The result was a lighter body and a glaze whitened by the inclusion of cobalt, which turned it from yellow toward blue. This new ware lent itself to transfer printing, an art rendered both appealing and inexpensive by John Sadler and his partner Guy Green of Liverpool in the 1750s.[31] By the close of the eighteenth century, transfer printing in blue had become the norm for just about every pearlware product, and chamber pots were no exception (Fig. IV.18).

As the British population grew, so did pottery production both upscale and down, the latter serving the lower strata of town and country society. The Collection's representative example of a mid-eighteenth-century, internally lead-glazed, redware chamber pot (Fig. IV.19) is by no stretch of imagination a thing of beauty, but it is undeniably practical and relatively well made. Indeed, it even retains the decorative ridge below the rim that is so often a feature of earlier pewter and earthenware forms. With nothing more in mind than utility, early- to mid-nineteenth-century pots over a wide range were as simple as they could be, and were reinforced only by an outwardly folded rim (Fig. IV.20). It is no accident, however, that the

FIGURE IV.17. Chinese export porcelain chamber pot from the *Geldermalsen* shipwreck, 1752. Photo courtesy of Christie's Amsterdam.

FIGURE IV.18. Transfer-printed pearlware chamber pot. The design shows Nuneham Courtney Mansion, Oxfordshire. Ca. 1810–1820. Ex Burnett Collection.

FIGURE IV.19. Red earthenware chamber pot with treacle-brown interior lead glaze, thickened and flattened rim, distinct shoulder cordon, and reeded handle. Mid-eighteenth century.

FIGURE IV.20. Red earthenware chamber pot with thickened rim. A type often used as paint pots, as this one had been. Ca. 1830–1860.

FIGURE IV.21. Detail from William Hogarth's *Strolling Actresses Dressing in a Barn* showing a chamber pot as a container for the scenic artist's paint. 1738.

FIGURE IV.22. A contemporary portrait of Hogarth at his easel with a small chamber/paint pot in the foreground.

example in the collection has several colors of paint smeared around its handle, for these easily held pots were used by house and theatrical scenery painters.[32] That rather obvious usage was documented by William Hogarth in 1732 when he engraved his *Strolling Actresses Dressing in a Barn,* which showed such a pot with a paintbrush protruding from it (Fig. IV.21).[33] Indeed, his own portrait shows a small (child's size?) chamber pot in the foreground, its paint contents suggested by brushes laid across it (Fig. IV.22).[34]

Small chamber pots are even rarer than large, so the discovery of a German stoneware example in the process of being auctioned on Ebay was an opportunity not to be missed. Two bids had been placed, but as neither had reached the reserve, whose figure remained secret, I had no choice but to put in a high bid in the hope that when the bidding picked up it would be tall enough to stay ahead of the game. On the auction's last day I stood poised to reenter the bidding if that should prove necessary. But the hours dwindled down to minutes without any change. However, I had been warned that clever bidders sometimes remain hidden in the underbrush until the last possible moment before putting in a topping bid too late to be capped. The tension became as taut as an overloaded sling shot—but for no good reason. There were to be no last-second bids, nothing more having been heard from the two early chamber-pot fanciers.

Not only was my new purchase unusually small, but it also retained its original brass lid, something I had never before seen (Fig. IV.23). Needless to say, a lid made excellent sense. One of Hogarth's drawn examples appears to have been covered, but the material is uncertain and it had no handle.[35] If, however, lids were normally made from sheet brass or cop-

IF THESE POTS COULD TALK

FIGURE IV.23. (*a*) Small Westerwald chamber pot decorated with oval wreathed and hatched medallions, found in Amsterdam with its brass lid *in situ*. (*b*) A standard-sized Westerwald chamber pot with similar side medallions along with the usual lions and rosettes. Mid-eighteenth century. (*b*) Ex Frank Thomas Collection.

per, the metal would have had some post-pot value or usage and so may rarely have found its way onto and into archaeological sites.[36] The seller told me that the pot had been recovered from an Amsterdam privy in a context of ca. 1675. I am reasonably certain, however, that the given date is some sixty-five years too early. You may ask, why so?

The answer comes from a Bermuda shipwreck containing wine bottles that could not date any earlier than the 1740s and possibly ten years thereafter. Found with the bottles was a small stoneware vessel from the Westerwald region of the German Rhineland resembling an oversized bird feeder, flat on one side and decorated with the same hatch-marked oval medallions as the three decorating the Amsterdam mini-pot (Fig. IV.24). However, there is some contrary evidence, but to make sense of it one needs first to have read about, and thought about, the much larger pot illustrated beside it.

Just as the accession of Dutch William and his wife Mary had brought with them a taste for chinoiserie, so the arrival of this foreign monarch seems to have heralded the mass importation of the Rhenish chamber pot. Made in gray salt-glazed stoneware decorated with sprigged-on lions and stamped rosettes enclosed within outlining bands of cobalt blue, these imports were known in the chinaman's trade as *grès-de-flandres*. From the frequency with which their fragments are found on archaeological sites both home and colonial, the Rhenish products seem to have cornered a sizeable share of the chamber-pot market through the first half of the eighteenth century. Common or not, however, I have never seen an intact example for sale—although there are two in the Collection.

In the early 1950s, while Audrey and I were working at the Guildhall Museum we came to know many distinguished collectors of glass and ceramics, among them Frank Thomas. He and his daughter Margaret were the premier English authorities on German stonewares. Their house in Highgate was ceiling high with glass cases filled with literally hundreds of specimens ranging in date from the second quarter of the sixteenth to the end of the eighteenth century, and from all the best known Rhineland and

FIGURE IV.24. Westerwald bowl flattened at one side and with wall suspension loop. The single medallion is akin to those of Fig. IV.23. The vessel is held by diver and artifact restorer William Gillies, who recovered it from a Bermuda shipwreck of ca. 1740–1750. William Gillies Collection.

Flemish factories. Frank kept impeccable records of his purchases, most of them from sales at Sotheby's and Christie's auction houses. He wrote careful descriptions of each piece along with a record of its source and the price paid. Alas, like so many collectors, he was content to amass and to satisfy his own interest and curiosity. He never considered publishing a book or catalog—until I came along and offered to help him with the writing and editing. However, Audrey and I left London for Virginia before a word was written—nor would it ever be. Frank died at some time in the 1960s, leaving daughter Margaret to decide what to do with the collection. Victoria and Albert Museum curator Robert Charleston had been a frequent guest at the house in Highgate and had expressed willingness to acquire selected pieces for the V & A collection, but just like David Burnett with his delftware, Frank had insisted that he wanted the collection to stay together. The British Museum, however, was anxious to acquire the collection and offered to publish a catalog. Although much of the collection went there, the century ended with no catalog in print.[37]

It was Frank Thomas's credo that his collection should reflect the very best of Rhenish craftsmanship, and from time to time he culled from it those examples that he had replaced with better or that he felt were not appropriate in a collection of its caliber. Our two Westerwald stoneware chamber pots were the product, or more accurately the victims, of that insistence on excellence (Fig. IV.25). Frank thought they lowered the tone of the collection and so gave them to us. So delighted were we to have them that we failed to see any personal criticism in the gift—and I doubt that any was intended.

FIGURE IV.25. Westerwald chamber pots representing (*a*) the common and (*b*) more rare decorative types used in Britain and abroad through the first half of the eighteenth century and beyond. These were auctioned together and probably had been found together. Ex Frank Thomas Collection.

One of the pots is of the standard lion and rosette variety, but the other is relatively unusual, having the mini-pot's hatched ovals as the side stamps rather than the rosettes. Whether this is indicative of an earlier date or a different and less productive factory, no one yet can say. It does seem, however, that in general the German stoneware types most common on British and British colonial sites in Virginia are less common elsewhere. Nevertheless, one might expect an adjacent colony like Bermuda to be supplied, just as would Virginia. But that appears not to have been so. Dr. Edward Schultz, who heads the emergency-room department of the island's main hospital, is also an archaeologically oriented diver who has forty or more broken Westerwald chamber pots in his collection from a single harbor dump site, three of them with the figure "$1/2$" painted in cobalt below or beside their handles, presumably a capacity indicator that I had previously seen only on Rhenish stoneware tavern bottles, mugs, and jugs (Fig. IV.26).[38]

FIGURE IV.26. Westerwald chamber pot with "$1/2$" painted beside the handle. Shown by Dr. Edward Schultz, who found it in Hamilton Harbour, Bermuda. Mid-eighteenth century. Edward Schultz Collection.

I could detect no difference in size between the $1/2$-marked pots and those that were not, but while seeking one answer I ran into another question. Although I had handled Westerwald chamber pots by the score in the course of my career, it was only in Bermuda that I discovered that chamber-pot lions came in two sizes: standard with crowns and small without. One group of fragments in the Schultz collection yielded a total of forty-eight lions, of which nine were of the smaller size. Whether these should be seen as the product of a single, out-of-step factory or an odd-ball matrix maker is anybody's guess. But as my illustration (Fig. IV.27) suggests, the cobalt decorator when confronted by a nonstandard lion was at a loss to know how to outline it and so elected to give it the big-lion treatment.[39]

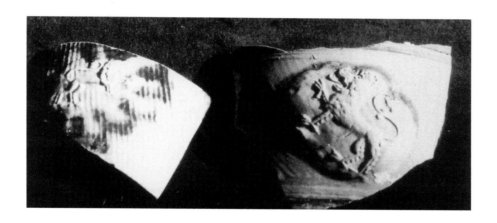

FIGURE IV.27. Westerwald chamber pot shards illustrating (*a*) small uncrowned and (*b*) large crowned lions. Mid-eighteenth century. Edward Schultz Collection.

In 1966 or thereabouts, I was shown a small fragment of a medallion from a Rhenish gray-and-blue stoneware vessel of uncertain shape that had been found on a plantation site in northern Virginia. What made this shard important was the encircling inscription, which, though somewhat blurred, appeared to include the date 1632. I promptly sent a photograph to Frank Thomas, excitedly telling him that it had to be the earliest date so far found on German stoneware in Virginia. Instead, Frank replied that it was impossible for a medallion of that style to be of so early a date, and that the "3" had to be an "8." Two months later a colleague passing a roadside utility trench in Frankfurt, Germany, picked up an even smaller fragment from an identical medallion with the same 1632 date.[40] I took both photographs to England and showed them to Frank, but he was adamant: The date had to be 1682. When I somewhat tremulously asked him why that had to be

FIGURE IV.28. (*a*) Westerwald bottle decorated in cobalt and manganese with "chamber pot" lions and three medallions dated 1634; (*b*) another painted only in cobalt with "chamber pot"–style impressed rosettes. Mid-eighteenth century. (*a*) American private collection.

so, he replied, "I have never, in a lifetime of collecting, seen this type of decoration dating as early as the 1630s." As Frank was a person of vast experience, there could be no further argument. So that was that, or so it seemed.

A year later and only a couple of weeks after Frank's death, I received a photograph from a New England collector who had recently bought a stoneware bottle (Fig. IV.28 *a*) decorated with twin "chamber-pot" lions. It had evolved from an earlier, squatter bottle in plain gray Siegburg stoneware of the 1560s, a type the Germans call a *kugelbauchkrug* (globular-bellied jug). Made in the Westerwald district, the taller, blue-on-gray versions continued into the first half of the eighteenth century (Fig. IV.28 *b*). The New England bottle, however, though of late shape is decorated with medallions almost exactly the same as those from Virginia and Frankfurt, but dated 1634.

Thirty years later the final proof entered our collection in the shape of a Rhenish chamber pot decorated with the lions and two of the medallions, both of them unequivocally dated 1632. This was by no means the earliest date on Rhenish blue-and-gray stoneware; to my own satisfaction, it was

FIGURE IV.29. (*a*) Westerwald chamber pot with central, sprig-applied double-headed eagle flanked by crowned lions, and with side medallions (*b*) dated 1632. Found in Amsterdam.

IF THESE POTS COULD TALK

the earliest dated stoneware chamber pot (Fig. IV.29).[41] That pot's everted rim is reflected in the miniature from Amsterdam (Fig. IV.23 *a*), as is the shape of its oval medallions. One might argue, albeit without much conviction, that the latter pot's alleged 1675 context is correct and that its hatched medallions when found on mid-eighteenth-century vessels represent only a continuation or revival of a much older decorative technique.

In addition to the lions and ovals, the 1632 pot has as its central ornament a sprig-applied medallion featuring a double-headed eagle, the emblem of the German Hapsburgs, a detail not seen on run-of-the-mill Westerwald pots found in Britain. It might be thought curious, therefore, that nearly two hundred years later, satirical artist James Gillray, in drawing a cartoon lampooning the gross eating habits of Germans resident in London, had included under the chair of the principal glutton a chamber pot adorned with a double-headed eagle (Fig. IV.30).[42] Whence came

FIGURE IV.30. Detail from James Gillray's *Germans Eating Sour-Krout,* showing an eagle-decorated chamber pot beneath the chair. 1803.

Gillray's inspiration for this detail? It could hardly have been from an early-seventeenth-century pot of a type hitherto unrecorded in England. The answer would seem to be that although unaware that seventeenth-century Rhenish chamber pots had been eagle decorated, Gillray independently settled on that device to show that he had put a German pot under the German's chair.

Fragments of several Westerwald pots of the 1632 shape have been found in excavations in the East Anglian town of Norwich, but none (to my knowledge) has the same eagle medallion.[43] Among the Norwich examples is one whose rim is gently concave on the inside, a detail exhibited by another reportedly recovered from a Dutch shipwreck in New York

Harbor and now in a private American collection (Fig. IV.31). I have argued that being more squat (or perhaps I should say wider) this is a more evolved shape and attributable to the second half of the seventeenth century. The form is paralleled by yet another excavated in the Lower Rhine city of Duisburg, with its oval side cartouches dated 1677—which (if correctly read) supports the date so vehemently argued by Frank Thomas.[44]

I do not recount my exchanges with Frank in any sense of superiority or one-upmanship, for I was privileged to learn from him and am forever grateful to him for his forbearance in sharing his knowledge with a young man still celadon green behind the ears. From time to time I have caught myself saying to a student or colleague "I know this to be so because I've never seen . . ." and then I remember the 1632 medallion and give a less rigid answer. Amid the shifting sands of artifact research, fifty years of experience has proved a frail buckler against the arrows of new information. All too often I have quoted Frank in saying that manganese purple was not used until about 1660 and then principally on highly decorated "star" jugs.[45] The New England collector's 1634 bottle not only dated the medallion but also proved that by that early date gray German stoneware potters were already coupling cobalt with manganese. In venturing into the field of seventeenth-century ceramics, one must constantly be prepared to be proved wrong and to emulate Hogarth by throwing out the slops of old certainties in favor of new possibilities (Fig. IV.32).

V Of Mugs and Jugs Both Large and Small

And he took him a potsherd to scrape himself withal.

Job 2:8

FIGURE V.1. A face from the past. Who saw it last?

BEAUTY, WE ARE told, is in the eye of the beholder, a platitude usually uttered in a condescending tone by someone who thinks that whatever it is you happen to like is as ugly as sin.[1] Porcelain people are usually too polite to say so when invited to admire a stoneware collection, but one can tell what they are thinking by the slight pause and pained expression as they grope for a less damning response. For my part, I make no excuses for being amorously drawn to stoneware. Let me tell you why.

As a long-time historical archaeologist with an equally long fixation on the sixteenth and seventeenth centuries, when I uncover the neck of a Rhenish graybeard bottle I see a face from the past staring up at me out of the ground (Fig. v.1). Not only that, stoneware repels dirt. A light brushing reveals it in exactly the color and condition it was in when buried. Unlike other less highly fired wares, stoneware and dirt do not cling to each other, nor does the glaze flake. What you see is what it was. Be it the mottled brown of the graybeard or the brilliant blue of the Westerwald wares, it shines in sunlight. Its discovery provides a moment of exaltation that is rarely experienced by finding, say, a chunk of lead-glazed earthenware or something as antiseptic as white salt glaze or even creamware. Better yet is the certainty that we can find a Dutch or Flemish genre painting in which a mug or jug exactly like it will show us where it belonged—on the table or in the hands of real people. It's a safe bet, too, that those people appreciated the color and the heft of their stonewares—just as I do. Thus is one drawn into the picture and toward a growing awareness of what life was like in seventeenth-century Katwijk-aan-Zee, at East Grinstead, or in Jamestown, Virginia.

No one knows the exact date when the first Rhenish potter learned to make stoneware, but like many discoveries it may well have happened by accident when a kiln overheated to a temperature in excess of 1,200°C while using clay that could withstand it without warping. Whether that supposition be right or wrong, ceramic historians agree that the new ware went into production in the latter years of the thirteenth or early in the fourteenth century. About a hundred years later, potters discovered that salt thrown into the kiln would vaporize and impart a hard, shiny but pitted glaze. At first the products were salt-glazed but uncolored, and therefore remained gray (Fig. V.2), but due to atmospheric variations in the kiln some emerged with patches of brown, a color that would have been appealing had it not been in isolated blobs. The next step came at the end of the fifteenth century, when stoneware potters took to coating their products with a thin, iron oxide slip, which achieved uniformity and the same brown color (Fig. V.3). This mastered, the potters were able to market three varieties of their wares: unadorned gray usually associated with the town of Siegburg and plain brown with Cologne (Fig. V.3 *b*), whereas Raeren became famous for the third variant, namely, vessels featuring relief decoration outlined in cobalt blue atop a gray ware.

Six of the seven principal brown stoneware production centers of the fifteenth and sixteenth centuries were widely scattered in the region lying between the Meuse and Rhine rivers.[2] Other lesser centers had been in operation further south in the vicinity of Coblenz in the fifteenth century, beginning at the village of Höhr by 1402 and somewhat later at Grenzhausen and at eight more locations of lesser renown. Due to civil, religious, and territorial conflicts that ravaged the Rhineland from the 1580s through to the end of the Thirty Years War in 1648, potters moved from one supposedly safe haven to another. Thus in the late sixteenth century potters from Siegburg and Raeren settled in the vicinity of Höhr and continued to produce quality wares indistinguishable from those they had made earlier. As many as ten stoneware potting centers sprang up to the south in the Westerwald region, and by the end of the seventeenth century there were several hundred potters at work there. Most of their products were of the kind we loosely describe as *Westerwald*, and are a familiar presence on archaeological sites from Nova Scotia to South Africa and beyond.

FIGURE V.2. Typical salt-glazed but uncolored stoneware drinking vessel with weakly frilled foot and poorly formed strap handle. Siegburg, ca. 1475–1525.

FIGURE V.3. Two small brown stoneware mugs and a can. (*a*) Attributed to Raeren; (*b*) a waster from a Cologne kiln dump. Both first half of sixteenth century. (*c*) An unusually shaped can, another kiln reject, Raeren or perhaps Bouffioulx in Belgium, late sixteenth century.

Although Rhenish stonewares are known to most of us by their later products, there is no doubt that throughout the sixteenth century, brown stoneware mugs, jugs, and bottles were the ware of choice in every Rhineland and neighboring town, village, and home. When such artists as Bosch or Brueghel wanted to depict a drinking vessel it invariably was a frilly-footed, Rhenish brown stoneware mug, several examples of which are included in the Collection. The earliest dates from ca. 1450–1475 and exhibits the lateral ridging of the dull gray wares found in waster dumps at Siegburg (Fig. v.2).[3] By no stretch of imagination is this an attractive mug, and it is no surprise that the skilled Rhineland potters soon produced more pleasing shapes, eccentric though some may seem to us (Fig. v.4 *a*). The tall, funnel-mouthed type is typical of its period and is the successor to the same shapes that previously came unglazed from Siegburg. It evidently was thought sufficiently practical and attractive to be copied by English potters in Surrey, who made a version whose funnel mouth more closely resembled that of a sixteenth-century wine goblet (Fig. v.4 *b*).

FIGURE V.4. (*a*) Cone-mouthed, partially browned in firing, but unslipped salt-glazed stoneware drinking vessel. The frilled foot is well formed and the short handle at the shoulder is typical of the type. Siegburg, ca. 1475–1525. (*b*) An English Border Ware drinking vessel, its goblet profile perhaps inspired by the Rhenish shape, ca. 1500–1550. [Mouth reconstructed.] (*b*) Ex Burnett Collection.

A ceramic detective looks for clues wherever they might be found, but more often than not they fall into one's lap while looking for something quite different. The British Museum's David Gaimster learned that the laterally-ribbed vessels were sometimes made by women when he found one at work on the back of a ca. 1450 playing card.[4] She appears to be in the

IF THESE POTS COULD TALK

FIGURE V.5. A German playing card from a set depicting contemporary crafts, showing a female potter at her wheel throwing a drinking vessel similar to Fig. V.4, and deliberately creating lateral ridges with the aid of a cut-down animal metacarpal. Mid-fifteenth century. Collection of Kunstkammer, Kunsthistorisches Museum, Vienna.

process of deliberately creating the ribs with the aid of a tool cut from a long leg bone of an ox (Fig. V.5). My own experiments with such a bone (actually a pin-maker's bone found in the Thames) did a fair job of reproducing the ribbing characteristic of most stoneware drinking vessels of the fifteenth and sixteenth centuries (Fig. V.6).

The Collection's examples illustrate the evolution of the mug from its rustic beginnings to its sophisticated and evenly fired version in the late sixteenth century after frilly feet had lost their appeal (Fig. V.7). This last used to be attributed to Cologne but is now considered to originate in Frechen and to a date around 1580. At the same time that plain mugs and gorges were being exported, Siegburg potters introduced a range of tall tankards in white, unsalted stoneware that the Germans call *schnelles,* and that were decorated with elaborate, sprig-molded panels, usually armorial in nature, but sometimes in carefully delineated Biblical scenes. The Collection's rare example is one such, with its three abutting panels depicting the

FIGURE V.6. Duplicating Siegburg grooves and ridges using a trimmed animal metacarpal.

FIGURE V.7. Typical Rhenish brown stoneware mug (gorge) with straight collar neck, sharp shoulder cordon, and well-formed foot—a vast improvement over the frilly feet common earlier in the sixteenth century. Probably from Frechen, ca. 1560–1590.

FIGURE V.8. Siegburg white stoneware schnelle of ca. 1570–1595, with original lid but Victorian pewter mounts. The three sprig-applied, vertical panels tell the story of the Crucifixion, the Entombment, and the Resurrection. The crucified Christ wears a curiously wind-blown loincloth, a feature paralleled though somewhat more stylized on the fragments in Fig. v.9.

FIGURE V.9. Fragments from a Westerwald stoneware jug (or bottle?) decorated with a sprig-applied Crucifixion image reminiscent of the schnelle, of Fig. v.8. Found on the Pickleherring site not far from Southwark's Crucifix Lane. Ca. 1610–1630. Ex Burnett Collection.

Crucifixion, the Burial, and the Resurrection (Fig. v.8). Handles on these tankards are usually rather thick and end in a none-too-attractive lower terminal lump. This example, however, has something to add that ties to David Gaimster's playing card. The finger that pressed the terminal to the wall left an impression too small to have been that of an average man.

The Siegburg *schnelle* entered the Collection within weeks of my receiving fragments from David Burnett's Southwark collection that portrayed Christ crucified in such detail that it showed the driven nails, his face bearded and mustachioed, and a loincloth curiously windswept (Fig. v.9). Those who seek and believe in religious symbolism may think it miraculous that from a fairly large vessel only four fragments survived, two of them those that make up the Christ figure.[5] Although the wing-like loincloth is paralleled on the schnelle, the two Crucifixions are thirty or forty years apart, with the fragmentary figure having decorated a blue-on-gray Westerwald-style jug made as late as perhaps 1630.

Like the Christ figures, additions to Audrey's and my collection often resulted from outside stimuli and unexpected sources. Thus the recovery of two small, Rhenish brown stoneware drinking or dispensing jugs by diver E. B. "Teddy" Tucker from an unidentified Bermuda shipwreck site prompted us to add one exactly like them to the Collection (Fig. v.10). Although fairly precise dating might have resulted had there been other objects from the wreck site, in this instance nothing else was found. Indeed, the jugs may not have been on a wreck site at all, but may have come from cargo jettisoned when its ship was escaping the clutches of the treacherous Bermuda reefs. No example of this strange shape is illustrated in David Gaimster's major work on German stonewares, but he did include a page of drawings of such wares found in a ca. 1518–1550 context in Bergen-op-Zoom that included a fragment of one such jug, thereby putting it distinctly earlier than I had supposed.[6] However, an intact specimen in the collection of the Rheinisches Freilichtmuseum at Kommern is there attributed to Raeren at the end of the sixteenth century.[7] Which is

IF THESE POTS COULD TALK

FIGURE V.10. (*a, b*) A pair of Rhenish brown stoneware gill measures (quarterns), found on a Bermuda reef; (*c*) the Collection's parallel. All probably Raeren, ca. 1580. (*a, b*) E. B. Tucker Collection.

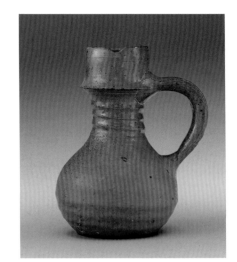

correct only time and more research will tell, but a date around 1580–1600 seems a fair bet. Unfortunately, neither source told us what purpose was served by these tiny jugs.

In 1999 I bought a comparably small blue-on-gray Westerwald jug dating from the second half of the seventeenth century that looked for all the world like a toy or mantle-shelf ornament (Fig. V.11 *a*).[8] The question I asked myself was whether smallness was significant for some practical reason or whether, like glass makers, the potters made miniature items after working hours to take home to amuse wives and kids. Alternatively, might they not have been young potters' masterpieces demonstrating the skills that, if sufficient, made them freemen of their guild? That, however, could hardly be true of this little Westerwald jug on whose base was carefully glued its provenance (clipped and pasted from the sale catalog) stating that it had been found during building site work in London's Fleet Street

FIGURE V.11. (*a, c*) Westerwald stoneware quarterns, (*a*) perhaps twenty years later than (*c*), the latter with stamp-impressed roundel decoration and "rope" cordoning at the shoulder and above the foot; (*c*) decorated with sprigged, spiraling roundels akin to metal buttons of the early seventeenth century, label on base reading "Excavated in Fleet Street, London during extensive re-development at the turn of this century." Both ca. 1630–1660. (*b*) Westerwald jug decorated with arms and profiles of the seven Electors of the Holy Roman Emperors, dated within the sprigged frieze, 1585. (*b*) Ex Frank Thomas Collection.

early in the twentieth century. This, then, had been a *working* pot, so it occurred to me that capacity might have been more significant than size, shape, or decoration.

On filling our parallel for the Bermuda jugs to its lip with water, I found that it held exactly five fluid ounces and that pouring the water from it into the Westerwald juglet showed them to be of the same capacity. Clearly, therefore, these mini-jugs, though from different centuries, were made for the same purpose, a standardized capacity achieved by potters so experienced that, allowing for kiln shrinkage, their jugs gave full measure. Subtracting the space that could be taken up by stoppers, both capacities were reduced by one ounce, proving that these small jugs were gill measures known in the tavern trade as *quarterns*, a measure used for dispensing brandy, aqua vitae, and other distilled spirits.[9]

Within a week of acquiring what on the basis of my experience I believed to be a juglet of infinite rarity, I came upon another of the same size but complete with its original pewter lid (Fig. v.11 *c*). Although this was a sobering reminder that even at the age of seventy-two I still had much to learn, the second jug entered the collection riding on the admittedly flimsy justification that two of anything make a pair.

Having belatedly discovered that quartern-sized stoneware mini-jugs were not as rare as I had supposed, my next step was to seek them out in contemporary paintings of still life or convivial life. After going through the paintings and engravings of the usual suspects—Brueghel, the David Teniers young and old, Jan Steen, Vermeer, Adrian van Ostade, and a small host of others—I found not a single parallel for either the early brown jug or the later blue and gray couple. Having found virtually every other Rhenish stoneware type common in the sixteenth and seventeenth centuries, why not these?

I have two explanations—neither of which may be sound: First, the jugs, being so small, would occupy so minuscule an area of a large canvas as not to be worth including. The second theory seems the more plausible, to wit: Most Dutch and Flemish convivially bucolic scenes feature rustic figures swilling from larger stoneware mugs and jugs—imbibers of beer, ale, and cheap wines. Rarely, if ever, does one find scenes of revelers downing the hard liquor characteristic of the lone tippler. For reasons best left to psychologists to figure out, images of rowdy horseplay and lechery evoke indulgent smiles while the sight of the solo sot makes one shudder—as we shall see when we come to the ceramics of gin in the nineteenth century.

When the British government passed a series of acts designed to restrict and even prohibit foreign trade, German stonewares were excluded. This may be explained by the supposition that in the waning years of the seventeenth century they posed no threat to British potters, who were thought to be incapable of producing comparable stonewares, and that patents given to the latter would be helped by also bestowing a monopoly on the importation of such wares. We now know that at least one British factory could, indeed, produce creditable copies of the imports.

IF THESE POTS COULD TALK

At his factory beside the Thames at Fulham, John Dwight, who had studied at Oxford under the tutelage of the "father of chemistry" the great Robert Boyle, had mastered "the Mistery of the Stone ware vulgarly called Cologne ware" and in 1672 obtained a royal patent to commercially produce it. Although samples of Dwight's German-style stoneware products had been found during building construction on the Fulham site in the late nineteenth century and were obtained for the famed Schreiber Collection that was absorbed into London's Victoria and Albert Museum as long ago as 1884, they were seen as little more than amusingly experimental copies.[10]

Excavations on Dwight's Fulham factory site in the 1970s revealed for the first time the scope of his achievement and showed that his reproductions of the current Rhenish covered mugs and jugs had advanced to greater perfection than had hitherto been supposed. However, the excavated evidence also demonstrated that production emphasis had been on utilitarian brown stonewares on the one hand, and on the other to experiments to emulate Chinese red ware and the making of Oriental porcelain. In his 1672 patent Dwight described the latter as "Earthen Ware commonly knowne by the name of Porcelaine or China and Persian ware."

Although John Dwight and his secret-stealing rivals revolutionized the English potting industry and paved the way for the worldwide impact of Staffordshire in the following century, it is best to pursue that connection down another avenue of Audrey's and my ceramic collecting. I return, therefore, to the blue and gray Rhenish stonewares that were to enjoy a major share of the British ceramic market until the early 1770s. Working mostly in the Westerwald district of the Rhineland, the potters of these wares did nothing to compete with the English taste for delicate tea wares or even for dinner plates, tureens, sauce boats, and cruets. Like the Germans themselves (or so the insular English believed), theirs was heavy stuff that traveled well and was destined for a hard life in the taproom and kitchen. Along with the previously discussed lion-decorated chamber pots, the trade was in bulbous gorges and later cylindrical drinking vessels, as well as in jugs or pitchers in graduated sizes. Both mugs and jugs were mass produced to standard capacities identified by numbers adjacent to their handles either incised or more often painted in cobalt—as on the chamber pots found in a Bermuda harbor.

The numbering began with 1 as the largest and worked its way down to 10 as the smallest, and their approximate equivalents in British 20-ounce pints went like this:

    1 = 1 gallon   2 = 3 quarts   3 = 2 quarts   4 = 1 quart   6 = 1 pint
    8 = 1/2 pint (or 8 Dutch "mussies")   9 = not found
    10 = 1 gill, noggin, or quartern

Those capacity marks coincide to some degree with the blue bands below the rims and above the bases of straight-sided Westerwald mugs: triple blues for 3's, doubles for 4's, and singles for all those of lesser capacity.

However, it is likely that the number of blue bands had more to do with proportionate design than with capacity.

Because the American archaeological study of seventeenth- and eighteenth-century domestic life in Virginia was in full throttle before the British came to realize that what they termed the "postmedieval centuries" were worthy of their attention, it follows that dating for ceramics from colonial sites is often closer than it has been for comparable material from Old World excavations. Thus, as already noted, the excavation of the palisaded fort at Jamestown (1607 to ca. 1619) has produced a wealth of tightly attributable data whose impact has yet to be fully absorbed and appreciated. In the 1970s the Colonial Williamsburg Foundation's excavations on the several sites of Martin's Hundred beside the James River were able to isolate ceramics that reached there in the two years prior to the Indian assault of 1622 from others used in its aftermath. Thus, for example, the largest (if not the finest) Westerwald jug yet found in the Virginia colony (Fig. V.12) was discovered in a pit in association with a locally made slipware dish in the Metropolitan style dated 1631.[11] Other jugs of this class were decorated in relief with panels made from strips of clay first pressed into molds; then, after sufficient drying and shrinking, the body-encircling frieze was transferred from the mold and luted to the jug's wall.

IF THESE POTS COULD TALK

The master matrices ranged from Biblical scenes and rustic amusements to—and these were very common—the armorial shields and portrait busts of the palatinate's seven archbishop electors who chose the emperors of the Holy Roman Empire. The Collection's early jug is one such specimen and is dated 1585 in the last of the panels (Fig. v.11 *b*). But there being no knowing how long a mold remained in use, one cannot be sure that any jug or bottle so ornamented was actually made in the stated year.

Through the late sixteenth century into the first half of the seventeenth century, most jugs exported into England from the Rhineland were of shapes akin to the Martin's Hundred example, though varying considerably in sizes—none of which, to our knowledge, exhibit capacity-defining

FIGURE V.13. (*a*) Westerwald gorge with sprigged and incised decoration, its key feature the reeded, blue-painted neck. Ca. 1680–1700. (*b*) Gorge with incised and stamped decoration and sprigged GR medallion, its reeded neck manganese painted. Attributed to Grenzhausen, 1720–1750. (*b*) Ex Margaret Thomas Collection.

numbers. Beginning in the 1630s, some blue-on-gray Rhenish wares were decorated in often combined yet distinctly different techniques. First the leather-hard walls were scored with knives or two- and three-tined rakes to create foliate and other incised ornament; then, while in the green stage, the scoring was overlaid by separately applied flowers that range from daisies to rosettes and tulips. These relief-decorating details were next painted in cobalt blue and often in manganese purple (Fig. v.13 *a*). The same style is illustrated in the Collection by an unpainted, grayish stoneware jug that combines the combed stems with lozenge-shaped individually sprigged tulips (Fig. v.14). Nineteenth-century collectors believed that these unpainted jugs were the product of Höhr in the Westerwald, but it is now known that they were made in more than one factory. Our specimen's principal ornament is its central, sprig-applied medallion displaying the arms of the Archbishop of Cologne and the date 1700. By the close of the seventeenth century the time-consuming application of individually stamped blossoms was giving way to a greater reliance on scored ornaments whose curls and swirls could be speedily infilled with cobalt.

In less than a hundred years Rhenish stoneware decoration had advanced from scratching funny faces onto the sides of Siegburg beakers to applied portrayals of the greatest detail and delicacy—as is demonstrated by the Collection's Crucifixion schnelle (Fig. v.8). Among the most attractive of

FIGURE V.14. Westerwald gray stoneware jug with incised and sprigged decoration akin to that of Fig. v.13 *a*, and with a sprigged central medallion bearing the arms of the Archbishop of Cologne and dated 1700. Both neck and foot are heavily cordoned. Such gray wares without cobalt enrichment are usually (but ill-advisedly) attributed to the town of Höhr. For the handle detail see Fig. v.24.

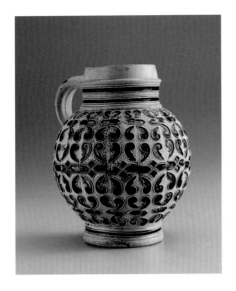

FIGURE V.15. Westerwald gray stoneware jug decorated with sprigged vertical panels with incuse parenthetic marks alternatingly in-filled in cobalt and manganese The jugs of this period are characterized by pairs of blue decorated cordons at the neck and another above the base. Ca. 1680–1700.

FIGURE V.16. Westerwald stoneware jug fragments decorated with vertical sprigged panels in a geometric foliate design shown in both large and small versions. This was the sprig-molding motif copied by John Dwight at Fulham in his attempts to simulate the Rhenish wares. Both shards from the Pickleherring area. Ca. 1680–1700. Ex Burnett Collection.

Westerwald jugs of the last third of the seventeenth century were those carefully decorated with applied, vertical strips, whose molds were pre-shaped to fit the curvature of the vessel to which they were being pressed (Fig.v.15). The ornamental panels, once attached to the leather-hard or "green" ware, were then carefully in-painted in cobalt blue and manganese purple, and came in designs both large and small (Fig. v.16). This was the Rhenish product that John Dwight tried to emulate at his Fulham factory, where carved chalk molds for comparable panels have been found in contexts dating between 1665 and ca. 1675.

Along with the rapid decline in the use of separately molded devices came another feature of mass production, namely, the use of templates either hand held or attached to the frame of the wheel. This shaping tool established both size and the sharp cordons characteristic of German stone-wares in the eighteenth century. But rather than creating a smoothly shaped surface, the template caused a chatter that imparted a multitude of very shallow vertical ridges, which, though concealed beneath applied rosettes, medallions, and cobalt painting, remained visible in undecorated areas flanking the handles (Fig. v.17). Chatter is even more visible in rare brown stoneware tankards, where it seems to have been considered a dec-orative asset (Fig. v.18). Thus, the presence or absence of chatter provides an important clue in determining to which century a vessel belonged.[12] However, most examples of Westerwald wares found in Britain and in her erstwhile American colonies need no such scrutiny to determine their age.

From the reigns of Dutch William on through the Hanoverian Georges, Rhenish potters deliberately catered to the export market by featuring the reigning monarch in the central, sprig-applied medallions. On small and medium-sized gorges, William III is usually represented by a front-facing portrait in a style established when he was Prince of Orange-Nassau prior to winning the English throne in 1689. Thereafter he would be shown crowned within a circlet proclaiming his royal titles as king of England, France, and Ireland—which, needless to say, continued to irk the French.

FIGURE V.17. Typical Westerwald stoneware tankards made for home and international markets, each illustrating the degree of "chatter" visible with and without applied central zone decoration. No capacity marks; pewter lids original. (*a*) ca. 1700–1730; (*b*) ca. 1690–1720; (*c*) ca. 1700–1750.

FIGURE V.18. A fragmentary Rhenish stoneware tankard, salt-glazed over a pale, ginger-brown firing slip. The central zone is plain save for a frontal medallion depicting a city gate, and takes advantage of the template chatter to provide its ornament. A simple, sprigged band of raised dots creates an upper frieze, and below are zones of cordoning. This rare mug fabric and form was recovered from Hamilton Harbour, Bermuda. First half of eighteenth century. Edward Schultz Collection.

FIGURE V.19. "AR" (Anna Regina) sprig-applied medallion on a fragmentary blue-on-gray stoneware mug of pint capacity. Westerwald. 1702–1714. Ex Burnett Collection.

In 1672, to protect the English delftware industry, the British government had banned the importation of "painted wares," but it said nothing about Rhenish stonewares, whose influx increased dramatically in the early eighteenth century and would continue to enter the country and its colonies (albeit aboard English ships) into the 1770s.[13]

William III died in 1702, to be succeeded by Queen Anne (1702–1714), who had to settle for her Anna Regina initials on the exported Rhenish stonewares (Fig. V.19), as did the three Georges, whose GR (Georgius Rex) medallions are indistinguishable one from another (Fig. V.20). However, there are dating clues, some more reliable than others. The most obvious is the treatment of jug necks, with the earliest being relatively short and encircled by a pair of molded and incuse cordons painted in blue. Those that came later abandoned the cordons and substituted a wall of laterally incised grooves washed with manganese. Unfortunately, rules of thumb are four digits short of a hand, as Audrey and I were reminded when we purchased a small bulbous mug or gorge with all the right attributes for a date around 1690 but possessing a laterally grooved (reeded) neck washed with cobalt (Fig. V.13 *a*). On that evidence it seems fair to conclude that such necks were in production simultaneously with the

FIGURE V.20. Westerwald stoneware mugs both with sprigged "GR" medallions, flanking incised scroll and foliate ornament, and with double blue banding between the cordons above and below. (*a*) "3" incised on rim (2 quart), and (*b*) blue-painted "4" beside handle (1 quart). (*a*) ca. 1730–1760; (*b*) 1714–1730.

FIGURE V.21. Westerwald stoneware jug with sprigged "GR" medallion and incised flanking tulip and foliate decoration; double blue cordon above and one below. Blue-painted "3" capacity mark beside the handle (2 quart). 1714–1730.

blue-banded ones and eventually replaced them. The key word, of course, is *eventually*. But are we talking about years or decades?

The Collection's example of blue-banding on a GR jug (Fig. V.21) puts its date of manufacture no earlier than 1714 and probably no later than 1727, when George I was succeeded by the more popular George II. A couple of gallon-sized jugs joined the Collection as classic examples of the danger of reading too much into too little. The neck of one is blue banded and the other purple reeded, yet both are adorned with GR medallions that appear to be from the same mold (Fig. V.22). At first sight, therefore, one is tempted to conclude that both are of the same date. But are they? The medallion on the blue-necked jug is distinctly sharper than that of its companion, implying that the master mold became worn over time, resulting in softer and inferior casts. The problem, of course, is knowing whether the mold was in constant use over a short period of time or less frequently over a longer one.

Three more Westerwald jugs further muddy the chronological waters (Fig. V.23). None dates earlier than 1714. That much is certain. If we assume that, in general, blue-banded necks are earlier than manganese reeding, the large, bird-decorated example came first. Its smaller companions certainly look later on the evidence of their more standardized petaled surround to their GR medallions. But when we look back to the big pair of Fig. V.22, we find the same "late" petaled surround on the blue-banded jug. The explanation for all this contradictory evidence may be that although blue banding certainly began in the late seventeenth century (e.g., Fig. V.15), it may have continued throughout the life of one factory while another, from its outset, made only manganese-painted necks. But is there a flaw in this reasoning?

Of course there is. I have already linked together the jugs of Figure V.22 claiming that both their GR medallions came from the same master matrix and so, by extension, from the same factory. An alternative explanation, however, is that mold-making was a separate craft whose proprietors sold to several factories unhampered by modern collectors' hang-ups over banded or reeded necks.

FIGURE V.22. Westerwald stoneware jugs with "GR" medallions apparently from the same master mold; (*a*) sharper than (*b*). Neck and foot decoration of (*a*) as for Fig. v.21; (*b*) has manganese reeding at the neck and no coloring at the base. Neither jug has a capacity mark, but both are of 1 gallon capacity. The small foreground jug or gorge is present only to provide scale (see Fig. v.13 *b*). Ca. 1725–1750.

FIGURE V.23. Westerwald stoneware jugs of 2, 3, and 4 capacities, all with "GR" medallions of decreasing quality. (*a*) incised with "2" (3 quarts) below the handle and decorated with elaborate pelican medallion-flanking motifs; neck as Figs. v.21 and 22 *a*. (*b, c*) Incised "petal" treatment around their medallions, and necks as Fig. v.22 *a*. (*a*) Ca. 1715–1740; (*b, c*), ca. 1730–1760.

Yet another feature of Rhenish stonewares has been the subject of debate, namely, the nail-punched holes usually present in the crests of handles of both jugs and mugs. Some collectors have explained them as a safety valve to prevent warping in the kiln. But that is not the reason. The holes were made (usually one, but sometimes two and even three) to enable pewter lids to be added. The 1700 jug (Figs. v.14 and v.24) provides proof by possessing a ghost image of a lost pewter mount whose rattail extremity had left its stain on the handle, and whose securing pewter lug remains in the hole.

The German stoneware industry had an incredibly long life, outlasting most of the ceramic wares produced in England and Europe, so long, in fact, that it continues today and provides traps for novice collectors of its earlier products. The Gothic revival of the mid-nineteenth century proved a godsend to an ailing craft, creating a market for antique-appearing jugs and mugs (steins) to decorate the shelves of neo-baronial halls.[14] Several Rhineland factories deliberately copied shapes common in the sixteenth and

FIGURE V.24. Detail of the upper handle terminal of the gray Westerwald jug of Fig. v.14, revealing the ghost image of a lost pewter handle mount and showing the securing lug still in its hole. 1700.

FIGURE V.25. Rhenish brown stoneware candle holder and separate tinderbox, shaped and rotated in a three-piece press mold, with the latter imparting in sharp relief an Empire-style male profile flanked by six different but unidentified shields of arms, one of them featuring three jugs. The bottom is impressed with the ligatured monogram HS and the number 48. This is the mark of Hubert Schiffer, who went into business at Raeren in 1885 to make copies of Renaissance-era German stonewares.

seventeenth centuries, sometimes using original sprig molds. Although advertised in contemporary catalogs as reproductions, once parted from that documentation many Siegburg-style and Raeren-type vessels passed through famed collections and auction houses, acquiring impressive pedigrees as they went. Even collectors as savvy as Frank and Margaret Thomas did not escape the occasional bad apple in their barrels—as I had reason to discover when I came close to paying a princely sum for a splendid schnelle that beguilingly bore the rare arms of Elizabethan England along with a "Thomas Collection" label. It was only through the British Museum's David Gaimster having given me a copy of an article on Siegburg-style fakes that I escaped the trap. David gave me the offprint on a Thursday, but being on a tight London schedule I did not have time to read it. On the Saturday I was offered the schnelle, but at a price sufficiently daunting for me to ask the dealer to hold it until I returned to London a week later. In my Portsmouth hotel room on the Sunday, having nothing better to do, I sat down to read David's articles—and there found an illustration of a fake that looked incredibly like the mug from the Thomas Collection. The next day I called the dealer and asked whether he would allow David to examine it on my behalf. The dealer agreed—on two alternative conditions: I could buy the mug at the stated price without authentication, or I could have the jug evaluated by my British Museum authority. But if he accepted it as genuine, the price would double! The moral to this story is simple enough: Never examine any antique in a poorly lit shop.

Because ours is a teaching collection, I have always found it useful to be able to show students examples that illustrate the differences between those that are "right" and those that are not. In some instances objects made as unassuming reproductions, and marked on their bases with the initials or logo of the manufacture, later exhibit worn patches where unscrupulous vendors have filed or sanded away the marks. Figure V.25 shows an example that escaped such a disguise and bears on its base the ligatured initials HS for the Westerwald factory of Hubert Schiffer, who was one of several retrospective manufacturers working in the last quarter of the nineteenth century. The object (which may have been designed as an inkwell or candleholder) is decorated with authentic-looking shields of arms reminiscent of the Raeran wares of the late sixteenth century. But there is an important difference. Those were ornamented with separately molded and applied friezes, whereas Schiffer's was made entirely in a three-piece mold, faint traces of whose joins are discernible to anyone who really looks for them. The same is true of most German stonewares of the latter part of the nineteenth century. In the twentieth century, on the other hand, more sophisticated reproductive techniques as well as the careful use of original methods can result in copies that only a person used to handling originals may recognize (Fig. V.26 *a*). Produced in the same Höhr-Grenzhausen that had been the source of so much of the salt-glazed stonewares of earlier centuries, the Grenzau reproductions of Siegburg, Frechen, and Westerwald wares are of fine quality, though somewhat too

FIGURE V.26. (*a*) A mid-seventeenth-century Frechen graybeard with the arms of Amsterdam; (*b*) a good-quality Grenzau reproduction; (*c*) the multi-marked base of the modern copy.

uniform in their color. Produced in limited editions of only 5,000, each is individually numbered and its source clearly identified, but even if it were not, the base betrays its lack of age. The pulling striations imparted when original graybeards were separated from the still-revolving wheel with a cutting wire invariably left swirling marks that were off center and drawn to one side. The illustrated reproduction, however, exhibits a tightly wound central spiral never found on seventeenth-century examples (Fig. v.26 *c*).

On nineteenth-century Westerwald copies or adaptations, handles are an easily recognizable clue to age, most of them having been shaped in a two-piece mold. From the sixteenth through the eighteenth centuries, handles were drawn out from measured strips of clay either flattened or rolled and tapering in width from top to tail. On being luted to the pot's rim or shoulder, the handle was looped down and pressed to its lower wall, leaving a small tail needing either to be broken off, smeared away, or converted into a decorative terminal. Although, in the eighteenth century, the usual practice was to draw the surplus clay down into an elongated V (rat-tail),[15] in the previous centuries it was either folded back on itself or rolled into a scroll that left lateral space between the loops. In reproducing this detail in the nineteenth century, the shape of the previously hand-made roll was cast in the mold, and in consequence the open scroll became mere indentations on either side of the terminal (Fig. v.27).

Distinguishing between pieces that are "right" or "wrong" depends in part on having studied a sufficient number of those that are genuine to recognize when some detail appears to be amiss. No less necessary is having seen enough pieces that provably are not what they claim, to recognize their details when they show up where they shouldn't. The handsome

FIGURE V.27. Examples of handle terminals on Rhenish gray stonewares: *left*, hand-drawn and rolled, ca. 1585; *right*, molded, ca. 1885.

FIGURE V.28. (*a*) Frechen-style brown stoneware mug with late silver mounts in the Elizabethan manner with marks identifying them as being from Chester in 1911. Subsequent revelations were to shift the mug forward to that date and to a Doulton attribution. Determining clues: (*b*) The interior potting rings characteristic of comparable vessels from Rhenish kilns of the sixteenth century are absent from the mug. (*c*) The other clue, at *left*, shows the sharp and complex basal cordoning of an original un-matched by the reproduction (*right*), whose ridges are softly rounded as was common among English brown stone-wares in the late nineteenth century.

Raeran style stoneware jug with its Elizabethan mounts helps explain what I mean (Fig. v.28). It was sold at Christie's auction rooms in April 2000, and was described in the catalog as follows:

> 99. A German brown-glazed stoneware silver-mounted jug and hinged cover with globular body and cylindrical neck, the silver mounts embossed in the Renaissance style, the jug 17th century, the mounts hallmarked for Chester 1911 . . . 27 cm. high. £300–500.[16]

I bought it three months later in the United States, and without seeing the catalog entry recognized the mounts as essentially Victorian in feeling though exhibiting pleasingly Elizabethan details. My independent check of the date letter and hallmark came up Chester, 1911. So far, so good. The mug itself was extremely well made and wonderfully uniform in its redbrown mottling. Nor was there any doubt that it was brown slipped and salt glazed. Indeed, salt had piled on the inside of the base as so often happens among sixteenth-century Rhineland stonewares. Nevertheless, I had an intestinal feeling that something was wrong. The glazing was just too splendid, and I was therefore mindful of the adage that if it looks too good . . . well, you know the rest.

It seemed very odd that a silversmith in the northwest of England would in 1911 be attaching silver mounts to a plain, sixteenth-century German mug, no matter how good a specimen it might be. There was relatively little interest in such plain wares in England at that time, and with the Rhineland factories turning out highly decorated and ornamented reproductions and adaptations of their ancient wares, the who and the why moved to front and center of my growing concerns. Was it not strange, too, I asked myself, that the Chester silversmith neglected to include his own punch along with the city guild's lion passant regardant and the cursive "𝓛" of 1911?

FIGURE V.29. Typical Frechen stoneware ale jugs with characteristically sharp-tooled shoulder cordons, another detail absent from the Doulton mug (Fig. v.28 *a*). (*a*) Retrieved from the North Sea, ca. 1590–1640. (*b*) Ca. 1630–1660.

With questions burgeoning and no answers forthcoming, I asked the doyen of stoneware authorities, Jonathan Horne, why he had not put in a bid for so desirable a mug. Jonathan replied that he invariably left the silver-mounted pieces to be fought over by the silver dealers. Then he asked, "Are you sure it isn't Doulton?"

For me that was one of those memorable "Oh, my God!" moments. I had no idea that either of the Doulton factories had ever made authentic copies of undecorated German stonewares. But once Jonathan said he had seen them from time to time and knew them to be so marked on their bases, I sensed that he was right. However, there was no way that I could expose such a mark without ruining the silver foot mount. Worrying about the mount resulted in my looking with greater care at the upper cordoning of the foot itself, at the ridges that I realized were far softer and more rounded than was usual on sixteenth-century pieces (Fig. v.28 *c*). They were, however, consistent with ridges and collars on later nineteenth-century Doulton-style stonewares.

Worrying about the outside ridges made me think about the more uneven and usually pronounced ridges or potting rings to be found on the interiors of genuine sixteenth- and seventeenth-century drinking mugs and jugs (Fig.v.29). Inside the Chester mug, there were none. Nor was that all. The more I looked the more I saw. My new treasure's so-splendidly mottled neck sloped gracefully down into its bulbous body. But it had no business doing so. The straight necks of original sixteenth- and seventeenth-century jugs terminated at their shoulders in a sharp cordon (Fig. v.29). There could be little doubt, therefore, that Christie's was wrong in its identification, that the dealer who sold it was wrong, and worse—I was the mug who bought it!

Had I known what Jonathan Horne knew about Doulton reproductions, I would have seen the warning flags as soon as they were hoisted. But I hadn't. And that brings me back to my point about experience of handling enough pieces to readily tell the good from the bad. The tale also points to the need to have access to fragments that unashamedly reveal their insides and those small details so readily missed when the vessel is seen intact and, worse still, when one is only allowed to view it through the protective armor of its museum case.

With the Chester mug's pedigree substantially rewritten, one more question remains hanging. Why Chester?

Why did the Chester silversmith, who had done such a good job, omit his name stamp? Was it possible that he knew that were he to apply it, the work could be traced to him? If the mug was made in a Burslem or Liverpool factory, was there collusion between it and the mount maker to create a deliberate fake to sell at high price to a well-heeled North Country businessman anxious to emulate the connoisseurship of the aristocracy? I doubt that I shall live to learn the answer. But the question and the quest make the "wrong" Chester mug far more interesting than it would be had it been "right."

Now and again one comes upon an object that rings no bells at all, but looks as though it should. The badly chipped and horribly proportioned jugs (Fig. v.30 *a* and *c*) belong in that category. Horrid or not, being an obvious pair made them interesting in that they must have been together from birth until 1965 when we found them in a junk shop near Salisbury. On being questioned, the proprietor could (or would) tell us only that they came from "hereabouts." He obviously thought even less of them than we did, for he priced them at 1s.6d each—or about 40 cents. Although no exact parallels have been found, their small bases and elongated, pinched-lipped necks belong to a class loosely attributed to somewhere in the second half of the eighteenth century or early in the nineteenth. Nevertheless, they have their place in the Collection as a last gasp of the traditional Rhenish stoneware before the factories of the Westerwald-Hessen district turned to reproducing and adapting the best of their past to feed a new and retrospective market.

Between the anomalous pair stands a third jug that owes its kinship to possessing a pinched spout, a detail that in general points to a late date, but in this instance not quite as late as its companions (Fig. v.30 *b*). Rarely are such jugs considered worthy of illustration—which is a pity because they reflect the degradation of old decorative techniques and shapes at the end of the eighteenth century before the potters shifted to the neo-Gothic adaptations that became the hallmark of the Rhenish stoneware industry in the nineteenth century.

FIGURE V.30. (*a, c*) Pinched-spouted pitchers with incised free-style foliate ornament in-filled in dark-blue cobalt; Westerwald Hessen, early nineteenth century? (*b*) Westerwald spouted pitcher with more traditional decoration, second half of eighteenth century.

FIGURE V.31. In 1993, posing for the *AARP Journal* had unexpected consequences. Photo: William K. Geiger.

In 1996 I was made painfully aware that America is home for legions of German stoneware mugs and vases—a lesson learned in the aftermath of agreeing to be interviewed by a feature writer for the newsletter of the AARP—the American Association for Retired People. In the accompanying photograph I was shown with several antique objects beside me, among them our 1585 Westerwald jug (Fig. V.31). A flood of mail followed the profile's publication, none of it expressing interest in me, but all the writers wanting me to know that they had a pitcher just like it. Some had been brought by emigrating grandparents and others by soldiers returning from Germany at the end of World War II. Many of my hopeful correspondents included photographs of their heirlooms from every angle—including the initials and numbers impressed on their bases, which left no doubt of their late nineteenth-century date. Indeed, out of all those examples, only one was an actual copy of a sixteenth-century tankard, with the rest being typical, latter-day German beer steins. One cannot deny, however, that if these not-so-old treasures are put back in the attic for another hundred years or so, collectors may be eager to pay breathtaking prices for them. But I wouldn't bet on it. Anything that copies something else and does it less well has little laudable or evocative to say about itself or about the era wherein it was made. A copy never aspires to being anything more—unless, of course, it hopes to become an undetected fake.

VI   Broomsticks and Beer Bottles

It is with narrow-souled people as with narrow-necked bottles;
the less they have in them the more noise they make in
pouring out.

Alexander Pope, 1741

THROUGHOUT CERAMIC HISTORY as in any
other, different craftsmen were developing and trading different products
in different markets—which is probably why most collectors prefer to focus
on one ware, one shape, or one period. Archaeologists, on the other hand,
are unable to so specialize. We dig up whatever anyone has left behind and
try to make sense of it. Consequently, Audrey's and my ceramic collecting
was the reflection of that enforced eclecticism. It also makes writing about
it akin to a juggler with too many balls in the air.

In the last chapter I looked in some detail at the evolution of blue-on-
gray German stonewares, but said little about the brown salt-glazed wares
that were their ubiquitous contemporaries. My reasoning was this: With
one minor exception, and in spite of John Dwight's experiments, the gray
wares had no lasting impact on the evolution of English ceramics, but the
brown would give rise to the British brown stoneware industry that was
to embrace every aspect of national need from bed pans to sewer pipes—
which, upon reflection, is not as broad a gamut as I intended.

Although the shipping of liquids had been efficiently handled in the
classical centuries by the manufacture of large, bun-shaped and elongated
amphorae as well as in square glass bottles, the Dark Ages caused containerization to take several steps backward. Throughout the medieval centuries, wines and oils were shipped either in barrels and pitch-coated
leather flasks or later in large jars from Spain and Italy. However, it was to
compete with the coopers and tanners that Rhineland stoneware potters
went into the bottle business.[1] Had it not been for the glass industry being
slow to develop a sturdy wine bottle that could be shipped without the
protection of wicker casing or compartmented caskets, German stoneware
bottle production might never have grown into an international necessity.

But it did, and once rolling, it kept pace with catching-up glass makers, who were to become increasingly successful rivals in the third quarter of the seventeenth century.

Wherever the English, Dutch, French, Spaniards, and Portugese put down colonial roots, the German bottles were there, destined to show their faces to dirt-shifting archaeologists who until the 1990s were content to call them *Bellarmines* on the grounds that the neck of each bears a molded face once thought to satirize the Jesuit cardinal Roberto Bellarmino. William Chaffers, the nineteenth-century antiquary who made that connection, saw the bottles as a Protestant potters' way of embarrassing the hated Catholic cardinal. Chaffers was unaware that the brown, salt-glazed stoneware bottles and mugs bearing a bearded human face were in production by ca. 1540, at least two years before the cardinal was born and twenty-eight years before he came to theological prominence. Bellarmino died in 1616, but Rhenish potters continued to apply the bearded face to their large stoneware bottles until at least 1767.[2] By then, however, their legitimate export trade to Britain had long since ceased.

The Bellarmine appellation was never adopted by European collectors, who preferred to know them as bearded-man bottles (*bartmannkruegs*), a term recently partially Anglicized into *Bartmanns*, though why the eighteenth-century English term *grey beard* has not been retained is, as they say, a puzzlement.[3] An English dictionary of slang first published in 1785 had this to say of greybeards:

> Earthen jugs formerly used in public house[s] for drawing ale: they had the figure of a man with a large beard stamped on them; whence probably they took the name . . . Dutch earthen jugs, used for smuggling gin on the coasts of Essex and Suffolk, are at this time called grey beards.[4]

For simplicity's sake and to use a single definitive noun rather than two words that together have more to do with longevity than with stoneware bottles, we elected to use the term *graybeard* in preference to the German Bartmann or the baseless British Bellarmine.

FIGURE VI.1. Graybeard (Bartmann) masks realistic and comical, both from the late sixteenth century; found in the Thames at London.

In 1951, antiquary and London Museum assistant curator Martin Holmes attempted to classify and date the evolution of the bottles' applied masks, a typology too readily adopted by collectors and archaeologists. In simple terms, the progress was from fine and realistic to coarse and cartoon-like. Fifty years later, we know better, largely as the result of a vast range from good to really bad masks on bottles discovered on the wreck of the Dutch East India Company ship the *Batavia* that sank off the west coast of Australia in 1629. Although it remains true that well-defined portrait masks are undeniably early rather than late and that the crude ones continued to the last, there is an almost century-long overlap. Two neck fragments in the Collection make the point, both of them characteristic of the mid- to late sixteenth century, one of them benignly realistic and the other leering and cartoon-like (Fig. VI.1). Our finest intact example of the bearded mask oc-

FIGURE VI.2. A classic Rhenish flagon with sprigged ornament comprising a benign graybeard mask, male portrait roundels, and acanthus fronds above a girth-girdling band inscribed thrice in relief ~ALAF FVR EINEN GOTEN DRUVNCK~ [Hooray for a good drink!]. The pewter lid is original and marked on the inside with "A" of Antwerp or Amsterdam over a male profile to left, a flagon (?), and the initials HS over a star. Frechen, ca. 1550–1570.

curs, not on a bottle but on a pewter-lidded flagon that I had long thought to date around 1580 but that is now considered to be at least twenty years earlier (Fig. VI.2).[5] As the last object Audrey and I purchased before emigrating to the United States, it has an important memory-evoking place in the Collection—not the least being the fact that in 1957 it cost us only 10 pounds!

The vast majority of sixteenth- and seventeenth-century graybeards are decorated by means of a second sprig mold from which came a usually heraldic medallion to grace the front of each bottle. In some instances, particularly at the beginning of the seventeenth century, large bottles (as well as some small ones) were enriched with three medallions—usually, but not always, from the same mold. At least one surviving specimen displays

FIGURE VI.3. Fragments from a large graybeard akin in size to Fig.VI.5, showing one of three medallions bearing the arms of Amsterdam and with separately sprigged grotesque face paralleled by an example in the Museum of Applied Arts at Cologne, there loosely attributed to the seventeenth century. Frechen, second half of seventeenth century. Found in Bermuda. Edward Schultz Collection.

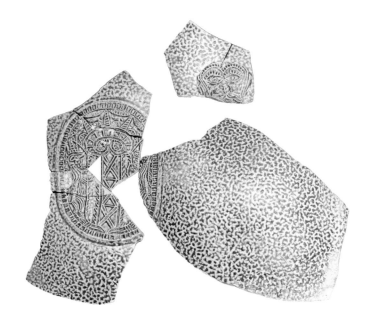

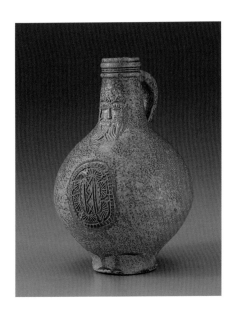  

FIGURE VI.4. (*a*) Standard graybeard with arms of Amsterdam in their simplest form. Frechen, ca. 1645–1670. (*b*) Rhenish salt-glazed stoneware bottle decorated in blue and with sprigged medallions displaying the arms of Amsterdam and the date 1630. From a Susquehannock grave in Washington Boro, Pennsylvania. (*c*) A matching fragment from the Pickleherring site in Southwark. (*a*) Ex Douglas Walton Collection; (*b*) photo courtesy of The State Museum of Pennsylvania, Pennsylvania Historical and Museum Commission; (*c*) ex Burnett Collection.

different shields of arms, one dated 1607 and the other 1608, demonstrating that once carved the master matrix could have had a misleadingly extended life.[6] Fragments of another three-medallion giant have been found in Bermuda, and although the bottle dated from ca. 1630, it must have been in use there at least fifty years later (Fig. VI.3).[7] The three crosses are the heraldic emblem of Amsterdam and are the most commonly found on mid-seventeenth-century graybeards and occasionally on Westerwald stoneware bottles earlier in the century (Fig. VI.4).[8]

As I explained in the preceding chapter, my collector friend Frank Thomas had an eye for quality and a conviction that his collection should contain nothing but the best. Audrey and I, however, had no such aesthetic hangups, arguing that excellence is best recognized in the company of the not so great. When Frank told us that he planned to dispose of the

FIGURE VI.5. Graybeard with twisted "rope" handle, three sprigged, crowned-rose medallions, and double-headed eagle roundels in groups of three. Reputedly among the largest specimens of its period in existence, height 47.62 cm. Frechen, ca. 1640. Ex Frank Thomas Collection.

largest graybeard in his collection on the grounds that it failed to meet his standards, we promptly forked out the requested eight pounds and carried it triumphantly home unwrapped on the long subway journey from Highgate to Wimbledon (Fig. VI.5). The bottle stands an impressive 18 3/4 inches in height and has an admittedly less than fine mask and three not-so-great primary medallions, shortcomings made up for by the presence of six small, double-headed eagle disks and by its extremely handsome twisted clay (rope) handle. Of technical interest is the means the potter employed to ensure that his thinly cast medallions did not break away in firing. He pricked or punched very small holes into each, thereby bonding these points of contacting clay into the wall of the bottle. It is not a technique that we have noticed on other large graybeards, nor, indeed, have we found another of anything approaching that size with the rope-style handle.[9] Although wild speculation is always in danger of being taken by others as gospel, we have wondered whether our bottle's potter could have been influenced by faience-making confreres at Nevers in central France, where twisted handles were featured.[10] However, considering that Nevers is a long way from the Rhineland, it seems more likely that with the bottle being of such size and so heavy, it demanded a heavyweight handle—and got it. As for its date, ca.1640 seems reasonable, but only until a fragment turns up in some archaeologist's excavation to prove us wrong.

We have long recognized that collectors who shy away from specimens that are even slightly damaged find no merit in the bits and pieces that archaeologists unearth. Indeed, I shall always remember the edict proclaimed by Colonial Williamsburg's Curator of Collections, John M. Graham, who ordered his assistants to have no truck with the department of archaeology and "all its junk." That was more than forty years ago. Today most curators recognize that potsherds provide an opportunity to learn more about how an object was made than was possible from only studying intact "museum quality" specimens.[11] A classic example was provided by a large but broken graybeard found in excavations at Martin's Hundred and whose interior showed that the potter had pressed outward with his fingers from the inside as the medallion was being externally applied. That meant, of course, that, in this example at least, the medallions were attached while the vessel was still at an "open bowl" stage in its shaping. We had hitherto believed that all sprigged decoration was added after the bottles were in their green state.

That revelation prompted a question that in the stillness of the night or the warmth of the bathtub I have often been prompted to ask: "who the h—— cares?" What possible merit can there be in spending a career studying our ancestors' trash and figuring out—sometimes wrongly—how it was made and what they did with it? There is no denying that I could have been a lot more useful to society as a brain surgeon or a tax collector, but the truth is that I have been content to leave it to others to take giant steps for Futurekind. Instead, finding and finding out have been the principal joys of my life—which brings me to witchcraft.

In 1954, my Guildhall Museum colleague Ralph Merrifield published a short paper titled "The Use of Bellarmines as Witch-Bottles," describing how late-seventeenth-century graybeards were used to deflect evil spells from witches' intended victims.[12] The bottles usually contained something sharp such as nails and/or pins, a heart-shaped piece of cloth, and sometimes a trimming of human hair, all topped up with urine. More than twenty such bottles have now been recorded, most of them found under cottage hearths, but a few have been fished out of rivers—perhaps in recognition of the then current practice of "finding" a witch by dunking her in a river or pond (Fig. VI.6). If she sank and drowned she was innocent, but if she floated she was guilty. Either way the village elders had one less nuisance to worry about.

There are two witch bottles in the Collection, both of the same later period (ca. 1660–1685), but one better documented than the other. The former was discovered in 1967 during renovations to the hearth in a cottage in the Suffolk village of Stratford St. Mary and found to contain rusted nails, bent brass pins, and blackthorn spears (Fig. VI.7 b). The attached label stated that when its contents were decanted, the bottle was found to

FIGURE VI.6. Ducking or drowning a witch; detail from a mid-seventeenth century woodcut.

IF THESE POTS COULD TALK

FIGURE VI.7. Typical brown salt-glazed stoneware graybeards used as "witch bottles." (*a*) From the Thames at London; (*b*) from beneath the hearth of a cottage at Stratford St. Mary in Suffolk. Frechen, ca. 1660–1685.

hold "about a teacup full" of thorns. Today only five remain, along with two bent pins and the rusted conglomerate of iron nails. Microscopic examination showed that earthy dust in the plastic bag containing what remained of the contents included tiny fly and parasitic wasp wings. However, the presence also of a few minute wood shavings suggested that the insect traces had been swept up from the dirty floor after the builder's renovating carpenters had emptied the nails, pins, and thorns onto it, and so had nothing to do with the original anti-witch assemblage.[13]

The second witch bottle was reportedly found in the Thames mud near the north end of Blackfriars Bridge at some time between 1953 and 1955, and was retrieved by one of my archaeological volunteers whom I had first met in 1950 when I, too, was scouring the river's tidal shores for antiquities. I knew him only as "Johnny" Johnson, a strange, saturnine man reminiscent of one of the lost souls drawn by Gustave Doré in his studies of the destitute of Victorian London. Johnny's volunteering was always erratic, and I remember him as a man who kept himself pretty much to himself. I forget what I paid him for the bottle, but it cannot have been more than two or three pounds. Being severely cracked, it would have commanded only a few shillings had it not contained witch-related pins, a cloth heart, and a wisp of brown human hair (Fig.VI.7 *a*.)

Although coincidences are more common than some people suppose, it has long worried me that Johnny's bottle should be found in the Thames at about the same time that Ralph Merrifield drew the public's attention to another from the river, one found perhaps as little as a hundred yards downstream at Paul's Pier Wharf—by another Mr. Johnson. Ralph's

FIGURE VI.8. (*a*) Standard graybeard of poor proportions, with its mask and crowned floral medallion crudely applied. The cork reputedly original. (*b*) Rare pint-sized graybeard with stylized mask and no girth medallion, otherwise well made save for its extremely thin and consequently punctured base. Both Frechen, mid-seventeenth century.

FIGURE VI.9. Graybeard made for Dutch exporter Jan op de Camp, whose initials and trading mark provide the medallion source. The mask is unusual by reason of being crowned. Frechen, ca. 1660.

account made it clear that this could not have been our Johnny Johnson, his being a Charles Johnson who found his bottle in 1926—several years before Johnny was old enough to become a Thames "mudlark."

Evidence supporting Johnny Johnson's claim is provided by another such bottle, this one found in a silted stream at Westminster in 1905. Although I have found no documentation for drowning a witch bottle and its protective magic, it seems a reasonable hypothesis. All in all, therefore, the Suffolk bottle's usage can be accepted without question, while the Thames example had best shelter behind the old Scottish verdict of "not proven."

Other graybeards have no such dramatic tales to tell yet are of interest to us for quite different reasons, not the least of them being the example illustrated in Fig. VI.8 *b*. That bottle became the foundation of our German stoneware collection as it was given to me in 1949 on the occasion of my twenty-second birthday by my Guildhall Museum mentor Adrian Oswald. More pertinent is the bottle's rarity by reason of its unusually small size and the absence of any decoration other than its late-style graybeard mask. Another initially unrecognized gem was purchased in 1950 for 7s.6d while visiting the town of St. Albans to view the Roman ruins of Verulamium (Fig. VI.9). The bottle had lost its handle but possessed an unusual, crowned mask, and a girth-displaying medallion bearing the mercantile sign of Jan op de Camp, a ceramic exporter of Frechen in the Rhineland, and almost certainly it was found in England. Conveniently, a fragment with the same medallion has been found on a Frechen kiln site, leaving no doubt where these bottles were made. Another Jan op de Camp medallion variant excavated in Tidewater Virginia is helpfully dated 1664.[14]

Pieter Van den Ancker, another Dutch export merchant, took his business to London in person, having moved there from Dordrecht in 1654 to sell French and Rhenish wines and the stoneware graybeards in which to store them. His bottles are represented in the Collection by two fragments, both bearing his trademark AA with a loop on the right side of the first "A" to represent the "D" of Den, while the abutting of the two "A"s created the "V" of Van, all this above the Ancker (anchor) rebus. The better molded of the two examples has his name spelled out in upper case letters around the central device, and exhibits the even, rich brown speckle that caused the fabric to be known to early collectors as *Tiger Ware* (Fig. VI.10 *a*).[15] The second specimen has nothing but the AA and anchor, and its salt glazing has left it a muddy, greenish yellow (Fig. VI.10 *b*).[16] Together, these fragments graphically demonstrate that color variations are an unwise criterion for separating early and good from late and bad. The variations in the masks applied to Van den Ancker graybeards are equally diverse and play havoc with the Holmes typology.

As the German stoneware bottle market declined in the late seventeenth century, the regular quart-capacitied graybeards disappeared and were replaced by large lozenge-shaped bottles, some decorated with a mask but most of them plain save for a rouletted number such as a "3" or a "V" on their weakly sloping shoulders. The typical example shown in Fig. VI.11 was purchased in 1959 from a local Williamsburg antique shop and probably had been in a neighborhood house since the eighteenth century.[17] Another just like it was discovered in the 1950s by a Dutch amateur antiquary, who found it in an aboriginal chieftain's hut in Surinam's jungle interior, where it reportedly was greatly prized.[18]

By 1700 in England, the supremacy of the glass wine bottle had made serious inroads into the importation of Rhenish graybeards, which by then had become heavy and crude. The Collection includes an example of that grotesquery (Fig. VI.12). It retains its late-style mask, but the erstwhile girth-adorning medallion has been replaced by a small "daisy," perhaps

FIGURE VI.10. (*a, b*) Medallions from graybeards made for Pieter van den Ancker, a Dutch exporter of both wine and bottles, resident in London. His initials and rebus provide the medallion device. Both fragments found in Southwark. Frechen, ca. 1655–1665. (*c*) An intact Van den Ancker bottle in the Chipstone Collection. (*a, b*) Ex Burnett Collection.

FIGURE VI.11. The last phase in the decline of the large-sized, Rhenish salt-glazed stoneware bottle. Bought in Williamsburg ca. 1959 and thought to have had a local history. Frechen, mid-eighteenth century.

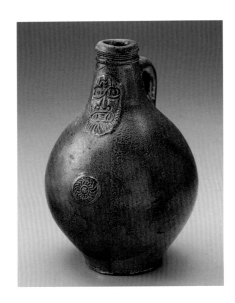

FIGURE VI.12. Graybeards similar to this example continued to be made into the mid-eighteenth century. The central, sprigged ornamental belly button was quicker to apply than had been larger medallions that required care both in application and in subsequent trimming. Frechen, ca. 1695–1730.

FIGURE VI.13. A Japanese stoneware copy of a mid-eighteenth-century graybeard emulating the shape and size of those recovered from the 1752 wreck of the *Geldermalsen*. Cast rather than thrown, the lateral mold mark is clearly visible at the girth. Chipstone Collection.

salvaged from a late seventeenth-century sprig mold originally intended for multiple use in conjunction with combed stems.[19] It is, undeniably, a pretty sorry apology for a graybeard, but it has its place in the Collection for precisely that reason.

One tends to think of graybeards, particularly those of large capacity, being for ale or wine. But as the previously cited 1811 *Dictionary of the Vulgar Tongue* reminds us, that though "formerly used in public house[s] for drawing ale," they were later "used for smuggling gin on the coasts of Essex and Suffolk." Lest there should be any dispute, an example in the museum at Kommern is impressed GENEVER under a roundel bearing the name of distiller TOBIAS SYBENHAGE.[20] That graybeards were also for other spirits is proven by William Hogarth's *A Harlot's Progress,* Plate VI, wherein he shows such a bottle in the foreground as a container for French brandy and labeled NANTS.

As is invariably the case, the testimony of shipwrecks provides the most accurate dating of all — indeed, more reliable than that to be gleaned from dated graybeard medallions. The previously mentioned *Geldermalsen* that sank in 1752 is one such example. Recovered from it were at least forty-three such bottles, a few with applied masks but most without, all evidence of the shapes and sizes being made and transported in the mid-eighteenth century.[21] One might wonder why a Dutch East Indiaman would be carrying so many Rhineland stoneware bottles that could be expected to have been traded away before returning home. The explanation may be found in a 1797 Danish ordinance controlling the ships of its own East India trade. Amid a plethora of instructions was a section on import duties imposed on the hard liquor called Arrack, made from the juice of the cocoa palm or from rice and sugar fermented with coconut juice. Popular in the Mohammedan countries but also drunk in Europe as a punch, the ordinance required that Arrack "immediately on Importation from the East Indies, is to be paid a duty of ½ Skill per Pott." It was popularly known as "Rack," and the Danish authorities encouraged its re-exportation, saying that "the Consumption Duty will be refunded on the exportation of the Arrack." It seems likely, however, that most of the potted or bottled liquor would have been sold at ports of call on the homeward voyage.[22] Indeed, had the returning *Geldermalsen* sunk in the Bay of Biscay, few if any of the bottles might have remained aboard.

That Dutch traders continued to use debased versions of the graybeard may have had another explanation besides their obvious advantage of being stronger than glass bottles. Funny-faced bottles may have had an unexpected appeal for the Oriental consumer and might even have developed their own "Bellarmine-like" iconography. But no matter what the reason, Japanese stoneware potters tried their hands at mold-producing the graybeard, an example of which has a place of muted honor in the Chipstone Collection (Fig. VI.13).

Our archaeological excavations in Virginia would lead us to believe that by the second quarter of the eighteenth century, English stoneware bottle potters had the home and colonial market virtually to themselves—which only goes to show that archaeological evidence is easily negated by a few words in a ledger. English Custom House records reveal that in 1717, 894½ dozen "earthenware stone bottles" were imported into England from Holland, and that in 1741 the number had increased to 1,110 dozen. Even as late as 1771, 993 dozen were taxed. Five years later still, 36 dozen arrived from Flanders.[23] An incomplete bottle from London and comparable to the mid-eighteenth-century *Geldermalsen* group serves as an example of the appallingly shoddy wares that the Rhenish potters of that era were able to market abroad (Fig. VI.14).

From the days of M. L. Solon who published his pioneering two-volume work in 1892,[24] until the mid-twentieth century, age and source attributions for Rhenish stonewares have been based on dated specimens, datable paintings and drawings, and collectors' often dogmatic yet sometimes unreliable opinions. Furthermore, as Solon's book title makes clear, he (and most museums) saw these objects as "Ancient Art" and by that criterion showed little or no interest in the vast majority of utilitarian products that kept the master potters in business. Not until Rhineland kiln sites began to be archaeologically excavated and their spoiled products chemically analyzed could anyone be sure which pots came from where. A single example in the Collection made that point (Fig. V.3 *b*). Conventional wisdom would almost certainly have attributed that split and squashed brown stoneware mug to Raeren,[25] but in truth it came from a waster dump near Cologne.

Just as Westerwald potters of the late seventeenth and eighteenth centuries made a hole in their handles to secure pewter lids, so others of the late Elizabethan era expected their straight-necked plain wares to be enriched with silver mounts both at their rims and often at the bases—the latter not possible had frilly feet persisted. A scarcely studied group of larger straight-necked drinking vessels has sometimes been perceived as another stoneware type so shaped in the expectation of silver embellishment, and therefore datable to the late Elizabethan years (Fig. V.29).[26] However, its discovery in archaeological contexts in Virginia as well as in England leaves no doubt that it was common in the 1640s and had no higher social aspirations. There are discernible dating trends among these undecorated and straight-necked vessels; the later examples (by which I mean ca. 1620–1645) are usually wider at the base of the neck than at the top, whereas those of the Elizabethan era are not.

Only very rarely did English silversmiths apply silver or silver gilt mounts to wares other than those imported from the Rhineland. It has long been supposed, however, that notable exceptions are the dappled blue and manganese–decorated tin-glazed tankards or jugs similar in shape to the Rhenish and popularly known as Malling Ware. That, however, is another of those misleading terms with which ceramic history abounds. The prototype example was owned by the parish church at West Malling in Kent, and not having previously been identified, it gained that name along with the false assumption that it was made near the village. From this seed grew

FIGURE VI.14. (*a*) Exterior and (*b*) interior of a mid-eighteenth-century Rhenish brown salt-glazed stoneware bottle from Southwark, showing the extent of distortion in the kiln considered insufficient to preclude the bottle's export to England. Ex Burnett Collection.

FIGURE VI.15. Tudor porringers from Southwark representing their evolution from (*a*) a tripod-footed bowl that may be Dutch, ca. 1500–1550, to (*b*) English redware, mid-sixteenth century, and (*c*) the standard Border Ware type, late sixteenth well through the seventeenth century. Ex Burnett Collection.

the notion that if it wasn't made at West Malling, it had to have come from another sixteenth-century Kentish pottery. No such factory has yet been identified, but it is tantalizing to recall that outside the medieval wall of the one-time port town of Sandwich is a road named Delph Street. Several authorities have parroted each other in saying that delftware potters were working at Sandwich by 1582 (the date of the Malling jug's mount), and it certainly is true that Dutch potters working in the early delftware factory outside the London city wall at Aldgate had lived in Sandwich before 1567.[27] All that became moot, however, when the sacred-cow–devouring NAA (neutron activation analysis) proved that the Malling jug was made with Low Countries clay and therefore was not made in Kent or anywhere else in England.[28]

The semantic and practical question of whether a heavily silver-enriched vessel like the Malling tankard was intended to be poured from or drunk out of (or maybe both) has not been resolved. Lower down the ceramic scale, however, it seems that English drinking habits were changing in the late fifteenth and early sixteenth century, for it is then that we first encounter the single-handled porringers that would become ubiquitous by the early seventeenth century both in Britain and in her fledgling colonies in both pottery and pewter.

The term *porringer* is derived from potage, which meant any kind of soup and became more specific as a container for porridge, which in the sixteenth century was made from stewed vegetables and meat, sometimes thickened with barley. By and large, however, it was a soup to be drunk, not necessarily with the aid of a spoon. The earliest earthenware porringer form that we have discovered is copied from a late-fifteenth-century Siegburg stoneware shape but differs to the extent of standing on three feet (Fig. VI.15 *a*).²⁹ By the mid-sixteenth century, porringers were being made in lead-glazed London redware and characterized by their shallow profile that could be cupped in one hand while being tipped with the other by means of the single, side-hugging handle (Fig. VI.15 *b*). It was only while restoring the Collection's example that I realized how comfortably the bowl nestled in the palm of one hand while the other used the handle to guide it. I had not previously realized that the handle was intended for tipping rather than lifting. Later, the much larger, projecting handles found on delftware and pewter porringers were equally useful for either purpose.

Porridge aside, English potters had entered the ceramic drinking mug game in the early sixteenth century, producing black, lead-glazed, often multiple-handled drinking vessels that collectors used to call *Cistercian Ware* in the belief that it was made in Cistercian monasteries prior to the Dissolution. The early squat, flaring-mouthed cups evolved into much taller versions that continued to be made at least into the mid-seventeenth century. These came in various sizes, but always with triple ridges or cordons above the base and below the rim (Fig. VI.16). The popularity and

marketability of these vessels (today generally known as *tygs*) was such that in the 1620s the potter of Martin's Hundred, Virginia, made not very successful attempts to copy them. The presence of two and sometimes three handles is explained by the following unsubstantiated legend: In the sixteenth century the French Dauphin stopped at an inn and called for a mug of water, whereupon a serving girl (whose name wasn't Cinderella) came out and held up the mug by its handle to the still-mounted prince. He told her that the next time he came by she should find a mug with two

FIGURE VI.16. (*a*) A typical black-glazed redware drinking mug usually known as a tyg, paralleled by fragments from the Pickleherring area of Southwark in both single and double-handled versions (*c, d*); (*b*) a shorter mug but retaining the cordoning of its companions. All early to mid-seventeenth century. (*a*) Photo courtesy of the Museum of London; (*b–d*) ex Burnett Collection.

FIGURE VI.17. (*a*, *c*) Typical Rhenish salt-glazed stoneware mugs whose frill-footed types were common in British households in the first half of the sixteenth century. (*b*) A redware, slipped and lead-glazed copy made in the London area in the same period. (*a*) Ex Dwight Lanmon Collection; (*b*, *c*) ex Burnett Collection.

handles. This she did, but being more pretty than bright, she held it up with hands that gripped both handles. The prince, with fairy-tale good humor, advised adding yet another. But whether he ever returned to check on the girl's handles is a story lost in the mists of time—which is probably just as well.

Perhaps because these tall, distinctively shaped tygs have eye appeal and look good in museum cases, they are perceived as the seventeenth-century tavern counterpart of the subsequent century's brown stoneware tankards. Although there may be some truth in this, there is no doubt that they were but one facet of the black-glazed red earthenware potters' inventory. In addition, they used the same ware and black glaze to produce bottles, bulbous mugs, and the porringers, all of whose presence is more often identifiable among archaeologists' shards than in the cabinets of collectors.

Although the English tyg may indeed have been the poor man's drinking vessel of choice in the first half of the seventeenth century, it had been preceded by some woeful English attempts to copy Rhenish, frilly-footed stoneware mugs (Fig. VI.17 *b*). The Collection's lead-glazed, partially yellow and partly green mug has too much of its clay in its crudely cockled foot, leaving insufficient to pull up into the neck and rim. It may well be that the English potter was unaware that his (or her?) Rhenish opposite numbers usually formed their feet from separately applied strips of clay. Here, one might suppose, is a classic example of a pottery vessel that, by its very clumsiness, has something to teach us about the state of English ceramic craftsmanship early in the Tudor century and about the superiority and desirability of the German imports. Such generalizations are not only dangerous, but in this case downright wrong. The frilly-footed mug was a product of mid-sixteenth-century heavy-duty potting in the immediate

FIGURE VI.18. Jars in a sandy gray-to-pink earthenware coated with a thin yellow slip, and made for the exportation of Iberian olives, olive oil, or honey. Found together on Pickleherring property. Their strongly differing shapes illustrate the considerable variety of forms in use at any given time from the late sixteenth through the seventeenth and eighteenth centuries. Spanish, probably from Seville. Close dating unavailable. Ex Burnett Collection.

London area. However, at the same time other, more clay-friendly potters in Surrey (who, too, served the metropolis) were throwing much more sophisticated drinking vessels that also drew their inspiration from Rhenish stonewares (Fig. v.4 *b*).

The prevalence of German stonewares in the towns of southeast England is no surprise. On a clear day one could see across the Channel to the coast of France, and for exporters in Holland and Flanders the North Sea trip to Essex and East Anglia was *un morceau du gâteau*. For manufacturers and exporters in Spain, Portugal,[30] and Italy, however, the voyages were considerably longer and through the Bay of Biscay, often highly dangerous. Nevertheless, their ceramic wares found their way to England in considerable quantities, much of it arriving at the West of England ports of Plymouth, Exeter, and probably Dartmouth, thence proceeding in the seventeenth century to Virginia and New England.

Spain's exports to Britain and her colonies were principally in the form of jars for olives, olive oil, and sometimes honey, rather than shipments of salable pots. There are two such jars in the Collection, both presumably found together in Southwark and both dating from anywhere in the seventeenth into the eighteenth century (Fig. vi.18). When John Goggin of the University of Florida published his pioneering paper "The Spanish Olive Jar" in 1960, users of his data had reason to believe that in spite of caveats, his typology was as sound as a silver dollar.[31] In truth, however, it followed in the wake of Martin Holmes's study of graybeard masks, which, in the final analysis, accomplished very little beyond a false sense of security for those who swore by it.

Goggin had divided the buff-bodied amphora-style jars into three groups, the earliest from ca. 1500–1580, the second to from 1580–1800, and the third, his Late Style, from an indeterminate span after 1800. To this last group belonged a type distinctly different from all the others, being bulbous below the mouth and suddenly tapering down to a pointed base reminiscent of the "carrot amphorae" of classical Rome (Fig. vi.19). When, in 1970, Australian archaeologist Graeme Henderson explored the wreck of the barque *Elizabeth* lost near Perth in 1839, he found several examples of this distinctive jar, proving, he wrote, that "the presence of the jars on the wreck . . . presents an opportunity to give one form of the Late Style an exact date."[32] I had no reason to doubt him and so stored this information away in my memory bank until such time as some inquirer might have a use for it.

As I noted earlier, I had directed three excavations on Roanoke Island to confirm the alleged settlement site of Sir Walter Ralegh's failed attempts to establish an English colony there in 1586 and 1587. While our work was in progress, a tourist walking a beach further down the North Carolina coast found a shattered jar of the *Elizabeth* wreck type, and when I was asked by the National Park Service to date it I readily attributed it to the early nineteenth century. Thanks to Graeme Henderson's report I had the documentary evidence to back it up. I equally readily dismissed any

FIGURE VI.19. Globe-and-carrot-type Iberian olive jar made in a pinkish-red-ware with an uneven yellow to buff surface. Though reportedly found off Bermuda aboard the wreck of the Spanish *Vega* (1639), the shape is very similar to that of others recovered from an Australian wreck of 1839. E. B. Tucker Collection.

suggestion that the tourist's jar could have been a relic of Ralegh's "Lost Colony." Not until two years later did I learn that examples of the *Elizabeth* type jars had been recovered from the *Vega*, a Spanish ship wrecked on a Bermuda reef in 1639 (Fig. VI.19).[33]

Fortunately, the National Park Service retained the fragmentary jar, for had it not done so my attribution might have lost the Hatteras Island park one of its most historic treasures. Henderson's Australian report allowed that there had been speculation that his wreck site had been contaminated by artifacts from others, but as none of the salvaged objects predated the nineteenth century he remained convinced that the jars came from the *Elizabeth*. Sitting at a desk on the other side of the world I have no reason to doubt his conclusion. However, the *Vega*'s contradictory evidence suggests that the carrot and onion-type jars were made over a much longer period than either Goggin or Henderson had claimed. The explanation may well be that this peculiar shape was not simply a design quirk, but that it served a very specific transportational need, perhaps separating its upper buoyant contents from the liquid beneath.

Along with other unstratified finds from the same Southwark site that yielded the Spanish jars came a fragment whose shape I had never before seen (Fig. VI.20). It was made from the same coarse buff-to-yellow ware as the jars, and I thought at first that it was a hollow bung for one or other of them. It fitted the mouths, if not like a glove, closely enough to have been sealed with pitch and tied down around its small collar. The flaw in that reasoning was evident inside, though at the outset, with "bung" firmly in mind, I was reluctant to accept it. The interior was coated with a very thin vitreous glaze, which would neither have been necessary nor even possible had the object been a bung. Turned the other way up, the collar converted to a shallow foot and the tapering exterior to the lower wall of a small, waisted jar (*albarello*). Even closer examination revealed traces of glaze on the outside as well as a hint of a label in underglaze black or blue. Although I have found no parallel for it, there seems little doubt that this was another version of the thick-walled Spanish jars already in the Collection and believed to have been used for the carriage and dispensing of mercury (Fig. III.19).[34]

The clue of the thin, scarcely visible glaze leads me to another Spanish export and to another Bermuda shipwreck. She was the *Warwick*, an English

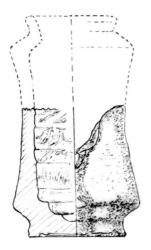

FIGURE VI.20. (*a*) Conjectural reconstruction derived from base and partial side (*b*) of a small, waisted jar (*albarello*) made from the same Spanish ware as that used for the olive jars (see Fig. VI.18). Because the wall is very thick and internally glazed, it is likely that the jar held mercury, as did other small imported jars found on the Pickleherring sites. Probably from Seville, seventeenth century. Ex Burnett Collection.

FIGURE VI.21. Ceramic treasures from the 1619 wreck of the *Warwick* came in very small pieces. Photo: Joseph Bailey/ NGS Image Collection.

FIGURE VI.22. Among the more commonly found ceramic objects on early-seventeenth-century colonial sites are double-handled bottles (costrels) partially tin-glazed and often marked with "stars" in blue or red. (*a*) Fragments from an unusually larger example with a blue star recovered from the 1619 wreck of the *Warwick* at Bermuda. (*b*) This intact example, bought in England, has no stars but is incised with the I E initials of its onetime owner. (*c*) An incomplete red-star version found in Southwark. Spanish, probably from Seville, ca. 1610–1640. (*a*) E. B. Tucker Collection; (*c*) ex Burnett Collection.

vessel dashed to pieces against a Southampton Harbour cliff in a 1619 hurricane.[35] Amid hundreds of potsherds recovered by diver Teddy Tucker (Fig. VI.21) were pieces of a soft, pale yellow earthenware bottle with two ear-like handles (Fig. VI.22 *a*). It was thinly tin glazed over its neck and upper body, and painted under it with a star created by five strokes of a cobalt-loaded brush. Fragments of these bottles are common on archaeological sites of the second quarter of the seventeenth century,[36] but having been fired at such low temperatures they were easily broken. Consequently, the opportunity to add an intact example to the Collection was

IF THESE POTS COULD TALK

one to be savored, and nigh on a quarter century later it still is (Fig. VI.22 *b*).

It was Audrey who found it. We were on our annual visit to London's Portobello Road antiques market, and while talking to a dealer about stoneware gin flasks I felt a sharp tug at my sleeve. When I turned I saw Audrey give an upward nod in the direction of a high shelf at the back of the stall. We had long since learned to avoid cries of *Eureka!* or any such price-hiking exhibitions of interest. "That . . . er . . . jug thing up there on the shelf . . . what's that?" I asked as casually as I could. The dealer said he didn't know—which was encouraging. I asked him where he got it and was told that he had bought it from somebody else. There was little doubt in my mind, however, that, like so much else, it had come from a London building site. The long and short of it was that this incredible rarity entered the Collection at an inappropriately modest price.

These double-handled Hispanic bottles came in at least two sizes, with ours being the smaller. Some are marked with a blue star and others in red (Fig. VI.22 *c*). No one has yet come up with a documented answer to explain

FIGURE VI.23. Tall-necked costrel with four lionesque suspension loops and spread, pedestal foot. The buff body is coated with an iron-red slip and subsequently marbleized with white, prior to lead glazing. This marbled ware is often further decorated with splashes of copper green, traces of which have attached themselves to this specimen. Northern Italy, ca. 1610–1640. Ex Harrison Weir Collection.

the purpose of the stars, though it seems likely that they identified different types of contents. Ours, however, is starless and so may indicate a third variety. What gives it greater interest is the fact that its owner thought it valuable enough to carve his initials into one side, cutting the letters I E through the glaze. Who was he? Or was it she? And who was the potter who left his or her fingerprints on the handles' moist clay? What was he thinking about as he applied them? Was his mind on his job? Was he happy in his work? And how did he spend his evening when the day's handle-attaching was done? Such questions will never be answered, but the asking of them takes us beyond the stark reality of a not very attractive pot into the world of 300 years ago—which I contend, and repeat, is what archaeology and collecting are all about.

From northern Italy (probably in the vicinity of the town of Pisa)[37] came another export into England and the Colonies,[38] namely, the distinctively colored marbleized dishes, bowls, and bottles whose shards when found in the ground tell us that we are in the second quarter of the seventeenth century.[39] The Collection's example (Fig. VI.23) is a distinctively shaped bottle usually described as a costrel, that is, a vessel containing liquid and meant to be carried about suspended from attached cords or thongs. In its Italian form the tall bottle has pairs of molded, lion-headed loops on either side, through which the hanger lines passed. The red earthenware was first coated with an iron oxide slip and then combed with a fine white slip using a feather or some such brush to create the swirling effect characteristic of marble. Bowls and jugs decorated in the same way were often enriched with patches of copper oxide that added green to the red-brown and white. The Collection's costrel lacked the additional color but was fired in a kiln adjacent to such green-splashed wares, for traces of it are visible on a small neck scar. A faded label attached by a frayed piece of green string reads "Marbled Pilgrim Bottle with mask loops. From Collection of the late Harrison Weir, Appledore, Kent." Weir was born in 1824 and died in 1906 at Poplar Hall at Appledore, and was a famed illustrator of natural history subjects. His special interest in chickens and pigeons prompted him to write several books; prominent among them (at least among chicken fanciers) was his *Our Poultry and All About Them* (1903). What, if anything, Weir's penchant for poultry had to do with Italian slipware remains food for not very productive thought.

Although, as I explained in a previous chapter, French ceramic exports had been a significant aspect of pottery usage in England during three centuries prior to the loss of Calais in 1558, Normandy potters of the sixteenth and early seventeenth centuries made their own contribution to the pre–glass bottle era by exporting ball-shaped bottles that had to be cased in wicker to enable them to stand. The globular flasks came in several sizes and went through three evolutionary stages, only the last of which is represented in the Collection (Fig. VI.24 *a*).[40] The first was made in a buff-colored, hard-fired earthenware, the second in gray (fired in a reducing

　　　　　　　　　　　　　　　　IF THESE POTS COULD TALK

FIGURE VI.24. (*a*) Globular flask in a hard, red ware, originally cased in straw or wicker as shown in (*b*) the 1641 woodcut. Many were imported into Britain and her colonies in the first half of the seventeenth century. Normandy, probably from Martincamp, where examples have been found in kiln excavations.

atmosphere), and the third in an equally hard red ware. I found fragments of the second period in our excavations on Roanoke Island where in 1585–1586 they had been used in scientific experiments to determine the potentially commercial properties of the region.[41] These flasks were long thought to have been made in two bowl-shaped halves subsequently luted together, but fragmentary examples found by South Carolina archaeologist Stanley South showed that the globular bodies were made as one. While they were still in the leather hard state a hole was punched through one side so that a separately thrown neck and mouth could be attached. Medieval pottery expert John Hurst has written that "Examples are so common in Britain that they may be regarded as much a chronological type-fossil of the 16th and 17th centuries as the Raeren drinking jugs of the early 16th century."[42] He noted that in 1974 wasters of all three flask types were found at the town of Martincamp, which lies between Dieppe and Beauvais. Whether, however, Martincamp was the sole source of these distinctive flasks remains to be seen. The similarity between the Phase II bodies and the large quantities of gray stonewares made elsewhere in Normandy in the eighteenth century suggests that there may have been more than one source for the flasks. Not only were they widely used in England but they turn up fairly regularly on American colonial sites from the late sixteenth century to the mid-seventeenth century.

While studying the shards from David Burnett's Thames-side construction sites I came upon fragments of more than one of these globular bottles made not in the Collection's redware, but in a pale yellow body that could easily be mistaken for first-fired biscuit delft—and it was. Consequently, although the source of these pale bottles has yet to be determined, their presence in Southwark seems to support my suspicion that they were made in more than one factory.

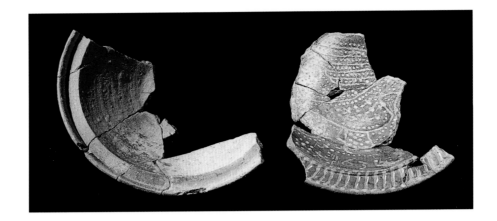

FIGURE VI.25. Waster earthenwares attributed to Martin's Hundred potter Thomas Ward (ca. 1620–1635). (*a*) an underfired deep red earthenware bowl characterized by a sharply upturned rim in the Dutch manner; (*b*) red-bodied slipware dish decorated with a bird in the Dutch style and dated 1631, probably a waster and the earliest dated example of American pottery. Colonial Williamsburg Foundation.

By the mid-sixteenth century the Netherlands, which had been the exporting source for most of the German stonewares, would be selling its own common, lead-glazed earthenwares in eastern Britain. Like the difficulty of distinguishing between Dutch delft tiles from "look-alikes" made in England by emigrant potters, so a problem besets us when we have to label a simple cooking pot as imported or home thrown. Thus, for example, potter Thomas Ward of Martin's Hundred[43] produced pipkins and slipware dishes whose rim forms were characteristically Dutch while at the same time looking remarkably like English Metropolitan wares. Most important among the Virginia-London look-alikes are fragments of three slip decorated dishes, one retaining the date 1631, making it the earliest, dated example of colonial American pottery (Fig. VI.25 *b*) so far discovered. If earthenware potter Ward took his lead from delftware potter Janson who had changed his name to Johnson, it is possible that Ward, too, had gone as a "stranger" to work in England and Anglicized his name before moving on to Virginia.[44]

The pursuit of Thomas Ward led us on numerous wild goose chases, one of them a reminder that history is strewn with coincidences that are precisely that, and so lead absolutely nowhere. When the names Potter and Thomas Ward turned up together in 1615 we thought we had made a memorable discovery. The reference came from the English Middlesex court records, which showed that Edmund Potter was put on trial "for cozening Thomas Ward, a simple country man, of 7s. in money at the game called decoy." Clearly our Thomas Ward was not the cheated simpleton of the court record—although ours may have deemed himself incredibly foolish to have committed himself to the life of a potter in the American wilderness.[45]

Tom Ward of Martin's Hundred was not in competition with importers other than the arriving colonists who brought English and European pottery with them. We know that at the nearby home site of Governor William Harwood, he had Westerwald stoneware from Germany, slipware from Pisa and North Holland, earthenware bottles from Spain, maiolica from Portugal, and high-quality Dutch earthenware. This last was represented by a buff-bodied and externally green-glazed pipkin paralleled

IF THESE POTS COULD TALK

FIGURE VI.26. Detail from Jan Steen's *The Poultry Yard* (1660), beginning a retrogressive series of Dutch pipkins in a pale yellow ware with external green lead glaze and internal clear (yellow) glaze. The type is characterized by triple feet and by handles sharply pinched at their junction with the rim. The late Steen example has only a single shoulder cordon, while the specimen in front of it (*a*) exhibits multiple wall grooving (ca. 1650), albeit less sharply defined than the more angular version (*b*) in the left foreground. This last, from Martin's Hundred (ca. 1625–1635), is more angular, and more distinctively ribbed. Colonial Williamsburg Foundation. Painting reproduced by permission of the Royal Cabinet of Paintings, Mauritshuis, The Hague.

in Dutch paintings such as Jan Steen's 1660 *The Poultry Yard,* which includes a similar trifooted pot with its handle pinched at its crest (Fig. VI.26). However, the painting is thirty to forty years later than the age of the Martin's Hundred pot, and although the basic features remain, Steen would paint a much taller and debased version indicative of declining quality as business became more important than ceramic art. The markedly angular and ribbed profile of the excavated example suggests that the potter was emulating a bell-metal cauldron, but over time both features softened and led to the version in Fig. VI.26 *a*; Audrey and I bought it for Colonial Williamsburg on one of our English research trips. Much later we purchased for the Collection a twin-handled variant of the early angular form, but in red earthenware and reputed to have been found in Holland (Fig. VI.27).

FIGURE VI.27. Lead-glazed red earthenware pipkin exhibiting details similar to Fig. VI.26 *b.* The handles are pinched, the rim everted in metallic cauldron style, the girth angled, and the wall above pronouncedly ribbed. Found in Holland. Ca. 1600–1640.

Jan Steen's *The Poultry Yard* was one of many Dutch and Flemish genre paintings being put to use by archaeologists and curators in the waning years of the twentieth century to help in the dating of pottery. But there is a caveat, one as worthy of attention as a torero's red cape. Taken at face value, one may think it reasonable to deduce that a stoneware jug paralleled, say, in Nicolaes Maes's 1655 *The Idle Servant* not only existed in 1655, but almost certainly belonged in the household depicted. At least it does until we look at the same artist's *The Listening Housewife* painted in the following year and there find the same jug in another woman's hand![46] The jug turns out to have been a studio prop and may have been around

FIGURE VI.29. An assemblage of largely sixteenth-century coarse earthenwares in the Dutch style, typical of English domestic pottery used in Southwark during the Tudor dynasty. Ex Burnett Collection.

for years, even decades. German stonewares had a great appeal to artists, particularly the blue-on-gray jugs and mugs from the Westerwald, one of which is to be seen in an 1861 English painting of a countryman and his family (Fig. VI.28).[47] The same painting also included a jug that almost certainly came from Spain and would never have been found in a mid-nineteenth-century cottage kitchen. To artist William Henry Knight, however, such foreign shapes and colors gave the picture greater interest and character than would their familiar British counterparts. Indeed, he may have been unaware that his prop jugs were German and Spanish.

Unfortunately, there are almost no British genre paintings from the sixteenth and seventeenth centuries, but had there been, the artists would not have to look abroad for exotic props; the coarseware pottery being made in Tudor England differed scarcely at all from the red wares being made in northern France or in the Netherlands (Fig. VI.29). Three examples of the latter were found in the Dutch province of Limburg (Fig. VI.30). Two we believe to date from the late fifteenth or early sixteenth century. However, the heart-shaped mini-cauldron may be much later, for an example in the Van Beuningen Collection in Rotterdam is of the same general shape, albeit differing in its rim profile, and is slip dated to 1663.[48] Although the pipkins' handles are similar to the English of the same period, their high-collar necks are characteristically Dutch. Also part of the Collection's Dutch element is a shallow dish with vestigial feet and a drawn-out handle (Fig. VI.32). Although such a handle is the simplest of shapes and could easily have been made by any novice potter anywhere, I include it because I know this dish to have come from Holland, where such handles were common.

Until relatively recently there has been little American interest in Dutch household wares, but they were here, not only on such Dutch colonial

sites as Fort Orange in up-state New York, but also among the English settlements of seventeenth-century Virginia—as the pinched-handled pipkin from Martin's Hundred attests. Collectors and archaeologists have devoted so much time to British wares that European parallels and their design influences have been woefully neglected, and in consequence this is a vast area of study about which we still know all too little. That English potters learned and adapted from continental imports there can be no doubt. Thus, for example, the addition of hollow, heat-resistant handles to tri-footed pipkins seems to have been a Border Ware development (Fig. VI.31).

I do not doubt that finely focused collectors will condemn any collection that includes items for which one has little or no knowledge, but I cannot repeat too often that the pleasure of Audrey's and my collecting has been the quest—the hope that one day we should find out. For us, were we to know all the answers there would be no point in collecting. Consequently, we have avidly sought the pieces that baffled us—and some still do.

FIGURE VI.30. Dutch pipkins (*a, c*) and a small cauldron (*b*), all in lead-glazed red earthenware and types that as yet defy close dating. Reputedly found in Limburg. Ca. 1550–1650.

FIGURE VI.31. Typical English redware pipkin with characteristic hollow handle, but retaining the ribbing common to Dutch kitchen wares ca. 1640–1675. A faded paper label states that it was found in "Upper East Smithfield New Goods Depot, 5 ft. from surface in gravel while excavating for foundations. Stated to be 15th century manufacture."

FIGURE VI.32. A small, handled saucer or patera in lead-glazed redware with vestigial pinched feet. Found in Dutch Limburg. Probably seventeenth century.

FIGURE VI.33. Slip-decorated mugs and a jug in lead-glazed redware, a concept reminiscent of Metropolitan slipware. Although all three have decorative features in common, their shapes differ sufficiently to suggest a datable evolution. All were bought in London, but are not English and may be from the north Netherlands. Probably eighteenth century.

A small red earthenware cup decorated with white slip in the manner of Metropolitan wares[49] is of a shape that might well be English, and yet there was something indefinably wrong about it (Fig.VI.33 *a*). The shape was right, as was the decorating technique, but there was a strange thickening around the rim that was new to us. Then along came another that was one size larger—both from stalls in the Portobello Road but found a couple of years apart (Fig. VI.33 *b*). Later still came a third (Fig. VI.33 *c*). The rim was the same as the others and so was its handle. But the base had become much larger, thereby rendering the overall proportions less pleasing and reminiscent of jugs from France. All three pots have one key feature in common: Beneath the handle of each is a circle of slip-applied dots with another at its center. There is reason to believe, therefore, that all three emanated from the same factory at approximately the same time. But did they? Could the shape differences point to the pots being from the same factory but perhaps a century apart in date? On the other hand, could they be of the same period and in the same decorative style but made in more than one factory?

Nobody ever said that dating and attributing common earthenwares was easy!

VII   Calcutta, Ballast, and Anti-clockwise Hunting

Mr. Josiah Wedgwood returned to Burslem, about 1760, and commenced Business alone, at the small manufactory (at that time thatched, as usual) to be seen from the bar of the Leopard Inn.

Simeon Shaw, 1829[1]

IF ASKED TO name the most significant individual in the history of English ceramics, few would hesitate for even a second before nominating Josiah Wedgwood. In truth, however, Wedgwood's genius was in selling both himself and his wares. Ceramic historian Simeon Shaw, writing in 1829, described the provincialism of many of the Staffordshire potters who were content to argue over who had invented what while sitting "on the ale benches at home"; meanwhile, Wedgwood "was making arrangements in London, by which all the merit of the improvement attached itself unto him."[2] No one could ever accuse Josiah of conservatism when it came to self-promotion. However, the cream-colored earthenware with which he is most closely associated had been developed at least ten years earlier by another Staffordshire potter, Enoch Booth.[3] The hard, dry-bodied (unglazed) earthenware that Wedgwood was to call *Rosso Antico* had been developed by the brothers Elers at the beginning of the eighteenth century in imitation of Chinese red stoneware teapots. The use of clouded glazes was an innovation first produced by Thomas Whieldon in the early 1750s. Whether Wedgwood was the first to whiten creamware into pearlware is equally in doubt, though there is no denying that it was he who elected to name it "pearl or Pearl White."[4]

My apparent assault on the good name of the best man in British pottery is an attempt not to tear down an ikon but rather to elevate that of the already introduced John Dwight of Fulham. His fairly successful attempts to copy blue-on-gray Westerwald stonewares have been noted, but in his original patent he claimed much more. The authorization from Charles II in 1672 referred to Dwight having discovered "the Mystery of Transparent Earthen Ware commonly knowne by the names of Porcelane or China & Persian ware As also the Mystery of the Stone ware vulgarly called Cologne ware."[5] Excavations on the factory site left no doubt that Dwight's primary goal was to produce a transparent ware capable of competing in the English marketplace with Oriental porcelain. In this he was never successful, but his brown stonewares—gorges, mugs, and gray-beard bottles—went into production in a big way, with London tavern keepers his principal customers.[6]

Although Dwight was the first in England to make brown stoneware the economic cornerstone of his business, he was by no means the first to seek an exclusive license to produce it. That distinction seems to have belonged to one Henry Noell, who was granted Letters Patent by Queen Elizabeth in 1593. His Royal Warrant gave him the sole right to import and manufacture "all manner of stone pottes[,] earthen pottes[,] stone bottles and earthen bottles" and to sell them wherever he liked. However, in the absence of evidence to the contrary, it seems probable that a monopoly on every pot and bottle brought into the realm was advantage enough without having to bother to try and reproduce them. Indeed, the authority to manufacture could have been no more than a politically correct ploy to secure control over a profitably imported commodity. Noell's patent expired in 1608, and six years later one Thomas Browne and his two partners were granted the sole right to make "all manner of stone pott stone jugg and stone bottles not heretofore usuallie made . . . within this Realm."[7] Nobody knows whether they were successful. Browne does not appear in the records as a potter but rather as a "tyler and bricklayer" of whose guild he was a member. Stoneware authority David Gaimster has noted that none of Browne's ten apprentices "between 1614 and 1633 has been traced as a potter."[8] So what, if any, was the connection between bricklaying and potting?

That was the kind of question that in Audrey's lifetime would set us off on the hunt like hounds after a fox, crying, "Tallyho!" or, as Sherlock Holmes would have exclaimed, "The game's afoot!"

Although having the appearance of an astonishing coincidence, the recent discovery of two letters written from Martin's Hundred in 1623 signed by "Thomas Ward pottmaker" and "John Jackson bricklayer" suggests a links between these seemingly disparate crafts. Had Browne and Jackson been identified as brickmakers rather than bricklayers, the relationship would have been more obvious—brickmaking, like pottery, involving both clay and kilns. Writing in the mid-seventeenth century, heraldic encyclopedist Randle Holme stated, "Brickmakers crist and tyle makers [were] a peculiar trade from Bricklaying."[9] The bricklayers and tilers were granted an incorporating charter in 1586, and supposedly the brickmakers received theirs in 1681. However, in 1753 the compiler of a tradesman's directory stated that brickmakers employed neither apprentices nor journeymen and were never incorporated.[10] From this one might argue that the lowly craft of brickmaking was a subsidiary to the bricklayers, who did train both apprentices and journeymen. Some suggestion that the bricklayers were superior to the brickmakers is provided by the

IF THESE POTS COULD TALK

fact that in 1864 there were twenty-seven London pubs named "The Brick-layers Arms" but none under the sign of the brickmakers! Unfortunately, neither superiority nor public-house popularity necessarily equates to control, and I have yet to find the reference that ties the two together. But there are hints. The Bricklayers' Company[11] arms comprised a chevron with two brick-axes above it and "a Bunch of Laths or faggots" below. Richard Neve's *Builder's Directory* (1736 ed.)[12] stated that 600 faggots would be burned to fire a kiln or clamp of 10,000 bricks. He also provided a copy of a bricklayer's bill listing the provision of 12,000 bricks at a cost of nine pounds sterling, leaving no doubt that bricklayers had responsibility for obtaining the right bricks for the job. How better, one might ask, to ensure that the bricks were the best available than to control their production—a responsibility requiring a knowledge of that craft? My argument is not helped, however, when in 1696 one of the most influential names at the beginning of the stoneware industry was described in a court affidavit as "a Brickmaker & no Pottmaker."[13]

Bricklayer Browne's patent theoretically remained in force until 1635, and in the previous year he had described himself as "Potter to King Charles"—which is odd because in 1626 the same King Charles had granted a patent to two wealthy Dutch merchants, Messrs. Thomas Rouse and Abraham Cullen, authorizing them to make stone bottles in England—which they may well have done.

The earliest archaeological evidence comes from a small kiln site down-river from London at Woolwich Ferry, where brown stoneware gray-beards were being made at some time in the third quarter of the seventeenth century.[14] Discovered in 1974, the retrieved specimens were poorly fired and no competition for the Rhenish imports. Further afield, at Southampton, in 1666 or thereabouts, one Captain William Killigrew had imported a Rhenish potter named Symon Wooltus and set him up in business to produce "stone bottles and blew canns"—the latter almost certainly copies of blue-on-gray Westerwald-style, straight-sided drinking mugs.[15]

The Killigrew-Wooltus factory site has not yet been located, but two graybeards having medallions with the initials WK and found in the Southampton area are believed to be theirs. There being no English gray-beards in the Collection, none of this would have relevance were it not for the presence in the Chipstone Collection of one of the worst examples, if not *the* worst example of such stoneware bottles (Fig. VII.1). There is so much clay in the body that it appears to have been dragged down by its own weight much as would mid-seventeenth-century glass wine bottles when still on the blowing iron. The analogy is, of course, a purely visual one, as stone bottles were drawn up and not down! What makes this monstrosity of particular interest is that neither its shape nor applied decoration matches the excavated Woolwich fragments or the WK graybeards from Southampton. Nor is it matched by a third possibly Killigrew gray-beard in the British Museum Collection that, when sold at Christie's in

FIGURE VII.1. Graybeard of abominable proportions and with mask and medallion of comparable crudity. Believed to be English from an unidentified factory. Ca. 1660–1685. Chipstone Collection.

1995, carried with it a pedigree that said it had belonged to Thomas Cartwright of Newbottle Manor in Northamptonshire.[16]

The previously cited 1673/74 committee hearing in the House of Lords regarding the regulation of foreign trade[17] had its to-be-expected conflicting testimony regarding the English manufacturing of stoneware as it had of delftware. Under discussion were "Dutch jugs and stone bottles, of which there had been no quantity made in England." The members were further advised that such bottles and jugs were "A commodity made at Cologne . . . and is not made to any perfection in any place in the world beside. Divers endeavours of imitating it here in England [have] all proved unsuccessful." That questionable assumption was made in spite of the fact that John Dwight had his patent and testified that he "could make as much Cologne ware as would supply England."[18]

Those red herrings aside, it seems clear that before John Dwight got his patent there were other English-made stonewares on sale here and there. Nevertheless, it is undeniable that he was responsible for transforming a few half-hearted attempts into a market-grabbing industry.

Dwight's experiments toward making porcelain yielded an important improvement over the German stoneware imports: coupling the iron oxide slip (which in a salt-glaze kiln produced the mottled brown wares) with a whitened body, creating a striking combination represented in the Collection by a single fragment. However, the Chipstone Foundation has an entirely white gorge that must rank as a prototype for the white salt-glazed wares that were destined to be the premier table dishes for most households through much of the eighteenth century (Fig. VII.2).

FIGURE VII.2. White salt-glazed stoneware gorge attributed to John Dwight of Fulham. Ca. 1680. Chipstone Collection.

IF THESE POTS COULD TALK

Among John Dwight's competitors were the brothers Elers, David and John, the former born in Amsterdam and the latter at Utrecht, both of them described as "chemists."[19] John had learned the secret of making stoneware in Cologne, and after working first at Fulham, the brothers set up a stoneware factory at Vauxhall and, as might be expected, found themselves on the wrong end of one of Dwight's many lawsuits. The Elers brothers' specialty was a thin, dry-bodied, red stoneware in the Chinese manner and focused on delicately sprig-ornamented teapots and other quality items. In 1693 or thereabouts, John moved to Staffordshire and began making red stoneware at his rented property named Bradwell Hall. Meanwhile, his brother David continued at Vauxhall. They were declared bankrupt in 1700, whereupon John moved to Dublin and there became a pottery and glass dealer. Consequently, their surviving red stonewares belong to a narrow date bracket of 1693–1700.[20] The Chipstone Foundation owns a second gorge similar in character to its Fulham example, but made in a fine brown stoneware of the kind usually associated with James Morley at Nottingham (Fig. VII.3).[21] This rarity is documented as having been excavated from John Elers's factory site at Bradwell Wood, evidence (one assumes) that he was making Nottingham-style stonewares akin to those made by Morley and of finer quality than the brown stonewares produced by the litigious John Dwight.

FIGURE VII.3. Thin-walled, brown salt-glazed stoneware gorge, perhaps by Elers. Ca. 1700. Chipstone Collection.

It was not the fine-quality salt-glazed wares that attracted Audrey and me, but the coarser brown stonewares that I first encountered, not at Dwight's Fulham factory but at another much closer to London, namely, the Gravel Lane site in Southwark, a location destined to house that skyline-piercing eyesore, the Bankside Power Station. There Adrian Oswald and I were finding fragmentary *saggers* for both brown stonewares and the soft, low-temperature yellow containers for delftware known in the trade as *slugs*. The latter were bottomless cylinders, with their walls punctured with triangular holes to receive the similarly shaped pegs that supported and separated plates stacked in them in the kiln.[22] The brown stoneware saggers, on the other hand, had bottoms, were much thicker, and when found are heavy with salt-derived glaze. Each had two or three large, pear-shaped holes in their sides as well as a single vertical slot to accommodate the projecting handles of bottles, jugs, mugs, and gorges.[23]

Our discovery of kiln debris on the power station site was made in 1949 when the archaeology of postmedieval pottery making had yet to emerge from its Dark Ages, and I suspect that few people outside the still-operational pottery factories knew anything about saggers or would recognize their fragments. In 1956, while on leave from Guildhall Museum and serving as an artifact consultant to Colonial Williamsburg, I was invited to visit historian Wilcomb Washburn at his house in Yorktown. It so happened that workmen installing utility lines outside the house had dug a trench that cut through a layer of broken pottery. Among the fragments I noticed sagger parts identical to those I had seen on the Gravel Lane site. I later saw many more such saggers (some of them almost whole) in the

FIGURE VII.4. An incomplete, quart-tankard capacity stoneware sagger, with a Swan Tavern pint mug seated within it. William Rogers's pottery, Yorktown, Virginia. Ca. 1724–1739. U.S. National Park Service Collection.

Yorktown collection of the National Park Service stored at Jamestown. With them were fragmentary brown stoneware mugs decorated with sprig-applied swans in high relief, their presence easily explained by their having been recovered from the site of Yorktown's Swan Tavern scarcely a hundred yards up the main street from the Washburn house (Fig. VII.4). Through another of those coincidences that have so frequently peppered my career, I was seeing and recognizing the products of a brown stoneware-producing factory that had existed at Yorktown between about 1724 and 1739. Operated by the previously mentioned Virginia brewer and businessman William Rogers,[24] the industry was in direct violation of the English Navigation Acts administered by the august-sounding Lords of the Board of Trade, whose duty was to prevent the development of any manufacturing business that competed with British exports and imports.[25]

The inventory made at the time of Rogers's death in 1739 listed the in-hand products of his potting operation, which included "26 doz qt Mugs £5.4" and "60 doz pt Do 7.10."[26] One of the latter became part of our collection, not having been dug up in Yorktown but found on the work site of another potter, who may or may not have been one Edward Challis whose name appears as the tenant on part of the tract known as The Governor's Land and shown on a survey plat drawn in 1683.[27]

In 1960 Audrey and I bought our first boat, a purchase that enabled me to return to a childhood joy, fishing. Audrey, on the other hand, was declaredly not a "Compleat Angler," having had enough of fishing while spending much of our honeymoon bobbing about in a rowboat fishing for mackerel. She also hated worms. While on one of our hook-dangling trips up the James, Audrey decided that she would rather go ashore to read a book and walk our dachshund, leaving me to play Isaac Walton by myself. Stepping out of the boat onto the beach under a clay cliff 20 to 30 feet high, she saw potsherds scattered like pebbles along the water's edge. We traced their source to the eroding bluff where hundreds more pieces protruded just below the turf line. The property then belonged to the Pine Dell Hunt Club and was accessible only from the water. A year later, the roar of bulldozers and chain saws heralded the advent of civilization into the hitherto silent forest, but not before we had rounded up several volunteers who, with the blessing of the landowners, helped us salvage what we could before the graders came in to reshape the cliff.

Thousands of potsherds and assorted kiln debris lay in a tangle of poison ivy roots whose juices penetrated the pottery and years later still proved capable of inflicting its familiar welts and sores. Alas, the broken and warped pans, dishes, bowls, colanders, jugs, and cups were all that remained of this early Virginia enterprise, with the kiln itself presumably having long since been eroded into the river (Fig. VII.5). However, about 60 yards east of the main deposit we found a shallow pit containing a concentration of metal artifacts along with more wasters that appeared to be rejects from the work of a less skilled potter. Significant among other artifacts were wine bottle fragments of types attributable to about 1725–1740,[28]

FIGURE VII.5. Audrey repairing jars and pans from the Challis earthenware kiln site in James City County, Virginia. Ca. 1680–1700. On loan to Colonial Williamsburg's Archaeological Collections.

FIGURE VII.6. (*a*) Brown salt-glazed stoneware mug of pint capacity from the William Rogers pottery at Yorktown; (*b*) detail of the crowned WR excise mark impressed on the front and believed to double as Rogers's stoneware trademark. Found near the Challis kiln site. Ca. 1724–1739.

probably deposited after the secondary potting operation had ceased. Also recovered were a delftware porringer and a broken brown stoneware mug stamped below the rim with the rectangular crowned WR mark found on William Rogers wasters excavated at Yorktown[29] (Fig. VII.6 *a* and *b*). The presence of a Rogers mug in association with waste products from another potting operation seemed to be one more improbable coincidence. It is tempting to speculate that the junior Challis Site potter was an apprentice who worked for Rogers—although there is no similarity between the Yorktown stonewares and earthenwares (Rogers's factory made both) and the shapes we found on the bank of the James.

Rogers's use of the WR stamp was his version of the capacity mark used in England on tavern mugs from 1700 when an "Act for ascertaining the measures for retailing ale and beer" passed into law.[30] As so often happens, one law breeds another, and in this instance the legislation was the offspring of a temporary excise tax imposed on ale and beer by Parliament

FIGURE VII.7 Applied AR excise mark below the rim of a tortoiseshell lead-glazed earthenware mug. Found in Southwark. Staffordshire, 1702–1714. Ex Burnett Collection.

FIGURE VII.8. (*a*) London brown stoneware mug impressed DOULTON LAMBETH and with printed mark (*b*) reading PINT over a crowned oval inscribed VR 523 LCC, identifying it as having been made to London County Council specifications. Ca. 1890.

in 1643 to help pay for its civil war with the Crown. With the parameters of "temporary" not having been defined, to no one's surprise, the tax continues to be levied. The 1700 act included the instruction that all ceramic vessels used to serve pint or quart measures of ale or beer should be marked with "WR and a Crowne."[31] This means, of course, that surviving mugs and gorges so marked will not predate 1700—which is fine as far as it goes. But just as a London ordinance forcing hansom cab drivers to relieve themselves only on the off-side rear wheel has only recently been repealed, so nobody thought to revise the 1700 ale stamp act to reflect the reigns of subsequent monarchs. Nevertheless, some potters took it upon themselves to keep up with the times and purchased new AR (Anna Regina, 1702–1714) stamps. In 1992, on what was to be Audrey's last visit to the Thames foreshore at the Bankside, she found a rim fragment from a Westerwald stoneware drinking vessel with a sprig-molded crowned AR where, had it been English, a Queen Anne–era impressed stamp would have been in order.[32] The marking requirement was not limited to stonewares; it applied to any vessel intended for dispensing ale and beer in taverns. Thus, the Collection's fragment of a tortoiseshell-glazed Staffordshire mug has a crowned AR sprig-padded onto its rim (Fig. VII.7). It appears, however, that the use of the queen's initials was short-lived and that some petty, letter-of-the-law bureaucrat went after the potters and innkeepers, insisting that the ordinance had not been modified to reflect the new reign, and until it did, the WR stamp should continue to be used. And so it was—

all through the eighteenth century, dutifully ignoring the accessions of Georges I, II, and III. Although the order was repealed in 1824, another mug in the Collection (Fig. VII.8) carries a white-printed mark identifying its capacity as a pint, and bearing the VR of Queen Victoria over the initials LCC, that is, the London County Council, which was created in 1888.

An almost illegible mark that could be WR or AR is impressed below the everted rim of one of the Collection's most remarkable objects, a pitcher that is half brown salt-glazed stoneware and half delftware (Fig. VII.9). When we bought it, I knew of only one location from the late seventeenth

IF THESE POTS COULD TALK

FIGURE VII.9. Combination tin- and brown salt-glazed pitcher with an illegible excise stamp below the rim. Tin-glazed internally. London, ca. 1700? Ex Garner Collection.

and early eighteenth centuries where both wares were being made simultaneously—and that was where my archaeological career began. The Gravel Lane factory had been established in June 1694 by Luke Talbot and Mathew Garner to make brown salt-glazed mugs and bottles—until John Dwight found out about it and went to court to have them shut down. In 1697 Talbot was fined, and when he could not raise the necessary £66.8s., he borrowed it from a glove-maker named Nathaniel Oade. Unable to repay the debt, Talbot declared bankruptcy and mortgaged the factory to Oade who at first kept the original partners on as managers. However, they fared no better as managers than they had as owners, and before long the evidently odious Nathaniel had them thrown off the property along with their wives and children, electing to run the whole enterprise for himself. In the course of the related litigation, several pieces of important information emerged.

Adrian Oswald has noted that Oade's accounts at the time of the take-over cited both colors and salt, which Adrian deduced "suggests that the pottery was making delftware as well as stoneware."[33] By 1718 the factory was being run by Oade's three sons, at which time it was described as "the white and Stone-pot-house" where they had been making delftware through the previous six years.[34]

I was reasonably confident that the Collection's jug was made at Gravel Lane in the early Oade years, for as I have noted, it is half delft and half brown stoneware. The ware is a pale yellow, coated at the mouth and shoulder with iron oxide far more red than it would be had the firing temperature been elevated to stoneware intensity.[35] Instead, the color is akin to that of wasters from William Rogers's Yorktown kiln that were fired to biscuit and then painted with the iron oxide slip. From the girth down, the Collection's jug is pure delft, being thickly coated with an engobe of the tin-enriched lead glaze. The result would appear to be an attempt to emulate the white and brown stoneware mugs so successfully developed by Dwight at Fulham. Skeptics may question this assumption, arguing that if the jug had been fired in a salt-glaze kiln the white coating should have been pitted in the same way that true salt-glazed wares always are. However, experiments carried out in the early 1960s at James E. Maloney's Williamsburg Pottery showed that delftware-style glazes were unaffected by the salt. This also explains why, on German stonewares, those areas that are cobalt painted remain smooth while the gray body around them is salt pocked.

In reading the opening of the previous paragraph, "I was reasonably confident . . . ," you will have detected a degree of hesitation—for two reasons. Firstly, Chris Green in his magnum report on his excavations at the Fulham site included a drawing of a comparable pitcher in the Museum of London collection that he attributed to Fulham and to a date as late as the mid-eighteenth century. No one knows where it was found, but Green stated that "nominal pint jugs appear to have been a favored product, since two extant examples are known"—one of them in the Museum of London and the other in the British Museum. The latter was borrowed by Robin Hildyard for his 1985 *Brown Mugge* exhibition at the Victoria and Albert Museum. In his catalog Hildyard attributed the mug to the "early 18th century" and suggested that it was "an example of the Double-glaz'd Ware made at Fulham."[36] He also cited a 1754 announcement in the London *Daily Advertiser* stating that the late Samuel Dwight of Fulham had invented the double-glazed ware and that his son-in-law intended to renew its manufacture. Commenting on the advertisement, Robin Hildyard observed that although John Dwight's son Samuel owned the Fulham Pottery from 1709 to 1737, he was a practicing doctor in Fulham and had no known involvement in the wares made there. Hildyard was also skeptical that the half-delft/half-stoneware jugs were what was meant by the "Double-glaz'd Ware."[37] All in all, therefore, caution urges that the verdict remain in abeyance until we are presented with more definitive evidence.[38]

More importantly, we now know that the notion that delftware and stoneware manufacturing were separate crafts was incorrect. Indeed, by 1700, most of the London area potters were producing both. This was true of the Vauxhall potteries, which were established in 1682/83 by one John De Wilde, who emigrated to America in or before 1697.[39] Archaeological excavations carried out over several years uncovered more than twenty Vauxhall kilns ranging in date from the late seventeenth to the late nineteenth century. Both WR and AR stamps were found on brown stoneware mugs, leaving no doubt that they were being made there in the first years of the eighteenth century. But whether the half-delft/half-stoneware jugs were also made there remains an open question.[40]

That David Burnett's Pickleherring properties might have been a source of stoneware as well as delftware was a possibility that remained hidden for forty years in the crumbling and sagging cardboard boxes of unwashed pottery still on shelves in his Tandridge Hall scullery. When the last of it arrived on my doorstep, I found that it included half of a 2¾-inch cylinder coated with a greenish salt glaze that I recognized as a kiln pillar or prop (Fig. VII.10).[41] A curving line in the glazing matched the diameter of a pint mug.

One of the recurring problems in ceramic research, particularly of the archaeological kind, is that excavated information is all too often published in journals of which one has never heard or is stored away in inaccessible places and never published at all. Although to my knowledge there is no other archaeological evidence for stoneware manufacturing on the Burnett (Hays Wharf) properties, documentary evidence had been under Audrey's and my noses since 1990. It had been put there by delftware sleuth Frank Britton, who published the previously mentioned inventory of the stock of the Pickleherring potteries made at the time of its manager's death in October 1699.[42] In it, along with large quantities of delftware in various stages of production, was a listing titled "Perfect stone Ware," followed by "Stone Clay Ware." The latter clearly referred to the unfired greenware and left no doubt that John Robins, the deceased manager,

FIGURE VII.10. A tell-tale, stoneware stilt fragment from Stoney Lane, Southwark. Ca. 1690–1710. Ex Burnett Collection.

FIGURE VII.11. The Pickleherring, Stoney Lane, and Vine Yard area opposite the Tower of London as shown on a City map of 1793.

had been overseeing the production of both delftware and stoneware. The inventory began by identifying "two Pott Houses in Vine-yard and Stoney Lane Southwarke" (Fig. VII.11). As the map detail shows, Stoney Lane was only a block west of Vine Yard.[43] Britton stated that the "site of the stoneware kilns in Stoney Lane is unknown." However, the single stoneware cylinder fragment suggests that those kilns were just across the street from the delftware works and that Vine Yard served to keep the two operations and their waste products apart.

I have not been able to establish the date that Stoney Lane was first so named, but if Gravel Lane was named for the pebbles dug there for ships' ballast, it is not beyond possibility that the lane in which stoneware was made became known to the neighborhood as Stoney Lane.

One of the joys of working as an archaeologist is that people are constantly turning up with paper sacks filled with assorted artifacts asking "What's this?" In 1972 William M. Jones came up from Florida with a box of potsherds and asked that same question.[44]

Mr. Jones's trove comprised 320 ceramic sherds that he and his friends had found on the shore of Florida's Amelia Island. They included delftware kiln waste, fragments of stoneware saggers, and pieces from glassmaking crucibles (siege pots). The broken pottery ranged all the way from the late fifteenth century well through the eighteenth century and was undeniably English. It certainly was not the kind of assemblage one would expect to discover on the coast of once-Spanish Florida. The explanation was simple: The artifacts had been scooped up while loading ballast in England and dumped when a ship took on cargo or was beached at Amelia Island for careening. I knew of only one location where delftware, stoneware, and glass making all went on together, and that was at Gravel Lane.[45]

Several years after William Jones's visit, another much larger miscellany of shards reached my desk, brought there by a visitor from Charleston, South Carolina. These, too, had been found on a beach. They, however, were not English, but came instead from Portugal. Half of them were nineteenth-century waste products from a factory at Oporto (one tile was so stamped) while the rest came from a Roman era kiln site. It was apparent that although the two groups were about fifteen hundred years apart in date, both had been dumped into the same location on a shore of the Douro River and later scooped up as ballast. More recently, an amateur archaeologist walking the tidal shore of Virginia's Rappahannock River picked up several Roman era shards that included a Samian Ware cup base, evidently dumped there in the same way.[46] That gravel was being dredged up from the Thames to serve as ballast was further documented by my identifying other Samian shards amid ballast from the British ship *Warwick* wrecked at Bermuda in 1619, as well as another from the 1609 *Sea Venture*.[47]

By the close of the seventeenth century, regardless of John Dwight's efforts to prevent competitors from infringing his patent, English brown stoneware was becoming a familiar sight in British taverns and a cheap

alternative to pewter cans and flagons. Although the importation of Rhenish stoneware bottles had dwindled into insignificance, the new British ware had no adverse impact on the Dutch export trade in Westerwald-style mugs, which, with their GR medallions, remained popular into the 1760s. The majority of English Fulham-style brown stoneware mugs were without any form of decoration—a certainty provided by the evidence of archaeology. However, one would not think so from the examples to be seen in museums and private collections where virtually all are elaborately enhanced with bold, sprig-applied decoration (Fig. VII.12). The same sources would imply that most brown stoneware mugs were of huge, half-gallon capacity. That, of course, is a manifestation of the same false impression that has been inadvertently created by spring cleaners the world over. If it's pretty, keep it. If it isn't, dump it!

Much debate has focused on whether the large, decorated mugs were intended for taproom use or promotional decoration, and the probable answer is both. The earliest example in the Collection is of only quart size and decorated in a novel way not in the least like those that are embellished with sprig-applied medallions and panels (Fig. VII.13). The decorator first scratched the surface of the leather-hard cylinder, creating the trunks and branches of three trees. With that done, he used a sprig mold to give body to the trunks and then added pads of clay to represent the leaves. These he stippled with a tool about the diameter of a truncated toothpick to create a high-relief rusticated effect. However, his application of the handle had been less successful and in attaching the base of it his thumb slipped and punched a crack through the wall, which he successfully hid by smearing more clay over the outside to fill and hide it.

FIGURE VII.12. English half-gallon, brown stoneware tavern tankards dated (*a*) 1737, (*b*) 1722, and (*c*) ca. 1755–1765. London. (*c*) Ex Colonial Williamsburg Collection.

FIGURE VII.13. Brown, salt-glazed stoneware mug decorated with applied trees. Probably Vauxhall, ca. 1715.

FIGURE VII.14. Brown, salt-glazed stoneware mug fragment showing a crude clay repair to the junction of neck and handle, applied after slip coating and before firing. Raeren, mid-sixteenth century. Ex Burnett Collection.

Those are the kinds of details that span the centuries and breathe life into the long-dead potter. They echo both the expletive he must have uttered when he saw what he had done, and the sigh of satisfaction that followed when he knew he had effectively hidden the damage. Nor were German stoneware potters deterred from fixing the faintly fractured, as is shown by a sixteenth-century Raeren type mug fragment whose parting handle terminal had been "repaired" with clay *after* the brown-firing slip had been applied (Fig.VII.14).

Returning to the tree-decorated English mug, a parallel for its curious but effective use of punctured clay pads to create foliage is to be seen on a similar mug in the collection of the Museum of London, helpfully dated 1713 and attributed to the Vauxhall Pottery, where a matching waster fragment has been unearthed.[48] More historically significant than the early date (the earliest recorded on such tankards) is the incised inscription that reads "John Rose fill this with strong bear [sic] and we will fuddle our nos[e]."[49] There can be no doubt, therefore, that these large mugs were for use as well as for show. That the Collection's example is of only quart size yet has no impressed ale measure WR mark may be explainable by its having been made for private rather than ale house use, for, as I have noted, only commercially used tankards of above quart capacity were excluded from the 1700 tax.

The tree-decorated tankard came to us in a strange, roundabout way. While we were in London on one of our annual pilgrimages, dealer David Newbon showed us slides he had taken of a large American collection he was planning to buy. As he was a specialist in Oriental ceramics, he sought our opinions on some of the English pieces. When he showed a picture of the tankard, I told him that if and when he acquired it I would very much like to buy it. As months passed without hearing from Newbon, I assumed either that the collection purchase had failed to go through or that he had forgotten my request. I was surprised, therefore, when three or four years later he turned up in my Williamsburg office with a brown paper parcel in his hand. In it was *my* tankard—which he offered to me at a ridiculously modest price. I never saw him again, but learned that he had moved from London to New York, and thence to Bermuda where he died.

Another, larger brown stoneware tankard came into the Collection through an even more tortuous route. The annual Williamsburg Antiques Forum is renowned for bringing together a cross-section of America's wealthiest collectors (Audrey called them the "mink and drink brigade") along with many of the international dealers who supplied them. Among the latter was English brassware specialist Rupert Gentle, who, in 1967, showed me a brass-rimmed tankard he had recently acquired. "Why," he asked, "would such a tankard be impressed with the name of the Indian city of Calcutta?"

It was a good question. The clue to the answer was provided by a circular medallion above the CALCUTTA, its central element a quartered shield of "heater" shape blazoned with the English royal arms in the first

FIGURE VII.15. A brown, salt-glazed stoneware tankard or flagon made for the English East India Company ship *Calcutta*. The reinforcing brass rim is original. London, ca. 1755.

quarter (the others blank) with the legend in a ribbon above reading ENGL:E:IND:COMP.[50] These, therefore, were the arms of the English East India Company and hinted that the name was not that of a town, but of a ship (Fig. VII.15). The lettering had been deeply impressed using printer's type, a method that began to be adopted on English brown stonewares in the mid-eighteenth century in preference to freehand scratching. The *Calcutta* tankard almost certainly dated later than 1750. Its heavy brass rim covered no lip damage and clearly was original to the tankard, providing further evidence that this was a drinking vessel intended to weather rough handling aboard a heaving East India Company ship. She was indeed named *Calcutta,* and in 1759 was involved in a famous battle to save India from the Dutch. Taking advantage of Britain's preoccupation with its war with France,[51] on November 24, 1759, seven heavily armed Dutch men-of-war carrying a force of 1,500 men made their way up Bengal's Hugli River. Only three East Indiamen lay between the Dutch fleet and the lightly de-fended city of Calcutta, one of them its namesake commanded by Captain George Wilson. The others were the *Duke of York* and the *Hardwicke.*

Knowing that they would be outgunned, they nonetheless drew up in line of battle and prepared to give fire. The tactics of the ensuing battle are unrecorded, but the result was in no doubt. The Dutch flagship struck its colors, and five others quickly followed suit. The seventh escaped downriver only to be intercepted and seized by two newly arriving East Indiamen, thereby making the victory complete. It is tempting to think that if one were to hold the *Calcutta*'s tankard to one's ear like a seashell (something I do not recommend) one might hear the roar of her guns and the "Huzzahs!" of her crew as the invading Dutch surrendered.[52]

All this I explained to a grateful Rupert Gentle—but not sufficiently so that he would sell me the tankard at a price I could afford. Although it had been very poorly restored, it was, nonetheless, of great historical interest, and I was saddened to see it returned to England unsold.

Seven or eight years later Audrey and I were in London visiting antique dealer Alastair Sampson, who showed me an item from his stock and asked, "Why do you think it has the name of the city of Calcutta stamped on its side?" There, to our astonishment, was *our* tankard, now much better restored, its history lost, but available at half Rupert Gentle's price! As my illustration shows, it would not escape again.

The half-gallon *Calcutta* tankard carries a WR excise stamp, which may seem puzzling as by its size it should have been excluded from that requirement. But as it was made to order for the English East India Company, there had to be a reason for the stamp to be applied. A possible answer comes from the Danish East India Company's regulations of 1781, which specified who among the officers and official passengers was to sit at which table and how much was to be paid out for each in "Diet and Passage-Money to the East Indies."[53] It is likely, therefore, that a careful accounting had to be kept of how much ale was provided, and that doing so required the dispensing tankards to be of regulation capacity.

There seems little doubt that the *Calcutta*'s tankard, regardless of its large size, was used on the table of the officers' or passengers' mess, proof that in the eighteenth century half-gallon tankards of beer raised no eyebrows. On sea and land, ale and small beer were drunk in prodigious quantities, as an anonymous poet praising Yorkshire ale exclaimed:

> This moved Bacchus presently to call
> For a great Jug which will hold five Quarts,
> And filling't to the brim: Come here, my Hearts,
> Said he, wee'l drink about this merry Health,
> To the Honour of the Town, their State and Wealth.
> For by the essence of this Drink I swear,
> This Town is famous for strong Ale and Beer:[54]

Later in the same rambling paean in praise of ale the poet told how "Bacchus then took a great full Flaggon up, and drunk the Countess health, left not one sup." Bailey's *Universal Etymological English Dictionary* of 1749 defined a *flaggon* as "a Large Drinking-Pot." In another passage the poet described the sated sots lying down to sleep after "Bumpers and double Tankards did go round." The same dictionary defined a *tankard* as a "drinking Pot with a hinged Cover," while the *Oxford English Dictionary* equates *bumper* with anything unusually large and filled to the brim. All in all, it appears that large drinking vessels were well known and that they were passed around from one toper to another—which though weak on hygiene were strong on conviviality.[55] With tankards of these capacities excluded from legal controls, it seems likely that half-gallon-plus bumpers were in much more general use in taverns than some authorities have suggested.

A 1648 tract with an incredibly verbose title included a woodcut showing thirteen men (one perhaps the tavern keeper) cavorting, staggering, smoking, and throwing up, around a table on which stands a regular-size tankard and a huge, covered measure that probably contained the dregs of liquor previously dispensed into beakers and glasses (Fig. VII.16).[56] Further evidence of tankards or tankards of large capacities being considered more useful than ornamental is provided by several of William Hogarth's paintings and engravings. In Plate III of *The Harlot's Progress* we find a cluster of pewter ale measures, one of them twice the height of a standard pewter tankard. There is another in his *Strolling Actresses Dressing in a Barn*, and five more in *Beer Street,* suggesting that beer in bumpers was good for one's emotional and physical well-being.

In every facet of historical research we tend to believe that what our sources wrote (a) is true, and (b) meant what we think it did—which, of course, makes no more sense than believing everything we read in our morning papers. On October 29, 1663, diarist Samuel Pepys attended a Lord Mayor's Banquet at Guildhall. Today, that event is considered London's most lavish and prestigious dining experience of the year.[57] Pepys complained bitterly when it failed to live up to his expectations. He wrote that none but the Lords of the Privy Council were supplied with either napkins or knives, and at the meal he had to use the same trencher for each course and "drunk out of earthen pitchers and wooden dishes." So what

FIGURE VII.17. Green-glazed white earthenware ale mug or pitcher. Found in Whitefriars Street in London. Border Ware, ca. 1580–1620.

did Pepys mean by a pitcher? Contemporary dictionaries gave the primary meaning simply as a large vessel with a handle. Was he telling us that several people at his table drank from the same large vessel? If so, he provided documentation that it was not unusual for flagons of wine to be passed from mouth to mouth. However, the archaeologist in me questions why I have never found nor seen published any parallels for the massive stoneware tankards of the eighteenth century in contexts of the seventeenth.

There are several possible answers. First, until John Dwight came along, nobody was making stoneware tankards on any scale in England, and when he did, his output in tankards focused primarily on pints and quarts.[58] Second, the act regulating the sale of ale and beer did not become law until 1700; and third, in the seventeenth century, large drinking vessels were made in both wood and leather.[59] There is, however, another interpretation of Pepys's problem.

In excavations in and around the Inns of Court in the area known as the Temple, and where student lawyers and clerks ate together in halls, many examples of small Tudor-style, green-glazed jugs have been recovered (Fig. VII.17).[60] In 1594, they were described as "grene pottes usually drunke in by the gentlemen of the Temple."[61] Those green pots came either with simple cylindrical necks or with pinched spouts that turned a tankard into a small earthen pitcher. Among the many "grene pottes" found in Temple excavations were two examples of more goblet-shaped drinking vessels of the type illustrated in Fig. V.4 *b*. Nevertheless, if the legal eagles of the Inns of Court were being served their ale in little jugs, it seems likely that the Lord Mayor's penny-pinching caterers would have done the same. One can read Pepys's complaint, therefore, as relating not to wine being served in large vessels, but only to his being required to drink from earthenware rather than from the Venice glasses he considered his status deserved.

Most surviving examples of the massive, brown stoneware tankards seem to have been associated with taverns—as were their small cousins the pint-sized, swan-decorated mugs from Yorktown, Virginia. One of the earliest of the giants is in the Collection (Fig. VII.12 *b*). Dated 1722, it bears a sprig-applied portrait medallion of Queen Anne and presumably was made for a Queen's Head tavern—whose host doubtless suffered from being named "William Cheater."[62] Around the lower body, from right to left, a sprigged huntsman on foot and his eleven hounds pursue a single stag below trees of two varieties interspersed with button rosettes. On the base is a sticker marked Fulham, the date 1957, and the modest price of 65 pounds. It is my recollection, however, that on drawing attention to a chip on the rim I was able to pare the asking price down to a more manageable figure—one that by twenty-first-century values wouldn't pay for the chip. The young dealer from whom we bought the tankard rented a stall in the bustling Portobello Road market, where one could buy anything from a fake Rembrandt to a lettuce. His name was Jonathan Horne —and he would go on to become the doyen of British ceramic dealers and the publisher of several important ceramics-related books.

IF THESE POTS COULD TALK

In 1996 Jonathan mounted an exhibition of twenty decorated, half-gallon tankards and said of them that "they were rarely used, hence their survival," adding that "They were usually made as presentation pieces or to advertise a public house." Adrian Oswald has suggested that these massive tankards were made "as wedding or betrothal gifts,"[63] but the fact that several were made for known taverns as well as being decorated with images of masculine carousing would have made them less than ideal symbols of wedded bliss. Although the central panel on a tankard in the Chipstone Collection might conceivably be seen as a portrayal of the physical satisfaction of marriage (Fig. VII.18 *a*),[64] it is far more likely that the picture was intended as a reminder of the joys available upstairs in taverns like the Rose in Covent Garden. Support for such a conclusion was provided in 1962 during repairs to the Old Cheshire Cheese tavern in Fleet Street, where five explicitly erotic, plaster-of-Paris tiles were discovered behind the chimney breast of an upstairs fireplace.[65] From the style of the clothing, a date in the mid-eighteenth century is likely and fits well with that of the Chipstone tankard.

FIGURE VII.18. (*a*) Brown, salt-glazed stoneware tankard decorated with a clockwise hunt and a frontal brothel scene panel. London or Bristol, ca. 1755. (*b*) Sprigged cottage detail from the tankard, showing a post-built lean-to addition akin to the author's interpretation (*c*) of the 1620 John Boyse House in Martin's Hundred, Virginia. (*a*) Chipstone Collection; (*c*) detail from a painting by Richard Schlect, Colonial Williamsburg Foundation.

The tankard not only provided a unique yet very public canvas for activities usually limited to fan-fluttering and blush-promoting Parisian watercolors, it also offered an unexpected bonus for a less easily distracted archaeologist. I had been searching for English examples of small cottages with rear, lean-to additions, which, if and when found, would give credence to my interpretation of a pre-1622 Martin's Hundred dwelling whose post pattern pointed to just such an addition. Unfortunately, there are virtually no surviving paintings of English cottages of the seventeenth century, while those of the following century invariably show their fronts and not their backs. The Chipstone Foundation's erotic tankard was a most unlikely source for lean-to cottage architecture. Nevertheless, to the left of the central panel is a sprig-applied story-and-a-half thatched cottage with just the post-constructed shed I had been seeking (Fig. VII.18 *b* and *c*).

FIGURE VII.19. An adaptation of Hogarth's *Midnight Modern Conversation* on the 1737 tankard of Fig. VII.12 *a*.

The date and owner's name on the Collection's Queen Anne tankard were crudely scratched into the still moist clay, and the same is true of a somewhat later example, this one made for "John Sargent" and dated 1737 (Fig. VII.12 *a*). There the huntsman has acquired a horse and rides from left to right behind seven hounds in hot pursuit of a fleeing stag. The naturalistic trees of the 1722 tankard have been replaced by neatly defined palm trees and between them on one side a mill house and on the other a complex of buildings in front of which are a pig, a dog, and a cat. The principal ornament, however, is large, rectangular, and enclosed within a pillar-supported canopy (Fig. VII.19). On one side between the paired columns lurks a villainous-looking man who may have been a tavern drawer, while between the matching pillars on the other side stands an aproned maid who waits to serve six men, who sit, stand, or fall around a large gateleg table. On it are tobacco pipes, a punch bowl, and an ozier-wrapped flask. The first of the six men appears to be sober and sits on a high-backed chair smoking his pipe. Next to him another drinks from a straight-sided tankard while the third sits staring across the table, a full wig under his tricorn hat and a tobacco pipe clutched in one hand. Next to him stands another happier fellow, his arms raised with a glass in one hand and his hat in the other. Taking absolutely no notice, the fifth man is in the process of sliding off his chair onto a dog who has found something choice on the tiled floor. Front and center is the sixth reveler, who has already fallen, his legs tangled in the rails of his chair, his wig having preceded him onto the floor.

If this inebriated gathering looks and sounds familiar, it is because it is a simplified version of one of the most famous engravings surviving from the eighteenth century, William Hogarth's *A Midnight Modern Conversation*, which he drew in 1732 (Fig. VII.20). Clearly recognizable on the tankard is the fallen drunkard who has lost his wig, as are the punch bowl and the glass-raising toaster. However, the latter is shown with a glass in one hand

FIGURE VII.20. William Hogarth's *Midnight Modern Conversation*, published 1732/33.

IF THESE POTS COULD TALK

and his hat in the other, a misinterpretation of the engraving wherein the hat is not in the man's hand but hung on a wall peg and belonging to the cleric sitting beneath it. From that point onward the discrepancies are legion. Nevertheless, variations on Hogarth's bibulous scene were to become one of the most widely used on flagon-sized tankards into the 1760s, though some of the groups are far more sedate in their conviviality. Another example in the Collection is representative of the later, type-impressed variety and was made for a William Newman whose business was in Sarum, the old name for Salisbury.[66] In the central rectangular panel four men sit around a table strewn with pipes and bottles, but none are falling off their chairs or exhibiting any other signs of intemperance (Fig. VII.21). Two of the men have hung their hats neatly on pegs. Behind them is a square-paned window and a single, wall-mounted candle sconce. To the right of the panel a pot boy awaits his orders, while to the left stands an aproned woman reminiscent of the ballad singer in Hogarth's engraving of a convivial moment at the Rose Tavern.[67] The same panel is found on a tankard dated 1754 in the Colonial Williamsburg collection, but differs in that the corners are square cut. In the Collection's example the breaking away of one corner during application prompted the potter to trim off the other three, thereby turning a mistake into a decorative detail. Unfortunately, he wasn't much better at applying other molds or in cleaning up after himself. A tree lacks its foliage, and several dogs are applied with so much clay around them that they appear to be bounding over hillocks (Fig. VII.22).

Unlike the Collection's 1722 tankard whereon the stag is chased in a clockwise direction, the hunts on the 1737 example, as well as on Newman's tankard, chase anti-clockwise.[68] Eight hounds bound after one unfortunate rabbit, while two walking huntsmen blow on their horns as their master gallops along beside them, an oversized whip in his hand.[69] The anti-clockwise hunt tankards have been said to be characterized by an applied relief supposedly after Hogarth's previously discussed *Midnight Modern Conversation*, and have been attributed to a pottery known only as Factory B. However, as I have indicated, the panel on William Newman's tankard bears absolutely no resemblance to the chaos depicted in Hogarth's famed engraving. It is more likely that this tankard's central panel is the same as one described by Oswald as "The Punch Party," which he attributes to Factory C. Small wonder is it, therefore, that collectors throw up their hands in dismay and forget all about factories A, B, or C.[70]

A possible clue to the date, if not the manufacturer, of the Newman tankard is offered by the presence of a semicolon instead of a colon under the lower case "m" of W[m]. A tankard in the Colonial Williamsburg Collection has the anti-clockwise hunt, though this time in pursuit of a stag, and is type-impressed with the name "Rob[t] Paten"—with a semicolon under the elevated "t." The central panel is the same clipped-cornered "Punch Party" as the Newman tankard and under it is the location name "Alesbury" (a misspelling of Aylesbury) and the date 1762.[71]

FIGURE VII.21. More restrained than the *Conversation*, this panel from Fig. VII.12 *c* is sometimes identified as the "Punch Party." Ca. 1755–1765.

FIGURE VII.22. The "anti-clockwise hunt" in full cry around the Newman tankard (Fig. VII.12 *c*). Ca. 1755–1765.

An obvious question is whether the *Midnight Modern Conversation* or the "Punch Party" has any dating or factory-related significance, and the answer would seem to be that they don't. Nevertheless, one hook can snag another. If we cannot run William Newman to earth and thereby determine the name and nature of his business, we can fare much better with Robert Paten of Aylesbury. In 1793 he (or his son) was a resident of that Buckinghamshire town and there listed as "Grocer, Cheesemonger, and Bacon Factor." However, a portrait medallion above the party panel on the wall of the Paten tankard is shaped like a fireback decorated in relief with the head and shoulders of a king initialed GR. It seems reasonable to deduce, therefore, that in 1762 Robert Paten was landlord of an inn named the King's Head or the George. It so happens that the *Universal British Directory* for 1793 commented on Aylesbury's hostelries, noting that there were "several very good inns, the two chief [being] Mr. Sherriff's, the George, and Mr. Hicks's the White Hart."[72] Through this somewhat tortuous route one arrives at the conclusion that, like the Paten tankard, the Newman version dates somewhere between 1760 and 1765.

Because there are so many surviving examples of these massive tankards, one might expect that much more effort would have been put into finding exact parallels for individual molds for trees, hounds, huntsmen, and the like.[73] But apart from the not very conclusive clockwise and anti-clockwise hunts thesis, most remain tantalizingly mute.

The apparent demise of giant ale tankards in the third quarter of the eighteenth century did not spell the end of clockwise or anti-clockwise hunting, which, as we show in the next chapter, would continue to bound, leap, and *tallyho!* through another hundred years of beer-engendered good fellowship.

VIII   Stone Bottles and Other Puzzlers

How ever sore

the taxes gripe

there is always

pleasure ore a pipe

John Sayers, 1801

AUDREY AND I began our career-long fascination with the postmedieval centuries by following in the footsteps of Adrian Oswald, whose typology of clay tobacco-pipes had been hailed as the first step toward dating the buried remains of British life from the late sixteenth century onward. Little did I know that I would one day uncover the remains of Sir Walter Ralegh's Roanoke Island colony and hold in my hand Indian tobacco pipes smoked there by his men in 1585/86, thereby launching the Anglo-American tobacco industry. Independently, in the United States, J. C. "Pinky" Harrington of the National Park Service was exploring the same subject but along different lines. As fate had it, Adrian was responsible for bringing me into archaeology and Pinky for bringing me to America, neither of which outcomes would Audrey or I live to regret. But while tobacco pipes were to be a cornerstone of historical archaeology on both sides of the Atlantic and although more has been written about them by archaeologists than any other pottery object, ceramic historians and collectors have ignored them. Nevertheless, tobacco pipe makers were a significant arm of the ceramic industry across three centuries and in every European country (Fig. VIII.1).

While Adrian's and Pinky's pipe research provided valuable dating evidence for the seventeenth century, it was less effective in the eighteenth, thereby prompting us to seek another artifact category that went through a readily identifiable and datable evolution. We found it in the chronology of the glass wine bottle, whose shape changed rapidly from its introduction in the mid-seventeenth century through into the nineteenth century.[1] Because many had dated glass seals attached to their shoulders, they provided a "crib sheet" to keep us on the right track (Fig. VIII.2). As for everything else in our eclectic collecting, we immediately began our own

FIGURE VIII.1. Wares that ceramic historians forget. Tobacco pipe making was a major ceramic industry spanning three centuries. These examples range in date from ca. 1610 to 1800. Ex Burnett Collection.

FIGURE VIII.2 . A proliferation of English glass wine bottles through the eighteenth century would ruin the trade in imported Rhenish graybeards.

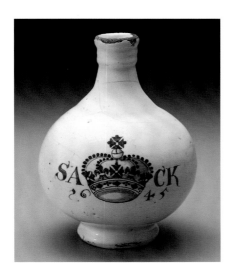

FIGURE VIII.3. In the mid-seventeenth century, English delftware bottle manufacturing posed no threat to the more durable Rhenish stoneware imports. Chipstone Collection.

collection of datable bottles, which in those days fetched prices far removed from those they command in the twenty-first century.

The earliest globular and tall-necked wine bottles seem to have appeared around 1645, prior to which time the bottle business had been almost exclusively a monopoly of the Rhenish graybeard potters. It is true that Dutch and Southwark delftware manufacturers produced bottles, but they were meant more for pouring than storing. Although definitive statements usually result in subsequent word eating, I think it fair to say that all ceramic bottles (excluding Oriental porcelain) of the seventeenth century had handles whereas glass bottles very rarely did.[2] The earliest of the delft bottles were elaborately cobalt painted in pseudo-Chinese bird-on-rocks motifs, and date in the late 1620s and 1630s. By the mid-1640s, however, plain white, handled bottles were in production, most of those surviving being painted with the names of their contents and a date ranging between 1645 and 1665 (Fig. VIII.3).[3] If the potters had a mind to compete with the graybeard imports, they must quickly have realized that glass bottles were becoming more and more popular and were easier and cheaper to make than were the twice-fired delftwares.

The eighteenth-century brown stoneware potters who turned out untold numbers of beer mugs were in obvious competition with Westerwald-style imports, but neither they nor the Germans had much of a chance when bottles were involved. That market continued to go to the glass sellers and remained so until the flip-top can usurped it after World War II.

FIGURE VIII.4. (*a*) The Carter's Grove mansion in James City County, Virginia, was completed by Carter Burwell in 1755. (*b*) That date is featured on shards of English brown stoneware bottles found there each with a sprigged inscription reading "G. Burwell / Edwd Atthawes." Atthawes was Burwell's London agent and involved with the Mortlake stoneware factory. Colonial Williamsburg Foundation.

There was, nonetheless, a small bottle market that remained open to the stoneware potters, namely bottles for porter and stout, which, in the minds of the aficionados, may have tasted better from clay than from glass. Besides, hard-fired clay was more resistant to the fermentation that could cause glass to explode.

John Dwight, as we have seen, produced large numbers of graybeard-shaped bottles for the use of taverns, but thereafter the market faded—or it would appear to have done so based on the evidence of surviving and excavated examples. Nevertheless, there are significant exceptions to question the value of negative evidence.

Beardless versions of Dwight's bottles were subsequently made across the Thames from Westminster at Vauxhall, which was renowned in the eighteenth century, not for its numerous kilns, but for its Vauxhall Gardens, London's up-scale playground after the decline of Southwark and its notorious Bankside. A Vauxhall bottle in the Stoke-on-Trent Museum is incised "John Price 1724," while others carry the date range into the 1760s.[4] From our excavations at Carter's Grove in Virginia came fragments of a similarly shaped brown stoneware bottle decorated with an applied panel reading "G: Burwell" over "Edwd : Atthawes 1755." The Burwell in question was Carter (not "G") Burwell, who completed his James River mansion in November 1755 only to die six months later (Fig. VIII.4). Edward Atthawes was Carter's London shipping agent, and it is tempting, but unwise, to speculate that Atthawes had the bottles made as a gift to his client on the occasion of the mansion's completion. But a gift there would be—though not for another 219 years. The first printing of my booklet *Digging for Carter's Grove* was read by Mrs. Joseph Moore of Virginia Beach, who gave Colonial Williamsburg an intact example of the Burwell/Atthawes bottle that had been in her family since the eighteenth century (Fig. VIII.5). The bottle gives no clue as to its contents, but we get one from Josiah Wedgwood's principal modeler, John Voyez, a man well

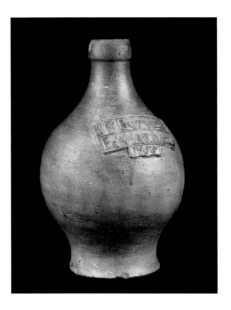

FIGURE VIII.5. This "G. Burwell, Edwd: Atthawes 1755" brown, salt-glazed stoneware bottle had been an heirloom in a Virginia Beach family until donated to Colonial Williamsburg to match the Carter's Grove shards. Colonial Williamsburg Foundation. Gift in memory of Joseph Porter Moore by his wife, Adelia Peebles Moore. Accession no. 1976-128.

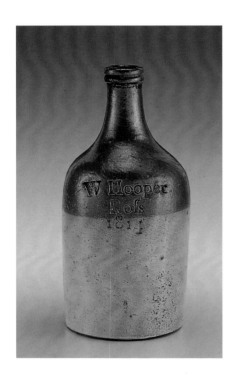

FIGURE VIII.6. An English brown, salt-glazed stoneware porter bottle, type-impressed with "W Hooper, Ross, 1814." Made for lawyer William Hooper of Ross-on-Wye. Probably Bristol.

known in Staffordshire as "a dishonourable and erratic character" famed for his "idle love of sotting." In 1768 he wrote to his master's London bookkeeper asking that "if it Suits you to send me a Stone bottle full of Good porter and Charge it as above you cannot oblige me more for I am just dead for want of it."[5]

Porter was a heavy and dark-colored beer and took its name from the working porters and farm laborers who drank it. Stout was an even heavier and darker version, and through the nineteenth century, bottling it in stoneware became the norm. The Collection's early and rare example of this kind of bottle (Fig. VIII.6) is dated 1814 and is a more or less faithful copy of the current shape in glass. However, the type-impressed name of its owner bears no relationship to produce porters, or farm workers, or, indeed, any other member of the laboring class. William Hooper was an affluent lawyer who lived at Ross-on-Wye in Hertfordshire.[6]

The largest surviving assemblage of brown stoneware porter and ale bottles was unearthed during road work in the market town of Dudley near Birmingham, where about a thousand bottles were exposed in a buried cellar of the Dudley Brewery. All could be dated within the second quarter of the nineteenth century, with several bearing the marks of the Belper & Denby Pottery in Derbyshire and impressed EX, the letters indicative of the excise tax on beer that would be dropped in 1834.[7] As the Collection's examples show (Fig. VIII.7 *a, b*), the lips and string-rims of these stoneware bottles were copying the shape common to glass beer and wine bottles after the invention of a mechanical means of blowing the glass in all-encasing metal molds.[8] Stoneware bottles continued to be made throughout the remainder of the nineteenth century, with porter usually (but not always) continuing in shouldered bottles like most from the "Dudley Hoard," while ale bottles resembled those of glass for French champagne. The latter shape (Fig. VIII.7 *d*)was included in Doulton & Watts's stoneware catalog of 1873 and is a remarkably close parallel to its glass cousin that Audrey

found on the Upchurch Marshes amid London trash of the 1870s. In spite of the fact that the stoneware bottle's bottom is flat and that the French glass has a high, basal kick, both are of 32-oz capacity. The origin and age of a second bottle (Fig. VIII.7 *c*), this one skittle-shaped in profile, raises more questions than it answers. The treatment of its string-rim, its color, and its general appearance are consistent with a date within the brackets 1830 and 1860. However, the rarity of the shape among known English bottles leaves the door open to its being from Holland or northern France. But in 1999 its cataloger at Sotheby's in London had no such doubts before it was sold as "An English saltglazed stoneware bottle early 18th century. . . . The string-ring neck is inkeeping [sic] with a similar Fulham sealed decanter, circa. 1680." With no catalog illustration to guide or warn him, the bottle's "sight-unseen" buyer paid a premium price for it and was less than delighted when eventually he saw what he had bought.

The dawn of the nineteenth century had seen a decline in the production of the mottled brown stone tablewares that a century ago were all attributed to Fulham but that we now know to have been produced in several other factories in the environs of London such as Stoney Lane, the Bear Garden, Gravel Lane, Vauxhall, Lambeth, and Mortlake, as well as in Bristol and elsewhere. Among the Collection's smaller pieces is a mustard pot that continued in the eighteenth-century "Fulham" mug tradition and helpfully sports a silver lid whose London hallmarks are dated to

FIGURE VIII.7. (*a*, *b*) Brown, salt-glazed stoneware porter bottles from the vast "Dudley Hoard," shown in the company of a typical, machine-molded glass porter bottle, whose lip and string-rim shape the stoneware potters copied. (*b*) stamped BELPER & DENBY POTTERI[ES] DERBYSHIRE / VITREOUS STONE BOTTLES, &C. / J. BOURNE, / PATENTEE. / Warranted not to Absorb / EX. The Denby Pottery separated itself from the older Belper Pottery in 1834, the same year the 1817 excise tax on beer bottles was abolished, thereby providing EX-stamped bottles with a firm *terminus ante quem*. (*c*, *d*) Champagne-shaped brown stoneware bottles accompanied by a comparable French glass bottle found on the Upchurch Marshes. Possibly French, ca. 1830–1860. (*a*, *b*) Ex Johnson Collection.

FIGURE VIII.8. Brown salt-glazed stoneware mustard pot with sprigged putti, windmill, and trees, its silver mount and lid with London hallmark for 1811. Probably Lambeth.

1811 (Fig. VIII.8). Decorated with sprig-applied trees, two of which are curiously crossed in a style that we have not seen anywhere else, the pot's principal feature is a pair of precocious putti (cherubs), one apparently forcing a goblet into the mouth of the other. To the left of the handle is a well-modeled windmill, a harbinger of a new era of decoration that was to continue into the present century. Oswald illustrated fifteen different types of windmill, the closest parallel being one attributed to Mortlake and to a date in the late eighteenth or early nineteenth century.

The Mortlake factory was among the later eighteenth-century ventures and did not open until 1740. Like Gravel Lane, it produced both stoneware and delftware, with the former becoming the more important as the fragile-surfaced delftware gave way to more durable wares. The business lasted until 1823. By another of those coincidences that littered my life and punctuate these pages, Carter Burwell's agent, Edward Atthawes, is buried in Mortlake church. The connection doesn't end there: Atthawes had been a witness to the will of Mortlake resident William Sanders, and Sanders was the owner of the Mortlake Pottery. So close was the relationship between these two men that Sanders bequeathed money to Atthawes's son Samuel.[9] Rarely do we find so much evidence pointing in a single direction, and it would be a rash critic (though there are plenty of

FIGURE VIII.9. Brown salt-glazed stoneware jug with reeded neck, pinched spout, and sprigged portrait of Horatio Nelson (see detail) flanked by putti representing the four seasons. Ca. 1805.

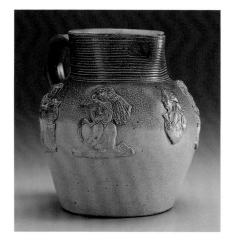

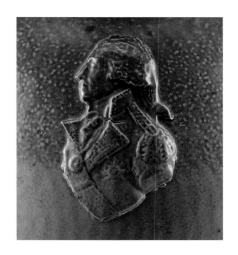

IF THESE POTS COULD TALK

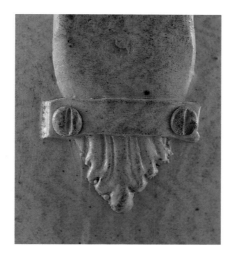

FIGURE VIII.10. Handle terminal details on *(a)* the Nelson jug (Fig. VIII.9) and *(b)* a Lambeth hunt jug (Fig. VIII.11 *a*), illustrating the evolution of a faux metal handle-anchoring device, as well as the deterioration of the acanthus leaf tail.

them around) who could argue that the Atthawes bottles that reached Virginia's Carter's Grove were made anywhere but at William Sanders's Mortlake Pottery.

Another jug in the Collection may also be a Mortlake product (Fig. VIII.9). Though decorated with what must be the grossest putti ever to take wing, its principal embellishment is a profile portrait of Horatio Nelson commemorating his death at the Battle of Trafalgar in 1805. Reading from the right side of the handle, the first naked (and doubtless shivering) cherub, representing the last of the four seasons, warms his hands over a Romanesque brazier while being goosed by sharp twigs protruding from a tree stump. The next has autumn's formidable sickle in one hand and carries a wheat sheaf over his left shoulder. Beyond the Nelson portrait the next putti, more modest than his companion, has a summer garland draped across his midriff. The fourth, and mercifully the last, is a pathologically obese lad who is either releasing a dove or grabbing it by its tail feathers. Regardless of whether or not one likes one's cherubs chubby, the jug is very well made and its foliate handle terminal is the most realistic that we had seen. Just as Oswald and Hildyard attempted a type-series of windmills,[10] so they did the same for nineteenth-century handle terminals, most of them characterized by a make-believe lateral bar held in place by two screws. The terminal on the Nelson jug, however, has no lateral bar, but does have a pair of mock screws "securing" the base of its handle (Fig. VIII.10 *a*). Oswald's earliest example is dated to ca. 1820, so it seems reasonable to assume that the Collection's jug of ca. 1805 is the first manifestation of this new handle style. Figure VIII.10 *b* illustrates this detail in its more developed form, by which time faux screws alone were insufficient in the curious game of pretending that the handle was metal rather than ceramic.

As I have hinted, beer jugs became increasingly gross as the nineteenth century progressed. But true to our credo that one cannot recognize the good until you see it alongside the bad, the Collection includes one example that can at least claim to be good of its type (Fig. VIII.11 *a*). This

FIGURE VIII.11. (*a*) Large brown, salt-glazed stoneware beer jug with lightly reeded neck, and multiple sprigged embellishments that include a clockwise hunt, and (*b*) a central panel in high re-lief featuring two men drinking at a table served by a potboy holding a large flagon of ale. Lambeth, ca. 1870. (*c, d*) Smokers and wavers; details (*c*) from the Lambeth jug (Fig. VIII.11 *a*) and (*d*) from an earlier Brampton puzzle jug (Fig. VIII.12 *a*). (*e, f*) The sleeping drunk: (*e*) from the Lambeth jug (Fig.VIII.11 *a*), and (*f*) from the Brampton puzzle jug (Fig. VIII.12 *a*).

massive beer jug still belongs to the class loosely known as "Hunt" mugs and jugs, retaining as it does the country squire's favorite sport, but where once the huntsman and his horn blower got their exercise on foot, here both ride. Reading from the left of the handle, the mounted horn sounder wears the kind of cap still worn by most hunters. Nine dogs pursue the stag, and in their midst gallops the master wearing a hat characteristic of the mid-nineteenth century, with his riding crop urging his horse to even greater exertion. Although the chase motif had its origins at the beginning of the eighteenth century, it remains subservient to the upper decoration, which by this time has isolated the *Midnight Modern Conversation*'s intemperate elements and brought them up to date—and in high relief.

Beneath the jug's pinched spout is a scene wherein two smokers sit at a three-legged table, one holding a large and presumably empty mug while the other reaches out to a potboy who has arrived with refills. The froth-capped jug he holds is akin to the one to which the scene is attached (Fig. VIII.11 *b*). To the right of the central grouping are three single figures (Fig. VIII.11 *c*). One sits behind a table made from a garlanded barrel, a glass in his left hand, and with his right hand waves his hat for attention. On his table are a carafe, two tobacco pipes, and a dish. A second man sits on a barrel smoking, while the third squats astride yet another barrel, a foaming mug in his right hand. To the left of center are only two scenes, with the first showing a man seated on an overturned barrel leaning forward and asleep across another (Fig. VIII.11 *e*). The last scene depicts six men gathered round a barrel in a tableau reminiscent of a seventeenth-century Flemish engraving. Unfortunately, the acanthus-leaf handle terminal with its lateral bar and naturalistic screws is not paralleled on Oswald's typology page,[11] but the neck's retention of the reeding that goes back to Dwight in the seventeenth century suggests a date ca. 1870, after which time most of the jugs had plain necks. A surviving 1873 catalog from the stoneware factory of Messrs. Doulton & Watts of Lambeth illustrates a plain-necked "Hunting Jug" and offers these in "Common Clay or Fine Clay" and in capacities that ranged from a quarter pint to one gallon.[12] But was our jug made by this famous Lambeth firm?

The answer may very well be that it came not from London but from Bristol, where William Powell set up a stoneware pottery in Thomas Street ca. 1816, a business that continued until it was destroyed by German bombs in 1941.[13] In 1834, William and his potters created an enormous jug almost thirty-three inches in height to celebrate the coming of age in January 1835 of his son, William Augustus Frederick. Using every mold in the shop, they sprig-applied a remarkable range of classically inspired figures and amidst them sneaked in the three right-of-center figures on the Collection's jug, namely, the hat-waving toper, the pipe smoker, and the guy with the foaming mug (Fig. VIII.11 *c*).[14]

In 1869, using a newly invented double glazing that created an appearance best suited to toilets, Powell's factory made a tobacco jar for Alfred Evans of Bristol, decorating it with, among other devices, the hat-waving man sitting behind his barrel, and on it the familiar carafe, two pipes and a platter. Beyond him is the barrel-sitting smoker. Both of these scenes are present on one of two puzzle jugs in the Collection (Fig. VIII.12 *a*) whose elaborate, cut-out neck decoration is paralleled by another stamped "R. Gilry 1837."[15] Further cementing our puzzle jug to Powell of Bristol—or so it might seem—is the inclusion of the sleeping drunk from our large jug, as well as the hat waver and the single smoker (Fig. VIII.11 *c* and *d*). But like red-herring clues planted in an Agatha Christie whodunit, the Powell association comes all too easily.

FIGURE VIII.12. (*a*) Brown salt-glazed stoneware puzzle jug with sprigged decoration drawn from similar mold designs used on nineteenth-century hunt jugs. (*b*) Detail showing the superior quality of the molding and the use of a less common design of the drunken master being helped home by his lantern-carrying servant. To its right, a second and better version of the "contented smoker" than occurs elsewhere on the same jug (Fig. VIII.11 *d*).

FIGURE VIII.13. Brown salt-glazed stoneware pint-capacity hunt mug with yet another version of the "contented smoker," this time with his cat-eared dog. Doulton, Lambeth, ca. 1869–1872.

FIGURE VIII.14. Uniform brown "Nottingham glaze" stoneware puzzle jug type-impressed STANLEY 1820, and with incised inscription common to such jugs. Probably Derbyshire.

The puzzle jug's almost orange-brown color, in tandem with the pale honey tone of the glazed body, closely resembles an anthropomorphic teapot in the Derby Museum attributed to a stoneware factory at Brampton in Derbyshire.[16] That distinctive coloration is thought to have been developed there around 1820, but it was not one characteristic of Bristol. Further evidence in support of a Brampton origin is an engraving of another puzzle jug so attributed, whose applied decoration includes a rarely used portrayal of two men homeward bound from a tavern, one clutching a bottle and evidently the master and the other his servant holding an oversized lantern, a scene paralleled on the Collection's puzzle jug (Fig. VIII.12 *b*).[17] The truth has to be that brass mold makers would sell their designs to any potter, anywhere. Furthermore, family relationships meant that fathers, brothers, and sons sometimes worked together but often on their own, no doubt borrowing from each other as the need arose. If further proof of that be wanted, we have found the whip-waving huntsman on our supposedly Powell jug on an oversized pitcher made in 1828 by the Caledonian Pottery at Glasgow in Scotland.[18]

That brass molds available in 1834 could still be in use in the 1870s should surprise no one, for the popularity of their images would wane long before the matrixes wore out. In consequence, the late jugs and mugs portray their countrymen in attire that was fifty and more years out of date. The Collection's pint mug made by Doulton of Lambeth between 1869 and 1872 is a good example (Fig. VIII.13). It retains the old hunting sequence, albeit scaled down to pint size, while above, in high relief, are three men. The first sits on a barrel and leans on a triangular table on which is a full and foaming mug of beer, but is too besotted to pick it up. The next sits beside a three-footed candle stand gripping a mug in his right hand and a pipe in his left. The third is more relaxed and with his dog beside him sits on a barrel beside a tree contentedly smoking.[19]

The Collection's second puzzle jug takes us into an entirely different facet of English stoneware, one whose chocolate-brown, high-gloss glaze is often, even usually, attributed to factories that began production in Nottingham in the first years of the eighteenth century and continued there for the best part of 200 years. But just as early collectors liked to attribute all mottled brown stonewares to Fulham, so Nottingham has enjoyed credit for many a piece made in Derbyshire. Our second puzzle jug is one of them (Fig. VIII.14).

James Morley, who in 1696 had been described as a "Brickmaker & no Potter," had opened a pottery in Nottingham by 1700 that stayed in business for a hundred years and was renowned for "its famous brown mugs for the use of public houses and the appellation of Nottingham ware is still in many villages attached to the better and more highly finished class of every description of salt glazed pots."[20] At about the same time, Morley, though not yet twenty years old, was buying land at Crich in Derbyshire, an area rich in excellent potting clays. Five years later he married Ann Mathews of Alfreton, another town in Derbyshire but only 16 miles from Nottingham. In 1793, a listing of the Alfreton tradesmen included "Smith. J. Manufacturer of Brown Ware," noting that along with a stocking manufactory, the two industries had an annual return of 50,000 pounds, which, as they say, "ain't hay!"[21] At the same date in nearby Chesterfield there were "Ten potteries, chiefly of brown ware," with all of their tradesmen identified. Perhaps indicating that some were lower on the social ladder than others, three are listed only by their last names: Cartledge, Ford, and the second of two Sanforths.[22]

There were so many brown stoneware manufacturers still at work in Derbyshire at the close of the eighteenth century that unless a pot bears a factory mark, source identification is well nigh impossible. Our second puzzle jug is type-stamped "STANLEY 1820" and hand-incised by someone with good writing ability to read

> Come Gentlemen and try your skill
> I'll lay a wager if you will
> That you drink this liquor all
> Unless you spill or some let fall.

But even that fairly long inscription gets us no further. The same invitation occurs on four other examples dated between 1775 and 1837, two with marks tying them to Chesterfield, one linked to Brampton, and another to Eastmoor.[23] Ours is featured in Oswald and Hildyard's *English Brown Stoneware, 1670–1900*, but only as a drawing and tentatively attributed to the Derbyshire village of Ilkeston.[24]

The Chipstone Foundation owns several puzzle jugs, one of them in brown stoneware and helpfully dated to 1751 (Fig. VIII.15). The rest of the inscription reads "E^d Linsdal, Thaxstead, Essex," which certainly points to a London source of manufacture, and the Chipstone catalog attributes it as "possibly Vauxhall."[25] A detail seemingly unique in puzzle jugs is this one's applied ornamentation of foliate and floral sprays. However, similar but better quality floral sprigging decorates a brown stoneware gorge attributed to Fulham and to ca. 1685–1695.[26]

I realize, of course, that some readers may be puzzled by puzzle jugs, and so a word or two of explanation are in order. These jugs were designed to get one idiot laughed at by a bunch of others. The jugs' handles were hollow and the challenge was to channel the contents toward one of three possible spouts. To succeed in drinking the contestant had to seal two and drain the jug by suction through the third—providing he chose the correct channel. Although three spouts was the most common arrangement, examples are known with five and even seven. Selecting the right spout was not enough, for the heart of the joke lay in the underside of the handle's crest where hid another hole through which the liquor would escape before reaching any of the spouts—as is the case with both of the Collection's examples.

The survival of so many puzzle jugs is explained by their having very obvious "keep me" appeal, so their number may be misleading. Nevertheless,

FIGURE VIII.15. Brown, salt-glazed stoneware puzzle jug with sprigged floral decoration and inscribed "E^d Linsdal, Thaxstead, Essex, 1751." Attributed to Vauxhall. Chipstone Collection.

it still seems likely that in their time they were relatively common. As we have seen in earlier chapters, most British potters (save those emulating oriental porcelain) seem to have obtained their ideas from western Europe, and puzzle jug may be no exception, The earliest thought to be English is a crude example in a green-glazed redware with applied numerals forming the date 1571, and when published was in the collection of London's Museum of Practical Geology and now, presumably, in the Victoria and Albert Museum.[27] Undated, but vastly more sophisticated, is a Westerwald stoneware puzzle jug of ca.1630 in the British Museum, as evidence suggesting that puzzle juggery was originally a German joke.[28] Making this specimen of particular interest is its stamped neck decoration, which is paralleled on a neck fragment from another Westerwald jug, this one found in the well at Virginia's Wolstenholme Town and deposited prior to the Indian attack of March 1622. One learns over time that impossible coincidences are more frequent than statisticians will admit.

Ranging as puzzle jugs do in various wares and dates from 1571 to 1866, it is astonishing that their "secret" would remain so through 295 years of dribbling and spilling. But I suppose we should put it down to their providing simple fun for *very* simple folk.

A second example in the Chipstone Collection is in delftware and carries the puzzle a step further by creating an S-curve to the base of the handle, which serves to hide the hollowness of the upper C-shaped curvature (Fig. VIII.16).[29] Both handle and daisy cut-out collar are in a curious dappled blue, but characteristic of at least two more late delftware puzzle jugs. Chipstone's is dated and its inscription reads as follows:

My Form has puzzled many a fertile Brain
The brightest Wits my Liquor could not gain
And still profusely spill it on the Ground
The Reason is no Suction they have found
Now honest Friend advance Thy Genius try
Spill Ne'er a Drop and strive to drain me dry
W.J. 1771

FIGURE VIII.16. Delftware puzzle jug, its blue-painted neck decorated with heart and lozenge piercing. This example has an unusual, S-scroll supported handle. The wall carries a long and finely written inscription and the date 1771. Probably Liverpool. Chipstone Collection.

IF THESE POTS COULD TALK

Most collectors recognize the need to have in their libraries the latest books on their subject, which means that over time they assemble a corpus of bafflingly conflicting information. Thus, for example, the Colonial Williamsburg Foundation owns a puzzle jug with the same sponged blue on its neck and handle as the Chipstone jug. However, the 1727 date makes it much earlier and the X-shaped cutting out of the neck is quite different. This Williamsburg jug is loosely attributed to London.[30] If we assume the neck coloring to be the determining feature, then London would be the likely source for the 1771 example. But now we add three delftware puzzle jugs in the collection of the Victoria and Albert Museum, all of them with the same daisy cut-outs made from alternating hearts and lozenges as the Chipstone jug.[31] These are all attributed to Liverpool, as was another, illustrated by Jewitt in 1878, that has Chipstone's dappled blue neck and handle, its daisy and lozenge cut-outs, but a single-element tubular handle. Its inscription read:

Here gentlemen, try y^r skill
Ile hold a wager if you will
That you Don't Drink this liq^r all
Without you spill or lett some Fall.[32]

Also attributed to Liverpool is another undated specimen in the Colonial Williamsburg collection that not only has the right cut-outs but also has the same inscription as Jewitt's example, complete with the same somewhat eccentric abbreviating. A fourth Victoria and Albert jug has quite different cut-outs (interlocking circles) but does have a double element handle paralleling that potentially significant feature of Chipstone's 1771 specimen. Furthermore, the handle is a similarly sponged a dappled blue.[33] Though undated, the jug's rococo-bordered body inscription puts it in the third quarter of the eighteenth century. But this one is attributed to Bristol, as is another in that city's City Art Gallery; it has the same interlocking circle cut-outs but lacks either the blue dappling or the double-element handle.[34]

One of the Liverpool jugs has the same inscription as Jewitt's, albeit without the abbreviations, but all three have their "dares" flanked by vertical gadrooning, which his does not.

Putting all this together, the Chipstone puzzle jug winds up with a blue neck and handle from London and Liverpool, cut-out daisies and blue neck from Liverpool, and a handle shape from Bristol! But when all the conflicting evidence is weighed, it seems to me that the Jewitt mug's abbreviated inscription is the determining factor, which, by extension, puts the Chipstone Foundation's delftware puzzle jug in the Liverpool column.

They say that a little knowledge is a dangerous thing, but sometimes a lot can be even more hazardous! However, I have plowed through the puzzle-jug evidence to a probably tiresome extent as a demonstration of the kind of tortuous thinking that is necessary to arrive at a ceramic attribution when no kiln-defining evidence is there to separate fact from speculation.

FIGURE VIII.17. Pearlware puzzle jug painted in "Pratt" colors, inscribed as having been made for *John Bloome* and depicting his ship *Hopewell* with its enigmatic figurehead. Probably South Yorkshire, ca. 1790–1800.

I hope I have shown, too, how the addition or subtraction of a single specimen can skew one's conclusion in one direction or another.

Unencumbered by the confusing and seemingly conflicting details surrounding any number of delftware puzzle jugs is the Collection's third example. In pearlware and decorated in so-called Pratt colors depicting the ship *Hopewell,* it bears the name John Bloome (Fig. VIII.17). This jug is by far the most elegant of any I have seen and appears almost egret-like in its extended neck and sense of lightness. Though undated, it is likely to be a product of a Yorkshire pottery between ca. 1790 and 1805. With the jug owner's name revealed, as well as the likelihood that he also owned the *Hopewell,* I thought it should be easy enough to track down a ship-owning merchant living in the Yorkshire area at the end of the eighteenth century. I felt certain that I'd find Bloome somewhere in my handy-dandy five-volume *Universal Gazetteer* for 1795—but I couldn't. And there was another mystery to be solved.

If you look very closely at the *Hopewell* you can see its most unusual figurehead—the carefully drawn head of an ass. Figureheads came as classical figures, buxom blondes, Neptunes, mermaids, lions, even dragons, but never as a donkey! Was this jug a gift to John Bloome from his wife reminding him that he had been a jackass to invest their savings in the *Hopewell*? Immediately we begin to ask such a question the ceramic jug fades from view and instead we find ourselves among the people of the past, sharing their emotions—real or imagined. How did John react when he unwrapped Mrs. Bloome's gift? Was he amused, contrite, angry? And what of her? Did she have the jug made as a gentle reproach to a misguided husband, or was it given in a spirit of malice and heartless pity? We shall never be sure—at least not until someone clearing out an attic finds a mouse-munched ledger containing an entry reading, "June 26, 1794, John Bloome for charter of the good ship Hopewell . . . £1,200 4s. 6d," and then parenthetically in another hand, "Lost at sea."

Belonging to much the same category as puzzle jugs were fuddling cups, involving three or many more small cups linked together, with holes at their interior bases that allowed the liquor to flow from one into another. Like so many other widely accepted ceramic names, the term "fuddling cup" seems to have been a late Victorian collectors' notion based on

the assumption that by drinking all three cups of intoxicating liquor one would find oneself befuddled.[35] If Llewellynn Jewitt is to be believed (and often he should not), fuddling cups go back to the age of Roman Britain. In his *The History of Ceramic Art in Great Britain* (1878) he illustrated such a set and described it like this:

> The triple, or triune vase . . . is an excellent specimen, the connecting bands being hollow tubes, so that when the liquor was placed in one, it rose to the same height in each.[36]

Several fuddling cups in English delftware are dated to the second quarter of the seventeenth century, one of them in the Chipstone Collection. Ours, however, is much later and dates around 1700 (Fig. VIII.18). Being made from a yellow body with red-ochre inclusions, and covered with a tortoiseshell mottled brown glaze, the ware is sometimes attributed to the Derbyshire village of Crich, but also was made in Staffordshire.[37]

In addition to Derbyshire puzzle jugs, the Collection includes three other comparable pieces of stoneware, yet of very different types. The first is a simple money box whose principal feature is its date-defining coin slot (Fig. VIII.19). This one was designed to accommodate the huge and unwieldy penny and twopenny pieces minted in Birmingham in 1797 in an effort to restore confidence in English copper currency, which, in the last quarter of the century, was represented by more underweight forgeries than genuine money from the royal mints. It turned out that with copper in an era of low market value, the coins had to contain a great deal of metal to be worth a penny or twopence. Needless to say, this bureaucratic expedient

FIGURE VIII.19. Money box in Nottingham-style brown stoneware. Its principal features are a spike or spire terminal and a wide money slot suitable for the reception of the large British penny and two-penny pieces (*right*) in use between 1797 and 1806, when a more manageable copper currency was introduced. Probably Derbyshire.

went with a dull thud into the citizens' pockets and purses, and was replaced with a more manageable copper currency in 1806. In theory, therefore, the brown stoneware money box should date between 1797 and 1806.

The date for another Derbyshire piece in the Collection is by no means as precise. This is a colander with strap handles reminiscent of Leeds creamware sugar bowls and the like (Fig. VIII.20).[38] Not being an object with evident "keep me" qualities, it has rarity value for that very reason. It belonged in the kitchen and was used there until it broke or was thrown away when a clean, whiteware version took its place. But why Derbyshire? Could it not as well be a relic from one of the Nottingham factories?

All are good questions, and I'm glad I asked them. Among general rules of thumb, it can be said that dark chocolate-brown wares are from Derbyshire and the lighter, evenly colored milk-chocolate or ginger-brown specimens are from Nottingham. But rules of thumb are not sculptured in marble, as our 1820 puzzle jug attests (Fig. VIII.14). Another dubious rule has it that "On the edges of the body fracture a thin white line is often found, due presumably to the nature of the clay since it occurs on both surfaces. This line," adds Oswald, "seems peculiar to products from Nottingham and Crich but is not universal among them." That sounds like a pretty sure clue—until one reads his footnote and finds that Oswald got the information from me in 1970![39]

Now, thirty years later, I wonder whether the exceptions are so numerous as to make nonsense of the rule. Nor is the dark-chocolate/milk-chocolate distinction all that reliable. The Collection's dark brown colander is decorated with two bands of beading applied with a roulette wheel, as are three rows of tiny cruciform impressions that run between them. I was to find an exact parallel for this device and those rows, but on a fragment

much more milk chocolate in tone. It came out of a flower bed in my father's garden at Sevenoaks in Kent! The tell- or tall-tale white line is not to be seen on the edges of the fragment. All I can add, therefore, is that both the colander and the design-matching fragment are cataloged into the Collection to be puzzled over by anyone with the urge to do so.

The last of the Collection's entries into the Nottingham/Derbyshire debate tosses in another more northerly location, that of Swinton in Yorkshire. The superlatively proportioned loving cup (Fig. VIII.21 *a*) was discovered by Audrey under a table in a small shop off London's Kensington Church Street whose proprietor specialized in Chinese porcelain rather than English pottery.[40] Although the cup spoke fairly loudly on its own behalf, the dealer said he had bought it in a sale lot and knew nothing more about it. Incised on one side is the date 1759 and on the other the names "John Lee and Sarah." The cup closely resembles another illustrated by Jewitt and dated to the same year (Fig. VIII.21 *b*). In discussing Swinton, my ever-helpful 1793 gazetteer tells us that "Here is an extensive earthenware manufactory, which employs a great number of hands, and at which are manufactured all kinds of earthenware, from the coarsest to the finest fabric." Among the listed tradesmen are "Brameld, John. One of the Managers of the Pottery, and Greens, Bingley, and Co. Proprietors of the Pottery, and Cinder-burners."[41] All this acquires pertinence when Jewitt tells us that his illustrated loving cup (which he called a "posset-pot") had attached to it "a fragment of a label, written at 'Swinton Pottery,' which authenticates it as having been made by, or for, John Brameld." Of the Swinton area, Jewitt wrote this in 1878:

> [At] the beginning of the last century, a hard brown ware, of much the same quality as that made at Nottingham and Chesterfield, was produced on Swinton Common, where clays useful for various purposes were abundantly found.[42]

We may safely accept that statement as correct, for if not, Oxley Grabham, retired keeper of the York Museum, would not have parroted it virtually word for word when he wrote his own book thirty-eight years later.[43] It seems highly likely that as the Nottingham and Derbyshire factories

FIGURE VIII.21. (*a*, *c*) Both sides of a brown salt-glazed stoneware loving cup made for John and Sarah Lee, dated 1759. This important vessel is believed to be from Swinton in Yorkshire on the evidence of the drawing (*b*) in Jewitt, *The History of Ceramic Art,* of an almost identical example documented as having been made by John Brameld and likewise dated 1759.

began making brown stoneware around 1700, similar wares would be in production in the neighboring county of Yorkshire very soon afterward. However, it was not until 1745 that the business named the Swinton Pottery was founded by one Edward Butler, who there "established a tile-yard and pot-works for common earthenware"—providing further documentation linking tile and brick making to the craft of the potter.

The Collection's Sarah Lee loving cup is illustrated in Adrian Oswald's book, but is attributed to Nottingham while at the same time noting Jewitt's reference to a possible Swinton association.[44] Oswald's reluctance to accept Swinton as the source is based upon a letter from a Mrs. A. Cox, who had excavated on the site of the Swinton Pottery and stated that she had found no stoneware in the early levels and knew of no examples from that pottery. One wonders, of course, whether Mrs. Cox was digging in the right place. Oswald, who is renowned for his impartiality and his cautious usage of documentary evidence, allows that although the excavations failed to support Jewitt's and Grabham's claim, "the incised decoration on the [Lee] cup does not compare with any on Nottingham dated pieces although it has some affinity with that of a loving cup at Lincoln."[45] However, the latter's decoration does not come within a country mile of the similarity provided by Jewitt's drawing of the Brameld cup.

Until more evidence for or against brown stoneware manufacturing on the Swinton Pottery site comes to light, we are left once again with the unsatisfactory Scottish verdict of "not proven." That does not, however, end the story of brown stonewares as told through the Collection. On the contrary, it opens the door to an era wherein the potters of Lambeth and Derbyshire callously catered to the nineteenth-century slum dweller's taste for the opiate whose "mother's ruin" nickname was all too apt. But before unlocking that Pandoric box, we must go back to the beginning of the eighteenth century to a time when the story of English pottery was about to enter a new and enlightened age of innovation and modernization, one that was to render the name *Staffordshire* synonymous with the best of the best.

IX   Potter to Her Majesty and Other Marketing Ploys

ABOUT *five miles north west and five miles south east of Newcastle-under-Lyme are the two extremities of that interesting and opulent district, named The* POTTERIES ... *not yielding in the elegance, beauty, and utility of the productions, to those of China; and in extent of operations exceeding all others in Europe.*

Simeon Shaw, 1829[1]

AT THE END of the seventeenth century, *rural* England remained almost medieval in character. Villages were scattered haphazardly through the shires and dominated by the old and new mansions of a changing gentry. Nevertheless, the medieval relationship between lord and tenant was alive and well and would stay so for many more generations. The farmers would still be eating off pewter and their workers off wooden trenchers and drinking from cups and bowls made from plain, lead-glazed earthenware. Indeed, the notion that any but the rich should be eating from plates shaped like those of silver-gilt or pewter was not seen as a market void eagerly waiting to be filled. That generalization is likely to be greeted with hoots of derision from ceramic historians, who will quickly assert that the seventeenth century's most famous English delftware plate was made in London in 1600 and reminded its owner that THE ROSE IS RED, THE LEAVES ARE GRENE and urged GOD SAVE ELIZABETH OUR QUEENE.[2] However, it is unlikely that this pious and patriotic invocation was expected to be smeared with beef gravy. Such plates (which were far less common than larger platters and chargers) were intended more for dresser decoration than for daily usage—at least at the lower levels of society. With that said, one has to add the caveat that most of what we know about seventeenth-century delftware is derived from the highly decorated and often dated pieces endowed with "keep me" potential. At the same time, it must also be said that although by the 1640s delftware potters were producing undecorated, plain white ointment and posset pots, candlesticks, and the like, undecorated white plates are rarely, if ever, found on contemporary archaeological sites either in Britain or in her American colonies. Not even those masters of merchandising, the Germanic potters of the Rhineland, saw a market for

FIGURE IX.I. (*a*) London delftware plate painted in polychrome with floral basket and flying bugs, the central design often seen on French faience in the second half of the eighteenth century (see Fig.IX.15). (*b*) A closely paralleling waster from the vicinity of the Pickleherring factory in Southwark. Ca. 1740. (*b*) Colonial Williamsburg Foundation.

stoneware dinner plates, and by the time they realized that they were wrong, it was far too late to carve out a share.

In England the shift toward 8½-inch table plates began around 1680 as earthenwares became cheaper and proved easier to clean than the treen trenchers that had been a staple tableware in most modest homes throughout the medieval centuries. It is true that blue-painted and polychrome dishes had been common throughout the first half of the seventeenth century, but these invariably stood on foot rings that elevated them above the table surface. By the 1650s, largely white plates first produced in Holland became increasingly in vogue, but it is not until the century's last decades that we begin to find delft plates decorated in the loose pseudo-Chinese style so well represented by the oddly placed and coffined example I discussed in a previous chapter (Fig. III.12). Thereafter, and almost to the end of the eighteenth century, delftware manufacturers saw plates as a major facet of their stock, yet omitted to list them by that name.[3] Because Audrey's and my collecting had always been driven by archaeology and the questions posed by it, the Collection's range of delftware plates may appear both eccentric and incomplete. The latter certainly is true. The range of designs produced by the London manufacturers alone was enormous, coming as they did from major factories strung out along the south bank of the Thames from Horseley Down and Pickleherring Quay to Vauxhall and Lambeth. Although, thanks to archaeology (mine and my successors'), Pickleherring is best known for its products of the Christian Wilhelm and Robins eras, it continued in business into the eighteenth century—but how far into that century is not entirely clear. Ceramic historian Frank Britton has determined that the old Pickleherring factory was acquired in 1708 by Richard Grove and James Robbins,[4] who packed up and moved two fifths of a mile downriver to Horsley Down Lane. However, a plate in the Collection that dates to ca. 1740 parallels an undeniable waster found by Sir David Burnett on Hays Wharf property abutting Vine Lane—a location too far removed from Grove and Robbins's new premises for the fragmentary plate to have strayed (Fig. IX.1).

In case a reminder of the definition of a *waster* will be helpful, it can be said to be a ceramic vessel that emerged from the kiln so warped, cracked, or otherwise damaged that nobody would buy or even use it. Whenever possible, potters did their best to hide or sufficiently repair the damage to enable their second-rate wares to be sold as *seconds* at much reduced prices.

IF THESE POTS COULD TALK

FIGURE IX.2. Queenhithe Dock in the shadow of St. Paul's Cathedral, ca. 1760. Both stoneware and biscuit delft shards were found on the shore to the right of the dock.

FIGURE IX.3. *(Top row)* Stoneware sagger shards. *(Below)* delftware biscuit fragments from a bowl, porringers, ointment pot, plate, and kiln pad. All from Queenhithe, early eighteenth century.

Josiah Wedgwood referred to these quick fixes as "tinkering" and was quite prepared to export them. In 1765, he wrote that "the bulk of our particular manufacture are . . . exported to foreign markets . . . the principal of these markets are the Continent and Islands of North America. To the Continent we send an amazing quantity of whiteware and some of the finer kinds, but for the Islands we cannot make anything too rich or costly."[5] Although Wedgwood's statement can be read as being either for or against sending the richest and costliest to the Caribbean plantation, the great wealth of the Island planters fosters the former interpretation.

For the archaeologist who sees virtually everything in its broken state, recognizing a second or even a waster is never easily done. Only when glaze covers a fracture can one be reasonably certain that the vessel could not have held water.[6] Finding unglazed (biscuit or bisque) wares does not make them wasters—factory discards, yes, but products of kiln damage they are not, at least not necessarily so.

I mentioned earlier that Audrey and I spent many an hour walking the shores of the River Thames at low tide in search of unusual or otherwise interesting potsherds. Much of the searching focused on a short stretch of the north shore between Southwark Bridge and a deep recess into the wharf line known since early medieval times as Queenhithe Dock (Fig. IX.2). On that shore we found a sufficient number of biscuit fragments to suggest the presence of a delftware factory where none is recorded as having existed, and these potentially informative fragments are now part of the Collection, all of them shapes common in the early eighteenth century (Fig. IX.3).[7] Had these clues been alone, I would undoubtedly have claimed their presence as

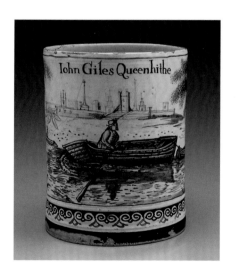

FIGURE IX.4. London delftware mug, probably made for a waterman operating from Queenhithe Stairs. Perhaps Montague Close, Southwark, or Thames Street. Ca. 1700–1730. Chipstone Collection.

FIGURE IX.5. (*a*) London delftware mug made for Joseph Piper of the London Blacksmiths' Company and dated 1752. Probably Lambeth. (*b*) Cutlery bearing the tobacco pipe rebus of IP [J. Piper], ca. 1725–1750. The cutler is believed to be Joshua Piper of Birmingham and the father of Joseph. (*a*) Chipstone Collection.

unequivocal evidence of a nearby, north-bank kiln, but found with them were fragments of stoneware waste and sagger fragments.[8]

Nothing is more embarrassing than rereading words that one wrote forty or fifty years ago and discovering them to be wrong. In my book *Treasure in the Thames* (1956), when I commented on these telltale fragments, I asserted that "There can be no doubt that I was dealing with hardcore brought, perhaps from potteries at Gravel Lane, Tooley Street, or even from Lambeth itself."[9] But maybe not. I later discovered that a delft, dish-spacing trivet had been found in nearby Thames Street in 1840 and is now in the British Museum.[10] Taken at face value, it is possible that somewhere between Queenhithe Dock and London Bridge a potter trained at a south-bank factory set up in business on the north in the first quarter of the eighteenth century.[11] Doubtless coincidental, but certainly serendipitous, is the presence in the Chipstone Collection of a fine London delftware mug of about 1720 bearing the name "John Giles Queenhithe" and depicting a waterman sitting in his wherry (Fig. IX.4). It seems likely that Giles was himself a waterman and that if he plied his trade from Queenhithe Stairs, a friendly nearby delftware potter made him that mug.

A second delftware mug in the Chipstone Collection brings us to yet another of those coincidences that punctuate our ceramic saga and which you may think stretch credulity as taut as a drawn bow string. The mug is painted with the arms of the Blacksmiths' Company, is dated 1752, and was made for one Joseph Piper (Fig. IX.5 *a*). A delft bowl in the Ashmolean Museum at Oxford also carries a rendering of the Blacksmiths' arms, is dated 1749, and has been attributed to Lambeth.[12] Consequently, it's fair to assume that both bowl and mug are London products and that Joseph Piper lived there and worked in the blacksmith's trade. Now we throw in some knives and forks to generate the promised coincidence.

Because cutlery styles changed through the seventeenth and eighteenth centuries, Audrey and I would buy representative examples to better illustrate the rusty blades found in our excavations. Among the purchases were table knives bearing the initials IP and a rebus in the form of a tobacco pipe—hence Piper, conceivably Joseph Piper and perhaps even the owner of the Chipstone mug (Fig. IX.5 *b*).[13] But there were snags. The mug showed him to have been a member of the Blacksmiths' Company and not of the Cutlers. Furthermore, we had attributed the IP knives to the period ca. 1720–1740. If Joseph's mug commemorated his acceptance into the Blacksmiths' Company, he is unlikely to have been old enough to have been making knives in the 1730s. Besides, had these been London knives, they would have carried the mark of the London Company of Cutlers. As they did not, it is safe to assume that they were of provincial origin. But where?

No greater service has ever been done to social history than by the Mormon Church with its extensive genealogical research and record keeping. Searching them for a Joseph Piper in London drew a blank, but there was one who was christened in Birmingham on October 1, 1736, and *Bremischam*, as the town was then called, had long been known as an iron-working center. Indeed, it still is. When, in 1535, John Leland embarked on his celebrated fact-finding tour around Britain, he noted that "There be many smithes in the towne that use to make knives and all manner of cuttynge tooles. . . . So that a great parte of the towne is mayntayned by smithes."[14] Although several craftsmen were still identified as Birmingham cutlers at the end of the eighteenth century, by then most had moved to Sheffield and closer to the sources of coal and ore. Nevertheless, the records indicate that in Birmingham cutlers were still separate from blacksmiths.

The Mormon records show that the father of Joseph was Joshua Piper (another IP), and it seems reasonable to conclude (though documentation is lacking) that Joshua was a cutler by trade and the maker of our knives, and that his second son, Joseph, moved from the iron-working center of Birmingham to London, where at the age of about sixteen he became apprenticed to a blacksmith. Be that scenario right or wrong, the relationship between the mug's Joseph Piper and the IP of our knives is too remarkable to be ignored.[15]

Back on, or *in* firmer ground, while excavating in Williamsburg behind the public gaol in 1959, Audrey and I found a splendid delft punch bowl and several plates from the 1720s. Among the latter was one decorated in blue with a helmet-wearing man performing a balancing act while steadying himself with the circus acrobat's mandatory pole (Fig. IX.6 *a*). When I showed a photograph of the plate to Robert Charleston, then keeper of

FIGURE IX.6. (*a*) London delftware plate, excavated in Williamsburg, Virginia, ca. 1710–1720. (*b*) Dutch delftware tile parallel for the acrobat design, ca. 1650. (*a*) Colonial Williamsburg Foundation.

ceramics at London's Victoria and Albert Museum, he told me that these kinds of images were almost always borrowed from Dutch delftware tiles. A few days later we were driving with David Burnett from Hays Wharf down to his home in Surrey when we passed a small junk shop with piles of tiles in its window—one of them the Dutch parallel to the Williamsburg plate (Fig. IX.6 *b*). Being in a hurry to get out of the seedy side of London before dark, we didn't stay long in the shop and I have no memory of asking the owner where he acquired the tiles—although it would have been a very obvious question to ask. We hastily bought the acrobat tile and half a dozen others, and hurried back to the car—leaving behind a hundred or more unexamined and, evenly more stupidly, unpurchased!

FIGURE IX.7. Squirrel and "croquet-hoop" design on a delftware plate paralleling fragments found on the property of Williamsburg tavern keeper and cabinetmaker Anthony Hay. London or Bristol, ca. 1750.

FIGURE IX.8. (*b*) Christiana Campbell's reconstructed tavern in Williamsburg, for which the Collection's squirrel plate became the hotel china design source. (*a*) A squirrel saucer or ash tray used there until too many were stolen.

I have ever since been kicking myself for not having invested our last shilling in buying the entire stock and squirreling them away like nuts for our old age. They could have been ours at slightly under 5 dollars apiece and in the twenty-first century would sell for upwards of 300.

Colonial Williamsburg reproduced both the punch bowl and the acrobat plate for sale in its Craft House. For more than thirty years the bowl continued to sell, but the acrobat plate was an immediate flop. The design had no appeal, and so today a remaining reproduction aspires to a place in the Collection, with its presence made the more desirable thirty years later after we found new copies made by another potter being sold in Boston's Museum of Fine Arts gift shop!

Another delftware plate in the Collection had its genesis in a Williamsburg excavation. We found it and fragments of two others in a stream behind the remains of a building that had served colonial cabinetmaker Anthony Hay as his workshop. The plates dated from around 1750 and featured a squirrel, which among rodently challenged collectors is known as the *rat and vine* design. Beneath the squirrel are a pair of inverted U-shaped devices that we referred to as the *croquet-hoop* motif (Fig. IX.7). Hay's occupancy of the shop building began in 1756 and ended ten years later when he leased the premises to another cabinetmaker and bought the Raleigh Tavern on Duke of Gloucester Street. As he continued to live in

the house next door to the cabinet shop, it seems likely that the squirrel plates came from that home. However, when we found the broken squirrel plates we believed them to be cast-offs from Hay's ownership of the Raleigh, but as they would not have been bought new as late as 1766, that conjecture now seems groundless. Nevertheless, the squirrel design copied

IF THESE POTS COULD TALK

FIGURE IX.9. (*a*) Large, delftware squirrel and croquet-hoop dish, on its back the paired dashes and crosses typical of Bristol dishes in the period, ca. 1710–1730. (*b, c*) Both sides of a large delftware dish variant of the squirrel and croquet-hoop motif sometimes referred to as the "rat and vine" design. Bristol, ca. 1710–1730.

from the intact parallel we bought for the Collection became the basis for the hotel china made specially for use in Colonial Williamsburg's Christiana Campbell's Tavern on Waller Street (Fig. IX.8 *a* and *b*). If one cares to be picky about it, the design was no more appropriate for Mrs. Campbell's emporium than it had been for Hay at the Raleigh, as she did not occupy the Waller Street premises until 1771. Our interest, however, was not in its appropriateness for use in a reconstructed Williamsburg tavern, but in the origin of the squirrel and croquet-hoop design elements. This prompted us to buy two large dishes made in Bristol in the 1720s, one of whose squirrels is backing up in a rather indelicate way against a bush (Fig. IX.9 *a* and *c*). These examples demonstrate that squirrels came in a variety of shapes and sizes, as did the croquet hoops. It is tempting to say that on the evidence of those two dishes, the Anthony Hay squirrel plate is both earlier than we supposed and attributable to Bristol. However, ceramic historians F. H. Garner and Michael Archer have illustrated an almost exact parallel and captioned it to Lambeth.[16] But on referring to the text, one finds that "it could equally easily have been made at either centre"—which dumps us back on square one. Retired Colonial Williamsburg ceramics curator John Austin in his invaluable delftware catalog attributed two variants of the croquet-hoop design to Bristol, but curiously made no reference to the Hay site squirrel plates. He also illustrated a soup-plate version of the Collection's Bristol dish and attributed that to Liverpool or Bristol and to a date as late as 1760.[17] A bowl with the croquet hoops but no squirrel is among the previously cited collection of delft and other

FIGURE IX.10. English delftware bowl with rudimentary croquet-hoop decoration, with the hoops and beads in dark blue and the foliage in pale. This is a later manifestation of the squirrel design, which itself occurs on bowls of this shape and date. Found in Hamilton Harbour, Bermuda. Bristol or London, ca. 1735–1750. Edward Schultz Collection.

wares recovered from Hamilton Harbour in Bermuda (Fig. IX.10). Unfortunately, the ceramics are thought to be trash from a nearby tavern and range in date from the end of the seventeenth century onward to the mid-nineteenth century. Although no closer contextual dating is possible, stylistically the Bermuda bowl dates somewhere between 1735 and 1750.

If, having read all this, you have no better idea where the squirrel plates were made than you did at the outset, you are not alone. Ceramic attributions are reliant on two factors: the few inscribed with the name of the factory, and those that are paralleled among wasters from kiln sites. Neither, however, is infallible, for as we saw when dealing with brown stonewares, potting families tended to scatter their offspring about, and as a result skills and styles learned at one factory would be duplicated at another. Consequently, in the absence of anything more tangible to cling to, the old children's game of "Follow the Leader" is continually played out by collectors and curators, each relying on the word of the last "expert" to risk putting something on paper. Unfortunately, any publisher or labeler of antique ceramics who fails to give a date or a source in each caption is liable to be stripped of his credentials and drummed out of the fort. Consequently, fear of that degradation can be a spur to our providing both—even when we aren't absolutely certain of either.

Several of our delftware plates were bought because they matched fragments from our Virginia excavations, and others simply because we wanted to learn more about them. The plate illustrated in Figure IX.11 rated in both categories. One of the first things about delftware I thought I had learned was that the so-called *mimosa* pattern was characteristically

FIGURE IX.11. Delftware plate in "mimosa" pattern, with the leaves painted with square brush strokes in underglaze blue and the red flowers added in a second glost firing. Probably Bristol, ca. 1725–1745.

IF THESE POTS COULD TALK

a Bristol product of the early eighteenth century and so, too, was the use of square brush strokes. I had also learned that the red was applied in a separate firing and consequently was raised above the surface of the primary glaze. While there is no denying that the red is usually recognizable by touch, neither the spatula-shaped brush strokes nor the dating and factory attributions hold up. The late F. H. Garner illustrated a much repaired mimosa patterned saucer and attributed it circa 1700 and to Lambeth.[18] However, Michael Archer noted that fragments have been found at kiln sites in London, Bristol, Wincanton, and Liverpool—in a word, everywhere. He also stated that "The fashion for the 'mimosa' pattern seems to have been around 1740."[19] Another respected pot pundit, in his catalog of the Robert Hall Warren Collection, attributed a plate with the mimosa pattern as "Perhaps Bristol or Wincanton (or Dutch?)" He also noted that the pattern "is often found on English delftware of the period 1700–1740."[20] Garner, however, stated that the design in blue and red was found "throughout the greater part of the century." Small wonder is it, therefore, that novice collectors and archaeologists who find fragments have a hard time learning what was made where, and when.

When writing her report on the contents of a Williamsburg well wherein we had found an almost complete mimosa plate (thus prompting our purchase), Audrey suggested that the manufacture date lay somewhere in the first quarter of the eighteenth century, then added this:

> As the painters in London, Bristol, and subsequently Wincanton are known to have used this design, it would be unwise to attribute these plates to a specific area, let alone a factory.[21]

FIGURE IX.12. Delftware plate with "pinwheel" central element and stylized floral elements painted first in underglaze blue and green and in a secondary firing in red and yellow. The plate differs in its thickness and resulting weight from most others displaying variations on this central device. Probably Bristol, ca. 1760–1775.

FIGURE IX.13. A pair of shallow delft-ware fruit bowls with elaborate peony patterning in blue, and the rims edged in orange. London or Liverpool, ca. 1780.

Another plate in the Collection (Fig. IX. 12)came aboard when we were studying ceramics unearthed on the Caribbean island of St. Eustatius, where we were finding examples of its pinwheel central decoration on faience plates we knew to be French.[22] However, Michael Archer attributes this color combination, shape, and design to a specific factory, namely, that of William and Abigail Griffith. They operated a potworks in Lambeth High Street in the third quarter of the eighteenth century, and William was described as "the most considerable potter in England."[23] His central roundel device, like so much else, can be traced back to the Netherlands at the beginning of the seventeenth century.

Although the Collection includes several more English delft items of no great consequence, it does have a pair of orange-rimmed bowls of later eighteenth-century date that are sufficiently unusual to be worthy of illustration (Fig. IX.13 *a* and *b*). They are so shallow that none of the exterior walls are seen; consequently, all the decorator's effort went into the interiors and to producing a very pleasing, peony-centered design against a pale blue ground that may point to a Liverpool origin. That they are, indeed, a pair, provides an opportunity to study the degree to which the original pounce-defined design differed when the freehand brushwork took over. To find a pair of such unusual bowls is in itself remarkable, and to find them undamaged was even rarer. Unfortunately, subsequent examination in the hands of the U.S. Customs Service ensured that they did not remain so.[24]

IF THESE POTS COULD TALK

FIGURE IX.14. Red-bodied French faience dish painted in purple with a stylized basket of flowers, manganese coated on the back. This heavy kitchenware with its purplish-brown back was characteristic of Rouen throughout the second half of the eighteenth century.

At one point, we had speculated that the bowls might be of European origin, but being unable to find any parallel, and recognizing that the decoration looked very "English," we did not pursue that possibility. Nevertheless, the Collection's foreign faience examples do have an important evidentiary role to play.

Soon after taking over the archaeological arm of Colonial Williamsburg I discovered that sites dating from the last quarter of the eighteenth century yielded numerous fragments of dishes and bowls in a red-bodied earthenware coated with a heavily crazed, bluish-white tin glaze on one side and painted with a manganese wash on their backs and exteriors (Fig. IX.14).[25] The Victoria and Albert Museum has one of these dishes helpfully impressed ROUEN, and on November 23, 1778, a firm of importers advertised in the *Maryland Gazette* (Baltimore) that they had for sale in Gay Street a variety of "china, Glass, and Rhoan ware." Another importer, this one in Philadelphia, advertising on May 5, 1784, offered amid much else "Delph and Roan wares, Dishes, Plates, tureens, bowls, fruit baskets, etc." That Rhoan and Roan were anglicizations of Rouen there could be no doubt, nor could we doubt the negative archaeological evidence that failed to yield any specimens from Williamsburg excavations dating prior to the Revolutionary decade.[26] Another lesson learned from this study was that publishing the evidence was a form of monetary masochism. Rouen dishes had hitherto been of no antiquarian or collector interest, and in 1960, before I wrote an article for *Antiques* magazine, they could be bought for 2 dollars apiece.[27] Afterward I was being offered identical dishes at 200 dollars. Alas, they have never reverted to their "nobody wants me" price. The same is true of heavy dishes tin-glazed on both back and front and tentatively attributed to Moustiers in southeastern France (Fig. IX.15).[28]

FIGURE IX.15. Heavy, bat-molded French faience dish, tin-enameled on both sides and painted more realistically than Fig. IX.14. Moustiers or Rouen, ca. 1760–1790.

FIGURE IX.16. Fragments of Rouen faience porringers illustrating the color of the body, the use of mold-cast handles, and the characteristic manganese exterior common to mugs, pitchers, covered tureens, and others in the second half of the eighteenth century. These examples from a French shipwreck on a Bermuda reef, ca.1760. E. B. Tucker Collection.

The Rouen wares were already standard French kitchen crockery by the middle of the eighteenth century, but they did not reach the British American colonies until the onset of the Revolution, when trade restrictions against foreign imports became meaningless. Many examples have been found on the site of the French fortress of Louisbourg in Nova Scotia, which surrendered (for the second time) to the British in 1758, thereby halting any further imports from France. About two years later a French ship sank on Bermuda's northern reef. Aboard, along with the officers' pewter, was a wide range of Rouen-style wares that included jugs, covered bowls, and porringers (Fig. IX.16). Whether this large assemblage of Rouen and other wares was for trade or for shipboard use there is now no telling. One thing is clear, however, namely, that this was the finest assemblage of tightly datable French earthenwares and Normandy stonewares ever found together in America. Indeed, it is doubtful that they have so rich a parallel in France itself, for the French are only marginally interested in the archaeology of so late a period.[29]

In preparation for writing a book on historical ghosts, Audrey and I went with David and Betty Burnett to Versailles and to Marie Antoinette's palace, the Petit Trianon, whose gardens provided the venue for one of the best-authenticated ghost stories ever published.[30] Legend has it that the Queen was sitting in a small pillared kiosk or belvedere beside a lake when word came to her that the Parisian mob was on its way to seize the royal family (Fig. IX.17 *a*).[31] Two hundred years later, beside the step to this historic little building I saw a fragment from a Rouen dish lying in the dirt. It seemed a most unlikely place to find so humble a shard, and I have no explanation for its presence beyond the possibility that soil from the palace kitchens was moved there during landscaping repairs (Fig. IX.17 *b*).

FIGURE IX.17. (*a*) Marie Antoinette's belvedere near the Petit Trianon at Versailles, where (*b*) Rouen faience and Normandy stoneware shards were found.

The Rouen fragments were not the only example of French faience to turn up in a most unlikely location. Among the thousands of fragments from the Bermudian French wreck came faience shards from two or more small cruet jugs, each with its lid secured by a pewter hinge and thumb plate. Florally decorated in red, blue, green, and yellow, these little pitchers were among the most attractive objects from the ship. Less than a year after first studying the shards I found their twin on a Portobello Road stall-holder's shelf (Fig. IX.18 *a*), there described by the dealer as a foreign bottle of maybe the mid-nineteenth century. I neglected to disillusion

FIGURE IX.18. (*a*) French, polychrome-decorated faience cruet bottle with pinched spout and pewter lid mount. (*b*) Matching fragments from the ca. 1760 French wreck off Bermuda. (*b*) E. B. Tucker Collection.

him. Another slightly larger faience jug of the same date, but in colors limited to blue and purple, was added to the Collection by David Burnett after he learned of our Portobello Road discovery (Fig. IX.19).[32]

As I noted when discussing our possibly French Metropolitan slipware-style mugs and jug,[33] we often bought items simply because we did

FIGURE IX.19. French faience cruet bottle painted in blue and manganese, its shape less elegant than Fig. IX.18 *a* but possessing the same pinched spout. Ca. 1750–1780. Ex Burnett Collection.

not know what they were and thought we could learn by finding someone who knew the answers. A supposedly French faience plate in the Collection is one such item (Fig. IX.20 *b*). With its tin-glaze thick and heavily crazed, and with its painting equally heavy, one might be forgiven for thinking it to be nineteenth-century Portuguese. However, the fleur-de-lis decorated shield points more toward Bourbon France and a date of manufacture prior to the ousting of the French monarchy. On the other hand, it might have heralded the restoration of the monarchy in 1814, although the flange decoration would have looked distinctly old-fashioned in France at such a date. Although I have been unable to find any visiting ceramics expert able to provide chapter and verse for this striking example of "French" faience, the Smithsonian Institution long ago provided me with photographs of six more plates in the same style. Unfortunately, the Smithsonian has no knowledge of their present whereabouts and can offer no opinion regarding them. Eventually, with the benefit of a little computer legerdemain, I was able to separate the colors of the mark, and found that under the heavily blue-painted Bourbon fleur-de-lis were the painter's initials P B. But for whom did he work?. After ruling out the royal porcelain factory at Spain's Buen Retiro, which used the same mark, my process of elimination led to the Marseilles factory of Honoré Savy, a faience manufacturer who, between 1764 and 1782, enjoyed a flourishing export business with the French colonies.[34] Alas, that

FIGURE IX.20. (*b*) French faience plate in "Royal" shape, polychrome-painted with Bourbon arms. (*a, c*) Faience plates in the same ware and decorative style. Probably Marseilles, late eighteenth century. (*a, c*) Photos: National Museum of American History, Smithsonian Institution.

"Eureka!" moment was short lived. I almost simultaneously learned that the fleur-de-lis mark adopted by Savy in 1777 was not his alone but "appears on many specimens of faience of an obviously different provenance."[35] No doubt European faience authorities will wince at reading that it took me twenty years to get this far; but it only goes to show that when a collector ventures out of his field, he becomes quickly (and sometimes disastrously) lost and an easy victim of fakery.

The Collection has its own homemade fake—although it was never intended as such. While working at the Guildhall Museum in London I made a rubber mold from a white salt-glazed stoneware figurine of a female servant holding a cloth,[36] and from it made a plaster copy that came with me to Virginia. On learning that Jim Maloney was making reproduction salt-glazed stoneware at his Williamsburg Pottery, I asked him to cast several of the figures for me to give to friends as Christmas presents—which he did (Fig. IX.21). Because clay shrinks by as much as 10% in firing, the copies came out smaller than the original, but otherwise they looked pretty good. Twenty years later one of the recipients of the gift sent it to New York to be auctioned as a copy of the original in the London museum's collection. Instead, it appeared in the catalog as an eighteenth-century female figurine in salt-glazed stoneware with no indication that it was, indeed, a copy. Fortunately, the owner read the description and quickly withdrew the figurine from the sale, but had to pay a penalty for so doing.

Maloney's figure had been slipcast in a plaster-of-Paris mold, a fact clearly evident when the open base revealed an inside whose indentations mirrored the exterior. Part of a salt-glaze teapot in the shape of a camel with a howdah strapped to its back has been found in Bermuda and well illustrates the exterior and interior appearance of a slip-cast object (Fig. IX.22). In this process liquid slip is poured into the mold, whose porous walls draw out the water pulling the clay particles toward it. The sculptured master original (known as the block) was usually made in salt-glazed

FIGURE IX.21. (*a*) Plaster cast of a white, salt-glazed stoneware figure of a female servant, rubber-molded from the original found in London and attributable to the mid-eighteenth century. (*b*) White salt-glazed copy demonstrating the resulting degree of shrinkage. Original in Guildhall/London Museum Collection.

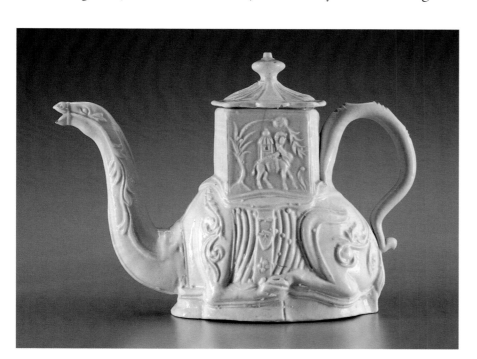

FIGURE IX.22. (*a*) English white salt-glazed teapot slip cast in the form of a camel with a howdah on its back, ca. 1745. (*b*, *c*) Exterior and interior of a comparable camel teapot illustrating the modified mirror image visible on the interiors of slip-cast objects. The fragment was found in Hamilton Harbour, Bermuda. (*a*) Chipstone Collection; (*b*, *c*) Edward Schultz Collection.

stoneware and thereafter used to shape the interiors of any number of plaster molds.[37] Simeon Shaw described how these were filled "by pouring in a very thin slip, and letting it remain a few minutes, then pouring it out, and refilling with a thicker slip which instantly assimilates with the former, and more than doubled its thickness."[38] That process went on until the object being cast had reached the needed thickness. The mold was then set near a fire until the clay dried and the several elements of the casing could be taken apart.

The alternative method, particularly prior to ca. 1745 and the introduction of plaster-of-Paris slip casting, was to use molds of metal, fired clay, or alabaster,[39] and as those were nonabsorbent, the clay had to be pressed into them by hand. The original figurine was made in that way, and in consequence the inside showed only the impressions of the worker's fingers and not an incuse image of the exterior. Included in the Collection are three figurines from the Thames, all made solid from two-piece press molds, one a boy's torso believed to be second-century Roman,[40] and a redware dog and a pipeclay lion, both thought to be Elizabethan (Fig. IX.23).

FIGURE IX.23. Examples of ceramic toys cast in two-piece molds: (*a*) lion fashioned in white pipe clay, (*b*) boy holding a dove in a hard gray clay, and (*c*) dog in finely modeled red earthenware with a chain-link collar round its neck. (*a*) Late sixteenth century, (*b*) second-century Roman, (*c*) early seventeenth century; all from the Thames near Queenhithe.

The question of who was the first to make and sell white, salt-glazed stoneware has been debated ever since John Dwight brought suit against half a dozen alleged competitors, three of whom were Wedgwoods, Aaron, Thomas, and Richard. If one can accept the word of John Dwight, white salt glaze had its origins in his Fulham factory, although as I have previously stated, his output was limited to ferruginous-dipped brown mugs, and tea and coffee pots—in short, all sorts of hollow wares, of which the gorge in the Chipstone Collection is a fine example (Fig. VII.2). One of Dwight's notebooks gave a 1691 formula for a body "to make a bright red Cley wth Staffordshire red Clay—Take sifted Staffordshire Cley thirty pounds. ffine dark twenty pounds. Mingle & tread."[41] It is evident, therefore, that there was intercourse between Fulham and Staffordshire during the lifetime of Dwight's second patent (1684), and that no matter how secretive he chose to be, his apprentices and other talkative factory employees would be flattered to meet with his competitors in the taproom at the Wheatsheaf or the Anchor.

By 1700, salt-glazed stoneware was being made in Staffordshire that closely resembled Dwight's tavern gorges and cans, examples of which are in the Stoke-on-Trent Museum, as well as the fine specimen attributed to John Elers of Bradwell Hall (Fig. VII.3).[42] These, unquestionably, were the sires of the Staffordshire trade that would eventually reach every corner of the English-speaking world. Moving on and away from the half-brown/half-white fabric borrowed from Dwight, Staffordshire potters experimented with an all-white ware created by coating a gray-firing body with a thick white engobe inside and out. All too often, however, the coating slid away from mug rims, spouts, and the crests of handles, revealing the unattractive gray core. The potters solved that problem by dipping or painting a brown-firing ferruginous slip around the rims and handle crests, creating a distinctive product that some collectors used to call *Crouch ware*.[43] This they attributed to the first teething years of Staffordshire salt-glaze production—and indeed it was (Fig. IX.24). The origin of the term *Crouch* has also been a subject for spirited speculation.[44] The answer would seem to be that the name is a corruption of Critch in Derbyshire, which, as we have seen, was an important source of clay. The dipped whiteware continued in production through much of the eighteenth century, as is testified by a mug recovered from one of the British ships scuttled at Yorktown in 1781.[45] In the previous year an advertisement for the sale of a pothouse in Prescott near Liverpool described two kilns, "the one for burning the Crouch or Nottingham ware and the other for the mottled or Brown ware."[46] Clearly, therefore, the brown stoneware mugs and tankards made at Fulham, Lambeth, Gravel Lane, and elsewhere belonged to one group, while the even, high-gloss, brown-coated wares characteristic of Nottingham and its darker cousins in Derbyshire and Yorkshire were sometimes sold under the name of Crouch ware. The only problem with this is that it leaves us with no generic name for the engobed and brown-rimmed pots.

While we are on the subject of Crouch ware, it may be useful to address another term that has sometimes been used as a variant, namely, *drab ware*. An unattractive term should describe unattractive pots, but it doesn't. It relates to a very thin, gray-bodied ware coated internally with an engobe of white-firing Devon and Dorset clay mixed with ground flint that rendered the body stronger and more refractory. The exterior is characterized by high-relief yet delicate decoration in the same white clay cast from metal (brass?) molds, and fired in a salt-glaze kiln (Fig. IX.25). The late Arnold Mountford attributed these drab tewares to ca. 1730, though some of the shapes suggested to us that they remained fashionable a decade and more later. Examples in the Chipstone Collection are without the shard's high-gloss glaze and so more readily lend themselves to the drab-ware description. Writing enthusiastically about others like them, Sir Arthur Church declared, "There can be no doubt that these things are far more worthy of preservation than many of the English porcelains and earthenwares which command high prices at sales and form the usual objects of

FIGURE IX.24. Engobe-coated, gray-bodied, white salt-glazed mug with iron oxide dip at lip and handle crest, representing the earliest form of Staffordshire white salt-glazed stoneware. The illustrated example was found at Wetherburn's Tavern in Williamsburg, Virginia, in a mid-eighteenth century context. Ca. 1710–1750. Colonial Williamsburg Foundation.

FIGURE IX.25. Gray-bodied stoneware teapot shard coated internally with a white engobe and externally with a brown slip under applied ornament from metal molds in a "grape and gnome" design combination. Called *drab ware,* the high-gloss surface exhibits the same salt-glaze pebbling characteristic of the plain whitewares. Staffordshire, ca. 1730–1745. Ex Burnett Collection.

worship among the devotees of bric à brac." In 1904, he proposed displaying this drab ware "upon the shelves of a cabinet lined with puce-coloured velvet."[47] To which I can only add—everyone to his own taste.

Chemical analysis showed that the early brown-rimmed wares contained flint in their engobe (as did the interiors of the drab wares) but not in the body beneath, and as usual there have been varying accounts of the beginning of ground-flint usage. In 1829, that always ready to help but not always right Simeon Shaw attributed it to one Daniel Bird, who, Shaw claimed, was known as the Flint Potter and who, having been killed in an unspecified accident at Twickenham outside London, had been brought back to lie under a subsequently dilapidated tomb in the old churchyard at Stoke.[48] Elsewhere in the same book, Shaw told that in 1720 or thereabouts, Jacob Astbury was on his way to London when his horse's eyes appeared to be failing. The hostler at the tavern where he was to spend the night ministered to the horse with a remedy that required flint to be heated red hot and then pulverized into a fine dust and blown into each eye. This greatly benefited the horse and gave Astbury the idea for mixing granulated flint into his salt-glaze engobe.[49] The truth, however, is that neither Bird nor Astbury was the first to experiment with flint-enriched clays. For that we have to go back to John Dwight, who in 1698 wrote that in creating a white body, "Calcin'd beaten and sifted flints will doe instead of white sand & rather whiter but ye charge & trouble is more."[50] He was quite right—and although blowing flint dust in the eyes of Astbury's horse may have wrought a minor miracle, it had the opposite effect on the lungs of the grinders.

In 1726 and 1732, Thomas Benson took out patents to remedy the respiratory problem by means of a crushing engine that did away with the hand hammering and sifting, "which hath proved very destructive to mankind, occasioned by the dust suckled into the body which, being of a ponderous nature, fixes so closely upon the lungs that nothing can remove it." Benson added that suppliers using the old method were having trouble attracting employees.[51]

Flint grinding would become a major and separate Staffordshire industry once the potters had access to West of England pipe clay as well as to

FIGURE IX.26. (*a*) Shard of transitional, press-molded, white salt-glazed stoneware, with its body clay coarse and slightly yellow under a white engobe, a style characterized by lower wall faceting comparable to that of a pitcher found in a pre-1728 context in Williamsburg, Virginia. (*b*) Transitional white salt-glazed teapot retaining the iron oxide detailing earlier, and by necessity, applied to dipped stonewares like the example in Fig. IX.24. Staffordshire, ca. 1720–1730. (*a*) Ex Burnett Collection; (*b*) Chipstone Collection.

IF THESE POTS COULD TALK

lesser sources in the northern part of their own county, for thereafter they made their salt-glazed wares entirely from those clays. Before the opening of the Trent and Mersey canal system (1772 and 1777), both flint and clay had to be brought overland in wagons or on packhorses, making raw materials expensive and conservatively used. Flints had to be brought overland from East Anglian chalk mines or by ship from the beaches of the south coast. The same was true, of course, of the white pipe clay and Cornish stone from Cornwall, which together formed the body for soft-paste porcelain. Only the common clay and salt were found in easy distance from the Staffordshire potteries, with the salt coming from Cheshire, where rock salt was discovered in 1670.[52]

The evolution of white salt-glazed stoneware, therefore, was governed in large measure by the cost of materials. At first the potters continued to coat a coarser, unflinted core under a flint-rich slip. I'm not sure whether it was I or someone else who dubbed these products *transitional white salt glaze*, but that is what they were. There is, I believe, a subtle distinction between the Staffordshire and London whitened wares, the former characterized by a very fine, black sand speckling, which shows through in the exteriors and cross-sections of those of the transitional specimens that are purely white. Examined under a magnifying glass, the black particles have levitated themselves upward through the glaze, leaving tiny tails behind them. These transitional salt-glazed wares are heavier and somewhat more yellow than the fully fledged white salt glaze that would follow it, and were in production by the 1720s. As these were thicker than the later true salt glaze, the potters often press molded vertical flutes around the pots' lower bodies that served both to give them a distinctive, even metallic appearance and to reduce their weight and bulk by thinning the lower wall.[53] Rare in any but archaeological collections, this transitional ware is represented in the Collection only by a single basal fragment but one that fairly closely parallels a jug in the Colonial Williamsburg collection deposited into a pit behind the John Brush House prior to Brush's death in 1728 (Fig. IX.26 *a*). Both shard and jug are characterized by a shiny surface and a matt interior. An extremely rare teapot in the Chipstone Collection exhibits the fluted lower wall, but at the same time retains the no-longer-necessary iron oxide rim, spout, handle, and lid finial details (Fig. IX.26 *b*). Once the all-in-one, flint-whitened clay became the norm, an entirely new world of ceramic art opened to a delighted public as well as to bevies of joyous potters and their equally happy salesmen. With so fine a body with which to work, it became possible for hollow wares to be press molded in bold relief in patterns that ranged from seashells to the dot-diaper-and-basket pattern that was destined to become the most familiar of all tableware designs from the mid-1720s to the 1760s.

For Audrey and for me, the same attributes that made white salt glaze such a hit in the mid-eighteenth century were the ones that made us dislike it. Our vicarious relationship with the craftsman who shaped the pot with his hands or painted the Wan Li designs on a delftware plate

FIGURE IX.27. (*a*) Rosewell, the Page family mansion in Gloucester County, Virginia, built ca. 1725. (*b*) Slip-cast house teapot of ca. 1745 paralleling a fragment found at Rosewell in a context of ca. 1770–1775.

could not be transferred to the slap-it-down and lift-it-off plate production of the new, increasingly mechanized age. We much preferred the fussy and folksy.

The Collection differed from most in that it was not limited to objects that we found aesthetically pleasing; it has tried to represent most of the ceramics that we found in our Virginia excavations. Those began, not in Williamsburg, but at the ruined mansion of Rosewell in Gloucester County, where, in the fall of 1956, we found a trash-filled pit, its contents dumped there around 1770 when improvements were being made to the mansion. Amid fragments of white salt-glaze mugs, teapots, pitchers, and the inevitable dot-diaper-and-basket plates, was a small fragment from the side of a slip-cast teapot in the shape of a house with the English royal arms over its door.[54] The house stood three stories over an English basement with a flight of steps rising above it to the first floor (Fig. IX.27 *a*). Was it just a coincidence that the teapot looked remarkably like the Rosewell mansion, or had someone given it to owner John Page for that very reason? This is, of course, a question that can never be answered, but it did prompt us to add a house teapot to the Collection (Fig. IX.27 *b*). Although the pots are much the same size, ours portrays a smaller house, having only three stories on one side and two on the other, but it is of interest in that it has its original lid, whose "chimney" knob and spout are shaped like the beak of a bird.[55]

The Collection's only example of slip-cast, pattern-molded, hollow ware is a three-footed open salt of great delicacy, and in spite of our lack of enthusiasm for white salt glaze in general, we could not deny its beauty

FIGURE IX.28. Slip-cast white salt-glazed stoneware salt cellar decorated with dot-diaper-and-basket-relief, standing on three zoomorphic feet. Ca. 1745–1760.

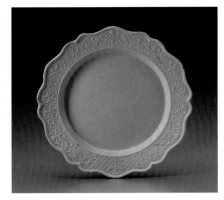

FIGURE IX.29. Typical white salt-glazed stoneware plates of differing shapes. (*a*) Octagonal dot and diaper pattern; (*b*) the standard dot, diaper, and basket design; (*c*) a relatively uncommon diaper and foliate flange combination. All Staffordshire, ca. 1745–1770.

(Fig. IX.28). Dinner plates and matching dishes were produced by the thousands, and being shaped over bat molds they required no throwing skill, making them as cheap as they were attractive (Fig. IX.29). With this development began the slow demise of the easily chipped delftware plate. Fussy and folksy was being replaced by clean modernity coupled with

FIGURE IX.30. Bat-molded white salt-glazed stoneware fruit dish featuring alternating basket and cut-out tracery panels within a central dot-diaper-and-basket design. Staffordshire, ca. 1750–1760.

durability. The manufacturers of these white salt-glaze wares went the whole hog in decorating their products, particularly in their sweetmeat and fruit dishes (Figs. IX.30 and IX. 31). Once they found that plates with rim decoration sold well, it was an obvious next step to cover the entire bat-molded upper surfaces with similar ornamentation and to add a new dimension by cutting out parts of the rim pattern to create a lighter and even lacy appearance.

Of more than average interest is a fruit-and-vine-decorated dinner plate that has its almost exact parallel in another ware of approximately the same date (Fig. IX.32). In 1759, Josiah Wedgwood was in business with Thomas Whieldon, and at that time he was experimenting with a new green glaze. Two months after perfecting it, Wedgwood dissolved the partnership and set up on his own to make the new green-colored ware. We found an example of it in the well at Wetherburn's Tavern in Williamsburg and realized that the plate had been shaped on a bat mold previously used to cast white salt-glazed stoneware. However, this green plate's body was not white but the pale yellow of the cream-colored earthenware developed by Enoch Booth around 1740 and thereafter much used by Thomas Whieldon and others. Coloring a salt-glaze plate green was not the extent of Wedgwood's ambition; he saw the green as an ideal background for oil gilding that would impart a hitherto unimagined richness—which it did when first purchased. But once in the hands of a dishwashing scullery maid the gilding began to come off, making the fine new ware appear prematurely old. By 1767, Wedgwood recognized that the gilded green wares were not as popular as he had predicted, and so wrote to his partner Thomas Bentley advocating a novel means of being rid of their unsold stock:

> I am rejoyced to know you have shipp'd off the Green & Gold—May the winds & seas be propitious, and the invaluable Cargo be wafted in safety to their destin'd Market, for the emolument of our American Bretheren & friends, & as this treasure will now no longer be locked up, or lost to the rest of the world, I shall be perfectly easy about the returns, be they much, little, or nothing at all.[56]

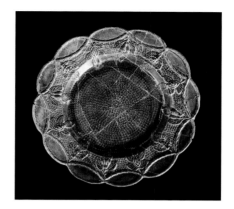

FIGURE IX.32. (*a*) White salt-glazed stoneware plate with fruit and foliage flange design around a deliberately pebbled center. (*b*) A cream-colored earthenware plate of the same bat-molded design but coated with Josiah Wedgwood's fluid green glaze developed in 1759. This latter plate was retrieved (*c*) from the Wetherburn's Tavern well shaft in very small pieces. (*b*) Colonial Williamsburg Foundation.

Josiah Wedgwood evidently had a sharp tongue and a sarcastic wit—which helps to make him something more than a face on a plaque or a name stamped on the bottom of a dish.

Just as white salt glaze had eroded the sales of delftware, so now the cream-colored earthenwares were whittling away at the market for the molded white wares. There is, of course, a considerable difference between marketing and owning. Just as today most homes have an assortment of old crockery that still gets used when no visitors are expected, so it was in the eighteenth century when chip-resistant salt-glaze plates remained in use long after they went out of fashion. While doing research for a book on the history of the supernatural, I came to the chapter dealing with a famous incident known as the Stockwell Ghost. On January 6, 1772, a Mrs. Golding who lived at Stockwell outside London was terrified out of her house by a poltergeist, at which time "the stone plates were falling off the shelf." Although this was an odd place to find a reference to white salt-glazed stonewares, there can be no doubting that those were what fell (or were pushed?) from Mrs. Golding's shelf.[57]

In Williamsburg the 1771 inventory of Anthony Hay (he of the squirrel plates) recorded his possession of "3 doz. white stone plates" worth 10 shillings and "34 do. dishes" valued at 40 shillings. He also owned "38 stone cups and saucers" worth 5 shillings.[58]

FIGURE IX.33. A rare "scratch-blue" decorated salt-glazed stoneware plate turned bluish gray in firing and exhibiting no great skill on the part of the lion tamer. Ca. 1760–1770. Chipstone Collection.

FIGURE IX.34. Examples of Staffordshire salt-glazed stoneware teapots slip cast with scenes showing Admiral Vernon and his victories at Porto Bello (1739) and Fort Chagre (1740): (*a*) all white; and (*b*) a similar body mold to (*a*) but with the details touched in blue, a precursor to the wide use of cobalt to enhance individually decorated white stonewares. Both ca. 1740–1745. Chipstone Collection.

There being nothing more inviting than a blank sheet of paper, the same thought must have occurred to the appliers of brown-slipped rims when presented with expanses of otherwise unadorned whiteware surfaces. It shouldn't surprise us, therefore, that before long someone would be inspired to use the same ferruginous color to paint a bird, add initials, or apply a date — all of which a Staffordshire potter did to one 1723 tankard now in the Stoke-on-Trent Museum. However, to discourage the brown lines from running, the decorator incised much of his pattern into the engobe and then filled those lines with color. A small flask in the British Museum was treated in the same way to inscribe initials and the date 1724. Within the next decade came a phase of applied sprigging, followed quickly by the raised decoration being highlighted in brown. By 1735 someone had suggested that not all customers might like brown as much as they would blue. All those German stoneware imports were decorated in cobalt, so why not do the same for Staffordshire salt glaze? Thus was born the class of white salt glaze that we now know as *scratch blue*.

IF THESE POTS COULD TALK

FIGURE IX.35. White salt-glazed stoneware scratch-blue and relief-decorated tea caddy made for "Mary Coall" by "Thoˢ Proufe September ye 26ᵗʰ 1767." Chipstone Collection.

Blue-decorated white salt glaze is well represented in the Chipstone Collection, which includes an infinitely rare dessert plate decorated in scratch blue with a crowned but possibly inebriated lion (Fig. IX.33). Particularly informative are two slip-cast teapots commemorating Admiral Vernon's Porto Bello victory of 1739, one pot plain white and the other cobalt highlighted. As for desirability, one pays one's money and takes one's choice, although in this instance it was a case of "Penny plain or Twopence colored"(Fig. IX.34).[59]

Among the several other scratch-blue examples in the Chipstone Collection is a relief-molded caddy with as much incuse information as we could ever hope to find. Dated "1767" on one shoulder with the name "Mary Coall" on another, it is marked on the base "Made by Thoˢ Proufe September ye 26ᵗʰ 1767" (Fig. IX.35).[60] The Collection's sole example of the scratch-blue technique is another tea caddy of about 1765 (Fig. IX.36). Some scratch-blue decorating was done with great skill, but more was poorly incised and unevenly blued. Nevertheless, it continued to be made from the late 1740s to about 1775, and in America examples have been found in Revolutionary War contexts.[61]

From the early dipped stage in the evolution of white salt-glazed wares, tavern mugs were a staple of the business, but as the decorating choices evolved from brown to blue, the Staffordshire stoneware potters' emphasis was on scratch-blue tablewares such as pitchers, bowls, teapots, caddies, cups, and saucers. They were content to leave the heavy and coarse ware market to the Germans. That is not to say that the entire chamberpot business was ignored. It wasn't, as the white salt-glazed example in the Collection testifies (Fig. IV.16). In the 1750s, it was still common for china shops to be advertising Dutch stonewares alongside the latest Staffordshire wares and designs. Although it took a long time for English entrepreneurs to realize that they were missing out on major sales opportunities, it was not until the 1760s that Staffordshire potters began to make their own versions of Westerwald stonewares that Audrey and I named *debased scratch-blue,* among them numerous jugs and mugs adorned with sprig-applied profile portraits of George III (Fig. IX.37).[62] The Germans, on

FIGURE IX.36. White salt-glazed stoneware tea caddy with incised scratch-blue decoration. Probably Staffordshire, ca. 1760–1770.

FIGURE IX.37. Typical examples of "debased scratch-blue" white salt-glazed stonewares. (*a*) A Rhenish jug shape with sprigged portrait medallion of George III, and (*b*) a can with an applied crowned GR cipher. Both Staffordshire, ca. 1775–1800.

FIGURE IX.38. Debased scratch-blue white salt-glazed stoneware chamber pots: (*a*) From Wetherburn's Tavern in Williamsburg (ca. 1765–1785), and (*b*) from Alexandria, Virginia, in a context of ca. 1800–1815. (*a*) Colonial Williamsburg Foundation; (*b*) photo: National Museum of American History, Smithsonian Institution/Alexandria Archaeology Museum, City of Alexandria, Virginia.

the other hand, had been content to apply a crowned GR (e.g., Fig. v.21).[63] Perhaps out of deference to the Hanoverian Georges, the Rhineland potters were never so indelicate as to put royal monograms on their exported chamber pots. The English, however, had no such scruples, as an example we excavated in Williamsburg attests (Fig. IX.38 *a*). Others coupled the GR with a portrait of the monarch (Fig. IX.38 *b*), a juxtaposition that continued at least until 1837, when the accession of Queen Victoria was commemorated with a VR and a portrait medallion on a whiteware chamber pot found in Jamaica.[64]

David Gaimster in his seminal work on German stonewares illustrated two English debased scratch-blue mugs and deduced that they were in production for only a short period between 1770 and 1780, but also called attention to the existence of a mug bearing a version of the Great Seal of the United States of America, which was not designed until 1786 (Fig. IX.39). At the other end of the bracket, Gaimster reported that wasters had been found at Burslem in a context of ca. 1760–1770.[65] At least one previous writer had dated this distinctive ware as early as 1750. In 1966 I wrote that from literary sources and archaeological associations, "the group's popularity continued through the period from about 1765 to 1790, with fragments turning up in contexts dating as late as 1820." More than thirty years later I still agree with myself.[66] Sir Arthur Church had said as much as long ago as 1904, when he wrote that at Burslem salt-glazed stoneware production was "said to have lingered on so late as the year 1823."[67]

American newspapers attest to the longevity of white salt-glaze sales, and it is always worth noting how and in what order the wares are listed. Thus, for example, on January 6, 1772, the *New-York Gazette and the Weekly Mercury* advertised "cream colour, stone, Nottingham, delft and other earthen-ware." Cream-colored had been steadily growing in popularity since the 1750s, when Thomas Whieldon and Josiah Wedgwood took their salt-glaze formula of ball clay and flint, fired it to biscuit, and then coated it with a fluid, transparent white- or red-lead glaze before firing it a second time at a lower temperature in a kiln free of salt.[68] Before dipping the biscuit ware in the glaze they spattered it with color, mainly manganese, copper, and antimony. The plates had been shaped on the old salt-glaze bat molds, so it was at first only the color and the shiny glazed surface that were new (Fig. IX.40).[69] Although those novel products gained almost immediate popularity, Wedgwood and others were not about to burn either their boats or their bridges, and through the 1760s they went on hedging their bets by continuing salt-glaze production.

FIGURE IX.39. Debased scratch-blue salt-glazed mug with applied seal of the United States of America. Staffordshire, ca. 1786–1795. Lloyd Hawes Collection, National Museum of American History, Smithsonian Institution.

FIGURE IX.40. (*a*) Front and (*b*) back of a cream-colored earthenware plate with flange in the barley pattern. The front decorated with clouded glazes and the back in tortoiseshell sponging. Staffordshire, ca. 1755–1765.

The big shift came around 1763, when Wedgwood decided that coloring salt-glaze shapes and patterns was no longer the way to go. Perhaps he remembered the success of the first flush of salt-glaze whiteness that hit so hard at the delftware industry; whatever the impetus, Wedgwood decided that clean and decent was to be the vogue of the 1760s. But fashion doesn't generate itself. It has to be pushed and prodded to the fore, and in Josiah's mind there was only one sure-fire style setter, and she was the Queen of England. As Simeon Shaw told it, Wedgwood presented the Queen with a caudle set[70] made from his best cream-colored ware apparently enameled by his two Daniels, Thomas Daniel and Daniel Steele. It seems likely

FIGURE IX.41. Creamware plate in the Queen's shape, with Liverpool, brownish-black transfer print. Staffordshire, ca. 1770–1785.

FIGURE IX.42. Creamware plate in the Royal shape, hand-painted with a Chinese house scene in underglaze blue. Staffordshire, ca. 1770–1780.

that at the time of the presentation, Wedgwood mentioned his eagerness to make her a complete dinner service, and when she accepted, he showed her several possible patterns taken from existing salt-glaze molds. This is an old sales pitch. One asks the Queen *which* she prefers, safe in the knowledge that regal courtesy requires her to make a choice and thus to accept one or other of them. So she chose the rims with panels of seeds known as the *barley pattern*, but said that she didn't like the roughness of it. Wedgwood took that as a royal command. He had the barley motif removed, leaving only the ridges that separated the panels, and this being approved by her Majesty, he called it the *Queen's Pattern* (Fig. IX.41). She then appointed him Potter to her Majesty, and Josiah Wedgwood was well on his way to living happily ever after.

Landing the Queen was a coup that made Wedgwood the envy of Stoke. But he could go one higher. So, as soon as her service was completed and delivered, he slung his hook for the King. The story goes that George III decided that he preferred a service that lacked the old barleycorn rim panels and told Wedgwood to make him one without them. The result was nothing more than a plain plate with a gently voluted rim. One can well imagine the exchange that led to its creation.

Says Wedgwood, "Sire, the Queen's Pattern is the talk of the town. It is only seemly that you, too, should have a pattern of your choice."

King George to his chamberlain, "What's this fellow talkin' about?"

"He's a potter, your Majesty."

"Is he, by God!"

"He made the service for her Majesty, the yellow one," the chamberlain explains .

"Oh, did he? Yellow, you say?"

"Indeed, sire."

"A good color, yellow." Then to Wedgwood, "So what is't you want, my good fellow?"

Wedgwood then explains that the Queen's Service is somewhat on the delicate side. "Perhaps your Majesty would like something a little different, something, shall we say, more robust? Maybe we could take out the partitions and then . . ."

"Good. Take 'em out. An excellent notion. Who's next?"

The audience is over. Wedgwood bows and retreats and never gets to explain his alternative design, and thus is born the *Royal Pattern* that would make Josiah an even bigger household name than before (Fig. IX.42). Wrote Shaw: "Now under Royal Patronage, Mr. W. had as many orders . . . as he could possibly manufacture."[71]

Although all this is usually thought to have occurred in 1763, and was independently so claimed as early as 1804, there is persuasive evidence that royal recognition came later. In June 1765 Wedgwood wrote that he had made a tea service for the royal household because "nobody else wo^d undertake it," which would have been odd if he was already the appointed potter to her Majesty. It was in that year, too, that he wrote about his export trade in whiteware (presumably white salt glaze) but made no mention of the yellow. His first surviving reference to his Queen's Ware dates from the autumn of 1767, when, in a letter to partner Thomas Bentley, he told him that "The demand for the s^d Cream-colour, alias

FIGURE IX.43. Creamware plates with feather-edge rim treatment. (*a*) Hand-painted with a version of the Chinese house pattern in underglaze blue; probably Staffordshire, ca. 1775–1785, tiny impressed seal mark much enlarged. (*b*) Plain creamware with pierced flange decoration; possibly Leeds, ca. 1780–1790.

Queen's Ware, alias Ivory, still increases."[72] Why, one might ask, would Wedgwood have thought it necessary to spell out the names if Bentley had been marketing Queen's Ware for the past three or more years? Furthermore, it was also in 1767 that we read of Josiah's first use of his royal warrant, but not until January of the following year do we hear of his London showrooms displaying the Queen's arms.[73]

The vogue for Queen's Ware (Wedgwood's generic name for his cream-colored ware) prompted many other potters to cash in. In 1770 he observed that there were as many as seventy factories producing it, and named the small town of Bovey Tracey in Devonshire as one of them. In 1968 Audrey and I went there to try to find the factory site, but arrived a few days too late. The remains of what was said to have been a mill related to it had been freshly cleared for new construction, and from the bulldozer tracks we recovered a few fragments of Bovey Tracey creamware of excellent quality.

The Collection's creamware assemblage is not large, but most of the pieces have something to say. The plates include examples of both the Queen's and Royal patterns, as well as the clouded ware usage of the barleycorn panels. There were, however, two more important steps in the evolution of creamware plate design, one of which would outlive its origins and continue throughout the next major phase in Staffordshire dinnerware production. The first, however, had a shorter life span. That was the curving, fronded rim that Wedgwood sold as his *feather edge* (Fig. IX.43 *a* and *b*). By 1773 he had introduced a variant on which, instead of the fronds all going in the same direction around the rim, his *new feather edge plain* had them in panels running both clockwise and counterclockwise (Fig. IX.44).[74]

FIGURE IX.44. Dessert plate in the "new feather edge" that Wedgwood proposed in 1773, the feathers enameled in pale green and the center with a single flower in purple. The combination of a very yellow body and the green enameling prompted us to purchase the plate in the hope that it was one of the then currently popular and sought-after products of the Melbourne Pottery in Derbyshire. And maybe it was. Ca. 1775–1785.

FIGURE IX.45. (*a*) Creamware lobed and pierced fruit bowl, and (*b*) a feather-edged dish for a similar bowl, both pierced in the manner loosely attributed to Leeds but equally likely to have been made in Staffordshire. Ca. 1780–1790.

The Collection's example of the new feather edge was not bought for that feature alone. It was the product of our embracing a new collecting fad—the pursuit of Melbourne. The name had nothing to do with the land of the kangaroo, but identified a small Derbyshire village where a kiln site had been discovered by a student looking for an iron-working site. The Melbourne factory had been in production from the early 1760s to about 1785, producing a deep yellow creamware, predominantly feather edged and often enameled in green and purple. Published by creamware authority Donald Towner in 1969, the discovery soon had archaeologists examining each feather frond on our creamware shards in the hopes of matching the arrangement of those on fragments from the Melbourne site.[75] The Collection's plate fitted the deep yellow requirement as well as being enameled in green and purple, but its new feather edge border was not paralleled among the designs illustrated by Towner. However, Towner noted that the excavated shards came from an area of only about 20 square feet and that many more still awaited discovery. The absence of a factory mark on any of the recovered fragments, or, indeed, on any of the complete examples Towner had tracked down, left Melbourne (and our plate) as something of a cipher.

Regardless of its source, the rarity of the new feather is proof enough that it was no great success. In 1783, Messrs. Hartley, Greens & Co., of Leeds in Yorkshire, offered four plate designs, namely *Queen's, Feather, Shell Edge,* and *Royal,* in that order. The Leeds Pottery was renowned for its use of lace-like piercing that made the plates, dishes, and fruit baskets appear much lighter than they are (Fig. IX.45), but although that connection stems from marked examples, it does not follow that all pierced but unmarked pieces should necessarily be attributed to Leeds. On the contrary, they were made elsewhere in Yorkshire as well as Staffordshire factories. All that can safely be said of most examples is that they are of late date, having been produced through the 1780s into the 1790s.

FIGURE IX.46. (*a*) Rim detail from a good-quality creamware dish decorated in the plain shell-edged pattern first produced by Wedgwood as a forerunner of the blue-edged pearlwares so common at the close of the eighteenth century. Impressed NEALE & Co. of Hanley, Staffordshire, 1778–1786. Found on the island of St. Eustatius. Ca. 1775–1790. (*b*) The mark made legible through computer enhancement.

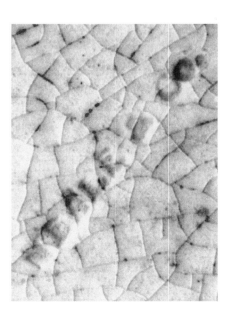

The same is true of Wedgwood's fourth creamware plate design, with its principal characteristic a cockled or bivalve-shaped edge (as in a cockle mollusc) highlighted by inwardly scored, shell-suggestive striations. It is evident that he intended the shell-edged rim to be additionally decorated, and in several instances he referred to the use of gilding. However, the only gilded example I have ever found turned up on a beach at the island of St. Eustatius in the Netherlands West Indies, evidence perhaps of Wedgwood's supposed belief that he should send his choicest and most expensive wares to the islands.[76] A pit exposed in an eroding cliff on the same Island yielded another shell-edged fragment that shows the rim treatment at its best, and on the basis of quality and color one might be tempted to attribute it to Wedgwood and to a date between 1775 and 1785 (Fig. IX.46). Wrong again! A faintly impressed mark (legible only as the result of computer-generated enhancement) reads "NEALE & Co," of Hanley in Staffordshire, a company in business under that name between 1778 and 1786.

Although as much as nine tenths of all creamware found in Williamsburg excavations has been undecorated, that ratio is by no means reflected in private and museum collections, where virtually every piece has some kind of ornamentation. The most common are in Queen's, feather, and Royal shapes decorated with black transfer printing applied, not in Wedgwood's own factory, but at the plant operated by John Sadler and Guy Green of Liverpool.[77]

The art of transfer printing on enamels has been attributed to a short-lived factory at Battersea (1753–1756) where it was developed by Robert Hancock under the auspices of Alderman Sir Theodore Jannsen. After the business failed in 1756, Hancock is believed to have gone first to the new Chelsea porcelain factory and thence to Worcester, where he eventually became a partner. At about the same time when Battersea was in production, Sadler and Green independently perfected the art of printing on delftware tiles and reputedly were able to turn out 1,200 in six hours. One of their least common prints on a delft tile was bought by Audrey in London with a view to proposing its use as the design for menus and the like in one of Colonial Williamsburg's tavern restaurants (Fig. IX.47 *a*). She was then chairman of the Foundation's tavern furnishings and food committee, making it a safe bet that her proposal would be adopted. And it was. The well-fed cook of the sepia-printed tile now adorns both the menus and the hanging outdoor sign at Shields Tavern.[78] This tile is known as "The English Cook" and was paired with another, "The French Cook," featuring an emaciated and frog-eating French chef, together a satire on food shortages in France during the Seven Years' War (1754–1763). However, once the war came to an end with the Treaty of Paris, it is surprising that any tile buyer would have cared enough to embellish his or her salon with so outdated a comparison.[79]

The same engraved prints that Sadler and Green applied to their delft and creamware tiles were often used to decorate the centers of creamware dinner plates, and "The Punch Party" is one of them (Fig. IX.48). Anthony

FIGURE IX.47. (*a*) Liverpool delftware tile transfer printed by Sadler and Green in black and sepia depicting "The English Cook." The rococo border is identified as the figure-eight type by virtue of its centrally placed side elements. Audrey bought this tile and used its central motif as precedent for the sign outside Shields Tavern (*b*) in Williamsburg, Virginia. Ca. 1765–1775.

FIGURE IX.48. Feather-edged creamware plate with black transfer print known as "The Punch Party," paralleled on a contemporary Liverpool tile with the same figure-eight border as Fig. IX.47 *a*. Staffordshire, ca. 1770–1780.

FIGURE IX.49. "Liverpool birds" transfer printed on a black-rimmed, augmented shell-edged creamware dessert plate. The paired-leaf flange ornament became common on early pearlware dessert plates (see Fig. X.6). Staffordshire, ca. 1780–1790.

Ray in his published paper "Liverpool Printed Tiles," which illustrated all but three of the 312 known designs, classified this one by its rococo border featuring figure-eight links on either side, and considered it among the late examples of the Sadler and Green partnership that ended upon Sadler's 1770 retirement.[80] On the Collection's creamware plate, the punch party is without the tile's date-defining border, and being unmarked, it offers no proof that it was one of those biscuit pieces that Wedgwood sent to Liverpool to be decorated and then returned to him to be glazed and fired again.

Among the most common of black transfers used on creamware dinner services were groups of pheasants and other birds, some standing and usually another in flight (Fig. IX.49). Because they were (a) printed in Liverpool and (b) birds, it is usual and, I might add, reasonable to call these designs "Liverpool birds." However, they should not be confused with the *liver bird* of Liverpool, a long-legged wader that was chosen in 1688 to feature in the heraldic arms of that city and that is sometimes considered to be the source of a metal, mold-applied bird that appears on dry-bodied redwares of the third quarter of the eighteenth century (Fig. IX.50). The Liverpool birds appear in miniature on a child's tea bowl in tandem with a much more interesting black print of a man and an elegantly dressed young woman passing a dolphin-supported fountain (Fig. IX.51). What makes this little print of above average interest is that it was borrowed and

FIGURE IX.50. Dry-bodied redware coffee pot with metal-mold applied example of the so-called Liver bird (detailed) along with its chinoiserie figures and rococo borders. There is a pseudo-Chinese stamp on the base in the manner of the redware teapots previously imported along with China tea. Staffordshire, ca. 1765–1775.

FIGURE IX.51. Miniature creamware tea bowl transfer printed in black with Liverpool birds on one side, and on the other a design adapted from a print by Robert Hancock while working for the Worcester porcelain factory. Staffordshire, ca. 1780–1790.

adapted from the same scene on Worcester porcelain, the engraving signed "R. Hancock fecit." Hancock was a principal engraver for the Worcester factory from ca. 1757 to 1775.

We look at prints on creamware dishes and on delftware tiles and delight in their elegance or their portrayal of folksy country life. They speak to us of times long past, so we rarely stop to think of them in their place in the age for which they were made. The punch party scene would equate with a twenty-first-century dinner plate printed with a photo image of a group of beer swilling good ol' boys watching football on TV. Then again, the naked cupids on a creamware can of the 1790s (Fig. IX.52) can be likened

FIGURE IX.52. Small creamware can with a transfer print in sepia titled "Cupids at Play." Staffordshire, ca. 1790–1800.

FIGURE IX.53. (*a*) Oil-gilded creamware saucer and (*b*) tea bowl bearing the name "Anne Boucant Page," with the saucer demonstrating the impermanence of overglaze gilding. Staffordshire, ca. 1770–1780.

FIGURE IX.54. Creamware (*a*) tea bowl, (*b*) saucer, (*c*) milk pitcher, and (*d*) slop basin enameled in the "blowsy rose" motif popular in the period ca. 1775–1790. Staffordshire or Yorkshire.

to a pedophilic coffee mug printed with pictures of nude children. Remembering the Sadler and Green tile with its figure of a cook, we might wonder, how many of us would want to surround our fireplace with tile pictures of Martha Stewart or Julia Child in their kitchens?

Printed decoration was by no means the only popular means of enriching eighteenth-century creamware, and the Collection deliberately included a range of them—beginning with the least successful, namely, the previously discussed oil gilding (Fig. IX.53). A plain creamware tea bowl and saucer had been gilded with the name "Anne Boucant Page" and was bought in Bath, not so much as an example of gilding but because the name Page had a good Virginia ring to it—as we well knew, having excavated at the aforementioned Rosewell in Gloucester County, the home of

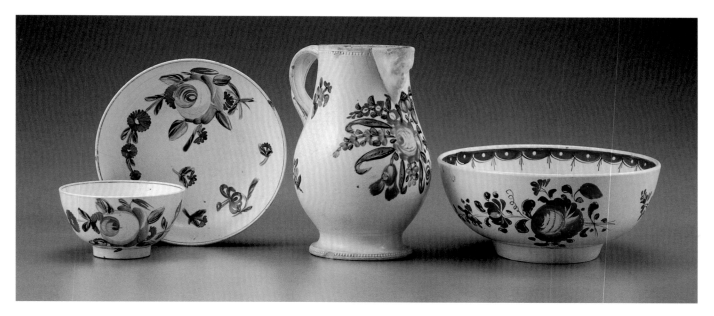

IF THESE POTS COULD TALK

FIGURE IX.55. Creamware sugar bowl with handle terminals attributable to Leeds and on which traces of black enameling survive. The lid is believed to be a fugitive from a coffee pot. Staffordshire, ca. 1775–1790.

that distinguished colonial family.[81] The gilding on the tea bowl survives better than it does on the saucer, which suffered from constant contact with the bowl's foot ring.

Much more durable, and for that reason more common, than gilding on creamware was overglaze enameling.[82] Once again the word *common* is misleading, as the undecorated ware represents at least nine tenths of all creamware found in Williamsburg excavations. Museums and collectors, on the other hand, focus on the ornamental wares of which the so-called "blowsy rose" painted in purple, red, green, and black is the most ubiquitous, a floral style usually, though not necessarily, associated with Leeds (Fig. IX.54). On occasion the colors were not as securely anchored as they should be. A small Leeds sugar bowl in the Collection retains only traces of black detailing around the handle terminals (Fig. IX.55). This "not as was" bowl had been paired with a lid that almost certainly came from a creamware coffee pot![83] Second only to the "blowsy rose" tea services are cylindrical teapots whose painters added yellow to the palette and generally show a red house flanked by Chinese-Chippendale style fences (Fig. IX.56 *a*). A good example was found in Williamsburg in 1955 and described by me in 1969 as being "in the style of David Rhodes of Liverpool, about 1765," which, I am ashamed to confess, is sheer nonsense! (Fig. IX.56 *b*).[84] Rhodes had been a partner in a Leeds enameling shop as early as 1760, at which time he advertised as follows:

FIGURE IX.56. (*a*) Creamware teapot in a style attributed to David Rhodes who worked for Josiah Wedgwood from 1769 to 1779. (*b*) A close parallel excavated on the Ravenscroft site in Williamsburg, Virginia. Staffordshire, ca. 1775–1785. (*b*) Colonial Williamsburg Foundation.

ENAMEL AND BURN IN GOLD AND COLOUR, FOREIGN AND ENGLISH CHINA, and match broken setts of enamel'd or Burnt-in China and Tea Ware, and make them complete to any pattern required—either Indian or Dresden. . . . They likewise enamel Stoneware, which they sell as cheap as in Staffordshire.[85]

Rhodes served as a decorator for Leeds products until he was hired away in 1769 by Wedgwood, for whom he worked until his death nine years later.[86]

It is clear that Leeds was a major player in the northern England ceramics industry by the early 1760s, but it took another fifteen years or so before the Yorkshire potters posed a serious threat to Wedgwood and his Staffordshire competitors. In 1783, the Hartley, Greens & Co's Leeds Pottery put out its first catalog offering its wares "Enamel'd Printed or Ornamented with Gold to any Pattern; also with Coats of Arms, Cyphers, Landscapes, &c. &c."[87] Neither the "blowsy rose" pieces in the Collection nor the Rhodes-style painted teapot are works of art, and they do not give a fair impression of the pot painters' skill, but they are representative of the kinds of tea wares used by the middle classes and rise one notch above the plain, unadorned creamwares.

One has only to thumb through a few English ceramics auction catalogs to get a better idea of the vast range of creamwares, which were far more diverse in shape and decoration than the few pieces in the Collection. Nevertheless, it does boast a few worthy pieces, among them a fine tankard of about 1780, painted with vertical panels of marbling in alternating maroon and brown (Fig. IX.57). On the front are four lines that remain as apt and topical today as they were when the mug was made:

Come drink a pot
w^t me kind friend
And tell me when,
the times will mend.

FIGURE IX.57. (*a*) Creamware tankard decorated with marbleized vertical panels around a melancholy message in verse. (*b*) Inside, a dark brown frog smiles up at the drinker. (*c*) The mug's handle terminals point to its Leeds origin. Ca. 1775–1785.

IF THESE POTS COULD TALK

Another tankard, almost certainly by the same hand, substituted a stag-hunting scene for the glum couplet. Both mugs have the same handle terminals, and it is this feature that draws us step by step to the drum-roll denouement. Both are products of the Leeds Pottery. The establishing steps are these: The handles match another on a different shaped mug in the Temple Newsam Museum, one decorated with a black transfer print titled "Love & Obedience."[88] By itself, of course, that tells us nothing; but there is more. In lettering so small as to be barely discernible, the print's copper plate was engraved LEEDS POTTERY. Both marbleized mugs have another detail in common: Each has a brown frog or toad at the bottom that becomes visible just before the drinker drains the last of his beer.[89] One might imagine that there once were many more such mugs, but that most got thrown aside and broken by the surprised toper. The frog-in-your-mug joke, like puzzle jugs, was another of the jolly japes played in taverns for the amusement of the eighteenth century's not-so-bright yokels. With that said, however, it does seem odd that so much decorative effort should be expended on these handsome tankards only to have them destined for usage best served by more durable brown stonewares.

The frog tankard particularly appealed to Audrey, I suppose because she had been a reptile fancier from early childhood, a fascination she explained in her book *My Family of Reptiles*.[90] She was also a dog lover and planned to make a collection of early dog collars—alas, a collection that never got beyond its first purchase. Nevertheless, one of the creamware

FIGURE IX.58. A miniature Dalmatian waits in its kennel, wakeful and ready for the hunt. Creamware and pearlware "fairings" were popular souvenirs of a day's escape from the simplicity and hardships of rural life. Staffordshire, ca. 1780–1810.

items that she bought for the Collection was a model of a Dalmatian puppy curled up in its kennel wearing a yellow (brass?) collar (Fig. IX.58). Of all the 400 or so pieces in the Collection, this little creamware kennel speaks to her gentleness, her goodness, and her love for all those creatures great and small—save for the previously mentioned earthworms, which for some unknown reason terrified her. Audrey was a very special person, and I confess that I am unable to look long at this little toy without a tightness in my throat and a slight misting of my eyeglasses.

I cannot stress more forcefully or more often that our collecting had far less to do with ceramic technology or economic history than it did with that intangible commodity we called "people stuff," the magic that visitors to historic places sense when they look through the very window that Thomas Jefferson stood at as he pondered the future of Monticello, or leave their cars to listen for the echo of the guns across the silent fields of Gettysburg. For us, this is what collecting, history, and archaeology are all about. However, the story of the Collection does not end with creamware and a Dalmatian in his (her?) kennel. We still, as they say, have a ways to go.

X   When the Public Eye Is Pall'd

There's a joy without canker or cark,
There's a pleasure eternally new,
'Tis to gloat on the glaze and the mark
Of china that's ancient and blue.

Andrew Lang (1844–1912)

FROM THE DAYS of John Dwight in Fulham onward to the willow pattern on truck-stop diners' blue-plate specials, the Anglo-American taste for chinoiserie has persisted, although never stronger than in the eighteenth century when it influenced the makers of everything from furniture, textiles, and fences, to wallpaper, screens, silver, and ceramics. Minor poet James Cawthorn wrote this in 1756:

> On ev'ry shelf a Joss divinely stares,
> Nymphs laid on chintzes sprawl upon our chairs;
> While o'er our cabinets Confucius nods,
> Midst porcelain elephants and China gods.[1]

From the early arrival of kraak porcelain in the sixteenth century, Portuguese, Dutch, and English potters strove to reproduce its underglaze blue designs, first on delftware and later on the porcelains of Bow, Chelsea, Worcester, and the rest. Underglaze blue painting on creamware was an inevitable step, although the result bore no resemblance to the whiteness and translucence of porcelain. Two examples in the Collection exemplify the most common designs, one long known to American collectors as the "Long Eliza" pattern[2] and the other that Audrey dubbed the "Chinese TV house" with its flanking Chinese-Chippendale fences. The former's principal feature is an elongated Chinese woman or man holding a parasol either walking toward or away from a house flanked by rocks and a willow tree (Fig. X.1).[3] The Collection's example is finely painted in underglaze blue on a Royal Pattern dinner plate that we bought very cheaply because, as the dealer confessed, it was dirty on the back. She was right. The plate wasn't clean on its underside; but what she didn't know was that we would gladly have payed several times the asking price *because* of that shortcoming.

FIGURE X.1. (*a*) Obverse and (*b*) reverse of a creamware plate in the Royal pattern painted in underglaze blue with a pleasingly conceived version of the *dame au parasol* motif that includes a Chinese building, willow tree, "hairy" rocks, and fence. Making this plate of above average interest is the fact that its back touched the front of another already pounced with the basic design and thereby transferred some of the color to itself. The result provides a rare demonstration of the degree to which a design differed in its free-hand details from one plate to the next. Staffordshire, ca. 1775–1785.

FIGURE X.2. Feather-edged creamware plate underglaze painted with the "Chinese TV house" and willow design. Staffordshire, ca. 1775–1785.

The back of the plate carries a mirror image of the Long Eliza pattern that we at first thought had been acquired through some volatilizing process in firing that lifted the image from the next plate down in the sagger. This would have required a brief time in which the pattern was in ghostly suspension before anchoring itself to the underside of our plate — which, of course, was impossible. The correct explanation was that while the biscuit-fired plates were in the painting shop, our plate was put down upon another before its cobalt paint was dry. As biscuit wares are highly absorbent, the color transferred and remained there when our plate was dipped in the lead glaze and fired. Making this anomaly of particular interest is the fact that it shows the extent to which the hand painting was guided by a pounced pattern and therefore was virtually identical from one plate to another. At the same time, the plate demonstrates how each differed in small details that were not dictated by the pouncing paper's charcoal-dotted outline. In this case the differences relate to plants sprouting from the rock as well as variations in the tree's foliage. The lesson one learns from this Long Eliza plate is simple but important: One should be wary of trying to read something major into minor design differences.[4]

Our second exercise in underglaze blue chinoiserie decorates a plate with a sharply molded Old Feather Edge rim (Fig. x.2). In the center we have the house with its aerial flanked by a willow tree, a disproportionately large flower, and the mandatory fences. Another version graces a mug whose profile and handle owe much to white salt-glazed stoneware tankards

FIGURE X.3. Creamware mug in a white salt-glaze shape, underglaze painted with a complex version of the Chinese house pattern. Staffordshire, ca. 1775–1785.

of the mid-eighteenth century, suggesting that this creamware example dates fairly early in the history of the Chinese house design (Fig. X.3). As we shall see, the motif was destined to become the principal decoration for English pottery through the closing decades of the century.

A much more striking creamware mug consciously and carefully pretends to be what it is not, a pretense so successful that an old collector's label on the bottom reads "Portobello Pottery" (Fig. X.4). To understand why, I need to digress long enough to explain what was meant by that identification.

Just as the last survivors of a jingoistic generation had a British victory to be proud of at the end of the Falkland Islands' War,[5] so in 1739, England made much of her capture of the Spanish American city of Porto Bello (Fig. IX.34). Suffice it to say that several locations in Britain named themselves Portobello, one of them a village near Edinburgh in Scotland. There, between ca. 1786 and 1796, two brothers appropriately named Scott acquired a factory that may then have been as much as ten years old. In it they produced a redware on which they transfer printed oriental scenes in yellow. To give their jugs a clean interior appropriate for milk dispensers, they coated them with white slip, and it is this combination of white slip, red body, and yellow-printed brown exterior that came to be known as Portobello Ware (Fig. X.5). As so often happens among experts, their conclusions do not always dovetail, leaving novices to pick the one whose book they happen to own. Thus, for example, Bernard and Therle Hughes, who for many years were *Country Life* magazine's experts on everything, wrote that the Portobello factory made "cream-coloured earthenwares from about 1770 under the proprietorship of Scott Brothers"—which puts them in business sixteen years earlier than have other writers.[6] Furthermore, the Hugheses seem to have been alone in declaring that the brothers made cream-colored earthenware.

With that background sketched in, the testimony of the Collection's tankard makes a little more sense. For want of a better term, it can be called an example of "mock" or "reverse" Portobello Ware. Using a finely potted cream-colored body, the potter had no need to coat the interior with white slip, but he did have to apply a brown coating to the outside on which to print the yellow chinoiserie design that we see on real Portobello Ware. This is one of those chicken or egg situations. If the Scott Brothers were the originators of the red-bodied ware and did not begin making it until 1786, where did the creamware potter get his prototype? I would be hard pressed to see the Collection's mug dating any later than 1785, and as it has the same Leeds handle terminals found on the "Come drink a pot" tankard (Fig. IX.57), both are likely to be of the same 1775–1785 period, thus predating the Scott brothers in Scotland. The Hugheses were wrong in putting them there in 1770, of that there can be no doubt, but were they also wrong in saying that cream-colored wares were made at Portobello in that decade? If not, could the tankard's "Portobello Pottery" label be correct?

FIGURE X.4. Creamware mug in imitation of Portobello ware (Fig. X.5), or perhaps the other way around. The mug is iron slipped to receive the yellow transfer print, but required no interior engobe to enhance the cleanliness of the ware. Staffordshire or Yorkshire, ca. 1780–1790.

FIGURE X.5. Portobello redware milk pitcher, the interior coated with a white engobe and the exterior transfer printed with a chinoiserie "willos-style" print in yellow. Scotland, ca. 1790-1810.

But then again, if that factory made such fine products in creamware, why in the world would it abandon them in favor of the much cruder transfer-decorated redware? The explanation that best fits the evidence seems to be that the latter was in production at Portobello before the arrival of the Scott brothers and that a designer at Leeds liked the idea and improved on it.

There is, however, another clue that does more to muddy than clarify. This is the blue transfer-printed band around the interior lip of the Collection's tankard. Pseudo-Chinese in style, the design incorporates what appears to be a spread-winged moth, a combination paralleled on another important piece in the Collection dated 1802.[7] However, the latter's principal motif is a partially developed willow pattern and so much later in style than the very individualistic oriental buildings portrayed on the tankard. One would like to be able to state that in the light of all these clues one can unequivocally pin down the origin and date of this Portobello-ish tankard. Indeed, you may be wondering why, if I don't know the answer, I've spent all this time laying out evidence that gets me nowhere. But to that question I do have a firm and categorical answer: The exercise provides another example of the kind of thinking that goes into the study of any enigmatic piece. It forces us to look past the impact of the whole to scrutinize its parts and to demonstrate that *thinking* that something is so is not necessarily the same as knowing it.

Even the revered Josiah Wedgwood could be wrong, and he was in his estimation of the popularity of the last great leap forward in the evolution of eighteenth-century earthenwares. Like others among his contemporaries, and beginning ca. 1765, Wedgwood made numerous experiments to perfect a whitened creamware, the product of which he dubbed *Pearl White*, but having done so he doubted the worth of producing it. Writing to partner Thomas Bentley on July 2, 1770, he said this:

FIGURE X.6. A pair of augmented shell-edged pearlware dessert plates painted underglaze in "Long Eliza" style but with differing "aerials." Staffordshire, ca. 1790–1810.

I have given over the thoughts of making any other colour but Queen's ware. The white ware would be a great deal dearer, & I apprehend not much better liked; and the Queen's ware, while it continues to sell, is quite as much business as I can manage.

Nine years later Wedgwood was still vacillating, not only about the marketability of a new whitened ware, but also whether by inclusion of Cornish china clay it might develop into porcelain and thereby cause him to be charged with infringing the porcelain patent held by Richard Champion of Bristol. On August 6, 1779, in another revealing letter to Bentley, Wedgwood wrote:

Your idea of the creamcolour having the merit of an original, & the pearl white being consider'd as an imitation of some of the blue & white fabriques, either earthenware or porcelain is perfectly right. . . . But you know what Lady Dartmouth told us, that she & her friends were tired of creamcolour, & so they would of Angels if they were shewn for sale in every chandlers shop through the town. The pearl white must be considered as a change rather than an improvement, & I must have something ready to succeed it when the public eye is pall'd.[8]

But the public eye was in no hurry to pall; instead, pearlware would dominate the genteel earthenware market until 1813, when Charles James Mason took out a patent to make his "Ironstone China."

Substantial evidence exists to indicate that just as cream-colored earthenware had been produced by other potters as early as the 1740s—long before Wedgwood came out with his Queen's Ware—so they had been working to get away from the yellow before he announced his Pearl White. Ceramic historian George Miller has pointed out that although creamware was more often than not undecorated and so required a generic name by which to identify it, pearlware rarely, if ever, was marketed without decoration, be it as minimal as a blue or green band around its shell-notched edges. Consequently, dealers knew that customers would readily recognize "a parcel of blue and green edge ware" as the bluish-white crockery that wasn't yellow, and so they had no need to identify it by the body color.[9]

Although Josiah Wedgwood is often seen as the forefather of modern marketing, neither he nor his Staffordshire and Yorkshire competitors were about to risk discontinuing products that had hitherto proved lucrative. Just as they had continued to produce white salt glaze alongside the new creamware, now they hedged their bets once again. Two plates that Audrey and I called *augmented shell edge* (Fig. x.6) illustrate that fact, being derived from molds intended for creamware[10] but used to shape pearlware hand-painted with a masculine version of the Long Eliza motif.[11]

The Long Eliza design came in several varieties but was no numerical match for the Chinese house (with or without TV aerial) and is represented

FIGURE X.7. (*a*) Tea caddy, (*b*) coffee pot with rococo spout, and (*c*) miniature teapot, all in pearlware and decorated with variations on the Chinese house design. (*a*) Staffordshire, ca. 1780–1790; (*b*) possibly Leeds, ca. 1785–1800; (*c*) Staffordshire, ca. 1790–1800.

FIGURE X.8. Pearlware teapot painted underglaze with the Chinese house design, and with twisted handles having Leeds-style floral terminals, ca. 1780–1795.

in the Collection by several examples ranging from a miniature teapot, through plates, a tea caddy, bowls, a fruit stand (Figs. X.7 and X.8), to a large oval dish whose interest is much enhanced by its similarity to another shown on the trade card of Bristol potters Joseph Ring and Henry Carter and attributed to a date between 1793 and 1810 (Fig. X.9). Carter became Ring's partner in 1793, joining an already existing manufactory specializing in creamware—as another trade card attests (Fig. X.10). The card is of interest in that it shows a lone potter at work, helped by a boy wheel driver and a girl clay preparator. This folksy-appearing operation cannot, however, be seen as the measure of Ring and Carter's business, for they were major exporters to the United States and the Caribbean.[12]

FIGURE X.9. (*a*) A fine oval serving dish in shell-edged pearlware painted in underglaze blue with the Chinese house pattern, the building here shifted to a secondary role left of center. (*b*) A similar dish shown on a trade card published by the Bristol Pottery of Messrs. Ring & Carter, ca. 1793–1813. Print source: Geoffrey Godden.

An example of that trade is provided by a saucer fragment recovered amid the reefs of Bermuda, albeit in an alleged context 200 years too early! Reporting on a wreck of 1594 that yielded Bermuda's famed "Tucker Treasure," the Smithsonian Institution's Mendel Peterson noted that "a particularly interesting find was a fragment of Japanese porcelain," adding that "ware of this kind will have come into Spanish possession as a result of Dutch trading via Manilla, Acapulco and Vera Cruz."[13] That would have been a much more exciting and evocative route to Bermuda in 1594 than the one that the saucer actually followed. It most likely set out around 1790 from Burslem in Staffordshire, via Liverpool and maybe Cork, to

FIGURE X.10. Another Ring & Carter trade card, this one showing a lone potter at work with two juvenile asistants, and by no means representative of the Bristol Pottery's manufacturing scope and capability. Ca. 1800.

Hamilton, Bermuda, there to become just another pearlware shard with its blue-painted Chinese house pattern. What it was doing in its alleged association with the treasure galleon is anybody's guess.

The Chinese house design is far less common in polychrome than in plain underglaze blue, but when it does occur the treatment is usually less heavy-handed. That certainly is true of the Collection's sole example (Fig. X.11). Possibly a Leeds product, this so-called loving cup is painted in orange, yellow, blue, and brown, a palette akin to those used to decorate the slip-cast hollow wares loosely described as *Pratt Ware,* which were most popular at the end of the eighteenth and beginning of the nineteenth centuries. Double-handled cups like ours were made both in cream and pearl wares.

In some instances, particularly in the last years of creamware production, it can be difficult to distinguish creamware from pearlware. The answer is almost always to be found on the inside of foot rings or at any sharp angle (such as the fold of a chamber pot rim) where the glaze has pooled. On creamware the thickened glaze appears a greenish yellow, whereas on pearlware it is blue. The plate and platter rim form of choice

FIGURE X.11. Pearlware loving cup with underglaze polychromatic version of the Chinese house pattern. Staffordshire, ca. 1795.

FIGURE X.12. Basic blue shell-edged pearlware plates. (*a*) Dessert plate impressed TURNER 5, a product of John and William Turner's factory at Lane End, Longport, that closed in 1806. (*b*) Dinner plate with pebbled surfaces, suggesting that it may have been fired in an old salt-glaze kiln, impressed ENOCH WOOD & SONS, BURSLEM. Post-1818. See rim details in Fig. X.13.

for virtually all pearlware potters was the cockled and notched shell edge, and it came predominantly blue painted, less frequently in green, and rarely in manganese purple (Fig. x.12). The presence here of these plates serves as a never-too-often repeatable reminder that the vast majority of ceramics, were they of salt glaze, creamware, or pearl, were no more embellished than were these unashamedly pearl white plates. I admit, however, that had not the name TURNER been stamped into the back of the smaller of the two, and that of ENOCH WOOD & SONS BURSLEM into the larger, we would not have bought either. The first provided us with another archaeological date—a *terminus ante quem*, a date before 1806 when John and William Turner's Lane End factory closed. The Wood stamp, on the other hand, gives us a *terminus post quem*, a date after July 1818 when Enoch and his sons began to use that mark. They would continue using it until 1848, a year far removed from the manufacture date of this pearlware plate, which was unlikely to have been made any later than 1825.

Although most shell-edged pearlware plates appear superficially the same, in reality not all bat molds were identical, and the Turner and Wood plates are good examples, demonstrating as they do that the edging is divided into panels linked by ornamental devices that are significantly different (Fig. x.13). The Staffordshire potters' choice of shell edge in preference to feather is likely to have been due to two factors: (1) it was newer

FIGURE x.13. Rim details from the Turner and Enoch Wood plates (Fig. x.12), (*a*) prior to 1806, and (*b*) between 1818 and 1846, together demonstrating that in pearlware the worst is not necessarily the latest.

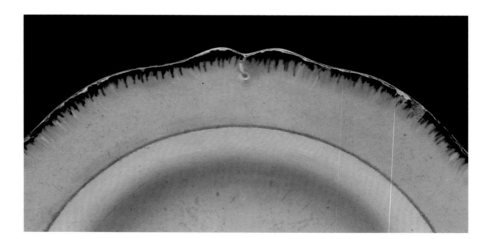

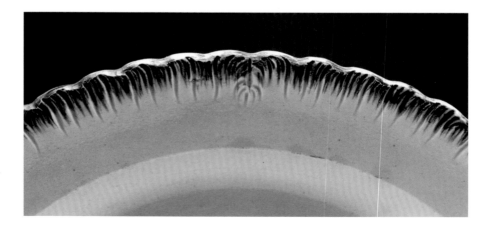

FIGURE X.14. Blue shell-edged pearlware sauceboat dish delicately painted in underglaze blue. Staffordshire, ca. 1785–1800.

and therefore more fashionable, and (2) it was infinitely easier to paint, there being no raised feather fronds to hamper brushwork or to create pockets where the color could pool in unsightly blobs. In the early and best periods of pearlware plate production the painter drew out her brush toward the edge, thereby reflecting the deepening shell notching as it reached the rim (Fig. x.14).[14] By the turn of the century, pearlware was everywhere. I even found shards of it amid the ruins of the great Ancient Egyptian temple at Edfu (Fig. x.15). But as worldwide demand increased, so did production, and so, too, did corner cutting. In place of the countless delicately applied brush strokes to color plate rims, the blue and green were applied with a single, lateral stroke as the bisque plate rotated on a slow wheel.[15] The result was a stripe around the rim in place of the feathery effect of the multiple strokes.

FIGURE X.15. An unlikely place to find pearlware shards: the temple of Horus at Edfu in Egypt, completed in 57 B.C.

As the eighteenth century neared its end and mass production aimed at worldwide markets replaced the handy-dandy small-output local potter, so hand painting gave way to mechanical decoration achieved on lathes and by simple wheel-engendered banding whose products have come to be known as *annular wares* and are found both in creamware and pearlware.[16] Much more significant was the widespread substitution of transfer printing to replace hand painting, a technique that, as we have seen, developed in the mid-eighteenth century among porcelain decorators and quickly spread to Liverpool for relatively unskilled application to fireplace tiles and creamware.

Transfer printing on good quality pearlware is represented in the Collection by a pair of cup plates decorated with pastoral scenes in black (Fig. x.16) and by another that pandered to the age's psychological need

FIGURE X.16. A pair of blue shell-edged pearlware cup plates with pastoral transfer prints in black. Staffordshire, ca. 1795–1810.

to make much ado about mourning (Fig. X.17). Two women in funereal veils are shown leaving a chapel, a scene embraced between doleful lines from Thomas Moore's *Odes and Other Poems,* first published in 1806. They read:

> Oh! breathe not his name, let it sleep in the shade.
>   Sad, silent & dark, be the tears that we shed,
>   As the night-dew that falls on the grass o'er his head!

That Moore's poem wasn't published until 1806 is the kind of information that archaeologists embrace with uncommon ardor, for to them (I used to say *us*) the ability to answer the "when" question can be the difference between success and failure. Let me reiterate. It makes no difference whether we are excavating a tel in Syria or a colonial house site in Virginia, the overlying ground is composed of soil layers that must be pealed away in the reverse order—last down, first out. You may remember that the most recent artifact found in each stratum provides a date after which it was laid down or disturbed. Only rarely do we find a coin or other artifact marked with its date of manufacture. However, like Thomas Moore's lines on a pearlware plate, every artifact, be it a shard of earthenware, glass, or whatever, possesses a date of birth to be recognized if we have the knowledge to do so. As a rule, the best we can manage is to come close—hence those abbreviated *circas* that so often precede a specific year.

For me, as director of archaeology for Colonial Williamsburg, learning in which layer we should expect to find creamware would provide an impor-

FIGURE X.17. Blue shell-edged pearlware cup plate printed with a melancholy moment in underglaze blue; the scene is embellished with lines by poet Thomas Moore. Staffordshire, ca. 1810.

IF THESE POTS COULD TALK

tant clue to aid in recognizing domestic activity in the years immediately prior to the American Revolution. The *Virginia Gazette*'s first reference to its being offered for sale was in 1769. Knowing that direct trade with Britain was curtailed during the 1776–1781 war years, and knowing, too, that pearlware was becoming popular during that period, it became of paramount importance to us to know whether the discovery of its fragments assured us that we were digging in the United States or could still be in colonial Virginia.

From the start of creamware production, newspaper advertisers had known how to describe it, not only for the benefit of their customers but also for the archaeologists who would be digging up their trash two centuries later. Either it was cream-colored or it was Queen's Ware. Thus, for example, in 1772 New York, "Davies and Minnitt at their Glass, China and Earthen-Ware Store" announced that they had just imported "a great variety of gilt and plain cream colour'd ware, red china tea pots and flower pots, china bowls and cups and saucers of all sorts, with a usual assortment of cream, aggitt, delf, black and white stoneware, and crates of flat and hollow ware for country consumption."[17]

That Messrs. Davies and Minnitt were still offering delftware in 1772 is a reminder that in spite of the increasingly damaging inroads into the delftware potters' business from white salt glaze, creamware, and the imminent dominance of pearlware, the old wheels kept turning, albeit to less and less purpose as their craftsmen vainly tried to emulate the new designs. The Collection's sole example of English delftware's last hurrah is a plate whose edge, though not cockled, is blue-brushed to resemble the shell-edge of the new pearlware (Fig. X.18). The rest of the decoration includes a somewhat limp peony, and a Chinese-inspired willow tree with an oddly geometrically shaped trunk that cannot make up its mind whether to grow inside or outside a fence and so settles for both. Dating for these pseudo-shell-edged plates is usually, and rightly, put in the decade 1780–1790. Several are decorated with a picture of Italian balloonist Vincenzo Lunardi, taking off from London's Artillery Ground in September 1785, thereby offering a convincing median date for the Collection's portrayal of a sorry end to a more than 200-year-old English ceramic tradition.[18]

One might argue, though not with much conviction, that in the mid-1780s pearlware was only beginning to capture the earthenware market and that the delftware potters still had a sufficient share of the trade to keep their kilns fired. By April 1786, New Yorkers who were prepared to let bygones be bygones could choose from "A large and general assortment of plain, enameled and blue and white earthenware." But was it pearlware? The description could just as well be of delftware. Two years earlier in England, china and glass dealer William Absolon of Yarmouth advertised that he had recently returned from London "with a large quantity of foreign and Salopian China, as well as some Blue and Green-edge Table services of two Sorts."[19] There could be no doubting that this was pearlware and that in 1784 it was available wholesale in London. The big

FIGURE X.18. Simulated blue shell-edged pearlware plate in late English delftware. Lambeth, ca. 1780–1790.

unanswered question was whether pearlware was available in sufficient quantities and at such attractive prices that it could have found its way to America before the 1781 surrender at Yorktown.

Direct ceramic trade from Britain, as I have already noted, was halted during the war years. But the key word is *direct*, for there were at least two ways in which it could reach her obstreperous colonies: in military baggage, or through a back door held open by devious Dutchmen. I was made aware of the military connection in 1966 when word reached Edward Alexander, Colonial Williamsburg's vice-president for research, that archaeologists digging at the site of the French and English fort at Michilimackinac in Michigan were finding "a Williamsburg on the frontier." I was duly dispatched to examine this surprising discovery and quickly realized that it wasn't surprising at all. It was true that good-quality ceramic shards matching others found in Virginia were being unearthed, but a 1750s Whieldon-style cream-colored teapot was just that—a teapot. Any officer who signed on for service in North America and wanted to bring one with him would almost certainly have bought the same kind that a genteel Williamsburg family would have wanted.[20] More to the point, fashionable ceramics bought in England would have been likely to have reached Michilimackinac *before* they were available in Williamsburg. Although a soldier bound for Michigan via New York would have arrived at his destination in about three months, in Williamsburg planters were reliant on the sale of their season's tobacco for credit, with which their English agents purchased requested supplies. But when, as factor William Norton said of John Page of Rosewell's crop, a large part "was dry rotten, perish'd and stunk like a dunghill and is not worth a farthing pr cwt,"[21] orders for goods in the latest fashion would go unfilled. Even if the tobacco did sell, the ceramic shipment could take at least twice as long as it would take a soldier to get from London to Michigan. Was it possible, therefore, that pearlware could have been reaching America before the war ended?

Evidence that it might have comes from the writing and digging of two members of the New-York Historical Society who, beginning in the 1880s, devoted much time and effort to unearthing artifacts from Revolutionary War military sites in the Manhattan Island area. William Louis Calver and his cohort Reginald Pelham Bolton were amateur archaeologists who began with an interest in the "Red Man" and then shifted to the White when they ran into debris from his forts. In the book that brought together a series of articles on their findings, Bolton contributed one on "Porcelain, Pottery and Glass Cast Away by the Soldiery in the War of Independence," and in it noted that "The familiar 'crinkled-edge' ware, colored green or blue, is a common accompaniment of camp débris."[22] One is naturally wary of archaeologists whose book is titled *History with Pick and Shovel* and not helped by murky black-and-white photographs of the pottery being described. But if Calver and Bolton's Revolutionary War collection does include pearlware shards, and if the last of the sites was vacated in 1783 and never reoccupied, then the arrival of pearlware in America has a *terminus ante quem*—a date before which it was discarded. Unfortunately, whacking away with pick and shovel is not an ideal means of separating the detritus of one occupation from another or even for being sure that there was no return to the site in the decades after the last British soldier sailed home. However, that suspicion has more recently been refuted by the discovery of pearlware shards on two Revolutionary War sites both reportedly abandoned in 1783.[23]

The second means of ceramics reaching the British American colonies was by neutral carriers, primarily the Dutch, who wisely stayed out of the war until 1781. Their West Indian island of St. Eustatius so profited from contraband business with the American colonies, particularly their Dutch brethren in New York, that this speck in the ocean came to be known as the Golden or Diamond Rock (Fig. x.19 *a*). When Audrey and I knew it in the 1960s and early 1970s, it had two guest houses, one run

FIGURE X.19. (*a*) The Caribbean island of St. Eustatius ca. 1775. (*b*) An engine-turned, lead-glazed redware coffee pot of similar date but still in use there in 1972.

by the Netherlands government and riddled with roaches, and the other, the Almond Tree Inn, roach free and hosted by two very engaging New Yorkers. Orange Town, the island's only settlement, stood on two levels, the Lower Town along the strand of the island's harbor, and the Upper Town atop the cliff and dominated by Fort Orange. The latter had its place in American history as having been the first to fire a salute welcoming the rebels' "Grand Union Flag" as it fluttered from the mizzen-mast of the brigantine *Andrew Doria* when she dropped anchor on November 16, 1776.[24]

Shortly before our first visit, much of the ruined Lower Town had been bulldozed as prelude to an ill-starred attempt to build harbor's-edge casinos. Artifacts were everywhere, from cannon to eighteenth-century wine bottles and masses of potsherds, most of them creamware, but with some good-quality pearlware mixed in. But as all this material had been wrenched from its archaeological contexts by the mechanical graders, we had no way of dating it. So plentiful were potsherds that in laying the modern concrete roadways in the Upper Town, numerous eighteenth-century ceramic fragments had been mixed into the cement like geological fossils. A local historian who had picked up shards from the Lower Town was anxious for us to comment on them. While doing so, we spotted an elegant engine-turned and brown-glazed, redware coffee pot similar to a teapot in the Collection (Fig. x.19 *b*). Though dating from ca. 1765–1780, the coffee pot stood on a tray amid several modern bottles and jugs. When I asked about it, the owner answered, "That? It's been in our family since way back. We use it all the time." Needless to say, we urged him to treat his ceramic treasure with more care. To our eyes, it confirmed Wedgwood's assertion that he and other traders found their most receptive markets among the rich planters of the Caribbean Islands. It was highly likely that if pearlware was reaching Statia on Dutch ships, it would have quickly been shipped on to the embattled British colonies.

Over a period of about twelve years, Audrey and I spent our vacations on different Caribbean islands doing our best to understand the range of English, Dutch, and French ceramics in use there in the seventeenth and eighteenth centuries. In 1969 we paid our only visit to St. Lucia, and while there spent a good deal of time on a narrow boot-shaped and uninhabited outcrop called Pigeon Island that lies only a few hundred yards from the mother island and was then reachable on foot at low tide across a silt-built

FIGURE X.20. (*a*) The shard-strewn scree below the high peak of Pigeon Island, St. Lucia. (*b*) The island seen across Gros Islet Bay in 1968.

isthmus (Fig. x.20 *b*).[25] On that northern end of Pigeon Island the ground rose steeply to a high bluff and to a ruined fort offering a commanding view of the Caribbean toward the French-held island of Martinique. The old fort retained several roofless, stone-walled buildings, and beyond them, cascading down the undergrowth-wrapped scarp to the sea, were more creamware and pearlware shards than we had ever seen: annular wares,

IF THESE POTS COULD TALK

mocha, creamware by the bucket; printed pearlwares, most of it blue but some in polychrome. There were cups, bowls, saucers, plates, milk jugs, crockery of every description left there by two generations of British naval garrisons (Fig. X.20 *a*). We were in pot heaven!

In the shallow lagoon between Pigeon Island and mainland St. Lucia the water was glassy clear, and snorkeling along peering at the bottom I could see more and more potsherds and bottle fragments glistening in the sunlight, for this was where Lord Rodney's British fleet rode at anchor in December 1780, waiting for orders to launch an attack on the French and Dutch whose ships rode so tantalizingly untouchable in Statia's neutral harbor. Snorkeling along hour after hour with the cool water caressing my shoulders was an experience I would never forget—the rays of the sun through the shallow film of water fried my back so thoroughly that it peeled away in bleeding strips and forced me to spend our last vacation days face down on my hotel bed.

The pre-agony enjoyment of imagining the English fleet riding on that blue-green water would prove to be the genesis of a fascination with Admiral Rodney, who in the 1780s became the most memorialized hero in the history of British ceramics and eventually a major focus of our pearlware collecting. Alas, no dating emerged from our days of exploring Pigeon Island. The pottery was jumbled together, having been tossed out of the fort over a period of ten or twenty years and subsequently pushed about by root growth and the activities of countless crabs.

If we were to learn the date when pearlware could first have reached the doomed British American colonies, we would have to find the documentation on dated pieces, specifically the earliest recorded example. We knew that what then passed for this benchmark was to be seen in the Victoria and Albert Museum, where a large pearlware jug bore an inscription that read "A. Butcher A.D. 1777." But we didn't believe it. The name and date was applied in overglaze black lettering and could have been added at any time, perhaps recalling a birthday or a wedding anniversary.

Since questioning the testimony of the Butcher jug as Audrey and I did in 1969, another pearlware jug proffered an even earlier date. The inscription reads: "Tidmarsh's Original Staffordshire Warehouse N 1775." What could be more conclusive, one might ask? It certainly was convincing enough for George Miller to declare the Tidmarsh jug to be "the earliest known example of China Glaze."[26] But, as they say in states south of Virginia, "wait just a cotton-pickin' minute!" If the Butcher jug is suspect, so too is the Tidmarsh evidence!

Consider the wording of the inscription: "Tidmarsh's Original Staffordshire Warehouse." We can deduce that *warehouse* identified a place where wares were housed and sold. It also meant that the business traded in wares not of its own manufacture, as Staffordshire was synonymous with all the products of that region. So why the word *Original?* The implication is that the Tidmarsh warehouse had the distinction of being well established, indeed, sufficiently so for longevity to have a degree of marketing

FIGURE X.21. (*b*) A massive whitened pearlware loving cup with "ear" handles, black printed with birds; and made for Thomas and Sarah Cook ostensibly in 1772, but in reality a retrospective inscription. (*a*) Detail of the central interior print known as "The Archery Lesson." Perhaps Liverpool, ca. 1795–1805.

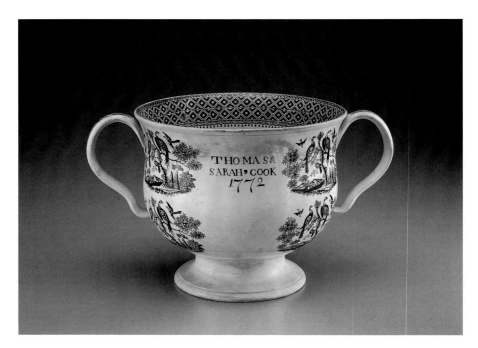

kudos. It was not unusual then (as today) for merchants to trade on it by proclaiming their age on their signboards and newspaper ads.

It remains a still-popular male historian's fallacy (or chauvinist wishful thinking) that most eighteenth-century businesses were run by men, and we are wont to think this way until proved wrong. Tidmarsh was actually Miss (or Mrs.) Margaret Tidmarsh, who in 1792 was listed as a "Potter and Glass-seller" of 123 Rosemary Lane near the Tower of London. Two of her relatives were also entered as potters, Joseph working at the other end of Rosemary Lane (No. 4) and another Joseph over the river on the Bankside in Southwark.[27] Members of the family had been in the potting trade in Cobridge in Staffordshire after moving there in the mid-century, having previously been London pewterers. All in all, therefore, it is as reasonable to argue that the Tidmarsh jug was retro-dated to proclaim the longevity of Margaret's warehouse as it is to assert that it was made in 1775.

With all that said, however, rejecting positive evidence simply because it fails to fit one's preconceived beliefs is a dangerous road to follow. Evidence is evidence unless and until you can prove otherwise. It turned out, however, that we could—at least we *thought* we could.

A Sotheby's catalog for a 1974 ceramics sale described a large pearlware loving cup, transfer-printed in black and inscribed "Thomas & Sarah Cook 1772." This was the evidence we had been waiting for! Five years earlier than the Butcher jug, it now made the authenticity of the latter's overglaze inscription of no importance. I asked London ceramics dealer John May to bid on our behalf, and the day after the sale he called to say that we had been successful. The earliest known dated piece of pearlware was ours! Several weeks later it arrived (Fig. X.21 *b*). It *was* pearlware, but a disappointingly anemic version that looked more like the whitewares that were to overtake pearlware in the 1820s. Nevertheless, it really was dated

1772. Around the outside were printed cartouches of Liverpoolish birds reminiscent of printing on Worcester and Caughley porcelain, and around the inside of the rim a familiar diapered transfer print that we would have expected to find in the *last* years of the eighteenth century. But this was not the key piece of dating evidence. In the center of the interior was another underglaze black print depicting two women wearing Empire-style clothing with feathers in their hats, being instructed in the art of archery by a man standing behind them (Fig. x.21 *a*). A well-known print, it is usually identified as the *Toxopholites* or *The Archery Lesson* and is to be seen in another medium on a tankard of John Turner's cane or bamboo ware that has a silver-mounted rim bearing the London date letter for 1794. Ceramic historian Minnie Holdaway illustrated the same transfer, albeit printed in brown, and noted that it is to be found in Ralph Wedgwood's *Ferrybridge Shape and Pattern Book,* which she dated between 1798 and 1801.[28]

The evidence against the validity of the loving cup's 1772 date seemed overwhelming. And there was more. Prominent among Audrey's acquisitions was a group of printed and polychrome enameled teaware that featured three figures commemorating the cessation of hostilities between Britain and France temporarily cemented by the Treaty of Amiens on March 27, 1802 (Fig. x.22).[29] Against the same checkerboard background as

FIGURE X.22. Pearlware (*a*) tea bowl, (*b*) saucer, (*c*) milk jug, (*d*) slop basin and its interior (*e*), and (*f*) teapot, underglaze transfer printed in brown and overglaze painted in blue and orange, a combination sometimes referred to as *Salopian.* The designs celebrate the Peace of Amiens in 1802. Staffordshire, 1802–1805.

FIGURE X.23. A matching, polychrome-decorated "Pax" tea bowl found in Alexandria, Virginia, in a context of ca. 1802–1810. Photo courtesy of Richard Muzzrole.

the loving cup's archers are a standing Victory holding a palm frond, next to her Britannia with her shield, and seated at right the female representation of France holding a staff topped by the Liberty Cap that epitomized the French Revolution. Inside the slop basin is a composition comprised of Britannia's shield, a medieval lance, and a palm frond. Together, all these elements were designed to laud Britain's supposed victory over her centuries-old enemy across the Channel. That was not an outcome likely to have found any favor in the fledgling United States, whose help from the French had made so much else possible. It is remarkable, therefore, that a "Pax" tea bowl identical to the example in the Collection was found in an excavation in Alexandria, Virginia (Fig. X.23). Nor was this the sole Anglophilic relic to be found in the 1970s excavations—as we shall reveal in a later chapter.

The "Pax" services and their variants became the standard tea-table ware of early-nineteenth-century families that could not afford porcelain and before the availability of competitively priced bone china. A tea bowl and saucer in the Collection reminds us that in the days before parents had to put up with the racket of guitars and bongo drums from upstairs, and before we had to suffer through "Here's another one of the duck" slide shows, families, friends, and neighbors endured the vocal and instrumental talents of their siblings (Fig. X.24). Equally laid back in their "visuals"

FIGURE X.24. Pearlware (*a*) tea bowl and (*b*) saucer with underglaze black print and overglaze enameling in red, green, and yellow. The "pluck, toot, and chortle" design differs from the more common political and martial motifs in being reminiscent of music as a family pastime.

were tea services decorated with the upliftingly righteous "Three Graces," the Misses Faith, Hope, and Charity, who adorn several more of the Collection's tea bowls and their saucers (Fig. X.25). Faith sits looking faithful as Hope prepares to whack her with an olive twig while Charity goes off with the wine and the Wheaties. Considering their admirable virtues, all three are rather negligently attired.

In poses closely reminiscent of the Graces, albeit more conservatively clothed, another Peace of Amiens–related design is represented in the Collection by an underglaze blue printed, pearlware dessert plate (Fig. X.26). There the trio approaches a seated Britainnia; the first bestows a victor's laurel wreath, the second holds a long rod topped with a Liberty cap, while the third seems distracted by something or someone off the edge of the plate. In each hand she holds an object that may be a trumpet but that at first sight resembles one of those spinning dinner plates that clever but ultimately boring Chinese acrobats hoist on bamboo canes. The plate is stamped IH, the mark of Joshua Heath of Hanley in Staffordshire, who reportedly was working there from 1770 to ca. 1800.[30] However, this Treaty of Amiens plate evidently pushes the *circa* on by two or three years.[31]

In the light of all that, it is safe to conclude that the "Thomas & Sarah Cook 1772" loving cup was actually made at some time between 1795 and 1810. If the cup commemorated the Cooks' twenty-fifth wedding anniversary, an addition of those years would put the manufacture date at 1797, which fits remarkably well within the brackets suggested by all the ancillary evidence.

After being presented with so tortuous an answer, you may well have forgotten the original question. It asked whether the overglaze date of 1777 on the Victoria and Albert Museum's "Butcher" jug could have been retrospective and therefore irrelevant to our quest for the earliest dated piece of pearlware. As the Cook cup proved, the answer was yes. Neither it nor the jug had anything useful to say — other than a warning that when dated pots look too good to be true, they probably are.[32]

With those red herrings out of the way, our search for the earliest legitimate date on pearlware went on. Our first acquisition was a half-pint can decorated with a transfer print in dark blue showing milkmaids with tubs on their heads, a scene borrowed from a design on Worcester porcelain

FIGURE X.25. Pearlware tea bowls and saucers printed in underglaze black and highlighted in overglaze green. The design is known as "The Three Graces" and was contemporary with the "Pax" series (Fig. X.22). Staffordshire, ca. 1800–1810.

FIGURE X.26. Pearlware dessert plate printed with the "Pax" design in underglaze blue. Impressed IH, which is believed to be the mark of Joshua Heath of Hanley and previously attributed to ca. 1800. The design that includes the figure of Victory and the breach of a cannon clearly relates to 1802 and thereafter. The central "Pax" design also occurs on a saucer attributed to Ralph Wedgwood of Ferrybridge between 1798 and 1801, again a year or two too early.

FIGURE X.27. A transfer-printed pearl-ware can, underglaze initialed and dated R C 1793. The milkmaids and haystall design was derived from a Worcester porcelain print by Robert Hancock attributed to ca. 1759. Staffordshire.

FIGURE X.28. (*a*) Front and (*b*) back of a pearlware loving cup made for Ralph Vernon, albeit misspelled, but with the 1780 beneath the glaze. This is among the earliest known dated examples of English pearlware. Staffordshire.

and there signed RH for Robert Hancock and attributed to ca. 1759 (Fig. X.27). However, our can was thirty-four years younger and painted with the initials R*C over 1793. Next came a standard loving cup dated 1787, and finally another marked "Ralph Vernon 1780." As with the others, we found it in the Portobello Road antiques market and have no reason to doubt that it was made for Mr. Vernon on the given date, thereby making it the earliest dated example of pearlware yet recorded (Fig. X.28). Nothing about it hoists a warning flag—and yet . . .

If the Cooks' giant loving cup is proved to have been made (not reglazed) to recall a twenty-fifth wedding anniversary, what is there to prove that the Vernon cup is not another such memento? The shape differs hardly at all from our second purchase, the loving cup of 1787. Who is to say, therefore, that the 1780 cup was not made for an adult, but to re-call the birthday of a ten-year-old Ralph Vernon? That possibility gains some credence when one notices that the "L" in Ralph had run in the firing and that the painter had misspelled the name as "Venon" and had to stick the missing "r" in over the top. All in all, it wasn't much of a gift and prob-ably should have been tossed onto the waster heap. Did it survive because the potter decided that it was "good enough for a kid"?

You may have noticed that I skipped quickly past the 1787 cup. I did so, not because it had no evidentiary place in the dating search, but because it had something astonishing to say in its own right. Audrey saw it on an open stall in the street-side section of the Portobello market where jostling crowds made reaching to examine anything difficult, even hazardous. The cup was chipped and cracked; its floral ornament was pretty standard for the period, and in spite of its dedication to "James & Lydia Vickers 1787," we decided to leave it unexamined (Fig. X.29). But just as we were about to move on, a break in the crowd left the stall reachable, so I changed my mind, leaned across the assorted bric-a-brac, picked up the cup, and turned it around. What I saw painted on the back was one of the greatest surprises in half a century of collecting. It had to be the work of an eigh-teenth-century Picasso! To the right stood an extraordinary creature that

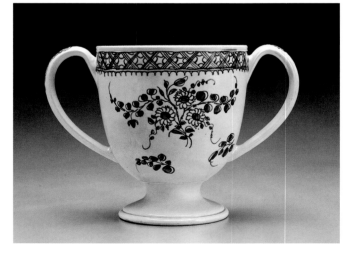

IF THESE POTS COULD TALK

looked like a pile of grass-sprouting rocks turned sideways. Its head had two eyes, and a huge slit for a mouth, and below it a torso with one female breast and a hairy posterior that seemed to be sitting atop an equally hairy rock. In front of her (it?) was a stand of three plants that might have been papyrus, and to the left of them a disk with a knob on top and stilt-like legs, that looked for all the world like a UFO buff's rendering of a spaceship. The scene seemed totally out of character for any eighteenth-century creamware or pearlware decoration. Indeed, it remains so today. What, we have wondered, must James and Lydia have thought when they received their cup? The front gave no hint of what they were to find when they looked at the back. Were they amused, appalled, puzzled, insulted? I liked to think that James and Lydia Vickers had had an extraterrestrial experience and wanted to preserve a record of what they had seen on a memorable day in 1787. It never occurred to me that the design might have been borrowed from another ceramic medium.

We visit museums, make notes, buy catalogs, and learn all we can about specimens on public show, and on that basis we draw our parallels and arrive at our attributions and dates. But those resources are a mere tip of a ceramic iceberg ever ready to sink us. We have only to skim through the auction catalogs of Sotheby's, Christie's, or Phillips to realize that significant objects are constantly rising to the surface only to disappear into someone's collection and may not be seen again for twenty or thirty years. Most collectors squirrel their acquisitions away and have no desire to write about them. Indeed, they are reluctant to let the world know that their collections exist, for fear that they may attract the attention of a nocturnal visitor wearing a black mask, striped jersey, and a sack labeled SWAG. Not until the collector dies and his executors need to dispose of all that "stuff" does it come to be cataloged, published, and auctioned. Some catalogs are handsome volumes, color illustrated and costly to produce—in the hope that sales will outrun the investment. But many of the past's ceramic treasures never receive that level of attention. Sold in local auction galleries by operators who must describe everything from an apple

FIGURE X.29. (*a*) Front and (*b*) back of James and Lydia Vickers's extraordinary loving cup. Hand painted in underglaze blue and dated 1787, the conventional frontal garlands did not prepare us for the Picasso-like Martian on the back. It turned out, however, that our interpretation was not shared by collectors of mid-eighteenth-century Worcester porcelains, who had prosaically named it the "windswept rock" motif. We preferred to see the much later loving cup as commemorating James and Lydia's 1787 extraterrestrial experience. Staffordshire or Leeds.

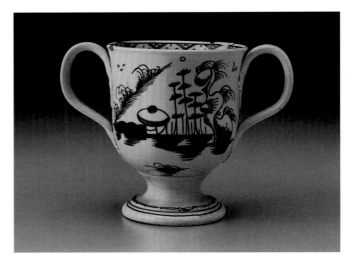

FIGURE X.30. Longton Hall porcelain sauce boat with underglaze-painted "windswept" motif, the design source for the 1787 Vickers's loving cup of Fig. x.29. Ca. 1755. Chipstone Collection.

peeler to a zither, a rare Astbury teapot may merit no more than: "Lot 431. A nice old red pottery teapot with lid, some chipping," in a catalog devoid of illustration and quickly run off on a Xerox machine.

Even if a coffee cup, tea bowl, and saucer were described in more detail, I am certain its relevance to my interests would have gone unrecognized:

> Each piece of plain shape, the cup with double scroll handle, painted in blue with the so-called 'Wind-swept' pattern of a hut by a rock and sketchily drawn plants on an island, a flock of birds in distance (chips to coffee cup and footrim of saucer) (3)   £300–350[33]

The auction catalog of the famed and revered English porcelain collector Dr. Bernard Watney was describing a Longton Hall porcelain version of my extraterrestrial visitation, made more than a quarter of a century earlier (Fig. x.30).[34] My spaceship had been downgraded to a hut and even my one-eyed, single-breasted Martianess had been mistaken (surely?) for a windswept rock!

Bernard Watney was the leading authority on the Longton Hall porcelain factory in Staffordshire, which began production around 1750 to make "a certain porcelain ware in imitation of china ware." Started by one William Jenkinson, it soon took in several partners, among them William Littler (of "Littler's blue" fame), Aaron Wedgwood, and a button maker named Samuel Firmin—whose later military buttons I was to find in the Thames mud. Why any of these men should have been inspired to supervise the production of the "so-called Wind-swept" pattern remains, for me, at least, a closed book. But so, too, does the reason for its being used to decorate the Vickers's pearlware loving cup in 1787. But if all question marks were eliminated in favor of periods, gone, too, would be the fun of collecting and the thrill of the chase.

IF THESE POTS COULD TALK

XI No Wind in the Willows

Turn, turn, my wheel! 'Tis nature's plan

The child should grow into the man . . .

The willow pattern that we knew,

In childhood, with its bridge of blue.

Henry Wadsworth Longfellow, 1878

AUDREY AND I had begun to study pearlware in the early 1960s when our excavations in Williamsburg were yielding quantities of shards about which we knew all too little. It quickly became apparent that we were not alone. Few ceramic authorities of the time had much to say about it, and one was left with the impression that it was no more than an insignificant variant along the road to better wares. One authority wrote that it was introduced by Wedgwood "about 1779 and adopted by several early nineteenth-century manufacturers," but added that "Queen's ware may be regarded as the staple earthenware of the period 1770–1830."[1] Another said that pearlware "was soon eclipsed by the kind of ware made by Spode and his followers."[2] Yet another thought it a bit more popular than the others had suggested, saying that it was "Made by Josiah Wedgwood in 1779 and in the early 19th century by many imitators."[3] Had these English authorities dug with us in Williamsburg, their suspicion would have grown that in the last twenty years of the eighteenth century, pearlware was much more common than they had suggested. If its breakage ratio was a valid archaeological guideline, by 1790 it was outcracking creamware by a measurable margin. In the early 1970s the Smithsonian Institution's self-trained Richard Muzzrole was excavating trash-filled wells and privy pits in Alexandria, Virginia. Dick was then the National Museum's sole historical archaeologist and had to rely on volunteers to help him dig down into silt and mud whose original components are best left to the reader's imagination. From these dumps he recovered prodigious quantities of imported pearl and other wares and in a multitude of hand-painted, printed, and later stenciled designs. Dick Muzzrole was destined to become one of the forgotten pioneers from the early days of American historical archaeology. Under sometimes dangerous and always filthy conditions,

FIGURE XI.1. Urban archaeology can be a dirty business, as Smithsonian archaeologist Richard Muzzrole knew in 1972 as he emerged from an early-nineteenth-century privy in Alexandria. Photo courtesy of Richard Muzzrole.

he opened our eyes to the range of ceramics in use in urban Virginia in the first half of the nineteenth century (Fig. XI.1). Unfortunately, his labors included trekking his privy dirt through the spotless halls and corridors of the National Museum, a trail that eventually convinced the powers-that-were to withdraw the museum's support for Muzzrole and his labors — but not before he had made a major contribution to the history of domestic pottery in Federal-era America.[4]

As with most ceramic wares in every period from Roman Samian to Dutch delft, the quality of pearlware declined as new products jostled for sales supremacy. Like Longfellow's poem about a little girl with a curl in the middle of her forehead, when pearlware was good "it was very, very

FIGURE XI.2. Pearlware at its worst. Condiment bottles from a cruet. Ca. 1800–1820.

IF THESE POTS COULD TALK

good, but when it was bad it was horrid."⁵ At the horrid end of the Collection's pearlware spectrum is the already discussed and truly awful Cook
loving cup as well as a couple of cruet bottles whose glaze has been fractured in attempts to clear their salt-clogged pouring holes (Fig. XI.2). The
very, very good, on the other hand, is represented by a polychrome-
decorated can featuring a wheat sheaf and the tools of the farmer's craft
(Fig. XI.3). Amid all the useful wares, this was Audrey's favorite acquisition, not only for the quality of its painting but also for the extreme thinness of the potting that made it as light as a handful of feathers. Between
those extremes are enough examples in the Collection to suggest the
breadth of the pearl body's usage and to remind us that the factories' designers and engravers were forever looking beyond their European neighbors to the Orient for designs to compete with porcelain's ever-fashionable
pagodas, bridges, and assorted mandarins.

Chinese porcelain exported to Europe in the mid-eighteenth century
often included tea bowls and matching saucers coated externally with a
brown slip and known in the contemporary trade as *Batavia* Ware on the
assumption that they were all first shipped from Canton to Batavia in the

FIGURE XI.3. Pearlware at its best.
Three views of a can of quite incredible
thinness painted with the tools and a
product of the harvest. Ca. 1780–1790.

FIGURE XI.4. "Batavian" Chinese export
porcelain (*a*) tea bowl and (*b*) saucer
from the wreck of the *Geldermalsen*, 1752.

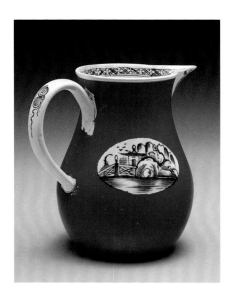

Dutch East Indies (Fig. XI.4). Most were plain brown slipped before firing, but some had reserves exposing the white background onto which were painted simple foliate patterns, sometimes in underglaze blue and at others with overglaze peony and suchlike floral and arboreal designs. In 1985, salvage diver Michael Hatcher found the wreck of the previously discussed *Geldermalsen* that sank in 1752, and from it salvaged approximately 150,000 items of porcelain from teapots to chamber pots. The Batavian brown tea bowls and saucers were so numerous that some were sold by Christie's in Amsterdam in lots of a thousand. With so much Chinese porcelain arriving in Europe in the mid-eighteenth century, it was only to be expected that English pearlware potters would try their hand at the Batavian style in which the porcelain's inherent translucence was obscured by the brown slip. The Collection's "Batavian" pitcher in pearlware is by no means a stellar example of the genre, but it is a relatively rare manifestation of it (Fig. XI.5). Before the reddish-brown slip was applied, the junctions for the yet-to-be-affixed handle were covered, in the same way that reserves were created for the decorative cartouches on the sides. Unfortunately, the handle did not precisely fit the prepared spaces and in consequence uneven patches of the pearl body spread out around it. Further minimizing the jug's aesthetic appeal is its lack of a foot so that it appears to squat rather than stand. Nevertheless, it provides yet another example of the late-eighteenth-century English taste for anything Chinese.

The second pearlware problem piece is a well-potted tankard decorated with an elaborately Anglicized version of the standard willow pattern—of which much more anon. Where the oriental-style willow print features a pagoda, this mug has a castle; a European stone bridge substitutes for the lightweight Chinese version, and the people crossing it are not fleeing Chinese but Europeans with, perhaps, the revealing inclusion of a woman carrying produce on her head (Fig. XI.6). The trees and boats, too, owe their origins to the basic willow pattern. Around the foot in black is an inscription that reads "Greenea hill Chappel." Several highly detailed gazetteers of the British Isles, both old and new, failed to identify Greenea hill—nor could I find any reference to it in the West Indies.[6] Why the West Indies? Because the woman on the bridge appears to be black; there are palm trees in the background, and the building in the distance looks more like a Caribbean "Great House" than it does an English Georgian mansion. Then, too, there has been my gut feeling that the name had a West Indian ring to it. I am well aware that intestinal sensations are about as reliable as Madam Zelda's crystal ball, but this one had been felt for so long that it just might have been correct—until I was writing this sentence. Only then did it dawn on me that the clue is to be found in the spelling of Chapel with two "p"s. All of us who have puzzled over this tankard have assumed that the person writing the name was spelling impaired. But when you think about it, beer mugs and Methodist chapels don't exactly go together! Was it possible, therefore, that Chappel was not a house of worship but a place in the vicinity of Greenea hill? A quick return to the gazetteers listed five places named Chapel in the British Isles, one of them in the county of Essex near Colchester cited as being "spelt Chappel." That seemed to clinch it. However, the exclamation of joy dried in my throat when I consulted another gazetteer and found a rural district in Derbyshire with the French-sounding name of Chapel en le Frith. The French for chapel being chapelle, it is not hard to imagine that the first written Anglicization came out as chappel. The Derbyshire district was divided into at least twenty-three parishes, with two of their names ending in hill, and one named Green. As Derbyshire became an important pottery county in the eighteenth and nineteenth centuries, it seems more reasonable to argue that the tankard was made for a relatively local someone living at Greenea Hill near Chappel.

I realize that only in school exams are math students required to show the workings that led to their answers, but in laying out the route that led me to Chapel en le Frith, I wanted to demonstrate how one can look at a ceramic object for years without recognizing the clue that has been staring one in the face all along.

The Greenea hill mug and its pastiche of the oriental willow pattern leads into an enormous range of blue, transfer-printed, pseudo-oriental designs that so often erroneously go by that name. Some authorities, such as Christie's cataloger of the *Geldermalsen*'s cargo, have called anything with a willow tree in its design a "willow pattern." That cataloger's usage extended to a variety of subspecies that included a fenced pine, the pine and bamboo, the blue pine, the latticed fence, or the scholar on bridge patterns. When, however, all these elements turn up on the same plate, clearly visualizable nomenclature becomes a problem.

Thomas Minton, who had been apprenticed to Thomas Turner of Caughley and later worked for Josiah Spode as an engraver, has been credited with designing the *English willow pattern*. Drawing on numerous examples of *Geldermalsen*-type porcelain designs, he is said to have arrived at a cluster of pagodas or temples, a bridge with people on it, a distant kiosk or pavilion, a couple of boats, doves in the air, and an assortment of trees dominated by the willow. An old Staffordshire ditty hooked them all together:

> Two pigeons flying high,
> Chinese vessels sailing by:
> Weeping willows hanging o'er,
> Bridge with three men, if not four:
> Chinese temples, there they stand,
> Seem to take up all the land:
> Apple trees with apples on,
> A pretty fence to end my Song.[7]

Minton's creation of the willow pattern design followed Spode's 1784 development of a reliable and quick method of blue transfer printing on earthenwares, at first almost certainly on pearlware.[8] Minton had previously

FIGURE XI.6. Two views of a pearlware tankard printed with an elaborately Europeanized version of a Chinese landscape, inscribed "Greenea hill Chappel" painted in overglaze black. Staffordshire, ca. 1810.

FIGURE XI.7. The more-or-less standard "willow pattern," its solid areas printed in stipple. Staffordshire, ca. 1825–1840.

been employed as an engraver in Spode's London warehouse, but moved to Staffordshire in 1788 or 1789, and it was there, and at that time, that the willow pattern was born (Fig. XI.7). The design was quickly followed by virtually every other blue-printing factory, using plates engraved by designers not necessarily in the users' employment. Because the majority of early willow style plates are unmarked, it is rarely possible to say that this was made here or that one there. By 1849, however, the design elements had become sufficiently standardized to prompt someone to weave a story around them and to publish it in a periodical suitable for the eyes of genteel young ladies called *The Family Friend*. As a result, the story of the flight of Koong-se and her lover Chang from the house of her tyrannical father has become so associated with Minton's design that some people have believed that the legend inspired the pattern and not the other way around.[9]

Messrs. Mankowitz and Haggar, discussing the willow pattern in their pottery encyclopedia, noted that "Dated examples are rare: a plate with this design in Hanley Museum, Stoke-on-Trent is lettered THOMASINE WILLEY 1818."[10] That statement gives importance to the Collection's only dated example of the modified, bridgeless, willow design (Fig. XI.8), there printed in black with the names POCOCK AND ALLEN and dated 1802. Then,

FIGURE XI.8. Two views of a pearlware beer pitcher printed with an oriental scene somewhat akin to the "willow pattern" featuring "staple-roofed" pagodas. Inscribed in overglaze black with the names of Thomas Pocock and Jeffreys Allen. The jug was made to help promote their successful reelection to Parliament for Bridgewater, Somerset, in 1802. Possibly Swansea.

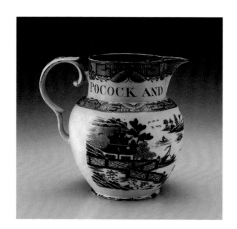

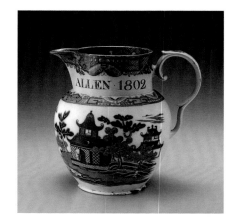

FIGURE XI.9. Influencing the voters is no new phenomenon, as William Hogarth showed in this detail from his *An Election Entertainment* (1755).

IF THESE POTS COULD TALK

as now, elected politicians' premier interest was in getting reelected using whatever means was necessary. As Hogarth showed in more than one picture, free booze was the way to many a voter's heart (Fig. XI.9). Our pitcher, therefore, was an election expense for George Pocock and Jeffreys Allen, who won reelection as parliamentary members for Bridgewater in Somersetshire in 1802. For several reasons, we believed the jug to have been a product of the Cambrian Pottery at Swansea in South Wales. First, the potting center of Swansea is a mere forty miles across the Bristol Channel from Bridgewater; next, several fragments of plates with the same design have been found in excavations in Williamsburg and have impressed diamond-shaped marks usually attributed to Swansea. The election jug's key detail is the inside and outside rim print, which features a diaper and spread-winged moth patterning. The same juxtaposition occurs on another of the Collection's pearlwares, this time on a willow style plate impressed DILLWYN & CO, the mark of Swansea's Cambrian Pottery between 1811 and 1818 during the partnership of Lewis Weston Dillwyn and Timothy and John Bevington (Fig. XI.10).[11] Another possibly pertinent detail to help in the identification of unmarked Swansea prints in the second decade of the nineteenth century is the pagoda's roof ridge that we have dubbed the "staple" type. It is to be seen both on the Dillwyn plate and on a small cup plate, which, in turn, is paralleled by a staple-roofed dinner plate with an impressed Swansea mark.[12]

FIGURE XI.10. (*a*) White earthenware plate printed with modified "willow pattern" featuring the "staple" roof line. Marked DILLWYN & CO. of Swansea, 1811–1818. (*b*) Whitened pearlware soup plate with chinoiserie print characterized by dart-shaped water and staple-roofed pagodas. Like the Dillwyn plate, its flange ornament includes a variant on the spread-winged moth motif. Ca. 1810–1820.

FIGURE XI.II. Pearlware dessert plates, with their early printed design, featuring a parasol-holding woman, her gardener (?), and a Buddha enthroned on the nearby temple roof. Ca. 1795–1815.

FIGURE XI.I2. Octagonal plate printed with "Lady with Parasol" design similar to Fig. XI.II. Ca. 1795–1815.

Along with the numerous minor variations on the willow pattern, several other pseudo-Chinese designs are often encountered on blue-printed pearlwares in the same general period, ca. 1795–1815. Three plates in the Collection, two round and one octagonal, belong to one of these groups (Figs. XI.II and XI.I2). They feature a standing woman with a parasol and beside her a man who seems to be surreptitiously departing. A. W. Coysh calls the pattern "Lady holding a parasol" and adds that it is also called *La Dame au Parasol,* which certainly sounds more up-market, but otherwise seems inappropriate—unless, of course, the lady was born in French Indo-China.[13]

Another popular design in the last years of the eighteenth century was a scene long known as the *buffalo pattern*. Four examples in the Collection comprise a pair of dessert plates, a soup plate, and a fruit stand (Fig. XI.I3). The key feature of all four is, none too surprisingly, a buffalo, on whose back rides the Chinese philosopher Lao-Tzŭ en route to the great beyond, apparently cheered on by a very small crowd.[14] Although Thomas Minton has been credited with engraving the design, its early production has been attributed to Josiah Spode the Elder who died in 1797.[15]

The buffalo-pattern engraving, like all others in the heyday of blue-printed pearlware, is characterized by the ground and water areas being depicted by laterally engraved straight lines. By 1830 or thereabouts, these areas were stippled. In brief, therefore, lines are early and dots are late. Early also are central designs that place the human figures in open white space. Some are actually round or oval reserves, but either way they date ca. 1790–1800. The Collection's example features a spear-carrying hunter and his dog in pursuit of a stag on a virtually clear ground so that they stand out as the plate's center of attention (Fig. XI.I4). Behind the hunting group, the building looks less like a temple than a Chinese castle, with a circular arch that lets us see into the interior. A not quite, but very close, parallel for this design is found on a plate impressed TURNER, the mark of John Turner, Jr., of Lane End used prior to 1803, at which date he went into partnership and changed his mark to TURNER & CO.[16]

FIGURE XI.13. (*a*, *b*) Pearlware small soup and dessert plate, and (*c*) a fruit stand (two views); all transfer printed with the design known as the "buffalo pattern." This version has been attributed to Josiah Spode the Elder, who died in 1797.

FIGURE XI.14. Pearlware plate printed with a chinoiserie design featuring a huntsman and fleeing stag within a reserve, and behind them a palace with a circular entrance. Ca. 1795–1810.

FIGURE XI.15. Pearlware plate printed in dark blue and featuring a fisherman with his catch. Possibly Longport, ca. 1790–1805.

FIGURE XI.16. Whitened pearlware plate printed with an Egypt-inspired scene and impressed RILEY. Burslem, ca. 1823–1828.

Along with the willow and buffalo patterns there was a third early design, the fisherman print. In it, one fisherman stands in an open area with his catch on a pole both fore and aft, while to the right beside a bridge another angler waits for a big one to bite (Fig. XI.15). This plate is unmarked, but others exactly like it were made by George Rogers of Longport who supplied Dublin retailer and decorator James Donovan, whose name is painted on examples of this fisherfolk pattern. George Rogers died in 1815, thereby helpfully providing the Collection's plate with a *terminus ante quem*—which, in case you've forgotten, is the erudite way of saying *before*.

The willow pattern would remain in production from then until now, satisfying every diner's taste for dinner-plate chinoiserie. Nevertheless, the makers of pearlware and the whitewares that succeeded it knew that there were other fish to fry, or rather other patterns to try. It was time to seek inspirations from sources closer to home. Napoleon's savants who went with him to Egypt in 1803 created a taste for things Egyptian. The Grand

FIGURE XI.17. (*a*) Whiteware soup plate printed with a "wild rose" border and a view of Nuneham Courtenay in Oxfordshire. The accompanying print (*b*) provided the source for one of the most widely used of English country house views on pearl- and whitewares. Ca. 1840–1865. (*b*) Ashmolean Museum, Oxford.

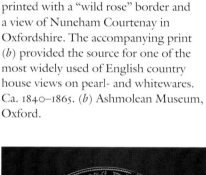

IF THESE POTS COULD TALK

Tour of classical Europe revived interest in mythology and chubby cherubs, and engravings of exotic animals provided inspirations for potters like the Riley brothers of Burslem (Fig. XI.16), whose factory was known as the Nile Street Works. It shouldn't surprise us, therefore, that the Collection's example manages to tie a distant view of the pyramids and a dragoman with his camel waiting for the next felucca-load of tourists to a Versailles-style kiosk, all within a border of very English wild roses. The border with its three-bloom grouping is relatively uncommon, but in this instance the printed mark RILEY pins it to a date between 1823 and 1828.[17] One might legitimately expect that unmarked wares with this border can confidently be identified as Riley of Burslem products. Unfortunately, in the study of early-nineteenth-century transfer-printed wares there are no legitimate expectations. John Riley's Egyptian plate's border also occurs on another Eastern scene (this one with an elephant and a lone pyramid) and is marked ROGERS and used by John Rogers of Longport between 1815 and 1842.[18] Just to make absolutely sure we are hopelessly confused, Riley, like Rogers, also used a camel print. When, as those did, two potters were using the same print at approximately the same time, we can at least be fairly certain of the dating brackets, but when as many as twenty different factories from Glasgow in Scotland to Bovey Tracey in Devonshire used the same pattern, an unmarked specimen has zero chance of losing its anonymity. Such was the fate of the Collection's soup plate, whose entire decoration is known as the *wild rose pattern,* a name more confusing than helpful since dozens of different central designs were ringed with roses in varying degrees of wildness (Fig. XI.17 *a*). This soup plate's pastoral scene involves a ferryman's cottage, his punt, a bridge, a Georgian mansion, and a tower that might be taken for a distant church. Ceramic historian William Coysh, whose scene sleuthing rivals the brilliance of the tenant of 221B Baker Street, has discovered that the engraving is based on a print titled *Nuneham Courtenay, Bridge & Cottage,* a mansion some five miles east of Oxford (Fig. XI.17 *b*). The home of the Earls Harcourt, Nuneham Park was redesigned by the great landscape architect Capability Brown, who is credited with destroying almost as many beautiful Tudor and Stuart gardens as Victorian restorers ruined churches.[19]

The Nuneham Park print was engraved in 1811, and there can be no denying the similarity between its bridge and cottage, and those of the *wild rose* pattern. However, there neither is, nor was, a tower to the right of the mansion, and there has been speculation that it was intended to be a Gothic folly, perhaps planned but never built when major changes were made to the mansion in 1832. However, when one looks carefully at the structure it turns out to have a columned portico, a bell tower, and another building half hidden in the trees beside it, none of it your standard Gothic folly. It seems much more likely that the first ceramic engraver had decided that there was too much woodland between cottage and mansion and so added other buildings whose elevation fitted neatly, though dominantly, between the two trees that occupy most of the sky.

FIGURE XI.18. A late pearlware milk
pitcher printed with a rustic village and
maypole dancing scene. Staffordshire,
ca. 1840–1850.

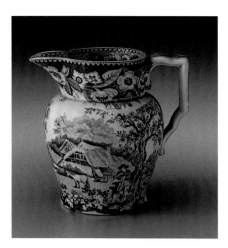 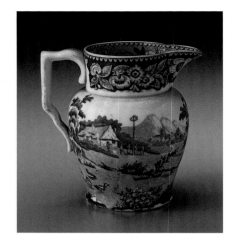

The Collection's plate is made from a whitened earthenware that no longer has the bluish tint of pearlware and therefore is unlikely to date earlier than the second quarter of the nineteenth century. The blue of its print is more strident than we expect of printing on pearlware and has a denseness that has a mechanical appearance, again a feature attributable to the later wares. But how late is later?

Knowing that the pattern was made by many factories, the *terminus ante quem* has to come from the demise of the first to use it, namely, William Hackwood and Son of Shelton in Staffordshire, whose business closed in 1855. Another firm, George Townsend of Longton, opened a factory in 1850 that lasted for only fourteen years. On balance, therefore, it seems reasonable to date the Collection's Nuneham Park plate to between circa 1840 and 1865. But that does not mean that all the wild roses have to date that late, the proof of which came not from a dinner plate but from a chamber pot (Fig. IV.18). As I explained in Chapter IV, Sir David Burnett had instructed workmen digging on his Hays Wharf properties to save him any potsherds that looked interesting. Consequently, along with vast quantities of shattered earthenwares came most of the pearlware chamber pot decorated with the wild rose design. However, this was not the same version used on plates and jugs, but one deliberately drawn larger, its wide-screen image showing buildings nowhere to be seen on the usual dinner plate versions. The mansion had another building to its rear, and in the foreground the two-part ferry house had acquired a third. There can be no doubt, therefore, that the engraver's intent was not to accurately portray Nuneham Park, but to create an attractive composition.

Here was yet another example of the kind of information that can be gleaned from the careful study of archaeological material that is rarely considered to be of museum quality and is all too often discarded. The Burnett chamber pot, being of pearlware and printed in a paler and much more pleasing blue, is clearly older than is the Collection's plate and, indeed, older than most of the wares produced by the twenty-odd factories known to be selling that design in the mid-nineteenth century. The chamber pot also differs from others in that the engraver has shown a weir beyond the bridge, presumably having misinterpreted the original print's faintly rendered stream bank. The weir is paralleled on a comparable plate impressed HEATH. The latter is almost certainly John Heath, who operated the Sytch Pottery in Burslem between ca. 1809 and 1823.[20]

Because plates large and small are akin to canvases whereon pictures are painted, collectors tend to pay less attention to cups and saucers or to jugs. The Collection's small pearlware pitcher has its place for both educational and personal reasons. The former relates to its angular handle, which is a style rarely, if ever, seen before about 1830 and thus makes this little jug a very late example of pearlware (Fig. XI.18). Unfortunately, I have been unable to trace its pastoral scene of milking, loafing, and maypole dancing, so it may have a rarity that escapes me. Its personal and sentimental significance, however, is well remembered, and it is simply this: When Audrey's home was destroyed by a flying bomb in June 1944, neighbors rallied around to provide her family with crockery and many other necessities.[21] This little jug was one such gift, and it was left to Audrey when her mother died. To hold it in one's hands is to look beyond it to the thousands, probably millions of cups, jars, plates, even chamber pots, all of them with their own stories to tell if only we had the key to unlock them.

Although most remain forever silent, some make no secret of at least part of their history, and these represent yet another aspect of the Collection. However, one such piece belongs here at the close of the pearlware saga. Just as creamware succeeded white salt glaze and pearlware ousted cream, so in the early years of the nineteenth century Charles James Mason was experimenting with ingredients that could make the cobalt-whitened wares whiter yet, and at the same time as durable as stoneware—or even iron. In 1813 he patented such a ware and called it Ironstone, claiming that it actually contained iron—which it didn't. Nevertheless, it was strong and just the thing for toilet bowls and the tables of military messes. The Collection's dessert plate (Fig. XI.19) is decorated in what Mason called his Japanese pattern, with the coloring in blue, red, puce, green, and gold applied partly at the biscuit stage and most of it thereafter to arrive at decoration of grandiose crudity. Why, then, did we buy it?

FIGURE XI.19. (*a*) Front and (*b*) back of an Ironstone dessert plate marked MASON'S PATENT IRONSTONE CHINA both impressed and printed. Made to order for the British 14th Regiment of Light Dragoons, the front's hideously drawn and clobbered interpretation of an oriental fence, rocks, and peony design says much about the taste of the officers of that cavalry regiment.

We bought it, not for its frontal design, but for its back. Centered within the elevated base is the impressed mark MASON'S PATENT IRONSTONE CHINA, and in case there should be any doubt, the plate was marked again with a crowned ribbon containing the words PATENT IRONSTONE CHINA and with MASON'S above the crown. The impressed, one-line mark is said to have been Mason's earliest and was used between 1813 and 1825, but the blue-printed marks were employed from about 1820 until he was declared bankrupt in 1848.[22] Using both brackets we arrived at a ca. 1825 date for this quite horrible plate. However, it was not its double marking that caught our attention, but the rest of the underglaze blue inscription that reads 14th Lᵗ DRAG. The plate evidently was made for the officers' mess of the British 14th Regiment of Light Dragoons, men who, one hopes, had better taste in horses than in china.

The cavalry officers' ironstone plate may loosely be considered *commemorative* because it recalls the existence of the long-gone regiment, but that was not Mason's intention. There is, however, a broad class of centuries-spanning ceramic products made specifically for that purpose. Closely tied to named people and events, it is no accident that those closely datable pieces, no matter what their ware, lie at the very heart of the Collection.

XII Memories, Fond and Otherwise

And every body praised the Duke,

Who this great fight did win.

"But what good came of it at last?"

Quoth little Peterkin,

"Why that I cannot tell," said he;

"But 'twas a famous victory."

Robert Southey, 1798

THE HISTORY OF commemorative souvenirs can be traced
back at least to the time of medieval religious pilgrimages and to William
Langland's lines from *Piers Plowman:*

> Ye may se bi my signes that sitten in myn hatte,
> That I have walked ful wyde in wete and in drye,
> And soughte gode seintes for my soules helth.[1]

The *signes* referred to the small pewter badges brought back and worn in
pilgrims' hats to prove that they had been to the shrines of their patron
saints—rather as society travelers in the 1920s and 1930s liked their steamer
trunks to be plastered with shipping labels. To my knowledge, however,
there are no surviving ceramic souvenir mugs or plates as mementoes of
medieval pilgrimages. It was not until the mid-seventeenth century that
the English penchant for memorializing great people and big events began,
and in the Judeo-Christian mind none came bigger than the nudist colony
in the Garden of Eden. But that was old history and really doesn't count.
Potters making large dishes looked to history-in-the-making for their inspirations, memorializing the beheaded Charles I and heralding the return
of his son. Those portrayals, however, may have been used less as memory
joggers than as evidence of one's politics or allegiance that could be displayed on the dresser. Such patriotism can be interpreted as the poor
families' version of the royal portraits copied from originals by Holbein,
Gheeraeds, or Van Dyck that graced the halls and walls of a sycophantic
nobility. In our collection of antiquities from the Thames foreshore are
sleeve-links decorated with portraits of Charles II and of Queen Anne, and
two others with a pair of hearts that are thought to commemorate the

marriage of Charles to Catherine of Braganza in 1662, all of which may have given rise to the expression "wearing one's heart on one's sleeve" (Fig. XII.1).

Charles, if not everybody's favorite, was sufficiently popular to prompt potters to set us on the long road to commemorative mugs for every occasion. They fared less well with James II, whose market value was small and short, but did great business with William and Mary. Queen Anne did best on stoneware tavern mugs—mostly after she was dead.[2] The Chipstone

IF THESE POTS COULD TALK

Foundation's Queen Anne charger is scarcely flattering, with the queen having been ejected upward out of her stomacher with such propulsion that her crown has been blown sideways (Fig. XII.2).[3] Nobody knew quite what to make of the first of the German Georges, so he is ceramically remembered by a few, none-too-well-painted Bristol delftware chargers and the occasional dinner plate with a half-hearted but mandatory toast of "God Save King George." The early-eighteenth-century potters soon learned that the market was in commemorating events rather than monarchs, and their first opportunity came in 1739 when, at the beginning of King George's War (1739–1748), Admiral Edward Vernon took a six-ship fleet into Spain's Porto Bello harbor and seized the Panama town, thereby becoming the British public's nine-day darling. By that date, as I have previously noted, white salt-glazed stoneware shaped in slip molds had been perfected, and numerous teapots, tankards, and bowls saluted the victory.[4] The example in the Collection, however, is not in salt glaze but in the fine redware commonly identified with John Astbury of Shelton (Fig. XII.3).[5] He is credited with creating a rich brown body using both yellow and red firing clays, to which he applied small metal-molded devices in white pipe clay reminiscent of John Dwight's Fulham products.[6] The Porto Bello bowl is decorated with very crude sprigged ornaments that include a rendering of the port, Vernon's ships, a small cannon, and two people, one of them presumably Vernon himself. Equally crudely applied are separated blocks of wording, which, when connected, read YE PRIDE OF SPAIN HUM[BLED] BY ADMIRAL VERNON HE TOOK [P]ORTO [B]ELLO WI[TH] VI [S]HIPS [ON]LY NOV YE 22 [17]39. Shortly afterward, Vernon sailed further up the Panamanian coast and captured Fort San Lorenzo at the mouth of the Chagre River.[7] Vernon evidently was rich in what we today would call "the right stuff," but his cantankerous nature and his tiresome trait of turning out to have been right did not endear him to his government. Emboldened by his earlier successes, Vernon and an army under General Wentworth set sail from Jamaica early in 1742, intending to land at Porto Bello and march across the Panamanian Isthmus to attack the city of Panama. However, on reaching Porto Bello the two commanders determined that (a) the troops were sickly, (b) backup supplies had not arrived, and (c) it was beginning to rain. Consequently, they abandoned the project and sailed back to Jamaica. Contemporary historian Tobias Smollett called the debacle "a ridiculous spectacle of folly and irresolution." In September the two commanders were ordered back to England, where "they lived to feel the scorn and reproach of their country."[8] For the Staffordshire potters to have continued to make Vernon souvenirs thereafter would have been akin to the Franklin Mint putting out a Nixon plate in 1975. Vernon's career ended in 1746 when, at the behest of the Admiral's enemies in Parliament, the king was "persuaded to strike his name out of the list of flag officers," thereby ignominiously concluding a lifetime of service that had been likened to those of Drake and Ralegh. Known to his seamen as "Old Grog," Vernon is best remembered

FIGURE XII.3. Thin-walled redware bowl of Astbury type, decorated with crudely sprig-applied devices in white clay, commemorating Admiral Vernon's capture of Porto Bello, Panama, in 1739. Ex Louis Gautier Collection.

for reducing drunkenness and improving discipline aboard his ships by watering his men's rum ration.[9]

There is a similar, but larger, Astbury-type Porto Bello bowl in the British Museum and another in the Manchester Gallery of Art. The history of the Collection's example is unknown until the 1920s, when, as one of its labels shows, it was bought by London's principal delftware dealer, Louis Gautier, who died in 1944. It subsequently passed into the hands of New York ceramics dealers Ben and Cora Ginsburg, and after them into a Washington, D.C., antiques fair where we bought it in 1980. I mention this trail because it behooves all of us who collect to do our best to trace the sources of our acquisitions and to ensure that their histories remain with them when they leave the safety of our cabinets.

Perhaps because Britain came to pride itself on being a seafaring nation, most of its eighteenth-century commemorative ceramics relate to naval exploits.[10] The dearth of terrestrial triumphs might also be occasioned by the fact that until the Napoleonic Wars, Britannia's land battles were more bloody than glorious, and with maimed and mustered-out soldiery begging in the streets, the citizenry had reminders enough. Naval engagements, on the other hand, were distant and clean. The blood and guts went down with the ship.

Like Admiral Vernon before him, George Bridges Rodney earned his first laurels in the Caribbean. In 1762, as commander of the British fleet that attacked the French on Martinique, he successfully assaulted their citadel at Fort Royal by lobbing mortar bombs over its defenses. He is said to have been the first to mount such heavy artillery on his ships, and a brass tobacco box in our collection attests to that method of attack (Fig. XII.4). Four warships are firing bombs while long boats disgorge files of musket-carrying soldiers onto the shore. The inscription below this

FIGURE XII.4. Brass and copper tobacco box lauding Admiral Rodney's defeat of the French at Martinique in 1762, his first step toward ceramic immortality. Dutch.

combined operation reads DER ENGELANDER GLORIEUSE EROBE RUNG MARTINIQUE D: 4: FEBRUARY 1762. That the Dutch should think Rodney's exploit sufficiently glorious to warrant portraying it on a tobacco box (albeit on the bottom) is a reminder of the shifting sands of European alliances in the eighteenth century. In 1743 the Dutch had joined Britain and Austria in an alliance against France, and in spite of their devious and disastrous exploit on the Hugli River in 1758,[11] by the 1760s anything that hurt the French sounded good to the Dutch. As I have noted earlier, in 1780 they were to change their minds after the English claimed the right to search foreign ships at sea, and by resisting were ill-advisedly pushed into war on the side of the French and the American rebels.

Although Rear Admiral Rodney succeeded in seizing Martinique as well as St. Lucia and Grenada, these early achievements went unnoticed by the British potters. They were to make up for this omission in 1782 after his humbling of the French admiral the Comte de Grasse, whose blockade of the British army at Yorktown had done such damage to English pride.

As I explained in the last chapter, Audrey's and my interest in Rodney was fired by our snorkeling visit to St. Lucia and Pigeon Island. Thereafter, we collected everything we could find that related to his exploits. Treasured among them is the letter he wrote on Christmas Day, 1780, aboard his flagship *Sandwich* as she and the rest of Rodney's fleet lay at anchor in St. Lucia's Gros Islet Bay (Fig. XII.5). Perhaps he remembered the fate of the outspoken Vernon, for in the letter Rodney complained about the un-readiness of the British fleet stationed in New England and questioned the wisdom of minds "unacquainted with the nature of the American Win-ters." Writing in evident frustration, he added, "I am extremely unwilling to complain. I must be supported *or I must speak out.*"[12]

Early in January 1781, Rodney was reinforced by the arrival of Sir Sam-uel Hood and a convoy of 120 sail, among them five heavily armed men-of-war ranging from ninety guns down to twenty-eight. Hood had been reluctant to serve under Rodney; indeed, he had at first declined the appointment. Nevertheless, Rodney wrote of him as his old friend, though privately saying that the Admiralty could have just as well sent him an old apple woman. But the wariness of both admirals was set aside when the sloop *Childress* arrived from England with news that Britain and the Dutch were now at war, and bringing orders instructing the combined fleets to move against their islands of St. Eustatius and St. Maarten. When the English armada bore down on Statia, the island that Rodney called "that nest of vipers" was haven for more than a hundred Dutch, French, and American ships. The shoreside warehouses of the lower town were filled with American tobacco and cotton bound for European markets, as well as huge quantities of food supplies, military materials, and the like going the other way. In the counting houses of the Dutch merchants, chests were heavy with gold specie. On February 3, it was all in Rodney's hands—as also was the problem of inventorying everything seized and securing it "to await his Majesty's pleasure." Needless to say, dealing with the outraged Dutch and the colony of British merchants whom Rodney considered traitors every one, was both time consuming and contentious. Eventually he sent Hood north to join Admiral Graves's fleet in the Hudson River, while he and a huge flotilla of heavily laden ships set sail for England.

The Golden Rock of St. Eustatius was left a scarcely inhabited ruin. Not only had the Lower Town warehouses been stripped of their contents,

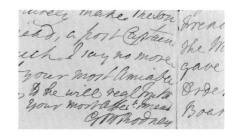

FIGURE XII.5. Signature of Admiral George Bridges Rodney in a letter written on December 25, 1780, aboard his flagship the *Sandwich* lying in Gros Islet Bay, St. Lucia.

FIGURE XII.6. After ravages by both Rodney and the sea, little is left to recall that St. Eustatius's colonial-era merchants had made the island among the richest in the Caribbean.

but their roof timbers, doors, window frames, indeed anything useful had been shipped for storage at Antigua (Fig. XII.6). News of Rodney's success had preceded him to England, and the populace was agog. Salutes were fired from the Tower, and the King toyed with the idea of making him an earl. Although popular adulation once charged was slow to cool, at the Admiralty, in Parliament, and at the court of St. James, voices of restraint were growing louder. English companies with roofless warehouses on Statia, as well as merchants brought home under arrest and charged by Rodney as traitors, were all running to their lawyers. To make matters worse, the first loot-laden convoy sent home in February had fallen into French hands when it reached the English Channel. Now the rich booty brought home by Rodney himself, whose share of the prize money was expected to set his family up for life, was impounded and likely to be legally entangled for years to come. Captured military stores were regarded as government property, and any possessions that might be proved to have been owned by British subjects and lawfully exported would not be released until title could be legally established or denied. On reflection, the King thought better of bestowing an earldom. Rodney, ill, frustrated, and feeling betrayed by friends and mauled by political enemies, retreated to Bath, where he spent the summer and fall recuperating.

Then came word of a huge French fleet under Admiral de Grasse being dispatched with 12,000 troops aboard to attack Jamaica. Soon afterward came the dreadful news of Admiral Graves's failure at the Chesapeake and the surrender at Yorktown. The unresolved Statia mess notwithstanding, the Admiralty called on Rodney to save England's Caribbean islands. Although still in poor health, he welcomed the chance to be back at sea and away from affidavits and depositions, and so accepted the new title of Vice-Admiral of Great Britain. He sailed from Plymouth aboard H.M.S. *Formidable* on January 9, 1782, with eleven more ships of the line strung out behind him.

Admiral Hood's fleet was already in the West Indies trying to wrest St. Kitts from the French, and there he forced de Grasse's fleet to withdraw, leaving his soldier garrison to fight it out with the British on Brimstone Hill.[13] Rodney's fleet reached St. Lucia without incident and lay once again in Gros Islet Bay, and from the little signal station fort atop Pigeon Island his lookout watched for the first French sail to clear the horizon. The to-ing and fro-ing that eventually brought the two huge fleets in range of each other's guns need not concern us, for it was only the eventual outcome that was to shape a significant part of our ceramic collection.

Rodney's ships of the line numbered thirty-seven and de Grasse's squadrons thirty-six. Before the battle began, two of the French warships had run into each other and suffered so much damage that they had to break away and head for Martinique, prompting de Grasse to forgo his up-wind advantage to protect his disabled vessels. The morning of April 12 found the French fleet grouped like a pod of whales south of a cluster of small islands known as the Saintes, while the British squadrons maneuvered off

IF THESE POTS COULD TALK

the northwest tip of Dominica. Both fleets then moved into line of battle, de Grasse aboard his flagship the *Ville de Paris* heading south, and Rodney on the *Formidable* and Hood on the *Barfleur* sailing north in the lee of the French, the broadsides of the British firing within pistol range of the enemy. The battle had begun at 7:40 in the morning; by 9:00 the French line had broken. But the cost in lives and damage to the ships of both sides was enormous and became more so as smaller battles were fought out through the rest of the day. Among the heavily damaged was the French flagship, which did its best to remain under way with only her foresail, mizen-topsail, and lower steering sail to keep her to the wind.

Alone and sorely wounded, the *Ville de Paris* stood cornered like a stag at bay, doing her best to defend herself from the hounding British aboard the *Marlborough*, *Russell*, and Hood's *Barfleur*. It was his raking broadside that gave de Grasse no choice but to sink or surrender. At 6:30 that evening, with the huge *Ville de Paris* dead in the water and the French admiral a prisoner, Rodney declared victory and refused to allow a disgruntled Hood to pursue the retreating but still formidable remnants of the French fleet (Fig. XII.7).

FIGURE XII.7. The victorious Rodney received the sword of the Comte de Grasse to end the Battle of the Saintes on April 12, 1782.

Meanwhile, back in England and in the aftermath of the defeat of Lord Cornwallis at Yorktown, Lord North's government fell and was replaced with another favorable to the St. Eustatius merchants, who were still clamoring for Rodney's head on a creamware plate. The new First Lord of the Admiralty, unaware of the victory at the Saintes, dispatched a letter recalling him, and sending out a replacement commander-in-chief. Both letter and replacement were on their way before news of Rodney's success reached London. England's Vice-Admiral immediately became a national hero and, regardless of the Statia cloud still hanging over him, the King granted him a peerage. Potters of both creamware and pearlware set their designers to work to make jugs, bowls, loving cups, teapots, anything that could be sold to feed the public's expected desire to own a piece of the action. Rodney returned to Bristol on September 15, 1782, and thereafter had to endure public adulation at levees and balls, endless speeches, and receiving keys to cities, all of it a drain on a sick, aging, and disappointed man. His Lordship's disposition was not helped by Hood, who continued to believe that he should have gone after the fleeing French warships, and who had not forgotten that it was he and not Rodney who had crippled the enemy's flagship. Furthermore, Hood bitterly blamed Rodney for the legal tangle that denied either of them the prize money that they believed to be their due.[14] Making matters worse was the news that the convoy bringing the *Ville de Paris* and other prize ships back to England had met with one disaster after another. The seventy-four-gun *Hector* ran into bad weather and sank off Newfoundland; the *César* with the same armament blew up, the similarly armed *Glorieux* sank, and on the following day the greatest prize of all, the 104-gun *Ville de Paris*, followed her to the bottom. Rarely in the history of British naval operations had there been so bittersweet a victory.

FIGURE XII.8. (*a*) Creamware mug decorated with annular reeding, tiger stipple, and sprigged portraits of Admiral Rodney and (*b*) its frontal cartouche incorrectly spelling the name of the French flagship *Ville de Paris* captured in the Battles of the Saintes as VILLA DE PARIS. Staffordshire, 1782–1785.

But a victory it was. The British citizenry, who had a long history of disliking the French for being French, saw the defeat of de Grasse as just retribution for his role in costing Britain her American colonies. Hastily engraved blocks, their images transferred to sprig molds depicting Rodney in a commanding stance, were soon on sale to potters eager to catch the moment. Best known among their surviving products is a creamware mug, leopard stippled over an ochre slip and with a pair of applied figures flanking an oval cartouche featuring a view of the captured French flagship identified as the *Villa de Paris* (sic). Evidently somebody couldn't read somebody else's writing (Fig. XII.8). The figures on either side of the mug are from the same mold and, lest there should be any doubt, they carry a banner inscribed "Lord Rodney." Two matching fragments have been found in the most unlikely of places, the first of them amid the ruins of the great French fortress of Louisbourg in Nova Scotia. The fort and township had been captured by the British for the second and last time in 1758, and their defenses were systematically demolished by a British garrison that remained there until 1768. After that, however, very little was standing and only a handful of British fisher-families remained at the desolate site. Who owned the Rodney mug and how it got there remains yet another unsolved mystery. It is, however, no more baffling than the discovery of the second fragment in a Federal-period privy in downtown Alexandria, Virginia (Fig. XII.9).

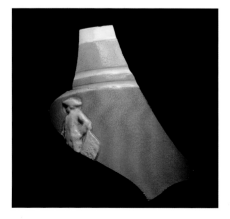

FIGURE XII.9. Fragment of an orange-slipped pearlware mug decorated with a sprigged portrait of Admiral Rodney wearing a hat different from that shown in Fig. XII.8 *a*. Found in Alexandria, Virginia, in a context of ca. 1790–1800. Staffordshire. National Museum of American History, Smithsonian Institution/Alexandria Archaeology Museum, City of Alexandria, Virginia.

FIGURE XII.10. (*a*) Pearlware teapot, iron-oxide slipped, cauliflower spout, and (*b*) its sprigged figures of Lords Rodney and Hood. The lid a replacement. Staffordshire, 1782–1785.

FIGURE XII.11. Redware loving cup with applied Rodney and Hood figures and unnamed portrait medallions. The standing figures appear to be from the same master mold as those on the pearlware teapot of Fig. XII.10. Staffordshire, perhaps Newcastle-under-Lyme, 1782–1785.

The designer of a black-slipped pearlware teapot, perhaps conscious of tension between Rodney and Hood and aware of the way the political wind was blowing, was more cautious than the maker of the *Ville de Paris* mug. Pairs of white pipeclay figures on either side are identified as Lords Hood and Rodney (Fig. XII.10).[15] Working in a different medium, a factory that may have been the Bell Pomona works at Newcastle-under-Lyme produced redware loving cups banded with white slip and with applied Rodney and Hood figures and cartouches (Fig. XII.11).[16] In addition, and unhesitatingly Rodneyesque, are press-molded portrait mugs or jugs in both creamware and pearlware, some painted in bizarre coloring and all wearing a headband lettered in relief SUCCESS TO LORD RODNEY (Fig. XII.12 *a*). Another souvenir of the great man's return is a standing pearlware statuette painted in Pratt-style colors and identified simply as RODNEY (Fig. XII.12 *b*).[17]

FIGURE XII.12. (*a*) Rodney portrait mug and (*b*) standing figure painted in "Pratt" colors. Both pearlware. Staffordshire, 1782–1785.

These pearlware commemorative pieces are important to the history of English earthenware evolution in that they demonstrate the sophisticated use of that body early in the 1780s and give additional credence to the Ralph Vernon 1780 loving cup. The Rodney wares cannot date earlier than his elevation to the peerage in July 1782, and there can be little doubt that their continued production would have been measured on the barometer of waning popular adulation. Apart from a crowd-gathering appearance at the Court of King's Bench in March of the following year, Rodney retired to Bath and for the most part remained there until the fall and winter of

FIGURE XII.13. (*a*) Press-molded feldspathic stoneware jug commemorating
Sir John Jervis's victory at the Battle of
St. Vincent, February 4, 1797. His name
is here spelled JARVIS. (*b*) Detail of the
matrix maker's idea of Jervis's flagship
with an apparently naked boy aft.
Castleford type, ca. 1797–1800.

1784, when he followed his doctor's orders and spent this time in the relative warmth of Italy. Rodney's distaste for public appearances, his lawsuits tied to the impounded Statia prize money, and his poor health made
it extremely unlikely that customers would be paying to wish success to
Lord Rodney so long after his retirement.[18] However, John and Grizelda
Lewis, the principal authorities on Pratt ware, have stated that "The earliest dated piece we have yet seen is a Rodney head mug, inscribed 1785,
and that was a transitional piece, part coloured glaze." The location of that
crucial piece of evidence is not cited, and the two Rodney head mugs illustrated in the Lewises' book are given ca. 1785 dates, presumably on the
strength of it.[19]

The next magic moment came on February 4, 1797, when a British fleet
commanded by Sir John Jervis defeated the Spaniards at the Battle of St.
Vincent. His flagship was the *Victory,* a ship that would later earn lasting
renown under the command of Horatio Nelson, who in 1797 was still a
commodore under Jervis. The latter was raised to the peerage as Earl St.
Vincent on the sixteenth of July, at which time he assumed commemorative ceramic status (Fig. XII.13 *a*). He also introduced a new ware to the
Collection, a dry-bodied feldspathic stoneware that is often referred to as
Castleford ware. Press molded in two pieces, each is slightly different in
its treatment of the Admiral and his attendant ships. Not knowing that he
spelled his name Jervis, the identifying ribbon calls him LORD JARVIS.
Odder still are two cannon-mounted, single-masted ships no bigger than
yachts; atop the stern cabin of one of them sits a naked boy holding a line
(Fig. XII.13 *b*).

Castleford ware is relatively common in the form of teapots decorated,
as in the Jervis jug, with highlighting in blue and green. As usual, more
than one factory produced this dry stoneware, but it is well established
that David Dunderdale, who had served his apprenticeship at Leeds, set
up his own factory ca. 1790 at Whitwood Meer in Yorkshire's Castleford,
and continued in production there until 1820. Although the Jervis jug is
unmarked, it seems likely that it is, indeed, a Castleford product and that
it was made in the months after Jervis became Earl St. Vincent. I doubt
that anyone would have disputed that assumption had it not been for a
red herring drawn across the trail when Sotheby's in New York auctioned

a larger jug decorated with much the same design and called it a "Pratt-ware Lord Jarvis Jug" and dated it to ca. 1810.[20] But why 1810? Jervis had had his day in 1797 and would fade from public adulation as new and more dramatic victories occupied the crowds' attention.

It seems likely that the collectors' and ceramic writers' penchant for identifying anything press molded and decorated in Pratt-style colors stemmed from an assumption that the Pratt in question was Felix Pratt, who began his Fenton business in 1810. However, Felix was preceded by his father William. Ceramic historian Geoffrey Godden has published the only two known jugs of this type marked with name PRATT and dates one to ca. 1790–1795 and the other to ca. 1790–1800.[21]

One might have expected that Pratt-style jugs with their relief decoration would have been made in slip-casting molds, but most were not. To create the final two-piece molds, the designer first made a solid, un-adorned block in the shape of the jug, and then sprig-applied the relief ornament to it. The fired block was subsequently used to create a final, decorated master matrix from which the factory-floor's press molds were derived. The resulting product was then painted in "Pratt colors" before being glazed.[22]

Throughout the eighteenth and early nineteenth centuries, the need for navy recruits was a major concern and gave rise to the press gangs who rounded up able-bodied drunks in port taverns and prodded or dragged them to ships from which they could not escape. However, the army's needs were not so easily served, for escape on land required no swimming skills. Consequently, recruiting by means of bribery and promises was the only solution. A Pratt-style pitcher in the Collection is molded on one side with a picture of a line regiment recruiting officer making his pitch to a simple soul, and on the other a hussar recruiter enjoying a beguilingly merry moment with another potential enlistee (Fig. XII.14). Grizelda Lewis, however, interprets the images very differently, calling them "smokers and drinkers," and believes that the civilian seated across the table from the line officer is holding a concealed dagger and that his face "wears a cunning expression."[23] Surprisingly, two of these Prattish recruiting jugs are impressed WEDGWOOD. Ours, alas, is not.

FIGURE XII.14. Slip-cast pearlware jug decorated in "Pratt" colors, and with an elaborate, "string-tied" handle. The scenes in relief are here interpreted as representing recruiting efforts in the era of the Napoleonic Wars. Staffordshire, ca. 1800.

FIGURE XII.15. Both sides of a press-molded pearlware jug decorated in "Pratt" colors, honoring Admiral Nelson and Captain Berry for their victory at the Battle of the Nile in 1798. Staffordshire, ca. 1800.

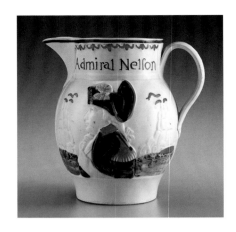

FIGURE XII.16. Both sides of a pearlware jug decorated under and over glaze, in commemoration of the Peace of Amiens in 1802. (*a*) A transfer-printed regal cipher is on one side and (*b*) a patriotic verse on the other. Staffordshire, 1802–1805.

Belonging to the same class is the Collection's next naval commemorative jug,[24] this in pearlware and molded with portraits of Horatio Nelson and his second in command, Captain Sir Edward Berry. Together they defeated Napoleon's Mediterranean fleet in the Battle of the Nile on August 1, 1798 (Fig. XII.15). Producing this jug seems to have been a rush job intended to catch the public fancy while the ink of the news was still fresh on the newspapers' pages. Berry's rank is given as CAPTARN followed by an unneeded period, while the lettering of both names is crude and uneven. The Nelson and Berry jugs are the most common of their genre, a prevalence resulting, perhaps, from their being reproduced at the Leeds Pottery beginning around 1888 and continuing into the First World War. The factory was then operated by W. W. Slee (a name suggestive of one of Charles Dickens's less admirable characters), who happened also to be in the antique dealing business.[25]

Of all the battles fought in the eighteenth and nineteenth centuries, those of the Napoleonic Wars were the greatest gift to the British commemorative potters. Trafalgar was the greatest of them all, and was made more so by coupling the joy of the naval victory with mourning for the death of Nelson. Tourists who feed insatiable pigeons in Trafalgar Square rarely pay any attention to the guano-spattered figure atop the central column, but in his day and in the days thereafter, Horatio Nelson was as close to being a god as Christianity would allow. The Peace of Amiens in 1802, which is recorded in the Collection by the so-called Salopian tewares[26] and by a polychrome pearlware pitcher whose message reads "May balmy peace And wreath'd renown Our virtuous Heroes Ever crown," came to an abrupt end on October 18, 1803 (Fig. XII.16). Two years later almost to the day, the French and English fleets faced each other outside the gateway to the Mediterranean and in sight of Cape Trafalgar.

The battle began just before noon on October 21, 1805, and was over in six hours of incredible carnage and destruction. Cuthbert Collingwood, Nelson's vice-admiral, declared that there "never was so complete an annihilation of a fleet." Out of the combined French and Spanish fleets of thirty-three men-of-war, eighteen too damaged to flee were captured, and eleven more made port at Cadiz so battered that they would never leave it. Two

thousand eight hundred were dead, and 20,000 sailors and soldiers were taken prisoner and would spend the next several years in British prisons and on hulks with nothing to do but make models from meat bones. By comparison, the English losses were minimal, only 429 killed, but among them the Hero of the Nile. Usual practice dictated that the dead should be sewn into canvas and ejected into the sea, but one of Nelson's dying requests had been that he should not be thrown overboard. However, with every ship's carpenter battling damage that could even yet sink the ships, none had time to build a coffin. Besides, there was no sheet lead aboard the *Victory* to provide the inner casing. Consequently, Nelson's body returned to England in a cask of brandy lashed to the flagship's mizzen mast. The French commanding admiral, Pierre Villeneuve, was taken prisoner and shortly afterward released. Blamed for the defeat by Napoleon, by his ministers, and by the French populace at large, he wrote a farewell letter to his wife from a bedroom in a Rennes hotel saying that he considered "life a disgrace and death a duty," then committed suicide.[27]

Admiral Collingwood's handling of the last hour of battle, and particularly his lack of punitive purpose thereafter that resulted in several of the captured French ships escaping after regaining control from token British prize crews, tarnished his career. Fellow officers compared him unfavorably to Nelson, and although he was granted a peerage he had to bear the burden of having lived while the better man died. Consequently, he was not imbued with solo ceramic immortality.

The national grief at the death of Nelson was kept alive by newspaper reports of his lying in state at Greenwich, his water procession up the Thames to London, his further lying in state at the Admiralty, and his eventual burial procession to St. Paul's Cathedral. All were manna to the memorializing potters. The finest *memento mori* were in transfer-printed creamware that would have been acceptable in the most affluent of homes, but other wares catered more to the humbler classes. Among the latter is a Portobello-style pitcher of redware internally white slipped and externally printed in yellow on the brown ground with portraits of both Nelson and Collingwood (Fig. XII.17). Dating for this pitcher is tight (ca. 1805–1806) on the grounds that, as noted earlier, when the public learned that Collingwood had let several of the French prizes escape, both his popularity and his marketability plummeted.

FIGURE XII.17. Three views of a red-bodied, internally white slipped pitcher, printed with portraits of Admirals Nelson and Collingwood and with a central medallion depicting the spoils of war within the victors' laurel wreath. A Portobello Ware commemoration of the Battle of Trafalgar, October 21, 1805. Scottish, ca. 1806–1810.

FIGURE XII.18. Three views of a pearlware jug with elaborate underglaze transfer prints borrowed from a larger vessel commemorating the death of Nelson and his victory at Trafalgar; the rim and handle are outlined in overglaze brown. The jug's "cut-to-fit" prints illustrate the applier's lack of concern for legibility. Staffordshire, ca. 1806–1810.

A small pearlware pitcher memorializing Nelson by means of three crowded transfer prints speaks both to the factories' haste in catching the market and the purchasers' inattention to fine detail (Fig. XII.18). Indeed, it is quite possible that the master potters' print-applying assistants were illiterate. The copperplate-derived prints used on this jug were made to fit a larger vessel and so had to be cut and lapped at several points, trimming that played havoc with the incorporated inscriptions (Fig. XII.19). The view of Nelson's flagship is titled VICORY, the portrait of the hero became NESON, and his famous signal to his fleet at the commencement of the battle reads ENGLAND [EXP]ECTS EVERY MA[N] TO DO HIS DUTY. Below, another garbled inscription reads "Shew me my Country's Foes [the H]ero cry'd, He saw, He fought, He conquered and he di'd."

England's greatest naval victory would be both preceded and followed by major land engagements, some more glorious than others. Five years

FIGURE XII.19. Printing thin paper impressions to be transferred to the biscuit wares, 1827.

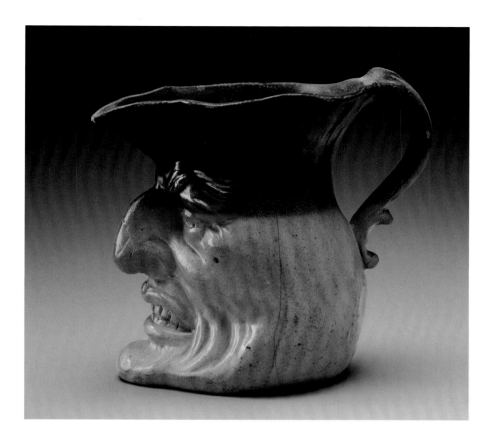

FIGURE XII.20. Press-molded brown stoneware jug caricaturing the victor of Waterloo when later an unpopular Prime Minister. Probably Lambeth, ca.1832.

of fighting the Peninsular Wars in Portugal and northern Spain resulted in several now scarcely remembered battles at Rolica, Vimeiro, Corunna, Talavera, Vittoria, and others, so it was not until the Peace of Paris of May 30, 1814, and after Napoleon surrendered and was shipped off to Elba, that the Duke of Wellington became the potters' safe-bet hero.[28] Even so, there was nothing like the amount of souvenir buying that had followed Nelson's death at Trafalgar. Indeed, when Field Marshall Wellington and the Prussians' General Blücher were victorious at Waterloo in June 1815, virtually no commemorative wares were forthcoming. Various explanations have been offered, but the most likely is that the British public had grown so used to victories that another, even though the most important of them all, evoked little more than a yawn.

Wellington's leadership qualities were unquestioned, and led him into politics in 1818 and from one administrative post to another, culminating in his becoming Prime Minister in 1827. However, his policies became increasingly unpopular, so much so that a mob threw rocks through the windows of his London mansion on the anniversary of his victory at Waterloo.[29] The Collection's sole Wellington relic is a brown stoneware pitcher cast in a two-piece mold that emphasized the feature that earned him the nickname of "Old Nosey" (Fig. XII.20). Although there is a matching jug shaped like the head of Napoleon that points to popular enthusiasm for Wellington as the 1815 victor, it is more likely to reflect the fickle beer-swilling, rock-throwing populace's later dislike of him as a parliamentarian.[30]

The Collection's last reminder of early-nineteenth-century English history has nothing to do with military or naval successes but much to do with scandal involving the Royal Family. It was one that would find its parallel in the storm in a large punch bowl that rocked the British establishment in 1937 and ended in the abdication of Edward VIII. The latter's intent differed, of course, in that he wished to marry an unsuitable woman whereas George IV was trying to rid himself of one. Not everyone thought either a good idea, and both scandals held the public enthralled until played to their history-making conclusions.

George, the eldest son of the sometimes looney George III, had taken over as Prince Regent in 1810. After being kept under close control throughout his boyhood, Junior George found the big chair surprisingly comfortable and discovered that leading rather than following was greatly to be preferred. He was not well liked. At the age of eighteen he had been involved in a seedy relationship with an actress; at twenty he went through an illegal marriage with the Catholic Maria Anne Smythe; and in 1795 he married the Princess Caroline of Brunswick. George soon wished he hadn't, and packed her off to a house out of London at Blackheath while he sowed his royal oats. The British public, ever ready to support an underdog (particularly if female), deplored the estrangement. In 1806, adverse public opinion prompted the still sane George III to have the Princess's conduct investigated in search of useful dirt, the results of which proved to be unbecoming a queen apparent, but not downright criminal. The public saw this as unwarranted harassment and increased its support for the wronged Caroline. In 1814 she moved to Italy and to the Villa d'Este beside Lake Como, and there entertained one of Royal history's least attractive appendages, the Count Bartolomeo Bergami.

Knowing that the old King could not last much longer, in 1818 the Prince Regent had sent a commission to Italy to scrape up sufficient evidence to enable him to divorce Caroline and have her safely out of the way before the accession. However, George III died too soon, and as the heir had feared, the Caroline matter moved to center stage where she immediately became a political football. The Whig Party leader, Henry Brougham, persuaded her to return to England, and she did so after turning down a 50,000-pound annuity if she would renounce the title of queen. Caroline's triumphant entry into London amid cheering crowds of well-wishers infuriated the new King and his political supporters. Brougham's Tory counterpart, Lord Liverpool, put before Parliament a Bill of Pains and Penalties using the 1818 commission's findings as evidence to deny Caroline the title of Queen Consort.

Several major ceramic factories began to put out supportive jugs, mugs, and plates, of which the Collection's pink lustered pearlware pitcher is a good example (Fig. XII.21). These wares, however, are not commemorative in the usual sense. They were the 1820 version of today's political TV ads, designed to promote both Caroline's rights and the Tories' wrongs.

FIGURE XII.21. Both sides of a luster-necked and transfer-printed pearlware jug from which to toast to the success of George IV's Queen Caroline during her "trial" in 1818. The verse refers to the green baize bag in which the evidence against her was taken in and out of the House of Lords. 1818–1821.

In August, the House of Lords began to review the evidence against the People's Queen, and in the process the intimate details of Caroline's relationship with Bergami became public knowledge. The saying about not washing one's dirty linen in public may have originated at that time, for dirty bed sheets, chamber pots, and similar unsavory details were part of the evidence brought against her. The documents relating to the Bergami scandal were taken daily into the Lords contained in a green baize bag, a reference to which appears on one side of the Collection's pitcher. The verse was written to be sung to the tune of the National Anthem.

> As for the Green Bag crew
> Justice will have it[s] due,
> God save the Queen!
> Confound their Politicks,
> Frustrate their knavish tricks
> On HER our hopes we fix,
> God save the Queen!

Unlike the Victorian prudery that would swaddle much of the century, in 1820 standards were far less rigid. In consequence, regardless of the fact that the Lords ruled against the Queen and that the King insisted that the matter should go to committee to secure approval from the Lower House, the public continued to side with Caroline. The Collection's jug had to have been made in the autumn of 1818 while the Tories and their Green Bag crew were dragging the unfortunate Caroline through the political mire. It turned out, however, that the committee concluded that there

FIGURE XII.22. Caroline being denied entry into Westminster Abbey to take her place as the Queen Consort at the coronation of George IV on July 18, 1821. Presenting the Queen's credentials is Lord Hood, one of her principal supporters. Detail from a contemporary engraving.

were insufficient votes to sustain the Bill of Pains and Penalties, and it was withdrawn. George IV still had his unwanted Queen Consort.

Several more pro-Caroline verses are to be found on other wares made to promote her cause, one of them evidently issued after the Tory effort was defeated. It reads

> I'll Sing a Song of Sixpence
> A Greenbag full of lies
> Four and twenty witnesses
> All proved to be spies,
> When the bag was open'd
> The Lords began to stare
> To see their precious evidence
> All vanished into air. [31]

The King had no intention of having "that woman" beside him at the coronation and ordered her not to attend, but Caroline insisted that it was her right to do so. For a fleeting moment two months before the crowning, George heard what he took to be most welcome news.

A courtier reported, "Sire, your greatest enemy is dead."

"Is she, by God!" replied the King.

The courtier had then to explain that he was referring to Napoleon, who had died in exile on May 5, 1821.[32] Caroline, however, was very much alive and, escorted by Lord Hood, arrived at Westminster Abbey for the coronation only to have the great doors closed in her face (Fig. XII.22).[33] Eleven days later, on August 7, the Queen was unexpectedly taken ill and died, thereby ridding the King of an embarrassment that otherwise would have haunted the rest of his reign.

Today, in a new millennium, the affair of the Green Bag crew is almost forgotten, save by those of us who own Queen Caroline's portrait on the side of a pearlware plate or a lustered jug. The poor, erring, yet wronged woman expected posterity to be kinder.

IF THESE POTS COULD TALK

XIII Clay, Cookworthy, and Targeting Ann Target

This is the porcelain clay of humankind.

John Dryden, 1690

I WAS WALKING, or, more correctly, shouldering my way through the mob crowding the Portobello antiques market one Saturday morning when I ran into Jonathan Horne carrying a laden yet crumpled paper sack. I asked him what he had bought and he told me that he had found four *Jackfield* jugs. He added that they were not at the high end of desirability, but that he bought them in the off chance that somebody might like them. It was a shrewd decision on his part, and five minutes later it was I who was carrying the scruffy paper sack. Like so many ceramic terms, Jackfield conjures up the right image—a thin, red- or gray-bodied, high-fired earthenware under a shiny iron-black glaze—but not necessarily the right location (Fig. XIII.1).

FIGURE XIII.1. Black-glazed and stoneware-hard "Jackfield" type jugs, illustrating the decline of a once more elegant shape. Staffordshire, ca. 1780–1820.

FIGURE XIII.2. (*a*) Jackfield-type jug in a salt-glazed stoneware form characteristic of the 1750s. Staffordshire, ca. 1755–1770. (*b*) A large jug in the same ware, elaborately enameled with family arms and supporters. The simplified handle suggests a date in the 1760–1770 period. (*b*) Chipstone Collection.

Jackfield is a town in Shropshire where potting is said to have begun at least as early as the sixteenth century, and may or may not have been producing black-glazed mugs and tankards of types that used to be known as Cistercian ware. They were so named on the grounds that monks of that order produced them at such abbeys as Kirkstall and Fountains in North Yorkshire. However, there seems to be no more foundation for that designation than has Jackfield for the later wares. Llewellynn Jewitt recalled that at some time in the mid-nineteenth century an abandoned Jackfield coal mine was reopened and "in it was found a small mug of brown earthenware, bearing the date 1634." He added that "The works were, probably not long after this period, carried on by a person of the name of Glover, who used the old salt glaze for his ware." Needless to say, one wishes we knew what happened to the 1634 mug and whether Jewitt was implying that it, too, was made from the old salt glaze. But no matter how you slice it, brown mugs aren't the same as black jugs. Those, according to Jewitt, were a speciality of Maurice Thursfield, who succeeded his late father John Thursfield, who had acquired the Jackfield factory from Glover around 1713. Wrote Jewitt, "Maurice Thursfield made at Jackfield a very superior black ware, highly vitrified and glazed; indeed, so highly glazed was it that it had all the outward appearance of glass."[1] It seems likely that this observation was the seed from which the Jackfield appellation grew. If Jewitt was correct in saying that Maurice inherited the business in 1751 and sold (?) it to a Mr. Simpson twelve years later,[2] none of Jonathan Horne's jugs could date within those narrow brackets. But another already in the Collection might conceivably do so (Fig. XIII.2 *a*). That likelihood is based on the pitcher shape's similarity to others in white salt glaze dating from the mid-eighteenth century, and on a parallel in a private collection dated 1760.[3] The later versions became more sleekly proportioned but not nearly as attractive. Nevertheless, the Collection's five jugs well demonstrate the degradation of a once pleasing form.[4]

Until my Saturday encounter with Jonathan, the Collection could boast—*claim* might be a better word—but one other example of Jackfield ware, and that a black-glazed teapot fired to stoneware hardness and with

a crabstock handle, typical of the mid-eighteenth century (Fig. XIII.3 *a*). More often than not, teapots of the so-called Whieldon-Wedgwood shape also had crabstock spouts, but this one does not. A handsome example of a Jackfield teapot with both crabstock handle and spout is in the Chipstone Collection (Fig. XIII.3 *b*). That it stands on three short legs rather than on a flat foot suggests a slightly earlier date than the teapot in the Collection, but in truth, both base types occur in the same general period between about 1735 and 1765, though more often toward the later date.

As we have seen, some ceramic terms (like *Jackfield*) convey their message regardless of their accuracy or origin. *Crabstock* is another of them. We use it whenever we see a spout or handle that fits it, but rarely, if ever, does anyone ask "why?" or take the time to find out. In truth, finding out isn't all that easy. Most books on ceramics use the term but provide no definition; indeed, I have found it in no one's index. The following, therefore, is an informational gem with which to amaze pot-collecting friends and colleagues:

The spouts and handles resemble tree limbs from which other small branches have been hewn away, and that is pretty much what crabstock means in one of its two nonceramic usages. It can apply either to a person of wild and untamed nature or to a wild crab-apple tree used as a stock on which to graft new limbs, with the latter connotation dating from ca. 1625.

Jackfield wares were ideally suited to enameling and to oil gilding, and the best of them were decorated with flowers, foliage, cartouche-contained initials, and even heraldic arms (Fig. XIII.2 *b*). The Collection's teapot had been gilded with an elaborate floral design, but like the Anne Boucant Page cup and saucer in creamware,[5] most of its gold either has turned to dull copper or has been eroded through constant usage, thereby leaving it looking worse than it would have had it been left undecorated (Fig. XIII.3 *a*). The pot dates from around 1760, and its body and lid closely resemble a mid-eighteenth-century white stoneware teapot coated overall with cobalt blue and known—and here we go again—as *Littler's blue* (Fig. XIII.4). William Littler is credited with the idea of coating white

FIGURE XIII.3. (*a*) Black-glazed, high-fired redware teapot with crabstock handle and plain spout, with its sides retaining the remains of once elegant floral designs in oil gilding. Staffordshire, ca. 1755–1770. (*b*) Similarly black-glazed teapot in an earlier form having both crabstock handle and spout, and standing on three splayed feet. The wall is rather crudely "personalized" in white slip for Mʳˢ GRIM: STONE. Staffordshire, ca. 1750–1765. (*b*) Chipstone Collection.

FIGURE XIII.4. White salt-glazed stoneware teapot, with crabstock handle and spout, and coated overall with the so-called "Littler's blue" slip. 1750–1765. Chipstone Collection.

stoneware with a dipped slip made from clay mixed with ground zaffer and flint, and to have done so around 1750.[6] That may or may not be true, but the notion of cobalt coloring salt-glazed stoneware (as I noted earlier) goes back to the Rhineland potters of the sixteenth century. Littler was in partnership with his brother-in-law, another of the Wedgwoods, namely, Aaron—of whom there were several—and together they owned a factory at Brownhills in Staffordshire, where from about 1745 on they made white salt-glazed stoneware.[7] Littler had bigger and better ideas, and twenty years later, believing that he knew how to make translucent porcelain from Cornish pipe clay, he moved to Longton Hall and there was both successful and unsuccessful. He did produce porcelain, but he did not develop a sufficient market for it, and having mortgaged the Brownhills works, he soon found himself penniless and forced to work for other companies.

Littler's blue wares are by no means common in archaeological contexts, but most of the examples known to us date between about 1745 and 1765—which happens to be the time span that William Littler ran the Brownhills factory. In the early 1970s, Audrey and I became interested in the process

FIGURE XIII.5. Chailey-style lead-glazed tobacco jar with brass-bound rim. The wall is type impressed with a none-too-encouraging verse and the name of its owner, JN.º SAYERS in the village of TARING in Sussex and dated 1801.

of manufacturing of Littler's blue on salt-glazed wares and prevailed upon master potter Jim Maloney to run tests for us. The earliest of Britain's ceramic historians, Simeon Shaw (1829), described Littler's process saying that he "dipped the clay ware [i.e. in the green state] into his liquid," but that a competitor, Enoch Booth, "fired his once, and dipped the Bisquet ware."[8] We had been led to believe that the body had first to be fired to biscuit before the dip glaze was applied, and were anxious to learn whether Littler's process really worked and was a match for the two-stage method. It turned out that Maloney was able to produce a successful imitation of Littler's blue-coated salt-glazed stoneware in a single firing. The samples, dipped in their green state and then fired alongside Maloney's regular salt-glazed wares, emerged without suffering any of the surface pitting characteristic of salt glazing.[9]

As is inevitable in generalist collections, Audrey's and mine has included several wares that were by no means in the mainstream of ceramic production, but that were nonetheless interesting in their own right. Foremost among these are the slip-decorated red earthenwares made in the county of Sussex from the late eighteenth into the mid-nineteenth century.[10] Their principal characteristic was the clever use of type-impressed lettering, which when filled with white clay appeared yellow after lead glazing. These wares come as bowls, harvest bottles, pig-shaped penny banks, kegs, spirit flasks, puzzle jugs, and tobacco humidors. Our example of this last is dated 1801 and was made for JNᵒ SAYERS of TARING (Fig. XIII.5). On one side, along with the name and date, are a pair of churchwarden tobacco pipes, two goblets, and between them a decanter. On the other side the somewhat melancholy verse with which I began Chapter VIII reads:

> How ever sore
> the taxes gripe
> there is always
> pleasure ore a pipe.[11]

The word "ore" looks at first glance to be a misspelling, but the *O.E.D.* cites it as an obsolete variant of "over"—thus pleasure over a pipe. In 1793 (eight years before the jar was made), one John Sayres, a maltster and corn merchant, was a prominent individual in the Sussex village of Tarring.[12] There can be little doubt that as the potter misspelled Tarring, he is equally likely to have turned John Sayres into John Sayers. If the potter was only *told* how to inscribe the jar, it is not hard to imagine that a broad Sussex accent would have made the names sound the same no matter how they were spelled.

This very distinctive earthenware is usually attributed to the village of *Chailey*, unless, of course, it is inscribed otherwise. Such is the case with our second "Chailey style" example, this one an oval-sectioned but round harvest bottle with the usual pair of lug ears through which to string it to one's belt (Fig. XIII.6 *a*). On one side an impressed-lettered inscription

FIGURE XIII.6. (*a*) A richly documented Chailey-style harvest bottle with white-slipped clock face on one side and impressed in type on the other JOHN SIGGERY / HERSTMONCEUX SUSSEX / GIVEN TO HENRY FUN- / NELL PIDDINGHOE / SUSSEX MAY 2 / 1836. (*b*) Piddinghoe has changed little since farmer Henry Funnel lived there in the mid-nineteenth century.

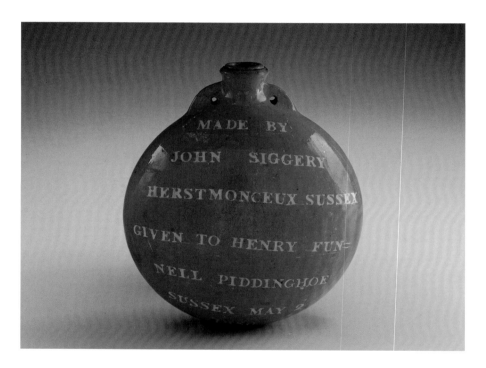

IF THESE POTS COULD TALK

FIGURE XIII.7. (*a*) Profile and (*b*) base of a miniature agateware pitcher, showing the body both lead glazed and unglazed. Staffordshire, ca. 1800–1840.

reads: JOHN SIGGERY, HURSTMONCEUX SUSSEX, GIVEN TO HENRY FUN-NEL, PIDDINGHOE, SUSSEX, MAY 2, 1836. That, of course, leaves absolutely no room for doubt or argument. What is not so clear—in fact, not clear at all—is the occasion on which John Siggery made this bottle for Henry Funnell. Our visit to the village of Piddinghoe and a check of the church records in search of Funnell's marriage, christening, or whatever proved fruitless (Fig. XIII.6 *b*). We learned only that he was a prominent local farmer. But more is known about the potter. John Siggery is thought to be the son of another John Siggery whose factory was at Lower Dicker from which a flask so identified is in the Victoria and Albert Museum and dated 1794. John Junior's kilns were at Herstmonceux (its castle now the Royal Observatory), and he married a domestic servant working in a household at Battle[13] whose name was Emma Goldsmith. A similar flask in the Glaisher Collection reads GIVEN TO EMMA GOLDSMITH BATTLE, SUSSEX 1835, and was probably made when Siggery was courting her. One wonders how she responded when she was given the kind of bottle that farm hands carried into the fields filled with ale or cider. But that question is typical of the wonderful journeys into imagination that make collecting anything so stimulating. Siggery's gift to a farmer carries with it no obvious flights of fancy. However, it might perhaps lay claim to being the most tightly dated ceramic item of all time, for not only does it carry the date May 2, 1836, but on the opposite side is a clock dial set at three minutes to three!

Not all Sussex red earthenwares were of this type, and several examples exist that blended white and red firing clays to create the previously discussed agateware. This process went on, not only in Sussex, but also in Staffordshire, well through the nineteenth century, and there are two small jugs in the Collection, one of them having a true agate body, but of a ca. 1800–1830 jug shape, and the other employing another red and white, sgraffito-paneled effect that had been popular in the mid-eighteenth century (Figs. XIII.7 and XIII.8). Some experts have dismissed other examples of these techniques as fakes. In reality, however, they are not, and instead are merely a much later return to old ornamenting methods.

FIGURE XIII.8. Miniature cream-colored pitcher, brown slipped and checker-tooled, and with reeded handle. Probably Staffordshire, ca. 1800–1830.

The Glaisher Collection at Cambridge includes two Sussex money boxes, one standing on a rectangular stem over a circular base, and the other in the form of a hen sitting atop her nest and surrounded by eggs.[14] Second only perhaps to chamber pots in their evocation of past usage are money boxes, which, of course, are not really boxes at all. They come, and did through the centuries, in a great variety of shapes, from those that looked like frogs to others made in the shape of balls on stalks, of cottages, of dogs, and eventually of pigs. A ball-shaped money box in the Collection (Fig. XIII.9 *a*) is likely to have been a Sussex product and is inscribed in cursive lettering "Pay Here, James Norman, D C 4 7899," which we have interpreted as December 4, 1899. Another in the shape of a circular house with a central chimney is of somewhat dubious antiquity (Fig. XIII.9 *b*). Under its eaves runs the inscription GUARD YOWRE PENCE AND YOWR POUNDES, with the lettering applied with printers' type. The box's high-gloss glaze and the too-bad-to-be-true spelling suggest that it is a relatively modern creation.

Although today we refer to money boxes as piggy banks, the porcine shaped containers are a relatively recent form and did not become popular in England until the late nineteenth century.[15] Considerably earlier is the more elaborate hen-and-chicken variety which seems to have had its origin in the latter years of the preceding century and presumably is an interpretation of describing one's rainy-day savings as a "nest egg," a term whose monetary usage dated as early as the year 1700. Unfortunately, the Collection's example looks a good deal more antique than it is (Fig. XIII.10). Others like it were made at several country potteries at Donyatt in Somerset, following a pottery-making tradition that goes back into the sixteenth century. These West Country wares are characterized by white slip

IF THESE POTS COULD TALK

that included patches of copper oxide over a red body with inscriptions and decorations incised through the slip. The result was a yellow box dappled with green and with red-brown lettering. The ancient-appearing sgraffito decoration has continued into the present century, as the Collection's example attests. Crudely inscribed through the slip are the name and date, "Ralph Coles, Xmas, 1905." Almost exact parallels have been found in excavations on Donyatt kiln sites, among them one "Wishing Edith a Merry Xmas" in 1893.[16]

The clays around Donyatt served at least ten different kiln locations, but regardless of their very considerable output, their wares are rarely encountered on American colonial sites. However, competitors to the northwest beside the Bristol Channel at Barnstaple and Bideford had a huge export trade beginning in the 1620s and continuing through to the Great Disruption of 1776. By comparison with the North Devon wares, Donyatt products were charmingly, but consistently and persistently, countrified. The Barnstaple-Bideford wares of the eighteenth and nineteenth centuries, on the other hand, were more accomplished in their decoration, and are best represented by elaborately slip-decorated harvest jugs in which the white slip is cut away and incised to create the shapes of ships, mermaids, and foliate designs; even the Hanoverian Royal Arms as is splendidly demonstrated by an example dated 1748 now in the Chipstone Collection (Fig. XIII.11).[17]

FIGURE XIII.10. Redware money box, slip-coated, and sgraffito inscribed "Ralph Coles / Xmas / 1905." Somersetshire.

FIGURE XIII.11. North Devon redware harvest jug, slip-coated and sgraffito-decorated with British royal arms and dated 1748. Probably Barnstaple. Chipstone Collection.

FIGURE XIII.12. Repairing with lead rivets had a long history. Roman-era Samian Ware bowl shards plugged and drilled. First to second century A.D.

Time and again we have asked ourselves, what value did the original owner put upon a Barnstaple harvest jug, or, indeed, any other ceramic object? In archaeology we encounter the relics of one domestic disaster after another, and every time we wonder, what retribution was exacted from the careless carrier? Then again, might the breakage have been deliberate, as was Ben Franklin's stoneware mug that he wrote about in the epigraph to this book? Why, we may wonder, were some broken pieces considered worth repairing and others not? In Roman Britain, Samian Ware was available in large quantities, yet it is not unusual to find examples of less than superb quality being repaired with rivets (Fig. XIII.12).

FIGURE XIII.13. A fluted delftware "Chinamen on rocks" dish mended with relatively inconspicuous frontal lead rivets but with many more highly visible on the back. Dutch, ca. 1680.

IF THESE POTS COULD TALK

The same method was employed to mend a late-seventeenth-century Dutch delftware dish which, thought handsome, in today's antiques world is considered no great rarity (Fig. XIII.13).

One can readily understand why a pearlware coffee pot with a chipped spout would be worth repairing simply for the sakes of hygiene and pourability (Fig. XIII.14)—though neither had prompted the owner of the St. Eustatius pot to have it repaired.[18] The explanation, of course, is that on a tiny Caribbean island nobody with appropriate skills was there to do the work. In a city like New York, on the other hand, one had only to consult the newspapers to find a professional repairer. In 1763 Nathaniel Lane of Warren Street assured customers that "if his Work gives Way, he will as often mend gratis."[19] Three years earlier James Walker, newly arrived from London, announced that with the aid of "Rivets and Cramps" he could mend more or less any pottery or porcelain. "Where Pieces are wanting in broken Bowls" he could supply "the Defects; and make Spouts and Handles to tea-pots, in the same Manner as is done in the East Indies" (Fig. XIII.15 *a*).[20] Depending on the value a customer put on her broken dishes, the repairers offered several levels of riveting. Nathaniel Lane's charges were spelled out in his ads: "The Price of the Rivets, he finding the Silver is 2s. each if the silver is found 1s. each Rivet, if Brass, is 1s. if white metal 6d."[21] In not-too-well-punctuated language Lane was saying that if you provided your own silver you paid for the work and not the materials.

FIGURE XIII.14. Pearlware coffee pot with replacement ferrous spout lip and lead cap securing the repaired lid finial. The waterside pier and brick bridge prints occur on a silver-mounted jar marked by potters T. & J. Hollins of Shelton, Staffordshire, ca. 1795–1820.

FIGURE XIII.15. (*a*) A nineteenth-century itinerant Chinese repairer using a bow drill and flanked by the work boxes he carried slung on a pole. (*b*) A Chinese export porcelain plate with "white metal" (ferrous) rivets visible only from behind (*c*). Ca. 1750–1780. (*a*) Robert Hunter Collection.

FIGURE XIII.16. Typical Chinese "Imari" style export porcelain bowls painted in underglaze blue and overglaze red and gold. Mid-eighteenth century.

Typical of mid- to-late-eighteenth-century riveting is a Chinese porcelain plate that we bought solely for that reason (Fig. XIII.15 *b* and *c*). Porcelain of any sort had never had much appeal to us. However, in a collection devoted to the useful wares common in their several periods, Chinese porcelain could not be ignored, representing, as it did, the average family's "company's coming" best. Cheapest were the solely underglaze blue wares, but they have less often found collectors' attention than have the more colorfully decorated, so-called Imari wares, which in our excavations have always been more prevalent than the porcelains of their English competitors (Fig. XIII.16).[22]

To students of ceramic history, the presence of Chinese export porcelain in a collection serves as a yardstick against which to measure the success or failure of its eighteenth-century English copiers. Eventually, of course, it became hard to determine who was copying whom. Another Chinese porcelain plate in the Collection almost certainly represents the Chinese exporters' attempt to copy an English "temple" design transfer printed on pearlware at the close of the eighteenth century (Fig. XIII.17). A close parallel is provided by a plate marked M. MASON, that is, Miles Mason of Lane Delph, 1806–1816. Here, then, we have Chinese designs being adapted by English potters whose fellow countrymen were sending transfer-printed examples to be duplicated by hand painting in China. The intent, of course, was to outsell the pearlware potters whose wares were being copied. This was the kind of aggressive business practice that would have had John Dwight of Fulham foaming at the mouth, but with so many factories making much the same thing, no one could be sure whose rights were being pilfered.

Until relatively recently, collectors' knowledge of Chinese porcelain was derived from reign-marked pieces and by information acquired by visiting the still-existing Chinese factories. Needless to say, therefore, the majority of museum pieces as well as those that sell at up-scale auctions are of superior quality and predate the run-of-the-kiln export wares of the eighteenth century or the later American Clipper trade in the blue-on-white wares

IF THESE POTS COULD TALK

loosely referred to as Canton. But then along comes salvage diver Captain Michael Hatcher to open doors hitherto sealed. An Australian based in Singapore, he set up a salvage company to examine (some would say, loot) shipwrecks in the South China Sea, among them an unidentified intercoastal trader and a ship of the Dutch East India Company (V.O.C.), both of which contained enormous quantities of porcelain. The earliest dated from the mid-seventeenth century and carried wares made for Asian consumption, while the later wreck's cargo was made for, and influenced by, Dutch merchants. Yet another Hatcher discovery led to the raising of 350,000 pieces of porcelain from a Chinese junk, the *Tek Sing,* that sank in 1822 with the loss of 1,600 lives. Sailing from the port of Amoy and bound for Batavia (now Jakarta), the ship was carrying porcelain intended, not for the European trade, but for oriental markets. Consequently, the *Tek Sing* sale in November 2000 provided a unique opportunity for porcelain students to study design differences that distinguish early-nineteenth-century oriental ceramic taste from the occidental.[23]

FIGURE XIII.17. Chinese export porcelain copy of an English chinoiserie plate design. Ca. 1795–1815.

Shipwrecks, no matter their age or contents, always retain an aura of excitement and romance, and the knowledge that one is holding a saucer that had been on the bottom of the China Sea since the 1640s has a *something* that porcelain handed down or passed in and out of sale rooms has not. Appropriate, we thought, was the acquisition of such a saucer from the cargo of that Asian merchant vessel, a mini-dish whose design incorporates several sea-bottom creatures, most prominent among them a jumbo shrimp (Fig. XIII.18).[24] For the same romantic reason, the Collection acquired the Batavia-style tea bowl and saucer from the *Geldermalsen* wreck of 1752.[25]

This may or may not be the place to comment on the ethics of salvaging and selling cargoes from shipwrecks—but this is my book, so I'll do so anyway. It is considered professionally correct for any archaeologist concerned with job safety to roundly condemn anyone who excavates on a wreck site who has not first been blessed by the underwater profession. Equally heinous is the notion that any of the recovered artifacts might be sold to help underwrite the cost of further exploration and recovery. Indeed, one underwater museum director has made it a rule to reject any gift of artifacts (no matter how important they may intrinsically be) if they were not brought up from the deep by a professionally accredited marine archaeologist. At the same time, major museums around the world have profited handsomely at their ticket desks by exhibiting relics mechanically snatched up from the *Titanic* that have no archaeological significance whatsoever.

FIGURE XIII.18. Chinese porcelain saucer, decorated under glaze with small sea creatures. From an unnamed wreck in the South China Sea. Sold in Amsterdam in 1984. Ca. 1645–1660.

Author C. J. A. Jörg was right when he bemoaned that Hatcher "had paid little attention to a detailed registration of his finds," adding that "Every minute a seemingly insignificant object may be a 'historical time capsule.' By lifting a find out of its context something of its tale is irrevocably lost and this detracts from its value."[26] No doubt Hatcher would argue that had he been required to substitute professional archaeological procedures for his cruder salvage methods, he could not have afforded to

FIGURE XIII.19. Part of the porcelain cargo from the 1752 wreck of the Dutch East India Company's *Geldermalsen* photographed before the boxes were disturbed and after the removal of a covering layer of tea. Photo courtesy of Christie's Amsterdam.

underwrite the greatly extended time needed to do so. In terms of ceramic history one can argue, perhaps, that half a cake is better than none—particularly when it contains most of the fruit (Figs. XIII.19 and XIII.20).

The key always is money, and, as in land archaeology, in underwater excavation somebody has to pay the bubble-blowing piper—and at far greater cost. If, as the archaeologists demand, all shipwreck sites are to be left untouched until such time as sufficient money is forthcoming to do the job properly (as they see it), most wrecks will never be studied at all. Furthermore, the dissemination of information to be derived from wrecks like the *Geldermalsen* would have taken years to get into print and then only in obscure journals with minimal illustrations. Instead, the *Geldermalsen* sale made possible both a fully color-illustrated catalog and an equally well illustrated book on the history of the ship and its cargo.[27] No less important was the opportunity for museums around the world, the revered Colonial Williamsburg Foundation included, to purchase samplings from the hugely repetitious inventory, and to use them in a variety of educational contexts. Had that cargo not been salvaged, there would be no books and no enhanced knowledge. The lessons learned about the eighteenth-century trade in oriental porcelain would still be waiting on the seabed until, in some utopian future, there might be sufficient money to be spent without any expectation of a bankable return. As there are

IF THESE POTS COULD TALK

FIGURE XIII.20. The *Geldermalsen*'s 1751–1752 cargo shelved in Amsterdam prior to its sale in 1986. Photo courtesy of Christie's Amsterdam.

thousands of shipwrecks in every ocean around the world, one wonders why the recovery of incomplete information from a few is not of greater value to our present generation than the dubious pleasure of knowing that there's stuff out there that some unborn generation of professionals may get paid to excavate and squirrel away in the attics of academe.

But back to porcelain, specifically to English porcelain.

Excavations in Williamsburg have yielded numerous fragments of English porcelain about which we knew next to nothing when we began digging there in 1957.[28] Consequently, we asked every porcelain pundit we could lure into our lab to provide us with dates and factory attributions. Audrey, however, complained that after each helpful visit she had to change the labels to reflect the latest opinion. Now, as more definitive evidence comes from excavations at Liverpool, Worcester, Bow and other kiln sites, her curatorial successors can be more confident in their conclusions.

Our prolonged study of blue transfer printing on pearlwares inevitably lapped over into porcelains whose painted and printed designs were duplicated and adapted to the later, cheaper ware. We needed, therefore, to

FIGURE XIII.22. Fisherman print from an original Caughley engraving plate published by Llewellynn Jewitt.

FIGURE XIII.23. Caughley porcelain "fat fish" (*a*) on a miniature porringer or taster and (*b*) on an asparagus tray. Ca. 1780–1790.

understand and recognize, say, the difference between fisherman prints on Caughley porcelain and very similar prints from Worcester (Fig. XIII.21). The answer to that question is to be found in the size of the catch, a short, fat fish for Caughley and a long skinny one for Worcester. Unfortunately, rules of thumb are never far from a warning forefinger. Worcester's skinny fish is sometimes to be landed on Liverpool porcelain of the 1770s–1780s.[29] But there are other clues: Caughley's background angler knows how to keep tension on his line, but the Worcester fisherman is unlikely to catch anything with a line that loose. Unfortunately, the loose-line test does not apply to other Caughley prints. A surviving Caughley copper plate is etched with a scene of a fisherman with the loosest line imaginable, possibly due to his lack of attention while listening to a girl-friend on the other side of a fence (Fig. XIII.22).[30]

A further distinguishing difference between a Caughley and a Worcester saucer can be found in the profiles of their foot rings. The Caughley saucer's foot ring is internally undercut and this permits one to lift it between finger and thumb, but the Worcester has a V-shaped foot that cannot be lifted.[31] I should add that this test is not infallible and can be disastrous if gravity returns the specimen to an unpadded surface. Yet another distinction between the two is that against a white light Caughley appears slightly orange while Worcester appears even more slightly green.

Audrey always had a fascination for miniature anythings, which explains the presence of a miniature porringer or taster from the Caughley (fat fish) factory. The same pattern occurs on our single example from a twelve-piece set of asparagus trays (Fig. XIII.23).[32] However, the smallest piece of English porcelain in the Collection is a child's toy tea bowl delicately decorated in green and brown, attributed to a date ca. 1790, though not to a known factory (Fig. XIII.24). At the other end of our size scale is a bowl that we at first thought to be Liverpool but that turned out to be from Worcester (Fig. XIII.25). Decorated with underglaze flowers and a tortuously rooted tree whose snake-like branches slither around the side, now and then erupting into flowers, the bowl is far more appealing than most of our

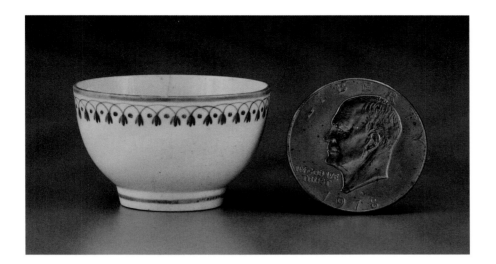

FIGURE XIII.24. Miniature English porcelain tea bowl with overglaze enameling. Factory unknown. Ca. 1790–1800. Eisenhower dollar as scale.

FIGURE XIII.25. The Collection's least costly purchase. A Worcester porcelain bowl with a basal workman's mark that attributes it to ca. 1758–1760.

later English porcelain. Furthermore, it has the distinction of being the cheapest ceramic object ever to enter the Collection. Its story is this:

In 1980 or thereabout, a nearby commercial building with a doleful history of its tenants providing the wrong services in the wrong place was purchased by a woman who had decided to try her luck in the antiques business. Knowing absolutely nothing about it, she invested in stock offered by a Philadelphia importer. All she had to do (besides part with money) was to select any one of several offered themes, so she chose the "Blue and White" package. Why she did so we never discovered, for she had no prior knowledge of English ceramics, were they blue, white, or purple. However, being a neighbor, the woman asked us to help her unpack and evaluate her blue and white treasures. They turned out (as we had suspected) to consist primarily of very late willow pattern plates, tureens, and so on; some so late that they were new. We did our best to be kind and admiring of each piece as it was revealed unto us. But after a while one runs low on superlatives: "What a great shade of blue!" "Wow, isn't that a beauty!" or "That's in real first rate condition" (none too surprisingly, as it was a 1976 Philadelphia commemorative). And so on. Amid everything in the shop, the Worcester porcelain bowl was the only piece with any real age to it, and the only one to which we would give house room. However, by the time it was unpacked we had waxed so enthusiastically about everything else that we had no topper with which to laud this genuinely eighteenth-century bowl. The shop owner was so grateful to us for our encouragement that she insisted that she would give us any piece from her new stock. After numerous polite demurrals, I told her that we would like to buy the Worcester bowl.[33] She adamantly insisted that it had to be a gift, and I equally adamantly said that we had to pay for it. The impasse was broken only when she agreed to sell it to us—for ten cents. So the dime changed hands and the bowl came home. I would like to be able to end the story by saying that from its humble start, our neighbor's blue-and-white antiques business went from strength to strength. But it didn't, and within six months the building was once again available to rent.

Another Worcester saucer and its cup have nothing to do with big or little fishes, but are still decorated in the Chinese manner. Although the subject emphasis has shifted from an angler and his boat to larger peonies, there is still a zigzagging fence, a stretch of water and beyond an island with a small Chinese building on it (Fig. XIII.26). However, the strength of the cobalt blue is noticeably greater on the cup and saucer than on the duo of saucers, and this color density is sometimes viewed as a later Worcester characteristic. Be that as it may, porcelain authority Roderick Jellicoe has suggested a 1775–1785 bracket for the former and 1775–1780 for the latter. Both cup and saucer are marked on their bases with Worcester's in-filled crescent—which also was used at Lowestoft![34] Worcester teawares like these are typical of the kinds of genteel yet cheapish English porcelain available in America toward the end of the eighteenth century.

It turns out that the Collection includes only one example of Liverpool porcelain, a can (demitasse) entirely different in every respect from all else (Fig. XIII.27). The little mug is pale-yellow bodied and overglaze decorated with standing Chinamen painted in a soft palette of red, green, yellow, and purple. Some thirty years ago the doyen of English porcelain scholars examined the can, agreed that it was from Liverpool, and dated

IF THESE POTS COULD TALK

it ca. 1765–1785. The upper date fitted well with an old dealer's label on the unglazed bottom that read "1775/85 Liverpool coffee can." The dealer evidently had had a pair of them as his label gave his price as "£4.10 / £8 pr." Much more recently, thanks to Roderick Jellicoe's input, the date has been adjusted backward to 1780 and the source to an enigmatic HP Group. I had guessed that HP was abbreviation for Hard to Place, but not so. It refers to a group of Liverpool porcelains with those initials on their bottoms and that have yet to be linked to any one of three Liverpool factories.

Considerably later is our lone example of New Hall hard-paste porcelain or bone china (Fig. XIII.28). The saucer's rim is enriched with silver luster, while the central decoration features a black transfer print of a Palladian mansion and to the right of it a summer house (?) in oriental style. This seemingly inappropriate structure reflects the taste for Indian and Chinese architecture fostered by the Prince Regent's garish pavilion at Brighton, work on which got under way in 1811. I think it almost certain that the design is taken from a contemporary print originally published in a book on English country mansions, but we have never been able to locate the right one. As with the engraving of the later pearlware willow patterns, the saucer's shading is created by stippling rather than by short, lateral lines, and thus points to its being a later rather than early example of the genre, to wit, ca. 1815–1825.

The evolution of English soft-paste porcelain toward the hard paste of oriental exports has been discussed in every porcelain primer. Suffice it to say, therefore, that at the end of the eighteenth century, porcelain manufacturing in England had taken another step toward the texture of Chinese hard-paste wares, an innovation usually attributed to Josiah Spode 1 of Stoke-on-Trent around 1790. He is credited with having added calcinated bone to the usual china clay base and thereby produced bone china, a combination that would be adopted and adapted by most English porcelain factories through the nineteenth century.[35] This ware has a slightly yellow cast and is represented in the Collection by a mug that does its best to hide its translucence by being black slipped on its outside (Fig. XIII.29). Indeed, so good was it that we bought it as Spode's white stoneware! The mistake was more easily made than some, for essentially the same hunting scene that was sprig-applied to the Spode mug is to be found on

FIGURE XIII.28. Bone china saucer with a black transfer print depicting a country mansion beyond a lake, with the rim silver lustered. This is the Collection's only example of New Hall hard-paste porcelain. Ca. 1815–1825.

FIGURE XIII.29. Two views of hunt mug in black-slipped and sprig-decorated hard-paste porcelain. Impressed SPODE. Ca. 1800–1820.

FIGURE XIII.30. Bat-molded and hand-painted Bow porcelain saucer or chocolate cup stand. Ca. 1775.

a black-necked white stoneware jug in the Glaisher Collection at Cambridge, dated 1811, a year comparable to that of our porcelain example to which we had given dating brackets of 1800–1820. Were it not for being porcelain rather than stoneware and being impressed with a Spode mark, a factory attribution would have been almost impossible, so many were the potteries producing similar hunting scenes on mugs and jugs.[36] In contrast to the delicacy and sharpness of our mug's scene, its two-piece cast handle retains mold marks. Although they may have been perceived as a decorative detail, in our eyes they detracted from the elegance of the whole.[37]

Josiah Spode I's vaunted discovery that the inclusion of bone ash could improve his porcelain was not as novel as the claim suggests, for bone ash had been used at the Bow porcelain factory half a century earlier.

There are two very different examples of Bow porcelain in the Collection, one a bat-molded saucer and the other a tea bowl. However, the saucer isn't really a saucer. I'm told that it is a chocolate cup stand—though the difference between a shallow, saucer-shaped saucer for a tea cup and a shallow saucer-shaped stand for a chocolate cup has eluded me. Be that as it may, the stand felicitously combines radiating ridged molding with hand painting of such precision that the rim motif fosters the erroneous impression of being printed (Fig. XIII.30). Roderick Jellicoe has dated the stand to ca. 1775—one year before the ailing factory was closed, having been taken over by entrepreneur William Duesbury in 1763 when the then owner, John Crowther, was declared bankrupt.[38] Although the cup stand is well painted, a glaze-robbed scar mars its surface, testifying to the widely held opinion that the quality of Bow's products had steadily declined as its management passed from one owner to another.

Our second example, the tea bowl, is a relic of happier days at Stratford-le-Bow, dating as it does from the factory's second phase under the management of Messrs. Crowther and Weatherby.[39] They renamed the business "New Canton," built a new factory structure in the style they supposed reflected the architecture of Canton in China, and employed close to 300 workers, ninety of them painters and the rest turners and throwers. Clearly, product sales needed to be enormous to keep pace with the cash flow of so large an enterprise. Whether the fear of failure hastened

IF THESE POTS COULD TALK

the death of Weatherby in 1762 (history has failed to preserve his first name), nobody knows; but we do know that John Crowther lived out his remaining years in Morden College at Blackheath, an institution founded in 1695 to house "decayed Turkey merchants" who had fallen on hard times. Later its sanctuary was extended to penniless businessmen of otherwise good character, Crowther among them. One of his old employees, painter Thomas Craft, would write in 1790 that he was "The only Person of all those employed there [at the factory] who annually visit him."[40]

What has any of this to do with a porcelain tea bowl? In our view, everything. Be it a tea bowl or any other ceramic ware or shape, indeed, any antique object, each has a history. Were it not for our two pieces of Bow porcelain, we would never have come to know and care about John Crowther. Passing his lonely years as a prisoner of charity, abandoned by all but one of his employees, one cannot but see in his plight the mirror image of thousands who today end their lives in nursing homes where care and kindness are in short supply.

Decorated in Chinese *famille rose* style, the Bow tea bowl is a small gem to those who like their colors muted, but to a Williamsburg smoker it was just another ashtray. It entered the Collection in a totally unforeseeable way, yet remains a far more historically valuable acquisition than all the rest as an example of documented early English porcelain. In the 1950s Craig Lupo, a young printer at the *Virginia Gazette* newspaper, lived with his mother in Williamsburg. Mrs. Lupo was a smoker and prone to using any available repository as an ashtray, the bowl among them. Its central feature is its over- and underglaze decoration in the form of a large peony accompanied by two short sections of oriental fence, a large rock with a hole in it, and a stand of leaning bamboo (Fig. XIII.31). The fence is red, the peony purple, and likewise the canes of bamboo. Other smaller flowers and leaves were painted in underglaze blue and overglaze enhanced in two shades of green and an orange-yellow. None of this would be worth relating were it not for the base's red, overglaze inscription reading "A. Target 1754," a distinction that placed Mrs. Lupo's ashtray among the earliest dated examples of English Bow porcelain. Like many an ashtray before and since, it was knocked off a table and broken in half. Rather than dumping the pieces into the trash, Mrs. Lupo gave them to her son, who, in turn, gave them to my conservator assistant, John Dunton, who had no trouble gluing the bowl together. When he left Colonial Williamsburg in 1962, he bequeathed the bowl to Audrey and to me. When we asked how it had come into the possession of Mrs. Lupo, all she could say was that it had been in the family a long time, but how long was *long* we never discovered. We did, however, learn a good deal about the bowl itself.

The "A. Target" was Ann, wife to Thomas Target, for whom another bowl was made in the same year and marked "Thos: Target 1754." That is in the collection of the British Museum, which also owns a Bow porcelain flowerpot that links Thomas and Anne together, being marked "Thos. & Ann Target July 2nd 1754." The museum also owns a cream pitcher inscribed

FIGURE XIII.31. Bow porcelain tea bowl with underglaze blue and overglaze enameling in green, yellow, and red, part of a set made for Ann Target in 1754.

"W Pether May 10 1754," evidence suggesting that in 1754 the Bow factory was featuring personalized tea sets. But whether this was its normal response to special orders or whether Pether and the Targets had a more than casual acquaintance with the owners of the factory, no one knows.

The Bow porcelain factory was launched in 1744 by a mineral merchant named Edward Heylyn and Thomas Frye, a painter and engraver,[41] who together secured a royal patent to protect their invention defined as "A New Method of Manufacturing A Certain Material, whereby A Ware might be made of the same Nature or Kind, and equal to, if not exceeding in goodness and beauty China or Porcelain Ware imported from Abroad." The patent stated that "The material is an earth, the produce of the Chirokee nation in America, called by the natives unaker."[42] Heylyn and Frye weren't alone in discovering the porcelain potential of American china clay. William Cookworthy of Plymouth, a pharmacist and an avid scientific experimenter, wrote to a friend in May 1745 saying that he had recently met a man who "hath discovered the china-earth" and who had brought with him "several samples of the china-ware of their making" and called them the equal of the Asiatic products.[43] Regarding the clay, Cookworthy wrote, "'Twas found in the back of Virginia where he was in quest of mines."[44] The intriguing question here, of course, is the identification of the chinaware samples. Who made them, when, and where? Taken at face value, one should assume that porcelain was already being manufactured in America, albeit at an experimental level, a conclusion for which there is no evidence.[45]

In the seemingly magical year of 1754, Cookworthy was to make his principal contribution to both the porcelain and earthenware industries by discovering massive deposits of kaolin clay in Cornwall, which thereafter became the source for many British wares. The year 1754 was also when the *Boston Evening Post* advertised "A Variety of Bow China, Cup and Saucers, Bowls, etc. . . . just imported by Philip Breadnig, and to be sold at his House in Fish Street."[46]

As will have become apparent from reading previous chapters, the life and interests of an archaeologist take unpredictable twists and turns as one discovery leads to another. Like our introduction to John Crowther, an affinity with William Cookworthy was the product of one such twist.

In 1963, while directing excavations behind Williamsburg's Wetherburn's Tavern, a colleague from the architects' office came to the site and told me that he had just witnessed an astonishing demonstration beside Bruton Parish Church, where power company electricians were tracing buried lines by means of divining rods made from bent wire coat hangers that crossed when they passed over metal. We had recently lost a pair of root cutters into our spoil heap that provided an opportunity to put this seemingly nutty process to the test. Feeling like an idiot and watched by my crew, who almost certainly thought I'd been hatless too long in the sun, I climbed onto the excavated spoil with my coat hangers correctly held. When they crossed, a little digging revealed the lost cutters. Ever

FIGURE XIII.32. Side and basal views of the companion Bow porcelain milk jug from Ann Target's tea service. 1754. Ex Clifford Larson Collection. Chipstone Collection.

since that day in 1963, a pair of bent coat hangers has been part of my archaeological kit, and I do not scoff at Cookworthy, who in the early 1750s fervently believed in the properties of a divining rod to find minerals. Because of it, his disbelieving friends called for a demonstration, having first, and unbeknownst to him, buried one of his large iron mortars in a corner of his garden. Cookworthy assured his audience that if there was metal there, the rod would find it. It made no difference, he said, whether the quantity of metal was large or small, shallow or deep, his rod would discover it. But it didn't. The laughing skeptics promptly dug up the mortar to prove that Cookworthy's procedure was nonsense. However, undaunted by what looked like a devastating failure, he declared that his mortar was an alloy and not being pure iron, his rod couldn't be expected to locate it.[47] I, too, have run similar experiments for skeptics, but usually with better results. In most instances (though not in all), the coat hangers have done their job of targeting telephone lines and electrical cables that might otherwise have been cut by my excavators. But now back to Bow in 1754 and that other Target.

In my 1972 book *All the Best Rubbish,* I illustrated Ann Target's tea bowl, the publishing of which prompted a letter from Clifford Larson, Director of the Laura Musser Art Gallery and Museum in Muscatine, Iowa, telling us that he owned Ann's Bow porcelain cream jug painted in the same pallet with peonies and the red fence, and marked "A ⋆ Target 1754" (Fig. XIII.32). Mr. Larson had bought the jug from a dealer in the small Wisconsin town of New Holstein, but knew nothing of its prior history. In 1970 he took the jug to the British Museum, where ceramic historian Mavis Bimson ran tests of the clay and determined that the jug was of phosphatic porcelain and unquestionably genuine. Mr. Larson ended his letter by expressing the hope that he would like some day to see the A. Target cream jug beside the A. Target tea bowl. After this chapter was already in proofs I received a phone call from Mrs. Larson, whom I had tried to track down after learning of her husband's death. She told me that although most of their collection of oriental antiques had already been auctioned, she still had the Target pitcher and would be pleased for it to be reunited with the bowl in the Chipstone Foundation's collection—thereby fulfilling a wish that had remained unanswered for twenty-eight years.

Throughout these pages I have stressed that the archaeologist has a distinct advantage over the collector and curator in that he or she rarely sees one example at a time, and instead finds them in their original associations either when discarded as domestic trash or as pottery-kiln rejects. The latter's potential is obvious, for like the delftware kiln material from Pickleherring Quay and the excavation of John Dwight's factory site at Fulham, every unfinished or overfired pot or pan tells us that this or that shape was made right there. In 1867, after the site of the Bow porcelain kilns had become a match factory, one of the latter's employees noticed children playing with potsherds beside a trench where a sewer line was being laid. The source of the toys was immediately evident. Fragments of biscuit and glazed porcelain were tumbling from the side of the trench. The observant young man, whose name is recorded simply as Mr. Higgins, Jr., obtained permission from his superiors to hold up the work long enough for him to do some digging on his own, and with the help of his sister (known to us only as Miss Higgins), he assembled a sufficient range of the factory's wares to be enthusiastically reported in the *Art Journal*.[48] Needless to say, Audrey and I had long felt an affinity with Mr. and Miss Higgins, for as salvage archaeologists for the City of London, we too spent much of our time peering into construction workers' trenches—though sometimes we went a step further and excavated *inside* the City's seventeenth-century sewers.

As you by now know, Audrey and I spent many hours searching the Thames's tidal shore for informative potsherds. One day when the tide was very low I was astonished to find fragments of high-quality English porcelain and several other wares being revealed as the water receded leaving the still-wet shards glistening in the sunlight (Fig. XIII.33).[49] What made this discovery different from any others I had come upon in close on half a century of searching was that the fragments all rested together in an area

FIGURE XIII.33. The north shore of the River Thames at an unusually low tide in 1991. The "Queenhithe Hoard" was found in the wet indentation in the foreground. An unidentified "mudlark" searches in the distance.

            IF THESE POTS COULD TALK

about two feet square. There was no doubt that they were associated with one another because they had been sealed beneath a layer of mud that was only then being washed away. Not only were the shards lying where they had fallen at some date within the brackets 1785–1790, but they were remarkably varied in their shapes and wares. Consequently, the salvaged group is cataloged as the grandiloquent-sounding "Queenhithe Hoard" (Figs. XIII.34 and XIII.35).

On American colonial sites there are usually two or three superior shards to every four or five hundred ordinary fragments. But this little Thames-side assemblage had nothing in it that could be dismissed as of

FIGURES XIII.34 and XIII.35. The "Queenhithe Hoard" of English ceramics deposited together in the last quarter of the eighteenth century, and of special interest by reason of the quality and variety of wares represented. Fig. XIII.34. (*a–c*) creamware bowl, Royal shape and feather-edged plates; (*d*) creamware saucer overglaze painted in red and black; (*e*) twisted handles from a creamware tureen; (*f*) notch-rimmed creamware bowl; (*g–i*) white salt-glazed stoneware plate in barley pattern, coffee cup, and cockle-edged plate; (*j*) dry-bodied redware teapot; (*k*) engine-turned, lead-glazed redware teapot (as Fig. XIII.36); (*l*) debased scratch-blue salt-glazed chamber pot; (*m*) Nottingham stoneware pitcher base; (*n*) dry-bodied and sprig-decorated redware punch pot lid; (*o*) Derbyshire or Nottingham brown stoneware bowl; (*p*) Nottingham brown stoneware pitcher base similar to (*m*). Fig. XIII.35 (*a–c*) Worcester sauce boat and fluted tea bowl; (*d*) small transfer-printed English porcelain bowl; (*e*) base of fluted tea bowl, possibly Bow; (*f, g*) rim and wall fragments from hand-painted, barrel-shaped Worcester mug; (*h*) base of marked Worcester porcelain tea bowl; (*i*) English porcelain punch pot spout, undecorated; (*j*) Chinese porcelain dish painted in overglaze enamels (*famille vert*); (*k*) white salt-glazed stoneware bowl with overglaze floral enameling; (*l, m*) creamware saucer and tea bowl painted in underglaze blue with Chinese house pattern; (*n*) pearlware bowl rim, hand painted in underglaze blue; (*o*) pearlware bowl base with internal underglaze transfer chinoiserie print. Context: Queenhithe, London, ca. 1785–1790.

FIGURE XIII.36. Engine-turned, lead-glazed redware teapot with characteristically conical spout. Staffordshire, ca. 1770–1780.

no interest. Among the pieces are the base of a marked Worcester porcelain bowl, parts of a barrel-shaped mug that may be of Liverpool porcelain (ca. 1755–1765) , the base of a fluted cup, pieces of a delicately fluted sauce boat whose border matches the late Bow stand, a shard from an overglaze-decorated white salt-glazed bowl, pieces from engine-turned teapots, one in dry-bodied redware and the other glazed, and a design parallel for a teapot in the Collection of ca. 1770 (Fig. XIII.36). Also included was a sprig-decorated lid from a dry-bodied redware punch kettle (?), along with fragments of underglaze-painted creamware and rare rim forms, two Nottingham brown stoneware mugs, a debased scratch-blue chamber pot, and the base from an early transfer-printed pearlware bowl. This last pushes the group to the late 1780s; otherwise, a date bracket of ca. 1775–1785 would be reasonable.[50] Realizing, as I do, that statistics can be made to support or refute virtually any premise, it nonetheless seems meaningful that the percentages provided by the group look like this:

English porcelain	30.5%
Creamware	23%
White salt glaze	13%
Nottingham	10.5%
Pearlware	7%
Dry-bodied red ware	7%
Engine-turned, glazed	3%
Debased scratch blue	3%
Chinese porcelain	3%

The intriguing and frustrating questions are these: How did this group get deposited together about 70 feet from the present shoreline, and what does it represent? In both the seventeenth and in the eighteenth centuries this was an area of warehouses and not of up-market homes (Fig. IX.2). Why does English porcelain run neck-and-neck with creamware? Why are nine different wares represented in a single group of only thirty-two fragments? That the questions remain unanswered should surprise no one, for in archaeology, alas, definitive conclusions are as scarce as were white whales to the crew of the *Pequod*.

XIV   Beyond the Gas Lamps' Glare

Poverty and misery are terribly concrete things. We find their incarnation everywhere. . . . The poet has admirable opportunities of drawing weird and dramatic contrasts between the purple of the rich and the rags of the poor.

Oscar Wilde, 1884[1]

AUDREY'S AND MY decision to collect intact and informative parallels for shards encountered in our excavations or while "mudlarking" on the Thames foreshores led us to commemorative wares because, as I have demonstrated, they were either marked with dates or linked to a specific event. At the same time, my own interest remained focused on stonewares both Rhenish and English—though I cannot deny that Audrey's early pursuit of Victorian ceramic pot lids and brown stoneware bottles from the Upchurch marshes, in preference to the nigh on two-thousand-year-old Romano-British wares, was a quirk I never understood (Figs. XIV.1 and XIV.2). I found it difficult to enthuse over an ironstone toothpaste pot lid or a brown stoneware ink bottle devoid of any source identification, but conceded that some have informative inscriptions and others pleasing shapes.[2]

FIGURE XIV.1. A selection of Audrey's Victorian ceramic pot lids from the Upchurch Marshes, ca. 1870–1880.

Most of the brown stoneware bottles date from the second half of the nineteenth century, and although part of British ceramic history, it is, alas, a pretty dull part. However, that cannot be said of the stoneware bottles and flasks of the century's second quarter, for these open the door to that dark side of Victorian life that has been described as the *legacy of the damned.*

"Drunk for a Penny / Dead drunk for two pence / clean straw for nothing" were words inscribed on an arch in the engraving by William Hogarth titled *Gin Lane* (Fig. XIV.3). In 1791, according to his biographer, John Ireland, there was "inscribed on a barber shop, in the vicinity of Drury Lane, 'Shave for a Penny, and a Glass of Gin into the Bargain.'" Gin, or geneva, took its name from the old French *genevre,* meaning juniper, and became the London poor's most affordable solace.

FIGURE XIV.2. Some of Audrey's brown stoneware bottle collection from the Upchurch Marshes, the transportation of which across the mud evinced minimal enthusiasm from the team, ca. 1870–1880.

FIGURE XIV.3. A detail from William Hogarth's *Gin Lane* (1751) depicting gin being fed to infants and the aged.

In 1690, in an effort to discourage the importation of French brandy, Parliament passed an Act encouraging the distillation of British brandy and spirits from home-grown corn. Early in the reign of Queen Anne (1702–1714), another Act of Parliament withdrew controls hitherto the prerogative of the Distillers' Company, and let anyone with a still make whatever spiritous drink he chose. The resulting effect on life and labor was disastrous and led to the Gin Act of 1736, designed to tax gin out of reach of the poor. The result: rioting in the streets of London. The Act's effectiveness can be judged by the following figures: eleven million gallons distilled in London in 1733 and twenty million in 1742.

In 1753, Chambers' *Cyclopaedia* reported that London's gin was no longer being made with juniper berries, "our rascally chemists" having taught the distillers that oil of turpentine would do as well.

So Quacks, for Cordials, filthy spirit sell,
Which soon dispatch the sick to heaven or Hell,
Not caring whether they are bless'd or curs'd,
Since they have pick'd the Patient's Pocket first.[3]

Several more legislative attempts to curb the drinking of spirits through taxation and licensing were made in the latter years of the eighteenth century, but none proved any more effective than attempts to curb drug addiction in our own time. Yet another Gin Act was voted up in 1830 to promote beer as an alternative to gin and permitting anyone to sell ale who cared to purchase a two-guinea license. The result of that was the birthing of countless legal backroom beer dives that made nonsense of existing laws regarding the licensing of taverns and ale houses. Needless to say, the latter's proprietors were not a happy band. No sooner had the two-guinea

IF THESE POTS COULD TALK

FIGURE XIV.4. Flat spirit bottle with the same sprigged profile on both sides. This is believed to be the ancestor of the next century's cast-in-the-mold gin flasks. Ca. 1780–1800.

premises acquired a clientele than the neo-publicans discovered that their customers still preferred gin. Being ever anxious to please, they promptly added illegally distilled spirits to their list of specials. In the decade that followed the 1830 Act, beer drinking went up 28% and gin sales by 32%. Although much gin was being consumed on the premises, it was the gin-to-go trade that fostered a new departure in the history of brown stoneware.

In October 1724, Joseph Blake, a pickpocket and burglar, was tried at the Old Bailey and confessed to numerous crimes that included the robbing of a woman in Threadneedle Street from whom he stole "37 shillings, and some half-pence, a silver snuff box gilt, a pocket bottle of geneva, and a tortoiseshell tobacco box." One might wonder why a respectable London lady would be carrying snuff, tobacco, and bottled gin.[4] The obvious conclusion, of course, is that she wasn't a respectable London lady. The point I am making, however, is that in the eighteenth century the carrying of small bottles of gin was no different from the pocketing of silver spirit flasks in more recent centuries. A small, flattened-sided, stoneware bottle in the Collection is one such portable container, and by the style of the mob-capped female profile sprig-molded on both sides, it should date around 1790 (Fig. XIV.4). Found on a construction site in Lambeth, this little bottle would seem to be an isolated example, for I know of no others of this period, and its claim to be the forerunner of the ubiquitous stoneware gin flasks of the nineteenth century has yet to be challenged.[5]

The 1830 Act selling two-guinea licenses not only increased rather than curtailed gin drinking, but it also heralded a novel means of selling gin, in reality pretty much the same one that Jim Beam Whisky latched onto a hundred years later. Making the bottles collectible, or at least sufficiently attractive for an already gin-soaked customer to be eager to take one home, continued to escalate the sale of bootleg gin. It would seem that the stoneware potters of Derbyshire were the pace setters for twenty years of gin-flask production, which very soon expanded to Lambeth. William IV had come to the English throne in 1830 and was considered a great improvement over the loathsome George IV, whose treatment of his erring wife had so enraged the British people. To my knowledge, William was the

FIGURE XIV.5. (*a*) Left: Molded brown stoneware William IV portrait flask, ca. 1832. (*b*) Modern copy of a rare Daniel O'Connell flask of ca. 1830. Both from the Bourne Pottery, Derbyshire.

FIGURE XIV.6. Molded brown stoneware flasks. (*a*) Representing Reform advocate Lord Brougham, impressed BROUGHAM REFORM CORDIAL, made by Oldfield & Co. of Chesterfield. (*b*) Large flask perhaps representing Reform party Prime Minister Lord Charles Grey, impressed THE TRUE SPIRIT OF REFORM. Unmarked. Both ca. 1832.

first reigning monarch to be honored with a portrait flask (Fig. XIV.5 *a*).[6] He is depicted wearing the Order of the Garter and looking resolutely ahead, and below, impressed with printers' type, we read WILLIAM, IV,TH'S REFORM CORDIAL. On the back is impressed BELPER & DENBY, BOURNES POTTERIES, DERBYSHIRE, an attribution that provides a *terminus ante quem* of 1834, when the Belper Pottery went out of business and the whole operation was taken over by William Bourne of Denby. Further narrowing the dating within the short reign of William IV is the flask's reference to Reform Cordial. Several portrait flasks were made in honor of individuals associated with the Reform Bill of 1832, among them Lord Brougham, whom we met earlier as the champion of Queen Caroline during the affair of the Green Bag (Fig. XIV.6 *a*). The smaller flask has a rather treacly color below the waist and a very dark and shiny surface above, both characteristic of the Oldfield Pottery, at Brampton in Derbyshire, whose name is impressed into the back. Lord Brougham is of the standard pint size, and stands beside the largest Reformer in the Collection, a flask that weighs 4¼ pounds and clearly had no intention of going in anyone's pocket. It may have been made as a taproom advertisement promoting the sale of the regular sizes. Although the portrait and related flasks may have been accepted as being of specific capacities, they clearly were not. It must, therefore, have been left to the honesty of the dispenser to ensure that what went into Lord Brougham's head or down the muzzle of a stoneware pocket pistol was a full measure. That, of course, put the customer at a considerable disadvantage, for who ever heard of an honest bootlegger?

The Oldfield Pottery is said to have opened ca. 1838 and continued in production until 1888.[7] It seems likely, however, that 1838 is several years too late, for the Reform leaders were no longer front and center in the minds of the average neo-Victorian sot once the Queen had come to the throne in 1837. The heavyweight bottle stands 14½ inches tall and bears no name, but the figure carries a scroll reading THE TRUE SPIRIT OF REFORM and probably depicts Lord Charles Grey, who was Prime Minister and head of the Whig Party until his retirement in 1834 (Fig. XIV.6 *b*).[8]

Among the rarest of all Reform-related flasks is one depicting the Irish firebrand Daniel O'Connell, who was elected to Parliament for County Clare in 1828, but who, as a Catholic, was barred from taking his seat. However, he was reelected two years later, after the Catholic Emancipation Bill had passed. For the rest of his often stormy life, O'Connell, known to his supporters as the "Liberator," fought for his countrymen through several Parliaments in a continuing effort to repeal the Anglo-Irish Union. Among collectors of stoneware gin flasks, "an O'Connell" is considered the greatest of all prizes.

In 1961 the Bourne Denby Pottery made some not-very-good reproductions of Reform flasks, among them Lords Brougham and Russell, as well as a Daniel O'Connell (Fig. XIV.5 *b*). An old friend from my theater days, Antony Oliver, ran a successful antique ceramics shop in Kensington Church Street a few doors down from John May, the latter being the principal London dealer in commemorative wares from whom many of our pieces were bought. With one of his sales in hand, I went into Oliver's shop and showed him our latest purchase. This prompted him to tell us that a few days earlier he had purchased a fine Daniel O'Connell—at least, he thought he had. The owner had brought the flask into the shop wrapped in newspaper, but while Oliver was at his cash register in the shop's back room, the seller switched the real O'Connell for the Bourne reproduction and left before Oliver discovered the deception. Needless to say, he was relieved to offset part of his loss by selling the copy to us at an honest price. As such, it has its place in the Collection as a further warning to collectors that unmarked but legitimate reproductions, once dishonestly sold, become fakes.

Belonging to the same general period as the Reform flasks is one impressed H R H DUKE OF YORK that shows him at full length, a sword in his right hand and his Garter robe draped over his left (Fig. XIV.7 *a*). We found His Royal Highness in an "antiques and collectibles" fair in Savannah, Georgia, the only flask in the Collection with an American history. The flask had been used as a container for varnish, and both the vendor's ignorance and the modest price made it highly unlikely that it had been bought as an antique in England. Had it been so, its true worth would

FIGURE XIV.7. (*a, b*) Two H R H DUKE OF YORK flasks made for a public house of that name. Neither marked; ca.1830–1835. (*a*) Found in Georgia.

have stayed with it. We concluded, therefore, that someone had brought it back to Georgia in the 1830s and that it remained unappreciated until it found its way into a yard sale or estate auction.

Regardless of the flask's varnish streaks, we were delighted to have found it, coming as it did from the same mold as another already in the Collection (Fig. xiv.7 *b*). The Savannah flask is iron-slip coated to the breast and a pale buff below, while the second example has no slip and is a mottled brown over all and presumably a product of a Lambeth kiln. Unresolved is the question of whether we are looking at two factories that bought molds from a single modeler or whether these very different surface techniques are variants from one pottery. There was a problem, too, about the identity of the Duke. Because he is shown holding a cavalry saber and wearing an armor breastplate, it is reasonable to deduce that he is Frederick, the second son of George iii, who made a heroic name for himself in 1793 by capturing the French town of Valenciennes, an achievement that earned him several commemorative mugs, jugs, and plates. In truth, the taking of Valenciennes was a joint effort with the Austrian army under the Prince of Coburg, and thereafter Frederick was responsible for numerous ignominious defeats that convinced his officers that "the duke was unfit for the command of an army in the field."[9] In 1808 he was forced to surrender his rank of Commander-in-Chief of the Army, due in part to his poor showing in battle, but more to his showing in bed with Mary Anne Clarke, who used her intimacy to promote the advancement of junior officers who had paid her for whispering into the duke's ear on their behalf. Like most scandals, it quickly blew over, and during George iv's reign Frederick addressed himself to improving esprit de corps in the army and seeing to it that the rank and file were better cared for. He died in 1827 at the age of sixty-four, and his passing was widely reported and regretted in the press. But whether that was sufficient to warrant the modeling of a commemorative gin flask several years later seemed to be an unanswerable question.

The vast majority of these brown stoneware flasks were produced between circa 1830 and 1856, and as yet there is no firm proof of their production any earlier—unless, of course, we were to accept the Duke of York flasks as having been made at the time of his death. There was, however, another possibility, namely, that he lived on for many years as the name for a public house. In 1864 there were at least thirty-two Duke of York pubs in London alone, although there is no certainty as to which Duke of York was thereby being commemorated.[10] Nevertheless, had Audrey and I visited Robin Hildyard's Victoria and Albert Museum exhibition of "Browne Muggs" in 1985, we would have known that our guess was at least half right. Furthermore, the mystery of how one of our bottles had wound up in Georgia would have been solved.

The V. & A.'s exhibition included a Duke of York bottle from the same mold as ours, but impressed "The Trade & Shipping Supplied. SAMUEL GARRETT Duke of York Wine & Spirit Vaults 29 High Street Shadwell."[11]

In the seventeenth century the Thameside village of Shadwell grew into an important maritime location for rope walks, wharves, chandlers' shops, and the like. By 1674 more than 8,000 people lived and worked there, most of them mariners and lightermen. Although the quality of life deteriorated in the first half of the nineteenth century to the point where Shadwell became one of London's most notorious slums, its connection with shipping persisted. It is safe to say, therefore, that one of Sam Garrett's Duke of York flasks boarded a Savannah-bound ship berthed at Shadwell at some time in the mid-1830s. Rarely do the pieces of a transatlantic ceramic puzzle fit so neatly together.

That our Duke of York flasks related to a wine and spirit purveyor and not to the a direct commemoration of the Duke himself, there can be no doubt. It does not follow, however, that all "prominent people" flasks were made for specific public houses or gin palaces, though another in the collection can claim that distinction. Molded in the shape of Elizabeth I's head and shoulders, it is labeled in a banner OLD QUEEN ELIZABETH HEAD (Fig. XIV.8). Above the ribbon is the publican's name G. BROWNE and under it his address at LOWER ROAD, ISLINGTON. More importantly, the flask's base is marked very faintly with an inscription that reads "F. Wetherill July 27 1830 [not fully legible]." Derek Askey has found an 1840 *London Directory* entry that identified one Francis Wetherall as a modeler at 3 Cleaver Street in Lambeth.[12]

The Old Queen Elizabeth Head Inn took its name from an event that occurred in Islington in 1581. One summer evening the Queen rode out from London to enjoy the still nearby countryside where she is said to have had a hunting lodge. While there she was beset by beggars who "gave the queen much disturbance." A footman hurried back to London and informed the Lord Mayor who sent out minions to arrest the beggars and to clap them into Bridewell prison. The roundup netted no fewer than "seventy-four rogues, whereof some were blind, and yet great usurers and very rich."[13] The subsequent fate of the seventy-four is not recorded. In those days, nobody sued for illegal arrest.

The Queen Elizabeth flask has been hailed as the only known specimen designed for a specific tavern. Whether this is true or not, the flask was the last of its category to enter the Collection, having cost twice the price of any other, a warning to us that we should shift our interest in another, less costly direction. By that time, however, there were thirty-nine flasks in the cupboard.

Possibly related to the Duke of York flasks are a pair of gray stoneware figures, both very well modeled, one an unidentified nobleman and the other presumably his wife, who stands taller by a hat (Fig. XIV.9). The man's features certainly resemble those of the Duke, but it seems unlikely that the death of a half-forgotten hero of questionable prowess would have resulted in the production of an unmarked full-length figure and even less likely that he would be accompanied by his wife, who had been dead for seven years. The Duke had married Charlotte, daughter of the King of

FIGURE XIV.8. Rare Queen Elizabeth portrait flask, made for G. BROWNE, publican of the OLD QUEEN ELIZABETH HEAD of LOWER ROAD ISLINGTON. Incuse on the base, a faint inscription identifies the maker as F. Wetherill and the date as July 27, 1830.

FIGURE XIV.9. A mystery couple in unslipped stoneware, probably originally with paper identifying labels on each of the flask's thick plinths. Possibly the Duke and Duchess of Kent, parents of Queen Victoria. Ca. 1830–1837.

Prussia, in 1791, but it was not a success and she soon retired to Oatlands Park in Surrey and remained there "playing with her dogs" until her death in 1820. The estrangement may have opened the door to the aforementioned Mrs. Mary Anne Clarke, who became a national celebrity when her relationship with the Duke became an issue during the investigation of charges laid against him for the misuse of his patronage. Mary Anne's popularity was short-lived, however, and ended when the Duke was acquitted. By 1816 she had moved to Paris and remained in France until her death in 1852. Highly unlikely is it, therefore, that the stoneware figure is actually the mercenary Mary, although she did merit a portrait on a late creamware jug.[14]

Regardless of any facial similarity to the dead Duke of York, it remains my own view that the stoneware couple are actually the parents of Victoria, the Duke and Duchess of Kent. Duke Edward was the fourth son of George III; he married Princess Victoria of Saxe-Coburg and would die in 1820. A portrait of him painted in 1818 bears a close resemblance to the male flask figure. In spite of his early death, it would make sense that accession promoters would create models of both the very much alive Duchess and her late husband. That neither figure is named in the clay is curious, but it is likely that the tall, blank bases originally were used to provide space for printed paper labels.

The accession of Victoria on June 20, 1837, spawned a plethora of gin flasks, among the most interesting being one we came to know as the "swan-necked portrait." She stands in high relief, an eagle-capped scepter in her right hand and her left resting on the cushion that supports the crown (Fig. XIV.10). She wears a coronet and, it would appear, a very tight corset, which so constricts her waist that it's hardly surprising that her neck is squeezed up like toothpaste from a tube.[15] On the opposite side of this pocket bottle are the royal arms in equally high relief and extremely carefully rendered—but wrong. The central charge incorporates the cap of Hanover, which had been part of the arms of William IV, but which could not be borne by the female line.[16] This flask leaves no doubt as to its date of manufacture or to the name of the potter. Incuse on the base is written in script "Published by S. Green, Lambeth, July 20th 1837," mean-

FIGURE XIV.10. Front and back of a Victoria accession flask. The swan-neck portrait is on the front, and on the back the Queen's royal arms are incorrectly charged with the horse of Hanover. Incuse on the base "Published by S. Green, Lambeth, July 20th 1837."

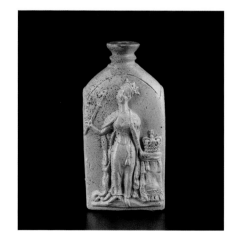

IF THESE POTS COULD TALK

FIGURE XIV.11. Two flask versions of the standing Victoria at the time of her coronation. Both ca. 1837.

ing that Accession gin flasks were modeled and in production a month after Victoria was proclaimed Queen. The importance of catching the market's mood is by no means a Madison Avenue concept.

Stephen Green of Lambeth did not restrict himself to pocket flasks—as is evidenced by another of his July 20 creations (Fig. XIV.11 *a*), but this time with the name VICTORIA on the front and below it the less regal 1/2, indicating a half-pint capacity. On the base in cursive script we read "Published, by S. Green, Lambeth, July 20th 1837." This one was made to order, for on the back is impressed B. COOPER COACH & HORSES, 4 HOSPITAL ROW, CHELSEA. A larger version, but with the same florid lettering of VICTORIA, lacks any factory identification, but claims royal preferment for its seaside-based customer (Fig. XIV.11 *b*). On the back of the plinth is the type-impressed inscription SAVAGE & AUSTIN WINE & SPIRIT MERCHANTS TO HER MAJESTY, CASTLE SQ BRIGHTON. As it is highly likely that this flask was made in 1837 it is less probable that by then the new Queen, with affairs of state suddenly demanding her attention, should be handing out preferments (by Appointments) to gin pedlars in Brighton. Far more likely is it that Messrs. Savage & Austin had been awarded their distinction in the reign of George IV, who, as Prince Regent, had promoted the building of the garish Brighton Pavilion, and that they continued to claim royal patronage until ordered to desist.

In 1840 the young Queen married Albert of Saxe-Coburg, giving gin-flask potters an opportunity to add another name to their stock of "Royals." The full-length figure of Albert stands 15 1/4 inches in height, and his name on the plinth is identical in style to that on Stephen Green's 1837 portrayal of the Queen (Fig. XIV.12). We archaeologists are always seeking connections that will enable us to use one artifact to date another, and were it not for the 1837 on the underside of Victoria one might very well be tricked into associating her flask with the royal wedding three years later. The connection, if indeed there is one, must surely be that the potter went to the same matrix modeler on both occasions. Although anyone buying a "big Albert" would have wanted a matching Queen, to date no companion Victoria has been recorded.

FIGURE XIV.12. A large portrait flask of Prince Albert for whom no matching Victoria is known. Unmarked, ca. 1840.

FIGURE XIV.13. A classic polychrome-decorated pearlware Toby jug that served as inspiration for cruder stoneware versions. Ca. 1825–1835. Chipstone Collection.

FIGURE XIV.14. (*a*) Toby as a brown stoneware bottle, shown holding the traditional beer jug. The boozer on a barrel design is derived from classical interpretations of Bacchus or Silenus, god of the grape. (*b*) Bacchanalian scene by Andrea Mantegna of Padua, 1431–1506.

The stoneware potters did not limit their flask casting to royalty and reformers. Over a period of about twenty years they repeatedly tapped into the popular pulse for inspiration. Particularly appreciated were versions of the standard Toby jug, a fine example of which is included in the Chipstone Collection (Fig. XIV.13) and serves as the geologists' type fossil for the Collection's brown stoneware Toby bottle. The ceramic origin of the so-called "Toby Jug" is accredited to Burslem's Ralph Wood I (1715–1772), who was followed by Ralphs II and III, all three of whom were styled "Figure makers." Like the legends of the willow pattern, there are several dubious histories attendant upon the inspiration to make jugs shaped like beer-guzzling fat farmers. According to one authority, the figure comes from an engraving of one Toby Philpot (fill pot) who was the subject of a song titled *The Brown Jug,* which had been translated from Latin, no less, and published in 1761.[17] Another writer stated that the song was actually titled *The Metamorphosis, or Toby Reduc'd,* and that the engraving was issued by chapbook and catchpenny print publisher Carrington Bowles,[18] who was in business as a London "Merchant and Printseller" in the 1780s and 1790s.[19] As Ralph Wood I was long dead, something is historically adrift. Nevertheless, regardless of their genesis, Toby jugs in a variety of guises continued to be popular throughout the nineteenth century, and any cottage mantle shelf that wasn't home to a pair of those awful Staffordshire dogs almost certainly displayed a Toby jug or two. The Collection's Toby bottle has him sitting on a barrel with its xxx (contents strength?) stamped on one of the staves (Fig.XIV.14 *a*). The modeling is sharp, and details such as his whiskers, eyes, teeth, coat buttons, and foam-capped mug are all well defined; so, too, are the buckles on his shoes. The Collection's second man on a barrel (Fig. XIV.15) was illustrated by Derek Askey in his book *Stoneware Bottles* as an example of inferior modeling.

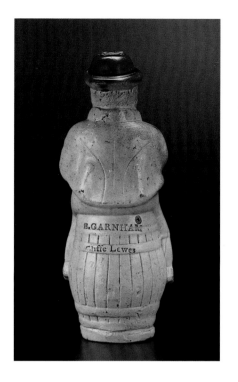

There are, however, a sufficient number of paralleling details to indicate that both this and the Toby bottle were the work of the same block maker and came from the same factory at more or less the same time.[20] The big question, of course, is: When was that time? The answer would seem to be hidden in the second figure's rounded- or rolled-brimmed hat, a type popular among the laboring poor in the 1850s. The man sits very awkwardly atop his barrel, which is impressed OLD TOM, a name to be found on barrel heads in gin-palace engravings. On his back is impressed the name of the liquor purveyor, B. GARNHAM, Cliffe Lewes.[21] Cliffe is a section of the Sussex county town of Lewes, and "The Cliffe" is one of six societies renowned for their breathtaking Bonfire Night parade, which each year on Guy Fawkes Day (November 5) celebrates the failure of the 1605 alleged Catholic attempt to blow up both king and Parliament (Fig. XIV.16).[22] Somewhere between 40,000 and 80,000 people crowd into Lewes's narrow streets that night to witness the studiedly politically incorrect parade of some 2,000 costumed participants of all ages, from babes in strollers to octogenarians in wheelchairs.

Political correctness as a denial of free speech was in no one's vocabulary in 1828 when a young American entertainer, Thomas Dartmouth Rice, his face blacked with burnt cork, performed Negro songs between the acts of plays, and thereby achieved considerable fame while appearing at the Southern Theater in Louisville, Kentucky. He was already a "name" when he took his act to England and to London's Surrey Theatre in 1836, and became the subject for another gin flask (Fig. XIV.17 *a*). In his act, Rice portrayed an old man he called Jim Crow, a name that became the title of his signature song. Sheet music printed to further promote his London success showed a ragged Rice dancing to the tune, its title reading JIM

FIGURE XIV.16. Lewes, the county town of Sussex, is divided into several parishes, one of them known as the Cliffe. The town is renowned for its annual fireworks parades that began in 1605 and that developed into separate societies in the mid-nineteenth century. The Cliffe Bonfire Society is the best known and is based at a Cliffe pub of which B. Garnham may have been the landlord. The Cliffe is seen here in full fire in Lewes High Street in the Guy Fawkes Night parade of November 5, 1997.

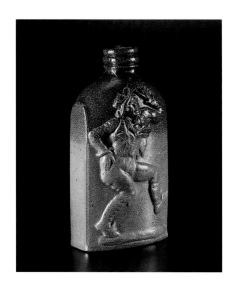

FIGURE XIV.17. (*a*) American black-face entertainer Thomas Dartmouth Rice was a hit at London's Surrey Theatre in 1836. The unmarked flask's design was taken from his sheet music cover (*b*).

FIGURE XIV.18. (*a*) Sir Marc Isambard Brunel (1769–1849) designed and, after many setbacks, built the first tunnel under the River Thames. (*b*) Brunel's signature on a letter in the Collection written in 1826 when all seemed to be going well. (*c*) Souvenirs from silver medals to stoneware gin flasks recalled the opening in 1843; this realistically three-dimensional flask derived from a contemporary engraving (*d*). (*a*) By courtesy of the National Portrait Gallery, London.

CROW, A CELEBRATED NIGGER SONG, SUNG BY, Mr. T. RICE, With the most unbounded Applause, AT THE SURREY THEATRE (Fig. XIV.17 *b*). The sheet music's portrayal (probably copied from playbills posted around London) became the source for gin flasks showing Rice in the same pose. Consequently, the Jim Crow flasks have a place in the history of theater as well as serving as a reminder of the origin of Jim Crow, the white man's subservient and often self-parodying black man.[23]

Dating for the Jim Crow bottle's master mold is provided by a handled example on whose base is inscribed "Pubed by F. Wetherill Novr 25 1836 25 Kennington Lane Lambeth."[24] This, of course, was the same Francis

Wetherill who, six years earlier, had modeled the Old Queen Elizabeth Head flask while at his Cleaver Street premises.

An entirely different flask commemoration related, not to royalty or to a vaudeville act, but to an engineering marvel, the tunnel under the Thames between Wapping on the north bank and Rotherhithe on the south. The first attempt was made in 1805, but the tunnel caved in, as would other later shafts. It fell to engineer Marc Isambard Brunel to invent a tunneling shield that could be augmented with every 4 1/2 inches of progress (Fig. XIV.18 *a*).

Whenever feasible, Audrey and I tried to augment the ceramics collection with related documentation. One such is a letter written by Marc Brunel on February 6, 1826, when the tunneling was in an early and still optimistic phase (Fig. XIV.18 *b*):

> I am much obliged to you for the notice you have taken of the Tunnel where I should be glad to see you, in about 3 weeks, rather than at present: as we are in great confusion for a few days longer, by the operation of removing the scaffolding for the first part of our proceedings.[25]

Parliament had voted to fund the project in 1823, but progress was slow and sometimes deadly, and by 1828 five inundations had sapped both the energy and the funding, causing the digging to cease until 1835. Supervised thereafter by Marc Brunel's son Isambard, the world's first underwater tunnel was finally completed in 1843 and opened with appropriate fanfare and hoopla. Although intended to be ramped and paved to carry horse-drawn vehicles, the funding took the project no further than a pedestrian walkway. It did, however, allow ample room for souvenir shops. Wrote American visitor William Drew in 1852:

> It is impossible to pass through without purchasing some curiosity. Most of the articles are labeled "Bought in the Thames Tunnel"— "a present from the Thames Tunnel." I purchased several of these souvenirs.[26]

Once the novelty wore off, the tunnel earned an unenviable reputation as a haven for thieves and for prostitutes who bestowed on their "gentlemen" souvenirs of a very different kind. However, the tunnel flasks, which skillfully provided a third dimension to several printed renderings, were almost certainly sold as legitimate reminders of the Brunels' engineering achievement (Fig. XIV.18 *c* and *d*). Indeed, the eventually knighted Sir Marc Brunel's protective casing has been the tunneling method employed in digging the twentieth century's Channel Tunnel and every other underwater highway.

In addition to flasks made to exploit specific events, there were others aimed to catch the fancy of readers of *Punch,* Victorian Britain's most popular current affairs magazine. A regular writer for it was the Surrey Theatre's sometime resident playwright Douglas William Jerrold, whose best

FIGURE XIV.19. (*a, b*) Two versions of MRS CAUDLE flasks capitalizing on the popularity of essays by Douglas Jerrold in *Punch* magazine that he called "Curtain Lectures." On the reverse of each the young woman labeled MISS PRETTYMAN was another Jerrold character. The concept of the woman berating her dozing husband was not Jerrold's alone, as the redrawing (*c*) of a woodcut published in 1646 attests. Flasks ca. 1846–1850.

remembered series of literary conversations was titled *Mrs. Caudle's Curtain Lectures*. In them, and from behind the bed curtains, she berated her long-suffering husband (Fig. XIV.19 *a* and *b*).[27] His weary request for her to desist drew the response NO MR CAUDLE, I SHALL NOT GO TO SLEEP LIKE A GOOD SOUL. Two flasks in the Collection carry that line, one of them with the addition of SEE PUNCH. The flasks are of two different sizes, but both almost certainly were the work of the same master modeler. Each shows the nightcapped and hen-pecked Mr. Caudle hunkering down in the bedclothes beside his wide-awake wife. On the backs of both flasks is a young woman holding a parasol and labeled in type MISS PRETTYMAN, who was another of Jerrold's characters. The larger of the two flasks is type-impressed STEPHEN GREEN, LAMBETH, but the other is stamped DOULTON & WATTS, LAMBETH POTTERY, LONDON. Green operated the Imperial Potteries in Lambeth from ca. 1820 to 1856, while his competitors, Messrs. Doulton and Watts, opened a few years earlier and continued their partnership until 1858.

Although the "curtain lectures" are widely considered to have been Jerrold's own invention, the concept is much older, as my Fig. XIV.19 *c* shows. It had been redrawn in the 1880s from a woodcut illustrating a book published in London in 1646 titled *Ar't asleepe Husband? A Boulster Lecture, Stored With all variety of Witty jeasts, merry Tales, and other pleasant passages,* and in whose pages the words "Curtaine Lecture" are used.[28]

Several flasks portray Mr. Punch, none of them, alas, in the Collection. He is there represented only by a stoneware inkwell on whose back is a registry mark that dates it to April 1, 1851 (Fig. XIV.20). Below the diamond-shaped mark panel is a scarcely legible retailer's address that should read GARDNER'S INK WORKS, LOWER WHITE CROSS STREET, LONDON. Unfortunately, in smoothing off the marks of the two-piece mold, the potter's not very able assistant also wiped away the beginning and end of the inscription.

FIGURE XIV.20. Mr. Punch as a brown stoneware inkwell, with a helpful registration mark molded into his back attributing the design to 1851.

The character of Mr. Punch goes back at least into the sixteenth century, when he was the star of live-action fairground plays, but over time the melodrama built around him degenerated, first into a marionette show, and later into a one-man glove puppet production. This last evolution began around 1800, and in the process rid the show of much of its earlier brutality that began by Punch throwing his baby daughter out of a window. He continued to be scolded and whacked by his wife Judy through the nineteenth century, during which time the performers introduced new characters whom Mr. Punch could wallop in return. Following the success of Thomas Rice at the Surrey Theatre, his alter ego Jim Crow was added to the cast, and in 1851 Henry Mayhew, in his seering essays on the life of the London poor, printed the text of a play that involved the black puppet. Modern social correctness prevents one from quoting the lines, but the puppeteer's complaint about the taboos of the times has an astonishingly current ring to it:

FIGURE XIV.21. (*a, b*) Two humpbacked old women whose identity remains a mystery. The answer may at one time have been printed on paper labels glued to their plinths. Ca. 1840–1850. (*c*) Detail from an 1825 London street scene by Robert Cruikshank showing a humpbacked and capped Judy, suggesting a similarity of origin for the stoneware figures.

> To these sentimental folks I'm obliged to preform werry steady and werry slow; they won't have no ghost, no coffin, and no devil; and that's what I call spoiling the preformance entirely. It's the march of intellect that's doing all this, he added with a deep sigh.[29]

To my knowledge, Mr. Punch does not occur in the round as a gin flask, but only in relief on the sides in the manner of the incompatible Caudles. However, humpbacked female figures sometimes identified as Judy did aspire to three-dimensional flask immortality (Fig. XIV.21 *a* and *b*). Engravings and woodcuts of the late eighteenth century show many humpbacked Mr. Punches,[30] but Judy is less frequently pictured and rarely from a helpful angle.[31] As a rule she wears a tall Welsh or witch's hat—which the flask figures do not. However, in a drawing by Robert Cruikshank for Charles M. Westmacott's *The London Spy* (1825), his street Punch and Judy show depicts her with both a hump and a white cap that reached to her chin (Fig. XIV.21 *c*). The stoneware women also wear fabric caps that tie beneath their chins. But if that is seen as the determining clue (as I suspect it is), why are there no pairing Mr. Punches?

Another candidate has been Mother Shipton, the Yorkshire witch who was born in 1488 and who is said to have prophesied several major moments in the reign of Queen Elizabeth:

> Great London's triumphant Spire
> Shall be consumed with flames of fire.
> More wonder yet! A widowed Queen
> In England shall be headless seen.
> The harp shall give a better sound
> The Earl without a head be found.[32]

The spire of the church of St. Paul was struck by lightning in 1561 and never rebuilt. On February 8, 1587, Mary Queen of Scots, the widow of Lord Darnley, was beheaded on orders from a reluctant Elizabeth, and Robert Devereux Earl of Essex, one-time governor of Ireland (hence the symbolic Irish harp), mounted the executioner's scaffold on Tower Hill in 1601.

Although witches are often portrayed as humpbacked hags, I have found no evidence that Mother Shipton was said to be deformed. Porcelain models of her were made by several Staffordshire factories between 1900 and 1920, and while she is shown with the mandatory broom and black cat, no deformity is suggested. Indeed, one model has the words GOOD LUCK painted on her plinth. The often voiced suggestion that the stoneware figure is simply a run-of-the-cauldron witch can be countered by noting that they invariably were depicted wearing tall, pointed hats. But then, of course, you cannot push a bottle-sealing cork into the apex of a witch's hat. When I illustrated this problem person in *Antiques* magazine, a reader generously sent me a parcel containing another flask of smaller size, albeit almost certainly from the same block modeler (Fig. XIV.21 *a*).[33] Alas, no name of maker or retailer was impressed into the flask's base, and so all one can say with certainty is that the Collection includes not one but two mystery women with back problems.[34]

The humpbacked woman is merely one among several debated identities in ours or any collection of nineteenth-century gin flasks. Another three-dimensional female figure has been thought to represent opera singer Jenny Lind, who was known on both sides of the Atlantic as "The Swedish Nightingale" (Fig. XIV.22).[35] That identification is based on the fact that on the flask she holds a bird to her bosom. However, atop a pilaster to her left rests what appears to be a crown. The figure's hair is in ringlets, and it might be argued that she is another version "in the round" of a Victoria portrait flask derived from an 1835 painting by George Hayter (Fig. XIV.23). A variant of the lady with bird flask has been recorded as being dated "August 19th 1836."[36] If that date is valid, it rules out Jenny Lind, who would not give her first performance in England until May 4, 1847.[37] Derek Askey in his book on stoneware bottles very wisely was content to label this enigmatic flask "Lady with Bird." Our example is impressed on its back DENBY & CODNOR PARK, BOURNES, POTTERIES. DERBYSHIRE, a factory amalgamation that began in 1834.

FIGURE XIV.23. Oval-sectioned flask molded on both sides with the figure of the young Princess Victoria, modeled after an 1835 painting by George Hayter. Unmarked, but almost certainly from Lambeth. Ca. 1837.

There seems no doubt that Joseph Bourne had a corner on the northern flask manufacturing market,[38] nor is there any denying that the Denby Potteries were able to compete with the Lambeth factories in the second half of the nineteenth century. As we have seen, the practice of dumping London's garbage on the Medway and Upchurch Marshes in the 1870s and 1880s left many Bourne of Denby ink and ginger beer bottles in the mud to await Audrey's attention seventy years later. It would have been one thing for Bourne to sell to retailers with London markets, but for Denby to make bottles to special orders from London merchants seems quite extraordinary. Nevertheless, there is proof that it did so. An ink bottle in the Collection is marked VITREOUS STONE BOTTLES, J. BOURNE & SON PATENTEES, DENBY POTTERIES NEAR DERBY, and below in a box P & J ARNOLD, LONDON and under the box ENGLAND (Fig. XIV.2, *second from left*).[39] We can narrow the dating to a starting year of 1841, when Joseph Bourne took his son Joseph Harvey into the business. Unfortunately, the closing bracket would be far distant, as the company continued to trade as J. BOURNE & SON until the death of the latter's widow in 1898.

Ever since we began collecting these flasks we have studied every engraving, every early photograph or painting, in search of an example in a bar, on a home mantle shelf, on the floor beside a bed, anywhere and anyhow their existence and usage could be documented. We read journals, newspapers, advertisements, court records, all to no avail. Here, it seems, is a widely made, and more widely sold, ceramic object that in documentary terms does not exist outside the flasks themselves—which, to say the least, is odd. Nevertheless, it is a fact that the majority of the decorated stoneware spirit flasks that carry the purveyors' names were located at addresses in the slums around the old City of London where few artists or early photographers ventured.[40]

FIGURE XIV.24. A beguiling assortment of stoneware gin flasks. (*a*) From the Fulham Pottery in the shape of a clock impressed RAILWAY CHRONOMETER and made for G. PERREN, Red Lion, Whitechapel Road. (*b*) An oval barrel with loop holes for belt suspension, and a blank panel above the bung hole perhaps intended to receive a paper label; unmarked. (*c*) Large barrel impressed on its head SHEPPARD, 130 BLACKMAN St BORO [Borough of Southwark], undated. (*d*) An unmarked woman's boot. All ca. 1840–1850.

Although there is no evidence to prove it one way or the other, it seems likely that the decorated flasks became children's toys and perhaps were resold as souvenirs and curiosities to amuse the next level up the social ladder—people who, like the gin swillers of the slums, remained outside the realm of polite and literate society. Nevertheless, the London and Derbyshire potters recognized that there was a market sufficiently savvy to recognize royalty, to respond to political events, and to appreciate amusing models of familiar objects like the Collection's "Railway Chronometer,"

FIGURE XIV.25 A splendidly modeled fox-head flask based on silver stirrup cups from the later eighteenth and early nineteenth centuries, but a form that goes back to the Greco-Roman ceramic rhytons of the first century B.C. The flask is impressed around its collar "Stephen Green Imperial Potteries Lambeth," with the inscription added after removal from the two-piece mold. Ca. 1840–1850.

IF THESE POTS COULD TALK

and a woman's boot (Fig. xiv.24). Nevertheless, there is a temptation to lump these nineteenth-century flasks and related objects together and to associate them all with abject poverty. But as the Thames Tunnel flask and the exported Duke of York demonstrate, that was not necessarily so.

Of the London potters, Stephen Green's gin flasks are far more common than are those of his principal competitors[41] Doulton & Watts, and were made in a wide variety of shapes that range from a beautifully modeled fox-head stirrup flask (Fig. xiv.25), and a fine VR tipstaff (Fig. xiv.26), to two poorly made and glazed flintlock pistols (Fig. xiv. 27). A third pis-

FIGURE XIV.26. Tipstaff flask with Royal arms in relief, impressed around the base with the same Stephen Green inscription as in Fig. xiv.25. Ca. 1840–1850. A tipstaff was a badge of office comprising a short, truncheon-like staff tipped with silver or brass. Carried by court-appointed bailiffs and constables, a tipstaff was easily recognized by the gin-drinking public. Ca. 1840–1850.

FIGURE XIV.27. Flintlock pistol flasks unconvincingly modeled by Stephen Green of Lambeth, both with the Imperial Potteries factory mark impressed on the stock behind the barrel. Ca. 1840–1850.

tol in the Collection has everything that the Stephen Green's Imperial Potteries models lacked, and takes us north again to Derbyshire and to Joseph Bourne's Denby Pottery (Fig. xiv.28). This specimen is so convincingly made that it could easily have been used as a criminal's persuader. Unlike

FIGURE XIV.28. The most realistic pistol we ever encountered. All "metal" parts from barrel and percussion lock to screws of all sizes are slipped a dark, iron brown, while the stock and ramrod have a lighter and convincing wood finish. The impressed mark on the left side of the stock reads J. BOURNE, DENBY POT-TERY, DERBYSHIRE. This fine example of the stoneware potter's art could very easily and successfully have been used in a homeward-bound holdup—and perhaps it was. Ca. 1840–1850.

FIGURE XIV.29. A relatively rare, overall-brown stoneware percussion pistol flask from the Fulham Pottery. Ca. 1842. Edward Schultz Collection.

the Lambeth flintlocks, the gun has a "modern" percussion-cap firing mechanism, every part not of wood on the original being colored and thereby given the appearance of iron. The nineteenth-century incarnation of John Dwight's Fulham Pottery was not a major player in the gin flask game, but it did produce at least one pistol, this with an uncocked percussion lock and therefore less effective as an intimidator than the Denby version would have been (Fig. XIV.29).[42] My illustrated example turned up in Bermuda, where it was purchased at a yard sale at the very unintimidating price of one dollar.

Stephen Green's flintlock pistols came in differing shades of brown but made no distinction between parts that were meant to be of wood and those that were not. It cannot be said, however, that the Imperial Potteries in their quest for maximum sales never tried to do better. A well-modeled powder flask in the Collection attests to that degree of care (Fig. XIV.30). The powder bag that would normally have been of leather is identified by a dark brown slip, while the metal nozzle (usually of brass) achieved a contrastingly light tan through the salt-glaze firing alone. Its impressed mark reads "Stephen Green Imperial Potteries Lambeth" in lettering almost too small to be legible, as does the collar of Green's fox-head stirrup flask.[43]

Guns and gunpowder bring us abruptly back to the people for whom the flasks were made. On the one hand, we can envisage a Denby pistol being pointed at a terrified pedestrian by a villainous Bill Sikes, and on the

FIGURE XIV.30. Powder flask bottle with glazing interpretation of embossed leather and brass pouring lock. The molded-in-relief hunting dogs on both sides evidently were originally created in separate sprig matrixes like those used on the hunt mugs, but here were incorporated into the flask's two-piece mold. Impressed over the mold junction at the base of the bag, "Stephen Green Imperial Potteries Lambeth." Ca. 1840–1850.

FIGURE XIV.31. Flask in the form of a leather-bound book, which, when hot-water filled, could serve as a hand warmer in church, or be gin filled to warm the heart. Unmarked. Ca. 1840–1850.

other, copies of women's purses and even a small book being concealed in a muff to provide the fortification to help endure long and tedious sermons (Fig. XIV.31). For anglers there was the catch of the day, be it soft-mouthed or sharp toothed fish (Fig. XIV.32). While admiring their variety, it is all too easy to lose sight of the fact that most, if not all, of these amusing ceramic relics had but one purpose, and that was to sell gin to anyone with a penny to spend, were they old man, young woman, or toddling child (Fig. XIV.33).

It fell to Blanchard, son of "curtain lecture" Jerrold, to put the plight of the London poor into literate perspective, with his vision made the more terrible by the drawings of his friend and illustrator, Gustave Doré.[++] They described conditions in the slums that Jerrold called "densely packed haunts of poverty and crime," where there existed an army of the poor and destitute—"the victims of Drink, illustrators of every horror, form of suffering, and description of crime, to which the special curse of our land leads

FIGURE XIV.32. (*a, b*) Fishes soft-mouthed and otherwise, the latter impressed T BALLANCE, Wine & Brandy Merchant, Red Lion, 197 Ratcliff Highway. Neither marked. Ca. 1840–1850.

FIGURE XIV.33. Beneath the gas lamps' glare, customers of every age from infant to dotage raised their spirits and drowned their sorrows in the London gin shops. Mid-nineteenth century.

FIGURE XIV.34. Social historian Walter Besant told his readers why gin was known as "blue ruin," and artist Gustav Doré looked into the faces of the damned and drew what he saw. London, ca. 1872.

the poor. At the corner of every tumbledown street is the flaring public-house lamp—hateful as the fabled jewel in the loathsome toad's head."[45]

Riding in a cab out of the city toward Smithfield, Jerrold described how "The progress of the cab becomes slow and difficult: angry words are exchanged with the driver; groups of gossiping or quarreling men and women block the road; the houses are black and grim, and only at the corners where the gin palaces light up their cruel splendours, can we obtain glimpses of the inhabitants."[46] Thirty-five years earlier, Charles Dickens described the same filth, adding that "You turn the corner, What a change! All is light and brilliancy. The hum of many voices issues from the splendid gin shop. Its profusion of gas-lights in richly gilt burners, is perfectly dazzling when contrasted with the darkness and dirt we have just left."[47]

Social historian and novelist Walter Besant, writing about London in the 1830s and 1840s, left us with an indelible image of the effect of gin on the hungry poor. "Do you know why they call it 'blue ruin'?" Besant asked. And then he told us.

Some time ago I saw, going into a public-house, somewhere near the West India Docks, a tall lean man, apparently five-and-forty or thereabouts. He was in rags; his knees bent as he walked, his hands trembled, his eyes were eager. And, wonderful to relate the face was perfectly blue—not indigo blue, or azure blue, but of a ghostly, ghastly, corpse-like blue, which made one shudder. Said my companion to me, "That is gin."[48] (See Fig. XIV.34.)

To leave brown stonewares on such a note would do their makers a grave injustice. As my mandate being limited to the scope of the Collection, I cannot launch into a survey of the range of wares that the stoneware potteries produced. Suffice it to say that the 1873 catalog put out by Doulton & Watts of Lambeth listed seventy-three different shapes that came in several sizes, and ranged from breast warmers (with screw tops) to telegraph

insulators.[49] The catalog illustrated bottles with paneled shoulders akin to one in the Collection impressed VEMUR, STOUT HOUSE, SHOREDITCH (Fig. XIV.35 *b*). These were listed as "Flat Bottles, Square Shaped" with capacities from a quarter pint to a gallon. Also illustrated were relief-decorated jars called "Shop Pots (For Tin Covers)" that came with or without royal arms and with or without labels. This last refers to the elevated blank panels to which the buyer attached paper identification (Fig. XIV.36).

By the mid-nineteenth century the brown, salt-glazed stonewares that had been a staple of the British household from the days of John Dwight were being challenged by a new vitreous stoneware that Audrey and I detested and considered fit only for the outhouse and would not accept into the Collection—the same elitism that we had deplored in earlier museum curators. The new ware's shiny white and dirty golden surface was invented by William Powell of Bristol in 1835 and became known (none too surprisingly) as *Bristol glaze*. This feldspathic slip-glaze could be applied to "green" wares both inside and out, and when fired to stoneware temperature it required no secondary firing, as had other glazed wares first fired to biscuit. To achieve the ware's distinctive two-tone finish, the bottles and pots had to be twice dipped, first into the white and then into the yellow, a process known as *double glazing*. So much for background.

As I have said, we didn't like it and we didn't want it. However, a visiting archaeologist working on a seventeenth-century site in Virginia came to us for advice, and on our giving it he presented us with a singularly unattractive pot lid thickly coated with the Bristol glaze. He thought it would be more in our line than his.

The lid was a twist-off type for sealing preserves jars and about as attractive as ceramic insulators that were to be produced in the same stoneware. That view was shared by traditional brown stoneware potter John Doulton, who scorned the new ware for its "aesthetic poverty."[50] Nevertheless, we kept the lid for the sole reason that it had that life-saving "keep me" factor that I have mentioned so often throughout these pages (Fig. XIV.37). In the center beneath the thick oily glaze were impressed the words

FIGURE XIV.37. Patented preserves jar cover, the Collection's sole example of the dirty gold colored "Bristol glaze" that began to dominate stoneware ginger-beer bottle production in the mid-nineteenth century. The lid has documentary value, being impressed under the glaze with the name SINGER, VAUXHALL, LONDON and around it REGISTERED N° 4138, DEC 17 1858. Found in Virginia.

REGISTERED N° 4138 DEC 17 1858 and SINGER, VAUXHALL, LONDON. On the strength of that date alone, the lid survived in our stoneware cabinet for more than twenty years, and was only fished out when I decided that I had better say something about the dreaded Bristol glaze. But who was Singer?

Whoever he was and whatever he did, he did it in Vauxhall, the pottery-producing area on the south bank of the Thames adjacent to the better known Lambeth. Both Audrey and I had assumed that Singer had invented and patented this particular type of locking pot lid, and that was all there was to it. Had it occurred to us that Singer had been a potter as well as an inventor, we would have put two and two together much sooner. But we didn't.

The Vauxhall delftware factory founded in 1697 had been moved to Mortlake in 1804, leaving the old premises to continue making brown stoneware, at which time it was run by one William Wagstaff and later by his nephew John Wisker, who patented a method of manufacturing stoneware pot lids. That was in 1833. Two years later, the Vauxhall Pottery was bought by Alfred Singer, who had a friend in William Powell, inventor of the Bristol glaze. Thus did the two ideas come together: patent pot lids and Bristol glazing.

In 1865 the new owner of the Fulham Pottery, Charles Bailey, bought Singer's Vauxhall works, and, in a manuscript discovered by archaeologist Chris Green, had this to say, first about his own business and then about Singer's:

> I have constructed to [two] kilns to burn the new fashioned "Bristol" "Double glaze" ware which has almost entirely superceded the Brown stone, and which is by far the most profitable part of the business. . . . It so happened that Mr. Singer is in very delicate health and quite unfit for business and that Mr. Blackwell [partner in Cross & Blackwell's Preserves] wanted Mr. Singer's premises for the purposes of his Trade.[51]

Alfred Singer is credited with having been the first to establish the Bristol glazing technique in a London stoneware factory and had a lucrative contract with Cross and Blackwell, which Bailey took over for his Fulham plant when he bought out and closed the Vauxhall Pottery upon Singer's retirement in 1865.

So much history in a single scorned pot lid from a Virginia corn field!

Brown stoneware pots had been used as containers for preserves since the early eighteenth century, but most relied not on fitted ceramic lids but on waxed paper and fabric covers tied down with string. In the home, only tobacco jars and tea caddies had tightly fitting metal lids. The Collection's scratch-blue white salt-glaze caddy (Fig. IX.36) is an early example, and the brown stoneware version in Figure XIV.38 is typical of the later usage and a reminder that throughout the Victorian era tea continued to be brewed at the table and so needed to be presented in a suitably decorated container.

The caddy retains its original "tin" lid—which is really sheet iron tin coated—and its sides demonstrate the use of relief decoration that was not sprig applied but shaped in the press mold. Beneath the arabesque upper element is a scene involving a goat apparently being fed by a small cherub while being sat on by another so large and fat as to warrant arrest on a

FIGURE XIV.38. Molded brown, salt-glazed stoneware tea caddy with original tin lid. The relief decoration, part rococo, part neo-classical, was created in the mold. Derbyshire, ca. 1825–1850.

FIGURE XIV.39. (*b*) Condiment pot or hairpin stand in skillfully modeled brown salt-glazed stoneware. Derbyshire, ca. 1780–1790. (*a*) Similar profile of Sarah Wedgwood, from a portrait medallion made in the 1780s by famed sculptor John Flaxman (1755–1826) while employed by Josiah Wedgwood.

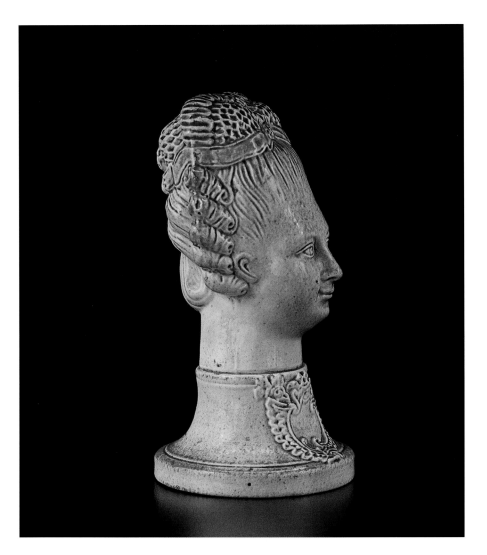

charge of animal cruelty. Like the vast majority of brown stonewares found on archaeological sites or preserved in public and private collections, the caddy is not marked with either the name of the factory or that of the customer. The Collection's finest specimen of brown stoneware modeling is similarly mute. This is a snuff caster, sander, or conceivably a hairpin holder, shaped as a 1790s-style head of an unidentified woman in a dappled, light brown salt glaze that I am tempted to attribute to Brampton (Fig. XIV.39 *b*). Adrian Oswald, however, was more cautious when he illustrated her in his book *English Brown Stoneware, 1670–1900*, there attributing the head only to Derbyshire and dating it to ca. 1780–1790.[52] His dating hinged on the existence of several rather similar heads made in Leeds Pottery creamware, each with a screw-capped base and holes in its hair. Those, in turn, are thought to owe their origin to a porcelain cane head in the Victoria and Albert Museum, which reportedly was attributed to Bow and to ca. 1765, but later cataloged as being from Lowestoft in about 1780.[53] Creamware expert Donald Towner agreed with the Leeds attribution for the creamware, but moved the date forward by another decade. Move it on another three years and an entirely new possibility

IF THESE POTS COULD TALK

emerges, namely, that this stoneware head memorialized the guillotining of Marie Antoinette on October 16, 1793, a step that appalled British royalists and later sent British troops to France under the Duke of York in a failing attempt to oust the revolutionaries and restore the French monarchy. If one cares to do so, the lace-like addition to the base can be seen at its top being intertwined with a tiny crown, a detail that, if it is truly there, provides support for the French connection.[54] But that is sheer speculation, as is the possibility that the head was sculpted by the celebrated modeler John Flaxman (1755–1826), who between 1775 and 1787 worked for Wedgwood and who, during that time, modeled a profile portrait plaque of Mrs. Wedgwood that bears more than a passing resemblance to the stoneware head (Fig. XIV.39 *a*).[55]

By the end of the 1980s, Audrey's and my decade-long focus on gin flasks was waning. Good examples were attracting higher and higher prices, and our ability to find shapes and subjects not already in the Collection resulted in too much fruitless hunting. Collecting anything you can't find is a singularly frustrating activity, and so by 1989 we were ripe for a new adventure, a new direction. And we found it in a French motel room.

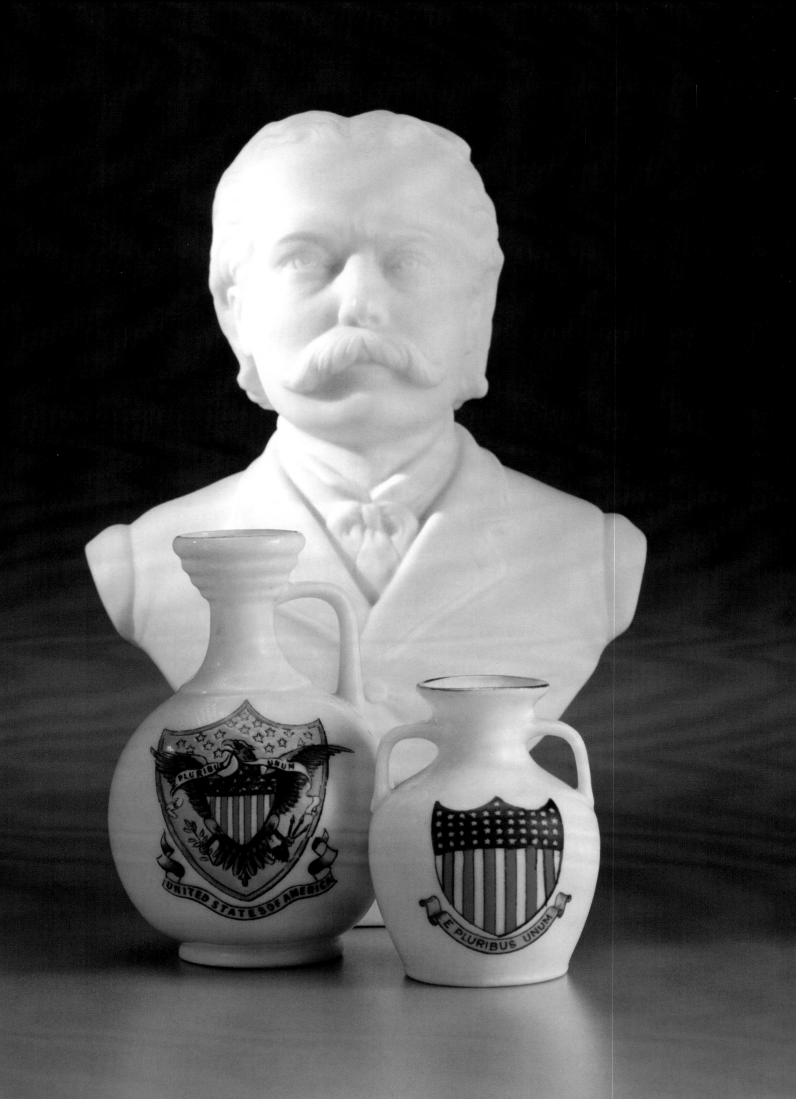

XV   In Remembrance, Staffordshire Style

In Flanders fields the poppies grow
Between the crosses row on row.

John McCrae, 1918

THE OLD SOLDIER was ninety-two but he walked ramrod straight as he carried the wreath to the foot of the monument and gently laid it down. Behind him, standing with Audrey and several others, I was elected to read the prayer for the remembered dead. Beyond us up a neatly mowed terrace the crosses stretched so far that they merged into a white sea. Behind them a marble wall, gray with carved names of men who were never found, stood sentinel over the vast cemetery at Passchendaele (Fig. xv.1). The sun had been shining as we approached the monument, but as I began to read the prayer it went behind a cloud and a chill wind blew across the graves. It began to rain, and for those of us not old enough to remember the War to End All Wars, we had a fleeting sense of what it must have been like in the trenches of the Ypres Salient in November 1917. Then, as suddenly as it had begun, the rain stopped and the wind died.

FIGURE XV.1. The wall of the unrecovered dead behind the British cemetery at Passchendaele barely hints at the magnitude of the losses suffered in the battlefields of the First World War.

Earlier in the morning, the old man had talked to me about his experiences, and one from among many remains implanted in my mind. He told us how he had received orders from company headquarters to pull back several hundred yards and dig new trenches. Captain Charles Austin, for that was the old soldier's name, telephoned back saying, "Sir, we are unable to dig in. There are too many bodies in the mud" (Fig. XV.2).[1]

FIGURE XV.2. A war artist's view of the mud and drenching rain characterizing the Third Battle of Ypres in 1917 that cost the British 310,000 casualties and the Germans almost as many. Painting from *The Illustrated London News*, Silver Jubilee edition, 1935. Courtesy The Illustrated London News Group Picture Library.

My father, a lieutenant in the Scots Guards, had enlisted at the age of seventeen and fought in Flanders through the last two years of the war, miraculously emerging unscathed. Like so many survivors, he rarely talked about it, but late in his life he began to write a history built around his own recollections, a project that was left in bits and pieces at the time of his death. I inherited the notes and the responsibility to do something with them. The notes were too incomplete to be shaped into a book, yet were so entertaining and so typical of the man and the war his generation fought that I decided that the best way to tell his story would be to put the notes in chronological order and turn them into an audio script.[2] Audrey, too, was anxious to learn more about that war, for her father had been gassed and died at an early age as the delayed result. Through the late 1980s and early 1990s, therefore, we joined several specialist tour groups and visited most of the battlefields and the places associated with them: Ypres, Armentières, Albert, the Somme, Thiepval, Sanctuary Wood, Beaumont Hamel, Vimy Ridge, as well as Verdun and the American killing fields in the Meuse Argonne sector.

On the first of these battlefield tours, the itinerary showed that after dinner on the second night at our French motel there was to be a speaker who would talk about "Gross China." But after a long day, Audrey and I were tired and decided that as we had no idea what Gross China might be, we would turn in early and excuse ourselves before the lecture began. However, our old Upchurch digging and antique-collecting friend, Douglas Walton, decided to stay, and therefore so did we—little realizing that we were about to be hooked on that neglected chapter in the history of English ceramics.

The speaker turned out to be Nicholas Pine, the principal dealer in what should have read "Goss" rather than "Gross." Neither Audrey nor I had ever given any thought to souvenir porcelain lighthouses, bathing belles, Mother Shiptons, lobster pots, and the like, which we remembered from our childhood as being sold in every seaside candy, tobacco, and newspaper shop. Those same shops also sold ribald picture postcards to the working-class vacationers (we called them holidaymakers), who would buy and take home a porcelain pin tray with a polychrome transfer print of the town pier over the message A PRESENT FROM BRIGHTON—or wherever. We quickly learned that from the 1880s to the 1930s, souvenir china was a major Staffordshire industry whose output was feeding the same desire to remember that had been served by the delftware, salt-glazed stoneware, creamware, and pearlware potters of the previous century.

Our speaker that night was not talking about recollections of walks on the promenade or of lazing in a deck chair while a brass band on the rotunda played "Sussex by the Sea." Nicholas Pine was focusing on a far more sinister aspect of china production and salesmanship, namely, the remembrance of daily horrors of the Great War, which were produced by the thousands—and sold to whom? But before I get to that, there's some background you need to know.

The memorializing china idea was the brainchild of William Henry Goss, who was born in 1833 and learned his craft in the factory of William Copeland, son of the Copeland who in that year had taken over the Spode works. After some early partnerships that need not concern us, Goss set up in business on his own making dry-bodied Parian Ware busts of famous individuals (including himself), whose quality is still admired (Fig. xv.3). William Henry came from a family sufficiently established to have its own crest, that of a spread-winged falcon, and in 1880 or thereabouts, he used it as his mark and named his factory the Falcon Works.[3]

Like Dwight, Cookworthy, Wedgwood, and others like them, William Henry Goss was a relatively well-educated man. He was fascinated by history and was a keen student of heraldry, both of which were to be driving factors in the development of his business. In his first ventures into souvenir ceramics, Goss concentrated on small ivory-yellow porcelain pots decorated with the crests of universities and public schools, the sort of thing that young men and boys might buy at local shops to take home to their parents. However, in 1883 William Henry's son, Adolphus, joined the company and quickly recognized that there were much wider markets to be tapped. Every town had its tobacconist shop, every pier its gift shop, and every country fair its souvenir stalls. Castles ruined and otherwise,

FIGURE XV.3. Parian Ware bust of William Henry Goss, founder of the Falcon Porcelain Factory, modeled in 1905 three months before his death.

FIGURE XV.4. The pyramid of Cheops as late Victorians saw it and as the Goss souvenir they bought in Cairo. Ca. 1887.

medieval abbeys, birthplaces, burial places, statues, memorials, all had sales potential. And then, enthused Adolphus, there were historic places in foreign lands where English travelers would be needing something small but tasteful to bring home (Fig. xv.4).[4] And what about the colonies, wouldn't they be proud to sell examples of their crests and arms on pots to expatriates who wanted to send an appropriate gift back to dear old England? The opportunities seemed endless, and when the aging William Henry muttered about lowering standards and cheapening the Falcon name, Adolphus said, in effect, "I'll drum up the business if you'll make the pots." And drum he did, and business he got.

Thanks to periodicals like the *Illustrated London News,* the literate Victorian and Edwardian English were fascinated by archaeology, and vicariously reveled in every new discovery from Nineveh, from Sakharra, or from the Roman camp on the outskirts of town. "Why not," urged Adolphus, "why not put the crests on miniature copies of historic relics like Roman pots, bronze cauldrons, leather mugs? Doesn't every local museum have something it would like to have copied and that folks could buy as reminders of their visit? A lot of people take the boat train to Ostend. We could find things there to copy and sell to the French for our people to buy and bring back!"

All that came to pass, and the Falcon Works prospered as never before. At the beginning of the twentieth century, one enthusiastic collector, J. J. Jarvis, started a society and called it the League of Goss Collectors and undertook to produce an annual news booklet called *The Goss Record.*[5] At first William Henry looked upon this venture as rip-off exploitation and would have none of it. After a few years, however, the

IF THESE POTS COULD TALK

firm realized that it was getting free publicity and additional sales, so Adolphus changed his father's mind. Thereafter, the Falcon Works cooperated closely with the League and each year produced a special piece available only to its members.

Meanwhile, Adolphus toured the country, visiting county and town museums to draw reproducible artifacts while at the same time signing up agents (one per town) to sell the Goss miniatures. By 1914 the firm had agents in at least 1,367 cities, towns, and villages in the British Isles, and 188 more around the world. Two were in the United States, one at Jones McDuffee & Stratton in Boston and the other at Marshall Field in Chicago. Adolphus's brother Godfrey had emigrated to America in 1882 and set up his own pottery at Kokomo, Indiana, making porcelain electrical insulators. The business did not prosper, but he was well placed to promote the old firm's American export trade.

There are several "American" pieces in the Collection, one of them a Bronze Age urn with the arms of Harvard (Fig. xv.5), another for the State of New York identified on the base as THE LINCOLN VASE, FROM ORIGINAL AT CATHEDRAL (Fig. xv.6), and two with the arms of Florida curiously charged with a "coin" depicting CHAMPLAIN and the date 1608 (Figs. xv.7).[6] One is identified as MODEL OF OAK PITCHER PECULIAR TO

FIGURE XV.6. The arms of New York State on a Goss copy of an undated vase in Lincoln Cathedral.

FIGURE XV.5. Goss porcelain MODEL OF CELTIC SEPULCHRAL URN FOUND AT LANLAWREN, CORNWALL, skillfully decorated beneath the glaze, and transfer printed and overglaze enameled with the badge of Harvard University. The "made for export" classification is identified by the mark EMBLEMATIC T ENGLAND. Ca. 1900–1914.

FIGURE XV.7. Models by Goss of (a) an OAK PITCHER PECULIAR TO DEVON, and (b) an ANCIENT CUP FOUND AT BRIXWORTH, NORTHAMPTONSHIRE, both with what purport to be the arms of Florida inexplicably charged with a "coin" portrait of Samuel de Champlain dated 1608, the year he founded Quebec. Ca. 1903.

FIGURE XV.8. Goss model of the Roman Portland Vase in the British Museum, decorated with the arms of the United States of America. First made for the League of Goss Collectors in 1904.

FIGURE XV.9. Heraldic porcelain copies of Roman ewers: (*a*) by Goss with the arms of Exeter, (*b*) by Swan China with the seal of the United States, presumably made to appeal to American tourists. Ca. 1910–1925.

DEVON and the other as a MODEL OF ANCIENT CUP FOUND AT BRIX-WORTH, NORTHAMPTONSHIRE. Others are decorated with the Stars and Stripes, one of them a model of the British Museum's famed Portland Vase (Fig. xv.8).

Over the last five years of Audrey's life, we joined the ranks of Crested China collectors and tried to obtain examples of all Adolphus's historical reproductions that matched objects in the Collection, were they copies of Roman pitchers and carinated beakers from the Upchurch Marshes, Tudor stoneware, or a seventeenth-century graybeard from Rochester in Kent

FIGURE XV.10. Romano-British carinated beakers from Upchurch representing the first- and second-century types, and copied by Goss models, (*a*) based on an example from Ramsgate, Kent, and (*b*) on another from Atwick in Yorkshire and first produced in 1908.

IF THESE POTS COULD TALK

FIGURE XV.11. (*a*) Goss model of a gray-beard found "spirit" filled in a pond at Horsgate in East Sussex, and made ca. 1914. The original of ca. 1670 may have been English rather than German. (*b*) Another Goss graybeard model, this one of an earlier shape found at Rochester in Kent. The copy's highly informative base (*c*) carries a registration number for 1903–1904.

FIGURE XV.12. A few Goss reproductions were made at full size, and this copy of a Rhenish stoneware mug from the sixteenth century is one of them. Its design number was registered in 1907.

(Figs. XV.9–12). This last is marked on its bottom MODEL OF BELLARMINE JUG 17th CENTURY FOUND IN ROCHESTER. PUB[LISHED] BY J. H. GOLDW [?], 31 HIGH ST.[7] In the eyes of collectors, examples with heraldic arms that match the place where the reproduced artifact was found are considered the most desirable. The rare inclusion of the name of the shop for whom the object was actually made adds another star.

The marketing acumen of Adolphus Goss was as developed as that of any modern business school graduate. He knew not only what would sell but where best to market it. In Cairo his agent was Charles Livadas, whose address was given as Opposite Shepheard's Hotel. Anybody who was anybody stayed at Shepheard's. At home the Market Place was every town's foremost business address; if it had no marketplace, the High Street was the next best location, and if it was a coastal town that had no High Street, then Fore Street or the Quay would serve as well.

Not all the information given to Adolphus on his museum visits has withstood the tests of time. Thus, for example, a gourd-shaped water cooler marked as being of "ancient oriental" origin is really from the eighteenth century, probably Spanish, and closely paralleled by another not-so-old

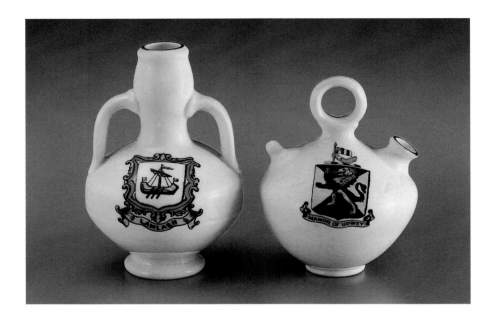

FIGURE XV.13. Goss "vase" (*a*) and "watercooler" (*b*) labeled as models of ancient specimens which, in reality, came from the Mediterranean and the Near East in the eighteenth century; (*a*) registered in 1909, (*b*) unmarked. (*c*) A *hidroceramo* of the same general type from a Bermuda reef, eighteenth or nineteenth century. (*c*) Photo courtesy of E. B. Tucker.

hidroceramo recovered from a Bermuda reef (Fig. XV.13 *b*).[8] Our second model of a less than ancient artifact was accepted by Adolphus Goss as an ANCIENT VASE DREDGED OUT OF THE THAMES NEAR ETON (Fig. XV.13 *a*). Another like it is marked as having been found in Greenwich Park, and a third as a model of a Roman ewer found in the Little Orme River in North Wales. I should add that in our early days as archaeological novices, Audrey and I were delighted by the modest price of one purchased for our collection. In reality, all are of Arab origin and probably had been brought home by Victorian tourists.

As I noted earlier, in 1950 we were working to establish a chronology of glass wine bottles that could help date the archaeological contexts in which they were found, and in consequence we collected bottles just as we would ceramics. That glass side of our collecting is represented by Goss porcelain reproductions of wine bottles, one of them dating around 1700 and the other specifically to 1735 (Fig. XV.14). The copy of the earlier of the two is marked MODEL OF SACK BOTTLE DUG UP IN CASTLE MOAT,

FIGURE XV.14. Goss models of early and later eighteenth-century glass wine bottles. (*a*) Found in the castle moat at Ludlow; (*b, c*) with seal dated 1735, dredged from the River Dart. Because (*b*) bears the arms of the town of Dartmouth, collectors consider it more desirable than is (*c*), with the unrelated arms of Belfast.

LUDLOW. NOW IN LUDLOW MUSEUM, while the other reads MODEL OF SACK BOTTLE DREDGED FROM THE DART FROM ORIGINAL IN EXETER MUSEUM. Although the latter bottle subsequently disappeared from the museum, the surviving catalog card reads "An old Wine Bottle dredged up in the harbour, Dartmouth, Devon, having on the back of it an embossed Medallion in molten glass with this inscription in relief: Thos. Holdsworth, Dartmouth, 1735." One of our three Goss examples has the arms of Dartmouth on one side, and on the other the glass seal so accurately modeled that the wording can be read. It survives, therefore, as the stand-in for a bottle whose shape would have been lost had not Adolphus Goss visited the Exeter Museum.[9]

The last decade of the nineteenth century and the first of the twentieth were the apex of Britain's global success. Everyone but the poor saw sunshine all the way, and business at the Falcon Works was never better. But every hilltop has a downward slope. On January 4, 1906, William Henry Goss died. He had quarreled with Adolphus for having bastardized the Falcon Works into a highly successful business, and although in his will he gave him £4,000, he left the factory to his two younger sons, Victor Henry and William Huntley, neither of whom had Adolphus's head for marketing. In 1913, an errant chicken fluttered cackling out of a hedgerow into the path of Victor's horse, causing it to shy and throw its rider onto his head. Thus, as war clouds gathered over Europe, William Henry's third son was left to run the factory in all its many facets.

King George of Greece was assassinated on March 18, 1913. War in the Balkans broke out for the second time in a year when a Bulgarian army attacked Serb positions, prompting the Turks to declare war on Bulgaria. In June of the following year, high school student Gavrilo Prinzip gunned down Archduke Franz Ferdinand and his wife in Sarajevo, and the European kettle boiled over.

FIGURE XV.15. Adolphus and Nellie Goss with their sons and daughters in 1913. All four sons went to war in 1914; two were killed and one returned wounded. Photo courtesy of Nicholas and Lynda Pine.

Adolphus Goss lived to be eighty-one and did not die until 1934, and although he was no longer in charge at the Falcon Works when the Great War began, he must surely have offered his advice on how best to profit from it. Like so many other families, the Gosses payed a heavy price for the prayed-for victory (Fig. XV.15). Of Adolphus's four sons, two were killed and a third wounded.[10] They had promised to go into battle proclaiming "Potters for Ever!" and no doubt they did. Within a year of the conflict, the Falcon Works had produced souvenir badges of 125 British regiments, and 46 Royal Navy ships, all adorning a miscellany of pots that did not, themselves, have any direct connection with either regiments or ships. In addition, the firm produced a small number of war-related artifacts—and it is these that bring us back to the beginning of this chapter and to the lecture on "Gross China." *The Goss Record* reported that "Trophies from the battlefields and the modern inventions of war provide many subjects of interest, and for long years to come the Goss War Models will be preserved as mementoes of the greatest conflict of history." In reality, the Falcon Works was to mold very few of these "Trophies," for its trade in heraldic porcelain was slipping away to competing factories that were manufacturing miniature copies of virtually every artifact of the war.

In 1902, the Carlton Company of Stoke-on-Trent had advertised "Carlton Heraldic China" and was the first to challenge the Goss monopoly. A Carlton salesman, Harold T. Robinson, set up his own heraldic china business in 1903 and named its products "Arcadian China." He would become a partner in the Carlton business three years later, and thereafter Arcadian and Carlton together seized a major part of the souvenir porcelain market and were leaders in the production of war souvenirs. Together, these factories seem to have specialized in ammunition and the guns to fire it. Several factories made models of Red Cross nurses, but Carlton was alone in memorializing the women munitions workers who kept the killing going (Fig. XV.16).[11] A worker stands, shell in hand, beside a pile of others ready to go, and to make sure that nobody misses the point, her plinth carries two inscriptions that read SHELLS AND MORE SHELLS and in smaller letters, "Doing her Bit."

FIGURE XV.16. Women at war: (*a*) nurse with bandage at the ready. Like all nurse models, she is identified as "Nurse Cavell," who was shot in 1915. The figure is by the little known Porcelle porcelain and earthenware company of Edinburgh (ca. 1910–1924). (*b*) Carlton China's smartly dressed munition worker with shell in hand, and a pile beside her ready to pound the hated Hun. The base inscription reads "Doing her Bit" and SHELLS AND MORE SHELLS, and is marked as being made for sale by Davy Stephens of Kingstown, whose civic arms are displayed.

IF THESE POTS COULD TALK

FIGURE XV.17. The Grafton china factory's realistic "The Bomb Thrower" with a separately cast box of grenades beside him. Dating is suggested by the fact that steel helmets were not issued to British troops until 1915.

FIGURE XV.18. Grafton was the only factory to issue an American doughboy. The design called for him to be smoking a cigar, but in this example it has not survived. The rare model shown is also known enameled with the Stars and Stripes, and in black.

FIGURE XV.19. (*a*) A Mills bomb from the Somme battlefield. (*b*) Grafton's porcelain copy complete with removable iron pin. The grenade was patented by William Mills of Birmingham in January 1915 and in use on the Western Front by the spring of that year.

FIGURE XV.20. (*a*) TOMMY AND HIS MACHINE GUN by Arcadian China, and (*b*) in battle-weary reality. The prototype was built by American Hiram S. Maxim in 1884 and was produced in Britain by Alfred Vickers, whose name the guns took after Maxim's patent expired. Photograph courtesy of the Imperial War Museum, London.

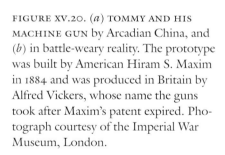

Another firm, the Grafton China Works, was in production by 1906 producing heraldically painted miniatures, and by 1909 was advertising several hundred shapes. It seems, however, that this pottery was late in the war artifact competition, waiting until the victory parades of 1919 to introduce most of its line of submarines, tanks, and artillery pieces. Grafton excelled in producing three-dimensional action figures like the Collection's grenade thrower (Fig. XV.17) and the war's only porcelain rendering of an American doughboy (Fig. XV.18), who is found in white, multicolored,

FIGURE XV.21. Food for the "soldier's friend": a clip of .303 bullets from Arcadian China.

FIGURE XV.22. The colorful tunics of lead soldiers in every boy's pre-1914 toy box went unreplaced when lead went toward the war effort and their fathers sailed for France in khaki. It therefore fell to the porcelain modelers to keep playroom wars in step with technology.

and black. Grafton also had the questionable distinction of being the only manufacturer of porcelain grenades that came with a realistic iron pin that could be pulled out (Fig. XV.19). Who, one might ask, would want so exact a copy of this lethal weapon; indeed, who would want one at all? Then again a model of a Vickers machine gunner or a clip of rifle bullets is not exactly uplifting (Figs. XV.20 and XV.21).

Although many of the war souvenirs were simply that, there was another likely reason for their popularity, namely, among children deprived of that ikon of the nursery and playroom, the lead-cast toy soldier. Introduced by the still-existing British firm founded by William Britain, Jr., in 1893, hollow-cast model armies refought the battles of then recent memory against the Zulus, the Boers, and the Mahdi in the Sudan (Fig. XV.22). But with the outbreak of a new war in 1914 there were to be far fewer tabletop recruits. Most of the available lead was diverted to making real bullets, and therefore it fell to the porcelain entrepreneurs to provide new models to fill the void and to keep pace with evolving military technology and news from the front.[12] That did not mean that lead soldier production ceased entirely, but no new molds were made to reflect Great War uniforms and equipment. Indeed, with the war ended and a weary and suffering nation's patriotism spent, Britains Ltd. focused on casting farm animals, haystacks, trees, and suchlike to augment model train sets.[13]

Like the grieving family of Adolphus Goss, there was no British town and scarcely a family that did not lose sons, fathers, brothers in the carnage of Flanders Fields. The numbers were appalling, 807,451 killed, 617,740 seriously wounded, and 1,441,394 "otherwise wounded." Although the United States did not enter the war until 1917, that nation's losses were proportionate, 107,284 killed and 148,043 wounded. However, Russian casualties were the highest: 2,762,064, killed, 4,950,000 injured seriously and otherwise. It is against that blood-drenched background that we find customers for countless porcelain weapons and war-related vehicles. A model Red Cross ambulance tells us in small but clear print, LOAD NOT TO EXCEED I. DRIVER, I. ATTENDANT AND PATIENTS—a euphemism for the limbless, blinded, and gassed (Fig. xv.23). On the bottom, between

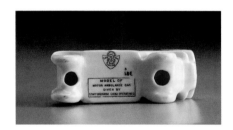

the wheels, we are told that this example of Grafton China is a MODEL OF MOTOR AMBULANCE CAR GIVEN BY STAFFORDSHIRE CHINA OPERATIVES. Regardless of the potters' motivation or, indeed, the mentality of their customers, the Great War porcelains have provided a remarkable history of the conflict and its hardware.

While ceramic souvenirs of previous wars stood alone and distant from the battles that would be recorded only in subsequently reconstructive paintings seen by relatively few, the 1914–1918 conflict was photographed from every angle and the pictures arrived every day on the pages of the morning newspapers. Thus, models of light and heavy artillery (Fig. xv.24) could be seen in context. Guns needed shells and the porcelain factories were quick to oblige, among them one captured from the Russians by the Germans and then fired at the British. That heavy howitzer shell was described by Goss as a shrapnel type and therefore designed for maximum casualty impact (Fig. xv.25). Hence the clean porcelain ambulance whose reality was to be found at a frail and vulnerable dressing station amid the shell holes of Flanders.

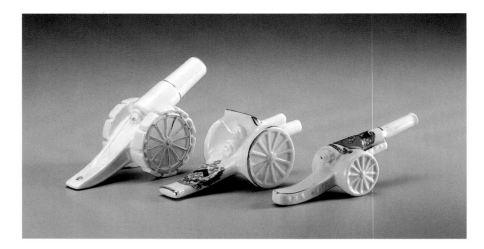

FIGURE XV.24. Models of artillery pieces were sometimes more accurately modeled than they appear. (*a*) A heavy howitzer from Arcadian China and made for one Hancock of Bamford in Derbyshire and enameled with the arms of nearby Hathersage. (*b*) A field gun by Waterfall China with the arms of Grimsby in Lincolnshire. Waterfall was a wholesaler in northeastern England for whom Willow Art China of Longton manufactured under contract. (*c*) By Carlton China with the cannonball-stacked arms of Aldershot.

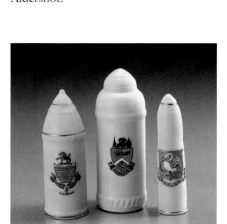

FIGURE XV.25. Artillery being useless without shells, the porcelain potters copied them in several sizes. Of these (*b*) is of the greatest interest, having been captured by the "Huns" on the Russian Front and fired at the British in Flanders. The frilled base shows that the model represents the projectile divorced from its brass case.

Until the first tanks lumbered up to the front line in 1916, their production had been a carefully kept secret. Developed under Navy and not Army aegis, they were first classified as Royal Naval Land Ships (R.N.L.S.); but it was the disguising name used during their secret development, "water-storage tank," that would henceforth identify these track-propelled fighting vehicles. The Mark I tank (known as "Mother") came in a male version with two 6-pounder naval guns mounted in its side turrets and a female version with machine guns fore and aft designed for straddling and enfilading enemy trenches (Fig. xv.26). Both sexes went into action for the first time on September 15, 1916, but not with conspicuous success.[14] Of the thirty-two sent out, only nine made it to the German lines; the rest either broke down or got stuck in the mud. Nevertheless, a shocked German prisoner observed that this wasn't war, it was bloody butchery! The Mark I had two large wheels at its stern that were supposed to help in steering. On the contrary, if one got shot off (as frequently happened), the other became more a liability than an asset.

FIGURE XV.26. The first British tank, the Mark I, had stern wheels to assist in steering, and went into action for the first time in September 1916 at the Battle of Flers-Courcelette, but without conspicuous success. The earliest Arcadian China model was based on the first published photograph of a wrecked Mark I, and was mistakenly given only one wheel. When it was learned that the other had been blown off, the mold was retooled to add the second wheel (*b*), as seen in this example. (*c*) Willow Art's version of the Mark I with the axle mounts correctly centered. (*a*) The Mark I in action as infantry support. Photograph courtesy of the Imperial War Museum, London.

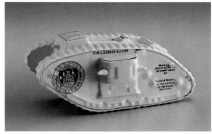

FIGURE XV.27. (*b*) Savoy China's model of the Mark IV heavy tank, with an inscription erroneously suggesting that it was present at the battle of the Ancre in September 1916. The Mark IV was not in service until March 1917. The model's number 515 indicates that it represents the "female" version, equipped with five machine guns, rather than the male's two six pounders. (*a*) A male Mark IV stuck in the Flanders mud. Photograph courtesy of the Imperial War Museum, London.

Once the word got out that this new secret weapon was about to win the war, Staffordshire porcelain modelers hastily produced souvenirs they hoped would be something like the real thing. The result was essentially an armored car that exchanged its wheels for a farm tractor's caterpillar tracks and bore no resemblance to the Mark I. Two months later the censors released the first photograph of "Mother" in action, or rather *out* of action. Within a week of the picture being printed on the front page of *The Daily Mirror*, Arcadian China registered its model complete with a trailing wheel—*one* trailing wheel. The newspaper's picture did not show, nor did its reporter explain, that the other wheel had been blown off. In consequence, "Mother One-Wheel" is the most desirable and the most expensive of all World War I commemorative objects. The Collection, alas, only aspires to the second Arcadian version wherein the original mold had been reworked to add the missing wheel (Fig. XV.27 *b*). By November, a modified Mark I without guiding wheels went into service and was followed by a heavier Mark IV, but among the porcelain copies there is some confusion. Examples usually cataloged as Mark IVs carry an inscription reading MODEL OF BRITISH TANK AS FIRST USED BY BRITISH TROOPS AT THE BATTLE OF THE ANCRE, SEP. 1916. The date of the wheels' removal is usually given as November 1916. It was not until a year later that the Mark IV was really to test its mettle, when 381 did so at the battle of Cambrai, cutting a slice through the Hindenburg Line 6 miles wide and 4,000 yards deep. But as so often happened throughout the war, the ground won was quickly lost when the Germans counterattacked.

The United States troops had no tank of their own and so used a light French Renault that was well suited for fast reconnaissance work and that also was supplied to British units. Delays in production (occasioned, in part, by using substandard British steel plates), and problems with its revolving turret, saw to it that the little French tank would not go into combat until May 31, 1918. Nevertheless, it did yeoman service through the last

FIGURE XV.28. (*a*) Victoria China's very accurate model of the French Renault light tank, which was supplied to the American Army early in 1918. Formed into a brigade under Col. G. S. Patton, Jr., they first went into action on September 12, 1918. Henry Ford's American-built version of the Renault reached France in October, and it may be one of his (*b*) that trundled down Williamsburg's Duke of Gloucester Street to help raise funds for the war effort. Photo: Colonial Williamsburg Foundation.

five months of the conflict and continued in production with only minor modifications until the Second World War. One of the lesser known heraldic porcelain manufacturers, Victoria China, made a remarkably accurate model of the Renault tank (Fig. XV.28).[15]

At the beginning of the 1914–1918 war, getting the troops to the front posed a major problem. The French solved it by seizing Parisian taxis and the British by using London double-decker buses, one of which survives in its Imperial War Museum. Carlton China miniaturized one of them and did so with such detail that legible advertisements on the sides read GLOBE THEATRE, JOHN BULL THURSDAY[16] as well as the bus's peacetime route: PUTNEY CHARING CROSS (Fig. XV.29).

FIGURE XV.29. (*a*) With trucks in short supply, London buses like this Carlton China model were commandeered to carry troops to the front. (*b*) One such veteran vehicle survives in London at the Imperial War Museum.

The British troops were collectively known as Tommies and the Americans as Yanks, but as the war progressed, soldier-cartoonist Bruce Bairnsfather created a single character who was to capture the wry, joking spirit that kept the troops steadfastly in their trenches. Everybody from general to private knew and loved "Old Bill," whose beery nose and walrus mustache were destined to make him the lasting image of trench war soldiering (Fig. XV.30 *b*). Bairnsfather was a lieutenant in the Warwickshire Regiment and went to France in 1914 thinking that the war would be tremendous fun and a marvelous adventure. When he learned better, he kept his nerve and his sanity by finding humor in the horror of the front-line experiences and did so by capturing those lighter moments in his drawings. He sent one home to the *Bystander* magazine, which bought it and asked for more, and thereby began a series known as "Fragments from France." The first of them became immortalized in Carlton China and showed a Tommy in his dugout with the label "Shrapnel Villa" over the entrance. The cartoon had shown five men peering out of their sandbagged shelter as a shell plowed into its roof, prompting one of them to ask, "Where did that one go to?" (Fig. xv.31).[17]

FIGURE XV.30. (*a*) The 1914 myth of the smartly turned out "Brave Defender" and (*b*) the reality of cartoonist Bruce Bairnsfather's battle-hardened survivalist "Old Bill." (*a*) By Willow Art; (*b*) unmarked.

FIGURE XV.31. (*a*) Bruce Bairnsfather's most famous cartoon, and (*b*) "Shrapnel Villa," Carlton China's interpretation, also labeled TOMMIES DUGOUT SOMEWHERE IN FRANCE. (*a*) Courtesy of Milestone Publications.

The First World War is remembered by the British primarily for the wire, the water, and the daily carnage in the mud of the Western Front; by the Australians for the disaster at Gallipoli, the French for Verdun, the Canadians for Vimy Ridge, the Newfoundland Highlanders for the slaughter at Beaumont Hamel, and the Americans for the First Army's drive between the Meuse and the Argonne Forest. Unlike World War II, the first was primarily a land war, and it would be no surprise, therefore, if the souvenir porcelain manufacturers had ignored the war at sea. But they didn't.

With the war scarcely begun, on December 16, 1914, a squadron of the Imperial German Navy crossed the North Sea from Heligoland and bombarded the English east coast ports of Whitby, Hartlepool, and Scarborough, killing 110 civilians and shooting a hole through the Scarborough lighthouse. One of the second-string potteries trading under the name of "Willow Art" was almost alone in expecting that the damaged lighthouse might sell well in Scarborough—and even further afield. The Collection's model of the shell-shot Scarborough light bears the arms of the distant Shropshire town of Church Stretton, proving that Willow Art's hunch was right (Fig. xv.32).[18]

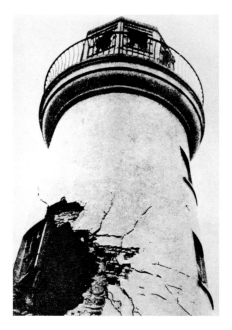

FIGURE XV.32. In December 1914, German cruisers shelled the Scarborough lighthouse (*a*), as well as killing more than a hundred people in the town. (*b*) An unidentified manufacturer (probably Willow Art) made this souvenir of the damaged lighthouse. (*a*) Photo: Hartlepool Public Library.

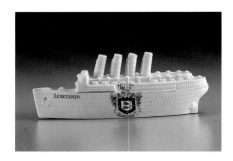

FIGURE XV.33. (*a*) The sinking of the liner *Lusitania* in 1915 became a defining moment in the war. (*b*) This model, one of several, was produced by Corona China; its funnels' gilding is worn away by playroom use. (*a*) Painting from *The Illustrated London News,* Silver Jubilee edition, 1935. (*a*) Courtesy The Illustrated London News Group Picture Library.

FIGURE XV.34. The propaganda value of the sinking of the *Lusitania* was not lost on the souvenir porcelain designers. These miniature vases by Carlton China give the number of lives lost as 1,275 and the saved as 703. Neither figure is correct.

Of all the ship models produced during the First World War, those associated with the R.M.S. *Lusitania* are of the greatest interest. The German warning that this New York-to-Liverpool luxury liner would be a target was ignored by virtually all the booked passengers, many Americans among them. On May 7, 1915, the German U-boat U20 fired one torpedo as the *Lusitania* came in sight of Ireland's Head of Kinsale. The explosion of the first impact was quickly followed by another, and eighteen minutes later the great ship went down, taking most of her passengers and crew with her (Fig. XV.33 *a*). Carlton China was the first to exploit the disaster, producing small pots and jars painted on one side with a polychrome transfer print of the ship and on the other the wording THE LUSITANIA, SUNK BY GERMAN SUBMARINE OFF THE IRISH COAST, MAY 7th 1915, LIVES LOST 1275, SAVED 703 (Fig. XV.34). The first figure is incorrect, as the drowned numbered 1,198, and would be corrected in later firings.[19] The same erroneous death count also appears on Carlton's model of the *Lusitania* herself (Fig. XV.35 *b*). Another, sleeker version with a very different silhouette was made by the Corona China company of the Bridge Works in Stoke-on-Trent (Fig. XV.33 *b*).[20] It seems evident that when ship models were needed, none of the factories concerned themselves with the level of accuracy bestowed on their land war souvenirs. Carlton used its *Lusitania*

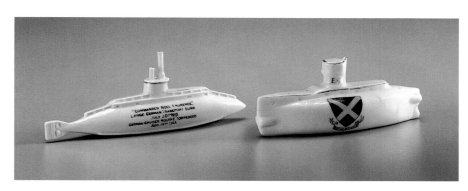

FIGURE XV.35. The same mold was used by Carlton China for both (*a*) its *Anglia* "Hospital Ship whose voyage was Disregarded on three occasions by the German Submarines," harassment of which no record seems to have survived, and (*b*) its *Lusitania*.

FIGURE XV.36. Although no German submarine models were made, several British versions were produced, among them (*a*) the E1 captained by Commander Noel Lawrence, which scored major successes in 1915, modeled by Savoy China, and (*b*) Botolph China's E5, sunk in March 1916.

molds to make the H.M.H.S *Anglia*, which needed only a changed name, a red cross on its hull, and an inscription that reads "Model of British Hospital Ship whose voyage was Disregraded [sic] on three occasions by the German Submarines" (Fig. xv.35 *a* and *b*).

The reason for immortalizing the *Anglia* remains a mystery.[21] Carlton was alone in so doing, registering the design as No. 662104 in 1917, although the *Anglia* reputedly had sunk in 1915 after hitting a mine. Adding to the confusion, Carlton used the same design number when it made a two-funnel version and applied the same information to the hull. The obvious inference (which is likely to be wrong) is that another *Anglia* made headlines in 1917 and that to cash in on public indignation, Carlton rushed into production using the old four-funneled *Lusitania* molds until it could learn more about the ship and how to represent it. The Bible of naval vessels *Jane's All the World's Ships* recognizes the use of hospital ships but says only that one was assigned to duty with the Atlantic Fleet and another to the Mediterranean, but has no information on either.[22]

Just as in World War II, in 1914–1918 the enemy beneath the waves was a constant threat to allied supply lines and capable of starving the armies of munitions and the Home Front of food. The magnitude of that menace would be measured by the numbers of lost submarines on both sides: The British lost fifty-eight, the French twelve, the Russians twenty-nine, and America two, a total of 101.[23] The Germans lost 203. Several models of British submarines were issued by the Staffordshire potters, one of which (Botolph China's E5) was sunk in the North Sea in March 1916, probably

FIGURE XV.37. Two tars: (*a*) casting off, by Swan China; (*b*) Wilton China's squatting sailor gripping a German submarine. On some the cap band reads WE'VE GOT "U" WELL IN HAND.

FIGURE XV.38. Mounted on a brick pedestal, Carlton China's porcelain mine commemorated the war's end. Decorated with the arms of the seaport of Ipswich, it served as a reminder of the hazards of war faced daily by its fishing fleet.

FIGURE XV.39. (*a*) A typical coastal minesweeper by Carlton China. (*b*) Savoy China's battleship H.M.S. *Queen Elizabeth*, launched 1912.

after hitting a mine (Fig. xv.36 *b*).[24] Much more realistically modeled was Savoy China's E1, whose inscription tells how, on July 30, 1915, its commander Noel Lawrence sank a large German transport and three weeks later torpedoed the cruiser *Moltke*. Savoy was quick to honor both achievements and on September 18 registered its model of the E1 (Fig. xv.36 *a*).

Along with miniature warships, several factories produced models of the men to man them, one squatting with a German submarine in his grip (Fig. xv.37 *b*). And then there were the mines. At least three models were produced, one of them by Goss. The Collection's example is from Carlton China and described as MODEL OF FLOATING MINE (Fig. xv.38).

Among war's more unenviable tasks is that of the minesweeper, a role represented in the Collection by a Carlton China example with an inscription recalling the surrender on November 21, 1918, of the German Fleet, many of whose ships subsequently scuttled themselves while in detention at Scapa Flow (Fig. xv.39 *a*). The illustration that shows one of the smallest of the war's fighting ships includes one of the largest, the dreadnought

Queen Elizabeth. Built in 1912, she became the flagship of the commander in chief of the British Grand Fleet in 1917–1918. In 1919, *Jane's All the World's Ships* called her class "the most successful type of capital ship yet designed" (Fig. xv.39 *b*).[25] Although Goss produced no model ships, the factory did apply Navy crests to its existing line of mini-pots, prompting the *Goss Record* to ask, "What English home is there that will not welcome a model bearing the crest of . . . H.M.S. *Queen Elizabeth* whose guns thundered out in the ill-fated Dardanelles Campaign?"[26] The *Record* added that the souvenirs were currently available from any Goss agent.

In the rush to keep pace with war-related technology, the dogfighting in the air over the trenches was not to be ignored—even though molding porcelain models of aircraft was far more difficult than was casting tanks and ships.

Since the Wright Brothers got their contraption off the sands of Kitty Hawk in 1903, aircraft design had raced forward with quite incredible speed, and by 1917 the Flemish sky was abuzz with aircraft of many shapes and sizes. For the British, the fighter of choice was the Sopwith Camel, a radial-engine biplane capable of flying at 113 mph at 10,000 feet.

FIGURE XV.40. Model of a Sopwith Camel, Britain's most successful fighter of the First World War. Though provided with a rotatable propellor, Shelley China's plane was not the most realistic of the several porcelain modelers' aircraft creations.

FIGURE XV.41. Several types of German hand-delivered incendiary and explosive bombs. (*a*) An incendiary by Arcadian China, examples of which occur inscribed, "Model of a Bomb that killed a Chicken at Southend"; (*b*) one of the Goss factory's few war souvenirs, marked as being an incendiary dropped from a Zeppelin at Maldon, Essex, April 16, 1915; (*c*) Carlton China's version of the Goldsmith incendiary bomb with the frilled loop at the top representing its coiled wire fuse detonating connector; (*d*) Arcadian China's model of an "Aerial Torpedo," and (*e*) the same company's canister bomb.

This is represented in the Collection by a lone example (Fig. XV.40). Though complete with rotatable propeller, the model is not very convincing, as the designers failed to find a way of separating the lower from the upper wings, and so settled for a box-like shape. They did a good deal better with bombs, and of the five Goss war entries, one was incendiary and the other high explosive. True to the company's educational policy, the bottoms were imprinted with relevant information. The first explained that it was a model of an incendiary bomb dropped from a German Zeppelin at Malden in Essex on April 16, 1917 (Fig. XV.41 *b*), and the other said that it was a model of a bomb dropped on Bury St. Edmunds two weeks later. Although Goss marked these products as copyrighted, other companies produced souvenirs that closely resembled the Bury bomb (Fig. XV.41 *a*). Arcadian China made a model of a "German Aerial torpedo" as well as a "Canister Bomb" without saying which side was using it, and Carlton came up with a fairly realistic version of a wire-fused German incendiary bomb (Fig. XV.41 *c*). There being no point in modeling bombs without bombers, Carlton also produced the black-crossed Zeppelins to drop them.[27]

The provision of useful, commemorative information was not confined to the Falcon Works or to Carlton, and throughout the war another company had a virtual monopoly on small pots and vases decorated with the arms of places associated with war-related events. Savoy China was a 1910 offspring of the Vine Pottery at Stoke-on-Trent and covered most battles from Arras to Verdun. Typical of the genre is the inscription that reads YPRES, GERMAN RUSH STEMMED BY THE VALOUR OF THE BRITISH TROOPS, OCTOBER. 27. 1914. 2ND BATTLE OF YPRES THE CANADIANS

FIGURE XV.42. Savoy China's mini-memorials to places the British Tommies and the French *poilus* knew and hated: Liège, Dunkirk, Ypres, Verdun, Arras, and Beaumont-Hamel.

FIGURE XV.43. Only Savoy's souvenir from Armentières seems to bear any artifactual relation to the soldiers' memories, namely, the wine that the town's mercenary mademoiselles encouraged them to buy.

FIGURE XV.44. (*a*) British troops arriving at Salonika on October 5, 1915, to take part in a futile campaign in the Balkans. Three months later, the Anglo-French retreat resulted in trenching that unearthed a broken Greek vase (amphora). (*b*) Carefully reproducing it to show its missing handle and broken neck, Shelley China provided us with the war's only memorialized archaeological relic. (*a*) Photograph courtesy of the Imperial War Museum, London.

GALLANTRY SAVED THE SITUATION, APRIL. 24. 1915 (Figs. XV.42 and XV.43). An archaeology-style *terminus ante quem* is thereby provided by the absence of any reference to the meat-grinding Third Battle of Ypres that began in the morning of October 4, 1917, and would focus primarily on the rain-swept Passchendaele sector. The latest recorded date on one of these Savoy battle souvenirs would seem to be August 27, 1916, suggesting, perhaps, that production began in 1915 and continued into mid-August 1916 before finding the market less receptive than expected.[28]

Small and fragile as these ceramic messages from the past are, it is surprising that so many have survived unbroken. One, however, was severely damaged before it left the mold, and yet should have a warm place in any archaeologist's heart. Made by the Shelley China company, the tall, stand-supported, amphora-shaped vase is characterized by a gilded but jagged neck and one handle when there should be two. Only when we read the inscription do these eccentric features make sense: MODEL OF ANCIENT GREEK VASE FOUND AT SALONIKA BY THE BRITISH TROOPS WHEN ENTRENCHING, JAN 1916. A relic of the disastrous Balkans Campaign, this little vase has pride of place in the Collection's heraldic porcelain assemblage for the very good reason that it stands as the only ceramic record of archaeological salvage (albeit inadvertent) in the midst of war (Fig. XV.44).

The victorious allies brought the war to an end at the eleventh hour of the eleventh day in the eleventh month of 1918 (although my father saw a

MODEL OF
ANCIENT GREEK VASE
FOUND AT SALONIKA
BY THE BRITISH TROOPS
WHEN ENTRENCHING
JAN 1916

IF THESE POTS COULD TALK

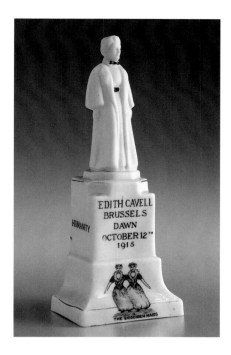

woman shot while milking a cow several hours after the cease fire, presumably by a frustrated and mean-minded German soldier). Although the news was received around the world with relief and knee-jerk exclamations of joy, the cost in lost and shattered lives could not be so easily forgotten. In 1919, memorials to the fallen began to be designed and built in virtually every British town and village, and the heraldic porcelain manufacturers obliged with models of many of them. Among the most frequently found is a memorial not to an army or to a single general, but to a lone, noncombatant woman. It stands in the heart of London in sight of Nelson's Column (Fig. xv.45 *a*). She was Edith Cavell (1866–1915), daughter of an English vicar, who served as a nurse in Brussels tending the wounds of both friend and foe alike. She also helped Belgian and allied fugitives, and for doing so was shot by a German firing squad on October 12, 1915. In her death, Edith Cavell replaced the Crimean War's Florence Nightingale as the epitome both of female courage and of the selflessness of wartime nursing. She also sired a hatred of the Germans that would not be surpassed until the gates of Bergen-Belsen, Buchenwald, and Auschwitz were opened in 1945. Models of the Nurse Cavell monument vary considerably in quality. One of the best has the base glazed but the figure left matt in Parian style and therefore more sharply detailed than would otherwise have been the case (Fig. xv.45 *b*). However, the Carlton China company that made it combined the dignity of Nurse Cavell's sacrifice with the hardly appropriate commemoration of an event that allegedly occurred 815 years earlier. Made for sale in the Kent village of Biddenden, along with details of Nurse Cavell's execution, the model features a pair of Siamese twins (Fig. xv.45 *c*). An inscription on the back explains: THE BIDDENDEN MAIDS WERE BORN JOINED TOGETHER HIPS & SHOULDERS IN THE YEAR 1100.[29]

FIGURE XV.45. (*a*) London's imposing memorial to the executed Nurse Edith Cavell stands in sight of Nelson on his column in Trafalgar Square. (*b*) The model of her monument in both bisque and glazed porcelain, by Carlton China, also commemorated a pair of Siamese twins (*c*) known as the "Maids of Biddenden." They left a legacy to their Kentish village (d) to serve an annual meal to the needy. It continues to do so after more than 400 years.

FIGURE XV.46. (*b*) The Cenotaph in Whitehall memorializes all who died for the country in "The War to End All Wars." The arms on the Willow Art model (*c*) are those of the City of London and bear the dates MCM/XIV and MCM/XIX, thereby including those who died of their wounds in 1919. (*a*) The Victory Parade passing the temporary Cenotaph in July 1919, an event having special significance for this collector. (*c*) Photograph courtesy of the Imperial War Museum, London.

FIGURE XV.47. Whiteware mug transfer-printed in sepia to commemorate the 1897 Diamond Jubilee of Queen Victoria. The faded black ribbon around its handle is thought to mourn her death in 1901.

The most common of all memorial models are those of the world famous Cenotaph at Whitehall (Fig. XV.46). Not completed in stone in time for the July 1919 Victory Parade, it was temporarily replicated in wood. But I doubt whether my father knew that as, with sword drawn, he proudly led a company of Scots Guards down Whitehall toward the joyously peeling bells of Westminster Abbey. Of that memorable occasion he wrote, "It's difficult to recall so much that happened during 1919—the march through London, brass bands stationed at various points, and we with the relatively slow long pace, would come round the corner onto a Rifle Brigade quick step band with disastrous results."

As generations pass and memories fade, the exploitive potters deserve a degree of gratitude for preserving not only the history of ceramics but also the world as they knew it. They speak to the cheering elation of coronations, the struggle for people's rights, the pride in architectural and engineering achievements, but also the sadness of personal and national loss. That, too, has its place in the Audrey and Ivor Noël Hume Collection, and in a shape that most collectors and museums may well dismiss as worthless. It is a simple tea mug printed in sepia with a portrait of an old woman who could be anyone's Victorian grandmother. But the inscription assures us otherwise. She was the "Beloved Queen of Great Britain, Ireland & the Colonies, Empress of India," celebrating her diamond jubilee on June 20, 1897. Around the handle is a short piece of faded black ribbon, tied there four years later when joy turned to grief with the passing of the Widow of Windsor (Fig. XV.47). From such fragile threads is the web of history spun.

XVI   A Mug's Game?

T H E   T E R M   *collectibles* means anything we care to hoard from string to Rembrandts, and several large companies best left unnamed make a killing manufacturing them to feed a kitsch-loving clientele. Whether their products will ever be fought over in high-end auction rooms by deep-pocketed collectors is something that future generations will have to determine. But having said that, one realizes that it was ever thus. The tinkers who sold buttons decorated with portraits of Queen Anne, the Staffordshire potters who glorified the successes of Admirals Vernon, Rodney, Nelson, and the like, and even the brown stoneware flask modelers of the nineteenth century were all exploiting the fleeting fancies of a fickle public. It is unlikely that they saw their products as enduring pieces of history—which, nevertheless, they have all proved to be. So we return once again to the question: How old must old be to be old enough? Which brings me to coffee mugs, perhaps the most common of late twentieth-century collectibles. Churches sold them to raise funds to add yet another annex; company salesmen gave them away to remind potential customers of their existence, and we all brought them home from vacations abroad. Their ready availability (regardless of having "Made in China" printed on their bottoms) saved us the trouble of searching for something more original to give to nieces, office colleagues, and dog sitters to prove that they had been constantly in our thoughts as we lived it up in Acapulco or Miami Beach.

But does that mean that all souvenir mugs are without enduring merit? The answer almost certainly is that some have that special "keep me" factor because they were made to commemorate something that affected the life of a nation and made its people proud, hopeful, relieved, or saddened. As you will by now be well aware, Audrey's and my ceramic studies took many

FIGURE XVI.1. (*a*) Whiteware Victory mug featuring Britannia, Admiral Beatty, and Field Marshall Haig. On the back, under the heading A SOUVENIR OF THE GREAT WAR, are the dates of its commencement, armistice, and peace signing. Made by Grimwade of Stoke-on-Trent, 1919. (*b*) Victory beaker with flags and badges of the allies under a peace dove and around a British bulldog; unmarked. (*c*) Pin box commemorating the British Empire Exhibition at Wembley in 1924; unmarked.

a curious turn, yet always fueled by caring about our predecessors, were they the burned-out and homeless citizens of Roman Londinium in A.D. 61 or victorious regiments marching past the Cenotaph in Whitehall at the end of the Great War (Fig. XVI.1). But why stop there, we asked ourselves?

Beginning with the simple mug I wrote about at the close of the last chapter that recalled the life and death of Queen Victoria, we extended that part of the Collection to include other great moments in British twentieth-century history. Though memorialized in a wide range of wares from

FIGURE XVI.2. (*a*) Porcelain mug honoring Queen Victoria's Diamond Jubilee, showing her at both her coronation in 1837 and her Jubilee in 1897; unmarked. (*b*) Porcelain mug by Royal Doulton for the coronation of Edward VII and Queen Alexandra in 1902.

fine porcelain (Fig. XVI.2) to the coarsest hotel china, each had a statement to make. Some recalled hopes fulfilled and others dashed. The coronation mugs and cups of George V and Queen Mary wished them long reigns—reigns that, in fact, lasted from 1911 to 1936. Our mug commemorating that event proudly called the new King and Queen "Rulers of an Empire

FIGURE XVI.3. Whiteware Coronation mugs honoring George V and Queen Mary in 1911. (*a*) Made exclusively for Harrods Ltd., but maker not named. (*b*) A very ordinary monochrome souvenir marked Doulton.

FIGURE XVI.4. (*a*) Cup and (*b*) egg cup in inexpensive whiteware commemorating the Silver Jubilee of George V and Queen Mary in 1935. Neither marked.

on which the Sun never Sets" and urged them to long continue a reign both happy and glorious (Fig. XVI.3). Their Silver Jubilee in 1935 was to be the last glittering assemblage of the rajahs and nabobs of Britain's globe girdling empire, a procession I watched from a seat in the grandstand in Piccadilly and that I have never forgotten—although my principal memory is not of the State Coach or the glitter of breastplates on the chests of the household cavalry, but rather of open-backed taxis carrying colonial potentates down Piccadilly to Westminster Abbey (Fig. XVI.4). A year later the King would be dead, and two years afterward the empire would begin to self-destruct under the pressures of a new Great War.

Before that could happen, however, the British public would go through the divisive trauma of another Royal scandal, one that took the Staffordshire potters by costly surprise. Expecting that Edward Prince of Wales would be crowned on May 12, 1937, they turned out mugs, beakers, and cups in profusion declaring "Long May He Reign" (Fig. XVI.5 *b* and *c*).

FIGURE XVI.5. (*b, c*) Whiteware handled beaker and mug intended to laud the coronation of Edward VIII. (*b*) Unmarked. (*c*) By Royal Doulton. (*a*) When Edward preferred Wallis Simpson to his duty, the only souvenirs of their wedding were canceled philatelic envelopes with nowhere to go.

FIGURE XVI.6. Whiteware mug commemorating the coronation of George VI and Queen Elizabeth. The mug's shape and color are typical of popular "modern" taste in the 1930s. Unmarked.

The world now knows that he preferred Wallis Simpson to the throne of England, thereby leaving its potters with souvenirs that nobody wanted. Following in the footsteps of Josiah Wedgwood, the ceramic merchants saw a marketplace amid the British islands of the Caribbean and so cynically shipped their Edwards there in the expectation that uneducated but patriotic islanders would not know the difference between Edward and his brother, who would be crowned George VI on the same May day (Fig. XVI.6).[1]

Although neither Audrey nor I had any sympathy for Edward and believed that he had dishonored himself and his country by quitting, we found his subsequent life chillingly fascinating. As Audrey was a stamp collector, it was only to be expected that we should acquire French souvenir envelopes recalling the thinly attended Edward and Wallis wedding at the Château de Cande at "Monts (France) le 3 Juin 1937—12 heures" (Fig. XVI.5 *a*). Regardless of the fact that the stamps were precanceled, allegedly at that very hour, the absence of anyone's written address suggests that the covers were not best-sellers. The wedding envelopes with their portraits of the happy couple represented to us the beginning of a pitiful saga that would end with the inevitable coffee mug on April 30, 1986. Produced in a wisely limited edition by commemorative ceramics dealer John May it recalled the birth of Bessie Wallis Warfield at Blue Ridge Summit, Pa., on June 19, 1896, and her burial beside her husband at Frogmore in the land from which she had been banned after becoming the despised Wallis, Duchess of Windsor (Fig. XVI.7).

Rarest among the latter-day monarchist souvenirs is a plate commemorating the visit of George VI and Queen Elizabeth to the United States in 1939 (Fig. XVI.8). That State Visit had been proposed by Canadian Prime Minister Mackenzie King at the time of the coronation in the hope

IF THESE POTS COULD TALK

of mending a widening crack between Franco-Canadian separatists and their Anglophile neighbors. With the threat of war with Germany looming ever darker, a broader North American tour assumed unexpected urgency. On May 5, 1939, the King and Queen sailed from Southampton

FIGURE XVI.9. Commemorative coronation mug for Elizabeth II, 1952, in a globular shape popular at that time. Bone china by John Aynsley & Sons of Longton.

aboard the *Empress of Australia,* nervous and uncertain about their reception in the United States. They had been informed that there was strong American suspicion that Edward had been robbed of his throne by an Establishment resentful of his populist leanings. A society had been formed in New York the previous year calling itself the "Friends of the Duke of Windsor in the United States," whose aim was to "urge his qualification as an international leader in the cause of human welfare and world peace."[2] Then, too, there were the anti-British rantings of the German American Bund as well as the influential Boston Irish, whose brogue-enhanced views on Britain were well known. Meanwhile, Edward paid a much publicized visit to the World War I battlefield of Verdun and there made a broadcast speech (aired live by NBC in America) aimed at putting himself back on the global stage in the guise of a peacemaker and friend to both Germany and Britain. Nevertheless, in spite of scattered opposition more needling than significant, the Royal visit to the United States did much to cement a bond between Britain and President Roosevelt that was to be crucial in the dangerous years ahead. In short, our commemorative plate has historical interest and importance never expected by its Staffordshire potters, Messrs. John Maddock & Sons of Burslem.[3]

The death of George VI in 1952 brought the young Queen Elizabeth to the throne, beginning a reign whose duration has rivaled that of Queen Victoria and matched that of her sixteenth-century namesake (Fig. XVI.9). Alas, the reign's coffee-mug–spawning great moments have been short-lived and a sad commentary on the House of Windsor as it tries to remain regal in the face of a press no longer shackled by traditional restraints of

FIGURE XVI.10. Expectations unfulfilled. Whiteware commemorative mugs made to celebrate the weddings of (*a*) Prince Charles and Diana Spencer in 1981, and (*b*) Prince Andrew and Sarah Ferguson in 1986. Neither marked.

compassion and respect. The marriage-commemorating mugs of Prince Andrew and Sarah Ferguson (July 23, 1986) and of Prince Charles and Diana Spencer five years earlier (July 29, 1981) speak now of heartbreak at the Palace rather than of joys remembered (Fig. XVI.10).

IF THESE POTS COULD TALK

FIGURE XVI.II. (*a*) London delftware royal portrait charger dated 1658. (*b*) Lady Burnett accompanied us to Buckingham Palace in 1992. (*c*) Another, somewhat less noble, delftware charger, this one by Michelle Erikson, 1992. (*a*) Colonial Williamsburg Foundation. Gift in memory of Joseph Porter Moore by his wife, Adelia Peebles Moore. Accession no. 1968-104; (*b*) photo courtesy of official investiture photographer, Charles Green.

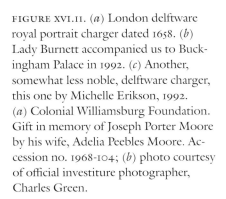

Accompanied by Lady Burnett, Audrey and I were received at Buckingham Palace on November 19, 1992, for the investiture that was to mark the pinnacle of our archaeological careers. I well remember how old and tired the Queen appeared as she pinned the badge of the Order of the British Empire to my lapel. She had no inkling that on the following day Windsor Castle would be burning, any more than I could have imagined that a year later Audrey would be dead. I venture to hope, however, that long after I am gone, the delftware plate made to commemorate the investiture will survive as a "keep me" antique prompting scholars and collectors to write erudite papers speculating on the identity of the crowned figure and the significance of June 14, 1992 (Fig. XVI.II).[+]

Eight years after Audrey's death the British Royal family finally had its moment of unbegrudged affection and gave Staffordshire one more occasion to pot about (Fig. XVI.I2). The widow of George VI, the truly beloved Queen Elizabeth the Queen Mother, celebrated her one hundredth birthday on August 4, 2000, thereby unwittingly bringing the Collection's 2,000-year odyssey to its crowd-cheering, band-playing, laser-flashing, fireworks-bursting conclusion.

FIGURE XVI.I2. Porcelain box by Royal Crown Derby commemorating the one hundredth birthday of Queen Elizabeth the Queen Mother, August 4, 2000.

Glossary

BECAUSE NOT ALL collectors, curators, and certainly not all archaeologists use the same descriptive language, and because the repetition of the same term can be jarring, alternative words are often needed. Knowing, too, that some readers will be dipping into the book without first having read introductory and explanatory passages in earlier chapters, I have included brief identifications of the most often named places of ceramic production. To make sure, therefore, that, be you novice or specialist, you have a means of knowing what in the world I'm talking about, the following etymology is humbly submitted.

AGATE: The product of mixing two or more clays of different colors together to create a marbleized effect, not to be confused with marbling. See Fig. XIII.7.

AMPHORA: A tall earthenware wine, oil, or olive storage and shipment jar, usually with a pointed base and two handles, predominantly of the Classical centuries (e.g., Fig. I.7).

ANNULAR WARE: Vessels with laterally banded decoration, usually used in reference to late creamwares, pearlwares, and whitewares.

ANTHROPOMORPHIC: Any ceramic detail such as a spout or finial having human form (e.g., Figs. II.22 and II.24), as opposed to ZOOMORPHIC.

ASTBURY: A generic term used to describe a hard, red, lead-glazed ware usually decorated with sprigged (q.v.) ornamentation, invented by John Astbury of Shelton in Staffordshire, but produced by several potteries (e.g., Fig. XII.3).

BADARIAN: Red and black gloss pottery made without a potter's wheel in that period of predynastic Egypt (e.g., Fig. I.1).

BARBOTINE: The application of hand-applied decoration, most often used in describing Roman-era wares (e.g., Fig. II.23).

BARTMANN: An abbreviation or Anglicization of the German *Bartmann-krug* (bearded man jug), long known in England, albeit incorrectly, as BELLARMINE bottles, also GRAYBEARDS.

BASALTES: A dry-bodied gray-black stoneware, originally the so-called ELERS Ware fired in a reducing atmosphere, but refined by Wedgwood and called *Black Basaltes* (1787). It was much used for vases and other ornaments as well as for mourning tea services popular in the period ca. 1790–1830.

BASE: The underside to a vessel that has no foot, an alternative to bottom.

BATAVIAN: The name given to British wares emulating the externally brown-slipped Chinese porcelains shipped in quantity via the clearing port of Batavia (now Jakarta) (e.g., Figs. XI.4–XI.5).

BAT MOLDING: Shaping a plate or dish over a former or mandril.

BEAKER: Any handleless drinking vessel.

BELLARMINE: An incorrect term, but one of some antiquity, identifying Rhenish salt-glazed stoneware bottles decorated at their necks with the sprig-applied face of a bearded man, and therefore known in Germany as *Bartmannkrugs* (bearded man bottles). Recognizing that to continue a supposed association with Cardinal Roberto Bellarmino makes no sense, curators now call these vessels BARTMANN bottles, an awkward name, part German and part English, that might just as well be fully converted to English as GRAYBEARDS, a term employed at least as late as 1811 (e.g., Fig. VI.7).

BISCUIT: The product of a first firing prior to glazing, synonymous with BISQUE, the latter also used to describe wares not intended to be glazed (e.g., Fig. IV.14).

BISQUE: See BISCUIT.

BODY: Used to describe the fired clay beneath the glazing.

BORDER WARE: The term relates primarily to white or buff-bodied wares either clear (yellow) glazed or copper-derived green glazed that had long been referred to as *Tudor Green*. But as each generation likes to make its mark by changing the name of something, the term (meaning kilns on both side of the Surrey-Hampshire county line) is the preferred revisionist usage (e.g., Fig. III.27).

BOUFFIOULX: One of several small centers near Liège in modern Belgium that produced brown stonewares in poor imitation of Rhineland forms. Production began around 1530 and continued through the seventeenth century.

BOWL: Any handleless, hemispherical or related vessel wherein to serve or store liquids or solids.

BRAZIER: An earthenware vessel constructed in two elements to enable air to reach burning charcoal whose heat is intended to keep food or feet warm, and which may also provide fire for smokers (e.g., Fig. II.32). See also CHAFING DISH.

BRISTOL GLAZE: See DOUBLE GLAZING.

CAN: A straight-sided mug or cup (e.g., Fig. IX.52).

CARINATED: A vessel prominently contoured, in-curving above and below its sharply defined girth (e.g., Fig. I.18).

CAUDLE: A drink made from thin gruel, spiced, sweetened, and mixed with ale or wine; commonly served to women bedded at childbirth and to other invalids. The *O.E.D.* offers a 1657 reference to "One Cawdell Cupp with a top," meaning fitted with a lid. However, all the Robins inventory's references are to "cawdle potts." It is likely that many of those described as caudle cups by collectors were wine rather than sickbed cups. The Robins inventory listed wine "cupps" (as opposed to pots for caudle), indicating a shape difference between the two.

CENTER: The usually flat, obverse face of a decorated plate or bowl.

CHAFING DISH: A portable grate holding burning coals to keep food or plates hot (e.g., Fig. II.32). See also BRAZIER.

CHAILEY: A Sussex village noted for the production of red, lead-glazed earthenware decorated by means of printer's type, its impressions filled with white, but yellow-appearing, slip. This is a generic term for a very distinctive product also made at Herstmonceux and other Sussex locations, in the late eighteenth and first half of the nineteenth centuries (e.g., Fig. XIII.6).

CHARGER: A large dish, a term usually restricted to those from the seventeenth century (e.g., Fig. III.6). A serving dish from which others are filled or charged.

CHINA GLAZ'D: Term used by late-eighteenth-century potters to describe the pearlware glaze. See PEARLWARE.

CLOBBERING: The crude application of heavy overglaze colors onto underglazed painting or printing, often, but not always, part of the original design intent (e.g., Fig. XI.19).

CLOUDED WARE: A term used to describe wares decorated with slips and coloring oxides commonly found on WHIELDON type cream-colored wares of the 1750s and 1760s (e.g., Fig. IX.40).

CRACKED: An item in the Collection thus damaged, but neither broken apart nor invisibly repaired.

COBALT: A blue pigment of cobalt oxide and alumina used for underglaze decoration, both free-hand and printed.

COIL-BUILT: Earthenware constructed with coils of rolled clay and shaped without the use of the potter's wheel.

COLLAR: A vertical section immediately below the rim or lip, usually intended to receive a lid. See PIPKIN.

CORDON: A ridge or series of ridges, sharp or rounded, often with space between, which on gray Westerwald stonewares may be painted blue.

COSTREL: A vessel intended for the personal transportation of liquids, usually with two or more carrying attachments (e.g., Fig. VI.22). Medieval versions are often referred to as *Pilgrim bottles,* while other globular, earthenware bottles used by nineteenth-century farm workers are called *owls*.

CREAMWARE: A yellow, lead-glazed ware developed in the 1740s as a successor to white salt-glazed stoneware, and frequently described as *cream-colored earthenware* or *Queen's ware*.

CUP: Any small, thinly potted drinking vessel having a handle, and of any shape other than straight-sided. See CAN, also GORGE.

DEBASED SCRATCH BLUE: English gray, salt-glazed stoneware decorated in imitation of Westerwald imports in the last decades of the eighteenth century, commonly found as chamber pots, mugs, and pitchers (e.g., Fig. IX.37). See also SCRATCH BLUE.

DELFTWARE: Tin-glazed earthenware, in England with a small "d" and when made at Delft in Holland with a capital "D." However, the Dutch call it FAYENCE. See also TIN GLAZE.

DONYATT: Red, slip-coated earthenware often copper-splashed, usually with sgraffito decoration and made in and around the village of that name in north-central Somerset from the thirteenth century but mainly from the seventeenth onward into the twentieth century (e.g., Fig. XIII.10).

DOUBLE GLAZING: Although used to describe eighteenth-century wares that were partly slipped with iron oxide and partly with an opaque ENGOBE (e.g., Fig. VII.9), the term generally applies to the vitreous slip glazes developed by William Powell of Bristol ca. 1835 (e.g. Fig. XIV.37), which achieved a highly commercial stoneware without the use of salt. The new product did much to diminish the subsequent marketability of old-style brown salt-glazed stoneware.

DRY BODY: Unglazed wares, often of stoneware hardness, such as those attributed to the brothers ELERS, most of which date much later (e.g., Fig. IX.50).

EAR: An ear-shaped handle, usually in pairs (e.g., Fig. X.21 *a*).

EARTHENWARE: Pottery fired at lower temperatures than were needed to make stoneware or porcelain.

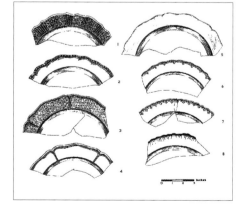

EDGE: The outer rim, primarily of plates and dishes, decorated in several relief patterns associated with eighteenth-century WHITE SALT GLAZE, WHIELDON ware, CREAMWARE, and PEARLWARE. 1, Dot-diaper-and-basket; 2, bead and reel; 3, barley; 4, Queen's shape; 5, Royal; 6, feather; 7, spearhead; 8, shell.

ELERS: The name of two brothers from Amsterdam who created a hard, dry-bodied redware usually decorated with sprigged ornament, making it first at Vauxhall in 1693 and later in Staffordshire. Their name used to be applied to all such tea and coffee wares, which, in reality, were made in several places through into the 1770s (e.g., Fig. IX.50).

ENGINE-TURNED: Wares lathe-turned while in the leather-hard state, and using jigs to create eccentric movement of the blade to cut geometric and other lateral patterns around teapots, coffee pots, and so on (e.g., Fig. XIII.36). The process was developed around 1765.

ENGOBE: A refined clay or thick slip used to cover another clay body of lesser quality or color; often of West of England white-firing clay strengthened with ground flint (e.g., Fig. IX.26).

EWER: Another name for a handled flagon, jug, or pitcher, usually of large size and used for the dispensing of liquids (e.g., Fig. I.7).

FABRIC: Alternative usage to WARE or BODY.

FAIENCE: European tin-glazed earthenwares from France and northward, excluding the Netherlands; similar to DELFTWARE and MAIOLICA.

FAIRINGS: A term to describe small objects such as toys and ceramic ornaments sold cheaply at fairs (e.g., Fig. IX.58).

FAYENCE: The term used by the Dutch to describe their post-maiolica tin-glazed wares that the English know as delftware—with a capital "D" when the city of Delft is the known origin. See also FAIENCE.

FAZACKERLEY: A term used to describe a pallet of soft-hued floral colors, principally red and green, used by Liverpool delftware potters. A mug so decorated and initialed T.F. 1757 is said to have been made by Thomas Shaw for Thomas Fazackerley.

FLAGON: A large mug or tankard, usually covered, and used as a serving rather than a drinking vessel (e.g., Fig. VII.16). See also EWER.

FLANGE: A flat and projecting collar as on pipkins (q.v.); also used to describe the flat area between the rim and the well of a plate or dish, sometimes called the MARLY.

FOOT RIM: The standing edge of a plate or bowl whose base is elevated within the circle thus created. This term is also often used (though not here) to describe a bowl or plate's basal collar here known as a FOOT RING.

FOOT RING: A collar sometimes V-shaped and sometimes square-cut on which a bowl or plate stands, not to be confused with a FOOT RIM (q.v.).

FRIEZE: A broad or narrow, relief-ornamented panel encircling the wall or neck of a vessel, usually separately applied (e.g., Fig. V.11 *b*).

FULHAM: The location of John Dwight's pioneering stoneware and porcelain manufacturing experiments on the north bank of the Thames opposite Putney. Founded in 1671; production of stonewares continued there until 1928.

GALENA: Lead sulfide, with the lead compound applied dry (sometimes secured by a flour-paste wash) in pottery glazing before fluid glazes were developed.

GALLEY WARE: A name common in the late sixteenth and seventeenth centuries to describe objects produced in tin-glazed earthenware. Thus, apothecaries' small ointment jars were called GALLEY POTS (e.g., Fig. III.3). The term is thought to be derived from the fact (or belief) that in the sixteenth century they were first shipped from the Mediterranean to the Low Countries aboard Portuguese or Venetian galleys. Netherlandish imitators were known as *galeyerspotbackers*.

GLAZE: A mixture, mainly of oxides (as silica and alumina), applied to the interior and/or exterior of a vessel to render it moisture impervious and to enhance its appearance.

GLOSS: A highly polished surface achieved without the application of a glaze, often employing a refined slip made from the same clay as the body. This term is commonly used to describe the so-called SAMIAN WARE of the Roman Empire, as well as the burnished fabrics used by the Medway potters; see UPCHURCH and Fig. I.4. The term is also used to describe any highly reflecting, glazed surface.

GORGE: A bulbous, handled mug with a straight, collar neck. The O.E.D.'s first citation is to John Dwight's patent of 1684. The term continued to be used by potters and retailers to the end of the eighteenth century (e.g., Fig. VII.2).

GRAYBEARD: The English name (and Americanized spelling) in use as late as 1811 to describe the imported Rhenish face-decorated brown stoneware bottles known to earlier collectors as BELLARMINES, and to new scholars as BARTMANNS.

GRENZHAUSEN: A German center for the manufacture of salt-glazed stonewares in the seventeenth and eighteenth centuries, usually gray-bodied and decorated first in cobalt and later also with manganese. The district continues in stoneware production today and is usually referred to as Höhr-Grenzhausen. See HÖHR.

GROG: A secondary clay mixed with the primary fabric to strengthen it and to reduce shrinkage in firing. See also TEMPER.

HARVEST BOTTLE: An earthenware, lead-glazed bottle usually with two pierced ears beside the neck to which a thong or string is attached to enable the farm worker to suspend the vessel from his belt; also known as OWLS (e.g., Fig. XIII.6). See also COSTREL.

HAYS WHARF: The company name for a firm of wharfingers owning river-fronting properties on the south bank of the Thames between London Bridge and Tower Bridge, among which was the site of the seventeenth-century PICKLEHERRING delftware pot houses.

HIDROCERAMO: The Spanish term for an earthenware flask with a carrying handle, a short tubular spout, and a flow-controlling nipple. The form was Islamic in origin and of considerable antiquity (e.g., Fig. XV.13 c).

HÖHR: A Rhineland center for making salt-glazed stonewares, a name often incorrectly applied to any Rhenish, gray-bodied, salt-glazed stoneware whose sprigged decoration is without cobalt or manganese enhancement (e.g., Fig. V.14).

HUNT MUGS AND JUGS: A collective term applied to all English brown stonewares of the eighteenth and nineteenth centuries decorated with sprig-applied hounds, huntsmen, and so on (e.g., Fig. VII.12).

IMARI: Correctly used, it means multicolored Japanese porcelain, but like so many other pirated terms, it is employed much more broadly to include Chinese porcelain whose underglaze blue is enriched with overglaze red and gold (e.g., Fig. XIII.16).

IN SITU: An archaeological term meaning an object discovered undisturbed in its original situation in the ground.

IRON OXIDE: Used to make a red slip or wash turning gray salt-glazed stonewares brown, and also used to blacken lead glazes.

JACKFIELD: A high-gloss, hard-fired, black-glazed redware often decorated with overglaze gilding, whose creation has been attributed to Richard Thursfield, who set up a pottery at Jackfield in Shropshire at the beginning of the eighteenth century. Sharp spouted jugs (e.g. Fig. XIII.1) and teapots in this lustrous ware were made at several Staffordshire potteries. Like ELERS ware, the name has been widely misused.

JUG: An alternative term for pitcher, having a handle and usually a spout.

KRAAK: Chinese porcelain first brought to Europe aboard Portuguese carracks, the term used to describe porcelain dishes in the Wan Li period that were without European prototypes or influence.

LAMBETH: A center for delftware production on the south bank of the Thames opposite to Westminster, beginning in 1676 and continuing through the eighteenth century in several factories that also made stonewares. The latter became Lambeth's principal ceramic output in the nineteenth and continued into the twentieth century.

LEAD GLAZE: A glaze made from lead oxide, although transparent, it imparted a yellow cast to whatever it covered. Thus, redwares become brown, and white slips yellow. A colorless lead glaze was developed late in the eighteenth century.

LEEDS WARE: The blanket term usually applied to creamware of high quality, often with pierced decoration and with intertwined and reeded handles with foliate and floral terminals (e.g., Fig. IX.45). Although there were several creamware- and pearlware-producing factories in the vicinity of Leeds in Yorkshire, the name is most often used to identify the products of the Old Pottery at Hunslet established ca. 1760 and in production until 1824.

LIP: The mouth-contacting edge of a cup or mug; also a V-shaped projection for pouring, but not sufficiently pronounced to be called a SPOUT.

LOVING CUP: Another of those much-used but not necessarily applicable terms used to describe two-handled, pedestal-footed cups of the eighteenth and nineteenth centuries that were sometimes passed from mouth to mouth to toast the health of newlyweds or the survival of couples who remained alive and together to reach a toastworthy jubilee (e.g., Fig. X.11).

LUG HANDLE: A short, usually solid handle projecting from the side of a vessel, as opposed to one looped and secured at both extremities.

LUSTER: Metallic decoration mainly derived from silver and gold (pink), and much used between ca. 1805 and 1875 (e.g., Fig. XII.21).

LUTE: Attached by the use of clay as opposed to any other securing device.

MAIOLICA (majolica): Tin-glazed earthenwares manufactured in the Mediterranean countries, and also used to describe such wares made at Antwerp and elsewhere in the sixteenth century by immigrant craftsmen from Italy and Spain.

MANGANESE: A metallic element resembling iron but not magnetic, and used, sometimes as the dioxide, to color slips and glazes to produce a purple color or to add its own tint to iron-colored, black lead glazes.

MARBLEIZED: The blending together of several colored slips and applied to the surface of earthenwares to give them the appearance of marble (e.g., Fig. VI.22). Not to be confused with AGATE, wherein the clays of different color clays are mixed together to create a marbleizing that extends through the thickness of the ware.

MARLY: The flat border to a plate or dish that lies between the rim and the wall below, a sector sometimes called the FLANGE (q.v.). Described in the *O.E.D.* as "the raised rim of a dish or plate."

MARVERING: A term most often used in glass making, meaning a slab or matrix over which the glass or clay is rolled and smoothed.

MENDED: Any object in the collection that has been broken and put back together without the need to reconstruct missing pieces, as opposed to RESTORED.

METROPOLITAN SLIPWARE: Yet another misleading term, originally coined to identify brown-glazed redwares of ca. 1630–1680, decorated with white (yellow) slip beneath the glaze, that have commonly been found in the metropolis (London), but that are now known to have been made near Harlow in Essex (e.g., Fig. IV.4).

MOCHA WARE: Decoration usually in association with lateral banding (see ANNULAR) creating a sea fern-like ornament by means of tobacco juice and urine.

MORTLAKE: The location of delftware and stoneware manufacturing on the south bank of the Thames below Brentford that began in 1745.

MUFFLE KILN: A low-temperature kiln used to consolidate decoration unable to withstand the first higher temperature firing.

MUG: A handled drinking vessel larger than a cup and usually straight sided.

NAA: Neutron activation analysis, a process involving multivariate statistics that include the tested pottery's principal components, as well as discriminant and cluster analysis, that is, the assembling and retesting of samples that exhibit the same composition.

OBVERSE: The up-facing surface of a plate, dish, or charger.

OLLA: A handleless earthenware jar used primarily for storage. In Spanish the term meant a cooking pot, and in the southwest United States a porous jar used to keep water cool (e.g., Fig. I.20).

OVERGLAZE: Enameling or other material such as oil gilding applied to the surface of an already glazed vessel.

OWL: An earthenware bottle, a West of England term synonymous with HARVEST BOTTLE, but usually applied to the larger and more globular vessels of the nineteenth century. It is not to be confused with slipware vessels made in the shape of owls with removable heads as lids.

OXIDATION: Meaning that the ware has been fired in a kiln in which oxygen is present, resulting in clays that turn red in the fire and remain so. See also REDUCTION.

PASTE: A term most often applied to porcelain; SOFT-PASTE ware is fired at a lower temperature than HARD-PASTE porcelain and achieves its luster through the application of a lead glaze and a second firing, while true porcelain, known as hard-paste, is achieved both with china clay and with china stone rendered fusible with a flux and fired at a high temperature.

PEARLWARE: derived from the name *Pearl White* given by Josiah Wedgwood in 1779 to a whitened creamware in imitation of oriental porcelain. The fabric would be widely used by most earthenware factories, where it was called CHINA-GLAZ'D and continued in production into the second quarter of the nineteenth century.

PEDESTAL: A truncated support attached to the bowl of a tazza, jar, salt, and so on (e.g., Fig. 1.24 *b*).

PICKLEHERRING STAIRS: A pioneering center of delftware production from ca.1618 begun under the management of Dutch emigrant Christian Wilhelm, and continued to ca. 1723.

PINS: Or pegs. Triangular-sectioned props inserted through holes in the sides of SAGGERS to support plates and dishes stacked within.

PIPKIN: An earthenware cooking vessel having three legs and a single handle that sometimes is solid and sometimes tubular, often with a collar below the lip to seat a lid (e.g., Fig. VI.31).

PITCHER: A jug, flagon, or ewer, sometimes used to define a pouring vessel smaller than a jug.

PLATE: A platter or dish, a term not used by the ceramic industry until the eighteenth century.

PORRINGER: A shallow bowl from which potage or porridge was imbibed, usually with a single handle, and in the sixteenth century designed more for tipping than lifting (e.g., Fig.VI.15). In the late seventeenth century, English delftware potters followed silver and pewter in making the handles large and more suited to lifting.

PORTOBELLO WARE: Wares reputedly made in that Scottish town from the late eighteenth century well through the nineteenth century. This has become another generic term, describing redwares white slipped inside, and externally transfer printed in yellow-orange pseudo-Chinese designs (e.g., Fig. XII.17). The name should not be confused with ASTBURY style wares made to commemorate Admiral Vernon's 1739 attack on that Spanish-American town.

POSSET POT: Usually a two-handled and lidded vessel with a long spout attached close to the bottom of the interior, enabling the potable part of the drink to be extracted without disturbing the floating curds. See also CAUDLE.

POTAGE: A medieval term for soups of all kinds (see PORRINGER), derived from the Latin *potabilis,* meaning drink.

POUNCE: A powder of charcoal or chalk marvered over a pricked template to transmit the basics of a design to tiles and vessels to provide the painter with guidelines to ensure that each copy would come out almost exactly alike (e.g., Fig. X.1).

PRESS MOLDING: The shaping of decorative wares by pressing soft clay into two or more molds and subsequently luting the parts together (e.g., Fig. XII.15). See also SLIP CASTING.

PUNCH BOWL: A term that seems to be indiscriminately applied to virtually any late seventeenth- or eighteenth-century, handleless bowl, regardless of size. In truth, the smaller bowls were used for all manner of purposes.

RAEREN: The name of a Rhineland town whose potteries produced predominantly brown, salt-glazed stonewares in the sixteenth and early seventeenth centuries, later including blue-decorated gray stonewares.

REEDING: Multiple lateral grooves and ridges around the neck of a vessel (e.g., Fig. V.23 *b* and *c*).

REPAIRED: A vessel broken to a greater or lesser degree and put back together without the replacement of any part. A variant of MENDED.

RESTORED: Items in the collection that have had lost fragments and have been replaced in another material, such as plaster of Paris.

REVERSE: The back or underside of a plate, charger, or dish.

RIM: The outer edge of a plate, bowl, and so on, not (at least not ordinarily) placed to the lips. See LIP.

ROSSO ANTICO: The name given by Wedgwood to his dry-bodied redware of stoneware hardness akin to those loosely attributed to ELERS (q.v.) and the opposite of similar wares fired in a reducing atmosphere, which he called BASALTES.

RIVETING: A means of repairing broken pottery and porcelain using lead and later brass and copper wire rivets. This was the principal method of repairing from Roman times to the end of the nineteenth century (e.g., Fig. XIII.15), and in the more recent centuries often used in conjunction with glues having various components.

SAGGER: A container wherein ceramic wares are stacked in the kiln. These are generally made from the same fabric as the preglazed pottery. Most of those for delftware were open-based cylinders that could be stacked one upon another. In the eighteenth century these were pierced to create triangular holes through which ceramic PINS were thrust to support each plate in the stack. Stoneware saggers, on the other hand, always had closed bases and had two or more pear-shaped apertures to allow the salt to reach the biscuit and iron oxide–slipped wares. In addition, there was a slot at one side so that a mug's or jug's handle could protrude. Sometimes the saggers were small and housed but a single mug, while others were much larger and could accommodate several vessels (e.g., Fig. VII.4).

SALOPIAN: Although this word means "belonging to Shropshire" and was used as a Caughley porcelain mark, it is also employed by some dealers to identify a range of pearlware, transfer-printed teawares, overglaze decorated with rather garish greens and orange, and dating between about 1795 and 1815 (e.g., Fig. X.22).

SALT GLAZING: The primary method of glazing stoneware from the Middle Ages into the present century. It involved throwing salt into the kiln when it reached its maximum temperature. The salt volatilized into the atmosphere and created an orange-peel pitting to the shiny surface of the vessels. However, cobalt repelled the salt, and in consequence one never sees the blue of Rhenish stonewares anything but smooth.

SAMIAN WARE: A red, high-gloss, mold-shaped earthenware made predominantly in central and southern Gaul between the first and third centuries, and imported into Britain in large quantities. The term *Samian* derives from the mistaken belief that the Gaulish products owed their origin to the island of Samos in the Aegean. Purists today call it *red gloss ware,* while older students retain the European term *terra sigillata,* the latter meaning adorned with little figures—which is true of some types (Fig. XIII.12), but by no means the majority of Samian products (e.g., Fig. I.4).

SCHNELLE: A tall tankard; in this context, a relief-decorated Rhenish gray stoneware manufactured at Siegburg in the second half of the sixteenth century (e.g., Fig. V.8).

SCRATCH BLUE AND SCRATCH BROWN: A means of decorating white salt-glazed English stoneware by scratching patterns into the still receptive clay and wiping the impacted areas with color, which, having filled the scratch marks, was wiped away from the rest of the body (e.g., Fig. IX.36). Cobalt provided the blue, and iron oxide the brown. In the late 1760s, in an effort to compete with the importation of blue-decorated Rhenish stonewares, the salt-glaze potters painted entire areas of previously outlined leaves and similar devices in imitation of the WESTERWALD jugs and chamber pots that had hitherto monopolized the market. These rather sorry English copies are known as DEBASED SCRATCH BLUE (e.g., Fig. IX.37).

SECONDS: Wares damaged in production but marketable at a reduced price.

SGRAFFITO (or sgraffiato): An Italian word meaning "scratching," and in ceramics a technique of cutting designs through a slip to expose the body color beneath, a method long popular in England's southwest counties (e.g., Fig. II.21).

SIEGBURG: A Rhineland location near Cologne where stoneware manufacturing began early in the Middle Ages, producing unsalted gray wares and later the ubiquitous brown salt-glazed wares.

SLIP: A coating of refined clay, usually firing to a different color than the vessel's body clay and applied either by brushing or dipping.

SLIP CASTING: The shaping of usually decorative wares by means of one or more pourings of slip into porous, water-extracting plaster-of-Paris molds (e.g. Fig. IX.22). See also PRESS MOLDING.

SLUG: A bottomless cylinder wherein plates were stacked in the kiln, separated by wall-piercing PINS.

SPRIGGING: The application of relief decoration to the walls of vessels employing separate molds into which the clay is pressed and then transferred (luted) to the moistened surface of the mugs and jugs. Products of that technique were reaching Roman Britain by the second century, were extensively used by the medieval and later stoneware potters of the Rhineland (e.g., Fig. VI.2), and were used among English stoneware and earthenware makers from the late seventeenth century onward (e.g., Fig. XII.3).

SPOUT: The entirety of any shaped device, be it hollow or open, designed to aid in the extraction of liquids from pitchers, teapots, and so on. The mouth of a spout is here described as a lip.

STRING-RIM: Sometimes called a "string ring." Defines the applied or molded collar around the neck of a glass or ceramic bottle to enable its cork to be tied down with wire or string.

TANKARD: A large mug of quart or more capacity, but here used interchangeably with mug when repetition palls. See also FLAGON.

TAZZA: A cup, vase, or incense burner on a pedestal base (e.g., Fig. I.24).

TEA BOWL: Any hemispherical cup without a handle (e.g., Fig. IX.53).

TEA POY: A tea caddy (e.g., Fig. IX.36).

TEMPER: The mixing of a secondary clay, fine gravel, ground up shell, flint, or even brick, to strengthen the clay used to make coarse utilitarian earthenwares (e.g., Fig. IV.11). See also GROG. In this book, grog is used to identify a fortifying clay, and temper to mean the addition of one or more of the ground-up solid ingredients.

TERMINUS ANTE QUEM: A date *before* which an object was made, thrown away, or whatever.

TERMINUS POST QUEM: A date *after* which an object was made, thrown away, or whatever.

TIGER WARE: A term used by early collectors to describe the surface of Rhenish brown stoneware bottles and mugs, apparently unaware that tigers are striped, not mottled.

TIN GLAZE: The term is somewhat misleading, for the basic ingredient is still lead. Consequently, some writers refer to it as *tin enamel*. In reality this is a lead glaze rendered opaque by the addition of ashes of tin, and in England the result is called DELFTWARE—with a lower case "d."

TINKERED: A term used by Josiah Wedgwood to mean products damaged in production but that could be repaired well enough to be sold, with the repairs usually made before the final firing (e.g., Fig. VII.14).

TORTOISESHELL: Glazing colored with dappled manganese or iron oxide, resulting in an appearance somewhat akin (but not very) to the coloring of the carapace of the hawksbill turtle from which commercial tortoiseshell was cut (e.g., Fig. IX.40). However, similar purple spattering occurs on the interior glazed surface of chamber pots and pipkins of seventeenth-century BORDER WARE, and evidently was unintentional. Deliberate tortoiseshell glazing is to be found on seventeenth-century redware mugs and on eighteenth-century chamber pots and bowls, and appears as dark brown or black elongated dots with an otherwise dark brown surface.

TRIVET: Or spacer, triangular in shape, and used to separate plates and chargers in the kiln. Just as sagger pins left marks on the underside of marlies of eighteenth-century delftware plates, so in the previous century the spacing trivets left three small, equidistant scars in the obverse centers of chargers and plates (e.g., Fig. III.10).

UPCHURCH: The name of a village in East Kent adjacent to the Medway marshes where, in the first and third centuries, large quantities of both fine and strictly utilitarian pottery was made. Because the same types have been found in deposits scattered across several miles of marshland south of the river Medway and near the village of Upchurch, I have preferred that as the generic name, although most of our finds came from one stretch called the Slayhills Saltings.

VAUXHALL: A location on the south bank of the Thames opposite to Westminster and adjacent to LAMBETH, and a center for delftware and stoneware manufacturing from 1683 through the eighteenth century.

WALL: The external side of a vessel, be it a plate, mug, or whatever, that stands between the base and the flange or neck. It is also used to describe the inner face of any vessel other than a dish, plate, or saucer See also WELL.

WELL: In flat wares (e.g., plates and dishes), the interior sides between the flange and center. The term also applies to cup-containing recesses in nineteenth-century and modern saucers.

WESTERWALD: A district of the German Rhineland in the vicinity of Coblenz that specialized in the production of blue-on-gray stonewares; among the factories were those of Grenzhau, Grenzhausen, and Höhr. Stoneware continues to be produced in this area.

WHIELDON: A class of lead-glazed, cream-colored earthenware developed by Thomas Whieldon of Fenton Low in Staffordshire, employing staining oxides that mixed greens, yellows, and purples to create what is often referred to as CLOUDED WARE. Popular among his products were those resembling tortoiseshell, for which dappled, purplish-brown glazing was often used on the backs of plates whose obverses were more brightly colored (e.g., Fig. IX.40). Whieldon opened his factory in 1740 and brought Josiah Wedgwood into partnership in 1754. A great variety of tea and coffee wares was developed during this partnership, among them pineapple and cauliflower, with some of the shapes employing salt-glazed stoneware molds (e.g., Fig. IX.40).

ZAFFRE: An impure oxide of cobalt used in ceramic coloring, as in Westerwald stonewares and "Littler's blue" salt-glazed stoneware.

ZOOMORPHIC: Decorative details such as spouts, handles, and feet in animal shapes (e.g., Figs. VI.23 and IX.27 *b*), as opposed to human form (ANTHROPOMORPHIC) decoration.

Scaling Measurements and Inscriptions

Unless otherwise indicated, *a, b,* and so on read
from left to right, then from top to bottom.

Fig. No.	Measurement	Inscription
CHAPTER I		
1.1	Ht.: 6.2 cm	
1.4 *a*	Diam.: 21.7 cm	
1.4 *b*	Ht.: 5.5 cm	
1.5	Diam: 2.7 cm	
1.10	Diam.: 10.5 cm	
1.12	Length: 2.5 cm	
1.15	Ht.: 11.4 cm	A. HENDERSON. / VETERINARY SURGEON. / NO. 8. PARK LANE
1.17 *a*	Diam.: 19.3 cm	
1.17 *b*	Diam.: 20.3 cm	
1.18 *a*	Ht.: 12.8 cm	
1.18 *b*	Ht.: 16.9 cm	
1.19	Ht.: 17.7 cm	
1.20	Ht.: 24.6 cm (largest)	
1.21 *a*	Lid diam.: 19.5 cm	
1.21 *b*	Ht. closed: 25.1 cm	
1.22 *a*	Ht.: 4.3 cm	
1.22 *b*	Ht.: 5.3 cm	
1.23	Ht.: 5.2 cm	
1.24 *a*	Ht.: 18.9 cm	
1.24 *b*	Ht.: 8.9 cm	
1.25	Ht.: 13.5 cm	
1.26 *a*	Projected girth diam.: 21 cm	
1.26 *b*	Projected rim diam.: 14.6 cm	
1.27	Projected rim diam.: 22.4 cm	
1.29 *a*	Ht.: 15.4 cm	
1.29 *b*	Ht.: 9.3 cm	

Fig. No.	Measurement	Inscription
I.29 *c*	Ht.: 35 cm	
I.29 *d*	Ht.: 9.2 cm	
I.29 *e*	Ht.: 12.5 cm	
CHAPTER II		
II.1	Ht.: 21.6 cm	
II.2	Ht. 26.7 cm	
II.3	Ht. 25 cm	
II.6	Ht.: 18 cm (approx.)	
II.7	Ht.: 28 cm	
II.8	Frag. ht.: 4.5 cm	
II.9	Ht.: 15 cm	
II.10	Ht.: 20.2 cm	
II.16 *a*	Base diam.: 10.4 cm	
II.16 *b*	Frag. ht.: 18 cm	
II.17	Ht.: 11.3 cm	
II.18	Ht.: 30 cm (approx.)	
II.19	Ht.: 30 cm (approx.)	
II.20 *a*	Diam.: 12.3 cm	
II.20 *b*	Ht.: 16 cm	
II.21 *a*	Projected rim diam.: 27 cm	
II.21 *b*	Projected rim diam.: 28.4 cm	
II.22	Ht.: 10 cm (approx.)	
II.23	Ht.: 9.5 cm	
II.24	Ht.: 14.6 cm	
II.25	Ht.: 8.2 cm	
II.26 *b*	Ht.: 30 cm (approx.)	
II.27 *a*	Ht.: 30 cm (approx.)	
II.27 *b*	Ht: 30 cm (approx.)	
II.27 *c*	Ht.: 26.4 cm	
II.30	Ht.: 12 cm	
II.31	Ht.: 6 cm	
II.32	Ht.: 16.7 cm	
CHAPTER III		
III.1 *a*	Ht.: 13.8 cm	
III.1 *b*	Ht.: 29.2 cm	
III.1 *c*	Ht.: 14.1 cm	
III.3 *a*	Ht.: 8.4 cm	
III.3 *b*	Ht.: 7.3 cm	
III.4	Panel width: 27 cm	
III.5	Rim diam.: 28 cm (approx.) (largest)	
III.6	Rim diam.: 34.4 cm	
III.7	Rim diam.: 35.6 cm	
III.8	Rim diam.: 34.6 cm	
III.10	Width: 11 cm (largest)	
III.12	Rim diam.: 21.6 cm	
III.13	Rim diam.: 15.6 cm	
III.14 *a*	Base diam.: 4.3 cm	

Fig. No.	Measurement	Inscription
III.15	Ht.: 11.7 cm	
III.16	Ht.: 13 cm	
III.17	Thick: 13 mm	
	Thin: 6 mm	
III.18 *a*	Ht.: 6 cm	
III.18 *b*	Ht.: 5.1 cm	
III.18 *c*	Ht.: 5.7 cm	
III.18 *d*	Ht.: 3.1 cm	
III.18 *e*	Ht.: 2.9 cm	
III.18 *f*	Ht.: 2.4 cm	
III.18 *g*	Rim diam.: 8.2 cm	
III.18 *h*	Rim diam.: 4.8 cm	
III.18 *i*	Ht.: 5.2 cm	
III.19 *a*	Ht.: 8.6 cm	
III.19 *b*	Ht.: 6.9 cm	
III.21 *a*	Length: 12 cm	
III.21 *b*	Length: 11.2 cm	
III.22	Center frag. width: 21.5 cm	
III.23	Ht.: 10.5 cm	
III.24	Thickness: .5 mm	
III.26	Left center base diam.: 10 cm	
III.27 *a*	Ht.: 8.1 cm	
III.27 *b*	Length: 16 cm	
III.27 *c*	Rim diam.: 22.2 cm	
III.27 *d*	Rim diam.: 12 cm	
III.27 *e*	Ht.: 15.3 cm	
CHAPTER IV		
IV.2	Ht.: 6.4 cm	
IV.3 *a*	Ht.: 16 cm (approx.)	
IV.3 *b*	Ht.: 18 cm (approx.)	
IV.3 *c*	Ht.: 15.8 cm	
IV.4	Rim diam.: 24.9 cm	
IV.5 *a*	Ht.: 13 cm	
IV.5 *b*	Diam.: 17.5 cm	
IV.7	Ht.: 15.9 cm	
IV.8 *a*	Ht.: 14.5 cm	
IV.8 *b*	Ht.: 14.2 cm	
IV.9	Ht.: 14.8 cm	
IV.10	Ht.: 16.8 cm	
IV.11	Ht.: 19.6 cm	
IV.13	Ht.: 13.2 cm	
IV.14 *a*	Ht.: 9.2 cm	
IV.14 *b*	Ht.: 9.5 cm (surviving)	
IV.14 *c*	Ht.: 5 cm	
IV.15	Ht.: 9.6 cm	
IV.16	Ht.: 12.9 cm	
IV.17	Rim diam.: 15.5 cm	

Fig. No.	Measurement	Inscription
IV.18	Ht.: 12.5 cm	
IV.19	Ht.: 13.8 cm	
IV.20	Ht.: 13.2 cm	
IV.23 *a*	Ht.: 9.5 cm	
IV.23 *b*	Ht.: 13.6 cm	
IV.24	Ht.: 9.5 cm	
IV.25 *a*	Ht.: 13.5 cm	
IV.25 *b*	Ht.: 13.6 cm	
IV.26	Ht.: 12.2 cm	
IV.28 *a*	Ht.: 22.5 cm	
IV.28 *b*	Ht.: 24.5 cm	
IV.29 *a*	Ht.: 15.25 cm	
IV.31	Ht.: 14 cm	
CHAPTER V		
V.1	Ht.: 7.7 cm	
V.2	Ht.: 18 cm	
V.3 *a*	Ht.: 10.5 cm	
V.3 *b*	Ht.: 8 cm	
V.3 *c*	Ht.: 10 cm	
V.4 *a*	Ht.: 23.2 cm	
V.4 *b*	Ht.: 17.8 cm (mouth reconstructed)	
V.7	Ht.: 12.9 cm	
V.8	Ht.: 22 cm	
V.9	Frag. ht.: 8 cm	
V.10 *a*	Ht.: 11 cm (approx.)	
V.10 *b*	Ht.: 13 cm (approx.)	
V.10 *c*	Ht.: 12.9 cm	
V.11 *a*	Ht.: 12.5 cm	
V.11 *b*	Ht.: 21.7 cm	
V.11 *c*	Ht.: 12.6 cm	
V.12	Ht.: 34.45 cm	
V.13 *a*	Ht.: 11 cm	
V.13 *b*	Ht.: 13.3 cm	
V.14	Ht.: 22 cm	
V.15	Ht.: 19.9 cm	
V.16 *a*	Frag. ht.: 9 cm	
V.16 *b*	Frag. ht.: 5.7 cm	
V.17 *a*	Ht.: 15.3 cm	
V.17 *b*	Ht.: 14.1 cm	
V.17 *c*	Ht.: 15.8 cm	
V.18	Ht.: 18 cm	
V.19	Medallion ht.: 4 cm	
V.20 *a*	Ht.: 17.5 cm	
V.20 *b*	Ht.: 15.1 cm	
V.21	Ht.: 22.5 cm	
V.22 *a*	Ht.: 32.5 cm	
V.22 *b*	Ht.: 29.8 cm	

Fig. No.	Measurement	Inscription
v.22 *c*	Ht.: 13.3 cm	
v.23 *a*	Ht.: 26 cm	
v.23 *b*	Ht.: 21.7 cm	
v.23 *c*	Ht.: 16 cm	
v.25	Ht.: 8.2 cm	
v.26 *a*	Ht.: 20.5 cm	
v.26 *b*	Ht.: 20.5 cm	
v.26 *c*	Base diam.: 6.5 cm	
v.28 *a*	Total ht.: 27.5 cm	
v.28 *b*	Max. ht.: 10 cm	
v.28 *c*	Base diam.: 6 cm	
v.29 *a*	Ht.: 27.2 cm	
v.29 *b*	Ht.: 22.5 cm	
v.30 *a*	Ht.: 27.5 cm	
v.30 *b*	Ht.: 24.1 cm	
v.30 *c*	Ht.: 27.2 cm	
CHAPTER VI		
VI.1 *a*	Ht.: 7.7 cm	
VI.1 *b*	Ht.: 6.5 cm	
VI.2	Ht.: 21.4 cm	
VI.3	Frag. ht.: 12.5 cm (largest)	
VI.4 *a*	Ht.: 20.5 cm	
VI.4 *b*	Ht.: 21.3 cm	
VI.4 *c*	Frag. ht.: 4.2 cm	
VI.5	Ht.: 47.6 cm	
VI.7 *a*	Ht.: 22 cm	
VI.7 *b*	Ht.: 22.7 cm	
VI.8 *a*	Ht.: 22.3 cm	
VI.8 *b*	Ht.: 17.1 cm	
VI.9	Ht.: 21.2 cm	
VI.10 *a*	Frag. ht.: 5.9 cm	
VI.10 *b*	Frag. ht.: 7.6 cm	
VI.10 *c*	Ht.: 22.2 cm	
VI.11	Ht.: 41.3 cm	
VI.12	Ht.: 22.6 cm	
VI.13	Ht.: 23.3 cm	
VI.14 *a*	Frag. ht.: 20 cm	
VI.15 *a*	Rim diam.: 12.2 cm	
VI.15 *b*	Rim diam.: 12.5 cm	
VI.15 *c*	Rim diam.: 14 cm	
VI.16 *a*	Ht: 21.4 cm	
VI.16 *b*	Surviving ht.: 7.5 cm	
VI.16 *c*	Surviving ht.: 11.5 cm	
VI.16 *d*	Surviving ht.: 6 cm	
VI.17 *a*	Ht.: 15.3 cm	
VI.17 *b*	Ht.: 10.5 cm	
VI.17 *c*	Ht.: 14.4 cm	

Fig. No.	Measurement	Inscription
VI.18 *a*	Ht.: 34.2 cm	
VI.18 *b*	Ht.: 31.5 cm	
VI.19	Not recorded	
VI.20 *a*	Ht.: 12.5 cm	
VI.20 *b*	Ht.: 8.2 cm	
VI.22 *b*	Ht.: 21 cm	
VI.22 *c*	Ht.: 16 cm	
VI.23	Ht.: 28.4 cm	
VI.24 *a*	Diam.: 12.5 cm (lip reconstructed)	
VI.25 *a*	Rim diam.: 25.4 cm (approx.)	
VI.25 *b*	Rim diam.: 27.75 cm (approx.)	
VI.26 *a*	Ht.: 13 cm	
VI.26 *b*	Ht.: 12.1 cm	
VI.27	Ht.: 11.5 cm	
VI.30 *a*	Ht.: 13.2 cm	
VI.30 *b*	Ht.: 14.8 cm	
VI.30 *c*	Ht.: 11.5 cm	
VI.31	Ht.: 17.3 cm	
VI.32	Rim diam.: 10.7 cm	
VI.33 *a*	Ht.: 9.7 cm	
VI.33 *b*	Ht.: 11.3 cm	
VI.33 *c*	Ht.: 13.4 cm	
CHAPTER VII		
VII.1	Ht.: 20.6 cm	
VII.2	Ht. 9.2 cm	
VII.3	Ht.: 12.7 cm	
VII.4	Ht.: 19 cm	
VII.6 *a*	Ht.: 23 cm	
VII.6 *b*	Stamp ht.: 1.3 cm	
VII.7	Frag. ht.: 6 cm	
VII.8 *a*	Ht.: 13.4 cm	DOULTON / LAMBETH (impressed)
VII.8 *b*	Mark ht.: 2.5 cm	VR / 523 / LCC (printed)
VII.9	Ht.: 12.7 cm	Mark illeg.
VII.10	Ht.: 4.5 cm	
VII.12 *a*	Ht.: 20.6 cm	John Sargent 1737
VII.12 *b*	Ht.: 20.6 cm	Wm Cheater 1722
VII.12 *c*	Ht.: 21 cm	Wᵐ NEWMAN / SARUM
VII.13	Ht.: 19.5 cm	
VII.14	Frag. width: 5.5 cm	
VII.15	Ht.: 21 cm	
VII.17	Ht.: 15.6 cm	
VII.18 *a*	Ht.: 23.5 cm	
CHAPTER VIII		
VIII.2 *a*		GR crowned. Ca.1750
VIII.2 *b*		W / H / M and Rose (ca. 1655)
VIII.2 *c*		T / WILLS / 1794
VIII.2 *d*		Ducal coronet over wolf (ca. 1715)

Fig. No.	Measurement	Inscription
VIII.2 *e*		Jnᵒ / Furse / 1823
VIII.2 *f*		John / Knottesford / 1736
VIII.3	Ht.: 15.6 cm	SA / CK / 16 / 45
VIII.4 *b*	Frag. ht.: 7.6 cm	G: Burwell / Edwᵈ: Atthawes / 1755
VIII.5	Ht.: 22.4 cm	As VIII.4 *b*
VIII.6	Ht.: 23 cm	W Hooper / Ross / 1814
VIII.7 *a*	Ht.: 23.2 cm	
VIII.7 *b*	Ht.: 23.8 cm	BELPER & DENBY POTTERI[ES] DERBYSHIRE / VITREOUS STONE BOTTLES, &c. / J. BOURNE, / PATENTEE. / Warranted not to Absorb / EX
VIII.7 *c*	Ht.: 27.5 cm	
VIII.7 *d*	Ht.: 32 cm	
VIII.8	Ht.: 7.5 cm	
VIII.9	Ht.: 19.5 cm	
VIII.11 *a*	Ht.: 23.8 cm	
VIII.12 *a*	Ht.: 20.3 cm	
VIII.13	Ht.: 12.1 cm	DOULTON / LAMBETH.
VIII.14	Ht.: 20.1 cm	STANLEY / 1820 Come Gentlemen and try your skill / I'll Lay a wager if you will / That you drink this liquor all / Unless you spill or some let fall.
VIII.15	Ht.: 18.7 cm	Eᵈ LINSDAL / THAXSTEAD / Essex / 1751
VIII.16	Ht.: 21.6 cm	My Form has puzzled many a fertile Brain The brightest Wits my Liquor could not gain And still profusely spill it on the Ground The Reason is no Suction they have found Now honest Friend advance Thy Genius try Spill Ne'er a Drop and strive to drain me dry W.J. 1771 . . . .
VIII.17	Ht.: 28 cm	John Bloome / Hopewell
VIII.18	Ht.: 7.7 cm	
VIII.19	Ht.: 15.6 cm	
VIII.20 *a*	Rim diam.: 21.7 cm	
VIII.21 *a*	Ht.: 20.3 cm	John Lee and Sarah / 1759
CHAPTER IX		
IX.1 *a*	Diam.: 22.2 cm	
IX.3	Ht. of largest frag.: 7 cm	
IX.4	Ht.: 18.4 cm	John Giles Queenhithe
IX.5 *a*	Ht.: 18.4 cm	Brother Vilckin Letus Drink Whilst Wee Have Breath / For There's No Drinking After death Joseph:1752:Piper
IX.6 *a*	Diam.: 21.5 cm	
IX.6 *b*	Width: 12 cm	
IX.7	Rim diam.: 21.4 cm	
IX.9 *a*	Rim diam.: 29.6 cm	
IX.9 *c*	Rim diam.: 29.5 cm	
IX.10	Ht.: 6 cm	
IX.11	Rim diam.: 22.3 cm	

Fig. No.	Measurement	Inscription
IX.12	Rim diam.: 22.4 cm	
IX.13 *a*	Rim diam.: 22.3 cm	
IX.13 *b*	Rim diam.: 22.3 cm	
IX.14	Max. rim length: 32.6 cm	
IX.15	Max. rim length: 31.8 cm	
IX.16	Rim diam.: 15 cm (approx.)	
IX.17 *b*	Ht. of largest frag.: 3.5 cm	
IX.18 *a*	Ht.: 11.6 cm	
IX.18 *b*	Ht.: 11.6 cm (approx.)	
IX.19	Ht.: 12 cm	
IX.20 *a*	Rim diam.: 33.2 cm (approx.)	
IX.20 *b*	Rim diam.: 33.2 cm	Mark: Mang. PB under blue fleur-de-lys
IX.20 *c*	Rim diam.: 33.2 cm (approx.)	
IX.21 *a*	Ht.: 10.7 cm	
IX.21 *b*	Ht.: 10 cm	
IX.22 *a*	Ht.: 11.8 cm	
IX.22 *b, c*	Width of frag.: 8.5 cm	
IX.23 *a*	Length: 5.5 cm	
IX.23 *b*	Ht.: 6.1 cm (surviving)	
IX.23 *c*	Ht. 3.9 cm	
IX.24	Ht.: 15.9 cm	
IX.25	Frag. width: 7.7 cm	
IX.26 *a*	Frag. ht.: 6.3 cm	
IX.26 *b*	Ht. w/ lid: 14.3 cm	
IX.27 *b*	Ht. w/ lid: 16 cm	
IX.28	Rim diam.: 5.8 cm	
IX.29 *a*	Width: 21.5 cm	
IX.29 *b*	Rim diam.: 23.9 cm	
IX.29 *c*	Rim diam.: 22.9 cm	
IX.30	Rim diam.: 26 cm	
IX.31	Rim diam.: 28.5 cm	
IX.32 *a*	Rim diam.: 22 cm	
IX.32 *b*	Rim diam.: 24 cm	
IX.33	Rim diam.: 24.1 cm	
IX.34 *a*	Ht.: 17.8 cm	
IX.34 *b*	Ht.: 13.7 cm	
IX.35	Ht.: 13 cm	Mary Coall Made by Thos Proufe September ye 26th 1767
IX.36	Ht.: 11.2 cm	
IX.37 *a*	Ht.: 15.5 cm	
IX.37 *b*	Ht.: 9.4 cm	
IX.38 *a*	Ht.: 12.1 cm	
IX.38 *b*	Ht.: 12 cm (approx.)	
IX.39	Ht.: 13.6 cm	
IX.40	Rim diam.: 23.8 cm	
IX.41	Rim diam.: 25.1 cm	
IX.42	Rim diam.: 23.5 cm	

Fig. No.	Measurement	Inscription
IX.43 *a*	Rim diam.: 23.7 cm	
IX.43 *b*	Rim diam.: 23.8 cm	
IX.44	Rim diam.: 22.7 cm	
IX.45 *a*	Rim length: 24.5 cm	
IX.45 *b*	Rim length: 28.5 cm	
IX.47 *a*	Width: 12.5 cm	
IX.48	Rim diam.: 25.5 cm	
IX.49	Rim diam.: 20.7 cm	
IX.50	Ht.: 18 cm	
IX.51	Rim diam.: 6.6 cm	
IX.52	Ht.: 8.7 cm	
IX.53 *a*	Diam.: 12.5 cm	Anne Boucant Page
IX.53 *b*	Rim diam.: 8.7 cm	Anne Boucant Page
IX.54 *a*	Rim diam.: 8.4 cm	
IX.54 *b*	Diam.: 13.2 cm	
IX.54 *c*	Ht.: 15 cm	
IX.54 *d*	Diam.: 15.5 cm	
IX.55	Bowl ht.: 6.1 cm	
IX.56 *a*	Ht. w/o lid: 11.5 cm	
IX.56 *b*	Ht.: 10.4 cm (surviving)	
IX.57	Ht.: 16.2 cm	[See figure]
IX.58	Ht.: 5.5 cm	
CHAPTER X		
X.1	Rim diam.: 24.1 cm	
X.2	Rim diam.: 23.7 cm	
X.3	Ht.: 12.2 cm	
X.4	Ht.: 16.4 cm	
X.5	Ht.: 14.6 cm	
X.6 *a*	Rim diam.: 20.1 cm	
X.6 *b*	Rim diam.: 20 cm	
X.7 *a*	Ht.: 10.7 cm	
X.7 *b*	Ht.: 16.6 cm	
X.7 *c*	Ht. w/ lid: 7.4 cm	
X.8	Ht. w/o lid: 7.5 cm	
X.9 *a*	Rim length: 47.3 cm	
X.11	Ht.: 10.7 cm	
X.12 *a*	Rim diam.: 17.9 cm	TURNER 5
X.12 *b*	Rim diam.: 22 cm	ENOCH WOOD & SONS / BURSLEM.
X.14	Length: 19.6 cm	
X.16 *a*	Rim diam.: 16 cm	
X.16 *b*	Rim diam.: 16 cm	
X.17	Rim diam.: 16.2 cm	Oh! Breathe not his name, let it sleep in the shade. / Sad, silent & dark, be the tears that we shed, / As the night-dew that falls on the grass o'er his head!
X.18	Rim diam.: 23 cm	
IX.19 *b*	Not recorded	
X.21 *a*	Ht.: 22 cm	
X.22 *a*	Rim diam.: 8.2 cm	

Fig. No.	Measurement	Inscription
x.22 *b*	Diam.: 12.6 cm	
x.22 *c*	Ht.: 6.4 cm	
x.22 *d*	Rim diam.: 15.7 cm	
x.22 *f*	Ht. w/o lid: 13.1 cm	
x.23	Rim diam.: 8.2 cm (approx.)	
x.24 *a*	Rim diam.: 8.3 cm	
x.24 *b*	Diam.: 13 cm	
x.25 *a–f*	Saucers' rim diam: 12.7 cm	
	Cups' rim diam.: 8.2 cm	
x.26	Diam.: 20.5 cm	
x.27	Ht.: 10.2 cm	R*C / 1793
x.28	Ht.: 15.5 cm	Ralph Vernon / 1780
x.29	Ht.: 12.8 cm	James & Lydia Vickers / 1787
x.30	Ht.: 11.8 cm	
CHAPTER XI		
XI.2 *a*	Ht.: 9.6 cm	
XI.2 *b*	Ht.: 10.6 cm	
XI.3	Ht.: 11.5 cm	
XI.4 *a*	Rim diam.: 8.5 cm	
IX.4 *b*	Diam.: 13.5 cm	
XI.5	Ht.: 16.9 cm	
XI.6	Ht.: 15.2 cm	Greenea hill Chappel
XI.7	Diam.: 21.7 cm	
XI.8	Ht.: 20.3 cm	POCOCK AND ALLEN 1802
XI.10 *a*	Diam.: 25 cm	DILLWYN & CO.
XI.10 *b*	Diam.: 24.2 cm	
XI.11 *a*	Diam.: 20 cm	
XI.11 *b*	Diam.: 20 cm	
XI.12	Width.: 22.4 cm	
XI.13 *a*	Diam.: 15.7 cm	
XI.13 *b*	Diam.: 20.4 cm	
XI.13 *c*	Length at rim: 28.4 cm	
XI.14	Diam.: 25 cm	
XI.15	Diam.: 24.3 cm	
XI.16	Diam.: 25.1 cm	RILEY
XI.17 *a*	Diam.: 24.4 cm	
XI.18	Ht.: 11.4 cm	
XI.19	Diam.: 20.1 cm	MASON'S PATENT IRONSTONE CHINA
CHAPTER XII		
XII.2	Diam.: 35.2 cm	
XII.3	Rim diam.: 13.3 cm	
XII.4	Length: 15.3 cm	
XII.8 *a*	Ht.: 12 cm	
XII.8 *b*	Ht. of cartouche: 5 cm	VILLA DE PARIS
XII.9	Not recorded	
XII.10 *a*	Ht. w/o lid: 9.2 cm	
XII.11	Ht.: 15 cm	

Fig. No.	Measurement	Inscription
XII.12 *a*	Ht.: 9.8 cm	SUCCESS TO LORD RODNEY
XII.12 *b*	Ht.: 16.6 cm	RODNEY
XII.13 *a*	Ht.: 13 cm	LORD JARVIS
XII.14	Ht.: 18.4 cm	
XII.15	Ht.: 15.5 cm	CAPTARN BERRY / ADMIRAL NELFON
XII.16	Ht.: 15.6 cm	May balmy peace / And wreath'd renown / Our virtuous Heroes / Ever crown
XII.17	Ht.: 12.6 cm	LORD NELSON / LORD COLLINGWOOD
XII.18	Ht.: 11.8 cm	HORATIO LORD VISCOUNT / NELSON / VICE ADMIRAL OF THE WHITE / Knight of the Order of the Bath / Duke of Bronte in Sicily, / Grand Crofs of the order of Ferdinand an[?] of Merit, and Knight of / the Imperial Order of the / Crescent
XII.20	Ht.: 17.3 cm	
XII.21 *a*	Ht.: 14.2 cm	Long live Caroline [see figure for detail]
CHAPTER XIII		
XIII.1 *a*	Ht.: 13.4 cm	
XIII.1 *b*	Ht.: 17.9 cm	
XIII.1 *c*	Ht.: 21 cm	
XIII.1 *d*	Ht.: 18.5 cm	
XIII.2 *a*	Ht.: 17.3 cm	
XIII.2 *b*	Ht.: 28 cm	
XIII.3 *a*	Ht. w/o lid: 9.2 cm	
XIII.3 *b*	Ht. w/ lid: 11.4 cm	Mrs GRIM: / STONE
XIII.4	Ht.: 8.9 cm	
XIII.5	Ht.: 11.1 cm	JN.^o SAYERS / TARING / 1801 How ever sore / the taxes gripe / there is always / pleasure ore a pipe
XIII.6 *a*	Ht.: 16.5 cm	J+SIGGERY Back: MADE BY / JOHN SIGGERY / HERSTMONCEUX SUSSEX / GIVEN TO HENRY FUN- / NELL PIDDINGHOE / SUSSEX MAY 2 / 1836.
XIII.7	Ht.: 7.7 cm	
XIII.8	Ht.: 9.1 cm	
XIII.9 *a*	Ht.: 19.8 cm	Pay Here / James Norman / D C 4 1899
XIII.9 *b*	Ht.: 13 cm	GUARD YOWRE PENCE AND YOWR POUNDES
XIII.10	Ht.: 14.3 cm	Ralph Coles / Xmas / 1905
XIII.11	Ht.: 30.8 cm	
XIII.12 *a*	Frag. width: 9 cm	
XIII.12 *b*	Frag. width: 5 cm	
XIII.13	Diam.: 35 cm	
XIII.14	Ht. w/ lid: 28 cm	
XIII.15 *b*	Diam.: 23.1 cm	
XIII.16 *a*	Rim diam.: 7.4 cm	
XIII.16 *b*	Rim diam.: 20 cm	
XIII.16 *c*	Rim diam.: 6.3 cm	
XIII.17	Diam.: 22.8 cm	
XIII.18	Diam.: 8.7 cm	
XIII.21 *a*	Diam.: 12.1 cm	
XIII.21 *b*	Diam.: 12 cm	
XIII.23 *a*	Rim diam.: 5.4 cm	
XIII.23 *b*	Length: 7.6 cm	

Fig. No.	Measurement	Inscription
XIII.24	Rim diam.: 5.3 cm	
XIII.25	Rim diam.: 15 cm	
XIII.26 *a*	Rim diam.: 7.6 cm	
XIII.26 *b*	Diam.: 12.4 cm	
XIII.27	Ht.: 6.3 cm	
XIII.28	Diam.: 13.8 cm	
XIII.29	Ht.: 8.2 cm	SPODE
XIII.30	Diam.: 14.3 cm	
XIII.31	Rim diam.: 7.6 cm	A. Target / 1754.
XIII.32	Ht.: 7.8 cm	A. Target / 1754
XIII.34	Width of largest shard: 14 cm	
XIII.35 *i*	Spout length: 9.7 cm	
XIII.36	Ht. w/o lid: 11.2 cm	
CHAPTER XIV		
XIV.1	Largest diam.: 8.5 cm	
XIV.2	Tallest: 18.5 cm	
XIV.4	Ht.: 12 cm	
XIV.5 *a*	Ht.: 19.2 cm	WILLIAM, IV,TH'S / REFORM / CORDIAL*
		Back: BELPER & DENBY / *BOURNES / POTTERIES / DERBYSHIRE*
XIV.5 *b*	Ht.: 19.1 cm	REPEAL / DANIEL O CONNELL ESQ
		Back: DENBY & BELPER / BOURNES / POTTERIES / DERBYSHIRE
XIV.6 *a*	Ht.: 19.4 cm	BROUGHAM / REFORM / CORDIAL /
		Back: OLDFIELD & CO.
XIV.6 *b*	Ht.: 37.6 cm	THE / TRUE SPIRIT OF / REFORM
		DOULTON & WATTS / (LAMBETH?)
XIV.7 *a*	Ht.: 20.5 cm	H R H DUKE OF YORK
XIV.7 *b*	Ht.: 20.5 cm	H R H DUKE OF YORK
XIV.8	Ht.: 17.9 cm	G. BROWNE / OLD QUEEN ELIZABETH HEAD / LOWER ROAD / ISLINGTON
		Base: F. Wetherill July 27 1830 [inscription not fully legible]
XIV.9 *a*	Ht.: 29.3 cm	
XIV.9 *b*	Ht.: 32.0 cm	
XIV.10	Ht.: 14.7 cm	Base: Published by / S. Green Lambeth / July 20th 1837
XIV.11 *a*	Ht.: 23.1 cm	VICTORIA / 1/2
		Back: B. COOPER / COACH & HORSES / 4 HOSPITAL ROW / CHELSEA
		Base: Published / by / S. Green Lambeth / July 20th 1837
XIV.11 *b*	Ht.: 26.5 cm	VICTORIA
		Back: SAVAGE & AUSTIN / WINE & SPIRIT MERCHANTS / TO HER MAJESTY /
		CASTLE SQ BRIGHTON
XIV.12	Ht.: 38.2 cm	ALBERT
XIV.13	Ht.: 25.4 cm	
XIV.14 *a*	Ht.: 18.1 cm	On barrell: XXX
XIV.15	Ht.: 22 cm	OLD / TOM
		Back: B. GARNHAM / Cliffe Lewes
XIV.17 *a*	Ht.: 17.5 cm	
XIV.18 *c*	Ht.: 18.2 cm	Thames Tunnel
XIV.19 *a*	Ht.: 18.7 cm	MR & MRS CAUDLE
		No Mr Caudle / I shall not go to sleep / like a good soul / See Punch

Fig. No.	Measurement	Inscription
		Back: Miss / Prettyman
		Base: DOULTON & WATTS / LAMBETH POTTERY / LONDON
XIV.19 b	Ht.: 20.5 cm	MR & MRS CAUDLE
		NO M R CAUDLE / I SHALL NOT GO TO SLEEP / LIKE A GOOD SOUL
		Back: MISS / PRETTYMAN
		Base: STEPHEN GREEN / LAMBETH
XIV.20	Ht.: 12.0 cm	Registry panel on back (1851) [see text]
XIV.21 a	Ht.: 21.0	Back: J. BROWN / Wine & Spirit Merchant / ADAM & EVE / 144 CHURCH ST / BETHNAL GREEN
XIV.21 b	Ht.: 24.6 cm	
XIV.22	Ht.: 21.7 cm	Back: DENBY & CODNOR PARK. / BOURNES, / POTTERIES. / DERBYSHIRE.
XIV.23	Ht.: 18.4 cm	
XIV.24 a	Ht.: 12.3 cm	RAILWAY / CHRONOMETER
		Back: G. PERREN / Red Lion / Whitechapel Road
		Base: Fulham / Pottery
XIV.24 b	Ht.: 10.7 cm	
XIV.24 c	Length: 20.2 cm	Head: SHEPPARD / 130 BLACKMAN St BORO
XIV.24 d	Length: 16.8 cm	
XIV.25	Ht.: 6.8 cm	Stephen Green Imperial Potteries Lambeth
XIV.26	Ht.: 28.2 cm	Stephen Green Imperial Potteries Lambeth
XIV.27 a	Length: 23.5 cm	Stephen Green / Imperial Potteries / Lambeth
XIV.27 b	Length: 21.3 cm	Stephen Green / Imperial Potteries / Lambeth
XIV.28	Length: 25 cm	J. BOURNE, / DENBY POTTERY / DERBYSHIRE
XIV.29	Length: 26 cm	FULHAM / POTTERY
XIV.30	Ht.: 23.7 cm	Stephen Green Imperial Potteries Lambeth
XIV.31	Ht.: 11.1 cm	
XIV.32 a	Length: 29 cm	T BALLANCE / Wine & Brandy Merchant / Red Lion / 197 Ratcliff Highway
XIV.32 b	Length: 17.9 cm	
XIV.35 a	Ht.: 13.7 cm	CHEESMAN / Wine & Spirit Merchant / 17 London St / TOTTENHAM Ct ROAD
XIV.35 b	Ht.: 18.4 cm	VEMUR / STOUT HOUSE / SHOREDITCH
XIV.35 c	Ht.: 13.6 cm	
XIV.36 a	Ht.: 7.3 cm	
XIV.36 b	Ht.: 9.8 cm	
XIV.37	Diam.: 7.9 cm	REGISTERED N O 4138 / DEC 17 1858 / SINGER / VAUXHALL / LONDON
XIV.38	Ht.: 16.7 cm	
XIV.39 b	Ht.: 11.8 cm	

Fig. No.	Measurement	Inscription	Maker	Badge
CHAPTER XV				
XV.3	Ht.: 16 cm	W. H. GOSS	Goss	None
XV.4	Width: 9.5 cm	MODEL OF / THE GREAT PYRAMID AT GIZEH / NEAR CAIRO, EGYPT / R^D. N^O. 602907	Goss	Cairo
XV.5	Ht.: 10.5 cm	MODEL OF / CELTIC SEPULCHRAL URN / FOUND AT / LANLAWREN, CORNWALL / EMBLEMATIC / T / ENGLAND	Goss	Harvard
V.6	Ht.: 6.2 cm	THE LINCOLN VASE, / FROM ORIGINAL / AT CATHEDRAL	Goss	New York State
XV.7 a	Ht.: 5.8 cm	MODEL OF OAK PITCHER / PECULIAR TO DEVON	Goss	Florida
XV.7 b	Ht.: 5.5 cm	MODEL OF / ANCIENT CUP / FOUND AT BRIXWORTH / NORTHAMPTONSHIRE / R^D. N^O. 413199	Goss	Florida
XV.8	Ht.: 5.1 cm	MODEL OF / THE PORTLAND VASE / IN THE BRITISH MUSEUM	Goss	United States
XV.9 a	Ht.: 11.3 cm	Back: SEE OF EXETER Base: MODEL OF / ROMAN EWER FOUND / AT FELIXSTOWE NOW / IN IPSWICH MUSEUM	Goss	City of Exeter
XV.9 b	Ht.: 7.5 cm	None	Swan	United States
XV.10 a	Ht.: 6.6 cm	MODEL OF / ANCIENT URN / FOUND AT RAMSGATE / COPYRIGHT	Goss	Chudleigh
XV.10 b	Ht.: 5.2 cm	787 / MODEL OF ROMAN VASE / FOUND AT ATWICK / NEAR HORNSEA / R^D. N^O. 5000864	Goss	Clacton-on-Sea
XV.11 a	Ht.: 7.9 cm	MODEL OF / ANCIENT BELLARMINE / FOUND FULL OF SPIRIT / IN A POND AT / HORSGATE. CUCKFIELD R^D N^O 647236	Goss	Paignton
XV.11 b	Ht.: 6.5 cm	MODEL OF / BELLARMINE JUG / 17th CENTURY FOUND / IN ROCHESTER / R^D. N^O. 403421 PUB. BY J. H. GOLDW[IN?] / 31 HIGH ST	Goss	Rochester
XV.12	Ht.: 13.7 cm	MODEL OF ANCIENT MUG / DREDGED FROM THE SEA / OFF GREAT YARMOUTH. NOW IN THE MUSEUM / R^D N^O 500870	Goss	Shanklin Isle of Wight
XV.13 a	Ht.: 8.1 cm	MODEL OF / ANCIENT VASE / DREDGED OUT OF THE / THAMES NEAR ETON / R^D. N^O. 539422	Goss	Lamlash
XV.13 b	Ht.: 7.6 cm	MODEL OF ANCIENT / ORIENTAL WATER COOLER / FOUND AT GRAVESEND / FROM THE ORIGINAL IN GRAVESEND PUBLIC LIBRARY. COPYRIGHT.	Goss	Manor of Upway
XV.13 c	No details			
XV.14 a	Ht.: 7.4 cm	MODEL OF SACK BOTTLE / DUG UP IN CASTLE MOAT, / LUDLOW. NOW IN / LUDLOW MUSEUM	Goss	Bromley
XV.14 b	Ht.: 9.1 cm	MODEL OF SACK BOTTLE / DREDGED FROM THE DART / FROM ORIGINAL IN EXETER MUSEUM	Goss	Dartmouth
XV.14 c	Ht.: 9.1 cm	MODEL OF SACK BOTTLE / DREDGED FROM THE DART / FROM ORIGINAL IN EXETER MUSEUM	Goss	Belfast
XV.16 a	Ht.: 16.6 cm	Nurse Cavell	Porcelle	
XV.16 b	Ht.: 13.5 cm	SHELLS AND / MORE SHELLS / Doing her Bit DAVY STEPHENS / KINGSTOWN	Carlton	Kingstown
XV.17	Ht.: 13.6 cm	The Bomb Thrower	Grafton	Cornwall
XV.18	Ht.: 8.2 cm	None	[Grafton]	Skegness
XV.19 a	Ht.: 10.5 cm			
XV.19 b	Ht.: 7.7 cm	The "Mills" Hand Grenade / REG^D. N^O. 657211	Grafton	Warwick
XV.20 a	Ht.: 7.4 cm	MODEL OF / TOMMY AND HIS / MACHINE GUN / R^D. N^O. 657214	Arcadian	Great Yarmouth

Fig. No.	Measurement	Inscription	Maker	Badge
XV.21	Ht.: 5.8 cm	MODEL OF / CLIP OF BULLETS / Rᴰ. Nᴼ. 657648	Arcadian	Thorpe
XV.23 a	Ht.: 5.5 cm	BRITISH RED CROSS SOCIETY / ST. JOHN / AMBULANCE ASSOCIATION / LOAD NOT / TO EXCEED / I. DRIVER / I. ATTENDANT / AND PATIENTS On base: MODEL OF / MOTOR AMBULANCE CAR / GIVEN BY / STAFFORDSHIRE CHINA OPERATIVES	Grafton	New Brighton
XV.24 a	Length: 11.6 cm	MADE FOR / HANCOCK / BAMFORD	Arcadian	Hathersage
XV.24 b	Length: 11 cm	None	Waterfall	Grimsby
XV.24 c	Length: 12.9 cm	None	Carlton	Aldershot
XV.25 a	Ht.: 10 cm	None	?	Eastbourne
XV.25 b	Ht.: 11.3 cm	MODEL OF RUSSIAN SHRAPNEL SHELL / THE ORIGINAL WAS CAPTURED BY / THE HUNS & FIRED BY THEM / AT THE BRITISH. / COPYRIGHT	Goss	Margate
XV.25 c	Ht.: 9.6 cm	None	Arcadian	Marlow
XV.26 b	Length: 12.2 cm	MODEL OF TANK / Rᴰ. Nᴼ. 658588	Arcadian	Bury St. Edmonds
XV.26 c	Length: 14.6 cm	MODEL OF BRITISH "TANK" / REG Nᴼ. 658588	Willow Art	City of London
XV.27 b	Length: 15.1 cm	MODEL OF / BRITISH TANK / AS FIRST USED / BY / BRITISH TROOPS / AT THE BATTLE / OF THE ANCRE. / SEP. 1916 H.M.S. DONNER BLITZEN 515	Savoy	Guildford
XV.28 a	Length: 17 cm	None	Victoria	Blackpool
XV.29 a	Length: 12 cm	PUTNEY CHARING CROSS / GLOBE THEATRE, JOHN BULL THURSDAY / GENERAL (ON GRILL) 10.N.999	Carlton	Southend on Sea
XV.30 a	Ht.: 13.3 cm	Our Brave Defender	Willow Art	Moffat
XV.30 b	Ht.: 13.5 cm	None	Carlton?	Southend on Sea
XV.31 b	Length: 6.2 cm	Schrapnel Villa TOMMIES DUGOUT SOMEWHERE IN FRANCE Rᴰ. Nᴼ. 660613	Carlton	Chatham
XV.32 b	Ht.: 13.2 cm	None	[Willow Art]	Church Stretton
XV.33 b	Length: 16.5 cm	LUSITANIA	Corona	Brighton
XV.34 a	Ht.: 7.8 cm	THE LUSITANIA / SUNK BY GERMAN SUBMARINE / OFF THE IRISH COAST / MAY 7ᵀᴴ 1915. / LIVES LOST 1275 / SAVED 703. Lusitania	Carlton	R.M.S.
XV.34 b	Ht.: 5.9 cm	THE LUSITANIA / SUNK BY GERMAN SUBMARINE / OFF THE IRISH COAST / MAY 7ᵀᴴ 1915 / LIVES LOST 1275 / SAVED 703. Lusitania	Carlton	R.M.S.
XV.35 a	Length: 16.8 cm	H.M.H.S. Anglia Model of British / Hospital Ship whose voyage was / Disregarded on three occasions by / the German Submarines / Rᴰ Nᴼ. 682104	Carlton	Galashiels
XV.35 b	Length: 16.8 cm	THE LUSITANIA SUNK BY GERMAN SUBMARINE / OFF THE IRISH COAST, / MAY 7ᵀʰ 1915 / LIVES LOST 1275 SAVED 703	Carlton	Swansea
XV.36 a	Length: 14.7 cm	"COMMANDER NOEL LAURENCE." LARGE GERMAN TRANSPORT SUNK / JULY 30ᵗʰ 1915 / GERMAN CRUISER MOLTKE TORPEDOED / AUG. 19ᵗʰ 1915	Savoy	Clackton-on-Sea

Fig. No.	Measurement	Inscription	Maker	Badge
xv.36 *b*	Length: 12.5 cm	E5 MODEL OF NEW SUBMARINE Rᴰ. Nᴼ. 658687	Botolph	St. Albans
xv.37 *a*	Ht.: 10.3 cm	MODEL OF / SAILOR WINDING / CAPSTAN / Rᴰ. Nᴼ. 356875	Swan	Lymington
xv.37 *b*	Ht.: 6.8 cm	None	Wilton	Leominster
xv.38	Ht.: 8.2 cm	THE VICTORY OF JUSTICE / ARMISTICE OF THE GREAT WAR / SIGNED NOV 11ᵗʰ 1918 Model of Floating Mine	Carlton	Ipswich
xv.39 *a*	Length: 11.5 cm	Great War 1914–1918. / The German Fleet Surrendered / 74 Warships. Nov 21ˢᵗ 1918 Model of British / Mine Sweeper whose / Splendid Work will Live / For ever in the annals of / British History	Carlton	Southend on Sea
xv.39 *b*	Length: 16.4 cm	H.M.S. QUEEN ELIZABETH / Rᴰ. Nᴼ. 652617	Savoy	Gosport
xv.40	Length: 15.0 cm	344	Shelley	Southwold
xv.41 *a*	Ht.: 7.9 cm	None	Arcadian	Southsea
xv.41 *b*	Ht.: 7.6 cm	MODEL OF / INCENDIARY BOMB DROPPED / AT MALDON 16 APRIL 1915 / FROM A GERMAN ZEPPELIN / COPYRIGHT.	Goss	Stratford on Avon
xv.41 *c*	Ht.: 8 cm	Model of German / Incendiary Bomb	Carlton	Birmingham
xv.41 *d*	Length: 8.3 cm	MODEL OF GERMAN / AERIAL TORPEDO Rᴰ. Nᴼ. 657601	Arcadian	Ventnor
xv.41 *e*	Ht.: 6.1 cm	MODEL OF / CANISTER BOMB Rᴰ. Nᴼ. 657700	Arcadian	Bolsover
xv.42 *a*	Ht.: 6.2 cm	LIEGE / INVESTED AND BOMBARDED / BY THE GERMANS / AUGUST 9, 1914	Savoy	Liège
xv.42 *b*	Ht.: 5.4 cm	DUNKERQUE / BOMBARDED BY LONG RANGE / GERMAN GUNS	Savoy	Dunkerque
xv.42 *c*	Ht.: 6.8 cm	YPRES / GERMAN RUSH STEMMED BY THE / VALOUR OF THE BRITISH TROOPS / OCTOBER. 27. 1914. / 2ᴺᴰ BATTLE OF YPRES THE / CANADIANS GALLANTRY SAVED / THE SITUATION / APRIL. 24. 1915.	Savoy	Ypres
xv.42 *d*	Ht.: 6.5 cm	VERDUN / GERMAN DEFEAT BEFORE / FORT DOUAMONT / FEBRUARY 26 1916	Savoy	Verdun
xv.42 *e*	Ht.: 5.2 cm	BATTLE OF ARRAS / BRITISH VICTORY / 13000 GERMAN PRISONERS / 150 GUNS CAPTURED / EASTER APRIL 9 1917	Savoy	Arras
xv.42 *f*	Ht.: 6.7 cm	BRITISH VICTORY / GERMAN FORTRESS OF BEAUMONT-HAMEL / BEAUCOURT AND Sᵀ PIERRE / DIVON, CAPTURED. / NOV 13–14 1916	Savoy	Beaumont Hamel
xv.43	Ht.: 8.8 cm	ARMENTIERES / DESPERATE BATTLES BETWEEN / BRITISH AND GERMANS / NOV. 1914 JUNE, 1915.	Savoy	Armentières
xv.44 *b*	Ht.: 6.9 cm	MODEL OF / ANCIENT GREEK VASE / FOUND AT SALONIKA / BY THE BRITISH TROOPS / WHEN ENTRENCHING / JAN 1916 / 170	Shelley	Evesham
xv.45 *b*	Ht.: 16.3 cm	EDITH CAVELL / BRUSSELS / DAWN / OCTOBER 12ᵗʰ, 1915 HUMANITY / SACRIFICE On back: THE BIDDENDEN MAIDS WERE BORN / JOINED TOGETHER HIPS & / SHOULDERS IN THE YEAR / 1100	Carlton	The Biddenden Maids
xv.46 *c*	Ht.: 14.2 cm	MCM / XIV / MCM / XIX THE GLORIOUS DEAD	Willow Art	City of London
xv.47	Ht.: 8.8 cm	VICTORIA R.I. DIAMOND JUBILEE / DOULTON BURSLEM / Rᴰ. Nᴼ. 293621		

Fig. No.	Measurement	Inscription	Maker	Badge
		IN COMMEMORATION OF / THE DIAMOND JUBILEE / OF VICTORIA THE / BELOVED QUEEN / OF GREAT BRITAIN / IRELAND & THE / COLONIES. EMPRESS OF / INDIA / JUNE 20th 1897	Doulton	None

CHAPTER XVI

Fig. No.	Measurement	Inscription	Maker	Badge
XVI.1 *a*	Ht.: 7 cm	BEATTY/ FOR FREEDOM AND HONOUR / HAIG / PEACE 1919 Back: A SOUVENIR OF / THE / GREAT WAR / COMMENCED AUG 4th 1914 / ARMISTICE NOV 11th 1918 / PEACE SIGNED JUNE 28th 1919		
XVI.1 *b*	Ht.: 9 cm			
XVI.1 *c*	Width: 6.8 cm	APRIL +WEMBLEY+ OCT / 1924 BRITISH EMPIRE EXHIBITION		
XVI.2 *a*	Ht.: 8.3 cm	V R / 1837 * 1897		
XVI.2 *b*	Ht.: 8.0 cm	Back: CORONATION / OF / KING EDWARD THE VIITH / JUNE 26TH / 1902 Base: ROYAL DOULTON / RG. NO. 228776		
XVI.3 *a*	Ht.: 8.8 cm	22nd JUNE / 1911 QUEEN MARY KING GEORGE V Back: RULERS / OF AN / EMPIRE / ON WHICH THE / SUN / NEVER SETS SEND THEM / VICTORIOUS / HAPPY AND / GLORIOUS / LONG TO / REIGN OVER US Bottom: HARRODS LTD EXCLUSIVE DESIGN / GUARANTEED ALL BRITISH Inside: Coronation Souvenir / 22 June 1911		
XVI.3 *b*	Ht.: 7.5 cm	CORONATION 1911 Back: CORONATION 1911 Base: ROYAL DOULTON / ENGLAND / COPYRIGHT		
XVI.4 *a*	Ht.: 5.8 cm	SILVER / JUBILEE H. M. KING GEORGE V. LONG LIVE THEIR MAJESTIES H. M. QUEEN MARY / 1911 1935 Base: Made in England		
XVI.4 *b*	Ht.: 6.2 cm	H.M. KING GEORGE H. M. QUEEN MARY SILVER 910 935 JUBILEE		
XVI.5 *b*	Ht.: 9.6 cm	CORONATION MAY 12th 1937 H.M. KING EDWARD VIII Back: LONG MAY HE REIGN Base: BRITISH ANCHOR / MADE IN ENGLAND		
XVI.5 *c*	Ht.: 7.3 cm	KING EDWARD VIII CROWNED 12th MAY 1937 Back: ER/ 1937		
XVI.6	Ht.: 8.6 cm	MAY, 1937. CORONATION. OF. KING. GEORGE. VI. &. QUEEN. ELIZABETH. Base: OFFICIAL DESIGN OF THE / BRITISH POTTERY MANUFACTURERS FEDERATION Bristol / POUNTNEY & CO. LTD		
XVI.7	Ht.: 8.6 cm	RIP WALLIS, DUCHESS OF WINDSOR: Born: Blue Ridge Summit PA 19 June 1896: Married: H.R.H. The Duke of Windsor, 3 June 1937: Died Paris, 24 April 1986: Buried Frogmore, 30 April 1986 HER HEART HAD ITS REASONS		

Fig. No.	Measurement	Inscription
		Base: J & J MAY
		The / Commemorators /
		40 Kensington Church Street. /
		London W84BX /
		British Made
XVI.8	Width: 22 cm	COMMEMORATING THE VISIT OF THEIR MAJESTIES TO THE
		UNITED STATES OF AMERICA 1939
		KING GEORGE VI / AND / QUEEN ELIZABETH
		Back: ROYAL IVORY
		JOHN MADDOCK & SONS LTD / MADE IN ENGLAND
		(Impressed: GVI / III)
XVI.9	Ht.: 10.4 cm	QUEEN ELIZABETH II. CROWNED IN WESTMINSTER ABBEY,
		JUNE 2, 1953.
		Base: AYNSLEY / ENGLAND / BONE CHINA
XVI.10 a	Ht.: 8.6 cm	H.R.H PRINCE CHARLES. LADY DIANA SPENCER
		TO COMMEMORATE THEIR MARRIAGE
		29th JULY 1981
XVI.10 b	Ht.: 7.9 cm	TO COMMEMORATE THEIR MARRIAGE 1986
		ANDREW SARAH
		Back: 23 JULY 1986
		Base: (embossed) Made in England
		Applied sticker: PRINCE WILLIAM POTTERY CO ENGLAND
XVI.11 a	Diam.: 32.1 cm	1658
XVI.11 c	Diam.: 35.1 cm	1992 / I.N.H. JUNE 14 O.B.E.
XVI.12	Diam.: 5.8 cm	TO COMMEMORATE / 100 WONDERFUL YEARS OF /
		HER MAJESTY QUEEN ELIZABETH / THE QUEEN MOTHER
		4th AUGUST 2000.
		Makers: GUILD OF ENGLISH MASTER POTTERS / ROYAL /
		CROWN DUCHY / FINE BONE CHINA / ENGLAND.

Notes

CHAPTER 1. KHNUM AND PTAH, AND THE CLAY OF LIFE

1. The first use of the slow wheel is attributed to the fourth-millennium Uruk Period in Mesopotamia, from which the knowledge spread to Egypt.

2. Veronica Seton-Williams.

3. The term *green* is used by potters to describe wares that have been air-dried but not yet fired.

4. The foot-rotated potter's wheel is thought have been in use in Egypt at some time around the beginning of the Christian era. Not until the seventeenth century was the cord-and-pulley (fast) wheel in general use, and it remained so until the development of steam power in the nineteenth century.

5. Wheeler was the foremost British archaeologist of his day, made so in the public mind by his television appearances on the museum quiz program *Animal, Mineral, or Vegetable.* In 1954, he was named the B.B.C.'s "Man of the Year."

6. *Sigillata,* meaning stamped or relief patterns, thus patterned earthenware. The term Samian Ware was adopted early in the nineteenth century by European scholars who mistakenly associated the red ware with the Greek island of Samos.

7. Bull-necked yet benign, Vespasian was one of the first century's most able emperors and a soldier of great experience. He was Governor of Judaea when proclaimed emperor by his troops on July 1, A.D. 69. His coin carries the figure of Peace on its reverse and is made from a brass-like copper alloy called orichalcum.

8. Meat-packer volunteer Charlie Lefevre, identified as a charge hand in a boot factory, gave his sage opinion that marks on the amphora "needed expert elucidation" (*Daily Herald,* March 6, 1950).

9. A newspaper reader writing from the south of France informed me that he knew where there was a Roman shipwreck loaded with amphorae and offered to sell me as many as I wanted.

10. Report to the Victoria and Albert Museum's Advisory Council by its subcommittee upon "the Principal Deficiencies in the Collections," 1913.

11. Such as Thomas and Ralph Toft, and Joseph Flower of Staffordshire.

12. Rheinzabern is located on the west bank of the Rhine north of Strassburg.

13. Verulamium, Camulodunum, and Calleva Atrebatum.

14. Donald Bailey, later a British Museum curator and the author of an important book on Roman clay lamps, and printer's assistant Peter Clark.

15. Over time, the marshland potters produced many different shapes and body types. Consequently, the Upchurch name, though still used, is not very helpful.

16. I have often been credited with being the first to promote the cross-mending process, but I have no idea whether that is a legitimate laurel.

17. Engine-turning is the term used to describe rotating the unfired, leather-hard pot on a special lathe that created uniform bands of irregular ridges and indentations. The machine was developed around 1764 and is attributed to Wedgwood.

18. According to the early (and sometimes unreliable) ceramic historian Simeon Shaw (1829), kaolin was first discovered in Cornwall by the Plymouth chemist William Cookworthy around 1745 (see chapter XIII, p. 296).

19. Report by R. Merlen, lecturer in anatomy at the Royal Veterinary College, appended to Ivor Noël Hume, "Ritual Burials on the Upchurch Marshes." The dog remains were donated to the Royal Veterinary College and the jars to the British Museum.

20. *Ibid.,* p. 164.

21. We were accompanied on this pilgrimage by our most loyal of volunteers, London timber broker J. Douglas Walton.

22. Note 8 given earlier, and *Archaeologia Cantiana*, Vol. LXVIII (1954), pp. 72–90, and Vol. LXIX (1955), pp. 69–74.

23. A miniature Roman amphora in lead that I found on the Thames foreshore beside Billingsgate fish market provides support for that likelihood.

24. Monaghan, *Upchurch and Thamesside Roman Pottery,* pp. 156–157.

CHAPTER II. IN AND OUT OF THE DARK AGES

1. Mortimer Wheeler, "Beginnings of Town Life in Britain," The Norman Lockyer Lecture, British Association for the Advancement of Science, 1937. Francis J. Haverfield, *The Romanization of Roman Britain*, Oxford: Clarendon Press, 1923.

2. In Eastern America the principal postnomadic Indian cultures break down into Early, Middle, and late Woodland, approximately 2000–1000 B.C., 1000 B.C.– A.D. 1, and A.D. 1–1500, and thereafter into the so-called European Contact phase.

3. Jewitt, *The History of Ceramic Art in Great Britain,* Vol. I, p. 2.

4. Lead glazing had been known in Egypt and Mesopotamia as early as the seventh century B.C. and had spread from Asia Minor to Gaul by the beginning of the Christian era.

5. Dunning, "Anglo-Saxon Pottery," p. 62, Fig. 23.

6. Potting rings are the ridges caused by pressure from the potter's fingers as the vessel takes shape on the turning wheel.

7. Bat molding is a process whereby a dish is shaped over a form or mandril either by hand or with the aid of an underside-shaping template.

8. Eraclius, *De Coloribus et Artibus Romanorum,* cited by Emmanuel Cooper, *Ten Thousand Years of Pottery,* Philadelphia: University of Pennsylvania Press, 4th ed., 2000, p. 144.

9. Shaw, *History of the Staffordshire Potteries.*

10. The word *biscuit,* meaning the products of a preliminary firing, was sometimes spelled *bisket* or pronounced *bisque.*

11. In the summer of 1956, while still an archaeologist for the Guildhall Museum, I had accepted an invitation from Colonial Williamsburg to come there on a three-month consultancy to report on its archaeological glass collections with special emphasis on eighteenth-century wine bottles.

12. The bare bones of that project were published by the National Geographic Society in its *Research Reports*, Vol. 17 (1984), pp. 653–676, neatly sandwiched between reports on hunting dugongs off Australia and gorilla language acquisition. The story of the Carter's Grove discoveries would be told in considerably more detail in Noël Hume, *Martin's Hundred.*

13. Beverley S. Nenk, "Post Medieval Redware Pottery of London and Essex," *Old and New Worlds*, Oxford: Oxbow Books, 1999, p. 236.

14. The *Oxford English Dictionary* suggests that the origin of the word *samel* comes from the Old English *samáeled,* meaning half-burnt.

15. The slipware dish was of paramount importance being dated 1631, thereby the earliest dated example of American-made pottery. It was also one of the earliest yet recorded in England. See Fig. VI.25 *b.*

16. Hurst, *Pottery Produced and Traded in North-West Europe, 1350–1650*, p. 76.

17. Among archaeologists, leaping to conclusions is a favorite acrobatic exercise.

18. The box is illustrated as Fig. III.27 *a.*

19. These braziers are of great interest in that they seem to relate to a patent secured by potter Richard Dyer in 1571 to make, among other wares, *"a kynde of earthen potte to holde fyre to seethe meate* [food] *uppon"* and which could be used *"for refreshing of houses in the heat of somer."* Dyer's pottery was located outside the London city walls beyond Cripplegate (Quinn, "London Pottery, 1565–1636," p. 58, citing Public Record Office C66/1077). These early food warmers were later developed into fuming pots used in sick rooms; examples of these have been found in London and were manufactured in Martin's Hundred, Virginia, prior to March 1622.

20. The Guildhall Library was founded in 1824, and two years later the Court of Common Council instructed the library committee "to consider the propriety of providing a suitable place for the reception of such antiquities relating to the City of London and suburbs, as may be procured or presented to this Corporation." The museum's first catalog was published in 1848.

21. The London Museum opened in 1913 at Lancaster House, a mansion originally built as the home of George III's second son, Frederick, Duke of York, who did not live to see it completed.

22. In 1975 the Guildhall and London museums were combined in an impressive new building built beside the last of the city's medieval defenses on the street appropriately named London Wall. For more details of the hectic postwar years see Noël Hume, "Into the Jaws of Death," pp. 7–22.

Chapter III. Adam, Eve, and a Bishop's Geese

1. Bernard Rackham, *Early Netherlands Maiolica with Special Reference to the Tiles at the Vyne in Hampshire*, London, 1926. At that date heads of museum departments, even of museums themselves, were generally identified as "keepers," a title today associated with zoos and prisons. Prior to the Second World War, the head

of the Guildhall Museum was just the "museum clerk" and answerable to the City's librarian.

2. Michel Hughes and David Gaimster, "Neutron Activation Analyses of Maiolica from London, Norwich, the Low Countries and Italy," in Gaimster, *Maiolica in the North,* pp. 57–90.

3. The London *Weekly Telegraph*, No. 429, October 13–19, 1999, p. 7. The Tate Gallery enters the twenty-first century split in half, with the traditional collections remaining at Millbank and the modern (and often controversial works) displayed in the old power plant renamed Tate Bankside. In a now all-too-familiar exercise in cultural puerility, the people's mind-molders renamed the old gallery Tate Britain.

4. *Saggers* were protective cylinders wherein ceramics were stacked in the kiln; *biscuit* referred to once-fired wares prior to glazing; *stilts* separated dishes stacked in saggers; *wasters* identified products that went hopelessly wrong in firing, and *seconds* those that went wrong but not so wrong that they couldn't be sold, albeit cheaply.

5. The property belonged to Sir William Gardiner, who leased "pte of a howse of myne in Southwark called Pickellherringe." For a more detailed summary of others' and my own research, see Noël Hume, *Early English Delftware,* pp. 2–12.

6. State Papers 39/25, No. 42, Public Record Office. See also Edwards, "London Potters," p. 121. There are minor spelling variations in the several readings of the Wilhelm patent, with the trailing "e"s interpretable as plurals.

7. The earliest known reference to galley pots (gallipots) dates from 1465. Similar usage occurred among bankers and merchants, who referred to Genoese coins of halfpenny value as *Galleyhal'pens.* Nathaniel Bailey, *An Universal Etymological English Dictionary,* 1749.

8. *Comfit* was a medieval word meaning preparations or sweetmeats and had nothing to do with chamber pots as comfort stations.

9. In 1610 Francis Bacon wrote that "It is to be known of what stuff galletyle is made" (*O.E.D.*).

10. The book titled *Early English Delftware from London and Virginia* was published by the Colonial Williamsburg Foundation in 1977.

11. Some writers refer to this motif as "The Temptation" in preference to "The Fall."

12. Rackham and Read, *English Pottery,* p. 48.

13. London 14 inches; Bristol 13½ inches. Because neither charger is completely round, much depends on where one chooses to take the diameters. When auctioned in 1931 the London example was listed as having a diameter of 13¾ inches, and the Bristol 13 inches.

14. Sotheby Parke Bernet sale catalog of *The Lipski Collection of English and Irish Delftware,* March 10, 1981, p. 12, Lot 6. Another, in a different pose, illustrated in Downman, *Blue Dash Chargers,* p. 52, is dated 1663.

15. Downman, *op. cit.,* p. 147.

16. At a year 2000 exchange rate the 260 chargers would have cost $7,583.68 (plus taxes, buyer's premium, etc.), a figure that in today's market would not buy a single good example.

17. The church was not restored after the fire, but its yard evidently continued to serve the parish, probably until the adjacent church of St. Michael Paternoster Royal was rebuilt in 1694.

18. These quotations are from Brand, *Observations on the Popular Antiquities,* Vol. II, pp. 234–235. Perhaps one may be forgiven for speculating that the dead man had

specified that his loved ones should make sure that he reached heaven with his favorite feature preserved.

19. Along with the Pickleherring factory there were others at Montague Close, Still Stairs, and the Bear Garden in Southwark and on the north bank of the Thames, Hermitage Dock in Wapping. The 1680s would see the industry spreading westward on the south shore to Gravel Lane and onward to three locations in Lambeth. For details see Britton, *London Delftware,* pp. 33–66.

20. The term *kraak* is believed to have been a contraction of the word *carrack,* used to identify the kind of Portuguese ship used in the Far Eastern trade during the reign of the emperor Wan Li (1573–1619) at the end of the Ming dynasty. However, the Dutch referred to *kraakporcelain* through much of the seventeenth century.

21. The Tutter's Neck base was donated to the Smithsonian Institution along with the rest of the excavated collection, in return for the Government Printing Office publishing the excavation report (Noël Hume, "Excavations at Tutter's Neck," p. 51, Fig. 11).

22. The location of Mr. Slater's fragment is not known to me.

23. Boulton, *The Amusements of Old London,* Vol. II, p. 164.

24. Britton, "The Pickleherring Potteries," p. 74. The word *eard* refers to vessels with two handles that protrude in the manner of ears from a human head.

25. Britton, *op. cit.,* pp. 61–92.

26. For reasons not immediately apparent (at least to me), all mid-seventeenth-century cups with a gentle ogee profile are called caudle cups, regardless of the fact that some of them carry inscriptions that have nothing to do with the drinker's health. One dated 1660, however, had much to do with toasting to the well-being of the newly restored king from the brush of an enthusiastic but educationally challenged painter, demanding: DRINK / UP YOUR DRINK AND LEVE NON IN / FOR HEAR IS HELTH TOO CHARLS OVER / RYOUL KING (Britton, *London Delftware*, p. 124, Fig. 75). In our view, the small size of the spouted pot, as well as the absence of decoration, together point to an association with sick rooms and the dispensing of warm gruel laced with wine and spices. Its spout's similarity to those of pap-boats, which undeniably served that recuperative purpose, seemed to us irrefutable. It is true that posset pots are spouted so that the potable liquid can be separated from the floating residue, but it can be argued, too, that caudle pots were also spouted. Thus John Robins's 1699 inventory lists consecutively "4 doz & half midle white possets" and "1 doz midle white Cawdle pots." Caudle cups were listed separately from caudle pots and were few in number (3 doz). Wine cups, on the other hand, were much more strongly represented (350 in one of several entries), prompting us to ask whether some of the cups identified by collectors as caudles were instead intended for wine.

27. The process is highly unscientific and we do not recommend it to anyone unused to handling acids. One places the vessel or dish in a deep basin of water and then pours concentrated hydrochloric acid into the water so that it floods over the blackened surface and immediately afterward is dispersed and diluted. The object is then removed and with the aid of soft soap smeared over the surface with one's fingers, the black comes off, exposing the original glazing and such colors as may lie beneath it. The item is then placed in a small, running water rinsing bath and remains in water until acid/alkali testing reads neutral, a process that may take several days.

28. Information from field notes for E.R. 161B, May 19, 1955.

29. van Beuningen, *Verdraaid goed gedraaid*, pp. 112–113, No. 551.

30. Catalog of the *Wine Trade Loan Exhibition of Drinking Vessels*, Vintners' Hall, 1933, p. 33, and Pl. XXXI.

31. *Ibid.*, p. 133 and Pl. LXVI. One of three such cups in the collection of the Worshipful Company of Clothworkers.

32. Taggart, *The Frank P. and Harriet C. Burnap Collection*, p. 44, No. 73.

33. Noël Hume, *Early English Delftware*, p. 67, Fig.VI, No. 13, and p. 69. The 1699 inventory of the Pickleherring factory's stock listed Oxes Eyes, and ceramic historian Frank Britton has equated that term with a "bulbous drinking vessel with two ring handles" (*op. cit.*, pp. 61–92).

34. That the pottery sellers' spokesmen should be named Sadler and Green would seem to be an astonishing coincidence, these being the name of the Liverpool developers of mass-production printing on Liverpool delftware tiles and other wares ca. 1750. However, there is no direct connection. In 1673 John Green (Greene) was Warden and later Master of the Glass Sellers' Company. Richard Sadler preceded him as Master in 1674.

35. Anonymous, *Ninth Report of the Royal Commission*, pp. 32–35.

36. Early-seventeenth-century London delftware tiles were square-cut and averaged from 13 mm to 16 mm in thickness. Those of the late seventeenth and eighteenth centuries averaged 6.5 mm and many were chamfered at their edges.

37. Anonymous, *Ninth Report, op. cit.*, p. 34.

38. It is, of course, entirely possible that the Commission's clerk, being unacquainted with potters' terminology, misheard what was being said.

39. The shape developed in fifteenth-century Italy, where the jars were known as *albarelli* and generally were somewhat waisted to better enable them to be taken down from the apothecary's shelf. That profile characterized Netherlandish maiolica jars and pots in the sixteenth century, but was not present among the many ointment pots (both biscuit and glazed) from the early-seventeenth-century London kiln sites.

40. See also chapter VI, p. 133.

41. F. N. L. Poynter (ed.), *Selected Writings of William Clewes, 1544–1604*, London: Harvey & Blythe, 1948, p. 73.

42. John Woodall, *The Surgeon's Mate, 1617*, facsimile, Bath, England: Kingsmead Press, 1978, pp. 31, 61.

43. By 1550 there were at least seven emigrant Dutch potters working further down the Thames at Greenwich (Edwards, *London Potters*, p. 6). On page 8 Edwards stated that "There is no evidence of any pottery [factory] across the river in Southwark before 1612."

44. In the late 1980s, excavations by the Museum of London on the site of the Cistercian Abbey of St. Mary Graces (east of the Tower of London) resulted in the recovery of 177 stove tile fragments, many of which were of the niche type somewhat akin to the Burnett fragment. Most of those, however, were made from a buff-colored ware with a film of white slip between body and glaze. The British Museum's David Gaimster reported at length on those discoveries and considered them all to be of German or Netherlandish origin and imported as parts of one or more stoves installed in the abbey in the early sixteenth century (Gaimster et al., "The Continental Stove-Tile Fragments"). However, the Burnett fragment, in its body clay, firing "sandwich" characteristic, and rich brown to green lead

glazing without any separating slip, renders it visually identical to many other early Tudor shards in the Collection believed to have been made in the London area. In view of the shard's importance, therefore, and at my urging, it has been donated to the British Museum on behalf of Sir David Burnett and the Chipstone Foundation.

45. G. Braun and F. Hogenberg, *Londinum Feracissimi Angliae Regni Metropolis,* 1574, reprinted from a German atlas of 1572, *Civitates Orbis Terrarum.*

46. Hoefnagel showed no water mill at the mouth of the sewer, though one had existed since the fourteenth century and would last until 1804. It may therefore be that there was another stream closer to Pickleherring Stairs.

47. Martha Carlin, "Four Plans of Southwark in the the Time of Stow," *London Topographical Record*, Vol. XXVI (1990), p. 33. The dunghill area was located south of the Bankside Power Station (Tate Bankside) in St. George's Fields, now Great Suffolk Street.

48. Edwards, *op. cit.,* p. 112.

49. *Ibid*. See also a paralleling reference regarding road maintenance at Yorktown, Virginia, in 1723; chapter 7, note 24.

50. *Ibid.*

51. Robert Morden and Philip Lea, *A Prospect of London and Westminster,* 1682, reprinted as Pl. 2A in Noël Hume, *English Delftware,* p. 6. It still showed (albeit within a built-up area) on John Roque's map of 1746.

52. See Fig. 11.16 *b.*

53. With London Bridge still the only dry crossing of the river, it is very unlikely that the pottery came from the City itself—though having said that, one cannot forget that in the 1870s London garbage would be barge-shipped all the way to the Medway marshes. The prevalence of chamber pots in the Burnett assemblage of later wares prompts a still small voice to whisper "dunghill fields" in one's ear.

54. Beverley S. Nenk and Michael J. Hughes, "Post Medieval Redware Pottery of London and Essex," *Old and New Worlds,* Oxford: Oxbow Books, 1999, pp. 235–245.

55. Excavations at the western corner of Horsleydown by the Museum of London in 1996 yielded large quantities of household earthenware from the period 1630–1680 but reported the recovery of "comparatively little 16th-century pottery." It also reported a second assemblage from the period ca. 1785–1830, a period only thinly represented in the Burnett material. See Steve Chew and Jacqui Pierce, "A Pottery Assemblage from a 17th-Century Revetted Channel at 12–26 Magdalen Street, Southwark," *London Archaeologist*, Vol. 9, No. 1 (Summer 1999), pp. 22–29.

56. Mary was the daughter of Henry's first wife, Catharine of Aragon, and reigned from 1553 to 1558. In her last three years, "Bloody Mary" was responsible, either directly or indirectly, for the burning deaths of at least 300 Protestant heretics.

57. One of the most disparaging epithets to hurl at an archaeologist is to call him or her a "pot hunter."

58. The transition from heavy reds and browns to lighter greens and yellows was a regional manifestation and a product of the factories supplying the London area from the counties of Surrey and Hampshire. In turn, early ships to America's two Virginias left England from the south and carried that southern English ceramic trend with them. Such wares have been found aboard the Bermuda wrecks of the *Sea Venture* (1609) and the *Warwick* (1619) and among the earliest finds from Jamestown (ca. 1607–1615).

CHAPTER IV. MENTIONING THE UNMENTIONABLE

1. Holme, *An Academie of Armory & Blazon*, Vol. II, Bk. III, chap. XIV, p. 2.

2. Barton, "The Buckley Potteries," pp. 1–23.

3. Haark, "Van Dubbels tot van Goyen," pp. 12–13.

4. A creditably broad-minded University of Keele provided "a small grant" toward this publication, but whether it was awarded to P. Amis or Francis Celoria is food for idle speculation. Nevertheless, in spite of a dismissively cute title page, his is a valuable (if early) contribution to an overlooked chapter of English ceramic history.

5. So called in the late nineteenth century because numerous examples of this ware had been found in metropolitan London.

6. Neither the revered *Oxford English Dictionary* nor any seventeenth- or eighteenth-century one that I have consulted cites any word that begins with the letters "p," "e," and "f." However, if we read the "e" as an overly exuberant "i" and recall that "s" was commonly drawn as an "f," a modicum of clarity emerges.

7. Hodgkin and Hodgkin, *Examples of Early English Pottery,* p. 9, No. 27.

8. My recollection is that the fragments came from a building site beyond the old city limits in the vicinity of Holborn. In the absence of any archaeological context, we could only assume a date somewhere between 1650 and 1670.

9. Postmedieval (albeit hyphenated) is the term used in Britain to separate the medieval centuries from those that came later. The magic date at which the population discovered that it was no longer medieval was 1485, when Richard III lost his crown and then his life on Bosworth Field. In America and other parts of the world that enjoyed the questionable fruits of colonization, unearthing the relics of the literate centuries is known as historical archaeology.

10. My editor assures me that few readers will know the meaning of the word *garderobe,* and therefore a word or two of amplification is in order. No medieval castle would be without several of the shafts so named. Pontefract Castle in Yorkshire, for example, had ten of them. Most dictionaries define the word simply as meaning a wardrobe (a room where clothing [robe] was stored or guarded), but, as the *O.E.D.* allows, it also meant a privy. Garderobes were drafty because they usually comprised a shaft within a tower whose top was open to the roof. Cut into the shaft's side were the vents of the latrines at each floor level, allowing the organic waste to drop into a basement cesspool from which it was occasionally extracted for use as fertilizer by picturesquely named *gong fermers* (Ian Roberts, *Pontefract Castle*, Yorkshire Archaeology Service, 1990, pp. 39–40). For a paralleling green-glazed chamber pot in a context of ca. 1702–1714, see Fryer and Selley, "Excavation of a Pit at 16 Tunsgate," p. 165, No. 41, and p. 175, Fig. 20, No. 41.

11. Celoria, "Some Domestic Vessels," p. 15.

12. Margaret Rule, "The Raising of the *Mary Rose," Country Life,* May 24, 1979, p. 1638. Celoria, *op. cit.,* p. 19, No. 21, Museum of London A 2736.

13. Quoted by Davis, *English Silver at Williamsburg*, p. 213.

14. *Wine Trade Loan Exhibition Catalogue,* 1933, Pl . VI.

15. Archer, " A relayton of the Discovery," Vol. I, p. liii.

16. That sometimes precarious venture to the "beak-head" is recalled to this day by ship's toilets being described as the head.

17. An example has been recovered from the 1609 wreck of the *Sea Venture* lying off the northeast tip of Bermuda as shown in Wingood, "*Sea Venture,*" p. 342, Fig. 12. The vessel is there described as a "Surrey ware jug with faded green glaze." The citation is attributed to Mathews and Green, "Pottery from the Inns of Court,"

p. 12, where the authors noted that the production of "green-glazed jugs continued to the close of the 17th century." In 1969, the term *Tudor green* had yet to be ousted, although a distinction was drawn between "Surrey wares" and "wares in the Surrey tradition."

18. As we find over and over again in the history of domestic pottery, many a supposed innovation was nothing of the sort. The Romano-British potters mixed gravel into the inside of their grinding and mixing bowls (*mortaria*) to create a deliberately rough surface. In the first century, Medway potters tempered their crudest wares with ground-up shell, a practice that would be used again by early medieval potters of the eleventh and twelfth centuries.

19. Watkins, "North Devon Pottery," pp. 17–59.

20. Wingood, *op. cit.,* p. 342, Fig. 10.

21. On occasion the untempered fabric would be combined with the gravel-mixed, and I have seen a fragmentary jug found in Londonderry, Northern Ireland, that had a plain body and a gravel-tempered handle.

22. Brown, *Plymouth Excavations,* p. 17, Nos. 38 and 39, and p. 59, Fig. 8.

23. Rogers's entire inventory of his possessions in 1739 was worth barely 7 pounds more than the ceramic stock of John Robins in 1699. Put another way, the relative value of the pound in 1999 to that of 1699 and 1739 made Rogers's stock worth £2,206.67 and Robins's £70,487.55. See Watkins, "The 'Poor Potter' of Yorktown," pp. 87–90. Also Britton, "The Pickleherring Potteries," pp. 67–80.

24. Biscuit examples from the Pickleherring site are frequently found partially pink and partly yellow, presumably, one might think, the product of localized oxidation within individual saggers. However, a delftware tile from the Pickleherring assemblage is quite clearly made from red-firing and yellow-firing clays wedged together.

25. The 1699 Robins inventory of the Pickleherring stock includes "8 Toy Nosegay potts att 9.0d" ready for sale (Britton, *op. cit.,* p. 69) and 150 more in their "clay" state and worth a miserable 4s.6d (p. 70). Clearly they were not difficult to make, and while the terminology may fit the Collection's example, one questions whether the inventory takers were counting paralleling objects.

26. Jörg, *The Geldermalsen,* p. 114. The capacity of a slop bowl is there said to have been one pint.

27. Christie's auction catalog, April 28, 1986, p. 26.

28. The previously cited 1699 inventory of Pickleherring potter John Robins contained no vomit pots but did list large numbers of both chamber pots and spitting pots—although the difference between them is uncertain.

29. See chapter VII, p. 143.

30. As with modern commemorative wares, there was money to be made by lampooning figures of popular favor or derision. Chamber pots containing a portrait of the allegedly Jacobite Dr. Henry Sacheverell (1674–1724) sold so well that a potter near Hackney north of London was able to build himself a substantial house that came to be known as Piss Pot Hall (*1811 Dictionary of the Vulgar Tongue,* London: Bibliophile Books, 1984, 1st ed. 1785). Functional humor has a history as long as history itself, and it should surprise no one that on the Thames during the Frost Fair of 1685 there was a temporary tavern named "The Flying Piss Pot" (cf. Larwood et al., *English Inn Signs,* p. 216).

31. Sadler and Green were primarily makers of printed tiles (see Fig. IX.47 *a*), but Wedgwood and others are known to have sent them creamwares to be transfer-decorated and refired in muffle kilns.

32. Some surviving examples have the names of their owners stamped on their sides (Celoria, *op. cit.*, p. 39, No. 50, marked J. H. SIMPSON / *Colorman* / *34 London Road*).

33. Another is to be seen in the left foreground of Hogarth's etched contribution to recruitment at the beginning of the French and Indian War (the Seven Years' War).

34. The undated portrait serves as the frontispiece to William Ireland's *Hogarth Illustrated* (1791/98). It is not, as might be otherwise supposed, a self-portrait. Ireland credited it to "Mortimer." John Hamilton Mortimer (1741–1779) was a respected but scarcely remembered painter who was only twenty-three when Hogarth died. Adding a touch of mystery is the fact that in another undated version of Mortimer's engraving, the mini-chamber pot and its brushes have been moved from the foreground to a location behind his chair and the pot no longer retains its distinguishing profile. (Sean Shesgreen [ed.], *Engravings by Hogarth*, New York: Dover Publications Inc., 1973, Frontis.).

35. *A Midnight Modern Conversation*, 1732.

36. Lidded chamber pots had became common by the mid-nineteenth century, most of them in transfer-printed Ironstone or other white wares.

37. The publication of David Gaimster's seminal *German Stoneware, 1200–1900*, is much more broadly focused than would be any catalog of the Thomas Collection.

38. In 1783, the stock ledgers of John Wood of Brownhills in Staffordshire listed chamber pots of several capacities: quart, 3-pint, 2-quart, also seventy "Blue holland" chamber pots, which almost certainly were Westerwald imports through Dutch factors. The entries also included "large coach pots," a reminder that bumping along rural roads in a poorly sprung coach not only stimulated "naturall necessity" but made large pots more practical than small (Celoria, *op. cit.*, p. 15).

39. On French colonial sites in America, the full range of mugs, jugs, and chamber pots differs in ornamentation from those found in England, although the ubiquitous GR medallions of the English Georges occur in the same French contexts. See, for example, Brain, *Tunica Treasure*, pp. 77–81.

40. Both shards are illustrated in Noël Hume, *All the Best Rubbish*, p. 109, Fig. 44a.

41. Within days of making that claim, the dealer from whom I bought the 1632 pot showed me another with the same oval medallions and the same date, but of slightly smaller size. It is one of the axioms of collecting that when one has paid a premium price for something that appears to be unique, several others turn up in rapid succession.

42. Hill, *Fashionable Contrasts*, Pl. 98. *Germans Eating Sour-Krout*, May 7, 1803.

43. Gaimster, *op. cit.*, p. 95.

44. *Ibid.*, p. 125.

45. Tall, usually zoomorphic-spouted jugs decorated on their fronts with star-shaped relief designs (e.g., Reineking-von Bock, *Steinzeug*, No. 506).

CHAPTER V. OF MUGS AND JUGS BOTH LARGE AND SMALL

1. That definition of beauty is attributed to Margaret Wolfe Hungerford, who coined it in 1878 before it sank to cliché status — along with "ugly as sin." For the latter we can blame another none-too-well-remembered name, that of Frederick Locker-Lampson (1821–1895).

2. Three were in the confluence of the Meuse and Rur rivers: Langerwehe, Aarchen, and Raeren; two more lay between the Meuse and the Rhine: Frechen and

Cologne; and closer to the source of the Meuse in modern Belgium was another brown stoneware center at Bouffioulx.

3. David Gaimster has cited a comparable example containing a hoard of silver coins, with the latest dating prior to 1442. See *German Stonewares, 1200–1900*, p. 166, Fig. 1.

4. *Ibid.,* facing p. 176, Fig. 2:1.

5. No less a coincidence is the fact that the Crucifixion jug fragments were found only a short distance from the Southwark byway called Crucifix Lane.

6. Gaimster, *op. cit.,* p. 57, Fig. 3–12, No. 81.

7. Zippelius, *Volkskunst im Rheinland,* p. 78, No. 225.

8. Probably ca. 1670–1690.

9. A quartern or gill was one fourth of an integer, which in turn was described as one fourth of a whole number, that is, a quarter pint.

10. Lady Charlotte Schreiber (1812–1895) donated her collection to what was then called the South Kensington Museum and did so "under certain conditions as to its being kept in its integrity." Having made the gift she was persuaded to prepare a catalog of it, and that she did (Archer, *Delftware,* p. 586). The Noël Hume Collection (though by no stretch of imagination comparable to Lady Schreiber's) followed the same sequence insofar as it related to the integrity of its preservation and the compilation of the catalog.

11. The dish is the earliest dated specimen of American potting so far recorded as well as being among the earliest made in England. Fragments of three such dishes were found at Site B (the home of potter Thomas Ward) in Martin's Hundred. See Fig. VI.25 *b.*

12. Neither the 1632 Westerwald chamber pot (Fig. IV.29 *a*) nor the small, lidded pot (Fig. IV.23 *a*) exhibits the results of template chatter. Its absence might be seen as evidence of the latter's early date, but it seems more likely that, this being an anomalous size, no such setup was installed. There is, however, a trace of the hand use of a slightly concave smoothing board.

13. English customs records show that "Pots, stone" were being imported into Britain from Holland in 1776, though in significantly smaller quantities than five years previously. Cf. Toppin, "The China Trade," p. 55: abstracts from the London Custom House Records.

14. In his masterly book *German Stonewares, 1200–1900,* David Gaimster discussed the revival of enthusiasm for Renaissance Germany and how the opportunity was seized by several Rhineland potters (pp. 325–343).

15. This was not true of most Westerwald chamber pots, whose handles continued to end in loosely rolled scrolls.

16. Christie's South Kensington, Sale 8734 csk, April 20, 2000, Lot 99.

CHAPTER VI. BROOMSTICKS AND BEER BOTTLES

1. Generalizations invariably get a writer into trouble, and this one is no exception. Although it is true that large ceramic containers were rare in northern medieval Europe, in Spain and Italy potters drawing on classical and North African precedents were producing large storage jars (*botijas*) and would continue to do so through the eighteenth century (Goggin, "The Spanish Olive Jar," pp. 3–37).

2. A bottle bearing that date is illustrated in Zippelius, *Volkskunst im Rheinland,* p. 111, No. 354.

3. Future historians may see this as yet another example of the Euroization of Britain at the end of the twentieth century.

4. Anonymous, *Dictionary of the Vulgar Tongue.*

5. On contextual evidence recovered by Dr. Martin Biddle from excavations at Henry VIII's Nonsuch palace in Surrey.

6. Noël Hume, "German Stoneware Bellarmines," p. 440, Fig. 3.

7. The fragmentary graybeard with its medallions depicting the arms of Amsterdam reached the Hamilton Harbor not from a passing ship but from residential dumpage.

8. Reineking-von Bock, *Steinzeug,* Fig. 444.

9. An ill-proportioned example in the museum at Cologne is attributed to Frechen and to a date around 1600. But this is only 15 cm in height, compared to the Collection's 47.65 cm (Reineking-von Bock, *op. cit.,* No. 324). Another very fragmentary bottle, excavated at Pemaquid in Maine, has one of its three medallions dated 1610 and stands about 38 cm in height (Wendy Cooper, "Seventeenth-Century Ceramics Used in New England," *The Decorative Arts Society Newsletter,* Vol. VIII, No. 2 [September 1982], p. 2, Fig. 2).

10. Solon, *A History and Description of the Old French Faience,* Fig. 11.

11. The term *museum quality* can be read in two distinctly different ways. To some curators it means the best of the best, but to others it denotes specimens that, though repaired, are sufficiently whole to serve an educational purpose regardless of the fact that connoisseurs would pay little for them. John Austin, retired curator of ceramics at Colonial Williamsburg, in his *British Delft at Williamsburg* (1994), was the first decorative arts museum scholar to use matching fragments as a major tool in the interpretation of ceramic antiques.

12. Merrifield, " The Use of Bellarmines as Witch-Bottles," pp. 3–15. Merrifield later expanded this study in a book he titled *The Archaeology of Ritual and Magic.*

13. The witch bottle was found at "Gooseacre," the home of Mr. J. Amies, who took it to the Ipswich Museum, where it was labeled and seems to have remained for an indeterminate time. It came into the hands of an American antique dealer in 1998 after being auctioned in London. But who sold it and where it had been through the previous thirty-odd years are questions still unanswered. A letter of inquiry to the museum elicited no reply.

14. Van Loo, "Pieter van den Ancker en Jan op de Kamp," pp. 22–29. Also Gaimster, *German Stoneware, 1200–1900,* p. 222, Fig. 71.

15. Collectors who had never been to a zoo may have been unaware that tigers were striped and leopards spotted.

16. There is an intact example of this Van den Ancker type in the Museum of London (MOL. A4287) illustrated in Gaimster (*op. cit.,* p. 221, No. 70). He dated that bottle to 1655–1665 on the evidence of Van den Ancker's 1654 arrival in London and the existence of dated rebus seals of 1660 and 1661 (Van Loo, *op. cit.,* p. 24, Figs. 1–3). Both medallions were found by Sir David Burnett or his workmen while rebuilding along the Bermondsey river front.

17. Although the likelihood that ancient anythings should escape the scrutiny of Williamsburg's restorers seems remote, we know that they did. A wine bottle of about 1690 (the earliest yet found in the city) was purchased in 1994 after it had been found in the attic of the Duke of Gloucester Street home of the "Armistead sisters" shortly before the house was moved out of the historic area.

18. Noël Hume, *op. cit.,* pp. 439–441.

19. For an example see Fig. V.II *a*.

20. Beckmann et al., *Volkskunst im Rheinland,* p. III, No. 359.

21. Christie's Amsterdam sale catalog, *The Nanking Cargo,* pp. 18–22, Lots 1014–1056.

22. Contemporary *"Translation of the Ordinance Relative to the East India Trade for the Danish European States, as well as for the Danish Settlements in India. Published on the 16th of June 1797,"* p. 5.

23. The cited references to the importation of stoneware bottles do not imply that in the years between them no bottles entered London or the English Out-ports. It means only that in some years the bottles were specified and that in others they were lumped together with other ceramic imports identified only as "Earthenware, several sorts" (Toppin, "The China Trade and Some London Chinamen," pp. 54–55).

24. Solon, *The Ancient Art Stoneware of the Low Countries and Germany.*

25. Zippelius, *op. cit.,* p. 77, No. 213, there attributed to Raeren.

26. This example was purchased in London's Bermondsey antiques street market and in all probability had been unearthed somewhere in the City.

27. I discussed this evidence in greater detail in *Early English Delftware from London and Virginia,* pp. 2–3, drawing on M. L. Solon and W. B. Honey. These jugs evidently were in use into the seventeenth century, as was demonstrated by my finding a fragment thrown up in the mouth of a crab burrow on the site of the ca. 1613 King's Castle, Bermuda.

28. Hughes and Gaimster, "Neutron Activation Analyses of Maiolica from London, Norwich, The Low Countries and Italy," *Maiolica in the North,* pp. 61–62.

29. Beckman et al., *op. cit.,* pp. 37–38, No. 55.

30. We tend to think of all seventeenth-century imported tin-glazed ware as being Dutch, but excavations at Martin's Hundred and elsewhere in Virginia have shown that Portuguese dishes were relatively common. However, in my book *Martin's Hundred* I put forward evidence from the Dutch island of St. Kitts to show that the Martin's Hundred dishes I had originally ascribed to Portugal were, in fact, Dutch. Twenty years later I have concluded that I was right the first time (cf. *Martin's Hundred,* pp. 99–100 and Figs. 5–9). That *volte-face* reversal is supported by the subsequent recovery of Portuguese maiolica in Amsterdam excavations (Jan Baart in *1600 Portuguese Faience 1660,* Holland: Amsterdam Historisch Museum, 1987, pp. 18–27).

31. Goggin, *op. cit.,* pp. 3–37.

32. Henderson, *The Wreck of the "Elizabeth,"* p. 25.

33. Noël Hume, *Shipwreck!* p. 56.

34. See chapter III, p. 68.

35. Southampton Harbour is now known as Castle Harbour.

36. Three complete or near complete examples were found at Site "A" in Martin's Hundred, all in contexts of ca. 1625–1640 (Noël Hume, *Martin's Hundred,* p. 52, Figs. 3–12). Two more are in the National Park Service collections at Jamestown where they were found in the cellar fill of the building identified as Structure 112 in a context attributed to ca. 1625–1650 (Cotter, *Archeological Excavations,* p. 184, Pl. 184).

37. Hurst et al., *Pottery Produced and Traded,* pp. 33–37. Hurst noted that no costrel wasters have yet been recovered from Pisa kiln sites, leaving the door wide open to the likelihood that they were produced elsewhere in northern Italy.

38. America's largest archaeological assemblage of North Italian marbleized slipwares was found in 1933 prior to enlarging a coal pier at Newport News, Virginia.

Known as the Knowles Collection, the material is now in the archaeological holdings of Colonial Williamsburg. The base of a costrel similar to Fig. VI.23 and several dish shards have been found at Jamestown (Cotter, *op. cit.,* p. 185, Pl. 83, there captioned as "English marbled slipware"). Jewitt had illustrated a damaged example in 1878, but evidently, knowing virtually nothing about it, he lumped it in with other "pilgrim's bottles" and noted that they "were much made in the Middle Ages" (Jewitt, *The History of Ceramic Art,* Vol. I, p. 86, No. 301). Also see Brown, "Iberian Pottery Excavated," p. 321, and Vince, "Spanish Medieval Pottery," pp. 329–331.

39. The term *marbleized* refers to wares whose decoration was achieved by the application of surface slips. When in the mid-eighteenth century that effect was created by the blending of red- and white-firing body clays, the striations went right through the wall, resulting in the truly marble-like product known as Agate Ware. See Fig. XIII.7.

40. The gift of a London building site workman, the flask almost certainly comes from somewhere in Southwark.

41. Ivor Noël Hume, "Roanoke Island: America's First Science Center," *Colonial Williamsburg,* Vol. XVI, No. 3 (Spring 1994), pp. 14–28.

42. Hurst et al., *op. cit.,* p. 102.

43. Ward made the chamber pots illustrated in Fig. IV.8.

44. It is, of course, equally possible that Ward was English but learned his craft in the factory of an emigrant Dutchman.

45. Le Hardy, *County of Middlesex Calendar,* p. 80.

46. See Fig. V.12.

47. One wonders whether artist Harrison Weir's "collection" had been no more than an assemblage of studio props that included the Italian costrel.

48. Renaud, *Rhodesteyn, schatkamer der middeleeuse ceramiek,* p. 49, Fig. 40.

49. For example, Fig. IV.3.

CHAPTER VII. CALCUTTA, BALLAST, AND ANTI-CLOCKWISE HUNTING

1. Shaw, *History of the Staffordshire Potteries,* p. 182.

2. *Ibid.,* p. 180.

3. *Ibid.,* p. 177. Shaw wrote that "In 1751, were made the last improvements of Cream Colour, (prior to those of the late Mr. Wedgwood,) by Mrs. Warburton, of Hot Lane."

4. Other potters were in production with a similar (?) ware that they called "China Glaze." According to Simeon Shaw, Enoch Booth's cream-colored body was "improved in quality by different persons, especially by John Greatbatch who made what has long been called the best China Glaze applied to cream colour" (Shaw, *op. cit.,* p. 184).

5. Haselgrove and Murray, "John Dwight's Fulham Pottery," p. 40.

6. Green, *John Dwight's Fulham Pottery, Excavations.*

7. Gaimster, *German Stoneware, 1200–1900,* p. 309.

8. *Ibid.;* Rhoda Edwards, "London Potters Circa 1570–1710," p. 41.

9. Holme, *An Academie or Store House,* Book IV, p. 408. No relevant dictionary definition for the word *crist* has been found.

10. Anonymous, *The General Shop Book,* n.p.

11. Holme, *op. cit.,* Book IV, p. 408.

12. Neve, *The City and Country Purchaser's and Builder's Dictionary*, n.p.

13. Luke Talbot referring to James Morley in answer to charges by John Dwight of Fulham, April 1, 1696 (Haselgrove and Murray, "John Dwight's Fulham Pottery," p. 121).

14. Dating is based on the insufficient evidence of a single clay pipe (Gaimster, *op. cit.*, p. 310).

15. William Killigrew applied for a patent in 1672 but was beaten to the post by Dwight who secured his own monopoly two weeks earlier (Green, *op. cit.*, p. 178; also Gaimster, *op. cit.*, p. 310).

16. Before claiming the name similarity as something more than a coincidence, it is best to reflect that there is another Newbottle in Durham County, and yet another in Gloucester County, Virginia.

17. Chapter III, p. 65.

18. Anonymous, *Ninth Report of the Royal Commission*, pp. 34ff.

19. I am advised that some readers may conclude that the Elers brothers ran an English drug store or chemist's shop. At the same time, the English are inclined to imagine that in America one goes to a drug store for supplies of crack cocaine. However, the reference here is to those who "make chemical investigations" (1626) rather than "one who deals or retails medicinal drugs" (1683). Thus sayeth the *O.E.D.*

20. Early collectors and dealers described any English unglazed red stoneware as *Elers Ware*, but in reality Staffordshire copycats were in production by 1740 (if not before), and the same body composition would become Josiah Wedgwood's *Rosso Antico*. See Fig. IX.50.

21. James Morley was another recipient of John Dwight's writs. As an apprentice he had learned the potting craft at the Montague Close delft and stoneware factory in Southwark and had set up in business at Nottingham by 1697.

22. Kiln cylinders *with* bottoms were used as the lowest unit of each stack, with the one at the top being covered with a disk of the same ware.

23. In contemporary terminology, mugs came straight sided and were usually called *cans*, while stoneware drinking vessels with globular bodies and straight necks were identified as *gorges*, that being the medieval term for neck or throat, that is, a collar narrower than the body of the vessel.

24. That Rogers's waste products were scattered up and down the main street of Yorktown is explained by his having been appointed in 1734 to be "surveyor of the Landings, Streets, and Cosways in York Town." He thus was doing his civic duty by disposing of his rejects as road fill (York County Records, Book 18, 1732–1740, *Orders, Wills, & Inventories*, p. 157).

25. Watkins, "The 'Poor Potter' of Yorktown," p. 82. See also chapter IV, pp. 84f.

26. *Ibid.*, p. 88; extracted from York County Records, Book 18, *Orders, Wills, & Inventories*, p. 553, William Rogers's will dated December 17, 1739.

27. The distinctive earthenware shapes are known as *Challis Ware*, although there is no documentary proof that he was the potter.

28. Noël Hume, *Here Lies Virginia*, p. 218. When I wrote this I dated the bottles to 1725–1730, a time span so narrow that it should be dismissed as the arrogance of youth.

29. When we secured permission to salvage what we could from the Pine Dell site, manager G. T. Brooks authorized me to do whatever I liked with whatever we might find. My original intent was to donate the collection to the Smithsonian

Institution in exchange for its publishing the report, as had been the case with my work at Rosewell, Clay Bank, and Tutter's Neck. But so great was the quantity of potsherds that the report was never finished. We loaned the Rogers mug to Colonial Williamsburg for exhibition in its James Anderson House archaeological museum. But when, as soon as we retired, that exhibit was closed and the building converted into offices, Audrey retrieved the mug to ensure that it would have a safe place amid the stonewares of the Collection.

30. Green, *op. cit.,* pp. 271ff.

31. *Ibid.*

32. She donated the shard to the British Museum, and it is illustrated in Gaimster's *German Stoneware, 1200–1900,* p. 119, Fig. 4.7.

33. Oswald et al., *English Brown Stoneware, 1670–1900,* p. 40. Oswald states that the Gravel Lane material was salvaged by us in 1950, but my notes made at the time were dated to the late summer of the previous year.

34. Britton, *London Delftware,* p. 48.

35. Above 1,250°C.

36. Hildyard, *Browne Mugges,* p. 33, No. 31.

37. Valpy, "Extracts from the *Daily Advertiser,*" pp. 209–211.

38. Green, *op. cit.,* p. 141, Fig. 115, and p. 284. For a more conventional usage of the term *double glazing* see chapter XIV, p. 324.

39. John De Wilde, master potter and wax chandler, moved to Burlington, New Jersey, and set up a delftware manufactory where he died in the spring of 1708. See Rhoda Edwards, *op.cit.,* pp. 54–55.

40. Roy Edwards, "An Early 18th Century Waste Deposit," pp. 45–56.

41. Chris Green in his *John Dwight's Fulham Pottery* includes a drawing of a comparable object that he describes as "wheel thrown pillars . . . probably designed specifically to level stacks" (pp. 181–182, Nos. 480–482). That these objects were found in seventeenth-century contexts and not in waste from the subsequent phases of Fulham's production helps confirm the seventeenth-century origin of the Burnett fragment.

42. Britton, "The Pickleherring Potteries," pp. 61–92. See also chapter IV, pp. 62ff.

43. Vine Yard is today known as Vine Lane.

44. Jones, "The Source of Ballast at a Florida Site," pp. 42–45.

45. In 1720 there were no fewer than three glass houses in the vicinity of Gravel Lane (Powell, *Glass-making in England,* p. 89).

46. For an intact example see Figure 1.4 *b.*

47. Noël Hume, *Shipwreck!* p. 15.

48. Oswald, et al., *op. cit.,* p. 49.

49. A large tankard in the Chipstone Collection (1972–75) bears a Queen Anne portrait medallion and the incised date 1731. The added silver rim is engraved "To the Pious Memory of Queen Ann. Drink all up & fill it again," clearly implying that the mug was to be used. There are several surviving, silver-mounted tankards bearing "Pious Memory" inscriptions, and these are considered to be early examples of Jacobite propaganda. This is further evidence that such large tankards were used—in these instances to toast the health of the Old Pretender (Anonymous, Catalog of the *Wine Trade Loan Exhibition,* p. 21, No. 11, tankard dated 1728).

50. In heraldry there are four basic shield shapes, this one so called because the field is narrow and shaped like the heater for a box iron.

51. The Seven Years' War (1754–1763), known in America as the French and Indian War.

52. Cotton, *East Indiamen,* p. 156. A ship of the same name made a hazardous voyage home from Bombay in 1775 (pp. 112–113), and another (or the same) *Calcutta* was lost with all hands off the coast of Mauritius on March 14, 1809 (p. 136).

53. *Translation of the Ordinance Relating to the East India Trade,* 1781, p. 14.

54. Simon, *Drink,* p. 165.

55. See note 49.

56. Anonymous, *A brown Dozen of drunkards: (Ali-ass Drink-hards) Whipt, and shipt to the Isle of Guls: for their abusing of Mr. Malt the bearded son, and Barley-broth the brainless daughter of Sir John Barley-corne. All joco-seriously descanted to our Wine drunk, Wrath drunk, Zeal drunk, staggering Times. By one that hath drunk at St. Patricks Well.* London. Printed by Robert Austen on Addlin-hill. The woodcut was discovered, copied, and illustrated by John Ashton in his *Humour, Wit, & Satire of the Seventeenth Century* (p. 286).

57. The guests would not think so, if they could have seen what Audrey and I knew about the banquet's traditional turtle soup being readied in the kitchen on the floor immediately below our lab!

58. Green, *op. cit.,* p. 334, citing a listing prepared by Excise Duty Inspector Thomas Bateman in 1696. Separated from these drinking tankards by other unrelated products was a series of "gorges" ranging in capacity from double gallon down to half pint. But in this context it could be applied to any vessel with a pronounced neck or throat, as was common among jugs large and small. The previously discussed 1699 inventory of John Robins's stoneware stock listed under "Perfect stone Ware" "4½ dozen pottle canns" valued at £4.10s and "13 pottle stone Canns att 8s." A pottle was a liquid measure equivalent to 2 quarts or half a gallon.

59. A leather tankard attributed to 1660 was exhibited in the Wine Trade Loan Exhibition of 1933 (No. 198) and was 9¼ inches in height and 5½ inches in diameter, measurements paralleling the standard large stoneware flagons of the eighteenth century.

60. The Collection's jug (Fig. III.27 *e*) has a faded label on its base that includes the name "White Friars Street," which bordered the Inns of Court to their east.

61. Cited by Mathews and Greene, "Post-Medieval Pottery of the Inns of Court," p. 4 (letter from Sir Julius Caesar, Treasurer of the Inner Temple, to Sir William More, August 1594). Mathews was of the opinion that the green-glazed "Surrey Ware" tankards and jugs were in production from the late sixteenth to well through the seventeenth century.

62. See note 49.

63. Oswald et al., *op. cit.,* p. 48.

64. The shape of the Chipstone Collection tankard (No. 1995.9) is unusual in that it has a sharply flaring base and multiple cordoning above it. It is neither named nor dated.

65. Henig and Munby, "Some Tiles from the Old Cheshire Cheese, London," pp. 156–159.

66. This tankard was deaccessioned by Colonial Williamsburg, presumably because it owned another very much like it (the Paten tankard discussed below). Thus C.W.1968-479 came into the Collection in trade around 1974.

67. This picture is sometimes called "The Orgy" and is the third plate in Hogarth's *A Rake's Progress,* a series painted in 1734 and issued as engravings in the following year.

68. The "Anti-clockwise Hunt" category was so named by the British Museum's Mavis Bimson in an unpublished lecture to the English Ceramic Circle in 1979.

69. The whip-holding huntsman may be from the same mold as several decorating a tankard attributed to Bristol and the Redcliff Pottery ca. 1750–1750 (Oswald et al., *op. cit.,* p. 91, Fig. 53).

70. *Ibid.,* p. 50. Two more versions of the "Punch Party" on brown stoneware are attributed by Oswald et al. to Benjamin Kishere's pottery at Mortlake in the last years of the eighteenth century (*ibid.,* p. 60, Fig. 25, and Plate D facing p. 113).

71. Illustrated in Askey, *Stoneware Bottles,* p. 7.

72. Vol. II, p. 79.

73. Oswald et al., *op. cit.,* pp. 280–283, did attempt a typology of windmills and trees on the later "hunting jugs," but did not extend to the eighteenth century's mammoth mugs.

CHAPTER VIII. STONE BOTTLES AND OTHER PUZZLERS

1. Although globular and later cylindrical glass bottles are conveniently described as wine bottles, they had many other uses that ranged from ale, paint, and lead shot, to oil and antidotes to witchcraft. For what may have been the first archaeologically published chronology, see Noël Hume, "The Glass Wine Bottle in Colonial Virginia," pp. 91–117.

2. Another exception is provided by a group of five handleless, brown stoneware bottles of globular form, two of which bore medallions with the ID initials of John Dwight and were found in his cellar. These have been described by Green in *John Dwight's Fulham Pottery* (p. 118, 121) as "Decanter bottles," although, among glass bottles of the early eighteenth century, handles were applied to those designed for that purpose: e.g., *Anonymous, Catalog of the Wine Trade Loan Exhibition,* Pl. XCIVA & B, one late seventeenth century and the other dated 1713, both now in the Museum of London.

3. Because the undecorated and therefore the cheapest white delftware bottles had no "keep me" appeal, they were discarded while those with dates survived, and in consequence the unadorned are infinitely more rare.

4. Hildyard, *Browne Muggs,* pp. 44–45, Nos. 71–75 (1740, 1749, 1753, ca. 1755, and ca. 1764–1774).

5. Jewitt, *The History of Ceramic Art in Great Britain,* Vol. II, p. 300. Also Meteyard, *The Life of Josiah Wedgwood,* Vol. II, p. 84; and Noël Hume, *Digging for Carter's Grove,* pp. 46–47.

6. Oswald et al., *English Brown Stoneware, 1670–1900,* p. 88, illustrated on p. 91 and attributed to Bristol. Other examples are in the collection of the Hampshire Museum.

7. Johnson, "The Dudley Hoard."

8. The method was invented in 1811 by Jacob Wilson Ricketts and his son Henry at their glasshouse in Bristol, and would revolutionize the industry.

9. Hildyard, *op. cit.,* p. 44, No. 74.

10. Oswald et al., *op. cit.,* pp. 281–283.

11. Detail in Fig. VIII.10 *b.*

12. This catalog is illustrated in Green, *op. cit.,* pp. 365–368.

13. The burning, bomb-shattered Bristol remains one of my childhood's most vivid memories. For reasons far beyond the scope of this book, my mother took me

on a tour of the ruins on the morning after the heaviest of the raids, with the car bouncing over hoses still pouring water into the smoldering debris. I recall being aware that we had no business to be there.

14. The Powell jug is in the collection of the Bristol City Art Gallery and Museum. (Oswald et al., *op. cit.,* p. 93, Fig. 55).

15. *Ibid.,* p. 286, No. 12.

16. *Ibid.,* p. 208, Fig. H.

17. Jewitt, *op. cit.,* Vol. II, p. 117, Fig. 97.

18. *Ibid.,* p. 225, Fig. 171 *b*.

19. Godden, *An Illustrated Encyclopaedia,* p. 214, mark No. 1340. The oval DOULTON LAMBETH mark on the base is one that was used only between the cited dates.

20. *Annals of Nottingham,* 1853, cited by Oswald et al., *op. cit.,* p. 104.

21. Anonymous, *The Universal British Directory,* Vol. II, pp. 29–30.

22. *Ibid.,* pp. 672–678.

23. The same inscription occurs on four delftware puzzle jugs described by Hodgkin, one of them dated 1733 and tentatively attributed to Liverpool. Two others (undated) were attributed to Bristol and one to Lambeth (Hodgkin and Hodgkin, *Examples of Early English Pottery,* pp. 137, 131, and 114, respectively). Another daisy cut-out, Liverpool delftware example ca. 1760, decorated in "Fazackerly" colors, was sold at Sotheby's (South), November 22, 2000, Lot 502.

24. Pages 263 and 286–287; his reasoning is unstated.

25. Chipstone Foundation collection, No. 1994.12. Another in a private Milwaukee collection bears a well-executed, sprig-applied Porto Bello scene and is dated 1741.

26. Illustrated by Green, *op. cit.,* p. 228, Fig. 228, from the collection of the Royal Ontario Museum, No. ROM 985.10.24.

27. Hodgkin and Hodgkin, *op. cit.,* p. 1, No. 1. The Museum of Practical Geology opened in London's Jermyn Street in 1851 as part of Britain's Great Exhibition of that year. Its content was a hodgepodge of anything that seemed inappropriate for the British Museum. When, in 1934, the Museum of Practical Geology was demolished, its collections were distributed to the Geological Museum, the Natural History Museum, and others.

28. Gaimster, *German Stoneware, 1200–1900,* p. 261, No. 115. The Wolstenholme fragments are part of the Carter's Grove archaeological collections: E.R.C.G. 3011H & 3161B [7241]. The crest of the handle is impressed with the initals WM, believed to be those of William Menniken, working at Driesch in the Rhineland ca. 1580–1590.

29. Chipstone Collection No. 1990.7.

30. Austin, *British Delft at Williamsburg,* p. 75, No. 31.

31. Michael Archer, *Delftware,* pp. 258–260.

32. Jewitt, *op. cit,* Vol. II, pp. 25–26, Fig. 16.

33. Archer, *Delftware,* pp. 259–260, D8.

34. Cleo Witt, *Delftware,* Bristol: City Art Gallery, n.d., Fig. 14, museum number N 6824.

35. The Hodgkins in their *Examples of Early English Pottery* illustrated a 1766 sgraffito slipware triple beaker and put the "fuddling cup" term in parentheses (p. 63, no. 222).

36. Jewitt, *op. cit.,* Vol. I, p. 52, Fig. 189. This fuddling cup and much more obviously Roman period material was excavated at the small Lancashire hamlet of

Wilderspool in the 1870s; the hamlet's only claim to fame is its "remains of a Roman Camp (141 yds. by 140 yds.)." Although no subsequent history of Roman Britain was to consider the camp and its pottery worth mentioning, Jewitt gave it three pages—evidence that immediacy or an author's personal interest does not necessarily translate into lasting importance.

37. They were also common in the West of England, being made in sgraffito slipware at Donyatt in Somersetshire, where dated examples ranged from 1697 to 1770. An early example of this tortoiseshell glazed Staffordshire ware turned up in Audrey's and my excavation on the site of a Virginia Plantation in a context of ca. 1700–1710 (Noël Hume, "Excavations at Tutter's Neck," pp. 68f., Fig. 19, No. 9).

38. This colander is illustrated in Oswald et al., *op. cit.*, p. 177, Fig. 145.

39. *Ibid.*, p. 106 and fn. 14. The colander is illustrated in Oswald's book (p. 177, Pl. 145) and is there attributed to Derbyshire (Brampton) or Nottingham, ca. 1800.

40. The term *loving cup* is defined in the *O.E.D.* as "a large drinking vessel, usu. of silver, passed from hand to hand, generally at the close of a banquet, for each guest to drink from in turn," and the *O.E.D.* gives the date of its source as 1808. This reference to the passing around of a communal drinking vessel reinforces the proposition that large brown stoneware tankards served a similar purpose, perhaps at weddings or other family gatherings.

41. Anonymous, *The Universal British Directory*, Vol. IV, pp. 527–528. That source added that there were "several smaller manufactories in the neighbourhood" and listed one at Rawmarsh named Button, Barker, and Co. Pot Manufacturers, as well as John Ward as a potter and Richard Wright as a pot maker. The Greens, Bingley & Co. partnership was dissolved in 1806.

42. Jewitt, *op. cit.*, Vol. II, p. 495.

43. Grabham, *Yorkshire Potteries, Pots and Potters,* p. 84.

44. Oswald et al., *op. cit.*, p. 121, Fig. 78.

45. *Ibid.*, pp. 212–213.

Chapter IX. Potter to Her Majesty and Other Marketing Ploys

1. *History of the Staffordshire Potteries,* p. 1.

2. Garner and Archer, *English Delftware*, Pl. 4.

3. The 1699 inventory of John Robins at the Pickleherring pothouse listed numerous dishes in various sizes but named no plates.

4. Britton has identified James Robins as an apprentice of John Robins who died in 1699 (see chapter III, p. 62), but acknowledges no family relationship.

5. Letter to Sir William Meredith quoted by Toppin, "The China Trade and Some London Chinamen," p. 37; after Eliza Meteyard, *The Life of Josiah Wedgwood,* Vol. I, p. 367.

6. There is a caveat even to this statement, namely, that when earthenwares are subjected to heat above the lead glaze's melting temperature (as can happen in a house fire), that glaze will liquify and run over a fracture just as it would if the vessel was broken in a kiln.

7. The Queenhithe fragments include a much used base fragment from a sagger, biscuit handle fragments from two porringers of one shape, and shards from two fireplace tiles, two examples of an early-eighteenth-century plate rim type (Britton, type H, p. 194), two bowls, one large pitcher(?), a basin, a cup, and something that may be the base of a twisted "rope" handle of a type used on jardinieres late

in the seventeenth century. Thomas Browne (see p. 144), who described himself as "Potter to King Charles," resided at Queenhithe where he had a pottery warehouse. Although a freeman of the Tilers' and Bricklayers' Company, in 1614 Browne had secured a patent to manufacture stoneware. At the time of his death at Queenhithe in 1634 he was a wealthy merchant with trading interests in Virginia. Rhoda Edwards, "London Potters Circa 1570–1710," p. 41.

8. Noël Hume, *Early English Delftware,* pp. 54 and 114.

9. Noël Hume, *Treasure in the Thames,* p. 193. For examples of such trivet spacers see Fig. III.10.

10. Noël Hume, *Early English Delftware*, p. 54, fn. 6. The Thames Street trivet is recorded as having been found in association with Roman Samian Ware—which helps nary at all!

11. In 1620, one Samuel Sotherne was accused by Southwark delftware potter Hugh Cressey of infringing on his galleyware patent and of luring his workers away to operate furnaces for the firing of "divers great quantities of paving tyles." This suit followed Cressey's raid on Sotherne's warehouse at the "Stilyard" on Thames Street, a location lying on the north shore between Queenhithe and London Bridge—albeit closer to the latter than the former. If Sotherne made tiles, it is entirely possible that he or his successors were involved in more general delftware production. Edwards, *op. cit.,* p. 104, citing Chancery Proceedings C. 3/305/47. P.R.O.

12. Ray, *English Delftware Pottery,* pp. 165ff., No. 75.

13. The knives and forks are most closely paralleled by a pair illustrated by J. F. Hayward in *English Cutlery,* London: Victoria and Albert Museum, 1957, p. 16, Pl. XVIa, and attributed to the early eighteenth century.

14. John Leland, *The Itinerary, 1535–1543* (Lucy Smith, ed.), Illinois: Southern Illinois University Press, 1964, Vol. II, p. 97.

15. A possibly fatal flaw in the reasoning is that one would not expect Joseph Piper to aspire to a mug decorated with the Company arms until he completed his seven years' apprenticeship.

16. Garner and Archer, *op. cit.,* pp. 40–41, Pl. 69c.

17. Austin, *British Delft at Williamsburg,* pp. 154–155, Nos. 237–240 and 242.

18. Garner and Archer, *op. cit.,* Pl. 52A and p. 25.

19. Archer, *Delftware,* pp. 174–175, Fig. B18.

20. Ray, *op. cit.,* p. 184.

21. Audrey Noël Hume, "A Group of Artifacts," pp. 5–6, Fig. 3, No. 2.

22. John Van Ness Dunton, "French Ceramics of the 18th Century," pp. 18–20, Figs. 8 and 10. For an engraving of St. Eustatius see Fig. X.19a.

23. Garner and Archer, *op. cit.,* p. 51.

24. The bowls were a gift from Sir David Burnett. Though of Lambeth shape, their interior design bears some resemblance to the peony motif decorating the back of a puzzle jug attributed to Liverpool and to a date ca. 1750. Garner and Archer, *op. cit.,* Pl. 100, state that most delftware puzzle jugs were made in Liverpool (p. 23).

25. There is a good example in the Chipstone Collection [1970.2], and being long and narrow it was probably intended for serving fish.

26. Negative archaeological evidence is undeniably the worst kind. Failure to find something need only mean that one is digging in the wrong place.

27. "Rouen Faience in Eighteenth-Century America," *Antiques*, Vol. LXXVIII, No. 6 (December 1960), pp. 559–561.

28. Moustiers in the Basses-Alpes became a potting center in 1686 and in the eighteenth century would rival Rouen and Nevers in output and importance.

29. Noël Hume, *Shipwreck!* pp. 18–29.

30. C. A. E. Moberly and E. F. Jourdain, *An Adventure,* London: Faber and Faber, 1955 ed.

31. There is some confusion between the terms *Le Kiosque* and *Belvédère*. The names are interchangeable in some sources, and in others are considered to have been separate but adjacent structures. *Ibid.,* p. 59.

32. The handle of this bottle is missing, but sufficient survives to indicate that it had been decorated with blue dashes similar those of the previously cited examples.

33. See Fig. VI.33.

34. Honoré Savy's painting was of infinitely higher quality than was displayed by PB on this armorial plate.

35. Solon, *A History and Description of the Old French Faience,* p. 119.

36. *Catalogue of the Collection of London Antiquities in the Guildhall Museum* (1908 ed.), Pl. LXX, No.1, and p. 210, No. 635.

37. Here again, nomenclature causes problems. Although molds were used both for slip casting and for pressing, most ceramic historians associate molding with pressing, and casting with the slip process. Thus, a slip-made piece is cast and a pressed one molded.

38. Shaw, *History of the Staffordshire Potteries,* p. 146. Historian/potter Michelle Erikson of Hampton, Virginia, has demonstrated that slip casting can be achieved in a single pouring, with the thickness dependent on the porosity of the mold and the length of time the liquid clay remains in it.

39. Alabaster is a mineral found in marl beds, principally in Britain's Midlands potting centers of Nottinghamshire, Staffordshire, and Derbyshire.

40. The Roman torso (Fig. IX.23 *b*) is paralleled by a boy's head and upper body almost certainly from the same mold but found in a Kent garden. In publishing it, archaeologist Frank Jenkins speculated that when whole the figure was no more than a half-length bust and that the bird in the boy's hands was a cockerel. The Thames torso, however, leaves no doubt that the figurine was full length and the bird a dove. Here is a graphic demonstration of the difficulty we face when we try to interpret a hitherto unrecorded ceramic fragment. Frank Jenkins, "A Romano-Gaulish Statuette from Cowden, Kent," *Archaeologia Cantiana,* vol. LXXXVI (1971), pp. 203–205.

41. Jewitt, *The History of Ceramic Art.,* Vol. I, p. 125.

42. See chapter VII, p. 147.

43. Most authorities describe this process as a dip, but examples are known that have the brown slip applied at different elevations, suggesting that on occasion the iron oxide was painted onto the to-be-affected areas.

44. Arnold Mountford in his *The Illustrated Guide to Staffordshire Salt-Glazed Stoneware,* pp. 21–22, postulated that Crouch ware was really a brown-slipped salt-glazed ware and in production through much of the eighteenth century.

45. *Ibid.* Mountford illustrated several examples of this ware and attributed them all to dates between ca. 1710 and 1720 [Pls. 51–58]. However, a mug or can fragment was found at Rosewell, Virginia, in a context of ca. 1770 (Noël Hume, "Excavations at Rosewell," p. 206, Fig. 27, No. 12).

46. Mountford, *op. cit.,* p. 22.

47. Church, *English Earthenware,* p. 57.

48. Shaw, *op. cit.,* pp. 63–64. Bird was a specialist in making agate knife handles and buttons as well as general earthenwares, but other writers have given him no credit for having pioneered the use of flint. Perhaps his soubriquet of the "Flint Potter" testified to his parsimony rather than his chemistry.

49. *Ibid.,* pp. 128–129.

50. Quoted by Mountford, *op. cit.,* p. 36.

51. Quoted by *ibid.,* p. 38.

52. Copeland, *A Short History of Pottery Raw Materials,* n.p.

53. These transitional wares were discussed at length in Noël Hume, "The Rise and Fall of English White Salt-Glazed Stoneware," pp. 248–255.

54. Noël Hume, "Excavations at Rosewell," p. 171, Fig. 8.

55. Arnold Mountford described his illustrated parallel as "unusual because of the bird chimney and shaped handle" (Mountford, *op. cit.,* Pl. 91). The Collection's teapot has an identical handle and dates to ca. 1745.

56. Meteyard, *op. cit.,* Vol. II, p. 86.

57. William Hone, *The Every-Day Book* (1826), Vol. I, p. 31.

58. York County Records, Wills and Inventories, Book XXII, p. 19. The white salt-glazed wares were not Hay's principal Raleigh Tavern crockery. The inventory listed "122 china plates" (Chinese porcelain) and "39 Queens china plates"—these last proving that creamware was available in large quantities prior to January 21, 1771, when Hay's inventory was made.

59. That probably alien phrase had its origin among Victorian street traders in children's cut-out paper theater characters that came in sheets either outline printed or infilled with colors at twice the price. Invented in 1811 under the title Juvenile Drama, the children's paper playhouses remained popular throughout the nineteenth century.

60. Chipstone Foundation Collection No. 1987.3. Unfortunately, neither Mary Coall nor Thomas Prouse has yet been identified.

61. Calver and Bolton, *History Written with Pick and Shovel*, p. 244, Fig. 5.

62. We had long believed that the narrow, straight-necked mugs or jugs so frequently found in debased scratch-blue salt glaze (Fig. IX.37 *a*) were an English shape developed there around 1760. However, there is evidence that like so much else in the history of salt-glazed stoneware, the shape came from the Rhineland. See Beckman, Reineking-von Bock, *Volkskunst im Rheinland,* p. 103, Fig. 301, where it is attributed to Westerwald from the second half of the eighteenth century into the early nineteenth century. The same shape occurs in English delftware and is attributed by Michael Archer in *Delftware* (p. 390, No. J.32) to London or Liverpool, ca. 1760–1800.

63. Foreign stoneware imports continued alongside home-thrown products. In 1771 "Pots Stone" were entered in the Custom House Records as arriving from Flanders, and 24,805 lb weight from Holland as well as 993 dozen stone bottles, but none of it directly from Germany (Toppin, *op. cit.,* pp. 54–55).

64. Noël Hume, "Mugs, Jugs and Chamber Pots," pp. 520–522.

65. Gaimster, *German Stoneware, 1200–1900,* p. 323.

66. Noël Hume, "Mugs, Jugs and Chamber Pots," p. 521. William Tunnicliffe's 1787 *A Survey of the Counties of Stafford, Chester, and Lancaster* listed, among many others, two Burslem potters making "white stone" pottery and another at Cobridge making "blue and white stoneware" (cited by Josiah Wedgwood and Thomas H. Ormsbee in *Staffordshire Pottery* [1947], p. 65).

67. Church, *op. cit.,* p. 56.

68. The fluid lead glaze was not a Whieldon-Wedgwood discovery. According to Simeon Shaw, that credit belonged to Enoch Booth of Tunstall, ca. 1750, who applied it to a cream-colored body developed by Thomas Astbury between 1720 and 1740. However, a fluid-glazed, cream-colored bowl with the initials E.B. and the date 1743 (now in the British Museum) strongly suggests that Enoch Booth made his major discovery a decade earlier than was stated by Shaw in his *History of the Staffordshire Potteries,* pp. 176–177.

69. The brown "tortoiseshell" glazing was not a Whieldon innovation. It occurs, for example, on early-seventeenth-century earthenware mugs as well as on chamber pots at the beginning of the following century.

70. Caudle was a warmed drink combining thin gruel with wine or ale, sweetened and spiced. The *O.E.D.* says that it was primarily served to the sick—which made it an odd choice to present to the Queen. For an earlier discussion of the identification and use of caudle cups, see chapter III, note 26.

71. Shaw, *op. cit.,* p. 186.

72. Meteyard, *op. cit.,* Vol. II, p. 56.

73. Noël Hume, "The What, Who, and When of English Creamware Plate Design," pp. 350–355.

74. This was not a widely used pattern, at least not in colonial America, although an almost complete example was found in a Revolutionary War context in excavations behind Williamsburg's Chiswell-Bucktrout House (*ibid.,* p. 355, Fig. 9).

75. Towner, "The Melbourne Pottery," pp. 18–30. Many of his illustrations closely resemble examples made at the Leeds Pottery and other centers, among them pierced dishes and twisted handles with floral terminals.

76. Noël Hume, "The What, Who, and When of English Creamware Plate Design," p. 355, Fig. 9.

77. The Chipstone Foundation owns a very handsome scratch-blue, white salt-glazed punch bowl dated 1759 incised with the name "Edward Saddler" (Chipstone Collection 1985.15). Although that ware was made in Liverpool and John Sadler's name was sometimes spelled with two "d"s, I have not found a family connection between John and Edward. Jewitt (*op. cit.,* Vol. II, p. 28) stated that John Sadler married Elizabeth Parker in 1748, but did not name their offspring.

78. A parallel is illustrated by Ray, "Liverpool Printed Tiles," Pl. 47, D3–5. The author placed the "English Cook" tile in his late category, that is, ca. 1765–1775.

79. The paucity of French food by comparison with the robust quality of English beef had been a popular English view of the French even before the Seven Years' War began, as is attested by Hogarth's 1748 painting and engraving whose title "O the Roast Beef of Old England, &c." was in turn derived from a popular song used in Fielding's *The Grub Street Opera,* Act III, scene 2. Fielding ceased writing for the theater in 1737.

80. Ray, "Liverpool Printed Tiles," p. 61 and Pl. 49, No. D5.20. The author suggested that the 88 border was first used in 1764. Sadler and Green's printed figure-eight tiles survive in several houses in South Carolina as well as in Massachusetts and Rhode Island (Bridges, "Sadler Tiles in Colonial America," pp. 174–183 and Pls. 87–93).

81. The name is unusual in that few women in the eighteenth century had more than one given name. Attempts to trace Anne Boucant Page have not been fruitful.

82. This term is misleading in that in some wares the decoration does indeed sit on top of the glaze, but in these enameled creamwares the ware is refired in a muffle kiln sufficiently to bond the colors. On June, 17, 1767, Yorkshire pothouse owner

John Platt wrote in his diary, "Building a muffle or kiln for ye painted or enamel ware pottery" (J. V. G. Mallet, "Rotherham Saltglaze: John Platt's Jug," *English Ceramic Circle Transactions,* Vol. 9, Part 1 [1973], p. 112).

83. Lost lids are commonplace, and so is the marrying of disparate elements by dealers who hope the buyer will not notice. It took us until we got home to realize that we had been had!

84. Noël Hume, *Pottery and Porcelain in Colonial Williamsburg's Archaeological Collections,* p. 24, Fig. 21.

85. *Leeds Intelligencer,* October 28, 1760.

86. Although pottery of one sort and another had been made at Leeds through most of the eighteenth century (tobacco pipe making had begun by 1715), it was not until 1770 that the business defined as the Leeds Pottery was begun. No named factory has been documented prior to the 1760s (Walton, *Creamware and Other English Pottery,* pp. 75–76).

87. Kidson and Kidson, *Historical Notices of the Leeds Old Pottery, Leeds,* following p. 32.

88. Walton, *op. cit.,* p. 233, No. 991, and p. 276, No. 14.

89. The hunt tankard passed through the hands of ceramics dealer Jonathan Horne and was illustrated in his booklet *A Collection of Early English Pottery,* Part V, No. 124, n.p., n.d. He dated the tankard to ca. 1775, whereas Walton (*op. cit.,* p. 233) gives looser and slightly later dating, that is, late 1770s–1780s.

90. Published by Frederick Muller Ltd., London, 1955. Audrey Noël Hume was also part author of *Tortoises, Terrapins & Turtles,* Foyle's Handbooks, London: W. & G. Foyle Ltd., 1954.

CHAPTER X. WHEN THE PUBLIC EYE IS PALL'D

1. James Cawthorn (1719–1761), schoolmaster and cleric. Quote from *Of Taste* (1756) (Honour, *Chinoiserie: The Vision of Cathay,* p. 125).

2. An Anglicized version of the Dutch *Lange Lysen*.

3. Jewitt in his *The History of Ceramic Art in Great Britain,* Vol. 1, Pl. III, facing p. 270, illustrated a group of images from original Caughley porcelain copper plates, one of them including the "Long Eliza" figure.

4. See Fig. X.6.

5. A generation to which Audrey and I unabashedly, and unapologetically, belonged.

6. Hughes and Hughes, *The Collector's Encyclopaedia of English Pottery,* p. 126.

7. Illustrated as Fig. XI.8.

8. Noël Hume, "Pearlware: Forgotten Milestone of English Ceramic History," pp. 390–397.

9. Miller has questioned the validity of calling pearlware "a milestone in English ceramic history." However, the ever-helpful Noah Webster defines *milestone* as "a significant point in development," and that it was—albeit not a cornerstone. By 1780, and perhaps half a decade before, call it what you will, the whitened ware was seizing the underglaze blue-painted and transfer-printed business from Wedgwood and his host of creamware-producing competitors (Miller, "Origins of Josiah Wedgwood's 'Pearlware,'" p. 85).

10. As in Fig. IX.32.

11. The term *Long Eliza* is an example of the English delight in deliberately mispronouncing foreign words and names. This one comes from the Dutch *Lange Lyzen,* meaning, oddly enough, Long Eliza.

12. The pottery-decorated card was discovered by ceramic authority Geoffrey Godden and published in his *An Illustrated Encyclopedia of British Pottery,* p. 278, Fig. 487. The earlier potworks card was published by W. J. Pountney in *Old Bristol Potteries,* Pl. XVII, and p. 88.

13. Bass, *A History of Seafaring,* p. 270, Fig. 16. The pearlware saucer provides a graphic example of the potential for contamination by later garbage when wrecks lie close inshore or in well-traveled sea lanes.

14. Am I saying that women were always the painters? Definitely not; but by suggesting that it might be so, I am hopeful that I may escape the gender bias that female archaeologists thought they had discovered in one of my earlier books.

15. The 1699 Robins inventory (Chap. III, p. 62) referred to the slow wheel as a "profileering wheel," presumably meaning a wheel used to finish the profile of a pot previously drawn up on the fast wheel. The order in which the potting equipment was listed, "6 wheels 8 benches 2 profileering wheels 3 painting tables and 7 chairs," suggests that the slowly rotating profileering wheels refined the profiles of the pots before they were transferred to the painting table. Distributing the chairs among the wheels, benches, and tables leads one to conclude that much of the work was performed standing.

16. Some collectors refer to annular wares as *Mocha Ware,* a term that belongs to but one variety of that banded class, namely, the yellowish-brown bowls and mugs decorated with a lacy pattern resembling fan coral and achieved by the unattractive association of urine, turpentine, and tobacco juice. Known to potters as "tobacco-spit ware," mocha was in production throughout the nineteenth century, with the earliest documented example being dated to 1799.

17. Gottesman, *The Arts and Crafts in New York,* pp. 88–89; *The New-York Gazette and the Weekly Mercury,* May 11, 1772. The reference to "red china tea" pots may be to imports from China or to the dry-bodied redwares first made by the Elers brothers and later by Wedgwood and other Staffordshire potters. "Aggit" meant *agate,* but whether the term meant to Davies and Minnitt what it does to modern ceramic collectors and curators is another question. The usage is almost certainly someone's phonetic spelling, which, if looked up in contemporary dictionaries, would not be found. In truth, the most commonly used dictionary (Nat. Bailey's *Universal Etymological English Dictionary*) would have been of very little help. Agate was defined therein as "a precious Stone of several Sorts and Colours."

18. Austin, *British Delft at Williamsburg,* p. 188, No. 364. It is not always certain whether the recorded ascent is that of 1785 or of his lofting from Moorfields on September 15 of the previous year.

19. William Absolon (1751–1815) is best known as having been an enameler of Staffordshire factories' wares, and he set up a glost kiln for that purpose at Yarmouth in Norfolk. That his name is sometimes painted on the backs of creamwares and related wares has led some collectors to conclude that he was himself a potter. There is, however, no supporting evidence for that interpretation of his mark.

20. As records show that at least one officer brought his billiard table in his baggage, packing a teapot would have been no more trouble than boxing his balls.

21. Mason, *John Norton & Sons,* p. 309; John Norton to John Hatley Norton, from London, March 20, 1773.

22. Calver and Bolton, *History Written with Pick and Shovel,* p. 256. In fairness to the authors, who died in 1940 and 1942, it was the Historical Society that coined the unfortunate title.

23. Miller, *op. cit.,* p. 85. The New York sites were Fort Watson and the New Windsor Cantonment, which had earlier been dug into by Calver and Bolton.

24. When naval historian Howard Shapelle referred to this ship in his *History of the American Sailing Navy* (New York: Bonanza Books, 1949), pp. 53 and 55, he called her the *Andrea Doria,* but both Dutch and English records called her the *Andrew Doria* and added that she was flying the "Congress Coulours." In 1777 she was set afire and scuttled in Delaware Bay (W. J. Morgan [ed.], *Naval Documents of the American Revolution,* Washington, D.C.: Naval History Division, Department of the Navy, 1976, Vol. 7, p. 214).

25. Today, Pigeon Island is linked to the main island by a permanent causeway and has been made into a tourist destination complete with audiovisual and assorted interactive exhibits. The "treasure island" we knew no longer leaves history to the imagination, and what was then known as Gros Islet Bay has now become the more history-promoting Rodney Bay.

26. Miller, *op. cit.,* p. 85.

27. Anonymous, *The Universal British Directory,* Vol. I, p. 312; also Elizabeth Adams, "Ceramic Insurances in the Sun Company Archives, 1766–1774," pp. 13–14 and Pls. 7 and 8. In her paper, Adams lists Margaret and the second Joseph only as china and earthenware dealers, but the *Directory* identifies all three as potters.

28. Holdaway, "The Wares of Ralph Wedgwood," p. 260, Pl. 162a & b, and Pl. 164b.

29. This printed and polychrome range of pearlware tea services has been identified by some dealers as *Salopian,* and, welcoming a name that embraces the entire range, we adopted it, albeit unaware of any evidence linking it to a Shropshire (Salopian) factory. As misnomers are so common in the history of ceramic studies, we felt that one more could do no harm. Products of the famed Caughley porcelain factory operated by Thomas Turner from 1772 to 1799 were sold as Salopian in contemporary advertisements, such as Robert Studwell in the *Norfolk Chronicle* (August 16, 1783), selling "a large Assortment of Foreign China, Worcester and Salopian Ditto" (Smith, "Norwich China Dealers of the Mid-Eighteenth Century," p. 201).

30. Geoffrey Godden, *Encyclopaedia of British Pottery and Porcelain Marks,* p. 318, No. 1991.

31. Minnie Holdaway noted that the border of a saucer matching the "Pax" plate was to be found in Ralph Wedgwood's "Ferrybridge Shape and Pattern Book," 1798–1801, a closing date at least a year too early for either plate or saucer (*op. cit.,* p. 261, and Fig. 164b).

32. Several delftware ointment pots of late-eighteenth-century shape turned up in the 1920s, each decorated in blue with dates in the second half of the seventeenth century. They were refired to seal the decoration under the glaze, and only the shape gave them away as fakes. Audrey suspected that on occasion white delftware wine bottles of the mid-seventeenth century were similarly improved.

33. Sandon, *The Watney Collection,* p. 42, No. 82.

34. In his 1973 book *English Blue and White Porcelain,* Watney insisted that "nothing can replace the knowledge gained by forming, cataloguing and living with a really representative collection." With that I fully agree. But as some sage once said, there's many a slip betwixt cup and lip. When Watney died, it turned out that "he never catalogued his collection or listed where he purchased it" (Sandon, *op. cit.,* p. 5).

CHAPTER XI. NO WIND IN THE WILLOWS

1. Godden, *British Pottery and Porcelain, 1780–1850,* p. 111.
2. Lewis, *A Collector's History of English Pottery,* p. 129.
3. Hughes and Hughes, *The Collector's Encyclopedia,* p. 121.
4. Having trekked more than a little dirt through London's Guildhall, I had great sympathy for Muzzrole, whose second-floor laboratory had no direct external access. He was an enthusiastic yet careful amateur archaeologist who had worked for Audrey and me on the Amelung glass factory site in Maryland and thereafter joined the staff of the Smithsonian, where he worked under the aegis of Malcolm Watkins, who was himself a leading authority on American pottery.
5. Henry Wadsworth Longfellow wrote "There Was a Little Girl" on March 15, 1882, and died nine days later.
6. The index to W. K. and K. Johnson's *Road Atlas of Great Britain* (1961 edition) lists a Greenhill near Dumfries in Scotland, but the map cites it as Greenmill.
7. Quoted in the anonymously written *The Story of the Willow Pattern Plate,* p. 5.
8. Jewitt, *The History of Ceramic Art,* Vol. II, p. 168.
9. For a Chinese porcelain source or parallel, see Fig. XIII.17.
10. Mankowitz and Haggar, *The Concise Encyclopedia,* p. 241. Coysh and Henrywood, in their *The Dictionary of Blue and White Printed Pottery, 1780–1880,* Vol. II, p. 211, note that the identity of Thomasine Willey has not been traced.
11. W. L. Little, *Staffordshire Blue,* p. 111. A comparable jug inscribed THOMAS KEEN 1797 can lay claim to being the earliest dated example of the basic willow concept. It came on the market early in 2001 and was promptly purchased by an American private collector. Illustrated by dealer Rita Entmacher Cohen in the 2001 guide to *The New York Ceramics Fair,* p. 32.
12. *Ibid.,* Vol. I, pp. 226 and 102. Our Swansea attribution is not without its critics, and the moth border has been claimed to be a Davenport characteristic. However, Coysh and Henrywood observed that John Davenport's blue printed wares (ca. 1794–1887) "tended to follow fashion" (*op. cit.,* p. 102). The staple-roofed pagoda is also to be seen on the 1802 jug.
13. Coysh and Henrywood, *op. cit.,* p. 207.
14. Lao-Tzŭ was the founder of the gentle philosophy known as Taoism (*ibid.,* p. 62).
15. des Fontaines, "Underglaze Blue-Printed Earthenware," p. 135 and Pl. 139f. See also Coysh and Henrywood, *op. cit.,* p. 62.
16. Coysh and Henrywood, *op. cit.,* p. 348.
17. John and Richard Riley marked their wares J. & R. RILEY until Richard's death in 1823, after which time John marked his wares RILEY until his death in 1828; hence the tight date bracketing for the camel plate. Its small flower border should not be confused with the wild rose rim pattern exemplified by the Nuneham Park plate in Fig. XI.17 *a.*
18. The son of George Rogers of Longport, d. 1815.
19. Brown's work at Nuneham Park was in progress between 1779 and 1782.
20. Coysh and Henrywood, *op. cit.,* p. 173.
21. Only three undamaged objects were retrieved from the ruins of Audrey Baines's house, her father's top hat, her teddy bear, and a whiteware chamber pot. This unexpected survival (often known in England as a "thunder mug") may have been the genesis of her interest in the ceramic history of these onetime bedroom essentials.
22. Geoffrey Godden, the principal authority on Mason's Ironstone China, shows several versions of the blue-printed mark, but in each instance the letters are

outlined, whereas those on the Collection's plate are blocked or lack the Mason name (Godden, *British Pottery and Porcelain, 1780–1850,* p. 39).

CHAPTER XII. MEMORIES, FOND AND OTHERWISE

1. The first version of what has been described as "the greatest poem of the Middle English" is thought to have been written between 1367 and 1370, after which the poet, William Langland (ca. 1330–ca. 1386), spent the remaining years of his life revising it.

2. Chipstone Collection, No. 1968.8.

3. There is a very similar Queen Anne charger in the Colonial Williamsburg Collection. It is illustrated in John Austin's *British Delft at Williamsburg,* p. 138, No. 181, and listed as "probably Bristol."

4. Fig. IX.34.

5. Although made from blended yellow and red firing clays, this Astbury-style bowl was not intended to be sufficiently variegated to make the agate effect ornamental. The yellow was, instead, a grog clay to help the body survive when thinly potted. In this example, however, the result was not as intended, for the wall cracked along the lines of the striations.

6. There is a fundamental difference between agate and marbleized wares, with the former involving the blending of two or more clays of different colors so that they run in veins through the thickness of the vessel. In contrast, marbleized wares rely for their appearance on colored slips applied only to the surface (see Fig. XIII.7).

7. The Chipstone Foundation's two salt-glaze Vernon teapots (Fig. IX.34) commemorate both the taking of Porto Bello and the attack on Fort Lorenzo westward at the mouth of the Chagre River. Each pot is inscribed BY AD/VERNON AND FORT/CHARGE. If these teapots are contemporary with most other Portobello souvenirs (as they almost certainly are), in the light of subsequent events they are unlikely to have been made any later than 1742. That date is incised beneath an applied Porto Bello medallion on the wall of a brown stoneware puzzle jug in the collection of Mr. and Mrs. Fred Vogel III of Milwaukee.

8. Smollett, *The History of England,* Vol. III, pp. 94–95. Although he omits to say so in his history, Smollett was a ship's surgeon with Vernon's fleet in 1741–1742, leaving little doubt that his comments were soaked in personal bias and animosity.

9. Vernon got his nickname for his perennially wearing a grogram cloak, grogram being a thick fabric made from a blend of silk and hair. The daily ration known thereafter as grog continued to be dispensed in the Royal Navy until 1994.

10. Though not represented in the Collection, there are a few jugs and mugs recalling Frederick, Duke of York's victory at Valenciennes in 1793. However, their scarcity speaks to their limited and short-lived popularity.

11. Chapter VII, p. 157.

12. The letter was addressed to George Jackson Esq., and sent regards to his "amiable Lady." Jackson was an official at the Admiralty whom Rodney believed to be supportive and a useful sounding board for his complaints against his superiors.

13. It was on Brimstone Hill that Audrey and I very nearly ended our careers. The roadway down from the fortress zigzags back and forth to reduce the gradient, but still descends abruptly with an escarpment at one side and a 600-foot dropoff at the other. Seated in a ramshackle taxi that proved to have lost its brake fluid, we sped ever faster down the slope toward a precipitous drop as the road turned.

Fortunately, our terrified driver had the presence of mind to steer up amid a scree of rocks and plowed into the back of a car parked just before the turn. Had there been no stationary vehicle, the Noël Hume Ceramics Collection would have stayed significantly smaller than it has since become.

14. Spinney, *Rodney,* pp. 419–420.

15. Hood was granted an Irish peerage, a subtle distinction being drawn between it and an English baronage.

16. Although William Bell, the founder of the factory, was long since dead, wasters from the Pomona site include white trimmed red wares at their biscuit stage.

17. Pratt ware is another of those names that serve their purpose without being accurate. The Pratt Family potters were in business in Staffordshire between about 1780 until the mid-nineteenth century, but molded figures and jugs made between about 1782 and 1815 were produced by as many as twenty different factories. The Rodney statuette has sentimental value, as it was the last gift from my father before his untimely death.

18. The ledgers and account books that Rodney seized from the English merchants on St. Eustatius and that were the proof of their complicity in trading with the American enemy mysteriously disappeared after Rodney passed them to the Admiralty. They were never found, and without their evidence he had no case.

19. Lewis and Lewis, *Pratt Ware,* pp. 14 and 144.

20. Sotheby Parke Bernet catalog for its sale of English pottery on May 7, 1974, p. 9, Lot 59.

21. Godden, *An Illustrated Encyclopaedia,* pp. 266–267 and Figs. 468 and 469, of which the former is in the British Museum and the latter in the Victoria and Albert Museum.

22. Press-molded but overglaze-decorated reproductions were made early in the twentieth century and advertised as such. However, I have seen one fake that was made by the slip-casting method; it thus behooves the novice collector to carefully examine the interior of any proffered "bargain."

23. Lewis and Lewis, *op. cit.,* p. 51.

24. The next naval triumph was Admiral Lord Duncan's defeat of the Dutch at the Battle of Camperdown on October 11, 1797. Although mugs and jugs in copperplate-printed creamware recall that victory, they are not represented in the Collection.

25. Lewis and Lewis, *op. cit.,* p. 67.

26. See note 29 to chapter x.

27. David Howarth, *Trafalgar, The Nelson Touch,* p. 239.

28. Arthur Wellesley, First Duke of Wellington (1769–1852). In 1809, following the Battle of Talavera, he was made Baron Douro of Wellesley and Viscount Wellington of Talavera.

29. Apsley House at Hyde Park Corner is now the Wellington Museum.

30. There is in the Collection a much later brown stoneware gin flask that has a profile of Dante (1265–1321) on one side and Napoleon (1769–1821) on the other. Although the connection escapes me, there is little doubt that the flask dates from the 1840s and demonstrates that not all Napoleons on pottery date before 1821. A more naturalistic Wellington face jug and a less generously rendered Napoleon are illustrated by Derek Askey in his *Stoneware Bottles,* pp. 132 and 169.

31. May and May, *Commemorative Pottery, 1780–1900,* p. 43. The Collection's Caroline jug was bought from John May, and is illustrated in his book on p. 40.

32. Quoted in *ibid.,* p. 110.

33. Another victim of the Caroline affair was circus strong man turned archaeologist Giovanni Belzoni, who having opened an exhibition of Egyptian antiquities in Piccadilly found himself pursued up Bond Street by an enraged mob that mistook him for Bergami.

CHAPTER XIII. CLAY, COOKWORTHY, AND TARGETING ANN TARGET

1. Jewitt, *The History of Ceramic Art in Great Britain,* Vol. II, p. 304.

2. Maurice Thursfield had business in the United States and reportedly died here.

3. Illustrated by Jonathan Horne as No. 309 in Part IX of his booklet series titled *Catalogue of Early English Pottery,* n.d.

4. In line with the revisionism fostered by ceramic historians in the late twentieth century, many favor dropping the name Jackfield in favor of "Staffordshire blackware" and the like. But as there is no certainty that all these distinctive vessels were made in that county rather than, say, Shropshire or Derbyshire, I see no advantage in abandoning one misnomer in favor of another.

5. Figure IX.53.

6. The Chipstone Foundation owns a fine "Littler's blue" coffeepot enriched with floral reserves and dates in the period ca. 1755–1765, No. 1983.6.

7. A Littler's blue teapot fragment found behind Wetherburn's Tavern in Williamsburg was made in a cream-colored earthenware and not from salt-glazed stoneware. This may have been a Whieldon product ca. 1750. The late Arnold Mountford in his book *The Illustrated Guide to Staffordshire Salt-Glazed Stoneware* (pp. 51–53) insisted that Aaron Wedgwood had as much to do with the invention of blued white salt glaze as did William Littler, and therefore the ware should be called Littler-Wedgwood blue. This seemed unnecessarily clumsy, and Audrey and I declined to subscribe to it.

8. Shaw, *History of the Staffordshire Potteries,* p. 176.

9. Independently, more scientific experiments conducted by the British Ceramic Research Association of Stoke-on-Trent came to the same conclusion (Mountford, *op. cit.,* p. 52). Like so many other *fin de siècle* restrictions on what one could not use, salting kilns was no longer allowed; nor, of course, was lead glazing.

10. Some factories, notably the Dicker Pottery, continued into the present century, and as the stamped and dated wares are highly collectable, fakes are relatively common (Brears, *The Collector's Book of English Country Pottery,* pp. 70–71).

11. The "bad times" message to be read into this inscription is reminiscent of that on the creamware "frog" tankard previously discussed (Fig. IX.57). Another Sussex humidor is in the Glaisher Collection in the Fitzwilliam Museum at Cambridge, this one dated 1812 and made for s. KEMLEY (Rackham, *Catalogue of the Glaisher Collection,* Vol. I, p. 53, No. 342).

12. Tarring (now West Tarring) lies nine miles from Arundel near the seaside town of Worthing.

13. The small Sussex town of Battle lies adjacent to the site of the 1066 Battle of Hastings, which was lost by England's Harold and won by William of Normandy, whose wife, Matilda, was my maternal ancestor on my father's side.

14. Rackham, *op. cit.,* Vol. I, p. 54, Nos. 352 and 353. They are not illustrated, and I have seen neither of them.

15. Brears, *op. cit.,* pp. 63–65. There is in the Museum of London, however, an allegedly seventeenth-century money box that was cited in the Guildhall Museum's *Catalogue of the Collection of London Antiquities in the Guildhall Museum* (1908) as "money box, in form of a Sussex pig, reddish glaze, with yellow patches; imperfect, XVII Cent.; perhaps made at Rye" (p. 206, No. 557). The Guildhall Museum's collections have since been absorbed into those of the Museum of London.

16. Coleman-Smith and Pearson, *Excavations in the Donyatt Potteries,* p. 274, Fig. 143, No. 22/12.

17. Chipstone Foundation Collection No. 1994.10.

18. Figure X.19 *b.*

19. *The New-York Gazette,* January 31, 1763.

20. *The New-York Gazette or the Weekly Post-Boy,* November 20, 1760.

21. *The New-York Journal or the General Advertiser,* July 9, 1767. The foregoing citations are from Gottesmann, *The Arts and Crafts in New York, 1726–1776.*

22. *Imari* is a term more properly reserved for polychrome-decorated Japanese porcelain made at Arita in the province of Hizan, but is more broadly used to identify Chinese wares first decorated in underglaze blue, with the designs then completed in red and highlighted with gold.

23. Sold by Nagel Auctions of Frankfurt, Germany, November 17–25, 2000, the *Tek Sing* collection was first published in a richly illustrated guide sponsored by the auction house, along with a thousand-page catalog of very little residual value.

24. Christie's Amsterdam sale of the Hatcher collection recovered from an unidentified Asian vessel, Wednesday, March 14, 1984, Lot 352. In a related lot (353) the cataloger identified the shrimp as a lobster, albeit one without claws.

25. Figure XI.4.

26. Jörg, *The Geldermalsen,* p. 51.

27. Christie's Amsterdam sale catalog of the *Geldermalsen's Cargo,* April 19, 1986, Lot 5626; also Jörg, *op. cit.*

28. The amount of English porcelain in use in eighteenth-century Williamsburg was far smaller than the quantities of Chinese wares, a few of which had been reaching the colony as early as 1620.

29. Sandon, *The Watney Collection,* Part I, p. 167, No. 341.

30. Jewitt, *op. cit.,* Vol. I, Pl. III, facing p. 270. It is possible, of course, that he is being berated by his wife, an interruption guaranteed to leave one's line wiggly.

31. Dating for the Caughley (fat fish) saucer design is suggested by a cabbage-leaf molded pitcher inscribed "Success To Trade 1793" (Godden, *British Pottery and Porcelain,* frontis.). Thomas Turner, who learned his craft at the Worcester porcelain factory, took over the Caughley works in Shropshire in 1772 and ran it until 1799. The Worcester factory began production in 1751, with physician Dr. John Wall a major player until his death in 1776. His apothecary partner, William Davis, continued the business until 1783, when he too died. The factory was then purchased by the Flight family, which remained at the helm until it closed in 1840.

32. Both date ca. 1780–1790.

33. A workman's mark on the base enabled porcelain expert Roderick Jellicoe to provide very tight dating: 1758–1760.

34. In the first years of the twentieth century, American collectors had described Chinese export porcelain as "Oriental Lowestoft" in the mistaken belief that the small factory opened at Lowestoft in Suffolk in 1757 made hard-paste porcelain—which it never did.

35. The bone of choice was the shin and knuckle of oxen, which was calcined in the same kind of kiln used to begin the processing of flint. Flint was loaded between layers of coal, whereas bone was separated by billets of wood that burned with less contamination than did coal. On reaching a temperature of 1,100°C, bone burned on its own (see Copeland, *A Short History of Pottery Raw Materials*, p. 15).

36. The Spode works was founded in 1770 by Josiah Spode I (1733–1797), leaving the business to his son Josiah II (1754–1827), with whose name improved bone china is always associated. However, like so many ceramic innovations, several other factories were making experiments along the same lines, as Stoke-on-Trent was a town where nothing remained secret very long. Josiah II was given a royal warrant by the Prince of Wales (later George IV) in 1806. After Josiah II's death in 1827, his son, another Josiah, ran it until his death two years later. In 1833 the factory was taken over by Spode's manager, William T. Copeland, who took into partnership Thomas Garrett, who had previously been a Spode salesman, and continued thus until 1847.

37. The mug's high-quality relief decoration was a technique most often associated with another Staffordshire potter, John Turner of Lane End, who used it with great effect on his blue jasper and black basalt wares. In 1784 John Turner (1738–1787) had preceded Spode II in being made Potter to the Prince of Wales.

38. William Duesbury (1725–1786) was an ancestor of today's Wall Street's merger *maesters*. Beginning as an independent porcelain decorator in London in 1751, he watched the decline of companies with the avidity of Uriah Heep, buying controlling interests in each, operating them for a while, and then shutting them down. He had his hand on the helm of the Derby Porcelain Works by 1756, Longton Hall about four years later, Bow in 1763, and Chelsea in 1770.

39. Stratford-le-Bow (now Stratford) was an early industrial area in Essex northeast of London. The Bow porcelain factory was located in the High Street adjacent to Bow bridge. In the year 1110, William I's Queen Matilda (my ancestor) is credited with ordering the bridge built and constructing a causeway that became the High Street.

40. Quoted by Jewitt, *op. cit.,* Vol. 1, p. 201.

41. Apart from their place in ceramic history as co-owners of the Bow Porcelain Factory, in 1750 Frye and Heylen had the added distinction of being the victims of a very modern-sounding crime. They were recipients of anonymous letters threatening to burn their place down if they did not take fifty pounds to a specified place at a given time. After the writer was caught and locked up in Newgate Prison, a second letter threatened to "put to Death the said Frye's Watchmen and other People" (quoted in the English Ceramic Circle *Transactions,* Vol. 11, Part 3 [1983], pp. 187–188).

42. Jewitt, *op. cit.,* Vol. 1, p. 112.

43. The man was Andrew Duché, then a resident of South Carolina, who subsequently moved to Philadelphia and there set up a Westerwald-style stoneware manufactury. Among shards recovered from the site was part of a chamber pot with the initials AD in a cartouche pressed against the base of the handle (Webster, *Decorated Stoneware Pottery of North America,* p. 31, Pl. 5).

44. Jewitt, *op. cit.,* pp. 320–321; a letter to surgeon Richard Hingston of Penryn in Cornwall, from Plymouth, May 5, 1745.

45. Graham Hood titled his book *Bonnin and Morris of Philadelphia: The First American Porcelain Factory, 1770–1772.*

46. *Boston Evening Post,* November 11, 1754; cited by Hood, *op. cit.,* p. 69, fn. 8.

47. Jewitt, *op. cit.,* Vol. I, p. 322.

48. *The Art Journal,* 1869, quoted by Jewitt, *op. cit.,* Vol. I, p. 203.

49. The appellation *high quality* is about as definitive as the much-used *affordable.* In this context I use it as it relates to finds from American archaeological sites of the same period.

50. In archaeology it takes but a single shard to provide a *terminus post quem.* Had this pearlware fragment not been recovered, we would have put the group ten years earlier; this demonstrates the fragility of much archaeological evidence. Small wonder is it, therefore, that traditional historians treat archaeological "evidence" with understandable caution.

CHAPTER XIV. BEYOND THE GAS LAMPS' GLARE

1. Quoted in Von Eckardt et al., *Oscar Wilde's London,* p. 154.

2. Of those on the outer row, the first two on the left are ink bottles, one impressed BOURNE, DENBY, the second marked J. BOURNE & SON (after 1841) and made for T & J ARNOLD, LONDON, ENGLAND. The third is an unmarked blacking bottle, and the fourth probably for stout. Continuing down the right side, (*e*) was for ginger beer and marked R. WHITE and REGISTERED TRADE MARK under St. George and the Dragon; (*f*) was probably for stout and stamped J. BOURNE & SON; while the contents of (*g*) are unknown. In the center in front of (*d*) is a small bottle of unknown purpose but stamped HOLLIS & SON, LONDON. The rest are desk-top ink bottles (listed as dwarf inks in the 1873 catalog of Messrs. Doulton & Watts of Lambeth) in various shapes and sizes, none of them marked. The deposition date for all would appear to be around 1870–1880.

3. Quoted by Simon, *Drink,* p. 138, from *The Quack Vintners.*

4. Joseph Blake is reported to have gone to the gallows "disguised in liquor and to reel and faulter in his speech at Tyburn," and it is safe to assume that the liquor was gin (Mountague, *The Old Bailey Chronicle,* London: R. Randall, 1788, Vol. I, pp. 328 and 331).

5. This flask is illustrated by Derek Askey in *Stoneware Bottles,* p. 54; the photograph is incorrectly attributed to Colonial Williamsburg. See also Noël Hume, "Stoneware Gin Flasks," p. 305, Fig. 2.

6. George IV had a maximum capacity of 12 fluid ounces.

7. Godden, *Encyclopaedia of British Pottery and Porcelain Marks,* p. 473.

8. Derek Askey in his catalog of the Reform-related flasks (*op. cit.,* p. 70) lists a Lord Grey bottle 11.2 inches in height, but none of 14.5 inches. The other possible identification of the figure would be as Lord John Russell, another of the Reform proponents, but Askey shows no Russell flask taller than 7.5 inches.

9. *The Compact Edition of the Dictionary of National Biography,* London: Oxford University Press (1975), Vol. I, p. 737.

10. Larwood, *English Inn Signs,* p. 26.

11. Hildyard, *Browne Muggs,* p. 51, No. 99. The telltale flask is in the Museum of London's collection, No. A20865.

12. Askey, *op. cit.,* p. 190. Another example of J. Wetherall's Queen Elizabeth flasks is in the collection of the Brighton Art Gallery and Museum. See Hildyard, *op. cit.,* p. 53, No. 105.

13. Anonymous, *The Universal British Directory,* Vol. II, p. 434.

14. Lincoln Hallinan, *British Commemoratives,* pp. 21–22, Pl. 23.

15. A distortion reminiscent of the Chipstone Foundation's delftware Queen Anne dish, Fig. XII.2.

16. The rush to exploit the accession fervor resulted in several false assumptions, among them a rare Bourne of Denby flask with the name ALEXANDRINA VICTORIA, presumably because no one at the time knew how the young Princess "Drina" would style herself.

17. Patrick Synge-Hutchinson, "Pottery and Porcelain, The Georgian Period," *The Connoisseur's Complete Period Guides,* New York: Bonanza Books, 1968, pp. 863–864. For what little it may be worth, I recall an unpleasant boyhood experience of sitting round a scout campfire singing stupid songs, one of which included the lines "Ha, ha, ha, he, he, he, little brown jug don't I love thee!" There was, of course, much more ho ho hoing! in the same vein, which, mercifully, I forget.

18. Mankowitz and Haggar, *The Concise Encyclopedia of English Pottery and Porcelain,* p. 221.

19. Bowles was so listed in the *London Directory* for 1793.

20. The most obvious parallel is the slip-dipping of the hats. But more significant, yet least visible, is the single waistcoat button below the right hand of each figure. The laborer's hat was the mid-nineteenth-century forerunner of the later Victorian hunter's hard hat and subsequently the English all-classes' twentieth-century bowler. Evidence that the modeling of this figure was better than the molded specimen may suggest is provided by the minute pairs of lace holes in his shoes. Thus, the difference between Master and Man is between shoes that buckled and those that laced.

21. B. Garnham of Lewes is almost certainly Benjamin Garnham, whose name (but not his address) occurs on another stoneware bottle described by Askey as "old woman in hooded cloak, holding bottle" (*op. cit.,* p. 76, No. R221). One wonders why Mr. Garnham invested in two varieties of stone spirit bottles in entirely different designs.

22. The Cliffe Bonfire Society is the largest of six such Lewes societies and was founded in 1852, and it is likely that B. Garnham was a member. I had the honor of being accepted into the society in 1997 as member No. 1444.

23. Thomas Dartmouth Rice (1806–1860) is reputed to have based Jim Crow on an old black man whom he saw singing and doing a shuffling dance while shoeing a horse (Hartnoll, *The Oxford Companion to the Theatre,* pp. 667–668). The Jim Crow name had its place in the American lexicon before the Civil War. Under the heading "Illustrations of Ornithology," *Harper's New Monthly Magazine* Vol. LXIVI, No. LXVIII, January 1856, p. 286, printed engravings of "Master Jim Crow" and his sister "Miss Dinah Crow."

24. Illustrated by Hildyard, *op. cit.,* p. 53, No. 107.

25. The recipient of the letter is not identified, but he evidently was a person whose support was of value to the project. Brunel told him that he had been unable to find a copy of the "Pamphlets describing the plan we are following," but he was prepared to lend his own.

26. Drew, *Glimpses and Gatherings,* pp. 247–248. Drew was then Commissioner of the State of Maine.

27. When I was growing up in the 1930s a scolding was still known as a "curtain lecture."

28. Ashton, *Humour, Wit, and Satire,* p. 193 and p. 443, Note 72.

29. Mayhew, *Selections from London Labour,* p. 54.

30. When Punch was first portrayed, the actor made or was supplied with a costume whose clumsiness visually contrasted with the cap and bells of the agile court jester. Thus, when "Punches youngest Son [sic]" was portrayed in a late-eighteenth-century woodcut, he, too, wore the same costume. But Judy, on the other hand, came into the story, not as a grotesque and unreal figure, but rather as a person all too familiar to audiences as a nagging wife. Requiring no special or bizarre costume, she also needed no hump.

31. A satirical election poster drawn by Hogarth in his 1757 *Canvassing for Voters* promotes PUNCH CANDIDATE FOR GUZZLEDOWN and shows what appears to be a humpbacked hag wearing a witch's hat to the left of the scene, and she, presumably, represents his avaricious wife.

32. Mother Shipton's "prophecies" were first published in 1641, edited and republished in 1791, and again in 1869. In spite of much printed "information" about her life, she is widely considered to have been a fictitious character. Nevertheless, in the seventeenth century her prophecies were taken seriously. Samuel Pepys wrote in his diary (October 20, 1666) that when Prince Rupert heard of the Great Fire of London, all he said "was that now Shipton's prophecy was out." See also, Askey, *op. cit.,* p. 64.

33. Noël Hume, "Stoneware Gin Flasks," p. 313.

34. In a listing of 27 different "Toby Jug" figure variants, Mankowitz and Haggar included one named "The Gin Woman" (*op. cit.,* p. 221). I have not seen this version, but it is possible that there is a connection between her and the humpbacked figures.

35. May and May in *Commemorative Pottery, 1780–1900,* p. 11, Fig. 19, note that "There is a gin flask of a lady holding a bird which is often, and probably correctly, ascribed to Jenny Lind."

36. Askey, *op. cit.,* p. 76.

37. She appeared in *Robert le Diable* at the His Majesty's Theatre in London and toured in the United States under the auspices of P. T. Barnum from 1850 to 1852.

38. Although the weight of evidence points to the retail market being in London and in direct competition with Lambeth and, to a lesser extent, Fulham.

39. This example is the Collection's only ink bottle not found on the marshes. Instead, it was purchased in 1998 in a Williamsburg flea market.

40. The Collection includes examples sold in London and the southeast, such as the Boro (Southwark), Whitechapel Road, Shoreditch, Tottenham Court Road, Bethnal Green, and the somewhat better Chelsea, and further afield in Sussex at Lewes and Brighton.

41. Stephen Green's Imperial Potteries in Lambeth opened around 1820 and closed in 1858, thereby providing a terminal date for all pieces so marked.

42. Another well-colored percussion-lock pistol impressed "Fulham Pottery" is illustrated in Robin Hildyard's *Browne Muggs,* p. 35, No. 37, there cross-referenced to yet another that had been auctioned at Sotheby's West Sussex establishment in 1983. That pistol's importance rests in its being the only known dated specimen. It is impressed "W Walker Windsor Berkshire 1842," further testifying to the fact that not all were made for the landlords of slum gin shops.

43. Another powder-flask bottle, almost certainly a product of the same master block maker, is impressed T. SMITH. Thomas Smith operated a stoneware pottery at 72, Prince's Street, Lambeth, between 1836 and 1847. See Oswald et al., *English Brown Stoneware,* p. 84, and Hildyard, *op. cit.,* p. 63, No. 145.

44. Doré and Jerrold, *London, a Pilgrimage.*

45. *Ibid.,* p. 138.

46. *Ibid.,* p. 142.

47. Charles Dickens, *Sketches by Boz,* 1835, cited by Massingham and Massingham, *The London Anthology,* p. 183.

48. Massingham, *op. cit.,* p. 182, quoting Walter Besant, *Fifty Years Ago,* 1888.

49. Green, *John Dwight's Fulham Pottery,* pp. 365–368.

50. *Ibid.,* p. 159.

51. *Ibid.,* pp. 337f. citing Hertfordshire County Records D/EAS 855; DS188, Charles Bailey, 1864.

52. Oswald et al., *op. cit.,* p. 167, Fig. 135.

53. This evolution of attribution occurred at a time when several successive experts came to Williamsburg and independently reviewed our excavated English porcelain, requiring an increasingly exasperated Audrey to relabel the collection with each succeeding opinion (Leon, "Yellow-Glazed English Earthenware," p. 35 and Pl. 40 d and e).

54. Without a French connection there would have been no collection and no book. My several times great grandmother was Princess Marie de Bourbon, who married into the Noël family of Caen. Her husband was executed on the guillotine in 1793, but aided by her coachman she escaped hidden under a wagon load of straw, settled on the island of Guernsey, and (as any reader of historical romance fiction would expect) there married the coachman.

55. Jewitt, *The History of Ceramic Art,* Vol. ii, p. 351.

CHAPTER XV. IN REMEMBRANCE, STAFFORDSHIRE STYLE

1. Charles Austin died in 1996.

2. After recording, the tape was accepted into the archives of the Imperial War Museum in London.

3. The Goss name and its goshawk mark continued to be used until the beginning of World War ii, although the business had left the Goss family hands in 1931.

4. Additional inscription and factory data on this chapter's Crested China are given in the measurements appendix.

5. Jarvis (ed.), *The Goss Record,* 1914. Reprinted by Milestone Publications, Horndean, U.K., 1973.

6. Samuel de Champlain founded the city of Quebec in 1608. I have found no evidence of his doing anything in Florida in that year, nor have I found any comparable badge and crest usage in Canada. Champlain's own flag had a blue field and the crown is French in character. Beyond that, this deponent sayeth not.

7. Jarvis (ed.), *op. cit.,* for 1914 lists E. Marshall as the proprietor of 31 High Street, Rochester, indicating that the graybeard was made prior to that date.

8. Another Goss *hidroceramo* in the Collection is described as an "ancient carafe" and as having been dredged up from the treacherous Goodwin Sands that stretch along the east Kentish coast, known since medieval times as the "shippe swalower."

9. In 1735, Thomas Holdsworth was Governor of Dartmouth Castle. The bottle was reported missing in 1922, and my own inquiries have confirmed that it has never been recovered. When Adolphus Goss visited the Exeter Museum, he was probably on his way to or from his Dartmouth agent, E. Lovel & Sons, The Quay.

While this book was already in press Dutch bottle collector Willy Van den Bossche published his *Antique Glass Bottles: Their History and Evolution (1500–1850)* and in Pl. 23 illustrated a silver-mounted bottle with the same seal and of similar shape. Now in his possession, it was previously in the collection of Florida collector Tom Floyd.

10. Adolphus's wife Nellie died in 1919, having never recovered from grief at the loss of her sons.

11. This Grafton figure is decorated with the arms of Kingstown, a location that may or may not be a village in Cumberland, albeit an unlikely venue for a munitions factory. Printed on the base is the name of the shopkeeper who invested in these figures: DAVEY STEPHENS / KINGSTOWN.

12. Proof of these models being playthings as well as mantel-shelf ornaments is provided by the Collection's miniature *Lusitania* having lost the gilding from both sides of its funnels as the result of being pushed about by a child's hand.

13. Andrew Rose, *The Collector's Guide to Toy Soldiers,* London: Salamander Books, 1997, p. 10.

14. Known as the Battle of Flers-Courcelette, the Mark I tanks were used there only as infantry support.

15. Victoria China was a product of James Reeves's Victoria Works of Fenton in Staffordshire, opening in 1890 and closing in 1948.

16. *John Bull* was a British weekly tabloid.

17. Bairnsfather was with his regiment in the Ypres Salient on April 22, 1915, when he was deafened by an exploding shell and sent home to England, with his nerves shot and his hearing impaired (Holt and Holt, *In Search of the Better 'Ole,* p. 38).

18. Willow Art was founded in 1905 by Messrs. Hewett and Leadbeater of Longton, and continued under several managements until 1930 when the poverty of the Great Depression ensured that no one had either the inclination or the money to spend on heraldic souvenirs.

19. American lives lost aboard the *Lusitania* have been cited as 124 or 128.

20. Corona Pottery was an offshoot of the Bridge Works at Stoke-on-Trent, begun by Sampson Hancock in 1858, which in the first years of the twentieth century manufactured "Art Trinket Wares." The firm joined the long list of companies unable to survive the 1930s Depression and was declared bankrupt in 1937.

21. There being no record of porcelain models commemorating ships lost in conventional warfare, the inference must be that the *Lusitania*s and *Anglia*s were produced as anti-German propaganda.

22. *Jane's Fighting Ships of World War I* was originally published as Jane's *All The World's Ships* in 1919. The reprint was published in 1990 by Studio Editions Ltd. of London.

23. The American losses were not combat related. In 1917 one (the F1) was rammed by another American sub (F3) in American waters, and the second foundered in Long Island Sound eight months after the war ended.

24. The Collection also includes the snub-bowed E4, which made headlines in August 1914 after rescuing survivors from a sunk British cruiser. The E5 model is inscribed MODEL OF NEW SUBMARINE and became a registered shape in December 1916, nine months after she was lost. Southall, *Take Me Back to Dear Old Blighty,* p. 92). Botolph China was a small Fenton Company in business from 1898 to 1926, one not renowned for the quality of its modeling (Andrews, *Crested China,* pp. 71–72).

25. Jane's *Fighting Ships of World War I,* p. 36.

26. Jarvis (ed.), *op. cit.,* War Edition, p. 4.

27. We tend to think of "Zeppelin" as a German name solely used for their lighter-than-air sausages such as the ill-fated *Hindenburg*. Instead, it was the name of the factory that produced both balloons and aircraft, among them a monster five-engine "giant" bomber.

28. Additional, not illustrated examples in the Collection include Antwerp, Boulogne, Bruges, Calais, Combles, Louvain, Malines, and Namur. One of the more significant battles of the war was the tank-led offensive at Cambrai, but I have found no Savoy pot to commemorate that somewhat iffy victory. In the Collection, therefore, it falls to a Goss product printed on the bottom with MODEL OF / ANCIENT COOKING POT / FOUND AT RAYLEIGH CASTLE ESSEX to stand in for that French town. The base of the pot has another inscription: IMPORTÉ D'ANGLETERRE. There being no battle inscription on the back, it seems safe to accept this as a relic of Adolphus Goss's prewar effort to expand his market into France.

29. A more reliable source, *AA Treasures of Britain* (1976 ed.), gives the Maids of Biddenden's life-span dates as 1500–1534. They are recalled by an annual distribution of food to the poor on Easter Day. One wonders how the beneficiaries of this largesse managed the rest of the year.

CHAPTER XVI. A MUG'S GAME?

1. A fine line exists between collecting ceramics as an aspect of the history of history and the study of stylistic and technical trends in pottery production. The Collection's 1937 coronation mugs made for Edward VIII and George VI were made only months apart and yet are entirely different in virtually every respect, yet the latter example is distinctively characteristic of its time. If they do nothing else, they warn us that design trends are difficult to date with any degree of accuracy.

2. Bradford, *The Reluctant King*, p. 284.

3. John Maddock opened his business as an Ironstone and "semi-porcelain" manufacturer in 1842, took his son into partnership in 1855, and thereafter continued under that combined name.

4. The Royal warrant was signed by the Queen on June 13, but the investiture did not take place until five months later—thereby making June 14 even more enigmatic.

Bibliography

Anon., Catalog of the *Wine Trade Loan Exhibition of Drinking Vessels*, London: Vintners' Hall, 1933.

——, *Dictionary of the Vulgar Tongue*, 2nd ed., London: C. Chappel, 1811, reprinted, London: Bibliophile Books, 1980.

——, *The General Shop Book: or, The Tradesman's Universal Directory*, London: C. Hitch and L. Hawes, 1753.

——, *Ninth Report of the Royal Commission on Historical Manuscripts, Part II, Appendix & Index,* London: H. M. Stationery Office, 1884, pp. 32–35, No. 130, Jan. 7, 1673/4, Draft of an Act for encouraging the manufactures of England.

——, *The Old Bailey Chronicle*, London: R. Randall, 1788.

——, *The Oxford Dictionary of Quotations*, 2nd ed., Oxford: Oxford University Press, 1955.

——, *The Story of the Willow Pattern Plate*, London: John Baker Publishers, 1970.

——, *The Universal British Directory of Trade, Commerce, and Manufacture*, 4 vols., London: 1793.

Adams, Elizabeth, "Ceramic Insurances in the Sun Company Archives, 1766–1774," English Ceramic Circle *Transactions*, Vol. 10, Pt. 1 (1976), pp. 1–38.

Andrews, Sandy E., *Crested China,* Horndean, U.K.: Milestone Publications, 1980.

Archer, Gabriel, "A relayton of the Discovery of our River . . . &c.," published in Edward Arber's edition of the *Travels and Works of Captain John Smith*, Edinburgh: John Grant, 1910, Vol. 1, pp. xl–lv.

Archer, Michael, *Delftware: The Tin-Glazed Earthenware of the British Isles*, London: British Museum, The Stationery Office, 1997.

——, *English Delftware*, Exhibition Catalog, Amsterdam: Rijksmuseum, n.d.

Ashton, John, *Humour, Wit, & Satire of the Seventeenth Century,* London: Chatto and Windus, 1883.

Askey, Derek, *Stoneware Bottles from Bellarmines to Ginger Beer, 1500–1949,* Brighton, U.K.: Bowman Graphics, 1981.

Austin, John C., *British Delft at Williamsburg*, Williamsburg, Va.: Colonial Williamsburg Foundation, 1994.

Bass, George F. (ed.), *A History of Seafaring Based on Underwater Archaeology*, New York: Walker and Company, 1972.

Barton, Kenneth J., "The Buckley Potteries," *Flintshire Historical Journal*, Vol. 16 (1956), pp. 1–23.

Beckman, Bernhard, Gisela von Bock, et al., *Volkskunst im Rheinland, Katalog*, Düsseldorf: Rheinischen Freilichtmuseum in Kommern, 1968.

Bergesen, Victoria, *Bergesen's Price Guide to British Ceramics*, London: Barrie & Jenkins, 1992.

Boulton, William B. *The Amusements of Old London*, New York: Benjamin Blom, 1969, reprint of the 1901 ed.

Bradford, Sarah, *The Reluctant King: The Life & Reign of George VI, 1895–1952*, New York: St. Martin's Press, 1989.

Brain, Jeffrey P., *Tunica Treasure*, Papers of the Peabody Museum of Archaeology and Ethnology, Vol. 71, Cambridge, Mass.: Harvard University, 1979.

Brand, John, *Observations on the Popular Antiquities of Great Britain*, 3 vols., London: Henry G. Bohn, 1849.

Brears, Peter, *The Collector's Book of English Country Pottery*, Newton Abbot, U.K.: David & Charles, 1974.

Bridges, D. W., "Sadler Tiles in Colonial America," English Ceramic Circle *Transactions*, Vol. 10, Pt. 3 (1978), pp. 174–183.

Britton, Frank, *London Delftware*, London: Jonathan Horne, 1986.

——, "The Pickleherring Potteries: An Inventory," *Post-Medieval Archaeology*, Vol. 24, (1990), pp. 61–92.

Brooks, Catherine M., *Medieval and Later Pottery from Aldwark and Other Sites*, York: York Archaeological Trust, 1987.

Brown, Cynthia Gaskell (ed.), *Plymouth Excavations: Castle Street, The Pottery*, Plymouth: Plymouth City Museum and Art Gallery, 1979.

Brown, Duncan H., "Iberian Pottery Excavated in Southampton," *Spanish Medieval*

Ceramics in Spain and the British Isles, BAR International Series 610 (1995), p. 321.

Bushe-Fox, J. P., *Fourth Report on the Excavations of the Roman Fort at Richborough, Kent,* Oxford: Oxford University Press on behalf of the Society of Antiquaries of London, 1949.

Calver, William Lewis, and Reginald Pelham Bolton, *History Written with Pick and Shovel,* New York: New-York Historical Society, 1950.

Cartwright, Frederick F., *Disease in History,* New York: Dorset Press, 1972.

Celoria, Francis (a.k.a. P. Amis), "Some Domestic Vessels of Southern Britain: A Social and Technical Analysis," *Journal of Ceramic History,* No. 2 (Stafford, U.K., 1968), pp. 1–35.

Chapelle, Howard L., *The History of the American Sailing Navy,* New York: Bonanza Books, 1949.

Charleston, Robert J., *Roman Pottery,* London: Faber and Faber, 1955.

——, (ed.), *World Ceramics: An Illustrated History,* New York: Crescent Books, 1968.

Christie's catalogues, *Fine and Important Late Ming and Transitional Porcelain,* Amsterdam, March 14, 1984.

——, *The Nanking Cargo: Chinese Export Porcelain and Gold,* Amsterdam, April 28, 1986.

Church, Arthur, *English Earthenware,* London: H. M. Stationery Office, 1905.

Coleman-Smith, R., and T. Pearson, *Excavations in the Donyatt Potteries,* Chichester, U.K.: Phillimore & Co., 1988.

Copeland, Robert, *A Short History of Pottery Raw Materials and the Cheddleton Flint Mill,* Leek, Staffs., U.K.: Cheddleton Flint Mill Industrial Heritage Trust, 1972.

Cotter, J. P., "The Mystery of the Hessian Wares: Post-Medieval Triangular Crucibles," in *Everyday and Exotic Pottery from Europe, c. 650–1900,* Oxford: Oxbow Books, 1992.

Cotter, John L., *Archaeological Excavations at Jamestown,* Washington, D.C.: Department of the Interior, 1958.

Cotton, Sir Evan, *East Indiamen: The East India Company's Maritime Service,* London: Batchworth Press, 1949.

Cox, Alwyn, and Angela Cox, "Recent Excavations at the Swinton Pottery: The Leeds Connection, 1785–1806," English Ceramic Circle *Transactions,* Vol. 11, Pt. 2 (1981), pp. 50–69.

Coysh, A. W., and R. K. Henrywood, *The Dictionary of Blue and White Printed Pottery, 1780–1880,* Woodbridge, U.K.: Antique Collectors' Club, 1982.

Davis, John, *English Silver at Williamsburg,* Williamsburg, Va.: Colonial Williamsburg Foundation, 1976.

des Fontaines, J. K., "Underglaze Blue-Printed Earthenware with Particular Reference to Spode," English Ceramic Circle *Transactions,* Vol. 7, Pt. 2 (1969), pp. 120–143.

des Fontaines, Una, "Wedgwood Blue-Printed Wares, 1805–1843," English Ceramic Circle *Transactions,* Vol. 11, Pt. 3, (1983), pp. 212–221.

Doré, Gustav, and Blanchard Jerrold, *London, a Pilgrimage,* 1872, reprinted, New York: Dover Publications, 1970.

Downman, Edward Andrews, *Blue Dash Chargers and Other Early English Tin Enamel Circular Dishes,* London: T. Werner Laurie, 1919.

Drabble, Margaret, ed., *The Oxford Companion to English Literature,* 5th ed., Oxford: Oxford University Press, 1985.

Drew, William A., *Glimpses and Gatherings During a Voyage and Visit to London and the Great Exhibition, in the Summer of 1851,* Augusta, Me.: Homan & Manley, 1852.

Dunning, Gerald (ed.), "Anglo-Saxon Pottery: A Symposium," *Medieval Archaeology,* Vol. III (1959), pp. 1–78.

Earle, Cyril, *The Earle Collection of Early Staffordshire Pottery,* London: A. Brown and Sons, 1915.

Edwards, Rhoda, "London Potters Circa 1570–1710," *Journal of Ceramic History,* No. 6 (Stafford, U.K., 1974).

Edwards, Roy, "An Early 18th Century Waste Deposit from the Vauxhall Pottery," English Ceramic Circle *Transactions,* Vol. 12, Pt. 1 (1983), pp. 45–56.

Engelmeier, Paul, "Westerwälder Steinzeugkrüge mit dem Monogramm GR," *Keramos,* No. 44 (April 1969).

Fairclough, Graham J., *Plymouth Excavations, St. Andrews Street, 1976,* Plymouth: Plymouth Museum Archaeological Series, No. 2, 1979.

Fryer, Kevin and Andrea Selley, "Excavation of a Pit at 16 Tunsgate, Guildford, Surrey, 1991," *Post-Medieval Archaeology,* Vol. 31 (1997), pp. 139–230.

Gaimster, David, *German Stoneware, 1200–1900,* London: British Museum Press, 1997.

——, *Maiolica in the North: The Archaeology of Tin-Glazed Earthenware in North-West Europe, c. 1500–1600,* London: British Museum Occasional Papers, Number 122, 1999.

——, "Renaissance Stoneware from the Rhineland: Continuing Problems of Authentication," in M. Jones (ed.), *Why Fakes Matter: Essays on Problems of Authentication,* London: British Museum, 1992, pp. 108–115.

Gaimster, David, Richenda Goffin, and Lyn Blackmore, "The Continental Stove-Tile Fragments from St. Mary Graces, London, in Their British and European Context," *Post-Medieval Archaeology,* Vol. 24 (1990), pp. 1–49.

Gaimster, David, and Mark Redknap (eds.), *Everyday and Exotic Pottery from Europe, c. 650–1900,* Oxford: Oxbow Books, 1992.

Garner, F. H., and Michael Archer, *English Delftware,* London: Faber and Faber, 1972.

Godden, Geoffrey A., *British Pottery and Porcelain, 1780–1850,* Cranberry, N.J.: A. S. Barnes, 1963.

——, *Encyclopaedia of British Pottery and Porcelain Marks,* New York: Crown Publishers, 1964.

——, *An Illustrated Encyclopaedia of British Pottery and Porcelain,* New York: Crown Publishers, 1966.

Goggin, John M., "The Spanish Olive Jar: An Introductory Study," *Yale University Publications in Anthropology,* No. 62 (1960), pp. 3–37.

Gottesman, Rita Susswein, *The Arts and Crafts in New York, 1726–1776,* New York: New-York Historical Society, 1938.

Grabham, Oxley, *Yorkshire Potteries, Pots and Potters,* 1916, reprinted, London: S. R. Publishers, 1971.

Grant, Alison, *North Devon Pottery: The Seventeenth Century,* Exeter: University of Exeter, 1983.

Green, Chris, *John Dwight's Fulham Pottery: Excavations, 1971–79,* London: English Heritage, 1999.

Grigsby, Leslie B., *English Slip-Decorated Earthenwares at Williamsburg,* Williamsburg, Va.: Colonial Williamsburg Foundation, 1993.

Grossman, Lloyd, *London Eats Out: 500 Years of Capital Dining,* London: Philip Wilson Publishers for the Museum of London, 1999.

Guildhall Museum (Frank Lambert?), *Catalogue of the Collection of London Antiquities in the Guildhall Museum*, London: Library Committee of the Corporation of the City of London, 1908.

Guthrie, Douglas, *A History of Medicine*, London: Thomas Nelson and Sons, 1945.

Haark, B., "Van Dubbels tot van Goyen, en weer terug," *Antiek*, No. 8 (March 1967), pp. 12–13.

Hallinan, Lincoln, *British Commemoratives*, Woodridge, U.K.: Antique Collectors' Club, 1995.

Hartnoll, Phillis (ed.), *The Oxford Companion to the Theatre*, London: Oxford University Press, 1957.

Haselgrove, Dennis, and John Murray, "John Dwight's Fulham Pottery, 1672–1978: A Collection of Documentary Sources," *Journal of Ceramic History*, No. 11, Stoke-on-Trent Museum publication, 1979.

Hawkes, C. F. C., and M. R. Hull, *Camulodunum: First Report on the Excavations at Colchester, 1930–1939*, Oxford: Oxford University Press on behalf of the Society of Antiquaries of London, 1947.

Henderson, Graeme, *The Wreck of the "Elizabeth,"* Studies in Historical Archaeology, No. 1, Sydney: Australian Society for Historical Archaeology, 1973.

Henig, Martin, and Katherine Munby, "Some Tiles from the Old Cheshire Cheese, London," *Post-Medieval Archaeology*, Vol. 10 (1976), pp. 156–159.

Hildyard, Robin, *Browne Muggs: English Brown Stoneware*, London: Victoria and Albert Museum, 1985.

Hill, Draper, *Fashionable Contrasts*, London: Phaidon Press, 1966.

Hillier, Bevis, *Pottery and Porcelain, 1700–1914*, London: Weidenfeld and Nicolson, 1968.

Hillis, Maurice, and Roderick Jellicoe, *The Liverpool Porcelain of William Reid*, London: Privately published, 2000.

Hodgkin, I. E., and E. Hodgkin, *Examples of Early English Pottery Named, Dated and Inscribed*, London: Privately printed, 1891.

Holdaway, Minnie, "The Wares of Ralph Wedgwood," English Ceramic Circle *Transactions*, Vol. 12, Pt. 3, (1986), pp. 255–264.

Holme, Randle, *An Academie or Store House of Armory & Blazon*, Vol. II, 1682,

reprinted, London: Roxburghe Club, 1905.

Holmes, Martin R., "The So-called 'Bellarmine' Mask on Imported Rhenish Stoneware," *The Antiquaries Journal*, Vol. XXXI (July–October 1951), pp. 173–179.

Holt, Toni, and Valma, *In Search of the Better 'Ole, The Life, the Works and the Collectables of Bruce Bairnsfather*, Horndean, U.K.: Milestone Publications, 1985.

Honour, Hugh, *Chinoiserie: The Vision of Cathay*, London: John Murray, 1961.

Hood, Graham, *Bonnin and Morris of Philadelphia*, Chapel Hill: University of North Carolina Press, 1972.

Horne, Jonathan, *A Collection of Early English Pottery*, Parts V, IX, X, and XI, London: Jonathan Horne Ltd., March 1990 and 1991.

Howarth, David, *Trafalgar: The Nelson Touch*, New York: Atheneum, 1969.

Hughes, Bernard, and Therle Hughes, *The Collector's Encyclopaedia of English Ceramics*, London: Abbey Library, 1968.

Hurst, John G., David S. Neale, and H. J. E. van Beauningen, *Pottery Produced and Traded in North-West Europe 1350–1650*, Rotterdam Papers VI, 1986.

Jane, *Jane's Fighting Aircraft of World War I*, 1919, reprinted, New York: Military Press, Studio Editions, 1990.

——, *Jane's Fighting Ships of World War I*, originally published as *Jane's All the World's Ships*, 1919, reprinted, London: Studio Editions Ltd., 1990.

Jarvis, J. J. (ed.), *The Goss Record*, London: Evans Brothers Ltd., 1914/1916, reprinted, Horndean, U.K.: Milestone Publications, 1973.

Jennings, Sarah, with M. M. Karshrer, W. F. Milligan, and S. V. Williams, "Eighteen Centuries of Pottery From Norwich," *East Anglian Archaeology*, Report No. 13, Norwich: Norwich Survey and Norfolk Museums Service, 1981.

Jessop, Ronald (ed.), *Curiosities of British Archaeology*, Chichester, U.K.: Phillimore & Co. Ltd., 1961.

Jewitt, Llewellynn, *The History of Ceramic Art in Great Britain from Prehistoric Times Down Through Each Successive Period to the Present Day: Being a History of All the Known Ancient and Modern Pottery and Porcelain Works of the Kingdom and of Their Productions of Every Class*, 2 vols., New York: Scribner, Welford, and Armstrong, 1878.

Johnson, Nicholas, "The Dudley Hoard," *The Web of Time* (www.theweboftime.com), Vol. III, No. 2 (Fall 2000).

Jones, William M., "The Source of Ballast at a Florida Site," *Historical Archaeology*, Vol. 10 (1976), pp. 42–45.

Jörg, C. J. A., *The Geldermalsen: History and Porcelain*, Groningen: Kemper Publishers, 1986.

Kidson, F., and J. R. Kidson, *Historical Notices of the Leeds Old Pottery*, 1892, reprinted, Menston: S. R. Publishers, 1970.

Klein, Adalbert, *Rheinisches Steinseug Des 15. Bis 18. Jahrhunderts*, Darmstadt: Franz Scheekluth, n.d.

Koning, D. A. Wittop, "Mineraalwaterkruiken," *Antiek*, Vol. 10, No. 9 (April 1976), pp. 853–862.

——, "Rigabalsem," *Antiek*, Vol. 15, No. 9 (April 1981), pp. 133–134.

Larwood, Joseph, *English Inn Signs*, London: Chatto and Windus, 1951.

Le Hardy, William Le (ed.), *County of Middlesex Calendar to the Sessions Records*, New Series, Vol. III, 1615–1616, London: The Guildhall, Westminster, 1937, p. 80.

Leon, Jack, "Yellow-glazed English Earthenware," English Ceramic Circle *Transactions*, Vol. 8, Pt. 1 (1971), pp. 31–41.

Lewis, Griselda, *A Collector's History of English Pottery*, New York: Viking Press, 1969.

Lewis, John, and Grizelda Lewis, *Pratt Ware*, New York: Leo Kaplin Ltd., 1994.

Little, W. L., *Staffordshire Blue*, New York: Crown Publishers, 1969.

Mankowitz, Wolf, and Reginald Haggar, *The Concise Encyclopaedia of English Pottery and Porcelain*, New York: Frederick A. Praeger, 1968.

Mason, Frances Norton (ed.), *John Norton & Sons, Merchants of London and Virginia: Being the Papers from Their Counting House for the Years 1750–1795*, Richmond, Va.: Dietz Press, 1937.

Massingham, Hugh, and Pauline Massingham, *The London Anthology*, London: Spring Books, n.d. (ca. 1950).

Mathews, L. G., and H. J. M. Green, "Post-Medieval Pottery of the Inns of Court," *Post-Medieval Archaeology*, Vol. 3 (1969), pp. 1–17.

May, John, and Jennifer May, *Commemorative Pottery, 1780–1900*, London: William Heinemann, 1972.

May, Thomas, *The Pottery Found at Silchester*, Reading, Berks.: E. Poynder and Son, Holybrook Press on behalf of the County Borough of Reading Museum and Art Gallery, 1916.

Mayhew, Henry, *Selections from London Labour and the London Poor*, London: Spring Books, 1969.

Merrifield, Ralph, *The Archaeology of Ritual and Magic*, London: B. T. Batsford Ltd., 1987.

——, "The Use of Bellarmines as Witch-Bottles," *Guildhall Miscellany*, London: Guildhall Library No. 3, February 1954, pp. 2–15.

Meteyard, Eliza, *The Life of Josiah Wedgwood*, 2 vols., London: Hurst and Blackett, 1865–1866.

Miller, George L., "Origins of Josiah Wedgwood's 'Pearlware,'" *Northeast Historical Archaeology*, Vol. 16 (1987), pp. 85–95.

Miller, Jefferson II, *English Yellow-Glazed Earthenware*, Washington, D.C.: Smithsonian Institution Press, 1974.

Monaghan, Jason, *Upchurch and Thames-side Roman Pottery*, Oxford: British Archaeological Research Series, No. 173, 1983.

Morgan, William James (ed.), *Naval Documents of the American Revolution*, Vol. 7, Washington, D.C.: Naval History Division, Department of the Navy, 1976.

Mount, Sally, *Price Guide to 18th Century English Pottery*, Woodbridge, Suffolk: Baron Publishing for the Antique Collectors' Club, 1972.

Mountford, Arnold, *The Illustrated Guide to Staffordshire Salt-Glazed Stoneware*, New York: Praeger Publishers, 1971.

Neve, Richard, *The City and Country Purchaser's and Builder's Dictionary: Or, The Complete Builder's Guide*, London: D. Sprint et al., 1736.

Nienhaus, H., "Mineraalwaterkruiken van grès met zoutglazuur, bron- en fabrikantenmerken," *Antiek*, Vol. 15, No. 9 (April 1981), pp. 489–509.

——, "Mineraalwaterkruiken van grès met zoutglazuur en de daarop voorkomende bronmerken," *Antiek*, Vol. 14, No. 9 (April 1980), pp. 567–582.

Noël Hume, Audrey, "A Group of Artifacts Recovered from an Eighteenth-Century Well in Williamsburg," *Five Artifact Studies*, Occasional Papers in Archaeology, Williamsburg, Va.: Colonial Williamsburg Foundation, 1973, pp. 1–24.

Noël Hume, Ivor, *All the Best Rubbish*, New York: Harper and Row, 1974.

——, *Archaeology and Wetherburn's Tavern*, Colonial Williamsburg Archaeological Series, No. 3, Williamsburg, Va.: Colonial Williamsburg Foundation, 1969.

——, *Archaeology in Britain*, London: W. & G. Foyle, 1953.

——, *Digging for Carter's Grove*, Colonial Williamsburg Archaeological Series, No. 8, Williamsburg, Va.: Colonial Williamsburg Foundation, 1974.

——, *Discoveries on Walbrook, 1949–1950*, London: Guildhall Museum, 1950.

——, *Early English Delftware from London and Virginia*, Williamsburg, Va.: Colonial Williamsburg Foundation, 1977.

——, "Excavations at Rosewell in Gloucester County, Virginia, 1757–1959," *Contributions from the Museum of History and Technology*, Paper 18, Washington, D.C.: Smithsonian Institution, 1963, pp. 156–228.

——, "Excavations at Tutter's Neck in James City County, Virginia, 1960–1961," *Contributions from the Museum of History and Technology*, Paper 53, Washington, D.C.: Smithsonian Institution, 1966, pp. 29–72.

——, "German Stoneware Bellarmines, An Introduction," *Antiques*, Vol. LXXVIII (November 1958), pp. 439–441.

——, "The Glass Wine Bottle in Colonial Virginia," *Journal of Glass Studies*, Vol. III (1961), pp. 91–117.

——, *Guide to Artifacts of Colonial America*, New York: Alfred A. Knopf, 1970.

——, *Here Lies Virginia*, New York: Alfred A. Knopf, 1963.

——, "Into the Jaws of Death . . . Walked One," *Collectanea Londiniensia*, No. 2, London and Middlesex Archaeological Society, 1978, pp. 7–22.

——, *James Geddy and Sons, Colonial Craftsmen*, Williamsburg, Va.: Colonial Williamsburg, 1970.

——, *Martin's Hundred*, New York: Alfred A. Knopf, 1982.

——, "Mugs, Jugs and Chamber Pots," *Antiques*, Vol. XC, No. 4 (October 1966), pp. 520–522.

——, "Pearlware: Forgotten Milestone of English Ceramic History," *Antiques*, Vol. XCV, No. 3 (March 1969), pp. 390–397.

——, *Pottery and Porcelain in Colonial Williamsburg's Archaeological Collections*, Colonial Williamsburg Archaeological Series, Williamsburg, Va.: Colonial Williamsburg Foundation, 1969.

——, "Rhenish Gray Stonewares in Colonial America," *Antiques*, Vol. XXVII, No. 3 (September 1967), pp. 349–353.

——, "The Rise and Fall of English White Salt-Glazed Stoneware, Part 1," *Antiques*, Vol. XCVII, No. 3, (March 1970), pp. 408–413.

——, "Ritual Burials on the Upchurch Marshes," *Archaeologia Cantiana*, Vol. LXX, (1956), pp. 160–167.

——, "Romano-British Potteries on the Upchurch Marshes," *Archaeologia Cantiana*, Vol. LXVIII (1954), pp. 72–90.

——, *Shipwreck! History from the Bermuda Reefs*, Hamilton, Bermuda: Capstan Publications, 1995.

——, "Stoneware Gin Flasks: Legacy of the Damned," *Antiques*, Vol. CVII, No. 2 (February 1975), pp. 304–313.

——, "The Who, What, and When of English Creamware Plate Design," *Antiques*, Vol. CI, No. 2 (February 1972), pp. 350–355.

——, *Treasure in the Thames*, London: Frederick Muller, 1956.

——, "'Twas the Night After Christmas . . . ," *Colonial Williamsburg Journal* (Autumn 1997), pp. 54–57.

——, "Wine-Bottle Treasures," *Wine and Spirit Trade Record* (May 16, 1956), pp. 580–586.

Oswald, Adrian, with R. J. C. Hildyard and R. G. Hughes, *English Brown Stoneware, 1670–1900*, London: Faber and Faber, 1982.

Oswald, Felix, and T. Davies Price, *An Introduction to the Study of Terra Sigillata*, London: Longmans, Green and Co., 1920.

Pearce, Jacqueline, *Border Wares, Post-Medieval Pottery in London, 1500–1700*, Vol. 1, London: H. M. Stationery Office for the Museum of London, 1992.

Pine, Lynda, and Nicholas Pine, *William Henry Goss*, Horndean, U.K.: Milestone Publications, 1987.

Pine, Nicholas, *The Concise Encyclopaedia and Price Guide to Goss China*, Horndean, U.K.: Milestone Publications, 1978 and subsequent editions.

Pountney, W. J., *Old Bristol Potteries*, Bristol: J. W. Arrowsmith, 1920.

Powell, Harry J., *Glass-Making in England*, Cambridge: Cambridge University Press, 1923.

Quinn, Kenneth, "London Pottery, 1565–1636," English Ceramic Circle *Transactions*, Vol. 8, Pt. 1 (1971), pp. 57–78.

Rackham, Bernard, *Catalogue of the Glaisher Collection of Pottery & Porcelain in the Fitzwilliam Museum, Cambridge,* 2 vols., reprinted, Woodbridge: Antique Collectors' Club, 1987.

——, *Italian Maiolica*, London: Faber and Faber, 1952.

Rackham, Bernard, and Herbert Read, *English Pottery*, New York: Charles Scribner's Sons, 1924.

Ray, Anthony, *English Delftware Pottery in the Robert Hall Warren Collection, Ashmolean Museum, Oxford,* Boston: Boston Book & Art Shop, 1968.

——, "Liverpool Printed Tiles," English Ceramic Circle *Transactions*, Vol. 9, Pt. 1 (1973), pp. 36–66.

Reineking-von Bock, Gisela, *Steinzeug,* Cologne: Kunstgewerbemuseum, 1971.

——, "Verbreitung von Rheinischem Steinzeug," *Keramos*, No. 87 (January 1980), pp. 11–48.

Renaud, J. G. N., *Rhodesteyn, schatkamer de middeleeuwse ceramiek*, Rhodesteyn Museum, Neelangbroek, Utrecht, n.d.

Sandon, John, *The Watney Collection of Fine Early English Porcelain*, London: Phillips auction catalog, September 22, 1999.

Shaw, Simeon, *History of the Staffordshire Potteries,* 1829, facsimile ed., Newton Abbot, Devon: David & Charles Reprints, 1970.

Simon, André, *Drink*, London: Burke Publishing Co. Ltd., 1948.

Smith, Sheenah, "Norwich China Dealers of the Mid-Eighteenth Century," English Ceramic Circle *Transactions*, Vol. 9, Pt. 2 (1974), pp. 193–211.

Smollett, Tobias George, *The History of England from the Revolution to the Death of George the Second,* 5 vols., rev. ed., London: T. Cadell, 1823.

Solon, M.L., *A History and Description of the Old French Faience*, London: Cassell and Company, ca. 1903.

——, *The Ancient Art Stoneware of the Low Countries and Germany,* 2 vols., London: Chiswick Press, 1892.

Southall Robert, *Take Me Back to Dear Old Blighty*, Horndean, U.K.: Milestone Publications, 1982.

Spinney, David, *Rodney*, London: George Allen and Unwin Ltd., 1969.

Stillinger, Elizabeth, *The Antiquers . . . &c.,* New York: Alfred A. Knopf, 1980.

Taggart, Ross, *The Frank P. and Harriet C. Burnap Collection of English Pottery in the William Rockhill Nelson Gallery,* Kansas City, Mo.: Nelson Gallery-Atkins Museum, 1967.

Toppin, Aubrey J., "The China Trade and Some London Chinamen," English Ceramic Circle *Transactions,* No. 3 (1935), pp. 37–56.

Towner, Donald C., *English Cream-Coloured Earthenware*, New York: Pitman Publishers, 1957.

——, "The Melbourne Pottery," English Ceramic Circle *Transactions,* Vol. 8, Pt. 1 (1971), pp. 18–30.

Valpy, Nancy, "Extracts from the *Daily Advertiser,* 1745–1756," with notes by Robin Hildyard, English Ceramic Circle *Transactions*, Vol. 11, pt. 3 (1983), pp. 195–211.

van Beuningen, H. J. E., *Verdraaid Goed Gedraaid*, Rotterdam: Museum Boyman-van Beuningen, 1973.

Van Dam, J. D., *Mededelingenblad Nederlandse Vereniging van Vrienden van de Ceramiek,* No. 108, Lochem Druk, 1982/84. English summaries by Patricia Wardle.

Van Den Bossche, Willy, *Antique Glass Bottles: Their History and Evolution (1500–1850),* Woodbridge, U.K.: Antique Collectors' Club, 2001.

Van Loo, J., "Pieter van den Ancker en Jan op de Kamp, handelaren in Frechense kruiken omstreeks het derde kwart," *Antiek* (Amsterdam, June–July 1986), pp. 22–29.

Vince, A. G., "Saxon and medieval pottery in London: A Review," *Medieval Archaeology*, Vol. XXIX (1985), pp. 25–93.

——, "Spanish Medieval Pottery from the City of London," *Spanish Medieval Ceramics in Spain and the British Isles,* Oxford: BAR International Series 610 (1995), pp. 329–331.

von Eckhardt, Wolf, Sander L. Gilman, and J. Edward Chamberlin, *Oscar Wilde's London: A Scrapbook of Vices and Virtues, 1880–1900,* Garden City, N.Y.: Anchor Press, 1987.

Walton, Peter, *Creamware and Other English Pottery at Temple Newsam House, Leeds,* Bradford: Manningham Press, 1976.

Ward, Roland, *The Price Guide to the Models of W. H. Goss,* Woodbridge U.K.: Antique Collectors' Club, 1975.

Watkins, C. Malcolm, "North Devon Pottery and Its Export to America in the 17th Century," *Contributions from the Museum of History and Technology*, Papers 12–18, Washington, D.C.: Smithsonian Institution, 1963.

——, "The 'Poor Potter' of Yorktown," *Contributions from the Museum of History and Technology*, Paper 54, Washington, D.C.: Smithsonian Institution, 1968.

Watney, Bernard, *English Blue and White Porcelain of the 18th Century*, London: Faber and Faber, 1973.

Webster, Donald Blake, *Decorated Stoneware Pottery of North America*, Rutland, Vt.: Charles E. Tuttle, 1971.

Wheeler, Sir Mortimer, *Alms for Oblivion: An Antiquary's Scrapbook*, London: Weidenfeld and Nicolson, 1966.

Wills, Geoffrey, *English Pottery and Porcelain*, Garden City, N.Y.: Doubleday, 1969.

Wingood, Allan J., "*Sea Venture*. An Interim Report on an Early 17th Century Shipwreck Lost in 1609," *International Journal of Nautical Archaeology*, Vol. 11, No. 4 (1982), p. 342, Fig. 10.

Woodall, John, *The Surgeon's Mate, 1617,* facsimile, Bath: Kingsmead Press, 1978.

Zippelius, Adelhart, *Volkskunst im Rheinland*, Düsseldorf: Rheinischen Freilichtmuseums in Kommern, 1968.

Index

Excluded from the index are glossary entries and photo or collection sources from the captions.

Goss Collectors, League of, 332
Goss Record, The, 332, 338, 348
Gothic Revival, 109, 115
Governor's Land, Jamestown, Va., 148
Grabham, Oxley, 181f.
Grafton China, 339ff.
Graham, John M., opinion of archaeology, 122
Gravel Lane, Southwark, 47, 147, 151, 154, 169f., 186
gravel temper, 84, 401n18
Graves, Robert, 25
Graves, Rear Admiral Sir Thomas, 261
graybeards, 166f.
    documentation for, 118
    English, 145
    Japanese, 126
    largest, 121
    last of, 125
    masks on, 118, 124
    medallions on, 119, 124ff., 145
    model of, 334f.
    reproductions of, 111
"green," definition of, 393n3
Green, Chris, 152
Green, Guy, 87, 213f.
Green, Mr., 65
Green, Stephen, 308f., 314, 320
Green Bag crew, 273f., 304
Greenea hill Chappel, 246f.
Greens, Bingley and Co., 181, 393n3
Grenada, 261
Grenzau, reproductions from, 110f.
Grey, Lord Charles, 305
Griffith, William and Abigail, 192
Grimstone, Mrs., 277
Gros Islet Bay, St. Lucia, 261f.
Grove, Richard, 184
Guildhall, 7f., 159
    laboratory at, 7f., 42f.
    Library, 43, 395n20
    Museum, 43

Hackwood, William, 254
Hadrian, Emperor, 6, 25
Haggar, Reginald G., 248
Haig, Field Marshal Sir Douglas, 354
hallmarks, silver, 112
Hancock, Robert, 213, 215, 240
Hancock, Sampson, 430n20
handle, French, 34
    terminals, 171
Hanover, Arms of, 308
Harlow, Essex, 79
Harrington, J. C. "Pinky," xviii, 165

Harrod's, Ltd., 355
Hartlepool, Durham, 345
Hartley, Greens & Co., 212, 218
Hartlip, Kent, 14
Harvard University, 333
Harwood, William, 138
Hatcher, Captain Michael, 246, 287
Hatteras Island, N.C., 133
Haverfield, Francis J., 394n1
Hay, Anthony (1771), ceramic stock of, 188f., 415n58
Hays Wharf, 48, 51, 68, 71, 84, 153, 184, 187, 254
Hayter, George, 316
Heath, John, 255
Heath, Joshua, 239
Henderson, A., 13
Henderson, Graeme, 132f.
heraldic china, 331ff.
Herstmonceux, Sussex, 280f.
Heylyn, Edward, 296
hidroceramo, 336, 429n8
Higgins, Mr. and Miss, 298
Highgate, 89f., 121
Hildyard, Robin, 152, 171, 175, 306
Hingston, Richard, 425n44
Hoefnagel, Joris, 72f.
Hogarth, William, 88, 126, 158f., 162, 248, 301
    portrait of, 88
Höhr, 97, 105
Holdaway, Minnie, 237
Holdsworth, Thomas, 337
Hollins, T. & J., 285
Holme, Randle, 144
Holmes, Martin R., 118, 125, 132
honey, 132
Hood, Graham, xiv
Hood, Admiral Sir Samuel, 1st Viscount, 261ff., 265, 274
Hooper, William, 168
Horne, Jonathan, xviii, 114, 160, 275
Horsgate, East Sussex, 335
Horsleydown, 72, 184, 399n55
Horus, temple of Egypt, 229
hotel china, 188
households, West of England, 83
House of Windsor, 358
Hughes, Bernard and Therle, 223
Hungerford, Margaret Wolfe, 402n1
Hunter, Robert, xvii
hunting scenes, 162ff.
Hurst, John, xvii, 35

Iceni, 6ff.
Imperial Potteries, Lambeth, 314, 318ff., 428n41
    see also Green, Stephen

imports
    Dutch, 65f., 70
    Flemish, 127
    French, 34
    Gaulish, 19f.
    to Plymouth, Exeter, Dartmouth, 132
    Rhenish, 207, 415n62
Indians, American, 26
Ink Works, Gardner's, 314
inns
    The George, Aylesbury, 164
    Kings Head, Aylesbury, 164
    White Hart, 164
Inns of Court, 160
Internet, 41
Ireland, William, 402n34
Iron Age, 23, 25
Ironmonger Lane, London, 3
Ironstone China, Mason's Patent, 10, 225, 255f.
    dessert plate, 255
    Japanese pattern, 255

"Jackfield" Ware
    enameled, 276
    jugs, 275f.
    teapot, 277
Jackson, John, 144
James River, Va., 31
Jamestown, Va., 74, 82f., 104
Jane's All the World's Ships, 347f.
Jannsen, Sir Theodore, 213
Jan Op de Camp, 124
Janson, Jacob, 47
jars
    butter, 85
    Italian, 117
    olive, evolution of, 132
    Spanish, 117, 131ff.
        carrot type, 132f.
    tobacco, 173
Jefferson, Thomas, 77
Jellicoe, Roderick, 292ff.
Jenkins, Frank, 414n40
Jerrold, Blanchard, 321f.
Jerrold, Douglas William, 313f.
Jervis, Sir John, 266
Jewitt, Llewellynn, 28, 177, 179, 181, 276
Johnson, Charles, 124
Johnson, "Johnny," 123
Johnson, Nicholas, xviii
Jones, Morgan, 30
Jones, William M., 154
Jones McDuffee & Stratton, Boston, 333
Judy, 315

Van den Ancker, Pieter, 125
Van de Passe, Crispin, 58
   engraver, 56
vases
   altar, North Italian, 46
   delftware pedestal, 86
Vauxhall, London, 147, 152, 155, 167,
      169, 175, 184
   delftware potteries, 325
   kilns, 153
   Pottery, 156
   stoneware potteries, 325
Verdun, 345, 357
Vernon, Admiral Edward, 206, 207,
      259f.
Vernon, Ralph, 240, 265
Versailles, 194
   Petit Trianon at, 194, 195
Vespasian, Emperor, 5, 393n7
Vickers, Alfred, 339
Vickers, James & Lydia, 240f.
Victoria, Duchess of Kent, 308
Victoria, Queen, 150, 308f., 354
   accession of, 308
   death of, 352
   Diamond Jubilee, 352
Victoria China, 344
Vimy Ridge, 345
Vine Lane, Southwark, 72, 184
Vine Pottery, 349
Virginia Gazette, 231, 295
Vogel, Fred III, xviii
Voyez, John, 167f.

Wagstaff, William, 325
Walker, James, 285
Walker, W., 428n42
Wall, Dr. John, 424n31
Wall Street crash, 58
Walton, J. Douglas, xviii, 53, 58,
      394n21
Wan Li, 51ff.
   "Bird on Rocks" design, 64
Wapping, London, 313, 397n19
Ward, John, 412n41
Ward, Thomas, 138, 144
wares
   Afghanistan, 45
   agate, 281
   Arab Spain, 45
   Black Basaltes, 3
   blue, 65
   Border, 41f., 82ff., 84, 98, 132, 160
   Cheam, 82
   Chinese, red, 103
   Donyatt, 83, 282f.
   dry-bodied, red, 143, 147, 215
   Gaulish, 4

gravel-tempered, 84
North Devon Plain, 83
Persian, 45, 103
Rosso Antico, 3
Samian, 4, 10f., 17, 19, 21
tin-glazed, 45
Tudor, 45
See also major wares, e.g.,
   creamware
Warren, Robert Hall Collection, 191
Washburn, Wilcomb E., 147
wasters, 31, 47, 51, 74, 83, 148
   ceramic, 11
   Challis, 407n29
   Cologne, 127
   definition of, 184
   dumps, 98, 127
   Portuguese, 154
Watkins, C. Malcolm, xviii, 83
Watling House, London, 35, 38
Watney, Dr. Bernard, 242
Weatherby, Mr., 294f.
Webb, Francis, 14
Wedgwood, Aaron, 198, 242, 423n7
Wedgwood, Josiah, 3, 10, 167, 204f.,
      209, 224f., 243, 267, 356
   exporter, 185
   Royal patronage, 210
   "tinkering" approved by, 185
Wedgwood, Ralph, pattern book
      of, 237
Wedgwood, Richard, 198
Wedgwood, Mrs. Sarah, 326, 327
Wedgwood, Thomas, 198
Weir, Harrison, 136
Wellington, Arthur Wellesley, 1st
      Duke of, 271
Wentworth, General, 259
West Africa, Portuguese, 80
Westerwald, 97ff., 103, 107, 207
   AR excise stamp on, 150
   chamber pots, 89ff.
      AR and GR medallions on,
         107f., 155
   handle terminal, 111
   imports, 166
   jugs, 140
      puzzle, 176
   mugs and tankards, 107
   neck types, 107
   spouts pinched, 115
   in Virginia, 138
Westminster, 124
   Abbey, 274, 352
Westmoreland County, Va., 30
Wetherill, Francis, 307, 312
"Weymouth Ware," 20f.
wheat, mildew on, 17

wheel, potter's, 25, 29, 393n1, 393n4
   "profileering," 418n15
Wheeler, Sir Mortimer, 4
Whieldon, Thomas, 143, 204, 209
whistles, bird, 35f.
Whitby, Yorkshire, 345
White Friar's Street, London,
      409n60
Whitwood Meer, Yorkshire, 266
"Wild Rose" pattern, 253, 254
Wilhelm, Christian, 48, 51, 59, 62,
      72, 184
Willey, Thomasine, 248
William III, 106
   and Mary, 258
William IV, 303f., 308
Williamsburg Pottery, 30, 152, 197
Williamsburg, Va., 31, 125, 188f., 204,
      208, 213, 296
   Duke of Gloucester Street, 344
Willow Art China, 342, 345
willow pattern, 247ff.
Wilson, Captain George, 157
Wilton China, 347
Wimbledon, 121
Wincanton, Somerset, 191
Winchester, Bishop of, 68
Windsor Castle, 359
Windsor
   Duchess of, 356f.
   Duke of
      at Verdun, 357
      wedding of, 355
      see also Edward VIII
"windswept rock" motif, 241f.
Wingood, Allan J. "Smokey,"
      xviii, 85
Wisker, John, 325
witch bottles, 122f.
witchcraft, 122, 316
Wolstenholme Towne, Va., 31,
      81, 176
Wood, Enoch, 227f.
Wood, Ralph I, 310
Woodfall, John, 69
Wooltus, Symon, 145
Woolwich, London, 75
Woolwich Ferry, 145
Worcester, 290
words, weasel, 23
World War I, 329, 337ff.
   Balkans Campaign, 350
   casualties of, 341
   cease fire, 350f.
   Gallipoli, 345
   Hindenburg Line, 343
   souvenir pottery
      Armentières, 350

A Note on the Photographer

If These Pots Could Talk combines the talents of two Englishmen, the author and his photographer, Gavin Ashworth, seen here in the process of creating the cover.

Gavin Ashworth is an internationally recognized photographer of museum objects and demonstrates his art in this book by turning even the most commonplace of objects into things of beauty. He earned a Photographic Diploma with Honours from Britain's Plymouth College of Art & Design in 1974, and subsequently worked with several distinguished photographic companies both in the United States and in the United Kingdom before setting up his own New York studio in 1991. He became a Fellow of the British Institute of Professional Photography in 1979 and the following year was honored with a fellowship of the Royal Photographic Society, one of the highest accolades the British photographic community can award.

Mr. Ashworth is photographer to the Chipstone Foundation and the principal photographer for its prestigious journals *American Furniture* and *Ceramics of America*. He has also photographed several major museum and private ceramics collections, among them the celebrated Longridge and Henry Weldon Collections.

THIS BOOK is set in Galliard, the typeface designed by Matthew Carter based on the 1503 drawings of Claude Garamond (1480–1561). It has been printed direct to plate offset lithography by Meridian Printing in East Greenwich, Rhode Island, on 115-pound Parilux Silk Text. The first printing is 4,000 copies, case bound in Natuurlinnen by Acme Bindery in Charlestown, Massachusetts. See preceding page for a note on the photography. Typesetting by Jo Ann Langone and Mary Gladue. Designed in the year 2001 by Wynne Patterson.